'DANCING IN CHAINS'

Narrative and Memory in Political Theory

Imagination and memory are but one thing.
—Thomas Hobbes

'Dancing in Chains'

NARRATIVE AND MEMORY
IN POLITICAL THEORY

Joshua Foa Dienstag

STANFORD UNIVERSITY PRESS

Stanford, California

1997

Stanford University Press
Stanford, California

© 1997 by the Board of Trustees of the
Leland Stanford Junior University

Printed in the United States of America

CIP data are at the end of the book

Stanford University Press publications are
distributed exclusively by Stanford University Press
within the United States, Canada, Mexico, and
Central America; they are distributed exclusively
by Cambridge University Press throughout
the rest of the world.

To my parents and their parents

Acknowledgments

A work concerned with the passage of time and our apprehension of it forces upon its author a deep appreciation for the many people and multiple accidents of history that went into shaping it. This project first took shape at Princeton University over five years ago. There I had the input and guidance of George Kateb and Alexander Nehamas, but I also received something else that I value much more: their display of an academic temper so judicious, restrained, and rigorous, and yet so good-natured, as to foster in me the belief (against much contrary evidence) that the institutionalized pursuit of knowledge could be a good thing. They teach, as Aristotle suggested, through the example of good character rather than the inculcation of doctrine. I hope it does not horrify them too much that I associate them here with that philosopher.

David Steiner, into whose office I stumbled many years ago, endured my first, embarrassingly grandiose attempts to discuss political philosophy seriously and managed to suggest some wise choices without any display of contempt. For this, and for his continually thoughtful advice and friendship at every later stage of my education, and throughout this project, I owe him a deep debt. John DiIulio has similarly counseled me for an even longer period than David, and he has my permanent gratitude as well.

Amy Gutmann, Alan Ryan, Elizabeth Kiss, Anne Norton, and Victor Preller all helped to realize this project with support both intellectual and material. My thanks as well to the "J-team"—Julia Faber, Judy Failer, John

Goldberg, Michael Jones, and Jeff Sacknowitz—for similar favors in more informal settings.

Several chapters in the book benefited from the learned readings of Paul Vogt and Pratap Mehta. Their generous comments helped me to clarify and deepen my own arguments, as well as improve countless points of presentation. Conversations with Judith Barish, Sammy Basu, Cheryl Hall, and Mark Brandon also undoubtedly improved the work. Early versions of several chapters were presented at annual meetings of the American Political Science Association and the Southern Political Science Association. I thank all the participants for stimulating conversations that helped to strengthen the chapters.

I also want to extend my appreciation to the students and faculty of the University of Virginia. George Klosko, Debra Morris, and Dante Germino each commented helpfully on portions of the manuscript. The students of my graduate seminar are also owed thanks, both for their comments and their patience as I tried to formulate some of the conclusions that appear here.

Princeton University, the Society of Fellows at Princeton, and the Charlotte W. Newcombe Foundation all supported the writing of this work with fellowships. Without their generous support, it could never have been completed in a timely fashion. A shorter version of Chapter 5 appeared in the *Review of Politics*; I thank the editors for their permission to reprint it here. Brief portions of Chapters 1 and 2 appeared in articles in the *American Political Science Review* and the *Journal of Politics*; I thank their editors also for permission to reprint these sections here. The index was prepared by Anna Kirkland with support from the University of Virginia's Rowland Egger Fund; I am indebted to both.

Stanford University Press and my editors there, Jan Spauschus Johnson, Peter Dreyer, and, especially, Muriel Bell, have been extremely patient and thoughtful in their efforts to make this a better book, and I am grateful to them.

Jennifer Mnookin withstood the grumpy self-centeredness of a first-time author and met it with unflagging support, love, good humor, and useful commentaries. My intellectual respect for her is surpassed only by my passion and my general feeling that she is the best thing that ever happened to me.

My debt to my family is embodied in the dedication to this work. It needs no embellishment here except to mention the constant delight my stepmother Jacqueline and sister Isabelle bring me, and my brother Jesse's consistent friendship, humor, and healthy disdain for all people and projects that take themselves too seriously.

J.F.D.

Contents

Abbreviations

The following abbreviations are used throughout the book. Numbers following the abbreviations refer either to numbered sections, when these are customarily used, or else to page numbers in the cited editions. Full publication details for these editions will be found in the Bibliography.

Very occasionally I have altered the translations from other languages given in these texts—this is usually indicated by the presence of the translated term in brackets. Emphasis in quotations is always original unless otherwise noted.

John Locke

E	*An Essay Concerning Human Understanding*
FCM	*Further Considerations . . . on Money*, in *The Works of John Locke*, vol. 5
LT1	*A Letter Concerning Toleration*, in *The Works of John Locke*, vol. 7 (the second *Letter* is *LT2*, etc.)
RC	*The Reasonableness of Christianity*, in *The Works of John Locke*, vol. 8
SCM	*Some Considerations . . . on Money*, in *The Works of John Locke*, vol. 5
STCE	*Some Thoughts Concerning Education*, in *The Works of John Locke*, vol. 6
1T or 2T	*Two Treatises of Government*

Friedrich Nietzsche

AC	*The Anti-Christ*
AOM	*Assorted Opinions and Maxims*
BGE	*Beyond Good and Evil*
BT	*The Birth of Tragedy*
CW	*The Case of Wagner*
D	*Daybreak*
EH	*Ecce Homo*
HH	*Human, All-Too-Human*
GS	*The Gay Science*
GM	*On the Genealogy of Morals*
OTL	"On Truth and Lying in an Extramoral Sense," in *Friedrich Nietzsche on Rhetoric and Language*
PTG	*Philosophy in the Tragic Age of the Greeks*
Z	*Thus Spoke Zarathustra*
TI	*Twilight of the Idols*
UM	*Untimely Meditations*
WP	*The Will to Power*
WS	*The Wanderer and His Shadow*

G. W. F. Hegel

AE	*Aesthetics*
LG	*Encyclopedia Logic*
IPH	*Lectures on the Philosophy of World History: Introduction: Reason in History*
PS	*Phenomenology of Spirit*
PH	*The Philosophy of History*
PR	*Philosophy of Right*

'DANCING IN CHAINS'

Narrative and Memory in Political Theory

INTRODUCTION

The Plotters of Political Theory

D'où venons nous
Que sommes nous
Où allons nous

On the eve of the twentieth century, in Tahiti, sick, destitute, Paul Gauguin resolved to kill himself. He determined that, before carrying out the act, he would paint one last canvas that would declare in the most definitive way possible his rejection of the modern condition and his embrace of the enchanted, custom-bound world of the South Pacific. He had come to the island, he said, hoping to learn from the natives as "a missionary in reverse." Now he wanted to send a final, unmistakable message back to Paris.

The suicide attempt was unsuccessful. But the resulting painting was to become one of Gauguin's best known. Over a scene of Tahitian women engaged in timeless and time-honored tasks, he scrawled the three large sentences, bereft of question marks, that appear as an epigraph above: "Where do we come from / What are we / Where are we going": "Not a title," he wrote later, "but a signature." Gauguin thus identified himself as one who had lost his place in time. The modern age, he thought, had wrenched humanity from its accustomed story, deprived it of past and future, and thereby, of its very identity.[1]

My efforts here are devoted to examining these three unmarked questions that Gauguin left as a name for himself and a last testament to modernity. More precisely, in the following pages, I examine the relation of the middle question to the outer two. For it is no longer obvious to philosophers or political theorists, as it was to Gauguin, that these three questions have anything to do with one another. It is no longer obvious, that is, that a sense of past and future, a sense of time, or a sense of history has anything to do with the human constitution or politics. Most recent attempts to answer the question "What are we?" do not consider it to be closely related to the questions of where we have been and where we are going. History and philosophy, it is felt, have different fields, or objects, of study.

Certainly it would be granted, in a loose sort of way, that our sense of ourselves, at least on an individual level, is somehow tied to our pasts—to our education, family, employment, or nationality, for example. But such ties, I think it is fair to say, have not been widely thought safe starting points for political reflections. Indeed, certain philosophers have taken it as a positive duty to detach their hypotheses from such conditions—to locate an account of human identity or human interests or reason that depends on no history in particular—and to use such an account as an Archimedean point for political philosophy. This is not a universal view, but it is widespread. And its opposite appears to be correspondingly rare. Few contemporary philosophers, that is, have taken as a starting point what Gauguin emphasizes, that human identity and a sense of past and future are closely connected. The role of the past is, at best, acknowledged in an ad hoc fashion. The role of the future receives even greater skepticism: how, after all, can that which does not yet exist contribute to the nature of existing human beings?

Etymology, at least, does not support this skepticism about past and future. The word *knowledge* derives from the Latin *gnarus* ("knowing" or "expert") and before that from the Indo-European root *gnâ* ("know"). But this ancient root has another line of descendants, which include the Latin *narro* ("relate"), from whence we have the English words *narration, narrative*, and all their related forms.[2] This common lineage suggests that at one time to know something or someone was closely linked to the ability to tell a story. Knowledge and narrative were thought to be the same sort of learning. Even self-knowledge, in this conception, would seem to require some element of story. The past of our language, then, suggests that the separation of philosophy and history is neither natural nor necessary. Of course, neither does it prove that they are "naturally" linked. It merely suggests that the extreme rejection of this link—the demand for a nonhistorical Archimedean point of self-knowledge—is itself not in accord with where we have been. Such a demand is not necessarily, then, the only way to begin reflections on politics. So while etymology cannot tell us much, it at least allows the possibility that Gauguin's intuition was not wholly mistaken.

The goal of this inquiry, therefore, is to explore the middle term in the three-sentence signature. And in considering the meaning of this middle term, in making Gauguin's central question *our* central question, I want to take seriously his suggestion that it be investigated in relation to the two other questions concerning past and future. To treat political theory from such a perspective is not to deny the utility of other approaches. It is merely to ask how our self-understanding may be improved by stressing the connection between the self and time. Nor do we have to start this project from scratch, for political theory has had much to say about this connection. Few, perhaps, state the problem as baldly as Gauguin. But neither do many wholly ignore it—although their thoughts on the subject may be submerged or not presented systematically.

What follows, then, is an attempt to examine the role of historical argument and narrative in political philosophy.[3] My primary contention is that political theory, rather than relying on concepts of abstract right and duty, often attempts to guide by giving its readers a particular sense of time. That sense of time persuades not only by logic but also by giving readers a more convincing account of history and of the particular roles they are to play. One principal consequence of this is that we put our own powers of interpretation in a straitjacket if we approach each book of political theory only in search of an abstract argument. Our readings will be more fruitful if we consider the possibility of historical argument alongside that of synchronic reason. Political theory speaks to questions of past and future more often than we are sometimes led to believe. To put it another way: the project of political theory is often not so much to reform our morals as it is to reform our memories.

The weight of my argument falls on extended interpretations of three figures in political theory: John Locke, Friedrich Nietzsche, and G. W. F. Hegel. Hegel's "historicism" is widely accepted, that of Locke is not, and as to Nietzsche, debate still waxes hot.[4] But in no case do I seek simply to prove that these authors make historical arguments. That conclusion would be trivially easy to arrive at in some cases, harder in others, but certainly pointless in all of them. If the larger value in locating each theorist's sense of the past cannot be articulated, then the mere detection of historical argument might simply be the detection of bad argument—or, at best, of supporting, inessential argument. My aim in each of the following chapters is to show that these theorists are at their most persuasive, and readings of their works are richest, when the historical element in their thought is foregrounded. Often, I think, the presence of historical argument and narration has been suppressed or unappreciated by commentators on the books I examine here. My purpose is not so much to refute these interpretations (although that is sometimes necessary) as to supplement them. We shall have a fuller appreciation of each of these theorists if we patiently examine their sense of time.

Taken together, however, Locke, Nietzsche, and Hegel do not provide a single "historical" viewpoint. Instead, they offer markedly different narratives, which rest on different notions of human experience. My goal is neither to identify one history as truer than another nor to describe a peculiarly historical philosophy. Indeed, I would deny the existence of such a perspective as surely as the existence of any single rationalist view. It is a question rather of how what we know of our past and expect of our future contribute to what we are. Each of these theorists has something to tell us about this question. Each, in his unique retelling of the past, has something to say about who we are. And in coming to appreciate this, we may come to see more broadly the importance of the question itself, of the relationship between the self and time. So before offering a short preview of these chapters, I shall attempt to articulate briefly where I believe this importance to lie.[5]

The Idea of a Role

A sense of one's place in a narrative might be seen as a piece of knowledge distinct from the subject or self who holds it. That is, we might think of ourselves as creatures that exist independently before we exist "in" time or "in" history. There is more than a little pride in this attitude. We do not like to think of our personality as in any way dependent on the sort of lives we have led or shall lead. Indeed, we prefer to think the opposite: "I have chosen to lead this life because I am such-and-such a type of person—even if I had been born in another country, in another century, I would still basically be the same person." And so, without really being able to test this hypothesis, we hold the idea of our "self" separate from our history. But Gauguin places his three questions together, as a signature, precisely because he thinks that a sense of time is inseparable from what we *are* at a fundamental level. In this section, I attempt to sketch out a vocabulary to discuss this condition. In the next, I attempt to give some substance to Gauguin's intuition. That attempt, I should say here, arises from my reaction to the hermeneutic tradition in philosophy.

For the purposes of a discussion of political theory, I have found it useful to describe the connection of identity and narrative through a vocabulary of drama based on the terms *role*, *character*, *plot*, and the like. When I describe the political identity bestowed on the reader by a work of political theory, I conceive of it as a "role," much like a role in a dramatic production. In learning a part an actor must think *both* of the subject's personality and of his or her particular place in the story enacted. The personality, the "character" of the role, will consist of values, attributes, loves, hates, obsessions, jealousies,

Roles of Actors

habits of mind, and indeed everything that makes up that person's outlook on the world—the terms in which the character sees the world in which she or he lives. An actor may rehearse for a part by imagining the character in scenes or situations apart from those in the play itself—trying thereby to imagine the reactions of such a character to events other than those of the role as written. This is useful rehearsal. But it is *not* the same thing as playing the role itself. For the role itself is not limited to its character but includes the plot as well—the series of events or episodes this character experiences. And from the perspective of characters, the plot is not just their own actions but also the setting, the other characters and the actions, or nonactions, that *they* engage, or do not engage, in. Every element of the story that reaches the character from the outside, as it were, is part of the plot.

But if we are tempted, here, to identify "character" with an ahistorical "self" and "plot" with "history," we miss the point: because there is no firm boundary between character and plot in the composition of a role. Events that occur in the plot may be taken up at a later time as elements in the character of those who participated in them. Purposes, needs, desires, hatreds, loves, loyalties, betrayals, and even habits of mind are all results in a character that have their origin in the plot. And yet the plot itself is composed of nothing but the interaction of the characters. Indeed, we often say that a drama is most successful when its plot flows directly from the natural interaction of its characters and not from events external to them. When lovers are separated, for example, by their own conflicting loyalties or personalities, rather than by happenstance, but then this very separation so saddens them that they attempt to reunite—*that*, we say, is a well-integrated drama, a great play: a comedy (e.g., *The Philadelphia Story*) when the reunion is successful; a tragedy (e.g., *Romeo and Juliet*) when it is not. It is this mutual influence, this constant back-and-forth motion between character and plot, on display most directly in drama, that captures the connection between identity and narrative that I want to explore in political theory. Not because this connection is good drama, of course, but because we judge such dramas good for the reason that they indicate something deeply human, using uncommon circumstances to reveal common human traits. That power is not, however, limited to theatrical works. It is, I argue, available to political philosophers too, even if they have not always used it, or if, when they have, it has been ignored.

When a philosopher offers a narrative, a sense of history, or even a set of memories to readers, it often has its effect through this connection between plot and character. The conjoining of these two elements into a *role* that contains them both, I maintain, is where much of the interest in works of political theory may be found. Rather than simply offering a set of values for the just person or good political judgment, the works I shall explore in this book link these elements of character to a narrative that locates them in time. Indeed, the temporal, historical element is inseparable from that of character. The two together, as a role, represent the core of any particular work's political understanding. That is why I say political theory attempts to reform memories as well as morals. To shape a role, a political theorist must work on the plot as well as the character. Put another way, the theorist must consider the past and future themselves and not just the beings who inhabit them. Or, at any rate, so I argue.

In exploring the role that a political philosopher creates, I shall often speak of vocabulary as well as of plot. It is in the vocabulary of a political philosophy that I find the element of character that contributes to a dramatic role. In its vocabulary I find the terms in which that philosophy sees the world, the categories into which the world is pre-organized. These vocabularies contain the values, the passions, and the habits of mind of the philosophy they are called upon to express. They compose the human character that enters into the plot these works also contain. In Locke, for example, I find an economistic vocabulary; in Hegel, an aesthetic one. The typical characters of these authors, then, are correspondingly different. In hermeneutic terms (about which more below), these elements of character represent the prejudices of a horizon of understanding that are distinguishable from the sense of time—even though it is the sense of time itself that holds the various terms together. The *role* then, that a work may suggest to its reader, embraces both character expressed as vocabulary and narrative employing that character in a plot.

History and Identity

Political theory, I have been arguing, attempts to put phenomena in a matrix of meaning that almost always includes, as one axis, historical time. It is principally to the hermeneutic tradition of philosophical inquiry that I owe this observation. Through its focus on the process of interpretation, philosophers in that tradition (principally Martin Heidegger, Hans-Georg Gadamer, Hannah Arendt, and Paul Ricoeur) have drawn attention to the same connection between human identity and a sense of time that Gauguin gestured at in his three-question signature. Rather than attempt to prove that connection in the abstract, I only want to argue here that the hermeneutic tradition suggests to us an approach to texts of political theory that may prove fruitful. What will validate this perspective is its productivity in practice—that is, in the specific explorations that constitute the bulk of this inquiry. If there is anything here that establishes the connection of the three questions in a definitive way, it will be the degree of success that the philosophies themselves achieve in fashioning a coherent answer to them as a set—and my own success in using the questions to fashion a coherent interpretation of these philosophies. The connection of identity to past and future is meant to be a stimulating hypothesis, not a certain proposition whose truth grounds further inquiry. Nevertheless, it will be worthwhile to establish here that this hypothesis is, at the least, a plausible one. In the concluding two chapters, I explore more directly the implications of this view, assuming it to have been substantiated, to some degree, by the intervening pages.

Hermeneutics suggests this hypothesis to us through its focus on the roles of prejudice and horizons of understanding in the process of interpretation. Originally concerned with the problems of reading associated with biblical exegesis, hermeneutic philosophy has, in the twentieth century, become a more general philosophy of human experience and identity. The proposition that unites the hermeneutic tradition is that no interpretation, no reading, can be made in a wholly neutral or disinterested fashion. In contrast to empiricism, which views experience as something that can precede understanding and knowledge, hermeneutics claims that experience always takes place within a preexisting horizon of understanding, which "conditions" it. An interpreter always begins with biases: prejudices (literally pre-judgments) that "constitute the initial directedness of our whole ability to experience. Prejudices are biases of our openness to the world."[6] Hans-Georg Gadamer means to indicate here both that biases are inevitable and that they are not necessarily something to be feared. Preexisting judgments do not just slant our reaction to a new experience. They simultaneously enable that reaction. Prejudgments form the terms of our understanding. They allow us to relate new features of the world to those we already have knowledge of: "This [condition of prejudice] is not a regrettable distortion which affects the purity of understanding, but the condition of its possibility."[7] The word *condition*, with regard to experience, thus carries both the positive meaning of "making it possible" and the negative meaning of "predetermining it." To understand a text, then, requires a prejudgment as to the meaning of its terms—but such judgments will always be in some sense incomplete, hence "biased." When, for example, we read in the U.S. Constitution that "cruel and unusual" punishment is forbidden, we draw, in our attempt to understand these words, on all manner of previous experiences. Previous written uses of the words may form the principal basis of our prejudgment of the meaning in this case. We know the words, not just from a dictionary, but from other documents and conversations that have made use of them. But surely also, modern hermeneutics argues, it is a lived experience in our culture that allows us to give this prejudgment depth: how, for example, could we understand what "unusual" means substantively without an understanding of what is "usual"? And if we had a firsthand experience of cruelty, say at the hands of a torturer, would this really distort our understanding of the constitutional prohibition of cruelty? Or would it, on the contrary, enrich it? Would we really want to say that a person without such experience but who had memorized a dictionary definition of the word *cruelty* understood the word better? It is in this manner that both prior texts and lived experience are held by hermeneutic philosophy to create a "horizon of understanding" within which prejudices condition our approach to new texts and experiences. Prejudgments are necessary for our understanding, while simultaneously limiting it.

It should also be clear both from the tenor of the observations by Gadamer quoted above and from the title of the article in which they appear ("The Universality of the Hermeneutical Problem") that, at least in its modern incarnation, hermeneutics no longer confines itself to textual exegesis but purports to give an all-embracing model of human experience. It does so by generalizing from what might be called the "reader-text" dyad to that of "observer-world": "What I am describing is the mode of the whole human experience of the world," Gadamer says.[8] The way in which this generalization is made is simple enough. In the previous example, the meaning of the written word *unusual* was held to depend on a predefined sense of the usual, which came in part from lived experience. But, one might ask, is the necessity of such prejudgments really limited to the case of writing? When we observe the world itself, can we really understand it outside of our prejudicial categories? Are we not constantly interpreting the world in terms of our own personal, as well as common cultural, prejudices as to what is usual? When we encounter something new, do we not come to grips with it precisely through differentiating it from that with which we are familiar? Such is Gadamer's argument for the universality of hermeneutics. We cannot experience life directly, but only through the lens of past experience.

It is in this manner that hermeneutics expands from being a model of reading to a general account of human identity. The relationship between experience and prejudice is no longer confined to the act of reading, but expanded to every sort of human activity. It is in this universal hermeneutics that an individual's sense of time or of the past can be analyzed as a primary—indeed even as the central—prejudice.

This notion that the hermeneutic problem is a universal one, and thus deeply connected to a sense of personal identity, is suggested most cogently by Heidegger.[9] That a sense of time or a sense of history is a central or necessary prejudice is also an idea that derives from Heidegger. Not only, he thought, do our set of prejudgments form a horizon within which we experience, but further, "Time must be brought to light and genuinely grasped as the horizon of every understanding and interpretation of Being."[10] The suggestion that every experience takes place within a preexisting horizon of understanding points to the idea that experience always takes place "within time." Experience cannot be modeled in an abstract, timeless way, but must always be conditioned by its place in time. One cannot ask what is unusual, for example, without an element of time as a boundary for a frame of reference.[11] And this suggests that time itself is the central category, the main axis, on which any particular horizon of understanding is founded. Heidegger called this the "elemental historicity" of the human condition.[12] From this, we can draw the hypothesis that any horizon contains within it an understanding, a judgment, a conception, of past, present, and future. Time is the vital prejudice, on which all other prejudices rely. Again, what I have outlined here is merely the thinking behind this hypothesis, not a proof of it. I should emphasize, too, that Heidegger draws certain conclusions from this thesis that I reject. These are discussed in Chapter 6.

For now, this conception of the horizon of understanding, besides being a model of human experience, may also suggest to us something about how we might approach texts of political theory. Gadamer famously describes the understanding that is conjoined to any experience of reading as resulting from a "fusion of horizons."[13] With this phrase he reminds us that books we read appear to us, not just as mute objects on our own horizons, but as works that contain *their own* horizons as well. Being efforts of the human spirit, like our own understanding, they bring, from their authors, their times and languages, and from any variety of sources, their own horizons of understanding, which it is our task as readers to comprehend. Like our horizons, these others must have their own senses of time, their own axes of history, on which whatever knowledge they contain is founded. The hint we glean from hermeneutics in our investigation of political theory is to beware the account of time that accompanies a horizon of understanding, whether it rests on the surface of the text or lurks beneath in its depths. The sense of time is as fundamental to the horizons of others as it is to our own—and we may best understand others' approaches to the world by exploring the temporal aspect of their perspective.

Sometimes, as in Hegel, an account of time lies on the surface of a text. In other cases, as with Locke and Nietzsche, one has to dig down a little further. But, as I said at the outset, it is not my goal here simply to prove that the texts I discuss contain a sense of time. Rather it is my contention that paying attention to the way they fashion time will lead us to the heart of these works. They will repay our attention most richly if we consider that their understanding of time is fundamental to their horizons.

So the hermeneutic tradition offers us a means by which we might reunite the understanding of knowledge and narrative. Hermeneutics suggests that every text that comes under our scrutiny contains an understanding of time—of past, present, and future—that is a fundamental element of its meaning. It is simply another way of stating this conclusion to phrase it in terms of narrative. What I shall be searching for in my exploration of a given political theory is an underlying narrative, a role, or an account of history, that lends coherence to the horizon of understanding that the work projects.

The hermeneutic tradition has directly identified the sense of time, or narrative with personal identity.[14] For this reason, I do not draw sharp distinctions between such terms as *time*, *history*, *the past*, and *memory*. Although it is undoubtedly often appropriate to differentiate among them, part of my purpose here is to show that there are broad areas of overlap in their meanings. I attempt to employ these terms in a fairly consistent manner. Since *time* is notoriously difficult to define, I use it least of all, referring instead to an author's "sense of time," by which I mean nothing more than the manner in which he or she describes past, present, and future. Are they, for example, to be divided up into distinctive eras, epochs, decades, episodes, or moments? And how are these periods to be marked off from and related to one another? *History*, therefore, will normally refer to the detailed account of the past that the author gives within this larger sense of time. *Narrative* is a term that describes many forms of speech and writing and refers to any description of events that occur over a period of time. Not all narratives are history, then, but all histories are narratives, for my purposes. Now, as indicated, it is part of my effort here to describe the relationship between such historical narratives and human identity. Insofar as this is the case, I argue, this history may rightly also be termed *memory*, which is therefore the key term—a porous membrane that connects the events of the past with the person who remembers them. Memory is the place where elements of plot meet up with elements of character and fuse themselves into the role. Just how memory performs this function receives further attention below—particularly in the pages on Nietzsche.

But the connection between memory and identity is present in Locke and Hegel as well. And the work of all three rests on a further understanding: that the border between personal and social memory is equally porous. Certainly, the two are not just the same. But in writing political narratives, Locke, Nietzsche, and Hegel have in mind, not just to alter us as individuals by reforming our individual memories, but to reform us as a people by altering our common memories. Our roles (since they contain the future) are larger than our memories, but our memories are an essential part of our roles.

The question arises at this point of whether I believe that political theory *must* contain a narrative element to qualify as such. In some sense, I do; but I also believe the question to be a red herring. My understanding of hermeneutics commits me to the position that whatever is expressed in language contains prejudgments, and that among these are prejudgments of time. Hence all political theory contains narrative whether explicit or hidden. But it would be equally true (and equally uninteresting) to say that all human speech contains narrative, or that it contains reason. Little is gained from such observations. And it is certainly possible for a political theorist committed to the idea of abstraction from history to travel far down the path of expunging narrative from his or her work (John Rawls might be an example here), although I would deny that the attempt to do so could completely succeed. Furthermore, it would be true that to insist on a narrative focus in reading such works would be, in large measure, to miss the point, or at least the intention, of the author (although such subversive readings would doubtless turn up interesting material). My meaning, though, is in a different register. First, I doubt whether political theorists have pursued this goal of abstraction as often or as thoroughly as contemporary histories of political thought would have us believe. This is the sense in which the modern commitment to abstraction becomes a self-imposed straitjacket when applied to the history of political thought. Second, it is not my goal to draw rigid boundaries around the field of political theory. It is not a question of whether a work of severe abstraction is "not political theory" but rather, of whether such a work has robbed itself of an element of the human condition. It is the time-bound nature of human life that directs us to the question of narrative in political theory, not vice versa. It is not that narrative makes something political theory, but that it makes that theory interesting and (occasionally) powerful, because it thereby addresses a central element of human life. Insofar as I have a claim to defend here, it is a claim for the *importance* of the question of narrative (and, yes, even its centrality), but not its absolute interpretive priority. I do believe we are diminished and endangered as political theorists and political beings insofar as we avoid such questions. But I could hardly hope to convince someone of this by eliminating other perspectives a priori. Rather, it is a conclusion toward which I hope to nudge the reader through the course of the book.

From this perspective, I want briefly to differentiate my inquiry from the most prominent recent attempt to theorize directly about the role of narrative in politics and political theory—that of Alasdair MacIntyre. Although I can offer nothing like a sustained critique of MacIntyre's philosophy, it may be useful to the reader to offer some account of my distance from it, since our vocabularies are superficially similar enough to arouse suspicion of a common source. While not entirely without foundation, such a suspicion might misdirect the reader. In capsule form, my differences with MacIntyre can be put quite simply: he allots far too little responsibility to individuals in determining their place in time. (The themes addressed here are revisited with greater depth in Chapter 6.)

Although his more recent works have moved somewhat away from this theme, in his book *After Virtue* (1981), MacIntyre attempts to articulate "a concept of self whose unity resides in the unity of a narrative."[15] MacIntyre has here clearly been influenced by the hermeneutic tradition (mainly through Jean-Paul Sartre, an astute student of Heidegger), yet, I would argue, his approach to narrative is so different from the one I have described above as to be largely incommensurable. MacIntyre grounds his account, not in hermeneutics, but, surprisingly, in speech-act theory. Starting from actions, rather than interpretation, he quickly identifies "intention" as the core of any action, and human life as the concatenation of many actions. Narrative is thus grounded in the ontological structure of the world, rather than growing out of the human experience of it. A sense of time, in this view, is less part of an interpretive landscape and more something that is simply "out there," waiting to be discovered by each individual as he learns his lot in life. "Narrative is not the work of poets, dramatists and novelists reflecting upon events which had no narrative order before one was imposed," MacIntyre writes.[16] Life, he holds, simply *has* narrative coherence, owing to the natural directedness (i.e., intentionality) of human action, rather than such coherence being a product of interpretation. Hermeneutics makes no such assumption about the structure of the world or of human behavior. It finds a sense of time only in human understanding of the world, not in the world itself, or even necessarily in human actions as such. Of course, it is possible that MacIntyre is right about the naturally directed quality of life—but the assumption is not necessary from a hermeneutic perspective and seems open to doubt.

Nor is the assumption a trivial one. MacIntyre's claim that Greek morality is superior to modern, rationalistic moralities rests on this assertion that life has a naturally narrative character. MacIntyre's quandary is this: he recognizes that no universal narrative for all human cultures can be found. Ancient Greeks lived in a web of stories about heroism and duty; medieval cultures had stories about sin, innocence, and Heaven and Hell; modern cultures have stories of accumulation, progress, and freedom. MacIntyre wants to assert the superiority of ancient forms of morality over modern ones, but what grounds, he asks, might there be for asserting the moral superiority of one story over another, if they are all simply confected by human will? Since none can be found, MacIntyre takes another route. He asserts that human life just *is* naturally story-bound, and Greek morality is superior because it *recognizes* this character of human action. All cultures are structured by narrative, he says, but Greek morality is the only morality that fully takes account of this fact; liberal morality certainly fails to do so.

MacIntyre's conclusions rely, then, in a strong sense on the premises of his version of speech-act theory: that human action has its start in intentions, and that intentions can only be formed inside cultural narratives. But MacIntyre cannot offer any true evidence for the assertion that speech-act theory correctly describes human actions. The assertion is based either on the traditional definitions of speech-act theory itself or, alternatively, on our own experiences of action. In the latter case, MacIntyre is bringing phenomenological evidence to bear on a question that demands an ontological answer. In other words, MacIntyre can, at best, assert that we experience life as a narrative (what hermeneutics maintains) rather than that it *has* narrative form. This latter assertion would be necessary to ground both speech-act theory and MacIntyre's claim for the superiority of ancient over modern morality.

Thus narratives, for MacIntyre, are important insofar as they present "a moral starting point," rather than an interpretive one.[17] Their existence is taken to be a given fact. And from an individual perspective, the most important narratives are those of the community in which one happens to find oneself born. They confront the individual as something separate to be experienced, rather than as something embedded in all experience. (MacIntyre's account thus partakes of something I shall later have cause to comment on in discussing Heidegger—a sense of "throwness.") MacIntyre believes that the narratives that guide our lives are those we are born into. Although not as extreme as Heidegger in his denial of authorship to individuals, MacIntyre denies that narratives can be radically rewritten. He finds our narrative nature to be a limit, rather than an opportunity.

One result of this approach is that it would seem an unlikely project to MacIntyre to search for a narrative element in texts of political theory. Narrative is something we soak up from community myths, not esoteric philosophy. Indeed, philosophy is largely to be reproached for not sufficiently valuing the narrative content of everyday life. Put most simply: MacIntyre views the narrative past of individuals as largely *given* in a way that my inquiry does not. For if our sense of time were as immovable as MacIntyre asserts, it would make little sense for political philosophers to attempt to reorient our temporal horizons in the way I claim they do. Yet philosophers *do* attempt to rewrite our narratives—they are not satisfied to be merely characters in a preordained plot. And whatever success they have in this endeavor constitutes an implicit criticism of MacIntyre's account.[18]

Clearly though, the differences set out here are ones of degree rather than of kind. One central point is the same: that narrative is central to human self-understanding. But this point leads to an important question: to what degree are living human beings prisoners of a history they did not create? This question deserves a more complex, and perhaps more political, answer than MacIntyre provides, I think, and this book seeks to address it. Here I can only indicate in a preliminary way my view that the idea of human beings as historical creatures has been wrongly associated (sometimes by opponents of this idea, sometimes by its defenders) with the idea that such beings live largely predetermined, prescripted lives. This has led to the view that, to the degree that we are historical, we are just so much less free. It is a mistake, I believe, to see these two values in a zero-sum competition. But to substantiate this position, it is necessary to see in more detail *how* history and narrative have come into play in the history of political theory. I believe we shall be better served by exploring the possibilities of narrative than by attempting to settle on some definitive ontology of time. When we return to some of these questions at the end of the book, we may no longer seek the same sort of answers from them.

The Political Narratives of Locke, Hegel, and Nietzsche

I have tried above to give a brief account of my approach to political theory in order to lay the groundwork for the investigations that form the bulk of this book. I argue that any political theory must contain a horizon of understanding that necessarily includes an element of time. This element often manifests itself as a "role" that is composed of both a sense of character and of the plot in which such a character is placed. Memory links such theoretical roles to human identity.

Thus far, then, I have been sketching an account of political theory that attempts to demonstrate the importance of its historical and narrative elements. But from a certain perspective, the attempt to establish the importance of history in abstract terms is ironic and futile. It is like trying to use mathematical formulae to justify poetry. That is why I have called my account merely a hypothesis. It can be a starting point and no more. It is only if I can use it to produce revealing readings of works of political philosophy that ring true that my approach will be validated, to whatever extent such validation is possible. To that end, I offer here a brief preview of the analyses that follow, as well as an explanation of what motivated my choice of subjects.

The philosophy of John Locke seemed to me to present one of the most significant challenges to my interpretive stance and, therefore, one of the best proving grounds. I have thus chosen to address it first (in Part I). There are many opinions about Locke's philosophy, but until recently these perspectives were united in their opposition to placing any weight on narrative elements in his writings.[19] Indeed, whether Locke is feted or pilloried for fathering liberal political theory, it is usually agreed that what he bequeathed us was a reasoned, abstract defense of a liberal system of government that rested on a postulate of natural rights. Narrative elements, if acknowledged, are usually treated as unwelcome obiter dicta. My view is the opposite: It is precisely Locke's narrative wherein his deepest secrets lie, and it is only by attending to them that we shall arrive at a fuller understanding of Locke's politics.[20]

In contrast to the prevailing view, I argue that what Locke has handed down to us is a narrative of government that locates its readers in a particular story as important characters. Locke's sense of character lies in the economistic vocabulary that grounds his discussions both of the mind and of the body politic. His consistent use of metaphors of money and contract creates a political actor with a distinctive outlook. The plot of the *Second Treatise of Government* places Locke's new characters in a story of government's rise and fall, leaving to them the role of inheritors, whose part in the drama is to renew a contractual trust through the act of revolution. This revolutionary role depends both on the economistic "character" of Locke's philosophy and on the plot against his liberty on the part of a greedy monarch.

In developing this interpretation of Locke, I want to make plausible my approach to political theory in the context of a "hard case"—that is, a text where the narrative elements are not obvious. If I dealt exclusively with writers such as Hegel and Nietzsche, who often make history the focus of their philosophy, I might be justly accused of choosing my subjects to suit my method. Since I want to avoid this immediate objection, it seems clear that I ought to explore either Locke or someone much like him (that is, someone who is commonly thought not to focus on history). That would be reason enough for Locke to appear and to appear first—but there is a further purpose. In bringing to light the narrative that lurks beneath the more familiar Lockean theory of property, rights, and revolution, I want to emphasize again that the relationship between history and liberal philosophy is not an either/or proposition. Emphasizing narrative does not mean approving of one kind of philosophy (or philosopher) rather than another. It often means appreciating lesser-known voices in books we are already familiar with.[21]

Such is also the goal in my examination of Friedrich Nietzsche's philosophy in Part II. There the key role appears to us directly in the figure of Zarathustra. But the content of this character is not to be found only in the book that bears his name. The overlap of character and plot that I spoke of earlier reaches its zenith, in some ways, in Zarathustra. The vocabulary of dreams, interpretation, creativity, and violence that I explore is, however, drawn from a wide range of Nietzsche's texts, although every element of it is, in some ways, an element of Zarathustra's character. The plot that I focus on is that contained in *On the Genealogy of Morals*: it deploys this vocabulary in a brutal history of "man's" separation from the animals and his subsequent "humanization" through an unbroken chain of violence. The focus of this plot is often on time itself—that is, on the human conception of past, present, and future.

So Nietzsche's philosophy, in my interpretation, is often concerned with the same questions that concern this inquiry as a whole. It will come as no surprise to the reader, then, that I did not begin my examination of Nietzsche in search of an "example" to validate my approach. It was rather in my reaction to Nietzsche that this work had its origins; and this special connection between Nietzsche and my project's overarching goals is reflected in the discussion. It is in Nietzsche's narrative, in his review of past, present, and future, that we find perhaps the starkest account of the alternatives facing a philosophy that takes the question of time seriously. The phrase "dancing in chains," which Nietzsche applies to Homer (*WS* 140) can be taken as shorthand for the response to such a question that Nietzsche deems most appropriate.

This is in part why I have chosen to address Nietzsche's work out of the order that ordinary chronology would suggest. Since Nietzsche is central to this inquiry, I have placed an examination of his views in the central position. The conclusion of this review is also central: that neither human memory in general nor any of our specific memories is natural in any sense. Rather, they are themselves products of history. It is through Nietzsche's discussion of the human condition, then, that we can learn the reason why Gauguin's three questions remain compelling, why it is that memory is often the object of politics and political theory. The analysis of Nietzsche is thus more complicated than that of Locke. In attending to questions of narrative here, we not only learn more about Nietzsche, but also about narrative itself.

Finally, it will come as no surprise that an inquiry concerned with the role of historical argument in political theory should look into the philosophy of G. W. F. Hegel. I hope, however, that my approach to Hegel, in Part III, will yield some unexpected conclusions. For while the plot of Hegel's narrative lies on the surface of his writings, in plain view, the *role* he describes to his readers is, I believe, a great deal more complicated than some simplistic interpretations of the *Philosophy of History* would have it. Indeed, I find that by turning to the lectures on the history of art, known as the *Aesthetics*, we get a much better sense of the vocabulary that grounds Hegel's grand narrative. The project of this section is thus more limited than those of the previous ones. Since less effort needs to be expended in reconstructing Hegelian history, the focus is largely on reassessing it. The outlines of that history are familiar to any student of political theory, but it takes on a very different coloration when viewed through the lens of the *Aesthetics*. Understanding the vocabulary of shape and beauty gives more substance to Hegel's past and present but, curiously, at the same time, denies that very substance to his future. Indeed, it is precisely on the question of the future (or the lack of one) that Hegel's narrative will be shown to differ from those of Locke and Nietzsche. The lack of a future is the largest disappointment in the plot of this most historical philosopher. For, as one works one's way through these three philosophers, the question of the future looms larger and larger.

Just as it might have been assumed that an approach to political theory centered on history would have little to say about Locke, it could also have been assumed that such an approach was, inevitably, "Hegelian." This is decidedly not the case. Although my time-centered approach might be expected to find the most in Hegel, my actual conclusion is that his theory is deficient in narrative resources. But the deficiency only becomes clear in comparison to what attention to historical argument can unearth in theorists such as Locke and Nietzsche.

That is one reason why Hegel's history is considered only after these other philosophies. Another stems from Hegel's philosophy itself: it asks to be taken last. That is, it conceives itself to mark a certain kind of culmination. So it seemed most appropriate to me to consider questions of the end *at* the end. At the same time, I hope that the attention paid to narrative will shed light on both the dangers and the possibilities of Hegel's philosophy of history. Political theorists have shied away too much from the subject of history, I feel, for fear of being tagged with the label "Hegelian," whose implications some find unsavory. There is much for a political theorist to learn about history from Hegel—but the latter holds no monopoly on the subject.

Breaking up the expected sequence of these philosophers, then, has several advantages. First, it points out to the reader how common and unstated prejudices about time are important in our automatic ordering of the world. The proper order, we assume until told otherwise, is the order the calendar provides. There is nothing wrong with this; the calendar is an excellent tool for organizing a history of political thought. It is just that we do not normally think of the calendar as a mere tool reflecting assumptions about time—we think of it as a marker of a basic reality. I would not discard such a tool for no reason—nor do I seek merely to make the (rather trivial) point that such assumptions are everywhere and can be disrupted whenever aesthetic or political concerns so dictate. But it *is* one of my central concerns here (one I draw from Nietzsche) that the organization of time is *not* a neutral background on which history may be mapped. The presentation of time, I argue, is precisely what is often up for grabs in political theory. So we should not accept the given chronology of political thought when there is good reason to amend it.

There is one further point to be made. All three theorists, I argue, engage in the politics of memory. They both use memory as a political tool and fear the use of such tools by others. But the cases of Hegel and Nietzsche differ in an important way from that of Locke. With these two, we shall be dealing, in part, with what I call the structural threats present in the politics of memory. We shall be dealing, among other things, with the possibility of the two extreme positions of memory: perfect recollection and complete amnesia. While the content of memory plays an important role in its political danger and power, these structural limits on the mnemonic represent special cases, which require particular attention. With Locke, we shall be dealing with the more ordinary, and therefore more common, politics of memory. The case of Locke might, for that reason, seem less dramatic than those of Hegel and Nietzsche, but just because of its quotidian nature, it should be equally interesting.

The Role of the Future

The role of the future is key to the attempt to explore the political implications of a sense of time, because, despite the white-hot intensity that often characterizes political debate about the past, Gauguin's last "name" ("Where are we going") is the most political.

In the revival of interest in narrative that has taken place in historiography and literary theory, writers have returned, almost obsessively, to Aristotle's account of narrative in the *Poetics*.[22] There Aristotle says, quite simply, that a narrative, to be whole, must have a beginning, a middle, and an end (1450b). The interpretations in this inquiry challenge that model. Or, at least, they challenge the assumption that such a completeness—"the sense of an ending," it has been called—is an important quality in a narrative.[23] For from Aristotle's perspective, some of the stories told here would seem radically incomplete. And yet, their incompleteness may be seen as one of the most attractive things about them. A narrative that ends is without a future. However satisfying the tying up of all plotlines and the fade-to-black may be at the close of a film, in politics, the idea of a final end point can be a dangerous one. To imagine a political narrative that ends may be to imagine a too-perfect satisfaction with the present and therefore an end to politics as the realm of conflict, change, and growth. An open-ended future, the lack of an end, may be as much an attractive feature in political theory as it is a shortcoming in fictions. At the very least, we should take care that an attention to narrative in political theory does not lead to a wholesale substitution of aesthetic values for political ones. The use of a narrative vocabulary is not meant to imply that all politics is simply theater and meant to be judged as such.

The precise task of the political theorist comes into sharper focus here. Whatever the broad affinity between narrative and knowledge indicated above, the philosophers studied here do not attempt grossly to equate the two. In fact, they undertake a much narrower project. They endeavor, in some sense, to design new plots for history. Now *plot* is a word with two clear meanings in English. It indicates, on the one hand, merely an ordering of things, whether on a chart or in a play. But a plot may also be a conspiracy, an intrigue, a scheme, an underground plan with certain steps designed to bring about a desired state of affairs. Political theory, I think, always partakes to some extent of this second meaning. Political theorists are all, in some sense, "plotters." In reaccounting for the past, a philosopher attempts to hatch a plot that is a surreptitious attempt to control the future. Citizens are cast in parts without their consent. Whether the intrigue succeeds depends on whether those citizens take up the roles a political theory casts them in: it depends, that is, on whether they join the plot.

Political theorists are plotters, then, in both senses of the word. They plot passively, as recorders of events; but they plot actively as well, with hidden or not-so-hidden plans for tomorrow. They describe politics with a sense of time—but also with the aim of altering the future. And these are not really two distinct projects but rather two ways of looking at one and the same activity. The political plots they write include, not just their sense of the course of past events, but also what they anticipate will come. Strictly speaking then, in scripting a conclusion to their story, they must know that in doing so, they offer a hope and nothing more. Perhaps the political theorist's sense of plot is not captured by Aristotle but rather by Ludwig Wittgenstein when he writes: "A plan as such is something unsatisfied. (Like a wish, an expectation, a suspicion, and so on.)"[24]

Political theory is not *of* the future—it is merely about it. The connection lies in the plotting character of the political theorist. The character who plots often plays a special role in dramatic productions. I think it is no less true that political theorists can also play a small but crucial part in actual history and politics—because of their special status as characters who plot. Plots are not incomplete when they lack endings, as Aristotle thought; unfinished plots are simply another kind of story. And a plot that has not yet been carried out retains its status as a threat in a way a completed story cannot. Political theory that plots contains an implicit challenge to the status quo that no well-ended drama can.

Political theory as narrative does not lose a critical capacity that it has when in the form of seemingly timeless principles. Its ability to disturb an unjust peace is just as strong as narrative—and it may even speak more directly to common politics in that form. It has been a continuing claim of privilege made on behalf of many modern philosophies (exemplified by various modern liberalisms, but certainly not limited to them) that the atemporal, Archimedian point from which they reason affords a critical moral perspective that no narrative writing can achieve. I do not believe this is the case, but I shall withhold extended reflection until Chapter 7, by which point the reader will have accumulated much of the evidence on this point contained in the interpretations of particular narrative thinkers. As to those who have recently suggested that all such plotting, indeed narrative as such, must issue in a kind of futility (Derrida in particular comes to mind here), my response is also contained at the end of the book.

Hatching a plot, then, is not executing it. That a political theorist qua theorist leaves to others.[25] The plot may only be carried out years or centuries after the theorist's death, or never. But the task is challenging enough. Political theorists are both active and passive plotters.

How complete a determination of the future should we expect, or desire, from a work of political theory? Is political theory like a dramatic performance, in which a lack of ending disappoints its audience?[26] Surely, it is in the future of the role a political theorist sketches out for his reader that he plots most actively. For whatever the retelling of the past, it is only the future that a political theorist (unless severely deluded) can hope to change. Re-presenting the past, altering its import, is not the same thing as changing events. The theorist has power over the past, but not a time machine. Whatever "prescription" a narrative political theory contains is held in its image of the future—but a future that is seen to flow from the past.

This inquiry reveals two interesting features of the responses that philosophers have given here. First, political theories need not "end" in the way Aristotle says a good narrative must end. To say that a narrative must end in order to be "complete" is unnecessarily to proscribe certain forms of story as unattractive. One of the conclusions of this inquiry is that narratives can be differentiated precisely on the grounds of how thoroughly they end. I occasionally refer to narratives that do not completely conclude as "open" and to others as "closed." All I mean to indicate by this is that some stories do not give a fully determined image of the future, while others do. I do *not* mean that some "open" narratives leave the future completely undecided. It is only a matter of painting a future with options or without. I argue in the conclusion that it is "open" narratives (incomplete from the Aristotelian standpoint), that make the most attractive political theories. Closed narratives, which Aristotle thought made for the most satisfying tragic theater, make perhaps the worst political theory. If a political theory were to end in the way that a drama must, the closing curtain would darken the entire world of politics. Equating politics and theater can be politically disastrous.

Second, and more fundamentally, the question of the future is not separate from that of the past. Even if my conclusion on the first point is not fully conceded, I hope the reader will accept that this inquiry has another purpose: pointing out the importance of recollection in the projection of the future. That is, I am trying to account for why Gauguin's three questions form a coherent set and not a random assemblage. The coherence does not come from metaphysical notions of the unity of time; rather, it derives from the project itself: the goal of recalling the past in order to care for the future. What the long chapters in this inquiry show, as examples, is that caring about the future, thinking about what we are, *means* being concerned about the past. In the particular theorists I discuss, this sort of care often emerges as a question of redemption. Whether offered in a strictly legal or a more mythical sense, the possibility of redeeming the past can be a temptation, a goal, a need, or a prize, but sometimes also a mirage of the politics of the future.

It might be thought that, in general, the very notion of redemption is so inherently religious that to read political theory in this way is to substitute Theory for the Book, and not in a healthy way either. But I prefer to look at these questions differently. It seems to me that we think of certain concepts, like redemption, as religious, not so much because of any inherent quality they possess as because modern philosophy has abandoned some fields of inquiry and left religion without rival there—the question of time is foremost among these. But to wonder about the meaning of time is a fundamentally *human* preoccupation, not necessarily a religious one, even if modern philosophy often abjures it. The question is generic and precedes the answers to it supplied by religion, answers that transform it in popular understanding into a "religious" question.[27] To reexamine the question without becoming religious in the process is difficult then, but not impossible and, I contend, some of the philosophers under discussion have given us great aid in this area.

Where the religious sense of *redemption* means almost "to rescue out of time," the term is used here to mean something quite different from the flight from temporality that this implies. *Redemption* can also mean "to buy back," "to ransom," and, hence, "to free." In the context of narrative political theory, this act can take on the sense of "to make good on the debts of the past" or even "to rescue the past by means of the future," with the implied connection to freedom taking on a political rather than a religious meaning. It is in this sense, I argue, that the question of time in politics can issue in a notion of redemption distinct from its religious meaning (one resolutely *within* time), even if it cannot shake all of the connotations that the term implies. The idea of redemption, then, is the tool a narrator can employ (as effectively as any timeless truths) to confront political evil. I address this theme more directly in the concluding chapters.

Again: any attempt to "prove" the importance of the past abstractly, without example, would always be self-defeating in some sense. That is why I have given a rather terse account of the connection between the three questions. I am only trying to point out that it makes sense to think of these terms together; that it makes sense in thinking about politics and the future to think about history or the past. Most of all I want to say (to repeat my earlier phrasing) that the project of political theory is not so much to reform our morals as it is to reform our memories.

PART I

John Locke

I have made this, I have forgotten
And remember.
The rigging weak and canvas rotten
Between one June and another September.
　　　—T. S. Eliot, "Marina"

CHAPTER I

A World Without Dreams

All the permanent—that is only a parable. And the poets lie too
much. It is of time and becoming that the best parables should speak.
—Friedrich Nietzsche, *Thus Spoke Zarathustra*

John Locke is the most important liberal theorist of revolution. Obliquely,
but unmistakably, he counseled the men of his time to rise up against unjust
authority and renew the rights of the people. We often lose sight of this amid
the intricacies of his theory of property or the arcane arguments about the
King's prerogative. Modern interpreters seem bent on confining Locke's revolutionary tendencies—either shutting them away with seventeenth-century
politics or burying them beneath the structure of Locke's system of government.[1] But his continuous appeal, I argue here, cannot be understood in either
of these responses. Rather, it is by attending to Locke's narrative that we can
learn the source of his theory's power.

I first examine Locke's model of experience in his epistemological writings and then, armed with an understanding of the typical Lockean "character," return to the *Second Treatise of Government* to describe its narrative of
revolution.[2] Locke confronts a memory that supports the status quo and attempts to replace it with one that leads to revolt. His "plot" is one that clearly
partakes of both meanings of that term: it is an organization of events—but it
is also an intrigue and a scheme to rescue the future from those who hold it
prisoner with their account of the past.

The memory he offers his readers and the revolution into which he projects them as the next chapter of their story contains a particular promise—a
promise of redemption. It is not a Christian redemption, to be sure (although
Locke had deeply held Christian beliefs), but a distinctly modern one. It is a

redemption of past generations on the grounds of a contract they long ago entered into. If this recovery seems short on moral salvation and relies too much on fiduciary duty, it is nonetheless what draws us to Locke long after the particular conflicts that motivated his writings have ceased to be relevant. His narrative functions as a political argument for revolution, but it is not, for that reason, merely seventeenth-century ideology.

In the *Essay on Human Understanding* and elsewhere, Locke develops an approach to human character that is at the same time theistic, economic, and legal. This leads him to describe each aspect of life in terms of "labor" and "contracts." Metaphors of economic activity allow Locke to present a consistent account of humanity, beginning with our innermost thoughts and proceeding to family life, religion, and political association. When he turns to politics, he does not simply present an ideal of government to aspire to; rather, he gives a narrative of contracts that describes the history of government. With this reading, I hope to contest long-held assumptions about the relation of history and theory in Locke. Rather than history providing evidence for a theory, it is the philosophy that supplies the vocabulary for a narrative.

In other words, it is *not* the case that the State of Nature is simply an abstract construct for determining what one ought to do in a situation of total freedom, where tales of American Indians then provide a verification that the construction is valid. Instead, it is the concept of contracts themselves, and the possibility of their redemption that make possible the narrative progression that takes place in the *Second Treatise*. The concept of contract is not just an apt metaphor that Locke hit upon to signify any human agreement. He thinks, rather, that we are contracting beings in a deep way. And he thinks that contracts we have already made bind the past to the future. While a time of pure freedom did perhaps once exist, it is not Locke's goal to return us to that freedom. Rather, he attempts to remind us of the obligations we have already incurred and the titles we already hold—obligations and titles that will only be enforced and upheld if we remember to do so. He attempts, in other words, to bring to light a hidden plot and remind us of the roles we are already playing within it.

In exploring Locke's economistic vocabulary, then, I shall be laying the groundwork for his narrative by exploring the kind of character that populates his story, as well as the world they inhabit. But the vocabulary does not completely ground the narrative. As I indicated in the Introduction, plot and character are always intertwined. In this case, the notion of contract, with its implied conception of past and future (i.e., contracts presuppose the passage of time) cannot simply be inserted into a story. It already contains a narrative element in itself. (I return to this problem below.) Nevertheless, it seems easiest to begin with Locke's vocabulary and then proceed to his history.

The Labor of Thinking

Locke begins the *Essay* with a determined assault on the notion of "innate ideas." Against the scholastics who argued that people were born with certain principles of religion or truth ingrained, Locke maintained that an infant's mind was like "white Paper" (*E* 2.1.2). He took several hundred pages to make this point, advancing a battery of arguments that are complementary, if not entirely cohesive. His reasoning is logical or empirical as suits his purpose. Even as he moves on to other subjects, he continues to fight a rearguard action against the theory of innate ideas and never misses an opportunity to disparage those who adhere to it.

The purpose of this attack emerges only slowly: it is a separation of the mind of man from the mind of God. This parting of ways, although it does not determine the shape of Locke's other writings, informs all of them. This separation is meant to liberate human reason for its own work.[3] It is not a denial of divine wisdom; it merely denies a particular form of access to that wisdom. Likewise, the separation does not deny the existence of God, merely a certain way of knowing him and, hence, a certain kind of divine guidance. Indeed, as we shall see, the continued presence of God is vital to other elements of Locke's political theory. But it never overwhelms the independence of the human mind.

The separation of minds also liberates Locke to reconnect knowledge and narrative in a manner that the theory of innate ideas had forbidden. If ideas were innate, then they had a timeless, unchanging quality. Whereas, if ideas are not innate then they can only appear in time and over time—not all at once but in some order, development, or plot. As we shall see below, Locke's account of education provides just such an order. Rebutting the theory of innate ideas, then, not only liberates Locke to develop a more empirical psychology but also enables him to give a diachronic, narrative element to his account of knowledge and self.

The unimprinted mind completes a particular understanding of the idea that human beings are created in God's image. Locke uses the metaphor of labor to describe both human and divine creativity. A free mind allows man to be a creator as well as God. It is well known that Locke always referred to men as the "Workmanship" of God (e.g., *2T* 6). As we examine the theory Locke replaced that of innate ideas with, working by what he called "Historical, plain Method" (*E* 1.1.2), we shall see him repeat this image for the products of the human mind. Ideas are the product of *human* workmanship. If it is not strictly physical labor, it is labor nonetheless. (Was God's labor in creating the world, after all, strictly physical?) The human mind, Locke holds, works in the same manner as the body.[4] But labor is only the starting point of the thought process. Locke describes this process as a complete economic system—in fact, as a peculiarly commercial system. As Locke sets out to describe his alternative psychology, he is trying to describe how the cupboard of our mind is stocked: "How comes it to be furnished? Whence comes it by that vast Store, which the busy and boundless Fancy of Man has painted on it, with an almost endless variety? Whence has it all the materials of Reason and Knowledge? To this I answer, in one word, from *Experience*" (*E* 2.1.2).

Just as God breathes life into a handful of dust, so do we come to animate the world around us by *working* on it. Although there are occasional artistic shades to Locke's metaphors, he hardly ever exploits them. (His notion of labor, we shall see below, is too Calvinist for that.) We take the simple ideas with which nature provides us, he writes, and we fashion them into our own product: "General and abstract ideas . . . are the Workmanship of the Mind" (*E* 4.12.3; cf. 2.22.1). Here Locke repeats the metaphor of labor used to characterize God's efforts in the Creation. Nor does he hesitate to carry this thought to its conclusion. Our thoughts are our own; God does not suggest them to us. In our own minor way, we possess the life-giving power of the Deity. "Creatures" spring from our labor as they did from God's: "No body can doubt, but that these Ideas of mixed Modes, are made by a voluntary Collection of Ideas put together in the Mind, independent from any Original Patterns in Nature. . . . Whereby it is plain, how much *the sorts of mixed Modes are the Creatures of the Understanding*" (*E* 3.5.5; cf. 3.3.12–14).

The image of the laboring mind pervades the *Essay* and forms the basis of both its religious and political conclusions. Only the latter receive attention here. But it is important to note that the separation of human and divine thought is not necessarily an insult to God. Indeed, for Locke it is the only way to spare man the incongruence of taking "Monsters lodged in his own brain, for the Images of the Deity, and the Workmanship of his Hands" (*E* 1.3.26). Our bodies and our brains are God's work, but not the thoughts they contain, whether good or evil. Nor does the metaphorical continuity necessarily mean that humans are exalted as gods or put on a par with the Deity. It is simply a way of being faithful to the notion that man is made in the image of God. Although we may be poor copies with diminished capacities, still, our powers are of the same *type*.

The parallel of mind and economy goes beyond that of thought and labor. The products of thought have many of the qualities associated with those

of labor. Once we have formed complex ideas from the raw materials provided by our senses, the finished products form a capital stock on which we
can draw. Thus, in the *Essay*, memory is characterized as a "Store-house." The
mind being in need of "a Repository, to lay up those Ideas, which at another
time it might have *use* of" (*E* 2.10.2). Later I argue that the capitalization of
thought products requires a direct parallel between ideas and money and even
between words and coins. For now, it is sufficient to note that the metaphor of
labor for thinking is not simply illustrative but follows every permutation of
Locke's argument. Thus, for example, in exhorting us to expand the frontiers
of knowledge, he urges "Industry and Labor of Thought" (*E* 4.3.6). The
independence of the human mind from the thoughts of God and our ability to
produce ideas through labor also explains the great stress that Locke puts on
education (*STCE* 1). Economy has replaced divinity as the model of mind.
Thinking involves neither flashes of insight or transcendence nor, on the
other hand, useless musings. Rather, Locke makes the mind appear as an
English shopkeeper, steadily building up a stock of goods by daily effort:

> The senses at first let in particular Ideas, and furnish the yet empty Cabinet: And
> the Mind, by degrees growing familiar with some of them, they are lodged in
> the Memory, and Names got to them. . . . In this manner the Mind comes to be
> furnished with Ideas and Language, the Materials about which to exercise its
> discursive Faculty: And the use of Reason becomes daily more visible, as these
> Materials, that give it Employment, increase. (*E* 1.2.15)

Interpreters of Locke have split rather sharply between those stressing the
role of labor (Leo Strauss and C. B. Macpherson) and those who emphasize
Locke's religious commitments (John Dunn and James Tully). Apparently, all
of these writers feel that there is some inherent tension between God and
labor, and that were Locke truly Christian, he could not have countenanced
the commercial world. But there seems no particular reason for this to be so.
If there were no other evidence, the term *workmanship* by itself ought to
indicate that, for Locke, *God labors*. If that disturbs our notions of divinity, it is
hardly Locke's fault.[5]

The Labor of Living

Locke's description of thought as labor forces us to consider his notion of
labor more thoroughly as a vital element of the Lockean character. It is
important, in this context, not to map our own idea of labor onto a different
understanding of it.[6] We commonly use labor as a counterpoint, almost an
antonym, to thought. This sense is not entirely absent in Locke. Indeed, he

often seems to think that those who labor in the fields will have little or no time to reflect on higher matters.[7] But his use of the economic metaphor for the mind does not allow this separation to be very thorough. Just as human labor is like divine Workmanship, so, for Locke, there is a strict continuity between the physical and mental labor of humans: "This shows Man's Power and its way of Operation to be muchwhat the same [sic] in the Material and Intellectual World. For the Materials in both being such as he has no power over, either to make or destroy, all that Man can do is either to unite them together or set them by one another, or wholly separate them" (E 2.12.1).

It is the mental and, as we shall see, moral elements of labor that interest Locke, rather than the purely physical. Locke's use of labor as a metaphor for thought should not lead us to conclude too quickly that his notion of work is strictly mechanical. The connection of thought to labor is not simply one-way.[8] We can best understand his approach to labor through the use of the well-worn concept of "the Protestant ethic." Rather than driving him from religion, Locke's notion of labor binds him ever more tightly to it. Weber's description of a set of religious beliefs and practices that prescribe self-denial and hard work for otherworldly rewards is readily discernible in Locke.[9] It appears most unabashedly in his book on education.

Some Thoughts Concerning Education, like some other Lockean works, takes the form of a letter to a friend. Although little read now, it was received quite seriously at the time of its publication (1694) and for some period thereafter. In composing *Emile*, Rousseau took himself to be responding (quite critically) to an agenda that Locke had set.[10] Only a third of Locke's essay is concerned with what we would now call formal education, and these pages come at the end. The first two-thirds are concerned with a kind of physical, social, and moral training that prepares one for the sort of existence described in the *Essay* and the *Two Treatises*.[11] Rather than book learning, it is the conditioning of the body and spirit that most concerns Locke. The best Lockean character is one who has endured (for an endurance it surely is) this sort of education and had his mental habits formed by it. Having established that ideas are not innate, Locke here prescribes what he takes to be the best temporal sequence for their creation. The fact that ideas can only be acquired over time ensures that Locke's prototypical character cannot emerge at once but requires an educational narrative.

It is often the only thing remembered about this book that it criticizes corporal punishment and cruelty toward children. So it does. But even a brief perusal of Locke's ideal education will find it to be quite harsh. In a child's physical education, he notes with some satisfaction that "the body may be brought to bear almost anything" (STCE 9). Children are not to be fed rich or tasty foods; indeed, if their fare is bland and dry, so much the better! (*STCE* 13–15). Although children shall be allowed to sleep, they should not enjoy it overmuch: "Let his bed be hard. . . . Hard lodging strengthens the parts" (*STCE* 22). Moral education, too, seems mostly to consist of endurance tests. Aristotle would have children become brave through imitation (*Nicomachean Ethics* 1103b). But where Locke repeats this advice, he gives it an ascetic gloss: "the way to harden and fortify children against fear and danger, is to accustom them to suffer pain" (*STCE* 115). Although milder in some respects than his contemporaries', Locke's regimen is strenuous and unforgiving—and it relies on the principle that this severity is necessary to foster good morals.

The purpose of this toughening is also recognizably ascetic. The virtue of self-denial is something Locke never doubts. When he condemns slavery as a political arrangement, he does not distinguish sharply between being a slave to a master and being a slave to one's own vices.[12] Among his few articles of faith, asceticism is prominent: "Whoever will list himself under the banner of Christ, must, in the first place, and above all things, make war upon his own lusts and vices" (*LT1* 6). This belief fed back into education, and from there to economics and politics.

For Locke, this is more education of the mind than of the body. Denial of desires is an intellectual ability as well as a physical one. And naturally so; otherwise it could hardly be considered a virtue. Labor is moral because it is opposed, not to thought, but to sin: "As the strength of the body lies chiefly in being able to endure hardships, so also does that of the mind. And the great principle and foundation of all virtue and worth is placed in this, that a man is able to deny himself his own desires, cross his own inclinations, and purely follow what reason directs as best, though the appetite lean the other way" (*STCE* 33).

Here Locke cannot cleanly separate mind and body when he considers where their virtues lie. What matters most is the suppression of vice. "Even from their very cradles," he says, children should be conditioned to this habit of self-denial. What the body does at the direction of another when young, the adult mind will practice on itself when older (*STCE* 38). Virtue is not fun. It is a labor (not rewarding work but toilsome effort) to suppress one's appetites. For a child, both body and mind need to be harnessed to such labor—with the goal that, as an adult, each person's mind will be able to harness its own body in the same way.

That this Protestant ethic of asceticism is connected to Locke's more strictly economic notion of labor is clear from the account of virtue in labor that appears in his economic writings.[13] Again and again, he writes of the financial rewards that result from industriousness and frugality (and not, say, genius or entrepreneurial daring). The opposite of these virtues is taken to be not mere laziness, but a self-indulgence that is morally censurable. In the first of his three tracts on money, Locke tells the tale of an upright and ascetic father who builds up a vast estate only to bequeath it to a wrongly spoiled (i.e., poorly educated) son. The young man's taste for fancy food, drink, and entertainment doom his inheritance: "This will tumble him down the hill the faster, and the stock, which the industry, frugality, and good order of his father had laid up, will be quickly brought to an end, and he fast in prison" (*SCM* 20). Material rewards accrue to the worldly, laboring ascetic. And they cannot even be maintained, much less increased, by the self-indulgent, no matter how bright or bold.

This distribution of riches according to moral worth is not limited to the individual level. It is, remarkably enough, the principle upon which Locke develops his ideas of international economics. Although it is easy enough to label his support of free trade "capitalist," it should also be noted who he thinks will win the contest of international competition. Not the strongest or the cleverest, but simply the most virtuous, where virtue is strictly defined as asceticism:

> Nature has bestowed mines on several parts of the world: but their riches are only for the industrious and frugal. Whomsoever else they visit, it is with the diligent and sober only they stay; and if the virtue and provident way of living of our ancestors (content with our native conveniences of life, without the costly itch after the materials of pride and luxury from abroad) were brought in fashion and countenance again amongst us; this alone would do more to keep and increase our wealth and enrich our land, than all our paper helps. (*SCM* 72; cf. 53–54)[14]

So, if Locke can be said to commercialize thought; he can be said equally to intellectualize commerce, and indeed, to moralize it. This crossing of mind and labor is the foundation on which the Lockean model of experience is built. Labor has a moral aspect and commerce, as the social result of labor, takes on that aspect as well. Indeed, it is a rather peculiar notion of commerce that receives Locke's blessing. An examination of it will eventually lead us to a description of political experiences that forms the basis for Locke's narrative in the *Second Treatise*. The man of labor is the main character of that story.[15] But even in Locke's epistemological works, the narrative element of this character has already appeared. It is not just that Locke tells little fables about the virtuous man—it is that such a person cannot be created with innate, virtuous ideas. His knowledge, his very self, is already the product of an educational narrative. The next step in our analysis is to develop this understanding of mind and labor into a general measure of worldly matters. We need, in other words, to lay out the setting in which the plot unfolds.

Usefulness, or, The Gray World

Locke is an important ancestor to the utilitarians. His is not a theory of utility, however, but a theory of usefulness. I call it "usefulness" because it is only partially captured by the opposition of pleasure and pain or cost and benefit that grounds utilitarianism. To this Locke adds his special understanding of labor and the mind within the ascetic framework. In order to be useful, it is not enough for something to be simply helpful or pleasurable. Rather, it must have come by its pleasant nature in the right sort of way—that is, by the application of honest labor. For something to possess usefulness, it must be the product of or capable of *use*. There are no passive pleasures in Locke's universe, at least no rightful ones. Usefulness is the amalgamation of utility with the work ethic. There is a gulf between interpreters who insist that Locke is a quasi-utilitarian, such as Karen Iversen Vaughn, and those such as Richard Ashcraft or James Tully who believe Locke's natural-law commitments prevent his acceptance of the individualistic or hedonistic elements of utilitarianism (see n. 13). The identification of usefulness as a value that, for Locke, has elements of both utility and asceticism is, I believe, the best way to settle this interpretive conflict. The divide between these views is much more a result of different interpretive frameworks than of any confusion in Locke's texts. From a modern perspective, usefulness may mix individual and communitarian elements illegitimately, but Locke found the mixture perfectly sensible, just as he did the notion of a God who labors. While usefulness may not be fully coherent as a moral doctrine, it is important because it is the measure of the universe within which Locke's narrative takes place. The question of usefulness is one that Locke's characters constantly pose to one another, as well as to the world itself.

In fact, Locke develops usefulness from a moral code into a measure of being (that is, something like an ontology). Since he believes himself to have found the true morality in usefulness—and since he cannot conceive that God would have created a world in violation of such a morality—he deploys usefulness against fantasy. To him, the latter is a useless element of the world. What exists must be useful. What is useless cannot exist. This is his main argument against innate ideas: not that they are impossible, but that they are useless. And useless mental fixtures we cannot suppose any to be; God would never have made them: "Principles not innate, because of little use, or little certainty: . . . I am fully persuaded, that the infinitely Wise God made all things in perfect Wisdom, [and] cannot satisfy myself, why he should be supposed to print upon the minds of Men, some universal Principles; whereof those *that* are pretended innate, and *concern Speculation, are of no great use; and those that concern Practice, not self-evident*" (*E* 1.4.21).

He relies on this theory in the question of language as well. When, later in the *Essay*, he argues for a form of nominalism, against the notion that words represent essences, usefulness again serves as both measure and weapon. Such essences, Locke says, would be "so *wholly useless*, and unserviceable to any part of our Knowledge, that that alone were sufficient, to make us lay it by" (*E* 3.3.17). Languages arise not from a correspondence of words to essences but from "the common use of the people" (*STCE* 168). Whatever humans have no use for, they give no name to, and it passes silently through the world (*E* 2.18.7). Locke even goes so far as to denounce poetry and poets as useless words and people, respectively. He counsels against raising children to be poets and counts it a failure when a child is determined for poetry against all efforts to the contrary (*STCE* 174; cf. 94). While the application of the standard of usefulness to language will, in fact, form the basis for his staunch defense of liberty, we must at least note here that it makes for a humorless and literal-minded account of speech, devoid of most of what we would call the pleasures of human discourse. Again, "useful" for Locke means both that something has utility *and* that it is the product of labor. And given Locke's joyless account of labor, it is not surprising that it results in a particularly grim ontology, such that poetry, in being useless, is morally censurable. "Labor" may include mental labor, but not the work of the poet. The gray setting of Locke's story is described by this idea of usefulness. He uses the concept as a moral caliper—both as a measure *and* as a tool to sketch the world.

It is much the same in Locke's description of the senses. While the harsh, simple measure of usefulness allows Locke to dispense with a lot of convoluted scholastic reasoning about the senses (large segments of the *Essay* are devoted to attacks on such earlier views), it is only at great cost to his sympathy for the human condition. Our senses are not for our pleasure but for our use: "The infinite wise Contriver of us . . . hath fitted our Senses, Faculties and Organs, to the Conveniences of Life, and the Business we have to do here. We are able, by our Senses, to know and distinguish things; and to examine them so far, as to apply them to our Uses" (*E* 2.23.12; cf. 2.9.13).

Our senses are exactly suited to our needs. If our eyes could be made more powerful, a man ought not to desire it "if such an acute Sight would not serve to conduct him to the Market and Exchange" (*E* 2.23.12). That such a sight could, say, reveal greater beauties and complexities in the universe does not count for anything here, unless it pays. Locke's characters inhabit a terribly colorless world and, like Dorothy in *The Wizard of Oz*, are much better suited to such a black-and-white reality, for that is all they can see.

If Locke can be said to demean our outer sight, he almost totally denies an inner one. The measurement of dreams by the standard of usefulness is one of the most striking ways in which the *Essay* flattens all experience onto a single axis and bleaches it of color. The subject of dreams frustrates Locke. He returns to it more than once, perhaps aware that none of his accounts are fully satisfactory. He compares dreams to reflections in a mirror, where images appear and then disappear with nothing remaining of them. No improvement to the mirror (that is, nothing useful), he notes, is obtained in this process. Like other experiences that he cannot well assimilate, Locke seems uncomfortable with the very existence of dreams. He offers testimony that many people dream infrequently or not at all. Finally, he attempts to banish the reality of dreams on account of their uselessness:

> *To think often, and never to retain it so much as one moment, is a very useless sort of thinking*: . . . Nature never makes excellent things, for mean or no uses: and it is hardly to be conceived, that our infinitely wise Creator, should make so admirable a faculty as the power of Thinking, . . . to be so idlely and uselessly employed, at least ¼ part of its time here, as to think constantly, without remembering any of those thoughts, without doing any good to it self or others, or being any way useful to any other part of the Creation. (*E* 2.1.15; cf. 4.2.14)

Although he admits at other points that dreams are composed of ideas like our regular thoughts (2.19.1), here he attempts to write dreams practically out of existence ("it is hardly to be conceived") since he can find no purpose for them. Although the experience of dreams makes it impossible to deny them in quite the same degree as innate ideas, Locke does attempt to deny them in the same *manner*. (As we shall see below, Nietzsche takes rather the opposite view of dreams. Where Locke makes them the most marginal of human experiences, Nietzsche makes them the most central.)

This insistence that thoughts, in order to be real, must be useful, is connected to Locke's approach to consciousness. He has depicted thought as a kind of labor, the utility of which has divine sanction. Dreams disturb this picture because they appear to have no purpose or use; they cannot be labor because they have no product. And for Locke this laborious thinking is not the most important thing, it is the only thing. He can conceive of no thought besides conscious, useful thought, and he tells us so quite plainly: "If the *Soul* doth *think in a sleeping Man*, without being conscious of it, I ask, whether, during such thinking, it has any Pleasure or Pain, or be capable of Happiness or Misery? . . . For to be happy or miserable without being conscious of it seems to me utterly inconsistent and impossible" (*E* 2.1.11).

Here again, Locke's drive for simplicity seems too ruthless. It does not require a full-blown theory of psychoanalysis to grant an unconscious or subconscious at least a modest place in an account of the mind. And we have all met people whom we imagine are miserable without being fully conscious of it. But when usefulness is made the sole measure of thinking, only consciousness will be able to contribute to that which we call "self" (*E* 2.27.9): we can see neither the labor that forms dreams nor the utility of the product. Locke's struggle with dreams marks the extent to which usefulness is for him an ontological as well as a moral yardstick. What does not register on this measure is not merely bad but unreal. Usefulness is the single axis on which experiences are ranged. Every kind of experience is, in the end, a product of labor. And labor provides a common measure for what we would now consider vastly different kinds of experience. Locke's characters never dream—and they inhabit a world without color. All their activity is labor, and their products, at best, are useful, but never beautiful. And the same goes for God's activity and the world He has created.

If anything more were needed to confirm the role of usefulness in Locke's work, we may note that this is also the standard he applies to himself. Often, in his notes to readers, he promises that he has labored to produce something of use to them. He even seems concerned to assure them that his books will be worth the money paid for them. In his epistle to the reader at the front of the *Essay*, he states that he has "aimed sincerely at Truth and Usefulness," and not merely truth alone (*E*, "Epistle to the Reader," 6).[16] More modestly, he describes himself as "an Under-Laborer . . . removing some Rubbish, that lies in the way to Knowledge." He describes his thoughts as the labor of the mind, and the products thereof as products in every sense, useful, not wasteful, and ready for market. I shall argue later that this measure of usefulness—utility combined with work—lies behind Locke's narrative of economics and politics. It forms the setting for his plot. To say that Locke offers a narrative, then, is not to say that he offers a colorful one. Indeed, it is easy to be misled by Locke's often dry and legalistic prose into believing that he produces only a lawyer's argument of abstract reasoning. But narratives need not be amusing, any more than lawyers' arguments need be dull. As we shall see below, the gray account of usefulness will provide a powerful, if controlled, defense of liberty. First, I want to describe how this measure grounds Locke's notions of freedom and slavery.

The Characters: The Free Thinker, the Slave of Belief

With an understanding of his idea of usefulness, we are now in a position to explore Locke's social theory. His concepts of freedom and slavery are closely connected to that of labor, both in thought and action. Indeed, slavery finds its most exact opposite in freedom of thought. And it is in thought that man can find an ultimate refuge from the most despotical, enslaving regimes.

It is not just the physical setting for Locke's characters that is described by usefulness—it is the political setting too, as well as the characters themselves.

Slavery is the political evil that preoccupies Locke most. It is the first word of the *First Treatise* and is there described as "so vile and miserable an Estate" as to be comparable to death (*1 T* 1). Indeed, when Locke describes just slavery, he can only imagine it as a death delayed. It is the interval between the pronouncement of a death sentence and its execution (*2 T* 23). Locke always characterizes political oppression as a form of slavery.[17] Although he attacks the royalist Sir Robert Filmer for identifying slavery with just political obligation, he is eager to consider *unjust* authority as enslavement of those it holds in its sway. Slavery he defines as the absolute, despotical power of one man over another.[18] What is unusual is not so much Locke's definition of slavery, as his understanding of freedom.

Since he has described the moral necessity of "crossing one's desires," Locke will not describe liberty as the capacity to do whatever one likes. The more fully developed the mind, in fact, the more one is able to counter one's inclinations. And it is this capacity to suspend desire, rather than freedom to choose or practice one's desires, that Locke calls free will (*E* 2.21.47). Aware that this may sound paradoxical, the author of the *Essay* nonetheless does not hesitate to call this self-restriction freedom and the opposite of slavery: "This is so far from being a restraint or diminution of Freedom, that it is the very improvement and benefit of it: 'tis not an Abridgement, 'tis the end and use of our Liberty; and the farther we are removed from such a determination, the nearer we are to Misery and Slavery" (*E* 2.21.48).

The self-restraint that was enforced on the child by his tutor is, for the adult, enforced on his body by his mind. Indeed, in this odd section, Locke says that the mind that can deny the body the most is, on that account, the most adult and the most free. What is prized most is independence of the mind. And this notion of liberty means that the mind should not be subject to the influence of pleasure and pain. This conception of freedom is what allows Locke to equate such threats to liberty as the physical temptation to pleasure with the threat of injury by an absolute government: both threaten to make concerns of the body overwhelm freedom of thought. Both desire and absolutism threaten the mind with "slavery."

That freedom of thought is the primary freedom is a point Locke makes again and again, even when he later comes to identify what ought to be respected by the government as property rights. He speaks of those under absolute rule as "degraded from the common state of Rational Creatures" and of the formation of complex ideas (which we previously saw was a kind of labor) as a product of liberty (*2 T* 91; *E* 2.28.7). Thus, the worst kind of subjugation is a mental one; "he is certainly the most subjected, the most enslaved, who is so in his Understanding" (*E* 4.20.6). This position is less surprising when it is considered that one of the contemporary issues that most concerned Locke was the protection of Christian dissenters from an enforced conformity to Anglican doctrine.

In the *Letters on Toleration*, Locke and his interlocutor engage in a long discussion as to whether force ought to be used in the promotion of religion. But since both agree that outward conformity is not sufficient for the saving of a Christian, this amounts to an argument over whether force can be used in order to make subjects believe "as they ought," or to force them to study the matter until their beliefs are in order (*LT1* 10–11). To this question Locke says no, while his opponent says yes. The latter, while claiming it should be a last resort, says unapologetically that nonbelievers must be forced into an outer and inner conformity if all forms of persuasion fail. But Locke maintains that freedom of conscience is the core of civic freedom. Using civil force against a citizen's conscience is the final assault on individual liberty. A similar concern motivated Locke during the Exclusion Crisis, which occasioned the writing of the *Two Treatises*. The main issue in that situation (besides the extent of royal authority and prerogative) was the concern that the new King would use his authority to enforce his Catholic beliefs. Locke's concern is, not so much wholesale seizure of property, as that "the Parties of Men, cram their Tenets down all Men's Throats, whom they can get into their Power" (*E* 4.3.20).

For Locke, this is the true slavery (whatever we may think of such a judgment), to which free thought is an antidote as well as an opposite. Seizures of property and involuntary servitude are undoubtedly violations of our freedom. But that liberty is one that takes freedom of thought as its ultimate reference point. The liberty of a Lockean character is ultimately found in his mind and not in his wealth or real property. Force may dominate conscience, but can never extinguish it: "The Subject part of Mankind, in most Places, might . . . with Egyptian Bondage expect Egyptian Darkness, were not the Candle of the Lord set up by himself in Men's minds, which it is impossible for the Breath or Power of Man wholly to extinguish" (*E* 4.3.20). This metaphor of conscience as the "Candle of the Lord" recurs in many of Locke's texts. It always refers to our capacity to reason in adverse circumstances. It is a capacity that can neither be torn from us nor bartered away (*E* 2.28.10; cf. 1.1.5; *RC* 132–33). Thought, and not action, is the fount of liberty, the opposite of slavery.

Freedom thus stands opposed to authority in both the political and literary senses. To be unfree in action means to labor unwillingly on behalf of another. To be unfree in thought means largely the same thing. A subjected mind is one that labors in the grip of another's spiritual authority. It forms ideas at the direction of another rather than on its own. Whether one acquiesces in another's beliefs at the point of a sword or out of one's own religious enthusiasm (which Locke calls tyrannizing over one's own mind), it is the most vile and miserable estate one can imagine (*E* 4.19.2). Taking the beliefs of others for one's own does not mean taking up the products of their thought—it means producing those thoughts in oneself by laboring (in thought) in imitation of them. Ultimately, some degree of acquiescence is always involved, since we cannot be forced to move our minds in a particular way (the way a body can be physically imprisoned or chained).[19] Yet we can be threatened with death—and our mind may often be swayed by this, as it is by the temptation of physical pleasure.

In sum then, Locke's account of the mind's activity as labor forms the basis for his critique of spiritual subjection and for his distinction between the free and the enslaved. His special understanding of the mind at work led him to take any attack on freedom of conscience as an attempt to enslave. The mind's liberty to labor in peace he saw as the source of liberty in action, which would not, however, mean giving full expression to desire, but in fact restricting it. So while Locke's account of human experience may seem especially grim to us, with its constant reliance on the image of a mind at work and never at play, it nonetheless provides a spirited defense of free thought. In divorcing men's thoughts from the mind of God, Locke finds the grounds for a defense of human freedom. Our thoughts do not come from God, but from our own labor. And if our more physical labor should be free from royal and ecclesiastical authority, so too should that of our minds. (I should emphasize here that I am not rejecting those interpretations of Locke that stress his opposition to seizures of property, I am merely emphasizing that that opposition is ultimately grounded in his model of the mind.) From freedom of thought, then, we need to work outward to consider Locke's idea of freedom in a social order. It is only because Locke pictured individuals as radically free to give or withhold their consent to an idea that he believed contract to be the central model of political association. No other sort of familial, ethnic, or social obligation could bind a free-laboring mind in the manner of a contract. Only on the basis of this sort of analysis can we then consider what narrative he created to ensure the realization of the freedom of his laborers.

We should also take care to notice the part that Locke's unusual notions of freedom and slavery play in the story of government that he tells. Characters who are free above all in the realm of ideas may face special sorts of threats. The threat of enslavement may come, not just from those who chain the body, but also from those who attempt to chain the soul. The Lockean character, it turns out, faces just such an attempt on his freedom—at the hands of the King. Both the danger to the citizen (from a plot by the King) and the freedom the citizen seeks (with his own counterplot) can be understood only from the viewpoint of the Lockean character, whose mental activity is conceived as a form of work. That is to say, Locke's historical narrative cannot be divorced from his ascetic, laborious, dreamless account of man—and of the world.

This account is connected to politics in a second way, in addition to the labor-bound understanding of slavery and freedom. This second connection concerns the relationship between money, as the token of physical labor, and words, the token (to Locke) of mental labor. An examination of this topic will also help flesh out the narrative introduced above in connection with Locke's ideas on education.

Words and Money, Money and Words

At times, Locke seems to us a man with a generous heart but a narrow mind. His magnanimity of spirit sits uncomfortably with the small set of concepts he uses to gauge human experience. The wide (although not universal) toleration he urged was the result of holding life within a narrow compass of thought, of imagining life as a gray labor, with little variety. No matter what aspect of human existence we examine through Locke, we shall not get away from characters who labor and work.

When Locke moves from matters of conscience to affairs of commerce, labor naturally remains at the forefront of his thought. The parallel of labor and thought is, in fact, carried a step further: words, as the units of thought, Locke holds to be particularly akin to money (especially coins), the units of wealth. The products of thought-labor are taken to be like the products of physical labor; both have the properties of a commodity. They can be quantified, itemized, accumulated, exchanged, and capitalized. And they have a particular unit in which they can be measured. The units (coins or words) are the specific forms that ideas and wealth take when they are exchanged or capitalized. Degrading the language therefore ought to be considered equivalent to the debasing of the currency, a crime Locke takes very seriously.[20] Both acts undermine the capacity for free exchange. This too is part of the setting in which Locke's narrative unfolds.

The coinlike character he attributes to words emphasizes the degree to which Locke considers reason and ideas to be within time, the subjects of narrative, rather than abstract entities. Money exists only in time. Not only does it take time to be minted and circulated, but its very reason for existence requires time. Money is a substitute for some item of value, and its substitution signals a readiness on the part of the owner to defer enjoyment of that value and a plan to redeem the currency for goods at some later date. Without the passage of time, these uses of money make no sense (i.e., there would be no such things as "plans" or "deferral" per se). That Locke discusses ideas and reason in monetary terms only strengthens the argument made above about the implications of the attack on innate ideas. If words are the coin of the intellectual realm, then ideas themselves will contain an inherently narrative element in the same way that money does. It will even be possible to give a history of the forging, accumulation, and degradation of ideas, as one might of a hoard of wealth.

The third book of the *Essay* is largely devoted to words—particularly to their conventional origin and their productive use. Locke first argues from the diversity of languages to their nonnatural status. If there were an essential link between objects and words, he says, mankind would all speak the same language. That this is not the case implies that it is "a voluntary Imposition, whereby such a Word is made arbitrarily the Mark of such an *Idea*" (*E* 3.2.1). In keeping with the rejection of innate ideas, Locke rejects the idea of innate language in favor of one developed in time. The labor of thought, begun with the manufacture of ideas through a joining of materials, is not complete when the idea itself is forged. The alloy must have a distinctive stamp set upon it before it is useful coin. It must be assigned a *word*: "The use Men have of these Marks, being either to record their own thoughts for the Assistance of their own Memory; or as it were, to bring out their *Ideas*, and lay them before the View of others" (*E* 3.2.2). Notice that Locke believes words to be helpful even apart from their role in communication. Just as a person with a pile of gold bullion would know its value more accurately if it were coined, so people with jumbles of ideas in their heads find them useful only when they have been formed into words. The thoughts of Lockean characters, formed by labor, take the shape of coins—which may be tarnished or cut.

The capitalization and marketing of ideas cannot begin until they have distinctive marks. But this requires more than that every person assign a word to every idea they have. That would result in a Babel even worse than the current variety of languages. Just as gold or silver is not sufficient for use in commerce, but needs a common coinage, so in the commerce of ideas, people need, not just any pottage of words, but a common language. Ideas are useful, but their common coinage makes them even more so. And this language, Locke thinks, can only be established by a kind of consent. It is not an explicit consent; rather, it develops out of the common use of words by a

society. Vocabulary arises out of common practices and the need to communicate about them. Words can thus vary according to use. Unlike the social
contract (which I discuss below), the original agreement is not binding.
Although it cannot be broken arbitrarily, it can be modified by common
agreement when people are so motivated by changing circumstances. And
so languages constantly change "because change of Customs and Opinions
bringing with it new Combinations of *Ideas*, . . . new names . . . are annexed
to them" (*E* 2.22.7). (Locke hardly seems to recognize words that are not
nouns.)

This mercantile account of language also points to the main obstacle to
reasoning in Locke's view. The productive use of the language depends on
maintaining a consensus about the meaning of words. To lose this is akin to
losing faith in one's currency; it becomes impossible to conduct human relations without it. And Locke does not believe this loss to occur gradually or
accidentally. He is particularly concerned that the currency is being abused by
those who want to turn it to their own ends. Certainty of meaning is threatened, he thinks, by people who use words arbitrarily. This threatens to disrupt
human society. A fascinating parallel can therefore be observed between
Locke's concern about the abuse of words in the *Essay* and his worries about
the fixity of actual English coin in his various writings on money. And both
prefigure the worry about the King's abuse of words in Locke's political
narrative.

The *Essay* repeats endlessly the theme that if speakers were simply a little
more precise about the meaning of their words, many intellectual and political controversies would be "at an end" (e.g., *E*, "Epistle to the Reader").
Locke also applies this charge to his opponent in the *Letters Concerning Toleration*. He often taxes his interlocutor with speaking unclearly and insists that
they would not have so much to disagree about if his opponent used words
more precisely (*LT3* 423). It is easy to get the impression from all this that
Locke thinks the indefiniteness of words results from too-casual usage or from
simple mistakes. But this is often not so. Such change comes in two varieties — consensual and arbitrary. Because language is a product of consent, it is
open to alteration. When such changes come about because of new circumstances, in a consensual way, they are legitimate. When one party to the
consent tries to arbitrarily alter meaning, however, for no good reason except
his own advantage, then such change is illegitimate. Slow changes represent
the renegotiation of an institution; quick ones are an abrogation or a fraud.

Locke views the abuse of language as being like the clipping of coins
(where someone shears off a bit of silver and then attempts to pass the coin off
at face value): "For Words, especially of Languages already framed, being no

Man's private possession, but the common measure of Commerce and Communication, 'tis not for any one, at pleasure, to change the Stamp they are current in" (*E* 3.11.11).[21] And, he asserts, " 'tis plain cheat and abuse, when I make [Words] stand sometimes for one thing, and sometimes for another; the wilful doing whereof, can be imputed to nothing but great folly, or greater dishonesty" (*E* 3.10.5). It ought also to be noted that Locke refers fairly consistently to the distortion of words as an "abuse" of them, that is, an ab-*use*, a degradation of their normal usefulness. "Abuse" is as much the opposite of use as is sloth or inactivity.

We can get a greater sense of the horror with which Locke viewed the possibility of such a "cheat" by turning briefly to his discussion of actual money. At first, as one reads these essays, one wonders why Locke spends so much time on an (apparently) minor concern: the clipping of coins. Even if it was a large practical problem in his day, this does not explain the almost existential anguish and fury Locke displays on the subject. No other financial matter preoccupies him more, even when he has been asked to write on other questions. Ultimately though, the reason for his concern becomes clear. Locke is concerned that without a fixed and dependable coinage, commerce, and therefore society itself, will be unable to continue. It will disintegrate in exactly the manner of Babel; and for precisely the same reasons: "But it is no wonder, if the price and value of things be confounded and uncertain, when the measure itself is lost. For we have now no lawful silver money current amongst us; and therefore cannot talk nor judge right, by our present, uncertain, clipped money, of the value and price of things" (*FCM* 158).

Our inability to "talk nor judge right" is the source of Locke's fear. It truly is, in this sense, existential. The harm only begins with the "shameful and horrible debasing" that "disorders trade and puzzles accounts" (*SCM* 127; *FCM* 189).[22] Locke believes the collapse in trade will be total (*FCM* 148). And the reason is that people will have lost faith in the very words they utter. For denominations of money are used as terms of contract. If all commerce were immediate exchange, the problem could perhaps be solved by everyone carrying a set of scales to verify the value of coin. But that is not the case: "Men in their bargains contract not for denominations of sounds, but for the intrinsic value, which is the quantity of silver, by public authority, warranted to be in pieces of such denominations" (*FCM* 144). If the content of coins is not fixed and known, the meanings of vital words such as *pound* and *shilling* (to say nothing of terms such as "equal value") will not be stable. No one will be able to contract. It would amount to the disruption of time itself, at least in the commercial sphere; no contracts, hence no commerce over time, would be possible.

In the case of human discourse, where the coin of the realm simply *is* sounds, the problem is that much more magnified (*E* 3.1.6). There is no set of scales that can be used to assure that words are not being "clipped"—abused of their original meaning and used in a "cheat" of some kind: "[T]o me it appears a greater dishonesty, than the misplacing of Counters, in the casting up a Debt; and the cheat the greater, by how much Truth is of greater concernment and value, than money" (*E* 3.10.5).[23]

Is it any wonder, then, that Locke found poetry morally censurable? The playfulness and arbitrariness of metaphors, the slipperiness of meaning, on which much poetry depends must have seemed patently dishonest to him. Although Locke's banishment of poets resembles that of Plato (who excluded them from his ideal city), there are, I should point out, significant differences as well. Plato abhors poetry's distortion of reality. But Locke, with his quasi-nominalist view of words, does not have this objection. His complaint is that poets violate the consent surrounding the use of language. Thus, for Plato, the poets' flaws are epistemological first and moral only as a result. For Locke, poetry's failing is primarily moral—it breaks a human agreement. (It should, perhaps, also be said here that, because of this difference, Plato is able to recognize and appreciate poetic achievement in a way Locke cannot.)

Locke similarly derogates the scholastics, whom he thinks are responsible for much of the mischief done to words, by calling them "Mint-Masters" (*E* 3.10.2; cf. 2.13.27). Their use of the language is to him nothing more than an abuse, which, rather than just depriving a few of the value they have bargained for, threatens the whole society with a collapse like that of the Tower of Babel. Rendering words uncertain is like diluting the mortar in such a tower. Our consent as to the meaning of words is what holds the structure of our society together, and it will crash to the ground without it. It only requires a few individuals, chiseling away at the units of commerce, to make those units useless for everyone.

As we shall see later, this power that a few abusers have to ruin a fair system for everyone takes on great importance in Locke's narrative of government—where the abuser turns out to be the King. For now, it is enough to note a key feature of Locke's colorless world. It may exist in either of two basic states: one in which there is a common currency (or words or coin) or one where such a currency has been abused to the point of uselessness. The collapse of the Tower would represent the end of the narrative of knowledge—all that had been built up would be lost. Putting knowledge "in time," then, exposes it to temporal dangers. Ideas that are innate can never be harmed or destroyed; ideas in a narrative, however, are exposed to the ravages of time.

It is the near-equation between words and money (see n. 23) that allows

Locke to make the kind of argument he does here, which ought to strike us as remarkable. By analogy, he makes what is essentially an economic argument into a social and political argument. The instability that besets the economic sphere when the currency is uncertain can attack the political and intellectual sphere as well only because thought is like labor, ideas are like gold, and words are like coined money (see *E*, "Epistle Dedicatory"; 1.4.23). In both spheres, human labor manufactures a product that is exchanged and stored in a particular commodity unit. What certainty we can obtain, in knowledge, economy, or politics, rests on the certainty of words, which are the coin of the intellectual realm. And the importance of this certainty to contracts in particular (as was hinted at above) will become clearer as we examine Locke's politics further.

The importance of contracts to a stable economy and continuing narrative is mirrored by their role in a polity. Locke's use of the contract to signify the origin of social organization was not just an apt metaphor for any kind of consent. This entire economic model of experience and social life stands behind it. And, in Locke's narrative of government, the main threats to the *social* contract resemble those that threaten in the economic sphere: "Mint-Masters" attempting to abuse the unit of political currency and thus alter the meaning of the contract. The greatest threat, we shall see, appears when the King becomes this kind of cheat. A full understanding of Locke's sense of history, including the episode of social contract, can only be reached with the aid of these concepts and characters.

At this point, then, we have a rough sketch of this cast of characters. Opposed to the laborer are, on the one hand, the lazy, and on the other, the cheats. As I argue in chapter 2, each of the last two present a particular kind of danger to the laborer, although it is largely the cheat who presents the political threat of tyranny.

History and Definitions

Locke's approach to contracts, through words and their abuse, leads to an examination of social compacts that at times focuses on particular terms (such as *prerogative*), rather than on broad outlines. One might expect, then, that with this attention to the meanings of words, Locke would insist on the importance of definitions. And so he does, often taxing his opponents for failing to provide them. But his understanding of definitions is not what we might expect. Because of his analysis of language as something that evolves over time, Locke does not consider the meanings of words to be firmly fixed. Although he is concerned about the abuse of words, this never leads him to say that a particular word has by nature a single meaning with some kind of metaphysical status. He rather thinks, as he argues here for substances, "to define their Names right, natural History is to be enquired into" (*E* 3.11.24). By this, he does not quite intend what we commonly mean by *history* or *natural history*, but neither is he far away from these ideas. For a definition of substances, I believe, he contemplates something like a history of their natures, what properties they have, and how they came to acquire them over time.[24] This is what Locke means when he refers to his epistemological enquiries as being carried out by a "Historical, plain Method" (*E* 1.1.2). His account is based on experience, rather than metaphysics; experience is time-bound in a way metaphysics is not. Definitions rooted in experience have a history. Experiential definitions can evolve over time, while metaphysical ones (if correct) are fixed.

This is the expression in etymology, if you will, of the separation of the human mind from that of God. Just as we have no innate ideas, neither do our words transcend our mortal station. Their meanings derive from human compact, not a metaphysical status. Locke does not equate his own *Essay* and, say, a chronicle of English kings, but he clearly does not think that his epistemology can be wholly isolated from history. In fact, if we are to have sound definitions, that would not be a particularly good idea. He even goes so far as to describe the *Essay* as a "true History of the first beginnings of Human Knowledge" (*E* 2.12.15). If history has this role even in the most immaterial branches of human knowledge, it can then be expected to have an even larger role in the study of political institutions. The best definition of government, we can perhaps say, is a natural history. Hence, while the terms I have outlined above form the vocabulary for the narrative in the *Second Treatise*, they do not ground it. That is, the meaning of these terms is, in some sense, bound to the story in which they appear. A common vocabulary only comes to be common by being experientially, narratively related. The character of Locke's laborers, then, is not wholly separate from the plot in which they participate. The natural history of government is tightly bound to the labor-based vocabulary in which it is recounted. Neither side of the role precedes the other.

In other words, the account of the Lockean character is *not* simply an account of an unchanging human nature, which is then neatly plugged in as a given for political reasoning. The central role of money and language in Locke's characters cannot be separated from the *story* in which such centrality arises. Locke does not simply postulate such centrality or argue for its natural status. Rather, he describes a natural history in which these structures come to have an increasingly large role in human affairs. It is this history that will be explored in Chapter 2.

In his essay on education, Locke specifically confirms the importance of history. A large portion of that essay is given over to attacking the forms of education then current in English private schools. Locke's recommendations often dispense with portions of the curriculum, previously taken to be sacred, because they are of no use to anyone but the narrowest of scholars. A man of affairs, for example, can do quite well without a knowledge of Greek. But history is irreplaceable. It is "the great mistress of prudence and civil knowledge; and ought to be the proper study of a gentleman" (*STCE* 182). Locke lays out a course of study for history more detailed than for almost any other subject he discusses, even going so far as to recommend particular authors. History is also the only subject of which Locke stresses that its study should not be confined to childhood. "This general part of civil law and history are studies which a gentleman should not barely touch at, but constantly dwell upon, and never have done with," he writes (*STCE* 186). All this suggests (but, of course, does not establish) the importance of the category of history to Locke's most explicit analysis of government, the *Two Treatises of Government*—a work to which we can now turn our attention. It suggests that a definition of a well-ordered government need not be a matter of deduction, but might well be a historical account. But such a definition must still use other terms, and the terms I have been emphasizing—*labor, usefulness, money, contracts*—are the ones Locke uses in his account of civil government. One term for which the historical character of definition is particularly crucial is *prerogative*. The extent of royal prerogative is a key question in the *Second Treatise*. It is a word that the King is said to have abused—and a proper understanding of it comes, not from an abstract analysis, but from historical inquiry. The whole social contract, in fact, is considered something to be examined historically, not a product of pure reason, but a faded memory, the terms of which need to be recalled.

CHAPTER 2

Plotting Liberty Under a Gray Sky

For man also knoweth not his time: as the fishes that are taken in an
evil net, and as the birds that are caught in the snare, so are the sons of
men snared in an evil time, when it falleth suddenly upon them.
—Ecclesiastes 9:12

Locke speaks only rarely of the "foundations" of government, but frequently of its "original." His search for the grounds of government took him
back to its beginning in time. Although he denies that he argues from the
rightness of what was to that of what is, in the process of describing government Locke came to write its history from the earliest scattering of humans,
through their association in a social contract, to their rebellion when the
terms of that contract were breached.[1] In doing so, Locke displaced several
other prominent histories, above all Sir Robert Filmer's biblical history of
patriarchal authority. To do so, he had to reject Filmer's account of the Bible's
story, but not so completely as to undercut his own view of the world, which,
as we have seen, had deep Protestant roots.

Locke accomplishes this by further separating man from God through a
segregation of reason and revelation. Building on this, he proceeds also to
argue for the separation of church and state and to deny the possibility of a
Christian commonwealth. Once the biblical story has been swept aside, the
field is free for the introduction of Locke's own narrative. This chapter thus
first discusses the Christian-patriarchal narrative that Locke declines before
laying out the "natural history" in the *Second Treatise*. Locke's history, we shall
see, takes its character from the economistic account of the world that the
previous chapter described. Only the man of usefulness described there can
be the focus of Locke's story. The "original" of government is a narrative in
which this character is the protagonist. And fraud and embezzlement are just
the sort of plot twists one would expect in such a story.

Christianity Retained; Christian Narrative Rejected

The separation of the minds of God and man requires the distancing of God's voice. This is reflected in the way Locke's argument downplays the role of revelation as a guide to human conduct. This is not to say that Locke is uninterested in Scripture, for he is quite interested in it. What his examination of it yields, however, is just the opposite of an authoritative account of government or politics. The independent biblical contribution to political theory, he claims, is practically nonexistent.

Locke's arguments about revelation are stated most directly in the essay entitled *The Reasonableness of Christianity, as delivered in the Scriptures*, in which he states without reservation that revelation is authoritative and cannot be defeated by reason or any other source of principles (*RC* 242–43). But he adds to this statement a caveat so large as to effectively render it inoperable. Although revelation is indefeasible, he says, the human mind must judge as to when it has occurred. "Whether it be a divine Revelation, or no, *Reason* must judge," otherwise, we would have no way to tell true revelation from false prophets (*E* 4.18.10). And since the mind of man has neither any direct connection to that of God nor innate ideas as to His purposes, we are left with the single tool of our minds, reason, with which to assess purported revelations. Even what Locke calls the "Traditional Revelation" of the Bible is always subject to the trump of reason, which has to authenticate it as divine in origin, although unable to alter its content (*E* 4.18.4).[2]

Nor does Locke think that revelation could contradict what reason has firmly established (although it might contradict a good judgment). "This would subvert the Principles, and Foundations of all Knowledge, Evidence, and Assent whatsoever" (*E* 4.18.5). And this is what he means when he says Christianity is reasonable. Not that its precepts can be entirely discovered by reason, but that, once revealed, they are perfectly compatible with reason and not in conflict with it (*RC* 145).

Locke thus makes use of Scripture in two principal ways: first, where he uses it to establish something where reason could not do so by itself, and second, where he uses the Bible to confirm something that he feels he has already demonstrated on strictly rational grounds. When attention is paid to this distinction, it becomes clear that Locke's fundamentally Christian orientation does not prevent his having a nonbiblical, and even antibiblical, approach to history and government.

Locke's own deepest engagement with the Scriptures (aside from his last work, a notation of Paul's Epistles) comes in the *Reasonableness*. But while this engagement undoubtedly establishes that Locke's Christianity was fundamental to his moral thought, it is important to consider what the content of that belief was. For if one were to describe that book briefly, it might most accurately be called a thorough investigation of the Scripture in order to establish its irrelevance to social and political questions. Locke counters the many political arguments that have been made out of the Bible, and offers nothing in their place. Indeed, he insists, there *is nothing* in their place. The only belief necessary to be a Christian, he argues, is "that Jesus was the Messiah; . . . salvation or perdition depends upon believing or rejecting this one proposition" (*RC* 26; cf. 102, 105). In so arguing, Locke may have hoped to deprive priests of power over the populace by denying them the right to read complicated political and social precepts out of Scripture that only they could comprehend.[3] Yet anticlericism is not antireligiousness. Indeed, a suspicion of clerical authority is a common Protestant theme. Locke also sharply reduced the scope of the Bible's authority and largely transferred its basis to reason alone. All the lesser rules of behavior, Locke thought, could be developed simply by reason, and did not need to rest on revelation (whose status seemed constantly in doubt in any case). Thus, except in the case of the divinity of Jesus, Locke preferred to rely on the authority of human reason and to cite Scripture only to confirm reason's conclusions—especially on political and social questions.[4] Even when Locke makes extensive use of Scripture, a careful reading will often show that he is using it to confirm what he already knows by dint of his own mental labor.

An important example of this type of discussion can be found in Locke's account of property in the *First Treatise*. There he derives man's right to the use of the animals, a property right, from his need to eat them for his survival. The human desire for survival and our capacity to use other things toward that end, Locke considers to be natural and God-given. And these are premises sufficient to establish our natural right to the use of other things. Thus, Locke declares that he is prepared to dispense with the biblical authorization of this use as redundant: "And therefore I doubt not, but before these words were pronounced, I Gen. 28, 29 (if they must be understood Literally to have been spoken) and without any such Verbal Donation, Man had a right to a use of the Creatures, by the will and Grant of God" (*1 T* 86). Locke's Christianity, however deep, does not prevent him from distancing his account of human society from the Scriptures. And although he does not want to contradict the Bible, neither does he want to reason from it.

Any reader of Locke will note that while some of his texts are replete with biblical references, others have them only sparingly. This contrast is most notable between the first and second of the *Two Treatises*. Where Locke is refuting Filmer's thesis in the first, he counters "Sir Robert" chapter for chapter and verse for verse. But when he comes to articulate his own views, the reliance on the Bible drops away and for long stretches is absent entirely. His tale of government is not spun entirely from whole cloth, but Holy Writ is not one of its more important sources. Christianity is never denied, but perhaps it is set aside where it does not speak to matters at hand (which it only does within a narrow compass of theological questions).

None of the foregoing is meant to dispute Locke's deep personal faith, which I believe John Dunn and others have shown beyond all doubt to be genuine.[5] My argument is simply that Locke takes his faith to tell him little or nothing about society and politics. Nor should this be difficult to accept: it follows in the best "Render unto Caesar . . ." tradition. Here, however, Caesar is replaced by Clio.

A further demonstration of this point can be seen in the *Letters Concerning Toleration*, which, as is well known, argue for the separation of church and state (*LT1* 9). Although Locke does not support the toleration of atheists or most Catholics, every other theistic religion (even Islam) ought, he thinks, to be tolerated. And the government should not require the profession of any particular creed. We can see now that this separation depends upon the disjunction of reason and revelation, and these both on the distance between God's ideas and man's. Christians are required to believe in the few things known directly through revelation (i.e., that Jesus is their Savior); but these things have nothing to do with government, which is the province of reason. Whereas even Hobbes spoke of a Christian commonwealth, Locke will have nothing to do with the concept: "There is absolutely no such thing, under the Gospel, as a Christian commonwealth. . . . [Christ] indeed, hath taught men how, by faith and good works, they may attain eternal life. But he instituted no Commonwealth; he prescribed unto his followers no new and peculiar form of government" (*LT1* 38).

Locke believes in Heaven and says repeatedly that everybody needs to believe the one true religion in order to be saved, but he nonetheless holds these questions firmly apart from that of a well-ordered government. One of the effects of this separation is that Locke takes the whole question of government more seriously than those who search for a religious ground for a polity. Whereas his opponent in the *Letters* is content to let civil authority be abused so long as God later punishes the abusers, Locke wants a self-limiting notion of government that prevents such abuses. He often points out the "uselessness" of his opponent's scheme—a not precisely theological condemnation (see *LT3*, ch. 1). Locke often uses the examples of Muslim countries to point out that the problem of government is distinct from religious questions, and that mixing the two ends up hurting both: "For the civil government can give no new right to the church, nor the church to the civil government. . . . The civil power is the same in every place: nor can that power, in the hands of a Christian prince, confer a greater authority upon the Church" (*LT1* 18–19). So, if Locke cleaves strongly to his Christian faith, he nonetheless puts religion and government in largely separate spheres and endeavors to keep them far apart in his political writings. What then, does he offer in place of religion for political reasoning? The same vocabulary of economy, it seems, that he uses to replace innate ideas as the model of the mind. And he uses as well the form of a natural history that he claims is most appropriate to worldly matters.

Having dispensed, in the *First Treatise* (and other works), with a biblical history of government where sovereign power is handed down from Adam to British kings, Locke offers, in the *Second Treatise*, not a nonnarrative, but a counternarrative account of the source of sovereignty. Although certainly not a conventional history, this account is hardly the geometric deduction that some have taken it to be.[6]

The Natural Story

Most readings of Locke's *Second Treatise of Government* depict the book, and especially its contentions about the State of Nature, as an abstract moral argument. This interpretation has two general forms. In the traditional secular, liberal version, it stresses the elements of liberty, equality, and contract as ideals that find physical expression in the concept of a state of nature.[7] More recent interpretations have stressed the religious roots of Locke's thought and the connection between Calvinist theology and his political position.[8]

It is not usually thought that Locke's efforts in the *Second Treatise* constitute an attempt to write a new history or to create new memories intended to supplant the existing ones of political authority.[9] My argument is that the *Second Treatise* provides its readers with an alternative to traditional histories of royal rule. It supplies a rival vocabulary and plot with which to constitute history. It challenges the prevailing account of the past with its own. As a result, its readers understand the present as a point in a different narrative—a sequence of events with a different direction. And *direction* here means both trajectory and injunction. This new history has the effect of changing its readers' understanding of their historical position—of changing, in effect, who they are. It lends historical, as well as moral, justification to the overthrow of an arbitrary and tyrannical ruler. The State of Nature is not meant merely as a physical incarnation of political ideals but as a representation of a past more "true" than the alternatives—and specifically truer than the ersatz biblical history that Filmer presented.[10] It is the political reflection of the developmental narrative apparent in Locke's epistemological and educational writings. In suggesting a past, furthermore, the *Second Treatise* also provides a view of what is to come.

The vocabulary and characters of this narrative are supplied by the account of experience I described in Chapter 1. Labor, usefulness, money, and contract are the basic concepts Locke employs to describe the moments in his political narrative. Once again, there is the paradox of a rather bleak and limited vocabulary of experience providing the grounds for a vigorous defense of liberty. The economic terminology provides the basis of a secular account of government that can evolve over time. Locke's abandonment of metaphysical definitions for a "Historical, plain Method" (*E* 1.1.2) (where ideas and words are of human coinage) requires such a time-bound vocabulary.

It is in this light, I think, that we should consider that famous sentence, "In the beginning all the World was America and more so than that is now" (*2 T* 49). This curious turn of phrase, often noted but little analyzed, has been construed either to indicate the special resonance of Locke for the Americas (a sentiment not misplaced) or to be simply a colorful depiction of the wilderness element of the State of Nature. But it seems to me that the most important element in this sentence is its formulation in the style of the first verse of Genesis. Indeed, Locke uses the formulation "in the beginning" repeatedly in the *Second Treatise*. This rhetorical connection of the State of Nature with Genesis labels the action that occurs within that state as a myth of creation, parallel to but separate from that of Scripture. Just as the story of the world's creation is told in Genesis, so is the story of the state's creation told in Locke's text.

The State of Nature is meant to be part of the true history of its readers and their political milieu, not a thought experiment in which ideals are simply given a concrete form.[11] And that history is meant to reconstitute its readers' self-understanding: with regard to both their character and to the role that character has in politics. The populace in Locke's history are not royal subjects by nature and history (as Filmer would have it) and, if the time is right, it may even be their role to revolt against a ruler who has broken a social contract. The countermemory Locke proposes is meant, not to establish abstract propositions, but to suggest and help bring about a particular future. It is a plot in both the passive and active senses described above: it provides a record of past events; but it also seeks to direct the course of the future.

But since Locke has declined to find in the Bible any detailed account of the story of government, he must look elsewhere to stock his history. He turns here to the vocabulary of experience that he has developed in the *Essay* and elsewhere: labor and product, words and money, freedom and slavery. To set these static concepts in motion, he employs the notion of contract and envisions society and government over time as a concatenation of contracts that leads from the earliest barter system, to the establishment of government, to the decline of that government and its renewal through revolution. The social contract is not of a different genre from the more strictly economic (and linguistic) contracts that order much of private life. Locke builds his account of government *up* from his economistic model of mental and social life, rather than inserting a model of political organization that is alien into his accounts of mind and economy. While some elements of this interpretation may not strike the reader as new, keep in mind that my attempt in what follows is to reverse the common understanding of history and theory in Locke. Rather than seeing history as contributing evidence to a theory, I want to suggest that it is the theory that provides the vocabulary of a historical narrative—and that it is this story that provides the unified theme of the *Second Treatise*. Its coherence is found in its account of time—not in a single strand of reasoning. This narrative functions as a political argument for revolution, but it is not, for that reason, a piece of ideology confined in its impact to seventeenth-century Englishmen. It is a story that can function as a political argument for current readers as well, for reasons that I hope will become clear as I proceed.

The Story of Property

The role of words in organizing mental labor was discussed in Chapter 1. We begin our discussion of Locke's political narrative by exploring the role of words in organizing the more mundane sorts of human labor. Language gives to people the ability to do more than conduct immediate exchanges. In providing the capacity for individuals to *consent* to explicit and complex conditions, it allows for the fashioning of long-term agreements—contracts. But what *is* a contract for Locke? Contracts are promises that bind the promising parties over time. Words, as we have seen, are like money: they can be stored in the "Storehouse" of memory (capitalization); they can be combined in complex ideas (investment, employment); they can be passed from one person to another while retaining their value (exchanged); and they can be abused (like clipped coins). A contract is possible only because words are durable and can be known and exchanged, like coin. Contracts are *not* simply possible because of human characteristics such as truth, honesty, or intent. The economic model of the mind and the resulting monetary characteristics of words and speech are contained in Locke's understanding of contract. A word can serve as a pledge and bond because it is like a coin (a) in carrying labor-created value (an idea) and (b) because it does not decay or spoil (although, like coin, it may be clipped). A contract is not, therefore, possible between just any two human beings, but only between those who have a common currency of words. This is an important point: a Lockean contract cannot be simply an "idea of Reason" like a Kantian one. And the State of Nature, for that reason, cannot simply be a diorama of pure human reason, as those who liken Locke's theory to geometry suppose. Rather, a social contract (or any other contract for that matter) can only be made between those who are at some middle point in time. They must already have had the common experiences necessary to desire a common language. The pages that precede the social contract in the *Second Treatise* are not merely preliminary reasoning, they describe the prior history necessary for such an agreement. Although the social contract is the "original" of government, it is not the earliest point in Locke's narrative.

Nietzsche asks how it is possible for a human being to promise—how the human mind can be dependable over time (see Chapter 4). Locke's response is rooted in the special durability of words and ideas, which he understands through the analogy to precious metals and currency. The permanence of our thoughts over time, our ability to contract, is described through the properties of gold and coin as well as our labor in "minting" them. So Locke's politics are bound to his economics and economistic psychology in form as well as content. The notion of contract is rooted in his economic vocabulary—even when the content of the contract is itself concerned with money, as in the designation of gold and silver as currency that takes place in the *Second Treatise*.

It is for this reason that I think many discussions of the role of "consent" in Locke, although quite important, somehow miss the point. Before the question of what constitutes explicit or tacit consent for Locke, or of what people consent to, there comes the question of how a consent that holds good over time is even *possible* for human beings as Locke has described them; and here we must turn to the durability of coin and the parallel to words that Locke draws. Without a firm coinage, the products of our mental labor would be like the products of physical labor without money—they would inevitably decay and ultimately spoil. A common language is as necessary for long-term promises and consent as a common currency is for the long-term storage of value.

Thus, Locke's argument that language is "the great Instrument and Tye of Society" does not rest strictly on its ability to facilitate exchange, but rather on its capacity to forge lasting bonds (*E* 3.1.1). This ability to contract explicitly plays a key role in the development of society that Locke describes in the *Second Treatise*. It is a narrative of contracts and their labor-content that he uses to refute Filmer's patriarchal story. Although I do not wish to repeat Locke's familiar story of property in too much detail, some discussion is in order.

The story begins with God's labor in the creation of humanity, "all the Workmanship of one Omnipotent, and infinitely wise Maker" (*2T* 6). Because of our status as God's creations, we are each bound to preserve ourselves and, where our own lives are not at stake, "to preserve the rest of Mankind" (ibid.). Further, we are created in such a condition that this preservation, of ourselves and others, requires our labor and the use of our natural surroundings. Fortunately, this is not difficult, since "God has given us all things richly" (*2T* 31).[12]

The model of labor, described above with regard to thought, is now deployed in the field of human history. Individuals create personal property by laboring on the Earth and bringing forth its useful fruits.[13] So long as they have no means of contracting, there are few disturbances between individuals and little interaction, other than procreation: "And thus considering the plenty of natural Provisions there was a long time in the World, and the few spenders . . . there could be then little room for Quarrels or Contentions about Property so established" (*2T* 31)."Thus *Labor*, in the Beginning [N.B.], *gave a Right of Property*, wherever any one was pleased to imploy it, upon what was common, which remained, a long while, the far greater part. . . . Men, at first, for the most part, contented themselves with what unassisted Nature Offered to their Necessities" (*2T* 45). Within this condition, bartering could take place, but extended associations, either economic or political, could not. (I return to the question of families later.) This was to change, however, with the introduction of money and the contract that took place to establish it as the medium of exchange.

Like all legitimate changes, Locke argues, money came about by general consent. The metals themselves have no intrinsic value save the durability that makes them useful as an instrument of exchange: "For mankind, having consented to put an imaginary value upon gold and silver, . . . have made them, by general consent, the common pledges, whereby men are assured, in exchange for them, to receive equally valuable things, to those they parted with" (*SCM* 22). This description of money as a "pledge" (which is repeated elsewhere) reemphasizes the congruence between words and coin. It is a general contract that introduces money; and money then serves to facilitate further, private agreements. Yet despite the agreement on gold and silver that takes place in the State of Nature, we cannot say that contracts are, in every sense, prior to money. As described above, contracts rest on a sense of words and ideas that presupposes the properties of money. Hence, the question arises: does money create contracts or do contracts create money? In the State of Nature, it seems to be the latter, yet it also seems that the only way to explain the function of words is through the metaphors of money and market exchange. This circle of meaning points even more strongly to the ungrounded status of Locke's theory. Neither the possibility of contract nor the story of money seems possible without the other. While the importance of narrative does not follow from this (and it might simply be that Locke is inconsistent on these questions), I believe that the most plausible interpretation of the text is one in which a narrative brings these two elements together and lends a coherence to the account that the elements do not possess on their own. The human character Locke describes will retain a fundamental ambiguity until located in a plot.

The convention of money is thus the first significant episode in this story after the pastoral stage of the State of Nature. The existence of the Lockean character thus relies on an element of the plot just as that plot would be impossible without the characters. Each requires the other in order for the account to be consistent. The invention of language is not discussed in the *Second Treatise*, just as the invention of money is not discussed in the *Essay*. Yet neither makes sense, or seems possible, without the other. What holds them together is time-bound experience. It is the *experience* of stability and surety that the use of words and precious metals brings about that allow them to take up their respective places in social life as the markers of mental and physical labor. The Lockean character cannot be defined or posited, he must be plotted. He can only exist within a story. The character's characteristics are acquired in a narrative. The invention of money and language are early episodes of this story. That is why the social contract cannot proceed strictly from reason, but requires these prior episodes. The social contract is the thickening of an earlier plot.

After the invention of money, then, individuals are now no longer limited to strict barter. They can accept money in place of valuable things because they have a general pledge, from all mankind, to redeem the money in goods at a later date.[14] Civil society develops as a network of contracts within a contract. Individuals contract out their labor; land and goods can also be rented, sold, or otherwise made the subject of contract.[15] And it is the use of a commodity that does not spoil that allows for these long-term agreements (*2T* 47). Only money allows for the fulfillment of agreements to be deferred over any length of time. Locke's greatest concern about altering the value of the coinage is that it will absolve parties to contracts from the duty of performing them and thus no long-term agreements will be possible (*FCM* 144). Each coin is a mini-pledge, and the fabric of society is maintained only through the integrity of such pledges. Without money, an integrated society would not be possible, and government, which follows upon it, would not be necessary. This transition from the "Golden Age" (as Locke calls it at *2T* 111) to something recognizable as an economy of yeoman or estate agriculture is encapsulated in the fifth chapter of the *Second Treatise*.[16] But far from being the climax of the argument, that section is only an overture. It introduces the theme of contract and sets in motion the narrative of civil association, which begins with the acquisition of property (in unequal amounts) and the development of commerce.[17]

And Locke is not without his doubts about this prelude, even if it does set the stage for the formation of government. At various points, he expresses a nostalgia for the earliest period in his history and his distaste for the commercial society that has sprung from it. In his advice on education, the one problem that seems to arise in children of its own accord (rather than as a result of bad schooling) is "covetousness" and the "love of dominion." Most of what Locke suggests is designed to endow children with traits and skills; here, and here only, he wants a trait "weeded out": "Covetousness, and the desire of having in our possession, and under our dominion, more than we have need of, being the root of all evil, should be early and carefully weeded out; and the contrary quality, or a readiness to impart to others, implanted" (*STCE* 110; cf. 103, 105).

Money has altered the natural distribution of things, and the possibility of having long-term property has made men more desirous of it and thus more covetous. Of course, the material benefits of commercial society are immense, but occasionally Locke seems to speak wistfully of that time "in the beginning, before the desire of having more than Men needed, had altered the intrinsick value of things, which depends only on their usefulness to the Life of Man" (*2T* 37; cf. 111). In part, this sentiment no doubt reflects Locke's concern that increasing wealth threatens the ascetic character of the labor that produced it. Perhaps, though, the muted character of this lament should be taken as a further indication of the chronological element in Locke's story. Advocating a return to a golden age is as vain as arguing for a return to Eden. Although the future may hold many possibilities, this is not among them. That time is past. And to understand our choices, we must continue the tale of society's development. From the licensing of the use of money, we move to the formation of government by contract.

The "Original" of Government

" 'Tis not every Compact that puts an end to the State of Nature," but only the one by which people pledge to make one "Body Politick" (*2T* 14).

The commercial dealings in the State of Nature are but the prelude to government and lay the groundwork for it. After the introduction of nonspoiling money, people increase their holdings farther than they could without such a store of value. Because of this accumulation, for the first time, conditions of scarcity occur, and this creates a competition between individuals unknown in the golden age. The disputes that arise in this competitive state vex the population, for there is no impartial judge to enforce their contracts and secure to each the product of his labor. A group therefore enters "into Society to make one People, one Body Politick under one Supreme Government" (*2T* 89).[18] This, in short, is the familiar episode of the social contract in Locke's story. The people contract to depute their right to judge to a central authority in order to secure their property claims more completely.

The important thing to recognize is the way in which this contract can only follow on the one that creates money. In the earliest period of the State of Nature, it is true, there is no judge to arbitrate disputes. But neither are there many disputes before the use of money. Since each person can only hold as much as will not spoil, little is hoarded. And so "economic" are Locke's characters that they never seem to commit crimes of passion or other non-pecuniary violations. Conflict over possessions only occurs as the use of money makes possible limitless holdings as well as interpersonal contracts. There is thus a brief period of conflict prior to the institution of civil government that secures to each the just reward of his or her labor (*2T* 101). The terms of the contract forming the government are that each person entrusts to the government the right to enforce the contracts that entitle each to the product of his labor. In turn, individuals are guaranteed that government will impartially secure them their due. So far, then, we have three stages of contracts: the first broad one that creates money; the second local ones that extend commerce but also engender conflicts; and the one creating government, which secures the first two.[19]

But while the broad outlines of this government are fixed by the requirement that it uphold the two sorts of contracts, the details of its design are not. It may be a monarchy, aristocracy, or republic, just as the people like (*2T* 106). Of course, some forms (such as absolute monarchy) are ruled out by the basic requirement (hence the executive and legislative ought to be separate [*2T* 90]). But the fact that Locke only rules out explicitly this one possibility indicates just how wide open it is for the founders of a political society to choose their form of government.[20] Concomitantly, while the basic rights of citizens derive from their property rights, other civil rights will depend on the style of political association chosen (*E* 2.28.2). These choices differentiate one polity from another and, remarkably, allow Locke to consider each almost as a private corporation within the community of mankind. Each citizen "joins in a private, if I may so call it, or particular Political Society, and incorporates into any Commonwealth, separate from the rest of Mankind" (2T 127).[21]

This unusual feature of the *Second Treatise*—that no one form of government is explicitly singled out as best—ought to reemphasize our understanding of the work as a narrative. If it were truly reasoning on the model of a geometric proof, as Ruth Grant would have it, then a single conclusion would be expected. In saying that the people may choose from a (slightly limited) variety of possible regimes, Locke emphasizes the degree to which the story of the government's creation is a contingent one. Only an actual history, not pure reason, could tell us what the people had decided in any particular case.[22] This is government by plot, not by proof.

But, if there are a variety of just political societies, this raises the question of how those who have not explicitly consented to participation in one are nonetheless said to be members of it. Or rather, it puts the question particularly strongly, for the following reason: any account of a social contract faces the question of how people who have not explicitly agreed to the contract can nonetheless be said to be parties to it. One standard reply is to establish that the terms of the contract are the only ones or the best ones to which a reasonable actor could have consented. By allowing that there are a variety of possible, legitimate social contracts, Locke forbids himself the use of this reply. He must therefore seek another way to join latecomers to the contract.

Put another way, we can say that the puzzle is how Locke can have his story continue. Having started from a natural state of relative separateness, he has brought humanity through commerce and strife to the formation of a government. He has done so with the economic yet spiritual vocabulary of human experience that I explored in the previous chapter. The challenge now is to continue the narrative of government across generations. This Locke also does with a kind of contract—this time a contract between the living and the dead, which we commonly call a testament—a covenant between generations. Although more than a little morbid, this notion of a contract with the dead endows the living with strong claims against absolute rule.

The casting of the social contract as a testament is the link between the founders of a political society and its later inhabitants. While in theory, Locke says, each individual is as free as the first generation and is not born into any political obligation, in practice, the consent of the later generations to a covenant with the preceding ones allows society to continue without interruption or the continual renegotiation of the contract. The question is how this occurs.

The key is, naturally enough, property. One holds property, Locke argues, within the laws of a particular political community and agrees thereby to abide by the terms of that polity's contract. In other words, while owning property is a natural right, which government is instituted to protect, by agreeing to join a *particular* political community and enjoy *its* protection, the original contractors agree to all the special conditions of government that state has. All just governments protect property; but whether they do it as monarchies or republics is another matter. And in order to enjoy the protection of a monarchy, say, one must consent to its governance.

While no man can oblige his children to join his political association, control over his property is another matter. If a later individual accepts an inheritance within a polity, Locke thinks, that person can only do so by accepting the conditions that come attached to the property. Just as any will can set conditions for an inheritance that a beneficiary must meet, so too does the social contract function as one large will for all the inheritors in its domain:

> For *Every Man's Children* being by Nature as *free* as himself, or any of his Ancestors ever were, may, whilst they are in that Freedom, choose what Society they will join themselves to, what Common-wealth they will put themselves under. But if they will enjoy the *Inheritance* of their Ancestors, they must take it on the same terms their Ancestors had it, and submit to all the Conditions annexed to such a Possession. (*2T* 73; cf. 116–17, 120)

Property, in the State of Nature, is held free and clear; within "Politick Society," however, an inheritance comes with encumbrances that it is the recipient's obligation to accept or else to forfeit the bequest. Thus, youths only come to be members of the commonwealth as they accede to the terms of testament, "separately in their turns, as each comes to be of Age" (*2T* 117). It is hard to imagine this system actually working as such. Not only does it leave women and children in a countryless void, but even those few who do accept an inheritance might be well past their majority when they receive it. Locke realizes this and tries to argue that conditions can be annexed to purchases as well as inheritance, but inheritance remains the basic model. It may be that Locke's attempts to stretch the model to include purchase render it inconsistent (especially in § 120). But this does not alter the conclusion that Locke attempted to order the narrative around this simple idea.[23]

Locke envisions the chain that holds society together over time to be a series of contracts whereby each generation accepts its inheritance with certain terms annexed, then engages in a series of contractual relations with others in order to improve their estates, only to turn their efforts over to the next generation with the same set of conditions. We might even say here that Locke is playing on the notion of "Inheritance" so that it includes both the wealth we receive from our ancestors and the form of government that secures it. Indeed, given the parallels between words and money that he has drawn, this double meaning can be made explicit: the words of the social contract (ideas stamped into a definite coinage) are themselves a precious inheritance. They are a valuable hoard—always in danger of being clipped—which we can only grasp by accepting them into our storehouse of memory.[24] There has been some disagreement as to whether there are two kinds of consent in Locke, express and tacit, the former of which results in a fuller citizenship than the latter. While there may be exceptional cases of tacit consent (e.g., resident aliens), it should be clear that express consent is the normal case. The language of §§ 116–17 leaves no doubt that Locke considers acceptance of an inheritance as full a consent to join the contract as could be desired:

> [The father] may indeed annex such Conditions to the Land, he enjoyed as a Subject of any Commonwealth, as may oblige his son to be of that Community, if he will enjoy those Possessions which were his Fathers; because that Estate being his Fathers Property, he may dispose or settle it as he pleases. . . . the Son cannot ordinarily enjoy the Possessions of his Father, but under the same terms his Father did; *by becoming a Member of the Society*: whereby he puts himself presently under the Government, he finds there established, *as much as any other Subject of that Commonwealth. (2T* 116–17, emphasis added)[25]

Society is thus envisioned as a concatenation of contracts, some among the living and some between the living and the dead. It is a story that preserves the freedom of every man to consent to his political obligations and still affords stability (perhaps too much) to political affairs. It is the sort of plot that could only involve a Lockean character with his particular labor-centered way of acting and thinking. The price is a unidimensional view of all human affairs as matters of labor, production, and contract. In his pursuit of a story of freedom, Locke has, perhaps, sacrificed much of what we commonly want to be free for: to have experiences rich and varied rather than economic and "useful." Still, we must see Locke's narrative complete before we judge it, especially its culmination in a call to freedom, with which, I argue, we often identify. We can do this, in part, by considering in more depth the narrative Locke wanted to displace. Although doing so will break up the recounting of Locke's narrative, it provides an opportunity for a more thorough discussion of an alternative use of history in political theory.

The Problems of Patriarchy

Now, Locke comments, quite curiously, about the social contract: "this is that, and that only which did, or could give *beginning* to any *lawful Government* in the World" (*2T* 99). This remark is most important to consider when we examine the chapter in the *Second Treatise* titled "Of the Beginning of Political Society." Several commentators have seen in this section nothing but "concessions" to Filmer, Locke's opponent and theorist of patriarchy.[26] I argue instead that Locke does not concede anything, but rather reappropriates the patriarchal story and, by setting it within his own vocabulary and narrative, turns it to his own ends.[27] Indeed, I think an examination of this question reveals the general limitations of contextual approaches to Locke—limitations typified by an inability to make distinctions between the first and second of the *Two Treatises*.

In the *First Treatise*, the subject of attention is Filmer's theory of monarchical authority by right of fatherhood, which he developed in his essay *Patriarcha*.[28] There Filmer attempted to account for all political authority as a matter of God's Donation to Adam of worldly dominion, and of the inheritance of this authority by Adam's descendants. On this basis, he maintained that the King of England had absolute power, and that in relation to the King, there was little difference between subjects and slaves.[29] In the context of the time, this amounted to defending the inheritance of James II (brother of Charles II) against Parliament's claim to a right to "exclude" James from the succession and pass the throne on to another heir.[30] Locke takes on this argument at several points, but chiefly as a matter of biblical interpretation, even going so far as to quibble about translations from the Hebrew.

Filmer based his argument largely on a reading of Genesis. For every verse he cited, Locke would develop an alternate interpretation that led to an opposite political conclusion. Thus where Filmer cites the anathematizing of Woman (Gen. 3:16: "Thy desire shall be to thy husband and he shall rule over thee") as proof of Adam's dominion, Locke counters with ridicule: " 'Twould be hard to imagine, that God, in the same Breath, should make him Universal Monarch over all Mankind, and a day Laborer [N.B.] for his Life; turn him out of Paradise, to till the ground, ver. 23, and at the same time, advance him to a Throne, and all the Privileges and Ease of Absolute Power" (*1 T* 44). Where Filmer argues that Abraham was the inheritor of Adam's power, Locke replies that " 'twas more it seems then Abraham himself knew" (*1 T* 135). Often Locke's arguments are far more detailed, as when he debates with Filmer the correct translation of the Hebrew words for "Beasts of the Earth" (*1 T* 25–27). What all of these arguments have in common, however, is that they are based on a particular understanding of Filmer.

Locke takes Filmer to be establishing a narrative of authority continuous from Adam to Charles II based on father-to-son inheritance. Locke attempts to break up this narrative at every point that he can, whether between God and Adam, Adam and Seth, Noah and Shem, or any other point of transmission Filmer tries to establish. But he never claims that it is an ill-conceived project to attempt to devise a narrative of political authority. Nor does he deny that political authority could be a matter of "inheritance." He attacks the specifics of Filmer's argument, but never its general form. Although capable of great arrogance and sarcasm toward Filmer, he never suggests that Filmer give up history and argue, instead, from reason alone. His overall point is, rather, that parental and political authority have different "originals," and that different rules of inheritance thus apply to each (1 T 97).

One target that appears repeatedly in this debate about inheritance is the practice of primogeniture. From the discussion above, it is clear that Locke's stake in notions of inheritance was large. It ought also to be clear why primogeniture in political authority represented a threat to his political theory: if inheritance fell naturally to the eldest, how would the younger children be incorporated into the polity? Thus Locke accuses Filmer of wrongly assuming primogeniture to be a natural or biblical pattern and describes in detail several cases from Genesis (Cain/Abel; Jacob/Esau; Jacob/Judah) to demonstrate the opposite (1 T ch. 11; cf. 74–77). He maintains that Filmer was wrongly reading a current practice back into the biblical text. Rightly understood, he argues, the Bible demonstrates that all children are eligible for an inheritance. With all these arguments then, Locke dismisses Filmer's account of royal authority passing from Adam to his eldest, male descendants in a patriarchal pattern without denying in general the legitimacy of narratives of inheritance.

For this reason, some of Locke's interpreters have been distressed to see him "concede" to elements of the patriarchal argument in the sixth, seventh, and eighth chapters of the *Second Treatise*, where Locke describes the emergence of government from family associations. My feeling, though, is that Locke concedes little if anything in these chapters, but that this has been obscured by contextual approaches that stress Locke's immediate political purposes. At a broader level, what I hope to show briefly in the following is that, although two political arguments may have the same immediate purpose (here, to deny that patriarchal inheritance determines the authority of the King), one may hold continuing appeal for us, whereas another may not. This is what differentiates the *First* and *Second Treatises*. Although both treatises are part of an effort to deny the crown to James II, the second offers something that the first does not—namely, a narrative account of political authority based on a special character that I have described in Chapter 1. It is this plot, I maintain, that has made the *Second Treatise* one of the best-known books in the history of political thought, while the *First Treatise* has, until recently, languished in largely deserved obscurity.

For contextual interpreters (particularly Peter Laslett and Richard Ashcraft), the overriding question is the immediate political use to which Locke's arguments were to be put. For this reason, they have revived interest in the *First Treatise* as equally pertinent to Locke's project of denying the crown to James II. For them, the purpose of the two treatises is the same, and the arguments merely differ in form, while making the same point—namely, that James can rightfully be denied the throne. Thus any admission on Locke's part that parental relations, of any kind, are related to political authority is a concession, jeopardizing his assault on the royalists. By these criteria, when Locke admits the existence of father-kings whose sons inherit their thrones, he gives ground. In considering this argument, it would be well, I think, to recall why the *First Treatise* was so neglected for so long.

Until Laslett republished it in 1960, the *First Treatise* had hardly had a fresh printing since the nineteenth century, whereas the *Second Treatise* had been published separately dozens of times and translated into a variety of languages.[31] If the political import of the two works were the same, it would be hard to understand this different level of interest. But reading the two treatises in succession, it is not at all hard to understand the relative attention they have received. While the *First Treatise* laboriously examines fragments of Scripture and seeks to establish from these only a refutation of another political doctrine based on Scripture, the *Second Treatise* starts not from Scripture but from what it claims to be natural history and principles of natural reason. Although undoubtedly Christian in its broad outline, the *Second Treatise* seeks an account of government wholly devoid of biblical proofs. Where it cites Scripture, it is only to confirm the conclusions of reason, and never to draw any conclusions based solely on biblical authority. Contextualists, focusing on the immediate purpose of denying James the crown, pass over in relative silence the vast differences between the two books in evidence and style.[32] Not only are they thus unable to understand the different appeals the two volumes have had over the centuries (of which more later), but they specifically misinterpret Locke on the question of paternal authority in the *Second Treatise*.

The focus on the immediate purpose of Locke's argument, rather than his style, evidence, and narrative, is what leads to this mistaken account. When Locke returns to the inheritance of rule in the *Second Treatise*, after demolishing Filmer's version in the *First Treatise*, it is with the purpose of setting it within his own narrative of inheritance through contract and within his own vocabulary of natural associations of usefulness and labor. His alternative Genesis offers a story of the incarnation of the family without divine intervention in the State of Nature. It follows the subsequent growth of that family into a political association in a manner quite consonant with his own narrative of contract, but quite at odds with any biblical narrative.

Locke describes marriage as an association for the production and support of children whose permanence is traceable only to the fact that, as with some animals, "the female is capable of conceiving, and *de facto* is commonly with Child again . . . long before the former is out of a dependency for support on his Parents help" (*2T* 80). This "de facto" account of marriage is totally at odds with biblical accounts of conjugal society and does not lead to a "patriarchal" account of family but rather to the one that stresses its usefulness. When Locke puts his account of the family after his account of property, his purpose is to *retell* the story of patriarchy from the perspective of natural history. By putting family and inheritance within his account, rather than leaving it to biblical theories, he captures the experience of family and patriarchal inheritance for his own narrative and further undercuts that of his opponents.

In Locke's version, political authority follows on parental authority, *not* as a matter of right or divine injunction, but as an unsurprising evolution in the early ages when children attain their majority but still respect the judgment of their elders. Notwithstanding that after a certain age children no longer owe their parents obedience, he thinks, they will often agree to make a common father the political head of a clan because he is the best-qualified candidate and the easiest to agree upon (*2T* 74–76; cf. 94). And so patriarchal government comes about "not by any Paternal Right, but only by the Consent of his Children." In this manner, Locke incorporates the figure of the father-king into his own *contractual* history, in which he plays an important role, but one that echoes the overall theme. Fathers are kings by consent only, and when they are not thought fit, that consent may be withdrawn: "if they find him any way weak, or uncapable, they pass him by and set up the stoutest and bravest Man for their Ruler" (*2T* 105). When Locke cites Scripture at length to buttress his account (109), it is in the manner of incorporating the Bible into his narrative, rather than conforming his own drama to biblical history. The story of contracts and testament is not countered by the existence of father-kings, and neither is Locke's discussion of them a concession; instead, his retelling the story of such kings brings them within the bounds of Locke's own narrative political thought.

Inheritance from father to son is *not* a matter of patriarchal right but of *contract* and contract alone. This is the point Locke is making in his pages on father-kings. If a son takes up his father's position, it is only because he has acceded to the terms of a testament, not because he has the right to do so by birth. Locke did not wish to deny the possibility of an inherited monarchy (indeed, he supported that of William and Mary). He merely wished to deny an unimpeachable blood-right to inheritance of the throne. His story cannot be understood simply as one promoting the people against the King. It also defends a (labor-defined) character and a (contractual) plot against the biblical-patriarchal account of authority. It sets out to reassess history and to reincorporate elements of the opposing history into its own. It is not a weakening of this narrative, but a strengthening of it, when it can utilize familiar and agreed-upon historical episodes.

Although Locke surely did want to deny the crown to James II, such immediate purposes are not a sufficient starting point for a thorough understanding of the *Second Treatise*. The contextual accounts fail to render the point of Locke's description of paternal authority because they only differentiate arguments according to immediate political purpose rather than by method and vocabulary. But if we are to understand the continuing appeal of Locke's defense of revolution (which, if anything, grew over time), I think it is incumbent upon us to account for the different reception of the two treatises. This is not difficult. Arguments from Scripture no longer carry the weight they once did because we simply no longer accept the authority of the Bible as the final arbiter of political debates. Arguments from natural history on the other hand, however much we may disagree with them, are not ruled out in this way *tout court*. The vocabulary and narrative of contract remain appealing to us even when the details no longer do. The difficulty contextualists have understanding the differences between the two treatises is an indication of the limitations of their style of interpretation. By focusing on narrative, we may be able to see political implications to which contextualism is blind. The account of father-kings, rather than being a concession to James's position, is Locke's attempt to bring past episodes of patriarchy into line with his alternate narrative—the economistic, ascetic narrative of contracts.

All this, then, by way of preface to the final stage of Locke's narrative, when the political argument becomes more pointed. His call to revolution is the culmination of his story and draws whatever strength it has from the drama he has developed.

The Decline of Government and Revolutionary Renewal

In the latter half of the *Second Treatise*, Locke turns away from Filmer and faces the question of authority more directly. What he describes is a degeneration of the government whose genesis he has chronicled. When the contract is broken by the executive, a new situation appears. The character of the people is tested as the rights they secured by consent come under assault. Finally, when they can take it no longer, the people reclaim their original

right to organize the government and, in doing so, return the society to its
original. The story ends, not with the destruction of government, but with its
renewal. Perhaps there is even a suggestion of circularity in the narrative. It
has been said that Locke cannot be a Christian because he does not believe in
the Fall of Man. But it might be better to say that he does not see a fall in any
one moment but in the whole process of history. From the introduction of
money, to the introduction of government, to the degeneration of that government, every step seems like a step away from the innocence of the State of
Nature. Revolution, in this pattern, seems like a way to recapture something
of that earlier time (although certainly not everything about it).

The first episode in the decline of government Locke charts is the abuse
of prerogative. An executive, he thinks, may well have a power of prerogative
to go beyond the letter of the law for the sake of the greater public good. But
if he acts against the interests of the people, then it is an abuse that ought to be
opposed. He hints at a justification of violence: "In all States and Conditions
the true remedy of *Force* without Authority, is to oppose *Force* to it" (*2T* 155).
This episode, like those before it, is only possible within a world of meanings
built up by labor and stored in mental warehouses. Abuse of prerogative is an
abuse of the very language of the social contract. The King is attempting to
make the term *prerogative* mean something that it does not mean—namely, an
absolute and arbitrary power (*2T* 163). He is trying to put the idea of prerogative to ill use, to clip the word it has become known by. (Recall Locke's
consistent use of *ab-use* to indicate this kind of language fraud.) That is why
the abuse of prerogative, even if it only affects a few directly, effectively
challenges the whole system of government. The words of the social contract
are like pieces of currency—the abuse of even a few of them can devastate the
entire system of which they are a part.[33]

Locke's objection to the abuse of *prerogative* may seem lawyerly and technical. In a sense, I suppose, it is. But we have seen before how Locke's account
of a gray and dreamless world is closely connected to an ardent defense of
liberty. His political theory is bound tightly to the ascetic, economistic account of his characters—so we should not be surprised if the threats to political freedom are similar to threats that Lockean man faces daily. The abuser of
the common currency, the King, in this matter is no different from a common
cheat. And his attempt to abuse the terms of the testament is no different from
a common fraud, except for the scale of its possible effects.

The people have their inheritance from their ancestors in the terms of a
testament. Although this is normally an inheritance to obedience, in special
times it can be a claim of privilege as well. The abuse of prerogative is one
such time, but not the worst. As Locke says, it often affects just a few people

and is not prolonged. It has not led (yet) to a general inability to "talk or judge right," as abuses of a currency can. So he hesitates. Casting the conflict as one between the executive and legislative branch, he weakens his conclusion by saying that it is hard in practice to determine abuses: "Between an Executive Power in being, with such a Prerogative, and a Legislative that depends upon his will for their convening, there can be no *Judge on Earth*" (*2T* 168). If this seems a quandary, Locke has a ready answer for it, and that is that the people should appeal to Heaven to confirm the justice of their cause. This tentative suggestion of revolt Locke buries, as is often the case, within convoluted sentences:

> tho' the *People* cannot be *Judge*, so as to have by the Constitution of that Society any Superior power, to determine and give effective Sentence in the case; yet they have, by a Law antecedent and paramount to all positive *Laws* of men, reserved that ultimate Determination to themselves, which belongs to all Mankind, where there lies no Appeal on Earth, viz. to judge whether they have just Cause to make their Appeal to Heaven. (*2T* 168)

But from there, Locke catalogues more dangerous conditions. His chapters run: Of Conquest, Of Usurpation, Of Tyranny, Of the Dissolution of Governments. At each step down this staircase, he renews his call for resistance, gradually shedding whatever inhibitions about it he has. The argument gathers steam: "Then they may *appeal*, as *Jephtha* did, *to Heaven*, and repeat their *Appeal*, till they have recovered the native Right of their Ancestors" (*2T* 176). This is a key point: *the people do not simply claim their own rights—* they redeem the earlier pledge of their ancestors. They reclaim what has been held in trust for them by the government: their right to judge. It is not so much their material inheritance that they seek, but the less physical one embodied in the valuable words of the social contract. They reclaim their liberty (their "native Right") as a property held in trust. They seek to enforce the terms of the testament. They not only seek justice for themselves, but redemption for their past. They want to ensure that their ancestors did not plot in vain. So now the word *rebellion* appears for the first time in a positive light at a key moment, to be often repeated thereafter. This comes at the very end of the second-to-last chapter: "Whence it is plain, that shaking off a Power, which Force, and not Right, hath set over any one, though it hath the Name *Rebellion*, yet is no Offence before God, but is that, which he allows and countenances" (*2T* 196).

The second half of the *Second Treatise* thus chronicles the story of a government's decline from its "original" to a degraded condition. The plot is one of increasingly severe challenges to the people's inheritance. This plot takes place in the setting established by the expansive notion of labor described above. Characters labor in mind as well as in body. The threats to their freedom are a spiritual subjection and an abuse of the currency of their thought. The degradation of government that Locke describes only makes sense in terms of this special vocabulary. The tyrannical plot of the King is only possible with Lockean subjects. Here plot and character cannot be separated—any more than they could be in the *Essay*.

With the subject of tyranny, Locke returns his story to where he began it in the first words of the *First Treatise*. The issue is not just the abuse of power, but its extent: "Tyranny is the exercise of Power beyond Right, which no Body can have a Right to" (*2T* 199). In so doing, a magistrate does not merely debase his post, he effectively abdicates it; a king in so doing "unkings himself." The prose becomes more apocalyptic: "he will by actually putting himself into a State of War with his People, dissolve the Government, and leave them to that defence, which belongs to everyone in the State of Nature. For of such things who can tell what the end will be?" (*2T* 205). It is unusual for Locke to sound as uncertain as he does here. I think it is safe to say that at this point, the narrative reaches a crossroads, and it is up to the reader to choose the way. Locke never tells his readers directly to revolt. But he hesitates only because he does not want to dictate to them what their situation is. He tells a parable of revolt and seems to say to them, "If this story sounds like your story, then it must be time to rebel":

> if a *long Train of Actings show the Councils* all tending that way, how can a Man any more hinder himself from being persuaded in his own Mind, which way things are going; or from casting about how to save himself, than he could from believing the Captain of the Ship he was in, was carrying him, and the rest of his Company to *Algiers* [a slave market], when he found him always steering that Course . . . ? (*2T* 210)

The suggestion that the King has embarked on a course of enslavement is not just hyperbole. Locke knows that the King will not sell his subjects into chattel slavery. But, as we saw above, Locke's notion of slavery as a political evil is more expansive than the idea of chattel slavery. His conception of slavery derives from his thoughts on labor. And these allow for slavery of the mind as well as of the body. If a Catholic king were to force his creed on the people, this would represent, to Locke, an attempt to force their minds to labor at the will of another. This is the slavery that threatens the Lockean character. If the King is successful in his attempts to abuse the terms of the contract by which he rules, the result will be the mental enslavement of the people—even if the King never touches their property. Degeneration of the government has come because it no longer respects the currency of words in which its social contract is written. It seeks to alter words to its own advantage. The fraud the King perpetrates is not against the property of his subjects (narrowly understood); it is against their minds and their inheritance from the past. The patriarchal narrative is part of that fraud; just as Locke's natural history of government represents a counterplot on behalf of the people.

In his last chapter, Locke lists in more detail just what abuses constitute a breach of trust on the part of the rulers, so that a people might be justified in revolt. When the chain of contracts is broken by the rulers, it is up to the people to reestablish it. It is no longer a question of the legislative versus the executive, but of the people against either or both (*2 T* 222).[34] And in this case, on nearly the very last page of his work, Locke expresses himself as he has not before. Although God in Heaven is the ultimate judge, yet this must not hinder one from taking action:

> Here, 'tis like, the common Question will be made, *Who shall be Judge* whether the Prince or Legislative act contrary to their Trust? . . . To this I reply, *The People shall be Judge*; for who shall be *Judge* whether his Trustee or Deputy acts well, and according to the Trust reposed in him, but he who deputes him, and must, by having deputed him have still a Power to discard him, when he fails in his Trust? If this be reasonable in particular Cases of private Men, why should it be otherwise in that of the greatest moment; where the Welfare of Millions is concerned . . . ? (*2 T* 240; cf. 171)[35]

The language of "Trust," which directly invokes the parallel between the "Cases" of individuals and that of the people versus the government, links the call to revolution to the characters, setting, and story that Locke has developed: the King has administered the testament in a cheating manner. He has failed in his duty to execute a "Fiduciary Trust" to the beneficiaries of that trust (*2 T* 156, 149). He must be replaced as Trustee.[36]

Although it has been suggested that Locke means the word *trust* in a sense more general than legal,[37] that sort of personal trust (between two people) is not usually termed "Fiduciary Trust," and neither does it issue in a "Trustee or Deputy." Locke's use of the term "Trust," as well as the parallel with individual "Cases," indicates that the King may be opposed by the people when he abjures his role in the testament between the generations. As J. W. Gough notes, it was often the claim of absolutist kings that their trust came only from God. Locke maintains that, although natural law bounds and shapes the governmental trust, the deputation of power takes place as a contract among the people only—hence only the people judge when their deputy is false to his duties. Normally, the people depute their right to judge individual cases concerning property to the government. But of this right the King only becomes a trustee and not an owner. Although it lies dormant and in trust, the people can reclaim their inheritance, the "native Right of their

Ancestors," when the government itself becomes a threat to the property held in trust, to the "Welfare of Millions."

It is hard to know what to make of John Dunn's assertion that "the metaphor of legal trust . . . was not original to [Locke]; and it carries little or no distinctive weight in his argument."[38] It is certainly true that Locke was not the first to use this metaphor. As Gough has shown, it was in widespread use during the trial and execution of Charles I.[39] But if this shows that the metaphor was not "distinctive," it only *adds* to the idea that it carries a great deal of *weight* in Locke's argument. Violation of a legal trust was, in Locke's day, a common way to describe a king's abuse of power and to justify revolt. It is odd that Dunn should so studiously ignore the implications of the historical evidence that Gough amasses on this point in trying to assimilate trust to faith.

Laslett's discussion has the merit at least of facing this question more squarely.[40] He argues that Locke is only trying "to make suggestive use of legal language." I hope my discussion has made clear that the use of "Trust" is not accidental but rather is linked to Locke's whole vocabulary of politics. Laslett says, "it is very difficult to make sense of what [Locke] says if you try to interpret the actions of people on breach of trust as those of defrauded beneficiaries under a formal trust." I leave this to the reader to judge—but it seems to me that Locke's meaning is perfectly plain under this interpretation: the people should reclaim their stolen inheritance. They should redeem the acts of their ancestors by holding the future to the terms agreed on in the past.[41] They should reaffirm the value of the currency. They should block the attempt at imposing slavery. And they must reject the story of patriarchal inheritance in favor of a story of inheritance by contract. They must join the plot that Locke has laid out for them and recall the memory of government's true original. If they lose this account of the past, then they will surely lose their "Case" as well and enter a future trapped in Filmer's plot, where their role will be that of slaves to the King. The Lockean character's true role is that of laborer-trustor and, when his deputy defrauds him, that of rebel-judge.

Locke quickly repeats his caveat that God is, in some sense, the ultimate judge, but he has already gone beyond that, at the last possible moment. The message to the public is unmistakable: *you* are judge. Are the times as Locke described things under tyranny? Have there been a long train of abuses and clear design to enslave the people? Has the government put itself at war with the people? Is it time then to reinitiate the cycle of government and establish a new pattern in the midst of the chaos of the State of Nature? What *time* is it?

Lockean rebels are not out simply to secure their own rights; they seek to reclaim an inheritance that is being withheld from them. They rely on an account of the past in order to pursue a future. Their claim is based on history as well as right. Their hope for the future grows out of their sense of the past, just as their sense of themselves relies on their historical memories.

Locke's Future

Locke's narrative ends dramatically: the curtain rings down on the heels of this call for the people to judge. In this brief moment, he suggests, although not very strongly to be sure, an element of circularity in his notion of time. In seizing authority from the rulers, the people return almost (but not quite) to the beginning of the process. In advancing the narrative, the revolutionary takes it back near to its start. The worst tyranny leads to the best revolution. But what Polybius described to his readers as an immutable, natural pattern, Locke presents to us as an open question, a crossroads, an unfinished story that we may participate in. To be sure, his story points us in a particular direction and paints the alternatives so as to color our choices. But he never chooses for us. That is his complaint against arbitrary power; and the consistency of his story is that he refrains from using his authorial power to choose how the narrative ends for us.

Locke's narrative is in this sense "open." It has a favored end, but not a definite one. It does not conform to Aristotle's requirement of completeness. But, in the context of political theory, such openness means that Locke offers his readers a choice rather than a creed. In theory, as he was in practice, Locke is a plotter, not a geometer. His theory moves in time, not just in space.

Yet the act of rebellion has a further power that submission does not. By rebelling against unjust authority, the people redeem Locke's narrative. Submitting to arbitrary authority means confirming Filmer's account, and the right of kings to unfettered power. The truth of Locke's account cannot be confirmed with reference to historical records—this he freely admits. The foundation of government always precedes such records, he says, and peoples "search into their *original*, when they have out-lived the memory of it" (*2 T* 101). The *Second Treatise* is Locke's attempt to restore to people the memory they have lost: the memory of the first of those many contracts that constitute the fabric of society. But the only way to test the accuracy of this narrative is by its connection to the future. If a revolt against unjust authority takes place, then the history of government is as Locke says it is; we can step into the future with our past intact. If not, Filmer or some other authority is the supplier of the unremembered original. The future determines the past, not causally, but through the consistency of narrative. The future must have its corresponding past. In fighting for a particular future, a Lockean revolutionary redeems a particular history as well.

This sense of redemption also further links the elements of plot and character. For if the victims of a royal fraud actually revolt, they will further confirm and develop their status as Lockean characters. In rebelling, they demonstrate that they are not Filmerian slaves, but Lockean free laborers. They establish the authenticity of their memories and verify the elements of their character by their actions within the plot. To ask whether Locke offers an account of human nature to ground the right to revolt is like asking whether Hamlet is a hero before the climactic final scene. He is the same man throughout. But his identity is confirmed by his final actions. And we can imagine another end to the play in which all of Hamlet's previous acts are the same, but then his final choices convince us that he has, after all, a different, unheroic character.[42] Here, in the redemptive moment, narration and knowledge are one.

Lockean rebels are no Hamlets. Locke's sense of redemption is too fiduciary for that. We cannot expect much more from a world without dreams. Where all thought is labor, even a concept as evanescent as redemption becomes heavy. What is remarkable is that Locke reaches such a concept at all. For a theorist so in the grip of the Protestant ethic, it is astonishing to see revolution appear as the redemptive moment in a narrative of ardor. But Locke is a theorist of revolution and not of obedience. Although we must make war on our own desires, we may make war also for the sake of the future. We must submit neither to our own lusts and enthusiasms nor to the King's slavery.[43]

The past Locke offers us, precisely because it is *not* bound to seventeenth-century politics but is based on a unremembered original, is one to which we still have access. It is still open to the victims of unjust authority, whether at the hands of a king or some other, to identify with the memories that Locke proposes to his reader. Among the many telling absences in his narrative, none is perhaps more revealing than the lack of reference to Magna Carta. Although later scholars would describe Magna Carta as the prototypical social contract, Locke declines the example. He has something more radical in mind. He means to replace British history with a deeper human history—and it is this, along with his refusal to provide an ending, that gives the book its open character, that allows us to identify with the historical role Locke has sketched for his reader.[44] Locke's message of revolution is carried in the direction of his narrative. The subversive plot he left us to redeem has proven much more effective than any of the revolutionary plots against Charles II (e.g., the Rye House Plot, the Monmouth Rebellion) in which he may actually have taken part. Locke's world may lack for dreams, but it does not lack for liberty—liberty under a gray sky.

PART II

Friedrich Nietzsche

If all time is eternally present
All time is unredeemable.
—T. S. Eliot, "Burnt Norton"

CHAPTER 3

The Reveries of the Solitary

The whole world is an omen and a sign.
—Ralph Waldo Emerson, "Demonology"

A gate called Moment stands between past and future in one of Nietzsche's most memorable fables. Whatever else our lives consist in, he thinks, we stand at such an opening at every instant. Nietzsche connects our every experience to an experience of time. The connection, I argue in this chapter, is not an abstract account of time, but a concrete history—"our" history. But if Nietzsche's political theory is similar to that of Locke in form, its tone and content are nearly as different as one could imagine. Instead of a dreamless landscape, we are confronted with a world where dreams are built into the warp and woof of existence. Instead of a generic natural history, Nietzsche offers a gruesomely detailed genealogy. Instead of a gray world, Nietzsche's is almost excessively colored.

The difficult image of Zarathustra will serve to open this subject. Next, we shall explore the use Nietzsche makes of dreams as a model of human experience. The connection between dreams and culture, which Nietzsche originally found only in the Greeks, forms the basis, in his mature works, for a general history of morality. Nietzsche's analysis of dreams reveals a tension between memory and creativity and a parallel tension between past and future. Exploring the past through these tensions, Nietzsche reveals a history composed of pain and violence. The role of violence in the creation of memory and the role such memory is to play in any possible future are key themes in my exploration of Nietzsche's philosophy. When we return to the "Present" in Nietzsche's story, to the gate called Moment, we find that the path

before us has changed as a result of our consideration of the past. The central
feature of the gate called Moment is that a path runs through it from the past
to the future. Nietzsche's narrative creates for its reader a historical identity
that propels him toward a future, a future constantly menaced by a "Present"
that threatens to engulf and annihilate it. Nietzsche encapsulates this project, I
believe, in *On the Genealogy of Morals*, discussion of which is reserved for the
next chapter. The goal of genealogy is not just a recovery of the past, but the
redemption of that past through the use of it in the creation of the future.

The idea that Nietzsche's works contain narratives at all has been contested by such postmodern critics as Jacques Derrida and Paul de Man, who
contend that the overriding feature of Nietzsche's writing is its self-deconstruction. My reply to this view is largely contained in the substance of the
chapter, in which I try to make Nietzsche's narrative a plausible construction.[1] But the postmodern view has, I think, already drawn a useful abstract
rebuttal from Gary Shapiro, who draws an apt distinction between Nietzsche's possession of a "critical narratology"—that is, a critique of narrative or
metanarrative in general—and an abandonment of narrative in practice. Just
as Kant, we might say, offers a critique of reason while still employing it, so it
is with Nietzsche and narrative. "The suggestion that none of Nietzsche's
texts are really narratives," Shapiro contends, "might have to rely on an
argument that would deny the narrative status of any writing whatsoever."[2]
Although there is undoubtedly a cogent postmodern reply to be made here,
all that I require at this point is that the reader keep an open mind about the
possibility of narrative in Nietzsche.

The Character of Zarathustra

Zarathustra stands astride Nietzsche's philosophy, at once his most challenging concept and character. At times, Nietzsche praises him so effusively
that we fear the author has repeated the error for which he chastises Western
culture: worshipping a god he forgets is his own creation. At other points,
Nietzsche discusses the purposes, elements, and sources of his character so
soberly that we are prepared to dismiss all doubts as to his authorial control.
Nietzsche's Zarathustra is a puzzle. Solving this will not reveal all of Nietzsche's philosophy to us. But it may prove a useful starting point in considering
his attitude toward history and narrative. First of all, then, let us consider
Zarathustra's status as a character.

In Zarathustra, it should not be forgotten, Nietzsche reanimates a real
historical figure. It may be that, following the examples of Plato's Socrates and
the Jesus of the Gospels, Nietzsche believes the most powerful messages

would be contained in such a rewritten character. But that still leaves us with the question of why Zarathustra is chosen. It could simply be a matter of timing. "The first wise man among the gentiles," was what Giambattista Vico had called the historical Zarathustra in distinguishing between the sacred history of the Bible and the secular history of the nonholy peoples, the gentiles.[3] From this perspective, Zarathustra stands at the starting point of the alternative to what Nietzsche calls "christian-moral" values—the first possible event in a non-Christian story. Then, too, Zarathustra is not only the earliest sage; he also stands in contrast to Socrates and Jesus as a champion of the aristocrats.[4] But there is more to it than that. In fact, the real historical Persian prophet and founder of Zoroastrianism plays an important role in the creation of Nietzsche's Zarathustra. Nietzsche's character is neither a repudiation nor an arbitrary rewriting of this figure but, rather, a continuation of him.

Nietzsche's portrait has more in common with the historical Zarathustra than is commonly recognized. Zarathustra did indeed leave his home at the age of thirty for ten years of solitude and revelation in the mountains (*Z* Prol.: 1). Like Nietzsche's version, the historical Zarathustra was identified with fire and laughter (*Z* 1.8; 2.6; 4.20); and he preached against asceticism (*Z* 1.4). The rejection Zarathustra experiences in Nietzsche's book is also in accord with Persian tradition.[5] While one might have expected the many parallels between Nietzsche's character and the historical Persian religious leader to lead to some investigation of the connection, most readers have preferred to identify Nietzsche's Zarathustra with the author himself. This too-convenient interpretation allows Zarathustra's pronouncements to be read straightforwardly as Nietzsche's views.[6]

Recently, interpretations of Nietzsche's Zarathustra that take his status as a character more seriously have at last opened up some distance between the author and the authored.[7] Discussions of Zarathustra as a character focus mostly on Nietzsche's brief comments about him in *Ecce Homo*. There (Preface: 4), Nietzsche denies that *his* Zarathustra speaks as a prophet and says that he preaches, in effect, the opposite of the historical one: "Zarathustra created the most calamitous error, morality; consequently, he must also be the first to recognize it" (*EH* 4.3). Like Manichaeism, which was descended from it, Zoroastrianism saw the structure of the world determined by the dichotomy of good and evil, with humans possessing the free will to choose between them. It appears from these passages that Nietzsche is simply attempting to have his earliest opponent repudiate morality. It seems as though Nietzsche invokes the past simply to reverse it.

The choice of Zarathustra, then, looks to be motivated by a sense of historical irony. It is that. But it is also much more than that. Nietzsche's views of morality and the history of morality do not simply suggest, but actually demand, the choice of Zarathustra as spokesman. They do so for the following reasons: Nietzsche's critique of morality is never that it is simply false. Not only does he deny the existence of universal truths, but he also states repeatedly that falsehoods may well be necessary or healthy.[8] His critique of morality is rather that it is poisonous and unstable: poisonous because it imposes unnecessary limitations on humanity; unstable because it eventually overcomes itself. It is this characteristic of instability that determines the choice of Zarathustra. More than its Manichaeism, it is the value Zoroastrianism placed on truthfulness that makes it significant for Nietzsche. Zarathustra's is the first religion to lay such stress on truthfulness. And Zarathustra himself, as prophet, must have been the first to live by such a code.

Truthfulness is the element of morality that initiates its self-overcoming. As truthfulness is developed, questions and doubts are pushed with more insistence until finally all the other elements of morality are placed in their shadow. The requirement to be truthful at last undermines its own roots in the dichotomy of good and evil, which had been accepted on faith. Truthfulness destroys that faith. Zarathustra recognizes his own error first, not simply because he made it first, but because truthfulness has been at work in him the longest: "[Zarathustra's] doctrine, and his alone, posits truthfulness as the highest virtue. . . . The self-overcoming of morality, out of truthfulness; the self-overcoming of the moralist, into his antithesis [Gegensatz]—into me—that is what the name Zarathustra means in my mouth" (EH 4.3).

The development of "Zarathustra" is made equivalent to the development of morality itself. Nietzsche's discussion here of "the name Zarathustra" thus slides, almost imperceptibly, between the character he has created and the historical figure himself. For the overcoming that takes place under the name of Zarathustra involves both the original views of the Persian prophet and the new ones of Nietzsche. In writing of Zarathustra, then, Nietzsche aims neither simply at an old moralist nor at a mouthpiece for his own views but at a single persona or character that contains both elements. Only as a character who stretches the span between the Persian Zarathustra and Nietzsche can "the name Zarathustra" represent, in its entirety, "the self-overcoming of the moralist." "The name Zarathustra" thus personifies the path of morality, not as a falsehood, but as a self-overcoming. It is, therefore, no coincidence that Nietzsche has chosen to take up this name in particular. Zarathustra says at one point that if Jesus had "reached my age," he would have recanted the doctrines of his youth (Z 1.21). Nietzsche's Zarathustra has "lived" even longer, indeed longer than anyone else has lived with morality.[9]

The overcoming of morality in the role of Zarathustra also suggests something of Nietzsche's approach to the past. It introduces a theme I shall take up below: that the path taken by centuries of human history may be encapsulated in a single human life. Nietzsche sought to elide the distinction between the substance of the past and the memory of it that we possess. As I shall argue later, Zarathustra's personification of human history is not meant to be so different from our own existence. Nietzsche is not as interested in the substance of the past as he is in what remains of it. What are our memories, he asks, and how do they contribute to who we are? For, however vague it may be, we do have *some* sense of the centuries that have preceded us. Like Locke, then, Nietzsche believes that our future will be deeply affected by our sense of this past. And, again like Locke, Nietzsche feels this to be a question of redemption: if the past is not recovered and made to issue in something good, then surely it will only serve to imprison us.

The thinker who thinks about the future (the "philosopher of the future") is a key figure in Nietzsche's story. Zarathustra's status as "prophet," therefore, should have been of great importance to Nietzsche. The prophecy of Zarathustra was not merely a prediction of future events, however; it was an eschatology. Zoroastrianism holds that the history of the world takes place in twelve thousand years, divided into four equal eras. The last of these commenced with the birth of Zarathustra, who was the first to relate the whole story to mankind. The purpose of this retelling was to inform men of the choice that would soon face them: in the apocalyptic final struggle, it would only be the aid of human beings that would allow good to triumph over evil. If Nietzsche's character is not a prophet, he nonetheless retains something of the prophet's purpose: "Zarathustra once defines, quite strictly, his task—it is mine, too— . . . it is Yes-saying to the point of justifying, of redeeming even all of the past" (*EH*, "Zarathustra": 8). Much of this is echoed in the Nietzschean history I sketch out below. Nietzsche's division of time shadows the four-part Zoroastrian chronology. Zarathustra's self-location at the opening of a fourth era (and a coming crisis), we shall see, are also repeated by Nietzsche.

His Zarathustra has another, related connection to Zoroastrianism: the prophet is an interpreter of dreams. Dream interpretation was a vital part of this ancient religion, and Nietzsche's Zarathustra spends a good portion of his time interpreting his own dreams and visions. The connection between prophecy and dream interpretation should be clear, but modern developments have obscured it. Since Freud, we inevitably think of the interpretation of dreams as an analysis that reveals our own emotions or suppressed events of the past. But in the ancient world, dreams were often received as portents of the future, and reading them was a magical power. Nietzsche straddles these two views. As we shall see below, he is clearly the main precursor of many of

Freud's views; but in Zarathustra, he continues the ancient ones as well. While at other points in his books, he discusses the ancient belief in dreams dispassionately (e.g., GS 3.152; HH, bk. 1), in *Thus Spoke Zarathustra*, he brings it to life. There, dreams often speak of the future. The striking vision that Zarathustra has of a snake crawling down the throat of a shepherd and his liberation through a "good bite" (Z 3.2) actually comes to pass in a later section (Z 3.13). After "the stillest hour" is declared the site of great events (Z 2.18), it turns out to be a dream, in which a voice insists Zarathustra proclaim his highest value (Z 2.22). Yet another dream results in the revaluation of the "three evils" (Z 3.10). In each episode, dreams signify something that later comes to pass.

The connection between the interpretation of dreams and the future captures something of the connection between the old and new Zarathustra. Although "the name Zarathustra" contains the self-overcoming of morality, it is not, for that reason, a dead end. We are not left empty-handed once morality has exhausted itself. If Zarathustra only signified the projection of morality into the structure of the world (the Manichaean ideal), then the end of that process would require his death. That he survives this self-overcoming, "glowing and strong as a morning sun," suggests that he contains something more (Z 4.20). Even when he becomes "Zarathustra the godless," he is still "heavier with future" (GM 2.25). The reading of dreams as prophecy suggests another way of giving meaning to the world (than morality) and a path for finding our way to the future. If the self-overcoming of morality in Zarathustra suggests that history is at some kind of end point, Zarathustra's dreams and his interpretations of them provide an element of hope for a future. Indeed, as we shall see, the greatest threat that Nietzsche sees to the future of mankind is that we shall lose the capacity to dream, that we shall lose the capacity to imagine a future, and that therefore we shall not *have* a future in a certain sense of that term. For Nietzsche, I argue, does not want to push us toward a particular future so much as toward the Future, as opposed to the Present. His fear, in other words, is that we shall tarry too long at the gate called Moment and never attempt to step through it. So long as we live in the present, the past will stand unredeemed. If we turn to Nietzsche's other works with these thoughts in mind, we shall discover that, like Zarathustra, he creates a past that impels us toward a future. He describes this project in a preface to the unwritten, abandoned "Will to Power": "He that speaks here, . . . a philosopher . . . a spirit of daring and experiment that has already lost its way once in every labyrinth of the future; as a soothsayer-bird spirit who *looks back* when relating what will come" (WP, Pref: 3–4)

Zarathustra is also another word for courage (Z 4.15). To interpret dreams with courage and thus to find the future is Zarathustra's project. Dreams are not of past or future solely. Instead, they bind the two together and thereby make both possible.

Dreams and Their Interpretations

The importance of dream episodes to Zarathustra is entirely in keeping with the attention paid to dreams in Nietzsche's other works. Nietzsche's material on dreams is not as well organized as that of Freud, but it anticipates the latter's theories in many respects.[10] Dreaming also affords a convenient entry point to Nietzsche's thoughts on the intellect and creativity. And it will eventually bring us to his thoughts on history and its contents. Rather than relegating dreams to the margins, Nietzsche puts dreams at the center of his philosophy. In addition to whatever else we find, we shall see in Nietzsche's work an implicit critique of Locke's dreamless world, and an attempt to replace it with one both colorful and unascetic.

Nietzsche's interest in dreams spans his entire career. From his earliest published writings to his last notes, the subject of dreams returns again and again.[11] In *The Birth of Tragedy*, Nietzsche's discussion focuses on the identification of dreaming and artistry (an identification that continues throughout his works). Dreams are given the most attention in the books of Nietzsche's "middle" period.[12] These culminate in (what is for him) an extensive essay in *Daybreak*.[13] The conclusions reached here are then put to extensive use in his next two books, *The Gay Science* and *Thus Spoke Zarathustra*. On this topic, there is no sharp break with the works of the earlier period. Indeed, as other elements of his psychology and metaphysics fall away, Nietzsche continues to develop the insights he first gained through the study of dreams, using them as the basis of his new image of the psyche. It is my purpose here not merely to show the continuity of Nietzsche's thought in this area, but also to demonstrate how his later accounts of history rest on these early conclusions about dreams. For Nietzsche, as for Zarathustra, dreams are the link between past and future. Rather than being an obstacle to a model of the mind (as was the case for Locke), dreams are a starting point.

Since the subject of dreams is never far away from questions of interpretation, creativity, and appearance, it is clearly a central element of Nietzsche's thought with which we are concerned. He is preoccupied at all times with creativity. The question of the artist's psychology appears in almost every one of his books. It is intimately connected to the perspective through which he views history. Yet despite this constant attention, his notion of creativity remains puzzling, and is even more so in his later books, when the distinctions between great artists and great philosophers fall. This often has the effect of making Nietzsche seem even more romantic than he is—with a hopelessly grandiose notion of creativity animating all the great intellects.

Yet Nietzsche's idea of creativity, we shall see, is not an abstract, but a highly physical process. Dreams, it turns out, are the purest form of this activity and constitute the paradigm case. When we dream, we create in the most unencumbered way. The work of the sleeper provides a map to guide one through the labyrinth of Nietzsche's psychology, both individual and social. The picture that emerges is of a creativity in productive tension with memory; each side feeds the other, while also serving as a restraint on it. Both creativity and memory are physical powers. By night, the power of creation is dominant; by day, the strength of memory. But neither completely subordinates the other at any time. Indeed, it is the threat of such subordination that most worries Nietzsche. We need the powers of both day and night, he argues, in order to be complete.[14]

And yet, from *The Birth of Tragedy* onward, Nietzsche is concerned to break down the firm wall that is held to exist between waking and dreaming. He replaces it with a difference of degree. He never holds that the two states are identical, but that "there is no *essential* difference" (*D* 2.119). He begins this project by identifying dreaming with the waking activity of artists: "The beautiful illusion of the dream worlds, in the creation of which every man is truly an artist, is the prerequisite of all plastic [*bildenden*] art, and, as we shall see, of an important part of poetry also. In our dreams, we delight in the immediate understanding of figures; all forms speak to us; there is nothing unimportant or superfluous" (*BT* 1). Here Nietzsche is describing the Apollonian element of artistry, which, in *The Birth of Tragedy*, is combined with the Dionysian in the creation of tragedy. Dreams are the metaphor he has chosen for the Apollonian state, and they are contrasted with the intoxication that symbolizes Dionysus. The metaphors are meant to be illustrative, but they are also something more. Since Dionysus is the god of wine, intoxication is naturally the Dionysian condition. But why is dreaming Apollonian (especially when it is Hermes who, in Greek tradition, actually brings dreams)? Nietzsche's answer reinforces the connection I drew earlier between dream reading and prophecy. Apollo is "the god of all plastic [*bildnerischen*] energies, [who] is at the same time the soothsaying god." Apollo is a soothsayer, hence, dreaming is Apollonian. In addition to their perfect forms, dreams are held to be portents of the future (at least by the Greeks).

Creativity, for Nietzsche, binds dreaming, art, and prophecy, but its nature is hard to fathom, hidden in such phrases as "plastic energy." The primary component of this activity seems to be the formation and contemplation of shapes and images: "the plastic artist . . . is absorbed in the pure contemplation of images [*Bilder*]" (*BT* 5). The opposite of this activity is Dionysian intoxication, a formless energy whose best expression is music. But what art does Nietzsche have in mind when he speaks of "images"? And how are dreams translated into the public realm? or into prophecies?

Nietzsche attempts to breach the wall between dreaming and wakefulness by making a connection between dreams and Greek mythology. He first describes the "dream-birth" of the Olympian gods as a general attribute of Greek culture, but then goes on to personify "a dreaming Greek" (*BT* 2): "How unutterably sublime is *Homer* therefore, who as an individual being, bears the same relation to this Apollonian folk culture as the individual dream artist does to the dream faculty of the people and of nature in general" (*BT* 3). Nietzsche takes the epic poetry of Homer to be the foundation of early Greek culture. And, if Homer's main inspiration is thought to be his dreams, the dreams of a typical Greek (see *BT* 2), then his dream images are clearly more than the inspiration for a particular artwork. They are the foundations of Greek culture itself. Somehow, these images embody the values of heroism, individuality, and glory around which Greek social life (in Nietzsche's interpretation) was organized. But how are the shapes of dream life translated into the values of the waking world? In particular, we might wonder how Homer—who was no plastic artist, of course, but a poet—could be called "a dreaming Greek." Nietzsche's answer tells us, not just about Homer, but about the typical Zarathustra-like character who dreams. This character grows in importance through Nietzsche's works, ultimately becoming the protagonist of *On the Genealogy of Morals*. What Nietzsche first explores as the special case of Homer, becomes, in many ways, his paradigm.

The broader significance of dreams Nietzsche finds in the *organization* of and the *relations* between their perfect shapes. Rather than any individual image having its own value, dreams convey their message through the ordering, accumulation, or interaction of the signs they contain. The perfect shapes of the plastic artist take their meaning only in a context of other shapes: "Our dreams are, on the rare occasions when they are for once successful and perfect—usually the dream is a bungled product—chains of symbolic scenes and images in place of the narrative poetic language" (*WS* 194). The isolated shapes do not carry the dream's significance; their composition and interaction do. Homer's "successful" dreams form the basis for his successful poetic narratives—which are not mere adventure stories, but "symbolic" of greater themes. Where Locke likened words to coins, Nietzsche compares them to dream images. And this means that, for Nietzsche, neither words nor images carry their meaning apart from the others with which they appear. "Narrative poetic language" cannot be compared to a stack of coins, but rather to a chain that takes its shape from the pattern linking its irregular units.

Interaction between shapes allows the transposition from the visual art to the verbal, and from there to social organization. That is, while individual shapes can be described, they cannot, in isolation, have the same sort of meaning that they can in the presence of other shapes. The relation between shapes has, beyond its beauty, a meaning that can be rendered more completely, if less elegantly, in language. In order to grasp the social implications of dream images, the relation of signs must be grasped linguistically, rather than visually. Take, for example, a simple two-shape image: the Soviet symbol of the hammer and sickle. Composed of two simple shapes, their combination could be considered solely on visual grounds. Comments on their balance, symmetry, color, and like qualities would then be appropriate. Yet a more powerful understanding of this symbol would surely refer to the alliance of workers and peasants that the superimposition of the two elements purportedly represents and reinforces.

This relation of signs represents the true cultural import of a work, for it conveys a meaning that, if powerful, both molds and captures the set of understandings shared by audience and author alike. It requires, as a base, a previous understanding of the signs on the part of the audience. The new composition may then alter those meanings somewhat by putting the signs in a new set of relations, and therefore in a new light. The combination of the hammer and the sickle suggested a potential political alliance and (because tools are used) evoked the possible power of such an arrangement. Originally, the visual composition was as novel as the coalition—a dream of Lenin, we might say. Once established, the composite symbol could itself be used in further combinations as the vocabulary of symbols grew. A dream image is thus a combination of symbols that make up a whole greater than the sum of its parts. The meaning of the individual symbols is culturally rooted. But the new composites created in dreams, Nietzsche suggests, can themselves feed back into our cultural understandings—at least when it is a Homer who so dreams.

The question remains then of how symbols acquire their simpler meanings in the first place. The pattern I have described suggests an infinite regress of composition. In fact, Nietzsche accepts this suggestion, or something very much like it. What is most important for Nietzsche is the long process of successive composition that builds up meanings rather than some original meaning-endowing act:

Dramatic music becomes possible only when the tonal art has conquered an enormous domain of symbolic means, through song, opera and a hundred

experiments in tone-painting. . . . It was the intellect itself which first introduced this significance [*Bedeutsamkeit*] into sounds; just as, in the case of architecture, it likewise introduced a significance into the relations between lines and
masses which is in itself quite unknown to the laws of mechanics. (*HH*, 4.215)

Even a simple composition in the present rests on the meanings built up in
previous generations. Although symbols may be ignored or lost by succeeding generations, the ones they retain will doubtless be based on many previous compositions. Even in our dreams, we manipulate symbols with a long
pedigree; we make new compositions with found objects.

   We can return, then, to the question of how the poet Homer could be
cast by Nietzsche in the role of a dreamer. Insofar as his verse is a composition
of signs, it resembles the work of a dreamer and plastic artist. We can now
make sense of an ambiguous passage quoted above in which Homer is said to
bear "the same relation" to folk culture as the individual artist does to the
"dream faculty of the people." He is neither purely a maker of culture nor
simply a representative of it. The "shapes" he takes from the existing milieu;
the composition is his own. When Nietzsche remarks that "three-quarters of
Homer is convention," this is what he has in mind (*WS* 122). Any artist uses
existing conventions, "the toilsomely acquired common language," to speak
to his audience (ibid.; see also *WP* 3.809). Homer did not fashion his epics out
of whole cloth, but this need not lead us to deny his remarkable originality.
For Nietzsche, to be one-quarter original is to be very original indeed.[15]

   Homer, the rarest of dreamers (*his* dreams are not bungled), brought
forth the most perfect, and therefore most powerful "chain of symbolic
scenes" and on this basis holds his particular place in Greek culture. Nietzsche
himself gives us the best way to evoke the continuity between dreams and
poetry in the case of Homer: "we can speak of [the Greeks'] *dreams* only
conjecturally . . . a certain pictorial sequence reminding us of their finest bas-
reliefs" (*BT* 2). The friezes of the Parthenon capture the elements of both
dream and poetry. Like a dream they are an ordered sequence of images, but
like poetry, each image carries a significance that derives from and contributes to the overall story—a story that is culturally constitutive. Each warrior
carved in stone is beautiful. But whether they signify good or ill, bravery or
cowardice is determined by their relation to the other characters. And the
story itself is not just some pleasant tale, but a national epic through which the
Athenians identify themselves.

   The bas-relief then captures Nietzsche's notion of the dream, but the
activity of the dreamer has still, perhaps, been left vague. The poet straddles
the line between dreams and waking life. Tragic theater mimics this defeat of
barriers by creating a field in which the dreams of a few become accessible to

many: "[The chorus] radiates this vision of the drama which is by all means a dream apparition and to that extent epic in nature. . . . But now we realize that the scene, complete with the action, was basically and originally thought of merely as a *vision*; the chorus is the only 'reality' and generates the vision, speaking of it with the entire symbolism of dance, tone and words" (*BT* 8). Here visions are merely waking dreams. As in monumental friezes, the perfect shapes of dreams are transformed into symbolic public statements. As the dreamer crafts his dreams, so the chorus projects the images that take place on the tragic stage. If Nietzsche has any "model of artistic practice," it is surely the activity of the Greek chorus and not that of the sculptor or the musician.[16] In tragedy, the work of the chorus is to bring to life a narrative that is at once familiar and unfamiliar to its viewers—familiar in that the events depicted rely on well-known history, unfamiliar in that the depiction reveals (or invents) a lesson of symbolic value not previously seen to attach to this history.

Nietzsche's early writing on dreams thus offers an intricate, complex account of what dreams are like, as well as describing a resemblance between dreaming and artistic creativity. Homer is described as the prototypical dreaming character. The connection between dreams and time I have begun to suggest, if only in outline. The images that appear in our dreams are bits of our history, shapes whose significance can only be explained in terms of our cultural past. The work of the dreamer, however, makes something new of those shapes. The narrative chain is reforged and (the invocation of Apollo the soothsayer suggests) that chain may lead to the future. How the likes of Homer can prophesy, however, has yet to be explained. Much about the Nietzschean character remains to be set out.

Dreamers and Sleepwalkers

What Nietzsche suggests through the example of the tragic chorus is that the figure of the artist may not be so rare as at first seemed. Through tragedy, it appears, an entire society was able to breach the wall between waking and dreaming. The Greeks, he believes, brought the simple beauty of their friezes into their real social lives. Tragedy enabled the many to experience (and thereafter to dream) the dreams of a few. "The waking day of a mythically excited nation, the ancient Greeks, for instance, is, by the constant action of marvels, indeed more like a dream than like the day of the scientifically sober thinker" (*OTL* 255). After *The Birth of Tragedy*, while he would continue to believe that Greek life held a sort of special perfection, Nietzsche applied his views on dreams, on the infirm barrier between waking and dreaming, to all peoples. As he gave up the distinction between "reality" and "appearance," his thoughts on Greek dreams and art moved to the center of his social psychology, although with a notably less romantic tone (see, e.g., *GS* 1.54; *TI* 4.1–6).

What seemed to Nietzsche, in *The Birth of Tragedy*, to be the specially Greek relation between dreams and social life came, in his later works, to be a general description of the sources and history of culture. Although this shift involved important changes in Nietzsche's philosophy, critical elements of the work on dreams are transferred to the later books more or less intact. When Nietzsche gave up the notion of a metaphysical truth or even a metaphysical emptiness standing behind dreams and tragedy (still in use at *UM* 2.10), this did nothing to lower his estimation of those phenomena. Indeed, the opposite happened. He came to value dreams for themselves, rather than trying to see through them to something more basic. Instead of discarding his analysis of dreams, he deepened it. He found he could continue to use dreams as the nexus of artistry, interpretation, past and future—all without the metaphysical backdrop.

But in doing so, Nietzsche shifts the basis of his account from metaphysics to something more mundanely physical. In the outline that follows, many elements of Nietzsche's view will seem crudely biologistic, if not downright bizarre. In fact, some of them bear a considerable affinity to the writings of Aristotle, not to mention the latest incarnations of neuroscience[17]—but this is really beside the point. Even if all of the physical elements of Nietzsche's account of dreams and related phenomena were demonstrably false, it would still be important to explore them. The value of such an exploration lies in gaining an understanding of the way these views underpin Nietzsche's account of memory and creativity, two concepts central to his notions of past and future, and, indeed, to his whole political philosophy.

Much of what Nietzsche wrote in his middle works on historical subjects is superseded by the *Genealogy*, but his thoughts on dreams span both periods. Although the connection with Apollo is put in abeyance, the link between dreams and the past is not. In *Human, All-Too-Human*, for example, men of a "primeval" period (*Urzeit*) do not distinguish, or are incapable of distinguishing, as we do, between what they see while waking and sleeping (*HH* 1.3, 5, 12, 13; also *D* 2.119). Unable to banish dreams to their sleeping hours, they suffered (or enjoyed) them all the time, as visions, and reacted to them as sleepwalkers do.[18] They could not perceive the "essential difference" between the two states that later people imagine. There was less mediation then, by the waking, conscious mind, between the artistic symbol chains of imagination and everyday life: "the perfect clarity of all dream-ideas . . . again reminds us of conditions pertaining to earlier mankind, in whom hallucination was extraordinarily common and sometimes seized whole communities, whole peoples at the same time. Thus: in sleep and dreams we repeat once again the curriculum of early mankind" (*HH* 1.12).

Here Nietzsche begins a theme that will be taken up most forcefully in the *Genealogy*. By postulating consciousness as the barrier between waking and dreaming, and as something that has appeared over the course of human history, Nietzsche argues that the wall between the two states has been *built* over time. In his early work, he accepted the division of waking and dreaming as natural. Later, rather than merely describing the differences between waking and dreaming, Nietzsche begins to wonder how these differences came about, how human beings came to possess consciousness. The historical account that responds to this query turns out to provide a narrative of morality and violence, a monstrous plot that is yet a redeemable past.

The levee of consciousness, erected between waking and sleeping, has not yet grown so high or so thick as to be impenetrable. Even today, Nietzsche holds, the activity of dream artists continues, even if most people hallucinate less frequently: "Oh, these men of former times knew how to *dream* and did not find it necessary to go to sleep first. And we men of today still master this art all too well. . . . It is quite enough to love, to hate, to desire, simply to feel—and right away the spirit and power of the dream overcome us . . . we somnambulists of the day! We artists!" (*GS* 2.59; see also *BGE* 5.193). The sleepwalking artists of today still resemble the Apollonian artists of the Greeks. They are led by the perfect shapes, symbols, and composition of their visions through a way of life others approach only in their dreams. Although there are few Homers to be found, and visions no longer seize "whole nations," they still lead a few to high mountains.

Or perhaps it is simply the case that conflicting visions do not seize nations in rapid succession—which is what would give the appearance of hallucinations to an observer. The rising wall of consciousness reduces the contact between the two realms, so that dreams disturb the stability of wakefulness less. This stability becomes a key feature of Nietzsche's account of morality, which centers on predictability and capacity to promise. In an early, unpublished essay, Nietzsche wrote: "Actually the wide-awake person is certain that he is awake only because of the rigidly regular web of concepts, and so he sometimes comes to believe that he is dreaming when at times that web of concepts is torn apart by art" (*OTL* 254). But for all this identification of dreaming and artistry and their opposition to consciousness, we still have only a fuzzy notion of just what the dreamer and artist are actually doing that sets them apart from those who are simply awake (or "more conscious"). Can we say anything more specific about their activity or are we to be left with only a vague idea of their "creativity"?

Creativity and Interpretation

Our first clue is contained in Nietzsche's frequent connection of dreaming and dancing. Why does Nietzsche so often resort to metaphors of dance? "[H]e has forgotten how to walk and speak and is on the way toward flying into the air, dancing. His very gestures express enchantment. . . . he feels himself a god, he himself now walks about enchanted, in ecstasy, like the gods he saw walking in his dreams. He is no longer an artist, he has become a work of art" (*BT* 1). To dance is to become the stuff of dreams; but we now know this means something rather specific—an ideal symbol chain. A dance is a series of movements and gestures, each of which might be isolated, but that together form a continuous expression far greater than the sum of its parts. The movements are integrated at a physical level, according to standards of grace and beauty. But a more powerful dance has an intellectual content as well. In such an effort, in addition to a physical, gymnastic display, each movement signs for an element related to the others in a narrative. A dance, then, even more than a painting or a sculpture of a single figure, corresponds to Nietzsche's idea of the unbungled dream as a symbol chain. Like tragedy or a frieze, the symbols come in a particular order, which constitutes the principal means of their organization. In plastic art, in contrast, the symbols are all presented simultaneously and the integration is simply spatial—while in dance it is both spatial and temporal. A painter, despite his best efforts, cannot compel an observer to take in the elements of his work in the right order in the way a dancer can.[19] Nietzsche's frequent invocation of dance is often taken as a sign of his hopeless romanticism. But he actually has a rather exacting view of what is required to make dance meaningful. As we shall see below, Nietzsche's description of dancing correlates precisely with that of dreaming. The creativity they describe is limited. In fact, it is highly regimented by the links between past, present, and future.

And what is required for the creative generation of meaning? What does it take to create a dance? In *Daybreak*, Nietzsche gives his most extended description of how he believes dreams arise. They are, he believes, a form of interpretation, but one where the dreamer's own creative capacities are clearly in the foreground. The text is simply our bodily sensations. The Apollonian images are the interpretations of these sensations by our drives:

These inventions [dreams], which give scope and discharge to our drives . . . , are interpretations of nervous stimuli we receive while we are asleep, *very free*, very arbitrary interpretations of the motions of the blood and intestines, of the pressure of the arm and the bedclothes, of the sounds made by church bells, weather-cocks, night revelers and other things of the kind. That this text, which is in general much the same on one night as on another, is commented on in such varying ways, that the inventive reasoning faculty *imagines* today a *cause* for the nervous stimuli so very different from the cause it imagined yesterday, though the stimuli are the same: the explanation of this is that today's prompter of the reasoning faculty was different from yesterday's—a different *drive* wanted to gratify itself. . . . Waking life does not have this *freedom* of interpretation possessed by the life of dreams, it is less inventive and unbridled—but do I have to add that when we are awake our drives likewise do nothing but interpret nervous stimuli and, according to their requirements posit their "causes"? that there is no *essential* difference between waking and dreaming? (D 2.119)[20]

There is no absolute difference between dreams and ordinary life;[21] what has shifted is the balance of text and interpretation. Dreaming is the piling up of great and wondrous interpretations on as minimal and (apparently) meaningless a text as can be imagined. When our feet are cold, we may dream we are standing on an iceberg; from noise outside, we might dream ourselves at a party; from the rustle of sheets, we could dream of the whistle of air as we fly (see also *HH* 1.13). Although our waking experience is also mediated by our drives, in sleep our drives come to dominate our sense impressions to the point where they are almost (but never quite) disconnected. Dreams are a commentary on our sense impressions, akin to a fairy-tale interpretation of a mundane, disorganized chemistry text.

But these interpretations are also our primary experience of these sense impressions and not something we experience separately, over and above them. That is, we do not, on Nietzsche's understanding, experience the bodily sensations *first*, and then afterwards *also* receive a dream image. Rather, before we experience the nerve stimuli at all, they are worked over by our drives so that they reach us in perfect Apollonian forms. This transformation is not added onto a baseline, ordinary perception; experience simply *is* this process—at least at night. As we shall see in a moment though, this model of experience (so different from Locke's) is meant to cover waking life as well.[22]

Before we explore how Nietzsche transfers this model to daytime, however, we must consider the meaning of the term *interpretation* in this context. Although Nietzsche continues to use it here, he does so in a particular way. In what sense can this creativity, which makes Homeric images from the contractions of intestines, be considered interpretive? It seems to be a pure expression, the crystallization of one of our drives into an Apollonian form. This process occurs as a reaction to or embellishment of a sense impulse. But, in sleep, the contribution of these impulses fades almost to insignificance. Here interpretation teeters on the brink of the seemingly impossible—to create something from nothing. Nietzsche held even Homeric verse to be largely convention. In dreams, he suggests, convention is at a minimum, and invention is at its strongest: "You are willing to assume responsibility for everything! Except, that is, for your dreams! What miserable weakness, what lack of consistent courage! Nothing is *more* your own than your dream! Nothing is more *your* work! Content, form, duration, performer, spectator—in these comedies you are all of this yourself!" (*D* 2.128).[23] Through discipline, we have made our waking lives more consistent; but our dreams have remained capricious and, on account of this discipline, have become even more so. Drives that are no longer allowed expression during the day, remain bottled up and have only the mundane text of the night on which to "comment." By the "drives" that interpret, Nietzsche does not simply mean instinctive, inborn motivations. Indeed, as we shall see when we come to examine the *Genealogy*, the creation of drives is a crucial element of human history: "The human and animal past, indeed the whole primal age and past of all sentient being continues in me to invent, to love, to hate and to infer" (*GS* 1.54). Nietzsche's notion of drives must be contrasted, not assimilated, to Freud's.

Our waking interpretations are less arbitrary, then, but less inventive as well. The title of section 2.119 in *Daybreak*, which contains the extensive discussion of dreams quoted above, is actually "Experience and Invention" ("Erleben und Erdichten"). Nietzsche uses the entire discussion about dreams here to make a point about experience in general, daytime as well as nighttime: "What then are our experiences? Much *more* that which we put into them than that which they already contain! Or must we go so far as to say: in themselves they contain nothing? To experience is to invent? ['Erleben ist ein Erdichten?']." Here Nietzsche is again reversing a common understanding. While experience, like interpretation, is normally taken to be a passive activity, a reaction to what is put before us, Nietzsche suggests that it is almost exactly the opposite of that.[24] Invention is the heart of experience, rather than its opposite. The interrogative formation ("To experience is to invent?") indicates that he recognizes the impossibility of this being wholly the case. Nonetheless, such a statement ("To experience is to invent") represents an asymptote toward which his thought tends—a conclusion toward which he reaches, but that would lose its force were he ever fully to achieve it (see also *GS* 2.87). I think it is often useful to approach Nietzsche's boldest questions as asymptotes and his thought on these matters as asymptotic. The statements have much more force when considered in this fashion. Clearly, a bald statement such as "experience is invention" can be as empty and tautological as "red is blue" or "freedom is slavery"—one is bound to face the objection that one simply has a deficient understanding of *experience* or *red* or *freedom*. When thought of as an asymptote however, when one tries to see how much invention can be *contained* in the concept of experience without denying some difference between the two, then the real power of the suggestion becomes clear.

The description of our experiences as containing invention might be illustrated by the idea of an enormous balloon. The sense impression represents the boundary or material of a balloon, which is then inflated to immense proportions by the inventions of its interpreter. The impression remains an inviolable border to the experience. Yet, as the size of the balloon continues to increase, it makes sense to ask whether the substance of the experience is the rubber sphere or the air inside it. As anyone who has inflated balloons knows, as the rubber stretches, it becomes more transparent. One can imagine a point where it is hard to discern at all, a point where the text disappears "beneath the interpretation" (*BGE* 2.38). Here I differ, although perhaps only in minor ways from Eric Blondel, who has asserted the priority of interpretation, for Nietzsche, over the body in the following terms:

> If, ontologically, Nietzsche maintains the body as a first reality, on the other hand, from the epistemological point of view (the only one he can support by virtue of challenging the in-itself), the ultimate principle is not the body, but interpretation, the "body" being merely the metaphor of interpretation, the human means of interpreting it. . . . Nietzsche's apparently biologizing texts, far from reducing the ideal to the body, are merely attempts to bring culture (conceived of *as* body) back to the fundamental interpretation, the physiological body being one case of interpretation among others.[25]

The texts I have quoted above, with their description of dreams as commentary on blood and intestine movements, make it difficult to accept Blondel's contention that Nietzsche is merely conceiving here of "culture as body." Nietzsche's descriptions seem too detailed and individual for that. In addition, Blondel's position slides over the question of *what* is being interpreted. Nietzsche may well believe that "there are no facts, only interpretations" (*WP* 481), but although he believes the mind supplies all the interpretations, he does *not* believe it supplies all the *texts*. *That* would be the solipsism into which many accuse Nietzsche of falling, but that he does not in fact succumb to. Indeed, if the mind supplied both interpretations and texts, there would be no reason for distinguishing the two, and the meaning of *interpretation* itself would be left empty. I can only reconcile myself to Blondel's view by stressing a modified version of his opening phrase describing the body as a "first reality." Without denying the epistemological priority of interpretation, we can still state that Nietzsche does not consider the body to be a mere metaphor for culture. He believes that the sense interpretations on which we comment are not themselves the product of the mind, even if we can never know the truth about them or about the body itself as a thing or, indeed, as a piece of some external reality. The body is what we call the medium through which we receive sense impressions—that is, through which we acquire texts. Thus the "body" *is* a metaphor, but only for . . . the body itself: the unknowable medium—the unknowable "x"—through which we receive impressions.

The connection with dreams and creativity is always present in Nietzsche's discussions of interpretation and experience. Several passages from *Beyond Good and Evil* make clear that he considered the interpretation that takes place in dreaming and waking to lie on a continuum of creativity: "What we do in dreams we also do when we are awake: we invent and fabricate the person with whom we associate—and immediately forget we have done so" (4.138). Nor is this model limited to the personal encounters described here. Nietzsche finds creativity even where we strive to be objective in recording information—that is, in our most scientific moments. In section 192, he describes the resistance in science to truly new information that would disturb our existing set of beliefs. Rather than being alone and asleep with only our drives and intestines to guide us, in science we make the greatest effort to look outside ourselves and take in new things. The scientific search for knowledge is in many ways our most wakeful, conscious state. Yet even here, Nietzsche says, our creativity cannot be constrained:

> It is more comfortable for our eye to react to a particular object by producing again an image it has often produced before than by retaining what is new and different in an impression. . . . Even when we are involved in the most uncommon experiences we still do the same thing: we fabricate [*Erdichten*] the greater part of the experience and can hardly be compelled *not* to contemplate some event as its "inventor" [*Erfinder*]. (*BGE* 5.192)[26]

When we look at a tree, he says, rather than really seeing all its particular attributes, we create "an approximation of a tree." In our dreams we do not experience the contractions of our intestines as such, but make out of them something quite different. Between waking and dreaming, only the balance of text and interpretation changes. Even philosophizing itself is not exempt from this condition: "Often I have asked myself whether, taking a large view, philosophy has not been merely an interpretation of the body and a *misinterpretation of the body*" (*GS*, Pref., 2). Approximating a tree is not the same thing as dreaming you are the king of Xanadu, but it is the same sort of process, the same invention on top of sense impressions. In whatever area of life Nietzsche looks, he finds this pattern.[27] What changes is the degree of freedom in interpreting. *Why* this is so, I shall examine shortly.

Yet if there is any doubt that Nietzsche sees this continuity between waking and dreaming, consider that he immediately follows the *Beyond Good and Evil* section above (about the invention of experience) with one of the few explicit discussions of dreams in his post-*Zarathustra* works. It emphasizes the sameness of dream images and ordinary perception: "*Quidquid luce fuit, tenebris agit* [that which happens in the light, persists in the dark]: but also the other way round. That which we experience in dreams, if we experience it often, is in the end just as much a part of the total economy of our soul as is anything we 'really' experience" (*BGE* 5.193). Just as for the "earlier" men whom "hallucinations seized," so for our most scientific spirits: dreams form the model of their experience. These sections indicate that Nietzsche never abandoned the model of experience that he worked out with reference to dreams in his middle period. Dreaming is, for him, the paradigm of all experience. The world he pictures is just the opposite of that of Locke. Where the latter wrote of a world without dreams, Nietzsche describes a world that is almost nothing *but* dreams. And the people in it are dreamers first and foremost.

Of Cause and Effect

Much of what I have been outlining here is illustrated in a remarkable section of *The Gay Science* (1.22). It contains both a stream-of-consciousness report of a dream and an immediate interpretation, along with a few significant sentences depicting the transition between dreaming and waking. The dream concerns the experiences of a retainer responsible for the schedule of a king. The king is in "bad weather," so the courtier is careful to plan appropriately: first, breakfast with only good news about the arrival of "M. Montaigne," a few people to receive, and then . . . the courtier's mind wanders before he can complete the schedule. The dream ends with the courtier being called back to attention by the bell that signals the beginning of the royal day:

> Listen! Wasn't that the bell? Damn! the day and the dance begin and we don't know the schedule! We have to improvise—all the world improvises its day. Let us proceed today as all the world does!
>
> At that, my strange morning dream vanished, probably a victim of the hard strokes of the tower clock which announced the fifth hour with all of its accustomed gravity. It seems to me that on this occasion the god of dreams was pleased to make fun of my habit of beginning the day by ordering it and making it tolerable *for myself*; and it is possible that I have sometimes done this too formally, as if I were a prince.

Here it is the drive to order that has commented on some sensations (we are only told of one) to build up the grandiose image of a king and a court that must cater to his whim. We might speculate that these scenes represent the way in which the dreamer has subordinated all the other elements of his life to his desire to have it regularly ordered. The frustration of the courtier unable to complete his schedule is the inability of these elements to comply wholly, resulting in the necessary improvisation. The entire story with all its images is the result of the expression of drives.

And to make the point that these images were the result of a commentary on our sensations, Nietzsche includes for us the short scene with the ringing bell. The striking of the fifth hour, heard by the sleeper, is *incorporated* into his dream without any interruption of the flow of the story. It is transformed into an element of the drama, rousing the courtier from his reverie—even as it is waking the sleeper. This short section, then, contains all the elements of dreamlike creativity that we have been discussing: the initial sense impressions and the interpretation of these by drives that transform the impressions into symbolic, Apollonian images.

But this dream contains something else as well that will help deepen the preceding discussion. We have seen that the fabrication of images is an ordinary part of both dreaming and waking experience. But we can go further than this and connect Nietzsche's ideas of creativity and interpretation with a certain element of that existence—our notion of cause and effect. Nietzsche identifies the symbol chain of dreams with the chain of causality,[28] which turns out to be one of the most important elements in the setting of Nietzsche's story. But, as we might expect, it cannot be wholly separated from the elements of character and plot. The construction of such a setting, the forging of the chain of causality is, in fact, one of the main threads of the narrative.

The ringing bell and its incorporation into the dream is our clue. The sound that is heard within a dream was one of two unusual psychological phenomena that led Nietzsche to question and eventually discount empiricist models of human experience (such as that of Locke) and the notion of causality. Although such incorporation is a common enough occurrence, Nietzsche thought, it cannot easily be accounted for by empiricism. What troubled him was this: how is it possible for a dreamer to hear a real ringing bell and at the same time see an image of a bell in his dream, if he could only start to imagine this image *after* initially hearing the bell? It must take some time to create the image—how then can it be synchronized with the bell? If experience were really immediate, should we not hear the bell and *then* see the image? Either we must first hear and later see or, if we hear and see the bell simultaneously, we must not be hearing the bell immediately—that is, exactly as it strikes our eardrums. Since we do dream in the latter fashion, Nietzsche took this evidence to mean that experience is *not* immediate. In fact, he thought, the mind mediates experiences and only permits them to rise to the level of consciousness, even dream consciousness, after an appropriate *cause* has been found and an image synthesized. We only "hear" the bell after we have had a moment to experience it unconsciously and invent a likely cause.

> To start from the dream: on to a certain sensation, the result for example of a distant cannon-shot, a cause is subsequently foisted (often a whole little novel in which precisely the dreamer is the chief character). The sensation, meanwhile, continues to persist, as a kind of resonance: it waits, as it were, until the cause-creating drive permits it to step into the foreground—now no longer as a chance occurrence but as a "meaning." The cannon-shot enters in a *causal* way, in an apparent inversion of time. That which comes later, the motivation, is experienced first, often with a hundred details which pass like lightning, the shot *follows*. . . . What has happened? The ideas *engendered* by a certain condition have been misunderstood as the cause of that condition.—We do just the same thing, in fact, when we are awake. (*TI*, p. 50).

In other words, the bell we have imagined, the image of it that we have in our dreams, is what we experience as a cause, regardless of what actually makes the noise. And, at the level of consciousness, we experience this cause first, in order for the whole experience to make sense. "We do just the same thing," Nietzsche says, "when we are awake."[29] The symbolic chain of scenes that a dream creates comes to serve as a chain of causality. In dreams we introduce causes to give meaning to the effects we perceive—that is, the sense impressions that we interpret. Our senses provide us with texts that, precisely do not make sense. In order to make sense of sensations, we interpret them—which often means "a whole little novel." We make sense of them, that is, by placing them within a narrative, a chain of cause and effect. Although Nietzsche does not take waking experience to be the same as dreaming, he thinks there is "no *essential* difference." The chains of causality that we perceive in the world, he thinks, may well be interpretive projections similar to dreams—only the degree of freedom in interpretation changes.

The other phenomenon that leads Nietzsche to this sort of conclusion is that of "phantom pain." This is the sort of pain an amputee feels in the missing limb. To Nietzsche this was further evidence that experience, as such, was largely created by the mind and not through an unmediated contact with the outside world.[30] "We have learned that pain is projected to a part of the body without being situated there—we have learned that sense impressions naively supposed to be conditioned by the outer world are, on the contrary, conditioned by the inner world" (*WP* 3.479; see also 3.490 and 3.699). Undoubtedly, some sense impression is creating the amputee's feeling of pain. But the amputee does not experience it "correctly." That is, his mind is creating a fictitious cause (e.g., his missing leg "hurts") and only then does he "experience" the pain as a "result" of an injury to a nonexistent limb. Like the cannon shot that becomes part of a dream, our unconscious mind receives a sense impression, goes to work on imagining a cause, and afterwards allows both cause and effect to rise to the level of consciousness. Normally, we do not notice this process. Only an unusual condition such as phantom pain allows us to see it in action. The amputee's hurting "leg" is actually a figment of his imagination—an image he has projected onto nervous sensations. But if this is so, Nietzsche reasons, does it not happen similarly when one's leg "really" hurts? It is not that our sensations are wholly imagined, but that we do not perceive pain or any other impression *directly*. And even more than our impressions, our perception of the objects or actions that we think *cause* these impressions is the outcome of an interpretive process—a process dominated more by our passions than by any reality. Although dreams are the purest case of this activity, the same process, Nietzsche holds, typifies conscious thought (see *WP* 3.479; also *GS* 3.112, *HH* 1.13).[31] There is always *something* that triggers this process, but there is no way for us to experience that something directly. Both dreaming and waking thought, Nietzsche contends, are to varying degrees the result of unconscious interpretation. And the most common of these is the creation of a causal narrative.

Nietzsche repeatedly attacked the idea of causality as a figment of the imagination. The widespread belief in this notion, he thought, was an important element in the last remaining faith—the faith in the existence and divinity of truth. Science, the keeper of this faith, attempts to explain the world in terms of cause and effect. Science considers truth to be found when for any effect the correct cause is located. To state the goal this way, Nietzsche thought, is to see its tautological nature, since the "correct" cause can be nothing other than the "true" or "effective" cause—that is, "the cause that caused it." In other words, the scientific search for causes presupposes that causes exist, that events themselves have a fundamentally causal nature, that the universe can be correctly described as an unbroken chain of cause and effect. To Nietzsche, this is science's leap of faith.

Nietzsche's attempts to debunk this idea always led him to hypotheses about mental activity that he had derived from the evidence of dreams: the real thinking takes place in our unconscious. From one sensation, we reason or imagine *backwards* to a possible antecedent. The conscious mind is fooled into believing the "cause" came first. While Nietzsche is not saying anything about the actual structure of the universe, he *is* saying that *our* experience of cause and effect is a product of our minds. That is, Nietzsche does *not* hold the positive view: "There is no cause and effect in the universe." He only holds that humans perceive causality for reasons having to do with their own psychology, not reasons having to do with the universe itself. In perceiving a chain of causality, a human being is actually experiencing a symbol chain that his or her mind has created, just as it does in dreams.

Indeed, we might rather say that in dreams the ordinary process of deducing causes from effects takes place in a more extreme fashion. The mind dreams up causes from effects in a more brazen way than usual. It piles these fanciful and extreme causes on top of the mundane effects as the freest "very free" interpretation possible. The only remaining puzzle is why this should be so. What restricts the mind by day? Or, for that matter, what separates us from earlier peoples who dreamed all day? To Nietzsche, the answer to these questions is the same.

Memory: The Root of Experience

Nietzsche's clear solution to this puzzle is *memory*. It is memory that conditions our imagination of cause and effect. It is the weakness of memory at night that frees the imagination for its boldest work. The coherence of our everyday experience is obtained for us by our memory, which conditions our interpretations of the "effects" we normally feel.

With memory, we stand at the border between what we might call Nietzsche's existential concerns and his historical concerns. It is our analysis of everyday (and everynight) human experience that has brought us to the subject of memory, but, as we pursue that subject, we retreat from present experience back into the sources of that experience in the past. Memory is not an abstract category or faculty for Nietzsche (like Locke's "white paper"), but on the contrary, inseparable from "our" particular memory. The development of memory and the development of consciousness are, for Nietzsche, largely historical questions, not biological (or even, strictly speaking, psychological) ones.

The question of memory is, as I have noted above, central to the broader themes of this book. For it is at the site of our memory that we can see the connection between plot and character, between a sense of history and a political theory, or between past and future. A memory is always an element of a person in the present, but it represents the mark left on that person by the past. We need to explore what Nietzsche says about memory in order to understand the rest of his political theory. But this exploration has a broader purpose—for Nietzsche's writings about memory will help us to understand the phenomenon more generally. Such exploration will, in other words, help us describe the broad role that memory plays in the writings of others. The subject of memory is central to Nietzsche's narrative of the human past. For this reason, it helps us to grasp just why history and narrative are so important to the human present. But (this bears repeating) memory is never, for Nietzsche, a generic human trait: there no memory before there is a memory of *something*. Memory itself has a history—even if, at any one time, nobody clearly remembers it.

Memory stands at the boundary of dreaming and wakefulness. Its presence or absence, Nietzsche contends, is the primary distinction between the two states. I have said that Nietzsche is concerned to break down the wall we understand to exist between these two parts of our lives. I have also said that he takes this wall between day and night to be a constructed, rather than natural, phenomenon. As we examine the development of memory, I shall argue that, for Nietzsche, this wall simply *is* memory.

We have seen that Nietzsche draws parallels between the dreaming portion of our lives and the waking lives of earlier humans. The idea that memory separates both dreamers and primitives from modern, waking people is also there from the start. Memory, Nietzsche holds, was weak in general among "earlier" humans, but is now especially so at night:

> *Dream and culture.* The function of the brain that sleep encroaches upon most is the memory: not that it ceases altogether—but it is reduced to a condition of imperfection such as in primeval ages of mankind may have been normal by day and in waking. Confused and capricious as it is, it continually confuses one thing with another on the basis of the most fleeting similarities: but it was with the same confusion and capriciousness that the peoples composed their mythologies. . . . But in dreams we all resemble this savage. (*HH* 1.12)[32]

The creation of the fantastic images and the symbol chains that are early human mythology was the result of an element of invention in interpretation that was much freer than that of the waking people today. This freedom we retain only in our dreams.

A strong memory, for Nietzsche, simply consists in a kind of discipline of "cause-creating." It had been particularly the puzzle in the case of dreams why the text of his sleeping sensations "much the same on one night as on another, is commented on in such varying ways." But now the question is reversed. The incredible variety of interpretation results from the multiplicity of drives; the question is why this variety does *not* exist during modern, waking life. And the answer is that *memory* of previous causal interpretations predominates over new ones: "The memory, which in such a case becomes active without our being aware of it, calls up earlier states of a similar kind and the causal interpretations which have grown out of them" (*TI*, p. 51). "But memory also retains the habit of old interpretations, i.e. of erroneous causality" (*WP* 3.479; see also *HH* 1.14).

Our creativity is nowadays held in check by our memory, which reminds us how we interpreted similar effects before. It is no surprise, then, that we "see" the same sequence of cause and effect taking place regularly in waking life. This regularity is purchased for us by our memory at the cost of a large measure of imagination and inventiveness.[33] Memory is a route (or rut) into which our waking thought is more and more likely to fall. This is why waking thought (seemingly, in its scientific form, seeking new evidence and theories) can often resist evidence that would disturb existing interpretations. "You are still burdened with those estimates of things that have their origin in the passions and loves of former centuries. . . . That mountain there! That cloud there! What is 'real' in that? Subtract the phantasm and every human *contribution* from it, my sober friends! If you *can*! If you can forget your descent, your past, your training—all of your humanity and animality" (*GS* 2.57).

This also explains the "hallucinations" of early or primitive humans. Unrestricted by memory, their ever-changing interpretations led them constantly onto different paths. Nietzsche argues that a measure of this undiscipline also held for the free-dreaming Greeks, whose undertakings were marked by "incalculability, even incredibility" (*GM* 1.11). Initially, our interpretations are no more correct or realistic than theirs; we invent chains of symbols and causality no less than they. But our memory keeps us from rapidly switching our chains. We have become disciplined, regular creatures; we have become boring—also safer and, in many ways, more powerful. The chains of causality only become binding chains for us when they are remembered. We become chained, so to speak, to a particular interpretive experience and then are bound to repeat that experience, like a ghost doomed to walk the same halls every night, so long as our memory is strong.

The inverse relationship between memory and creativity sheds some light on Nietzsche's praise of the "will to forget," first introduced in 1874 in his *Of the Uses and Disadvantages of History for Life*. Our memory constricts our creativity to well-trodden paths; it diverts attention away from new possibilities. Without forgetfulness, we should be forever stuck in the present and the past. If we are to have a real future at all—that is, something *new*—it cannot be a recollection. It must be freshly created if it is to exist at all. The wall built by memory against the chaotic creativity of the night isolates a few interpretations in daylight. It is a wall built against our savage, disordered past; but it is a wall that blocks our future as well. If memory is perfected, it will trap us in an eternal, unchanging present.[34]

Nietzsche depicts the power of memory to entrap us in a single interpretation at two levels: at the level of the individual and at the level of an entire society or culture. As usual, his sense of the creative individual emphasizes both the philosopher and the artist. Thus his sense of the over-memorious leads him to the idea of the *lost* philosopher as well as that of the *lost* artist: "Many a man fails to become a thinker only because his memory is too good" (*AOM* 122). "He who selects less rigorously and likes to give himself up to his imitative memory can, under the right circumstances, become a great improviser; but artistic improvisation is something very inferior in relation to the serious and carefully fashioned artistic idea" (*HH* 4.155).[35] As is often the case, Nietzsche's thoughts on the artist and the philosopher shed light on one another. A person who is too heavily schooled becomes incapable of developing original works, whether in philosophy or art. The over-memorious philosopher is like a dilettante: capable of a great variety of riffs or commentaries, but ultimately too steeped in past works to ever have any distance from them. In the same way, an artist of this type may be capable of creating good works in a previously established style. But too strong an attachment to the work done before makes it impossible for such an artist to break free and develop a new style. Memory restricts creativity.

We normally think of memory as an individual function, but Nietzsche is quite certain that social memory works in quite the same way to restrict the possibilities of life. In *The Gay Science*, he argues that often the memories we use in our disciplining of interpretation and experience are coterminous with morality—that is, the restrictions we all remember: "*How far the moral sphere extends.*—As soon as we see a new image, we immediately construct it with the aid of all our previous experiences. . . . All experiences are moral experiences, even in the realm of sense perception" (*GS* 3.114; see also *WP* 2.260, 294). Because of this close relation of memory and morality, Nietzsche's general critique of morality often strikes the same note as the attack on memory: both are restrictive and in the same manner. "The less men are bound by tradition, the greater is the fermentation of motivations within them [and] . . . the polyphony of their endeavors" (*HH* 1.23; see also *D* 1.9, 35, *WP* 2.363). Morality, in this respect, is no different from the memories separating us from early humanity. It is what restricts our interpretations in the day and holds back the chaos of the night. Once this question of memory becomes associated with social customs, it becomes increasingly clear why a genealogy of morals is necessary. Examining the development of the wall of memory means in large part observing, or uncovering, the development of morals. And, indeed, when we turn to *On the Genealogy of Morals*, we find that it announces its concern with the creation of memory in general. As with dreaming and waking, so with memory and morality: they are not the same, but nevertheless there is "no essential difference." Just as Nietzsche finds the key to consciousness in dreams, so he explores morality through the apparently tangentially related subject of memory.

Memory and Creativity

Yet before exploring Nietzsche's work in this direction, it is important to stress that he is not simply against the development of memory. He does not at all desire to return to the hallucinations of early men. At one point he even calls this the "greatest danger": "the eruption of madness—which means the eruption of arbitrariness in feeling, seeing and hearing" (*GS* 2.76).

In a certain sense, in fact, he does not want less memory, but more, since new interpretations would produce new memories. His concern is that memory is self-limiting; memory excludes new interpretations and experiences. But since memory is itself the strength of previous interpretations, this is as much as to say that old memories exclude possible new memories—old interpretations are excluding new ones. At the social level, this means old customs exclude new customs: "The *sense for custom* (morality) applies . . . to the age, the sanctity, the indiscussability of custom. And so this feeling is a hindrance to the acquisition of new experiences and the correction of customs: that is to say, morality [*Sittlichkeit*] is a hindrance to the creation of new and better customs [*Sitte*]: it makes stupid" (*D* 1.19).

While some view primitive cultures as custom-bound and our own as broad-minded and experimental, Nietzsche argues the opposite. It is primitive cultures, he feels, that are the most dynamic and inventive (if chaotic). Although certainly the Greeks, in his estimation, had a strong sense of custom, it is something that has intensified in modern thinking. Our cause-creating drive is "conditioned": "That something already *known*, experienced, inscribed in the memory is posited as cause is the first experience of this need. The new, the unexperienced, the strange is excluded from being cause.—Thus there [are] sought . . . the *most common* explanations" (*TI*, p. 51; see also p. 52).

Yet if Nietzsche is not against memory per se but just against the way in which it excludes new memories, what does his critique amount to? Is memory a restriction on creativity or is it not? And is this to be attacked or welcomed? Nietzsche himself sometimes describes the situation in ways that make it seem paradoxical: "Every habit lends our hand more wit but makes our wit less handy" (*GS* 3.247). To answer these questions, we must return once more to the dreaming Greeks and add a final twist to our analysis. I have been emphasizing that for Nietzsche, memory and creativity are opposing forces. But that analysis does not exclude the possibility that they may feed off each other as well. This too is an element of Nietzsche's view. It explains why he is not simply opposed to memory but views it as an element of dynamic creativity—an element that is also a continuing and growing danger.

The dreams of Homer formed the basis of Greek mythology and values. By their very power, they forged a deep memory in the people who lived by them, a morality. And this must have created a barrier to future dreams. Mythology, like science, created a rut that was more difficult for succeeding generations to avoid. Homer's great achievement made the next such achievement that much harder. Any attempt to breach the barrier between dreams and waking inevitably adds another brick to that wall.

And yet each such interpretation must build on the last.[36] Even Homer was, in Nietzsche's phrase, "three-quarters convention" (*WS* 122). Creativity cannot work without materials. It needs conventions. It needs memories. Nietzsche is fond of saying that each interpretation must "obliterate" previous ones (e.g., *GM* 2.12). This means to write *over* them (ob-literate; *auslöschen*)—not to replace them and start from scratch.[37] The image Nietzsche uses to describe this process is "dancing in chains." Although macabre, the metaphor captures just what he means to say about the mutual contributions of creativity and memory: " 'Dancing in chains', . . . that is the artifice they [Greek artists] want to demonstrate to us. Already in Homer we can perceive an abundance of inherited formulae and epic narrative rules *within* which he had to dance: and he himself created additional new conventions for those who came after him" (*WS* 140).[38]

Creativity and memory stand in tension then, but a tension born of a necessary, fateful, and possibly fruitful relation. Each constrains the other, but in doing so, each strengthens the other by providing it with new material. Each creation is another brick in the wall. But each piece of memory provides a new *tabula non rasa* over which new interpretations can be written. Chains of causality are not to be cast aside, but are to be part of the dance. It is actually better to be *partly* chained than it is to be either wholly chained or wholly unchained.[39] This pattern of mutual discipline and strengthening of different elements of the psyche is typically Nietzschean. To him it presents, not a paradox, but a prospect to be welcomed: "I have discovered for myself that the human and animal past, indeed the whole primal age and past of all sentient being continues in me to invent, to love, to hate, to infer. I suddenly woke up in the midst of this dream, but only to the consciousness that I am still dreaming and that I must go on dreaming lest I perish—as a somnambulist must go on dreaming lest he fall" (*GS* 1.54).

I have explored Nietzsche's thoughts on dreams and what follows from them in order to establish broadly how he relates past to present. But this has been done in an abstract way. I have not really explored *what* Nietzsche thinks our past is. What I have said might apply to any memory. But Nietzsche does not use such abstract categories. Memory is not, he believes, a natural human power; there is only *our* specific memory. Our memory is that which separates day from night, present from past. The creation of our memories is a very particular process. The reader having reached this point may feel dissatisfied that I have not yet said what memory "is," or that I have not really said where it comes from. Nietzsche answers only in terms of our memory. And the creation of our memories is the main subject of *On the Genealogy of Morals*.

CHAPTER 4

The Future of Pain

> If by eternity is understood not endless temporal duration but time-
> lessness, then he lives eternally who lives in the present.
> —Ludwig Wittgenstein, *Tractatus Logico-Philosophicus*

In *On the Genealogy of Morals*, Nietzsche provides us with the details of our history, which he does not sharply distinguish from our memory. Yet there must be some distance between the two, because it is exactly the history of our memory that, paradoxically, we seem to have forgotten. To understand the history Nietzsche gives us in the *Genealogy*, we have first explored the general way in which he relates the present to the past. The figure of Zarathustra and the phenomenon of dreams provided us with two important reference points. In Zarathustra, we saw a character who is neither wholly free of the past nor wholly trapped by it. His Nietzschean claims cannot cut him off completely from his Persian roots. Through Nietzsche's writing on dreams, we were able to obtain a more exact picture of this relationship of past and present. It is the chain of causality that binds us firmly to what was, fastening itself to us through memory. Yet neither is the uniqueness of the present possible without these chains. Our dreams are fresh because they manipulate items we already remember—reforge links in the chain—not because they create something out of nothing. Nietzsche's faith in artistic genius is not Byronic; his Homer is only one-quarter inspiration, three-quarters memory.

Before we can be open to Nietzsche's past, he wants first to disorient our sense of the present. He wants us to reconceive some of the givens of our lives as historical beings. Nietzsche is unlike Locke in the central role he ascribes to dreams for his typical character. He is quite similar to Locke, however, in strategy. He, too, has an alternative setting and plot that he wants to displace. Although not embodied in a single figure like Locke's opponent Filmer, Nietzsche's fears have a similar tone. Just as Locke feared a Filmerian would think himself justly enslaved to the king by a chain of paternity, so Nietzsche fears that the chain of causality, if misunderstood, will enslave us to the past. And, as with Locke, he would prefer to redeem the dead rather than abandon them.

The beliefs Nietzsche attempts to call into question are those concerning modern language, consciousness, and individuality. He feels we have a common understanding of these things, and he wants to attack both the substance of that understanding *and* the fact that we hold it in common. Indeed, its commonness will prove to be the very grounds on which it stands accused. In this, he is continuing his campaign against memory's capacity to imprison. Language and, above all, consciousness are coterminous with this memory and hold the same dangers. They provide us with a convenient link therefore, between memory in the abstract and our own memories.

Consciousness and Language

Nietzsche often identifies consciousness with interpretation. In *Daybreak*, he writes that, as is the case with dreams, "all our so-called consciousness is a more or less fantastic commentary on an unknown, perhaps unknowable, but felt text" (*D* 2.119). Likewise, he also links consciousness to memory. "There is in every judgment the avowal of having encountered an 'identical case': it [judgment] therefore presupposes comparison with the aid of memory" (*WP* 3.532). Given the creative tension between interpretation and memory that I have described above, there is no need to see any contradiction between these sentiments. The connection should even be expected. Consciousness partakes of the creative element in interpretation; but it can only do so on the basis of memory. Shapes must be preserved over time in memory before they can be repeatedly manipulated by the various drives. Further, it is not surprising that since consciousness stands in the middle of this tension, it, too, is concerned with matters of cause and effect.

Nietzsche links causal thinking to the appearance of language and consciousness.[1] It was the need for communication between individuals, he argues, that engendered conscious thought: "consciousness is really only a net of communication between human beings" (*GS* 5.354). Language has as its original purpose, not particularly the representation of human thought or truth, but communication between two or more individuals who are trying to coordinate their efforts against a common danger. Words are only "signs of communication, and this fact uncovers the origin of consciousness" (ibid.; see also *WP* 3.522, 524). That language has at its root a social, instrumental purpose severely limits its potential as an objective representation of the world. Its purpose is utilitarian, not epistemological. Neither the outer world nor the inner world of the unconscious is necessarily well described by human language. Modern language, Nietzsche believes, has the herd perspective embedded within it:

> My idea is, as you see, that consciousness does not really belong to man's individual existence but rather to his social or herd nature; that, as follows from this, it has developed subtlety only insofar as this is required by social or herd utility. . . . each of us will always succeed in becoming conscious only of what is not individual but "average." Our thoughts themselves are constantly governed by the character of consciousness—by the "genius of the species" that commands it—and translated back into the perspective of the herd. Fundamentally, all our actions are altogether incomparably personal, unique and infinitely individual; there is no doubt of that. But as soon as we translate them into consciousness *they no longer seem to be.* . . . the world of which we can become conscious is only a surface- and sign-world. (*GS* 5.354; see also *HH* 1.11)

It is the "commonness" and "regularity" of language that is for Nietzsche its most important feature. What is "incomparably personal, unique and infinitely individual" is trapped beneath it. This commonness is linked to our memory, which restricts the creativity of our interpretations. In order for sounds to function effectively as communication, Nietzsche holds, they need to have a fixed and regular meaning (see *BGE* 9.268; recall Locke's similar concern with a common currency of words). That way, all the participants in the conversation will understand what is being communicated. But, in Nietzsche's account, this goes against our inclination constantly to interpret the same impressions (such as sounds) differently, as we do from night to night in our dreams. If left unrestricted, our drives would constantly give the same sensory impression (such as the sound of a word) a different meaning. The assignment of meaning to sounds in language must be *remembered* if language is to function at all. But this regularity of language has nothing to do with the world of impressions about which we communicate. It is the strength of memory, not the constancy of the universe, that produces this regularity. Where Locke thinks that words, once coined, maintain their meaning until criminally altered by cheats, for Nietzsche the meaning of a sound is ordinarily as variable as the drives behind our interpretations. The wonder is that the meaning of terms in a language can achieve any stability at all. What limited regularity exists survives only on the strength of a *shared* memory. The result is that through language, we impose on the world (that is, on our conscious image of it) a regularity it may not contain. Again, Nietzsche is not making a claim about the structure of the universe (e.g., that it is chaotic). He merely argues for the limitations of our consciousness, and he specifically argues that the regularity we perceive in the world is a product of our own minds: "In this mirror—and our intellect is a mirror—something is taking place that exhibits regularity . . . —this we *call* . . . cause and effect—we fools! . . . For we have seen nothing but *pictures* [*Bilder*] of 'causes and effects'! And it is precisely this *pictorialness* [*Bildlichkeit*] that makes impossible an insight into a more essential connection than that of mere succession" (*D* 2.121; see also *GM* 1.13).

Like the shield of Perseus facing the Gorgons, language is a mirror in which we must reflect the world before we are able to see it, at least consciously (*D* 4.243). Nietzsche uses this metaphor of the mirror often, usually to point out the distortions that language causes.[2] The distortion results from the fact that the mirror ultimately has this social base, which must shape reality to serve its purpose of group communication.[3] Zarathustra faces this problem in trying to transmit his views: "I need clean, smooth mirrors for my doctrines; on your surface even my own image [*Bildniss*] is distorted. . . . There is hidden mob in you too" (*Z* 4.11; see also 2.1). What is most personal and individual about Zarathustra becomes distorted when he attempts to transmit it through the social medium of language. Still, Nietzsche does not give up on language because of this problem. Language does transmit meaning; it merely does so in a limited way—and the degree of limitation is directly related to the degree of "mob" in it.

> The dialogue [*Zwiegespräche*] is the perfect conversation [*Gespräche*]. . . . There is only a single refraction of the thought: this is produced by the partner in the dialogue, as the mirror in which we desire to see our thoughts reflected as perfectly as possible. But what happens when there are two, three or more fellow participants? The conversation necessarily loses its subtle individuality, different intentions clash with and disrupt one another. (*HH* 6.374)[4]

Many of Nietzsche's criticisms of modern society and modern morality spring from this argument about the distorting effects of language. Since language, for him, is coextensive with conscious thought, it is usually impossible for conscious ideas, arguments or decisions to be anything but directed toward the herd and its benefit.

> The great majority nonetheless do nothing for their ego their whole life long: what they do is done for the phantom of their ego which has formed itself in the heads of those around them and has been communicated to them;—as a consequence they all of them dwell in a fog of impersonal, semi-personal opinions, and arbitrary, as it were poetical evaluations, . . . this fog of habit and opinions lives and grows almost independently of the people it envelops; it is in this

fog that there lies the tremendous effect of general judgments about "man."
(*D* 2.105)

Nietzsche taxes language with suppressing "our true experiences" and "feelings" (*TI*, "Expeditions," 26; *AOM* 105). Our common words cover them all
up. Even when we think we are using language to express ourselves—we
express instead our shared, remembered generalizations.

   Indeed, much can be revealed about Nietzsche's ever-present critique of
pity by considering its roots in the critique of language. The German word
for pity is *Mitleid*, which literally means "with-pain." Etymologically, *Mitleid*
refers to the ability of the pitier to share the suffering of the pitied. Pity is
pain transmitted through the foggy medium of language and consciousness.
Through language, we are able to feel the pain of others, and they ours.
Simply put, because of language, we all feel a lot more pain, none of it
originally ours. It is like the phantom pain of a limb. We feel it as if it were
emanating from our own body. But this only confirms the degree to which
our pain is the result of the mediated character of experience. For Nietzsche,
this is one of the most horrible and debilitating elements of modern life. And
since communication of the herd is itself predicated on the need to avoid
pain, pity (the effort to relieve the pain of others) is the epitome of herd
emotion. Thus, the further we identify with the pain of others, the further we
are driven into the herd, into consciousness and away from individuality and
individual experience. The fog of consciousness, ostensibly developed for our
individual survival, ends up entrapping us in social relations. "Morality is herd
instinct in the individual" (*GS* 3.116). In my discussion of the *Genealogy*, the
central role of pain in the creation of memory itself (and, hence, consciousness and language) will be crucial.[5]

   But how did this state of affairs come about? We have seen the link
between the development of memory and consciousness, and now we have
further connected this to the development of language. Yet it now seems that
language develops the social impulse, but requires society in order to be
initiated:

> [W]hen human beings have lived together for a long time under similar condi-
> tions, there *arises* from this a group who "understand one another," a people
> [*Volk*]. In every soul in this group an equivalent number of frequently recurring
> experiences has gained the upper hand over those which come more rarely . . .
> —the history of language is the history of a process of abbreviation— . . . the
> continuing development of mankind into the similar, ordinary, average, herd-
> like—into the common! (*BGE* 9.268)

This question directs us to Nietzsche's *Genealogy*, where he explicitly addresses the question of how memories and society are formed. We shall see

that a single process forges both. In addition, we can already begin to see the danger that most worries Nietzsche. It is, in a sense, a more general form of Locke's fear. Where the latter was concerned that a particular memory would enslave us, Nietzsche anticipates a future where memory as a whole holds us in its thrall. His plot against this prospect, however, is not to escape from memory altogether but, like Homer, to dance in its chains.

The Genealogy of the 'Genealogy'

So far, I have skipped rather freely among Nietzsche's texts. Notwithstanding that I have occasionally described the development of his positions, the reader may think that essentially I view all his books as cut from a single cloth. Although I do think that many of his concerns and views are unchanged throughout, I must here indicate (very briefly) where he has shifted his stance. The genealogy he presents in 1887 is, I think, a significant departure from some earlier accounts he gives of the past. His method is also significantly different from any described in his famous meditation *Vom Nutzen und Nachteil der Historie für das Leben* (*Of the Uses and Disadvantages of History for Life*).

Many interpreters take this meditation to be Nietzsche's main statement on history. Walter Kaufmann, for example, argues that "Nietzsche, from his first book to his last, considered historical events less with an eye to literal correctness than 'to circumscribe . . . an everyday melody . . . , to elevate it, to intensify it into a comprehensive symbol' (*UM* 2.6)."[6] While Kaufmann's canonical status as an interpreter of Nietzsche is not what it once was, here many and diverse commentators have agreed with him. Writers as distinct as Phillipe Lacoue-Labarthe, Arthur Danto, R. J. Ackermann, and Mark Warren all take this essay to be Nietzsche's most definitive statement on the nature and method of history.[7] While the formulation Kaufmann quotes is especially poetic, this should not deter us from noticing that both the form and substance of Nietzsche's approach to history changed dramatically between the *Untimely Meditations* and the *Genealogy*. Kaufmann's view allows him (and others) to deal with the most gruesome parts of the *Genealogy* as so much metaphor and poetry. We owe Kaufmann a great debt for his tireless efforts to disprove any supposed connections between the *Genealogy*'s blond beasts and Nazi ideology, but the disadvantage of his approach is its dismissal of genuine historical claims in Nietzsche's work. If the denials of Nietzsche's fascism are really to stand the test of time, I think, we must be able to face Nietzsche at his most distasteful, as well as at his most poetic. And this cannot be accomplished without making some effort to compare and then to distinguish what Nietzsche says in the *Genealogy* from what he wrote earlier.

Without going into the details of that work yet, we can establish that he is actually abandoning some earlier views. Indeed, his attack on the "English psychologists" at the beginning of the *Genealogy* represents nothing so much as an attempt to distance himself from his previous incarnation, which he now sees as excessively "English." (This perhaps explains why the English psychologists are never named.) It is interesting too that this reversal comes on a topic of great importance to us, that of memory. In the opening sections of the *Genealogy*, Nietzsche criticizes the notion that morality could ever arise out of a kind of "forgetting." The "English psychologists" had held that things were called good on account of some benefit one received, but that one then forgot this association and called the things good in themselves. How, Nietzsche wonders, could one ever forget such an association when one is constantly reminded of it by receipt of the benefit? The only "psychologically tenable" history of morals, he now holds, is one in which such associations are remembered, not forgotten (*GM* 1.1–3). Yet in *Human, All-Too-Human* (1878), he had given precisely this "English" history of morals (2.39), indeed, in almost the same words he uses to describe the view he rejects in 1887.[8] Now he identifies the rejected arguments with Paul Rée, who had been his friend at the time of the earlier book and who had published his own book with similar views.[9] Rée was not English either, of course, but Nietzsche indicates that Rée had read Darwin—this is the source of the "English" taint (Preface, 4, 7). And if Rée could become an English psychologist by reading Darwin, it is not hard to imagine that the same thing happened to Nietzsche for a time—by reading Rée. He says as much in the introduction to *Human, All-Too-Human* that he wrote in 1886 (eight years after initial publication), in which he praises the book but says that it represents an earlier stage in his development (Preface, 8). In his middle works, Nietzsche had a positive attitude to Darwinian science and science in general. But in his later works, he has rejected all this as anglophilia.

A similarly brief comparison can show us that in the *Genealogy*, Nietzsche had also come some distance from the *Uses and Disadvantages*,[10] which prefigures many of the concerns about the conflict between memory and creativity discussed above. What is less clear, though, is whether Nietzsche has, in the earlier essay, arrived at an understanding of the positive relationship between these two forces—the way in which they feed off each other (see the section titled "Memory and Creativity" in Chapter 3). Indeed, there is evidence that he still has a quasi-romantic view of creativity as something that comes from nature, and of a simple tension between nature and culture (e.g., *UM* 2.10). He still seems to be in the grip of metaphysics. He also takes the gap between remembering "man" and the unremembering animals for granted and considers its effects, rather than its causes (*UM* 2.1).[11] Finally, we might note that the technique of genealogy as described in 1887 corresponds neither to any of the three historical techniques he outlines in the *Uses and Disadvantages* (the monumental, the antiquarian, and the critical) nor to a combination of them. The difference may perhaps be traced to the fact that, in the earlier period, he saw memory as a natural capacity that simply had to be fought. The *Genealogy* considers the origin of memory a question in itself and searches to reveal hidden processes in a way none of Nietzsche's earlier approaches sense to be necessary.[12]

In *Ecce Homo*, Nietzsche has surprisingly little (considering its later canonization) to say about the *Uses and Disadvantages*,[13] and what he says is revealing. He says nothing at all about the three types of history (or, indeed, about the bulk of the essay) and merely views the entire work as an attack on the "historical sense"—that is, the overstrong memory. This it certainly is, and this is consonant with his later work. But the essay is not nearly as subtle as the later work, and in it he considers the most significant bearers of the historical sense to be academic Hegelian historians (*UM* 2.5, 8, 9), rather than morality in general.[14] In sum then, the *Uses and Disadvantages* contains neither the method nor the object of study of the *Genealogy*. Neither can its conclusions be trusted as a sure guide to the workings of the *Genealogy*. I include these remarks, in large part, because I want to maintain that Nietzsche's thoughts on history find their true culmination in the *Genealogy*, and not in this early essay.[15] Of course, my assertion that genealogy is a different kind of history from those he had earlier described will only really be demonstrated when we have explored it in some detail.

It would be difficult to overemphasize the degree to which the secondary literature on Nietzsche (Michel Foucault and Gilles Deleuze excepted) has fled the bloody *Genealogy* for the calmer climate of the second of the *Untimely Meditations*. The second essay of the *Genealogy* in particular must be the least-commented-upon section of Nietzsche's published works. This is especially odd when one considers, as Walter Kaufmann notes in his introduction to the work, that the *Genealogy* is the least aphoristic, least allusive, most straightforward of Nietzsche's texts. Of course, it has everything to do with the frighteningly gruesome historical account that one finds in that essay. Even those eager to embrace the "method" of genealogy retreat from the *actual* genealogy that Nietzsche offers—and thus leave it as fodder for his critics.[16] It is this very un-Nietzschean separation of the form and content of genealogy that I hope to address here in order to show that Nietzsche is often at his most important when he is at his most frightening. We can now turn to the *Genealogy* and its problems directly.

The Attributes of Genealogy

One thing the *Uses and Disadvantages* shares with the *Genealogy* is the sense that the past continues to exist within us. Although Nietzsche distances himself from the Hegelian "historical sense," which finds a predetermined path in history, he certainly maintains a historical sense that sees a connection between man's present nature and his historical past. What the mature Nietzsche took this connection to be, I have elaborated at length above: it is the way in which memory determines our current consciousness. But this description is perhaps just the filling out or recasting of a historical sense that Nietzsche had from the beginning: "Direct self-observation is not nearly sufficient for us to know ourselves: we require history, for the past continues to flow within us in a hundred waves; we ourselves are, indeed, nothing but that which at every moment we experience of this continued flowing" (*AOM* 223; see also *HH* 5.272).[17]

The *Uses and Disadvantages* had also recognized that history could be written in a variety of ways, and that although none was more "correct" than the others, the choice had an enormous impact on the effect of the account given. Between that meditation and the *Genealogy*, Nietzsche radicalized this proposition. He came to argue that all accounts have this property, and not merely historical ones. He believes that any account of an object determines the perception of that object and thus its effect. What is more, such accounts appear to be more and more the sole subject of any historical writing; genealogy is an account of such accounts:

> This has given me the greatest trouble and still does: to realize that what things *are called* is incomparably more important than what they are. The reputation, name and appearance, the usual measure and weight of a thing, what it counts for—originally almost always wrong and arbitrary, thrown over things like a dress and altogether foreign to their nature and even to their skin—all this grows from generation unto generation, merely because people believe in it, until it gradually grows to be part of the thing and turns into its very body. (*GS* 2.58; see also *WS* 33)[18]

These aspects of genealogy I describe in advance merely for clarification; in practice, they cannot really be separated from the substance of the study itself. Just why the past continues within us and why reputations are more important than "reality" is something that genealogy itself is meant to prove. They are not assumptions on which it is meant to rest.

One further aspect of genealogy that it may be helpful to point out in advance is the importance of the human body in history. Although the focus on reputations might lead one to assume that the history Nietzsche gives is necessarily idealist or nominalist, this is not so. The mind/body dichotomy is one further distinction that Nietzsche feels to be socially created. Indeed, as we retrace the construction of the wall of memory, we shall see that it is the very same wall that separates mind and body. And that wall itself is distinctly part of the body. The record of accounts that Nietzsche takes to be the substance of history is kept in no other material but the body: "The human body, in which the most distant and most recent past of all organic development again becomes living and corporeal, through which and over and beyond which a tremendous inaudible stream seems to flow: the body is a more astonishing idea than the old 'soul' " (*WP* 3.659).[19] The past Locke explored turned out to be a series of contracts. Nietzsche also seeks to recall a forgotten, but recorded, past. The records are not contracts, though, and they are written, if it is not too much to say so, in blood.

The Origins of Memory

Nietzsche's obsession with Christianity sometimes gives the appearance of swallowing all of his other historical concerns. It may appear to the casual reader that all of Nietzsche's history is a study of Christianity, whether explicit or disguised. This is not quite right. While this latest stage of history dominates his attention (because it dominates us generally), Nietzsche is quite capable of distinguishing other, earlier stages in the history of morality. Indeed, his understanding of the Christian stage makes no sense at all without the grounding of these earlier stages. Quite often, Nietzsche speaks of the "Christian-moral" interpretation of the world. The two adjectives are not synonymous. He uses the term to indicate a Christianity that has its roots in a more general "morality" of an earlier period.

Nietzsche distinguishes quite clearly between the two periods. Christianity he identifies with the known past of Western civilization, whereas the earlier development of morality took place "long before the four thousand years we more or less know about" (*HH* 1.2). (Recall the Zoroastrian division of history into four three-thousand-year stages.) Greek civilization fits into the Christian period because of the identification of that creed with the philosophy of Plato. (Nietzsche once called Christianity "Platonism for the people" [*BGE*, Pref.].) But even Plato lacked "a history of the moral sensations" (*WS* 285). Even the wisest Greek was without firm knowledge, or memory, of the earlier era that Nietzsche is interested in.

Plato's fault was not simply that he had the wrong history of the moral sensations but that he lacked *any* history of them. Plato, and Christianity after him, took to be natural sensations what had actually been developed in the primeval period. This period Nietzsche calls that of the "morality of mores" or of "custom" (*Sittlichkeit der Sitte*), the *actual and decisive eras of history which determined the character of mankind*" (*D* 1.18; emphasis in original). In this period, man, who had previously been an animal without memory, learned for the first time to adhere to customs and mores. Memory was developed, along with the capacity of man to speak and act in a regular, "calculable" way and, hence, the ability to adhere to customs (*GM* 2.2). It was only on this basis, as we shall later see, that Christian morality was possible. In the preface to the *Genealogy*, Nietzsche states his intention to examine " 'the morality of mores' that much older and more primitive [*ursprunglichere*] species of morality" (Pref., 4). Nietzsche's narrative thus contains several distinct periods. Before the Greeks, there was another period, which he considers the decisive one for the human character. Nietzsche, like Locke, does not separate character from plot. Both have their origin, not in a human essence, but at some earlier point in time.[20]

He finds the opening of this period at the beginning of human history, the point where man is separated from the animals. The development of his memory and intellect begins "under the stress of the most fundamental change he ever experienced—that change which occurred when he found himself finally enclosed within the walls of society and peace" (*GM* 2.16). Here we stand at the ultimate temporal limit of human history, because we are also at the phenomenological limit of humanity itself. Before this, there was no "man," only what Nietzsche calls a "human animal." Nietzsche is always quite careful to refer to presocial, unremembering humans as animals. This is often taken as a romantic figure of speech. If anything, it is a relatively technical distinction between cultured, memorious man and the animals, which include the early-human-being animal. The separation of man from the animals is marked by the first brick in the wall of his earliest cities—which not incidentally is the same barrier of memory that separates waking and sleeping.

The development of memory, which we earlier identified as the key to human experience, is simultaneous with the beginning of the "morality of custom." By now, Nietzsche has reversed his position on memory from that of his earlier meditation on history. He now holds that, if anything, it is the faculty of forgetting that is natural to us, and memory that needs to be bred (*GM* 2.1). Indeed, Nietzsche announces that the entire second essay of the *Genealogy* is principally concerned with what he calls "mnemotechnics," the creation of memory. The main principle of this technique is quite simple: " 'If something is to stay in the memory it must be burned in: only that which never ceases to *hurt* stays in the memory' "(*GM* 2.3). This identification of memory and pain runs through the entire genealogy.[21] Not that memory is the result of pain simply, but that memory, as a faculty, as an element of the human psyche, is brought into being through pain alone.

In the middle of the second essay, Nietzsche locates the origins of society in primordial acts of violence and the pain they produce.[22] He envisions a shapeless, presocial mass of human animals. These suffer an incredible act or series of acts of violence at the hands of the "blond beasts." The mass is tortured and decimated until it is completely subordinated to the rule of the attackers. Nietzsche scorns the idea that any society begins with a contract or with an egalitarian association. He finds the opposite at the root of society, an uninhibited and unmoderated burst of violence and cruelty—the most unsocial and disagreeable origin possible:

> the welding of a hitherto unchecked and shapeless populace into a firm form was not only instituted by an act of violence but also carried to its conclusion by nothing but acts of violence—that the oldest "state" thus appeared as a fearful tyranny, as an oppressive and remorseless machine, and went on working until this raw material of people and semi-animals was at last not only thoroughly kneaded and pliant but also *formed*. (*GM* 2.17; see also *BGE* 9.257)

Although unconscious (the blond beasts are, after all, animals and not yet human), the assault is still of almost unimaginable cruelty. As animals, humanity had already experienced pain; that was not new. What was new was its scale and scope (and, perhaps, that some human animals were the objects of the cruelty of others [see *GM* 2.18]). Although cruel, these acts were not senseless. We have seen that in modern man, Nietzsche found the unconscious to be the site of much creativity. In dreams, the work of the unconscious is to create Apollonian shapes (*Bilder*), which carry meaning through the arrangement of symbols into a new whole. It was no different before: "Their work is an instinctive creation and imposition of forms; they are the most involuntary, unconscious artists there are—wherever they appear something new soon arises, a ruling structure [*Herrschaft-Gebilde*] . . . in which nothing whatever finds a place that has not first been assigned a 'meaning' in relation to the whole" (*GM* 2.17).

We can now locate the ultimate source for the process of creativity unfolded above. Nietzsche identifies the most primeval violence with the most primeval artistry: the creation of society from a shapeless mass. Memory has its origin in pain and violence; and humanity's earliest, most fundamental memories have their origins in the earliest, most fundamental pain and violence. Violence to the body can neither be separated from the formation of social groups, nor from the most subtle artistry. The permanence of forms (in memory)—social forms or Apollonian figures or chains of causality—is established by acts of violence.

In this interpretation, artistry is not made possible, maintained, or actualized by violence. Creativity simply *is* violence: no more and no less.[23] Nietzsche's point is that it is impossible to separate the two. The creation of forms, described so gently as dream work in *The Birth of Tragedy*, is seen in the *Genealogy* to be an inherently violent process. Harold Bloom's formulation, "the pain is the meaning," is a little simplistic, but makes the same basic point.[24] Bloom connects pain, meaning, and memory, but then reduces all of them to quantity: Nietzsche's insight becomes only that things are as memorable as they are painful. But Nietzsche's point is not that meaning is as monotonous as pain, but that pain is as variable in its effects as meaning and interpretation. The last thing Nietzsche wanted to do was reify pain, as my earlier discussion of phantom pain shows. The creation of forms has to be violent because the material must be hardened to give permanence to its shape where it previously had none.[25] Creating permanence in a field of impermanence is for Nietzsche the fundamental experience of man that separates him from the animals. Sometimes he calls this giving to an eternal becoming the character of being (*WP* 3.507, 617). More often though, it is an imposition of memory, a crystallizing of forms on an unconscious mind that previously invented causes at random and forgot them as easily. A memory is an interpretation that possesses staying power. It is a form that does not disappear in the sand as soon as it is drawn, but rather hardens into concrete, enduring.

> [F]undamentally, however, the eternally-creative appeared to me to be, as the eternal compulsion to destroy, associated with pain. The ugly is the form things assume when we view them with the will to implant a meaning, a new meaning, into what has become meaningless: the accumulated force which compels the creator to consider all that has been created hitherto as unacceptable, ill-constituted, worthy of being denied, ugly! (*WP* 2.416)[26]

We can see now why Nietzsche abandoned the romanticization of creativity that tinged *The Birth of Tragedy*. He came to realize at last that the artistic creation he valued as the highest product of mankind was inseparable from the cruelty that seemed the best argument against mankind. Violence and creativity make memory and interpretation: both are ultimately the imposition of forms (that is, *Bilder*).[27]

We can see as well how the imagery of dreams opens up Nietzsche's account of what he called "earlier" men. Both the blond beasts and their victims are dreamers. Both interpret their sensations in fantastic ways. The only difference is that the former use the latter as the material out of which they craft their Apollonian images. The dreamer who does not bungle creates a perfect symbol chain. That chain we later identified with the chain of causality. The blond beasts attempt to make their victims obey rules and behave regularly. This means, for Nietzsche, to conform, above all, to the law of causality. This is the fetter that binds us to the social order. What began as a dream, ends as a captivity. Ultimately, the dreamers will be trapped in this chain as well.

But this comes later. For now we can see the extent to which Nietzsche's account of dreams is meant to explain our past as well as our present. The connection, equation even, of dreaming and violence should give us pause. If Nietzsche continues to insist on the innocence of dreaming, he no longer does so in the light-hearted tones of *The Birth of Tragedy*. Violence, he acknowledges, is inseparable from the beauty of Apollo. Homer may have been blind, but he carried a sword.

The Earliest Memories

And what form was imposed on the "pliant," "kneadable" mass? What was it that violence caused that early generation of animals-turned-human to remember? The shape imposed was that of a society; and the memories created were the rules that had to be followed in order for that society to function: "With the aid of such images [*Bilder*] and procedures one finally remembers five or six 'I will not's,' in regard to which one had given one's *promise* so as to participate in the advantages of society" (*GM* 2.3). What needed to be introduced into the human animal was the ability to promise.[28] And what he had to promise was to obey the rules of society. This was so difficult because, before the imposition of violence, the human unconscious had simply dreamt up interpretations that led the human animal in a different direction at every moment. Early man "hallucinated"; he was not reliable. He did not see the world in a regular, ordered fashion. It seemed to change every moment; consequently, he changed every moment as well. Memory, however, disciplines interpretation, restricting creativity, but yielding, in return, the ability to promise. But in order for man to remember a few simple rules, large quantities of violence had to be employed.

The multifariousness of man's behavior had to be curbed in order for a society to function, for rules to rule. The multiple drives offering multiple interpretations of the world had to be curbed. Man had to adhere to one interpretation, and one in which he could promise to refrain from certain behavior. Nietzsche simultaneously calls this process "an extending of memory" and "a mastery of the desires" (*GM* 2.15). More famously, he calls it "taming." The wall of memory blocks out much of the multiplicity of drives and restricts them to sleep, to dreams, to the past. We "repeat the curriculum of earlier mankind" in our dreams because that is the only place where memory relaxes.

It is no accident which interpretation is left in daylight. Multiplicity is blocked so that a singular interpretation might dominate. But this is the content of the rule imposed by the beasts, as well as its form: the interpretation is simply *that* a single view dominates, that man is a regular, calculable being, capable of making promises. And this is no more than the idea *that* the world has the property of causality, that it is made up of a single chain of cause and effect—and that humans, too, are part of this world, that they are single, regular causes—and, hence, that they are predictable (self-predictable), unitary beings capable of making promises. Man's belief in the causality of the universe is a belief about himself as well. In this, our earliest waking thought, we are bound to the *one*, infinitely long, unbroken chain of causality.

This chain, the image of the universe *as* a chain of events, of causes and effects, is the bedrock interpretation. It is the first memory, but it is also the interpretation needed for memory to commence. It is not freely adopted. Yet, although it is imposed by violence, it continues to chain us through a kind of seduction. How, after all, can the mere image of chain be said to bind us? The answer is found in the shape and meaning given to lives that previously had none. Once in place, Homeric dreams create characters who choose to live so chained, and who view their earlier existences as so much hallucination and chaos. In part, this has to do with the irreversibility of time. Once characters have acquired memories, and hence histories, they can neither reverse the elements of their personalities rooted in the past nor would want to. Odysseus might acknowledge that the lotus eaters were happier and perhaps even freer than he, but would never choose to trade places with them. Once we are rooted in time, to choose timelessness and meaninglessness seems like a choice of nonexistence, a dissolution of self, a suicide.

The suppression of human multiplicity takes place as the necessary action that this interpretation entails and not "on behalf of" this interpretation. The suppression *is* the action, the violence, that is the substance of this interpretation. It is the interpretation itself, viewed from the perspective of the body, just as the idea of causality is the same interpretation from the perspective of the mind. The unity and regularity of man and the suppression of multiplicity are two sides of a coin. Or rather, they are the two sides of an interpretation, one of which faces the day and the other, the night.[29]

The substance of the wall of memory is thus simultaneously both pain and interpretation. From the point of view of pain, it is the violence of early conquerors; from the point of view of interpretation, it is the view that man is a calculable, regular animal. Even closer, perhaps, than the two faces of a coin, the suppression of drives is the pain and the interpretation. The memory of rules that tame the drives is built of both the violence and the view that holds them back. Here, at the early limit of human history, there is no distinction between mind and body. Violence is what we call the earliest actions from the point of view of the body; interpretation is what we call them from the point of view of the mind: memory is the result. Any ambiguity that remains is caused by our language, not by any doubleness of the original actions. We simply have no word that contains the sense of both "pain" and "interpretation" to use in a description of the first memory. Our language presupposes the separateness of mind and body. Indeed, it was this very violence that drove the wedge between mind and body, as it did between day and night. What remains in the daylight are the rules, the five or six "I will not's" that seem to be the reasons for which drives are suppressed. But they are simply the side of the wall that faces onto "reason." The opposite side, the night side, is the pain or violence that checks the multiplicity of our unconscious. "Ah, reason, seriousness, mastery over the affects, the whole somber thing called reflection, all these prerogatives and showpieces of man: how dearly they have been bought!" (*GM* 2.3).

Although genealogy lets us travel backwards in time, we can never imagine that doing so unravels all of its effects. We cannot get past the ambiguity of violence and creativity, because memory has been burned too deeply into us. It is the basis for the reason and language that empower genealogy itself. The first memory is thus genealogy's structural limit. Beyond it lies a realm that reason cannot grasp: the animal past and the human unconscious.[30]

Some Aspects of the First Memories

Before we complete the genealogy that Nietzsche gives us, a history composed of violence, it may be useful to state some findings that follow from the above. First, it should now be anything but surprising that Nietzsche thinks that language has at its root assumptions of cause and effect. The first memories, we have now established, were created for the purpose of making man regular, calculable, and capable of promising (on this, see also *HH* 2.59). What this amounts to is the view that man is the cause of his own effects. If a man can promise, it is because he can confirm that he will be the cause of a certain effect. He can only promise this because he is regular, and it is his memory that keeps him so.

Yet as we saw earlier, memory is also the source of language. In order to communicate (and, not incidentally, function as a society) humans must have a common memory of the meanings of various signs. Language does not grow out of a value-free environment. Its basis is the common memory we have, which keeps us predictable. It is no wonder that the assumption of a causal world is built into that language.[31] If dreams are best understood linguistically (as I argued in Chapter 3), it seems the reverse is true as well: language is built on the ideal symbol chains of dreams. Where Locke tried to write dreams out of existence, Nietzsche builds dreams into the very fabric of language. In this sense, the setting of Nietzsche's narrative is as dreamful as Locke's is dreamless.

The account of our earliest memories also illuminates many of Nietzsche's other statements about values. It clarifies Zarathustra's declaration that "soul is only a word for something about the body" (Z 1.4). Two important sentiments derive from this view. The first (already discussed) is that we must understand the soul, and the divide between waking and dreaming, as the product of a history of violence. The second is that this history is also a process of interpretation, and the violence inherent in interpretation can fall on the body politic as well as the individual body.

That interpretations are a violent and bodily action Nietzsche mentions at many points, although this is often taken as so much metaphor. "With your values and words of good and evil you do violence when you value," Zarathustra declares (Z 2.12; see also D 5.460). As interpretation, this violence can be transmitted through the fog of language to the larger body, the body politic: "[S]landers are other people's illnesses that have broken out on your body; they demonstrate that society is a (moral) body" (WS 264). The violence transmitted through language, through pity, has the same effect as the earliest acts of violence: it engraves memory, it carves a conscious soul out of a body.[32] This process begins with the violence of the blond beasts, but it continues and intensifies throughout history.

Yet we need not look for visible marks on the bodies of the victims of this violence. The capacity of language to transmit this pain as pity means that we experience as phantom pain what the earliest generations felt directly. This phantom pain may be less savage than that felt originally, but it may be all the more effective by virtue of its continuous presence. Indeed, our conscience may be considered, from Nietzsche's perspective, a phantom limb that constantly aches—and whose presence we are constantly adjusting ourselves to, like a missing arm or leg. It is as real a part of our body as any other (recall, though, the discussion in Chapter 3 about Nietzsche's use of the term *body*). The first episode in Nietzsche's plot is thus constitutive of the Nietzschean character, even at the level of his body. His first characteristic is his memory. This first episode is recorded *as* his memory; later ones will merely be *in* his memory. They will not, for that reason, be constitutive to the same degree. That is why Nietzsche claimed that the era of the morality of mores was the decisive one. Only there is the character who can *have* a history created; what comes later is coloring within pre-drawn lines. This is as far back as genealogy can go. The human animals had no history; but man is, for Nietzsche, a historical animal, or better, a historical no-longer-animal.

Continuing the History of Violence

Violence is the key unit in Nietzsche's history, but the narrative as a whole is composed of many violent episodes. The initial imposition of a social shape by violence is merely the first in the chain of events that compose human history. It has been important for us, not only for itself, but also because it illuminates the type of event central to Nietzsche's history. As we further navigate that narrative, we shall continue to find that episodes of violence (or, if you like, interpretation) continue to mark the way.

The second significant episode follows quickly on the first, still within the "morality of mores" period. Once the human animal was imprisoned within society, forced to remember, forced to become man, his drives, which he had previously expressed outwardly, in his actions, were held within. The purpose of memory had been to make humans predictable, to halt the effect that the drives had of giving man many interpretations and thus many conflicting purposes. But these drives did not go away simply because memory had stifled their outward expression. We know they continued to manifest themselves in dreams. But dreams are merely a symptom of and a window onto what really happened. The suppressed drives were directed *inward* with two main results: consciousness and conscience.

Although these two things are closely related in Nietzsche's analysis, we can trace their rise and their difference to two elements. Consciousness is the result of the general turning inward of the drives. The shapes, what would become the symbol chains of dreams and thoughts, previously engraved on the external world and forgotten, were now projected inside the psyche. Man acquired a mental life more complex and populated than he had had before— consciousness:

> All instincts that do not discharge themselves outwardly turn inward—this is what I call the *internalization* of man: thus it was that man first developed what was later called his "soul." The entire inner world, originally as thin as if it were stretched between two membranes, expanded and extended itself, acquired depth, breadth and height, in the same measure as outward discharge was *inhibited*. (*GM* 2.16)

The forms the drives could no longer impose on the outer world were reproduced inside. The establishment of peace fuels man's growing inwardness by pushing underground his unconscious drives (*WP* 2.376). In the end, they need to create an internal arena in which to express themselves. This arena is the consciousness, and the expressions are what we call thoughts (see *Z* 1.4, 2.8). In so arguing, Nietzsche is not claiming that he can predict every thought on account of knowing the origin of thought in general. He does maintain, though, that this origin tells us something about the parameters, possibilities, and sources of consciousness. If our animal past cannot tell us the details of our current mental world, it may nonetheless set limits to our future.

In the deepening process that is part of this past, all instincts are not created equal, and the instinct for cruelty dominates this process, creating what we call the bad conscience. Conscience is the element of consciousness that results from the internalization of cruelty. To be sure, in practice this is often a distinction without a difference, since the instinct for cruelty seems to dominate Nietzsche's history. But the existence of the distinction means that his condemnation of conscience and cruelty is not a condemnation of thinking as such.

> Hostility, cruelty, joy in persecuting, in attacking, in change, in destruction—all this turned against the possessors of such instincts. . . . The man who, from lack of external enemies and resistances and forcibly confined to the oppressive narrowness and punctiliousness of custom, impatiently lacerated, persecuted, gnawed at, assaulted and maltreated himself . . . who had to turn himself into an adventure, a torture chamber . . . became the inventor of the "bad conscience." (*GM* 2.16)

When cruelty dominates, the chamber of the mind becomes a torture chamber, and the only punishment allowed is self-punishment (see *BGE* 7.229). This is the origin of asceticism, indeed "the whole of asceticism belongs here" (*GM* 2.3). Asceticism does not originate with Christianity; the latter merely makes use of it. The conscience emerges as a phantom limb, created by self-directed cruelty. Once in existence, it can be used or made to mean any number of things, depending on who or what is interpreting. The third essay of the genealogy gives a long history of conscience, in which Christianity is merely one of its later inheritors. Although Christianity significantly altered the direction of asceticism, the older phenomenon is the basic "conscience-vivisection and self-animal-torture of millennia" (*GM* 2.24).

Conscience originates through the internalization of cruelty. This takes place shortly after the imprisonment of man in society at the opening of the period called "the morality of mores." Throughout this period, man is deepened and made more conscious and more pained by the continued internal festering of cruelty. The result is the further separation of "man" from the animals. A phantom organ, receptive to pain (or simply generating it), is the invisible mark of that separation. A man is created capable of deep thought and also deep suffering. Both are required for the next stage of human history.

The Christian Era

Nietzsche is famous for associating Christian mildness and pity with cruelty and torment. But this does not account for the origin of cruelty and torment themselves. As we have seen, these developed throughout the period known as the morality of mores and provided "a certain soil in which Christian values have taken root: [they are] not Christianity itself" (*WP* 2.174). What occurs in the Christian era is a fresh episode of violence and interpretation, which builds on the events of the earlier time. This era culminates in the present. In Nietzsche's history, we may say provisionally, the past contains three principal periods: our animal prehistory, the era of morality of mores, and the Christian era.[33] (Recall that the historical Zarathustra also claimed that the world had seen three eras prior to his birth.)

Throughout the period of customs, man's self-torture through the internalization of drives has continued. In the process, he has driven his pain to a fever pitch. In the second essay of the *Genealogy*, Nietzsche describes this process in terms of the increasing degree of debt tribal communities feel toward their ancestors, whom they eventually transfigure into gods. Their sense of having promised, the burden of their ever-growing memory, becomes increasingly heavy. The chain of causality binds them ever tighter as its length increases. Eventually, the pain associated with this debt reaches the point where something incredible happens. In what Nietzsche alternately characterizes as an event of violence or of interpretation, a Christian attitude replaces the morality of custom.

The motivating force behind this change is what Nietzsche calls *ressentiment*. This feeling is the result of both man's increasing pain and his increasing internalization or "deepening." In simple human animals, the pain would not have called forth any *feeling* at all (much less thought), but simply a reflexive defensive *reaction*, which Nietzsche calls "revenge." But since this reaction is forbidden by the rules of society, its force is internalized and intellectualized. It becomes "the ressentiment of natures that are denied the proper [*eigentliche*] reaction, that of deeds, and compensate themselves with an *imaginary* revenge" (*GM* 1.10; emphasis added). What separates ressentiment from simple revenge is its imaginary character.[34] Revenge is an action; ressentiment is always a *sentiment*, a feeling.[35] Christianity, for example, avenged itself on

Rome, despite the timidity of Christians, by *imagining* its destruction in a last judgment, "by imagining the sudden destruction of the world to be near at hand" (*D* 1.71). This last judgment did not come to pass, of course, but Nietzsche's point is that this development of the Christian imagination did indeed play a part in the fall of Rome. Equally powerful than an actual Last Judgment was the *idea* of such an event, the idea that Rome was not Eternal.

The Christian interpretation also depends on internalization in another way: our sense of responsibility is heightened. As I argued above, one result of the morality of custom was to inject the notion of causality into our basic view of the world. The cause-and-effect model is the bedrock of both our understanding of the external world and our self-understanding. During the period of morality of custom, the constant process of self-inflicted torture has the effect of further engraving this interpretation. The wall of memory is built ever higher. Alternate interpretations are pushed ever farther into the unconscious. We emerge more clearly into the daylight of consciousness. We become deeper, more "interesting," "cleverer" (*GM* 1.6, 10). The more this happens, the more the causal model becomes a self-fulfilling prophecy. Believing others to be dependable, we act as if it were so; they believe similarly, and the social world really does become more ordered and predictable. The evidence more and more comes to resemble the theory, thus reinforcing the theory.[36] We base our waking lives on this interpretation and become the cause of our own effects. We become "responsible."

The Christian interpretation combines these three elements of man that develop in the morality of custom period: our increasing pain, increasing imagination, and increasing sense of responsibility. Or rather, the latter two are directed against the former. The Christian interpretation tells us for the first time that we ourselves are responsible for our pain: "This is brazen and false enough: but one thing at least is achieved by it, the direction of ressentiment is altered" (*GM* 3.15). The innovation is to attach our sense of responsibility to our bad conscience to create the idea of guilt—that is, to moralize the concept of debt (*GM* 2.21, 22).[37] What had merely been painful, now becomes evil: " 'sin'—for this is the priestly name for the animal's bad conscience (cruelty directed backward)—has been the greatest event so far in the history of the sick soul" (*GM* 3.20).

The pain man experienced through the phantom organ of conscience in the morality of mores period had been severe. But it had been understood as part of an inevitable conflict between the individual and society. It was a fact of life to be regretted, but for which no one could be blamed, since human drives, which bring individuals into conflict with social rules, were taken to be natural. This conflict, Nietzsche might say, is exemplified by early

Greek tragedy. But Christianity interprets the pain of conscience otherwise. It claims the individual *is* responsible for his drives. Any pain he feels in the course of refraining from custom-breaking activity is thus his own fault. The phantom pain of conscience is thus reinterpreted as something the individual causes himself through sin; the interpretation of the morality of mores is obliterated. It is important to see, however, how the second interpretation builds on the first, how it builds on established conventions and existing symbols as each dream builds on the last. Without the notion of causality, carefully nurtured in the preceding period, sin would not be possible. And without the increasing imagination, or depth of soul, that also grew in the early era, the idea of a sinner, one who might have wished otherwise, would have seemed ridiculous.

Nietzsche associates this interpretation with a particular kind of violence. Where violence had been directed at suppressing certain activities, it is now directed at the very drives themselves. No longer content to block them, it now seeks their eradication. Violence is now directed not just at actions but at passions. "The Church combats the passions with excision in every sense of the word: its practice, its 'cure' is *castration*" (*TI* 5.1; see also *WP* 2.141, 248). It is not the acts so much as the passions associated with them that Christianity seeks to cast out. Where the morality of mores policed actions, the Christian-moral morality polices thoughts. Nietzsche links the sweet voice of Christianity to this particular kind of cruelty, which he also calls "moral castration-ism" (*WP* 2.204). Where once only outer experience was regulated by this pain-producing organ, now inner experience is also so controlled.

The Christian interpretation of asceticism alters the direction of its violence. It allows the blocked drives to express themselves again, but along only one narrow path, conditioned by the basic idea of causality. The path left is revenge against the "guilty." This interpretation continues to allow the self-punishment that existed in the morality of custom period (indeed, intensifies it), but also allows the attack on others that is typical of the Christian era—"the slave revolt in morality" (*GM* 1.10). In the concepts of "evil" and "sin," Christianity finds the tools that continue to permit the self-torture of the mores period, while at the same time permitting the venting of ressentiment on others in such a way that it does not violate the basic rules of all morality, obedience to custom and the associated orderliness and meekness. The victims of the original interpretation contained in morality *re*-interpret it so that it is now deployed against their oppressors. A new episode of violence re-writes (or ob-literates) the earlier chain of symbols rather than totally destroying or erasing it. The Christian exegesis of asceticism "read the highest meaning and value into it—and with this also the courage to despise every other way of life" (GS 5.353). Christians are able to disguise their cruelty beneath an interpretation of pity and mildness. The process of this revolt is what Nietzsche describes in the first essay of the *Genealogy*, where Christian values finally reconquer the barbarians who gave society its original shape (*GM* 1.11). The cruelty of Aquinas and Tertullian (cited at *GM* 1.15) merely reflects the redirection the church gives to the violence of the ascetic. "Christianity has made use of [the torments of the soul] on an unheard of scale and continues to preach this species of torture" (*D* 1.77; see also *TI* 7.2, *AC* 22). While the Christian interpretation heightens the self-torture by transforming "debt" into "guilt," the violence is no longer merely inwardly directed, as in the morality of mores; it relieves the pressure of this self-torment by directing its energy outward at others, the "evil" ones: nobles, Romans, sinners.

While it is the belief in guilt that haunts modern man, it was the belief in evil that allowed this interpretation to flourish by conquering those who opposed it. Guilt is the ghost of Banquo that haunts the murderers of the "good" kings, the instrument of whose death was the concept of "evil." The obliteration of the past does not mean that it is entirely forgotten. The Christian episode is contained in our memory, but the existence of our memory itself, like our conscience, is the mark of something older. By paying attention to these marks and to dreams, Nietzsche has been able to piece together this plot, deciphering the earlier meaning of symbols in older dreams. But Nietzsche's dreamscape is not an escape to a more tranquil reality. If anything, it focuses our attention on the inescapability of pain and violence.

The Three Epochs: The Course of History as the Course of Violence

To say it again, Nietzsche divides the axis of history into three eras: our animal prehistory; the period of morality of custom; and the Christian era. Each time has its own particular type of interpretation and violence. He sometimes calls these the three rungs on "a great ladder of religious cruelty" (*BGE* 3.55). In the animal period, interpretation is undisciplined and violence is unfocused. As beasts, blond or otherwise, we wreak havoc in a thoughtless manner; our every drive is instantly expressed (or impressed) upon the world. But these shapes disappear as soon as they are made, because the human animal has no memory. Like figures drawn in the sand, the shapes are erased by the next wave or breath of wind.

The second era starts with the violent conquest by one pack of these animals of another. The conquerors impose a shape upon human society by violently burning a memory into the flesh of those who cannot resist them. Thus initiated, the development of memory continues within society as the drives of those conquered turn inward and continue the torture begun by the conquerors. The shapes man had previously impressed on a meaningless world, and then on the body, are now internalized and begin to express themselves in the mind, *as* the mind. On this basis, language is created and the process of artistic development commences. In this process, the intellect is formed, but also bad conscience, the sense of debt. All the violence inherent in the creation and imposition of shapes must now be borne inside the soul rather than by an unfeeling world. We feel pain in our conscience much as we do in a phantom limb.

Finally, the Christian interpretation, born of the sufferings of the morality of custom, initiates the third era, which brings us to the present. The sense of responsibility is joined with the sense of debt to create the idea of guilt. This does not halt the process of self-torment, but it allows the drives to express themselves again, now in a highly disciplined fashion. The drives turn outward, not to create at random (to "hallucinate") but to impose one interpretation, the Christian one, on as much of the world as possible. Thus begins the long process by which the slave revolt in morals comes to shape the entire world. The Christians achieve permanence for their interpretation because they have been disciplined. The violence they suffered left a memory that blocked out all interpretations but one. The other drives are left largely to work themselves out at night. Dreams are all that are left of "the savage beast which, locked in the cellars beneath the foundations of culture, howls and rages" (*HH* 9.614). Christian meekness, paradoxically enforced by terrible cruelty, rules the day. It is not just that the truth hurts, but that our truths are inseparable from the pain and violence that created them, and that now maintain them through ascetic habits.

I should say here that I am probably collapsing too thoroughly many of the plot elements in the *Genealogy*, which perhaps should be allowed more freedom, in search of a particular kind of narrative coherence. Nonetheless, I think this is a necessary corrective to interpretations of Nietzsche that assert narrative incoherence to be his goal in writing, and that there is therefore no purpose in searching out his story. Many elements of the *Genealogy* that appear contradictory can be understood as rival versions of the narrative I have sketched, each with the same characters and plot, in different guises; just as Nietzsche held that all characters in Greek tragedy were always Dionysus in disguise.

And where has this history landed us? Nietzsche speaks often of the looming end of the Christian era. At last, one element of Christianity turns on the rest of it: the sense of Christian truthfulness draws "its inference against itself." The development of the sense of honesty at last renders the Christian

God unbelievable (*GM* 3:27; see also the opening pages of *WP*). The death of God is no accident but a murder (*GS* 3.125; *Z* 4.7). It is the final act of Christian cruelty. But since it is based on Christian values, it is by no means a liberation from them. Indeed, just as Christianity built on the eras that preceded it, so the demise of Christianity will not mean the end of its influence, or that of the earlier times. But without the dominance of the Christian interpretation, these accumulated wounds and memories lack an overarching purpose and man becomes a "motley cow," "with the characters of the past written all over you, and these characters in turn painted over with new characters . . . all ages and peoples peek out of your veils; motley, all customs and faiths speak out of your gestures" (*Z* 2.14; see also *WP* 2.260). In Nietzsche's meditation on history, however, the cow is his symbol of the unthinking, unmemorious animal. Why does he use the image again? How has man, who has suffered much pain to build memory to separate him from the animals come once again to resemble the animals?

The cows in the pasture live in an eternal present. They cannot think because they cannot remember from one moment to the next (*UM* 2.1). They have no memory and, hence, no language in which to think. But as I argued in Chapter 3, a surfeit of memory can have the same effect. Memory makes language possible; but it can also be a habit that we follow unthinkingly. It stifles creativity by forcing our minds into the same ruts again and again. The strength of a particular symbol chain prevents the appearance of new and different ones—even though new interpretations must build on the old. The paradoxical relationship of memory and creativity (simultaneously feeding and limiting each other) threatens to end in the overpowering of the latter by the former. Our history of violence has built the wall of memory to its highest point yet. Will it serve as our greatest canvas or as an impregnable prison, trapping us in the present? When Nietzsche says that mankind is becoming a herd, he worries that we are becoming a higher type of cow. Our thoughts develop to the point where we no longer have to think. The animal with an overpowering memory resembles the animal with no memory— neither thinks. We lapse into a new animality, contained in an eternal present.

Between Past and Future

I wrote above that Nietzsche sees three eras to history. Counting the future, it would be better to say that there are four. And one ought to count the future, because there is no writer to whom the future is more of a reality than Nietzsche.[38] No one has felt more in the vise between past and future. Nietzsche gives us his account of the past, not for our abstract edification, but in order to propel us to a future: "To impregnate the past and beget the future, let that be the present for me."[39] The alternative is really no future at all but an eternal present. The wall of memory, which we constructed to climb out of the past, will end up trapping us in the present. Memory will grow so strong that we shall be unable to imagine ourselves any differently, and shall thus never live any differently. Our interpretation of the world will become so fixed that no event will disturb it. Whereas Locke felt the future endangered by a particular past, Nietzsche feels the future *as such* threatened by the weight of memory in general. And yet his strategy is similar to Locke's. Rather than fleeing the past in search of the future, he attempts to *redeem* the former for the sake of the latter.

The strong links that Nietzsche sees between past and future (and his doctrine of "amor fati") have occasionally led to the view that he is a fatalist in the strong sense, seeing human beings as locked in a chain of causality, without free will.[40] More often, it is recognized that this would make nonsense of his other views, especially his dedication to creativity—but the response is often to subsume his views on past and future under "eternal recurrence." Yet his concern for past and future is almost constant, and we overdistill it if we maintain that it is wholly contained in the idea of recurrence (which actually occupies very few pages in Nietzsche's work).

Recurrence symbolizes the reunion of past and future in opposition to the present. In *Zarathustra* 2.20, redemption is defined as re-creating all "it was" into "thus I willed it." Redemption overcomes "the will's ill will against time and its 'it was.'" The will is frustrated and vows "revenge for its inability to go backwards." Recurrence is the solution to this frustration. How can the will, which can only will forward (as time runs forward), overcome its power-lessness against the past? By willing the past as the future, that is, by willing the past to recur again *as past*. That is the purpose of recurrence. It is to Nietzsche an element of mental health.[41] But since, as I have discussed, *the substance of the past is inherently mutable*, the idea of recurrence does not really determine the substance of future and past—it simply unites them. "There is no way of telling what may yet become part of history" (*GS* 1.34). The past is as unpredictable as the future. Even if one were to believe that the future must somehow repeat the past, this would tell one nothing about human history or the details of the human future. Knowing the form of time tells one almost nothing of its content. Recurrence is at best a seed, and certainly not the flower, of Nietzsche's account of time. It should be noted as well that in *Zarathustra*, the "cosmological" account of recurrence, where everything is repeated identically, is only given by Zarathustra's *animals* (*Z* 3.13, 2). Zara-thustra is silent in reply. It is one of those odd coincidences of Nietzsche interpretation that Arthur Danto and Martin Heidegger agree that Zarathustra's silence confirms the animals' expression; I see no particular reason to believe this, especially since Zarathustra has just predicted that the animals will turn his doctrine into "a hurdy-gurdy song" (*ein Leier-Lied*), that is, a simplified version of a more subtle tune that repeats itself eternally, and gratingly.[42]

In my discussion of creativity, I maintained the close relation of memories to the creation of new things. When Nietzsche instructs philosophers to create the future, he does so on the basis that "everything that is or has been becomes for them a means, an instrument, a hammer" (*BGE* 6.211). When such a philosopher addresses his soul, he asks "Where would future and past dwell closer together than in you?" (*Z* 3.14).

New things (the future as such) are created by writing over the past. The history of asceticism that Nietzsche gives in the third essay of the *Genealogy* is an account of such a pattern (and also, as I discuss below, an example of it). Ascetic practices served as the wall or canvas on which new creations were composed. Christian morality was merely the most recent of these compositions. It incorporated the past, reinterpreting it as leading to the Christian present. The history of the Old Testament became the prehistory of the Christian era (*AC* 42). Nietzsche believes the idea of causality is itself an interpretation—the very first, in fact, to be embedded in our memory, as our memory. Christianity merely fills in the substance of that chain with its own story.

Although Nietzsche speaks of the past as determining the future, he also holds that "there is no way of telling what may yet become part of history." It is quite wrong to say, as Joan Stambaugh does, that, for Nietzsche, "what has become is the only thing that is fixed, that is 'absolute'."[43] Zarathustra calls this doctrine "madness": " 'Alas, the stone *It was* cannot be moved: all punishments must be eternal too.' Thus preached madness." For those who are mad in this fashion, there can be no redemption or, at best, a false one, where willing becomes " 'not willing' " (*Z* 2.20). When the past is not held to be fixed, the absurdities that the cosmological version of Eternal Recurrence is said to entail become less relevant. Also, as we shall see, redemption of the past becomes more possible.

We are in a story that is of a piece. Each chapter must follow from those previous. If the earlier chapters are reinterpreted in the writing of a new chapter, it must be done in such a way that the consistency between past and future is retained. If not, the new interpretation will not stick in our minds—it will be forgotten as quickly as a dream. More than this is needed, of course, for a plot to succeed, but such consistency is a necessary starting point. Who would alter the future must begin with the past. But this is an opportunity as well as a burden. It holds open the possibility of redeeming the past, just as Locke sought to do, in pursuit of the future.

Nietzsche feels trapped between past and future. But he has hopes for the future based on the mutability of the past. We cannot flee from the wall of memory; if we are to have a future, we must reshape the past as Homer reshaped existing customs into new values. The past must be our bridge to the future. Zarathustra claims to have taught men "to work on the future and to redeem with their creation all that *has been*" (*Z* 3.12, 3; see also 1.16). Apollonian artistry redetermined the future by reshaping the past (*GS* 2.84). This discussion has finally given us some idea of the task of the philosopher of the future: he attempts to inscribe a new form on the wall of memory and at one stroke change past and future. He attempts to reinterpret the symbol chains that are there in order to write a new one. He attempts to do violence to the past in order to shape the future. Clearly, the *Genealogy* itself is just such an attempt. Toward what future does Nietzsche propel us?

Two Futures, or Future and Present?

Nietzsche often speaks, much like the original Zarathustra, as if we have two broad choices. One note in *The Will to Power* puts this explicitly: "The Two Futures of Mankind: 1) consistent growth of mediocrity; 2) conscious distinction, self-shaping" (*WP* 4.953). A more dramatic personification of this fork in our road is "Dionysus versus the 'Crucified'" (*WP* 4.1052). In this last section, I shall try to flesh out this alternative a little more, assimilating option (1) above to the threat I have already described of an eternal present. The second option represents, according to Nietzsche, the only real possibility of a true future.[44] There the past continues to serve as a canvas instead of as a prison wall.

The question is whether our memory has become so strong that it has finally succeeded in entirely enslaving our creativity. In *Zarathustra*, Nietzsche uses the image of the Last Men to help us picture this possibility (see the Prologue: 5). The Last Men embody this "growth of mediocrity." They are not the last because they are the final generation of men; indeed, "the last man lives longest." They are the last because they are the final, immutable form of man. Humans will no longer change; they will rather stay the same from generation to generation. History is arrested in the Last Man. Mediocrity grows in that it comes to capture all of humanity: "Everybody wants the same. Everybody is the same." Nietzsche has warned that memory is the rut into which conscious thought falls more and more often. We arrive at the position of Last Men when we can no longer think ourselves out of the rut. Our creativity is at an end. We can no longer create new forms, either of art or of life. The Last Man is the final version of man. He is without a future: "Thus all the past is abandoned: for one day the rabble might become master and drown all time in shallow waters" (Z 3.12, 11).

In discussing the downfall of Greek culture, Nietzsche gives, I believe, an account of something similar to the plight of the Last Men. The Greeks, he maintains, fell in love with their own capacity to play many roles. At last, they became nothing but pure actors. Thus they relinquished the possibility of being authors and were confined to a fixed set of preexisting roles: "another human type is disadvantaged more and more and finally made impossible; above all great 'architects'; the strength to build becomes paralyzed; the courage to make plans that encompass the distant future is discouraged" (GS 5.356). The Greeks enjoyed this life just as the Last Men enjoy their happiness—a happiness without end, but also without beginning or middle.[45] The dynamic tension of memory and creativity is stilled. Memory has won and we are irretrievably separated from past and future. There is no future, only an eternal present: we may shift roles, but nothing ever changes.

To this dystopia, Nietzsche offers the alternative of a real future, but a future that is no less an outgrowth of the past. "I love him who justifies the future and redeems past generations: for he wants to perish of the present" (Z, Prol., 4).[46] To will a future is just the opposite of willing the present. An eternal present is just the continuation of what exists now. The future represents that which is new, which does not yet exist, which has yet to be created, which is *not present*. The tension of memory and creativity is the tension between *present* and future, not between past and future. The past and future lie together on the other side of the wall.

Nietzsche's alternating optimism and pessimism about the future can easily be misunderstood. It needs to be interpreted through the tension of memory and creativity. Just as a strong memory poses a grave threat, it also opens the greatest opportunity. There exists, Nietzsche argues, "a magnificent tension of the spirit such as has never existed on earth before: with so tense a bow one can now shoot for the most distant targets" (BGE, Preface). In his cryptic note in The Will to Power, Nietzsche spoke of the alternative to mediocrity as "conscious distinction, self-shaping." This points us back in the direction of creativity and dreams.[47]

Nietzsche's concern is, from a certain perspective, like Locke's. He worries that we shall be trapped in an excessively "English" present, rather than a broader human one. But for Nietzsche this means that we shall be so chained by and to our notion of cause and effect that we effectively give up past and future for a castrated present. The narrative of causality is a dead end. Nietzsche's plot, on the other hand, is a dreamlike story. We are chained to the past, but this does not prevent us from dancing, which here means creating a future.

Daybreak ends with a dramatic "Or?" symbolizing our choice between the two alternatives.[48] There he invokes the image of Columbus as the symbol of creative possibilities (5.575). In another note, he further mixes the idea of discovery with that of creation: "Our new world: we have to realize to what degree we are the *creators* of our value feelings—and thus capable of projecting 'meaning' into history" (*WP* 4.1011).[49] The "new" world for Nietzsche is not that on the other side of the globe, but the world yet to be created. It lies in the future. It is new because it has not yet been. And the creation is, to repeat, a reinscription (an ob-literation) of the wall of memory. A new future is created by a rewriting of the past. It is a redemption of that past. It is the reshaping of the past to make a new value. Columbus, who had to reinterpret the globe before he could discover a new continent, is our modern-day Homer.

Many commentators who focus only on the second of the *Untimely Meditations* when discussing Nietzsche's views of history mistake him on this point. In that essay, the tension between past and future is already present, but it tends to be presented in an either/or way. Later, in the *Genealogy*, the question for Nietzsche is *how* the past can lead to the future, whereas in the *Uses and Disadvantages*, it is only a question of *how much* history can be withstood. Thus from the latter perspective, Lacoue-Labarthe writes that Nietzsche uses history "as a drug. . . . Absorbed in small quantity, it does not present any danger: it is even necessary. . . . But if one abuses it, it destroys and kills. It is a poison. One must therefore use history moderately."[50] The difference between *Uses and Disadvantages* and the *Genealogy* is thus one of quantity versus substance. In the former, Nietzsche is concerned with the *amount* of history; in the latter, he fills out the substance of history and is concerned with how that substance may either help or hinder the future.[51] "In your children you shall make up for being the children of your fathers: thus you shall redeem all that is past" (*Z* 3.12, 12).

But what is the special "tension of the spirit"? What makes those at the end of the Christian era stand apart? Our memory is stronger than that of any other era, the result of a continuous process of self-torment. This process Nietzsche now sees as a "discipline and preparation of the intellect for its future 'objectivity' ": the "latter understood not as 'contemplation without interest' (which is a nonsensical absurdity), but as the ability to *control* one's

Pro and Con and to dispose of them, so that one knows how to employ a *variety* of perspectives and affective interpretations in the service of knowledge" (*GM* 3.12). Memory came about with the purpose of disciplining the drives that through their too-various interpretations made ordered human life impossible. Now, Nietzsche says, that process has advanced to the stage where a new possibility has arisen. Man has achieved such self-mastery that the drives can be let loose from behind the wall of memory without destroying the structures built on that wall. The multiple "affective interpretations" can come forth without driving us to madness.

Our discipline can allow a passion to be expressed continuously, without breaking off suddenly in favor of another passion (as that of the *Urmenschen* did). This strength allows the creativity of the drive to be fully expressed. At the same time, the self-defeat of Christianity, with its associated notions of subjectivity and causality, means that the expression of one drive need not banish the others to the night. Passions will compete, no doubt, and attempt to obliterate one another, but they need not proclaim the nonexistence of other passions. Although they attempt to dominate, they do not do so by proclaiming the dominance of a single passion, regularity, to be a good thing. That was the tactic, and the interpretation, of morality.

This is Nietzsche's strategy of redemption: if we enter this future of disciplined creativity, the past will stand redeemed as its necessary prehistory. The attraction this possibility holds out is that of a "multi-stringed culture" (*HH* 5.281) in place of the monotonous life of the Last Man. The Last Man is the very opposite of redemption. All our history will be for naught if we return to the state of animals! Our discipline is now so great that the variousness we have consigned to our dreams and our past can once again be let loose. At the very end of *Zarathustra*, the sage and his followers emerge from their cave into *night*, the realm of dreams.[52] Their exploration has opened up the multiple possibilities of the night; they do not need the single interpretation of the day, for "night too is a sun" (*Z* 4.19, 10). Henceforth, Zarathustra has no need of the sun provided by custom. When he speaks to the sun at the end of the book, he speaks to himself (*Z* 4.20).

It should be clear by now that redemption is what is at stake here. For although Nietzsche argues for a dream-filled life, he does not believe the inverse, that life is but a dream. Indeed, he paints our past as a continuous plot of pain and violence, which desperately stands in need of redemption. Shall we have suffered all this, from the first blows of the conquerors to our most recent pangs of conscience, just to return to an animal herd, "fragments and limbs and dreadful accidents, but no human beings" (*Z* 2.20)? Or shall we, on the contrary, be able to make something of this wretched history, make it necessary and worthwhile so that we might even consent to it, will it to recur, as a required prelude to the future? Zarathustra seeks to redeem, not just his own life, but "to redeem those who lived in the past . . . that alone should I call redemption" (*Z* 2.20). To submit to the law of causality is to give up the chance of redemption. The past, in that case, cannot be recast, and it all appears as chance, as meaningless accident. The Christian narrative enslaves us because it deprives us of meaning. Although Nietzsche's genealogy is gruesome, it does offer a real future—a meaningful redemption: "All 'it was' is a fragment, a riddle, a dreadful accident—until the creative will says to it, 'But thus I willed it'" (*Z* 2.20). In dreaming a future, we redeem the dead, God included, by making their suffering an irreplaceable part of ourselves. "But," Nietzsche adds, "has the will yet spoken thus? And when will that happen?" (*Z* 2.20).

Although the political theory of Locke and Nietzsche differs in a thousand ways, they do at least share one purpose: they each seek an unreligious account of redemption. The redemption is similar in that they both seek to revive the memory of a forgotten original (recall Plato's contention in *Meno* that all knowledge is recollection), to show how that origin is constitutive of our present identity, and to present alternative futures in which the labor and suffering of previous generations are either made to bear fruit or to have been for naught. Although both describe the possibility of redemption, both do so, not out of religious concern, but precisely out of their concern to provide an alternative to a religious narrative. For Locke, this was the Filmerian account of biblical history; for Nietzsche, it was the story of the Last Man, brought to his untimely end by Christian morality. Locke's narrative may well be Christian (albeit in a more abstract sense than Filmer's), but it is surely not the notion of redemption itself that makes it so—it is the labor of preceding generations that is redeemed, not our immortal souls. As Nietzsche's account further demonstrates, the notion of redemption is not inherently religious, but has been taken over and moralized by Christian interpreters: human beings sought redemption long before they were offered a false one by the priests. In order to find it now, we must turn away from them, he contends, even more firmly.

The high wall of memory will be either our greatest barrier or our greatest canvas. If we follow our happiness, we shall surely end up in a cul-de-sac with the Last Men. Indeed, Nietzsche seems sure that this is the (non-)future for many, if not most, people. Nietzsche's history shows us that our every improvement has been predicated on the deepest pain. His *Genealogy* does not spur us to the future with a promise of joy. He only shows that our development up to this point leads to our present choice, a choice that faces us as a culture, but that each decides individually. Again as with Locke, the narrative is, at this point and in this way, open in the sense that it does not have a wholly determined future or end. Either we can become Last Men, returning nearly to the state of happy, unthinking cows, or we can continue on our path and complete our separation from the animals (see *WS* 350). The injunction to "live dangerously" (*GS* 283) is a reminder of the risk, indeed, the promise, of pain that accompanies the second path. To live dangerously is not to live masochistically; it is simply to judge that the avoidance of suffering should not be an exclusive (or even important) principle in the design of human life. Suffering can be redeemed. Animals have no past: they neither suffer nor stand in need of redemption. Does that make their lives worthwhile?

"He who discovered the land 'man', also discovered the land 'man's future'" (*Z* 3.12, 28). To choose the future with a future is essentially to affirm yourself as human, for it is choosing to *be* human, rather than an animal that registers pain and pleasure but makes nothing of them. It is choosing to make something, rather than nothing, of the past. It is choosing to dance in one's chains, rather than becoming another link in the chain of causality. As Locke did, Nietzsche believes the choice to be between moral slavery and true humanity. Dreams cannot redeem us, but redemption will only come if we plot as the dreamer does. Of all the various metaphors Nietzsche uses to present this possibility, I think this one is best: "Either we have no dreams or our dreams are interesting. We should learn to arrange our waking life the same way: nothing or interesting" (*GS* 3.232; see also 1.54).

PART III

G. W. F. Hegel

Or say that the end precedes the beginning,
And the end and the beginning were always there
Before the beginning and after the end.
And all is always now.
— T. S. Eliot, "Burnt Norton"

CHAPTER 5

The Temple of Memory

The truly apocalyptic view of the world is that things do not repeat
themselves.
          —Ludwig Wittgenstein, *Culture and Value*

Famished for history, nourished on history, Hegel's philosophy, without understanding that it did so, yet advocated fasting.
          —Benedetto Croce, *What Is Living and What Is Dead of the
          Philosophy of Hegel*

Where the burden of the preceding chapters on Locke and Nietzsche lay
in establishing that the arguments of those authors are best understood as a
kind of historical philosophy, with Hegel I take that to be a given. It is widely
accepted that Hegel attempted to marshal most of the human past into a
single storyline.[1] Indeed, Hegel's writings on history are often stereotyped to
the point where they seem too familiar to warrant serious investigation. The
loss that results from this unfortunate attitude, however, is not merely to one's
reading of Hegel, but also to one's appreciation of the role of history in
political theory generally, precisely because Hegel is assumed to typify such
theory. In the attempts of twentieth-century theorists, both liberal and conservative, to distance themselves from historical thinking, Hegel has become
the arch-villain of historicism.[2] This situation is compounded by the relative
neglect of Hegel's extensive discussion of the past in his lectures on the history
of the fine arts (hereafter, the *Aesthetics*).[3] By examining Hegel's aesthetics in
conjunction with his lectures on world history, we can discover an aspect of
his approach to the past that neither his critics nor his defenders have fully
appreciated.[4]

While the themes Hegel develops in these texts are echoed in all his
writings, their mode of presentation is sufficiently different there to warrant
consideration on its own. I shall therefore to some extent be reading elements
of Hegel's corpus (the *Aesthetics* and the *Philosophy of History*) against the grain
of other elements with the goal of indicating how the whole might be re-

imagined. In the *Aesthetics*, Hegel offers us a perspective on history at once powerful and fraught with dangers. Indeed, the dangers stem directly from its power—the capacity to view history from an aesthetic perspective. Beyond the integration of this perspective with the rest of Hegel's theory, then, there lurks the larger question of what this approach to history has to offer us of itself.

The "philosophy of history" has been linked with Hegel for so long now that the traditional associations it calls to mind (of reason and progress, of national spirit and historical purpose) seem almost impossible to dislodge. But these clichés, although containing a grain of truth, do not do much justice to Hegel's philosophy. What is worse though, and what often accompanies these clichés, is the thought that any philosopher who treats of history must end up with an approach like that of Hegel, who is held to be reductionist, schematic, and deterministic. Worse than a misperception about Hegel is the effect that this misperception can have in closing off an entire field of inquiry. Hegel is an important philosopher of history; but he is not *the* philosopher of history. Nor is there anything necessarily "Hegelian" about political philosophies of history or time. In fact, in this chapter and the next, Hegel's approach to time, his attempted reconciliation with it, will be set off sharply from the redemptive efforts of Locke and Nietzsche. (As I argue in Chapter 6, redemption and reconciliation are very different strategies for dealing with the past.) But before this is possible, Hegel's philosophy of history, long reduced to clichés, must be considered from a fresh angle.

Hegel's fundamental approach to history, I argue, is to aestheticize it. The vocabulary of his history correlates closely with that of his aesthetics. The study of art provides Hegel, at least to some extent, with both the form and the content of his study of history, because "in works of art the nations have deposited their richest inner intuitions and ideas" (*AE* 7). The history of art supplies a kind of template for the account of history proper. Once this is recognized, the implications of Hegel's history appear more complex than is often thought: it is neither the Victorian chronicle of Western reason and power that everyone loves to hate nor simply a thesis of the "end of history" in modern liberal democracy. It is, instead, an attempt to reconcile modern humans to their own past through an identification with that past's aesthetic qualities.[5]

To aestheticize, however, does not mean simply to beautify. In the same way as a decision to evaluate an action morally does not decide whether one judges it as good or evil, viewing an object from an aesthetic point of view does not predetermine the evaluation of it as beautiful or ugly; both are legitimate conclusions from the aesthetic perspective. Hegel's preliminary need, therefore, is to make history seem a fit object (or, rather, set of objects) for aesthetic judgment. Although he does ultimately find that there is a beauty to history, this conclusion does not follow directly from his use of aesthetics.

We need to reconstruct Hegel's history so that the strangeness of this perspective can once again appear for us. Without an element of strangeness, Hegel's history poses no challenge; it is easily summarized and dismissed. For this reason, among others, I have chosen to precede this chapter with distinctly un-Hegelian political histories in order to emphasize the variety of possibilities that exist within historical argument. If any readers thus far have been persuaded that historical argument is not what they have grown to expect, perhaps they can now be persuaded as well that Hegelian history is not what they have long assumed. In the section that follows, I shall further sketch out some introductory themes, which are then pursued more directly in the body of the chapter. Hegel's history is best understood, I contend, as an attempt to seduce us to life (to use a Nietzschean concept) and to the story of the world.[6] It is an attempt, I should add, that is probably unsuccessful. Its failure lies in its refusal to provide a future (and thus a politics), as Locke and Nietzsche do. Indeed, it is Hegel, above all, who must answer to Nietzsche's charge that modern thought traps us in an eternal present.

The Aesthetic Approach to History and the Seduction to Life

Despite the well-known Hegelian theme of dialectical development, the various civilizations depicted in Hegel's lectures on history are often remarkably static, indeed almost frozen in the statuesque poses of his favorite art. In fact, as we shall see, Hegel assigns to each period an art form that typifies it and represents it in his thought. And he evaluates each period both in terms of the art that typifies it and *as if* it were that art itself. For it is his principle that "at every particular stage on which the Ideal treads the road of its unfolding there is immediately linked with every *inner* determinacy another *real* configuration" (*AE* 300). Art does not just exemplify history, it embodies it. This "configuration" appears *both* as a form or genre of art (e.g., for the Oriental stage, architecture) *and* as particular works, both of which he uses to assess the era they mark out. In making the connection in this fashion, Hegel opens up for himself many possible lines of inquiry. He can explore, say, the meaning of the Oriental stage both through the genre of architecture and through particular structures such as the Pyramids. But after so doing, he will also be able to turn the critical vocabulary developed in these inquiries onto the state itself.

The historical dynamism that we associate with Hegel's dialectic does not disappear in these two sets of lectures (on history and art), but the historical stages described there are, I contend, as a consequence of the aesthetic perspective, considerably more fixed than those of the *Phenomenology*. In these texts, Hegel does not always view the state as a kinetic creature, but often describes a motionless shape or edifice, best evaluated in aesthetic terms.[7] The vocabulary that Hegel develops in the *Aesthetics*, he puts to significant use in the analysis of history. While the lectures on aesthetics attempt to confine their subject matter to the fine arts (and are hardly successful), the theory of aesthetics sketched there is not limited in its application to those arts. It is instead a general theory of beauty that can grapple with any kind of human activity said to have a shape.[8] From early descriptions of the state's "thinghood" or "mass" in the *Phenomenology* (e.g., *PS* 352, 420, 441) to a more consistent account of "shape" in later works, a continuous aesthetic mode of evaluation is present in Hegel's account of history (although it certainly becomes more prominent in his later works).

Although art itself, according to this mode of evaluation, is said to peak in the middle of history and to decline thereafter, the beauty of the state and citizen is on an ever-rising incline toward the present. Greek art is more beautiful than German art, but the German soul is more beautiful than the Greek soul was. The aesthetic standards Hegel elaborates tend to exalt Greek statuary above all other human artistic endeavor. But in the social realm, to which (as we shall see) these standards also apply, the modern Germanic state (as he conceives it) receives the highest endorsement. Indeed, its perfection is even greater than that of Hellenic statues. Attractive as the Greeks are, Hegel finds a higher beauty in his own time. And he does not find that beauty in art, even though his standards of beauty are derived from his study of art.

This static account of political units and the overall picture that they make up are linked to one of the most interesting elements in Hegel's narrative—the absence of a future. His identification of the present as the final episode of historical time (as well as other things discussed below) implies that his story is complete as it stands, and that history is at an end (*PH* 442). The existence of an end point differentiates Hegel's story from those of Locke and Nietzsche. It is the urge for an end itself that makes Hegel's narrative more of a theodicy (and more Christian even) than Locke's. We might call this urge "Aristotelian" in the sense that Aristotle (as I described in the Introduction) required every good narrative to have an end. But the lack of a future, I argue below, also makes the story seem emptier as a political theory than either Locke's or Nietzsche's history. The wealth of detail about the past (certainly much more than either of the other two provides) makes Hegel's silence about the future all the more troubling. This silence may cause us to question Hegel's achievement in crafting an aesthetic approach to history and time. To what sort of life, exactly, is Hegel seducing us?

By "seduction to life" I intend: to give meaning to the world and thus to block an interpretation of life that is world-denying. The seduction to life is the connection between aesthetics and Hegel's purpose in writing history. A seduction requires an attraction and an attraction requires beauty. Giving a beautiful shape to the past allows us to be attracted to what would otherwise seem disordered and repulsive. This beauty can then arouse a passion for life within us. Developing an aesthetics that applies equally to statues and states is thus crucial to Hegel's overall argument.

But the beauty of states is not necessarily visible to those who live within them, as the beauty of art is to those who see it. Those who live within states do not need to be attracted to them, as the person who views them in retrospect does, in order to be reconciled to them. Hegel desires us to embrace the past in a way that those who lived within it had no possibility (or need) of doing—we need to see the beauty of its whole shape. The seduction involves not so much a deception as a distraction. Our gaze has to be averted (or better, altered) so that the "slaughter-bench" elements of history do not cause us to turn away in disgust. Not that these are to be dismissed or forgotten, but that they should find a place in a whole that has a beautiful shape. Hegel does not try to hide history from us, but to make us see it in a particular light.

This does not mean that Hegel tries to beautify all of history. The Bible contains many stories of violence, irreligiosity, and heresy, but is still considered a text that attracts readers to religious devotion. In the same way, Hegel's history may attract readers to life without being beautiful in every chapter. Indeed, the overcoming of ugliness and evil is the basis, as in the Bible, for some of the most powerful episodes. So, for example, Hegel sees the violence of the French Terror overcome and made the basis for the beautiful modern state structured by the Napoleonic Code.

In the introduction to the *Phenomenology*, Hegel says that while he disagrees with the methods of the romantics, he shares their aim of recovering "that lost sense of solid and substantial being" (*PS* 7). This feeling of loss remains the principal focus of his work even in his laborious reconstruction of history. His fundamental worry is to win us back to the world, to have the details of the past, in their accumulated weight, provide us with a sense of "substantial being." He fears a condition that Nietzsche describes as occasionally necessary: the lightness that comes from the forgetting of history. But Hegel knows these details will not seem solid until they have a form, a shape, or some sturdiness. This shape will ultimately be recognizable as Hegel's

"Temple of Mnemosyne," or, more plainly, a Temple of Memory. The use of a building to symbolize human history is not Hegel's invention. Here, he drew on Kant's remarks in the "Idea for a Universal History with a Cosmopolitan Intent": "It remains perplexing that earlier generations seem to do their laborious work for the sake of later generations, in order to provide a foundation from which the latter can advance the building which nature has intended. Only later generations will have the good fortune to live in the building."[9] Not only does Hegel extend this metaphor of Kant's considerably; he puts greater weight on it than Kant would have thought possible. Where Kant was hopeful about the purposefulness of history, Hegel is certain.

But the real danger of Hegel's strategy is, not so much that we gloss over the ugly past, but that we fall so deeply in love with our own image (for Hegel thinks that history is nothing but the reflection of human spirit) that, like Narcissus, we become rooted to the spot, lost in admiration of and desire for our own reflection. The seduction is hazardous, not because we ignore the faults of the past, but because we become imprisoned in our memory of it. Even in the *Philosophy of Right*, where this project wears its most attractive face, there are many discordant notes that give the reader pause. The "system of right" described there is frequently likened to nature and, in fact, is called "a second nature" (*PR* 4), differentiated from nature itself only in that the latter is "mind asleep" (*PR* 258a). If the shapes of history are not sleep, they may yet remain in a kind of stupor that will seem something less than full wakefulness: a dreamless condition that is neither day nor night.

Philosophy and Reconciliation

Our exploration of Hegel's approach to the past begins with the attitude of reconciliation that he brings to it. As I discuss in Chapter 6, this approach is distinct from the redemptive one of Locke or Nietzsche. Since Hegel takes philosophy to be a process whereby human activity is reconciled with human thought, one who stands at the end of all historical activity, at the "end of days" is in a position to perform a special kind of reconciliation (*PH* 342).[10] Only when the past is something stable and complete, and not ever-growing, are we in a position to reach the highest realm of knowledge. Hegel's single most famous sentence—"The owl of Minerva spreads its wings only with the falling of the dusk" (*PR*, Pref., 13)—indicates the sense in which all knowledge is historical. Philosophy can only reflect on what already exists. Hence philosophy must tag along behind history and only evaluate what is already "grown old" (ibid.). The philosophy of history cannot reach its conclusion solely through the efforts of the philosopher, however wise; rather, it must be led there by events themselves. Philosophy, therefore, can only finish its reconciliatory task when history reaches a certain end point where, although events continue, a certain kind of meaningful activity no longer takes place.[11]

The situation is similar for art; indeed, the position of art illuminates that of history. Hegel's claim to stand at the end of history is well known. But it is also the case that art "is and remains for us a thing of the past" (*AE* 11). This likening of history to art will, in the pages that follow, allow us to gain a clearer sense of meaning of history's "end." As with history (indeed, for identical reasons), art has reached a special sort of completion and is therefore ready to be apprehended in a certain sort of way—that is, in a philosophy. Of course, Hegel knows that artists continue to labor and to produce works (just as he knows that states and politicians continue to act). It is not that artistic activity has ceased, but that the development of something called "art" is complete. This does not mean that philosophy (about either art or history) was impossible beforehand. It was simply bound to be incomplete. A philosophy composed at the end can achieve a more perfect reconciliation than one written any earlier. Such a work would contain all the actions of history or art and a perfect understanding of them: "the two together," he writes of history and knowledge, "comprehended History, form alike the inwardizing and the Calvary of absolute Spirit" (*PS* 808).[12]

But now we must complicate the picture. For Hegel does not really situate his philosophy at the "end" of history—this would mean that philosophy was within history itself. And here problems would arise: philosophy would not be able to know this last moment itself, a moment of supreme importance. In addition, Hegel wants philosophy to be in a position to survey all of history and value the process as a whole, rather than being tied to the last moment. As long as philosophy is within history, even at the end, both of these problems would impede Hegel's purpose. So Hegel postulates that a complete philosophy comes into being after history, standing outside it. He calls this temporal situation, the time in which the final reconciliation of philosophy takes place, "the Absolute Present" (*IPH* 24). It is important to see that Hegel claims this perspective in order to render judgment on the whole of history. "History," in this context, includes only the most significant parts of the past, a significance we can only detect from the absolute present. Only from this point of view can history be reconciled with knowledge, for only here can the former be freed from the clutter of details that clouds its relationship to the latter: "In our understanding of world-history, we are concerned with history primarily as a record of the past. [But] whatever is true exists eternally in and for itself—not yesterday or tomorrow, but entirely in the present, 'now', in the sense of an absolute present" (*IPH* 150).

From this point of view, philosophy "has no past." Rather, the entire course of history lies before it, each moment equally close or distant. While humans have to run through all of history before they can reach the absolute present, in a sense it was always there, as a perspective, waiting to be discovered. This perspective will ground Hegel's argument that it is the whole of history that is to be loved, and not simply the final, highest stage of it.[13] The philosopher comes after the Germanic stage and, qua philosopher, is not a part of it. History may come to an end in a modern European form, but it is the entire narrative, and not the final episode, that is the subject of Hegel's ultimate aesthetic judgment.[14]

In addition to standing apart from history, rather than at the end of it, the perspective of the absolute present has one other feature that will prove important. Hegel conceives of the relation of absolute present to past as a form of ownership. The past is the property of the present, and this in two senses. The first is the ordinary sense of property as possession. Hegel often notes that each nation has its own past as its property: "The history of their state, its deeds and the deeds of their forefathers, are theirs too" (*IPH* 102; cf. *AE* 272). As we shall see below, he believes this for a complex set of reasons. Briefly put, Hegel spiritualizes the Lockean model of labor-makes-property. In place of Lockean individuals, Hegel substitutes states. The products of these states are historical events, brought about by a certain kind of labor, which thus become the property of their producers. Spirit's activity is this "labor." While there is certainly no parallel to the State of Nature, the work of Spirit results in property much as it does for Locke, but with even greater significance. In Hegel's theory, it is an act of spiritual labor that makes for a true event of history.

When Hegel transfers this relationship to the absolute present, however, a different meaning of the word *property* emerges, that of "characteristic" or "quality."[15] Since the substance of a philosophy of history is nothing less than the past itself, elements of that past are properties of that philosophy in this second sense: "all the stages of the past still adhering to it" (*IPH* 151; cf. *LG* 125; *PS* 28). It is this sense of the past as something inherent in the present, rather than being simply possessed by it, that Hegel will later use to draw us closer to his narrative. Whereas a citizen of a state merely has that state's history as his own, the philosopher of history has the entire world's past to add to his sense of "solid and substantial being." Here again we see the mixing of character and plot that we noted in the philosophies of Locke and Nietzsche. Here the blending comes through the metaphor of property. Past events in the plot are said to belong to the present as property. But then these events are not just (or even primarily) objects but actually qualities of the character that holds them. This character is the unnamed one who lives in the absolute present. As we shall see, this character is also the one who inhabits the Temple of Memory, the "later generation," in Kant's words, "with the good fortune to live in the building."

It should be noted also that many of the things said in this section about history could apply to art as well. Art can also belong to the nation that produces it (*AE* 279). It is also a product of Spirit's labor. Indeed, national memorials, which Hegel mentions more than once, combine the ownership of the past by a nation as both art and history (see, e.g., *PR* 64n). We have already noted how the philosophy of art comes after art itself. Art is something that has ended much as history has. Not that art's beauty is diminished, but that we are its creatures no longer. Even Hegel's devout (if idiosyncratic) Christianity does not stop him from distancing himself from religious art. Although the highest art represents the essence of Christ, its time is past— before icons "we bend the knee no longer" (*AE* 103). Thus the philosophy of art, like that of history, combines a sense of standing apart from art itself with a sense of ownership over its evolution as a whole. The activity of art is complete, just as that of history is. These similarities between art and history hint at the deeper identification of the two that will be explored below. Through art, we can understand better how Hegel manages to overlap plot and character in the category of property.

History as a "Series of Shapes"

In exploring the convergence of history and art in Hegel's thought, we shall see that the former comes to resemble the latter far more than the reverse. Rather than art being examined historiographically, the past comes to be examined from an aesthetic perspective. Before going into the details of that perspective itself, it will be useful to establish in a preliminary way that Hegel considers history in a manner that requires an evaluation in terms of beauty.

When Hegel wrote of history in the most general way, he often relied on a vocabulary of "shape." Hegel's vocabulary of shape dates from the *Phenomenology*, where world history is described as a long labor of the World Spirit that "embodied in each shape (*Form*) as much of its content as that shape was capable of holding" (*PS* 29). The sequence of historical stages is characterized in the *Philosophy of Right* as a "series of shapes" (*Reihe von Gestaltungen*), and, Hegel says, "philosophic science must treat them accordingly" (*PR* 32). The various moments of Spirit's development appear in the actual world as historical shapes then and ought to be understood "accordingly." These shapes are the forms that Spirit takes within time—they are the units that make up the totality called history. If we are to be reconciled to our past, to that which takes place within time, it is these shapes that we must consider. Time, as such, is divided into episodes, each of which is, ultimately, a shape. More like a film than a play, Hegel's account of history is of a "series of shapes" with a particular order. In this, he is not so different from Nietzsche, who likened history to a Greek bas-relief.

In developing such a terminology, Hegel lays the groundwork for a later parallel of historical periods or moments with works of art. This identification takes place at several levels, each of which will receive more attention below. The most general level is the broad comparison between history and art. If both are "shapes," then both are open to an evaluation within aesthetic categories, as opposed to moral or epistemological ones (*IPH* 21). But further, particular historical periods can be compared to particular modes of art (e.g., Greece with sculpture, the East with architecture). At the most detailed level, historical moments can be connected to particular works. The Great Sphinx of Egypt, for example, is for Hegel both a great artwork and a representation of the culmination of the pre-Hellenic world. That history could be described in this way leads to further conclusions about the philosophy of history as well. As a collection of shapes, it comes to resemble a museum of enormous proportions, "a gallery of images" (*eine Gallerie von Bildern*) or, as I shall call it, a Temple of Memory (*PS* 808).

The "series of shapes" interests Hegel both as a whole and as individual moments. In this connection, two remarks that Hegel makes in the *Phenomenology* are of some import: "These shapes, however, are . . . actualities in the strict meaning of the word, and instead of being shapes merely of consciousness, are shapes of a world" (*PS* 441). This passage emphasizes that Hegel, when he speaks of "shapes," is referring to the historical past itself and *not* merely to our images of history.[16] He ascribes to the shapes of history the same degree of reality that he does to art or any other object. He is not simply *likening* history to a series of shapes.[17] Although we certainly interpret these shapes as we transplant them into a historical account ("a better and more exalted soil than the soil of transience in which [they] grew"), we do not create them (*IPH* 12). So while we do not make the shapes of history, we do manipulate them (as in a Nietzschean dream) into a new shape, "fashion[ing] a whole out of material from the past" (ibid.). Of course, the roles Nietzsche and Hegel assign to reason in this process are diametrically opposed. Whereas for Nietzsche, such creativity is a nighttime interpretation, separate from the reasoning of the day, for Hegel, this fashioning is the very work of reason. And the resulting form is, for Hegel, certainly not a dream. For him, this construct is the Temple of Memory itself, which, as we shall see, is composed from the different shapes of each historical stage. The single object called "art" or "history" is made by transplanting lesser objects from a transient soil to a more permanent place in the absolute present "thereby investing [them] with immortal life" (ibid.). In this passage, Hegel struggles, as we saw Nietzsche do, with the question of how much credit to give a composer of images who makes use of preexisting shapes. He resolves this question rather differently than Nietzsche, much less in favor of the artist. For this reason, Hegel is apt to view the philosophical historian, as I discuss below, not as a composing dreamer, but as one who merely unveils a preexisting image. The shapes are not the work of previous artists, but of history itself. The second remark from the *Phenomenology* tells us something about this process: "But the *length* of this path [*Weg*] has to be endured, because, for one thing, each moment is necessary; and further, each moment has to be *lingered* over, because each is itself a complete individual shape" (*PS* 29).

Hegel's lectures on history represent the "lingering" that he called necessary in the *Phenomenology*. With this one word, he manages to make the process sound both like a casual stroll through an art museum and like the bedrock of philosophy and life. The necessity of lingering is something Hegel finds in history itself, as well as its philosophy. It is the only real answer he provides to the question of why history takes so long, if it is just the development of a single idea.[18] Hegel views time as a succession of shapes. If we do not tarry in the single, long corridor of this museum, we could traverse it in an instant, just as we view a hundred frames of a film in the wink of an eye. But the World Spirit lingers over each shape, and thus so must any philosophy that attempts to comprehend it.

And linger Hegel does. For all the dynamism we normally associate with Hegel's history,[19] it is really a series of static portraits—much more static than Locke's or Nietzsche's history. Whereas those two trace change, Hegel largely describes each stage in copious detail and neglects the changes between them. Although he ridicules the "detailed portraiture" of Walter Scott's novels, no phrase could better capture his own approach to historical writing (*IPH* 19). And while he is fond of saying that each stage contains the image of past stages and the seeds of the next (*IPH* 82), when it comes to describing transformations in history, Hegel balks. He is more likely simply to say that the Idea "passes over" into its next form (*IPH* 148).

This hesitation at the point of transition is the clearest way in which the language of the *Philosophy of History* differs noticeably from that of the *Phenomenology*. Dialectical progression is the theme of the latter, but it is not the form that history takes in the former. Where Gadamer can maintain of the

Phenomenology that "Hegel's claim that the dialectical transitions are necessary is made good and verified again and again if one reads carefully,"[20] such a contention simply could not be made of the *Philosophy of History*. Gadamer's belief that an interpretation of a section of Hegel will lead naturally to the next section seems almost absurd in the context of Hegel's history. The discussion of China, for example, ends with a long discussion of the arts and sciences in that culture—everything from medicine and astronomy to metalworking and porcelain manufacture are described (*PH* 134–38). In no way is one prepared for the description of India on the following pages, which begins by designating that culture as Absolute Being, "presented here as in the ecstatic state of a dreaming condition" (139). This is hardly an isolated example. The constant connections that characterize dialectic are largely absent from the *Philosophy of History*, replaced by the "gallery of images." The transition between images is abrupt, not fluid. The shapes have *boundaries*, which demarcate and separate them from other shapes. What success Hegel may have in endowing thought with a sense of motion in the *Phenomenology* is not repeated (or even, I think, attempted) in the *Philosophy of History*.

That this lack of dynamism saddles the latter book with considerable weaknesses is best illustrated through a comparison with Hegel's best-known dialectical moment. In the *Phenomenology*, Hegel described a master/slave relation that typifies the dialectical advance of Spirit through opposites. In this parable, progress is said to occur in a paradoxical fashion. After a struggle for recognition between two equals, one finally submits to the other rather than facing death. But it is the ironic fate of the master to be the real loser in this situation. He settles into a repose that is ultimately enervating. The slave, because he continues to labor at the behest of the master, also continues to grow, and he eventually achieves a higher level of knowledge and power than his master (*PS* 178–96). The apparent defeat the slave suffers is transformed over time into a spiritual advance. This account of an ironic pattern of progress has long been held to be the paradigmatic dialectical episode.

By the time Hegel comes to lecture on the philosophy of history, this dialectic is considerably muted. Masters are masters and slaves are slaves. History is a succession of masters, and the slaves of one period never become masters of the next. Indeed, apart from one oblique reference (*PH* 407), this dialectic makes no appearance in his lectures on history; slavery is simply condemned, rather than interpreted as containing a silver lining for the slaves. Without this motor, there is little that drives Hegel's narrative from one stage to the next. Many commentators simply take Hegel at his word when he says in the *Phenomenology* and the introduction to the *Philosophy of History* that he has accounted for history in a dialectical fashion. Thus Charles Taylor, in his otherwise exemplary account of Hegel's philosophy, writes that in Hegel's history, "the motor force of movement is contradiction."[21] But the brief summary of this history that follows deals hardly at all with the stages other than the Greek and German and, more important, never quotes from the body of the *Philosophy of History* itself—because it would be impossible to prove this view of Hegel's history with reference to that text. History remains a succession of independent shapes, whose connection is found more in the philosophy that links them than in the empirical process that actually connects them in time.

The loss here is that the sense of irony that infuses the *Phenomenology* is missing from the *Philosophy of History*. The Greeks are crushed by "Roman power" (*PH* 277) and the Romans by "the might of the vigorous Turks" (*PH* 340). The irony of one's enemy developing in one's own house, which the master/slave episode described, is absent. Karl Marx, to be sure, found just such a relationship between the feudal lords and the bourgeoisie and then between the latter and the proletariat. And Alexandre Kojève then tried to reinsert Marx's history into the *Phenomenology* itself. ("History," he says, "is the history of the working Slave.")[22] But in Hegel's history, Egypt does not bear this relation to Greece, nor Greece to Rome. Historical stages appear as a succession of shapes—not as a series of transitions, and certainly not as the work of slaves. The sort of philosophy that investigates these shapes is the subject of the next section. If history is a series of shapes and not a flowing river of transformation, then philosophy must treat it "accordingly."

Aesthetics and Action

"Beauty can devolve only on the *shape*," Hegel writes (*AE* 124). Shapes are neither true nor false, neither good nor evil. They are only beautiful or lacking in beauty, ugly. To evaluate shapes, to philosophize about them, requires turning from epistemology or ethics to aesthetics. Hegel's approach to aesthetics bears enough similarities to that of Plato to make the differences illuminating. The parallels between the Hegelian Idea and Platonic Forms are strong enough to make their approaches to art similar. But Hegel resolves the ancient quarrel between the poets and the philosophers quite differently from Plato.[23] Where Plato's aesthetics includes an inherent denigration of the arts, Hegel's provides an inherent defense.

Plato thought art was twice-degraded: an inferior form of reality, which was itself an inferior form of the Forms. But Hegel sees in "action" the possibility for humans to purify mere existence and bring it closer to the Idea, rather than moving it further away. The status of art, a product of action, is thus between the mundane and the ideal, whereas for Plato it was beneath both. Those phenomena created by action (which includes history as well as art), Hegel terms "actuality" (*Wirklichkeit*): "Art liberates the true content of phenomena from the pure appearance and deception of this bad, transitory world, and gives them a higher actuality, born of the spirit. Thus, far from being mere pure appearance, a higher reality and truer existence is to be ascribed to the phenomena of art in comparison with [those of] ordinary reality" (*AE* 9).[24] So while Hegel and Plato both range art on a scale defined by the mundane and the ideal, they put art in very different places on that scale. Hegel welcomes poetry, which Plato had expelled, back into the city. He does so by incorporating art into the category of "actuality," which holds the middle position, between the quotidian and the ideal, in his metaphysics.

It must be emphasized, too, that Hegel parts company with Plato in emphasizing that it is human activity that brings the actual into existence. Indeed, in this matter, Hegel has more in common with Locke. His theory can even be seen as an attempt to integrate the Lockean and the Platonic perspectives. Hegel makes use of a spiritualized quasi-Lockean account of labor to explain the special status of actuality (and, hence, art and history). As we saw in Part I, Locke felt that labor infused objects with value. But since all labor was equally fungible for Locke, its effects were largely undifferentiated. For Locke, all labor is the same; its product is value. Hegel agrees that labor imparts value (*PR* 41–53), but he adds to Locke's formulation a parallel account of the idea being made manifest through human action. Ideas must "win their actuality by man's act in order to come on the scene in their proper shape [N.B.]" (*AE* 213; cf. 225). So while Locke's account of life in terms of labor is, as we saw earlier, colorless, for Hegel, the internal multiplicity of the idea means that labor will bring forth a variety of shapes rather than a monotony of value. True labor separates part of human existence (the actual) from the rest (the mundane, mere existence). That special part, whether art or history, because it is infused with human spirit, has the quality of actuality. It has been brought that much closer to the ideal.

But the Lockean side to Hegel's account of action also explains something else we noted earlier: the sense in which the present can be said to *own* the past. In Locke's account of labor, the products of work cleave to their producer as property. So, too, with Hegel's account of action. This holds both when individual human beings are involved and when "the individuals we are concerned with are nations, totalities, states" (*IPH* 36). Even Hegel's heroes only accomplish their aims by "arduous labours" (*IPH* 85). The products of a culture belong to that culture in a strong sense of the word *belong*.[25] Labor produces property in the Lockean sense, but the relation of the actual to the

Idea leads to a view of labor that emphasizes the particularity of acts, the specialness of every moment of labor. From Plato, Hegel draws the idea of a range between the mundane and the ideal form. From Locke, he draws the idea of human labor as that which produces the middling quality of actuality. Indeed, Hegel often describes this process in terms that stress the creative powers of the individual. Actualization is described as a process whereby "man as spirit duplicates himself" (*AE* 31). But the modifying phrase "as spirit" is important; the statement is far from a defense of individualism, even if those who labor are unavoidably individuals.

This connection to the Idea lends an odd flavor to the word *action* and dilutes its Lockean character. Since things created by action are supposed to be deeply rooted in the eternal Idea, it is hard to picture how they can be created by people. In fact, Hegel pictures action as a kind of "unveiling," in which shapes are ushered into the actual realm from the possible one (*AE* 93):

> Action alters nothing and opposes nothing. It is the pure form of a transition from a state of not being seen to one of being seen, and the content which is brought out into the daylight and displayed, is nothing else but what this action already is in itself. (*PS* 396)

> Action simply translates an initially implicit being into a being that is made explicit. (*PS* 401)

Action is that which funnels the ideal into the real.[26] *Labor* does not refer solely to physical toil, but to any activity that has this character of unveiling. Hegel construes things as disparate as the painting of Raphael's Madonnas and Alexander's conquest of Persia as spiritual labor. All such products are, therefore, "actuality." Both great history and great art are products of action, and their greatness is measured on Hegel's own scale of beauty. "And it is the same with the spirit of a nation; its activity consists in making itself into an actual world. . . . Its religion, ritual, ethics, customs, art, constitution, and political laws—indeed the whole range of its institutions, events and deeds—all this is its own creation, and it is this which makes the nation what it is" (*IPH* 58). The last clause of that quotation indicates one further potential direction to Hegel's philosophy of action: not only are individuals capable of action in his special sense; rather, it is *only* through such action that they can be said to exist. Nothing else counts. Although it is rooted in the Platonic notion that only that which partakes of the Idea is real, it is the Lockean account of the idea made actual by individual labor that gives this notion its radical edge:

> Action is the clearest revelation of the individual, of his temperament as well as his aims; what a man is at bottom and in his inmost being comes into actuality only by his action. (*AE* 219)

The *true being* of a man is rather his deed; in this the individual is *actual*. (*PS* 322)

[A] distinction is often made between man's inner nature and his deeds. This does not apply in history; the man himself is the sum total of his deeds. (*IPH* 57)

These remarks indicate as well the double-edged meaning of the term *property* discussed above. Not only are these actions owned by their doers, they are actually the *qualities* of these doers. They are the defining characteristics of the figures of history. Indeed, it would seem that a Hegelian character is almost *entirely* plot. Whoever one is, Hegel contends, will ultimately be revealed in the course of one's actions. This too lends an "Aristotelian" quality to Hegel's philosophy of history, since Aristotle (as discussed in Chapter 6) also found narrative to be composed solely of actions (*Poetics* 1450a).

Where Plato's idealism led him to value philosophical thought above all other human activity, Hegel's idealism, passing through a Lockean filter, leads him to an expansive notion of human action as the path through which the Idea becomes real. So it is the labor-minded side of Hegel that forbids him to settle the quarrel between poets and philosophers by banishing the former, as Plato did. Yet his poets, if that is what they are, are an odd sort. Locke, after all, did not think much of artists. And Hegel's decision to describe art and history as a kind of labor leads him to strange conclusions about creativity and beauty.

Beauty in Logic and History

Hegel develops his account of the Beautiful (the category through which the actual will be comprehended) by putting his defense of the poets into the framework of his logic. This emerges as an emphasis on the importance of the minor premise (or the "middle term," as he calls it) in the generic syllogism of logical reasoning. Hegel turns this middle term into the midway point between the pure realm of the Idea and its pale reflection in everyday existence. The middle term is the home of the actual, both in art and in history. The quality of the middle term that makes it akin to the actual is, for Hegel, its status in between the general and the specific.

Hegel's use of the middle term is idiosyncratic, but it is easy enough to understand. Take the following standard example of syllogistic reasoning: (a) All humans are mortal; (b) Socrates is human; (c) Socrates is mortal. The important thing here, for Hegel, is not how the conclusion follows from the premises, but how the middle term, (b), links the first and last statements. Statement (a) is a generalization. Statement (c) is a description of a single case. The function of statement (b) is to link the general to the particular. It does so by drawing together a particular individual, "Socrates," and a generic category, "human being." The general and the particular are thus linked by the "middle term." Hegel emphasizes this function of the middle term in his discussion of syllogism (*LG* 184ff.).

But now, this role of mediating between the ideal and the particular is, to Hegel, just another way of describing the "actual." It is not only in syllogisms that universal and singular must be mediated. Rather, man is "an amphibious animal, because he now has to live in two worlds," the ideal and the mundane (*AE* 54). Action funnels the Idea into the real world; it also lifts up the real world toward the Idea. This back-and-forth motion is what Hegel has in mind when he speaks of the mediating function of the middle term (*PS* 145, 231, 293, 444; *AE* 223). The statement "Socrates is human" unites the particular subject, Socrates, with the universal idea in which he participates, the human. Thus the universal (which is, after all, only an idea) is made real by being exampled, and the particular, Socrates, is made permanent, in a sense, by showing the universal idea of which he partakes. Furthermore, Hegel does not take this sort of example to be merely one of logic. Rather, the real life and actions of individuals like Socrates, insofar as they are labor, perform this mediating function in the world. What the minor premise does in logic, real artists and historical actors do in life. Where logic merely describes actuality, labor creates it.

Hegel rehabilitates the poets by finding that "art is the middle term" between "pure thought and what is merely external, sensuous and transient" (*AE* 8, 163). And Hegel means by this that such thought should be presented in art, "not in its universality as such," but in a form that has been "sensuously particularized" (*AE* 51). This means that individual works of art cannot represent concepts such as "Justice," "Love," or "Man" in the abstract, but must show them through individual examples. This is the meeting of universal and particular. To simply take reality as it is found would be to leave the individual and mundane untouched by the ideal. If a portrait is too accurate, Hegel thinks, it will be "disgustingly like" (*AE* 43). But the ideal cannot be directly represented. Generalizations must take particular forms in order to appear. So, for example, Raphael's Madonnas (one of Hegel's favorite examples), "show us forms of expression, cheeks, eyes, nose, mouth, which, as forms, are appropriate to the radiance, joy, piety, and also the humility of a mother's love" (*AE* 156). A representation of an individual here communicates a universal idea (see also *AE* 38, 70, 223, 227).[27] Love cannot be painted as a generic quality; it can only appear through a specific individual. Neither can mortality appear in the real world as a general quality, even though all men are mortal. It requires the mortality of an individual person, Socrates, in order for mortality to "actually" appear at all.

Hegel also uses the language of the middle term to describe history. Each of the cultures that Hegel describes in his history is also a shape that mediates between the ideal realm and the particular: "The state is actual. . . . Actuality is always the unity of universal and particular . . . where this unity is not present, a thing is not actual even though it may have acquired existence" (*PR* 270A). Thus, the middle term can also be "the system of structured shapes assumed by consciousness as a self-systematizing whole of the life of Spirit . . . which has its objective existence as world-history" (*PS* 295). Indeed, following the account of actuality above, it is more toward history than toward art that we would expect the account of the middle term to lead. For it is man's "amphibious" condition "between two worlds" that Hegel describes in that account. The case of the artist is only a special case within that description. The parallel between the two becomes more pronounced when considered through this lens of Hegel's logic.

Beauty, in fact, makes its appearance through the logic. It is the quality characterizing the middle term that performs its mediating function well. "[I]t is precisely the *unity* of the Concept with the individual appearance which is the essence of the beautiful" (*AE* 101; cf. 22). As such, beauty is the perfect category with which to evaluate the products of labor known as the actual. Beauty is that which appears through a good mediation of general and specific. The beautiful is the term of judgment that Hegel develops in the *Aesthetics* to cover the history of art. But it also covers the history of spirit that he gives in that text, as well as the parallel history in the *Philosophy of History*. "What is valid for the work of art as such is equally applicable to the external aspect of the historical reality there represented" (*AE* 273). Beauty is the measure of the actual. It exists when universal and particular are successfully brought together by a middle term, whether in art or history.

Just as truth is the highest value in the conceptual world, the quality against which things there are measured, so beauty is the highest value in the historical world. A middle term is that which draws the truth into actuality. Beauty is simply truth when it "exists"—that is, when it is made real or actual: "The true as such *exists* also. Now when truth in this its external existence is present to consciousness immediately, and when the Concept remains immediately in unity with its external appearance, the Idea is not only true but beautiful" (*AE* 111). Left in the realm of thought, the truth will remain true, but always unactualized, and thus, unreal. Brought down to earth by labor, it acquires the aspect of beauty, which comprehends, not just art, but everything that is "actual," everything that is real and contains the Idea (*AE* 114): "everything beautiful is truly beautiful only as sharing in this higher sphere" (*AE* 2). This is Hegel's first definition of beauty in the *Aesthetics*. Thus far, I have been elaborating the philosophy on which it relies. With an understanding of this beauty, we can say more about the works of art that "exist" in both art and history. And we can begin to see why their beautiful shapes mean so much to the overall project of Hegel's history: a seduction requires an attraction; an attraction requires beauty. In order for history to seduce us to life, it must first be known as beautiful. Hegel finds this attractiveness, not arbitrarily, but on the basis of the complicated philosophy of labor, actuality, and beauty just reviewed.

Artists and Works of Art

The strange character of Hegel's aesthetics is accentuated when we consider what he has to say on the character of the artist. Or rather, what he does not say. For in the entire thousand-plus pages of the *Aesthetics* as published,[28] scarcely twenty are devoted to artists (*AE* 280ff.). Scattered remarks in other places do not add substantially to this total. It is only the work of art that holds Hegel's attention, whether it is the shape of a statue or the shape of a nation. The curiously empty notion of action that he enunciates leaves him with little to say about the nature of artistry.

Hegel's aesthetics are embarrassed by the existence of artists. All his work to rehabilitate poetry cannot alter this. Hegel needs artists as passages, as it were, for the Idea. But if they threaten to call too much attention to themselves, they detract from the notion that beauty comes from the universal. It is their labor that brings the beautiful into existence. But since the beauty itself is said to derive from the Idea, it cannot be the product of the artist's inspiration. The artist, then, can be no more than a midwife, and not a true parent, for the birth of his or her own works. Thus, when Hegel pays homage to great artists, it is an odd sort of reverence indeed. Rather than emphasizing their creativity, he describes artists as "the living corridor for a work of art perfect in itself. . . . To have no manner has from time immemorial been the one grand manner, and in this sense alone are Homer, Sophocles, Raphael, Shakespeare, to be called 'original'" (*AE* 298). One wonders whether this spooky image of artists, hollow in themselves, mere passageways for preformed perfect works, would have satisfied any of these artists as a self-image. What other art critic would be satisfied with an evaluation of Raphael and Shakespeare that concludes that they have no style in particular? Hegel has welcomed back the poets for the sake of their poetry; but with their *poiēsis*, with their creativity, he will have no truck. The artists' contribution is their lack of contribution. Their originality is invisible to Hegel; he sees only a "living corridor": "[O]riginality is identical with true objectivity" (*AE* 294). He writes similarly of his historical heroes, "[T]hey are the living instruments of what is in substance the deed of the world-spirit" (*PR* 348). Hegel's artists (and heroes) have all the personality of a magnifying glass—that is their only function.

So it is not surprising that Hegel often seems to confuse artists with the cultures in which they live. Art reflects whatever stage has been reached in world history. But if the artists do not create the content of the work themselves, they must find it in the world in which they live. Thus in the Classical period (which, in Hegel's view, had the highest art), "the artist seems only to execute what is already cut and dried on its own account" (*AE* 439). It was Greek culture, not artistic originality, that was responsible for the achievements of Greek sculpture. Its beauty sprang directly from the beauty of Greek civilization. Neither can the artist be faulted for failing to achieve beauty when his culture did not supply it for him: "[T]he defectiveness of a work of art is not always due, as may be supposed, to the artist's lack of skill; on the contrary, defectiveness of *form* results from defectiveness of *content*. So, for example, the Chinese, Indians and Egyptians, in their artistic shapes, images of gods, and idols, never got beyond formlessness or a bad and untrue definiteness of form" (*AE* 74; see also 171, 256). An artist only counts as a transmission belt; as a personality, he is literally nothing: "[W]hat remains buried in his heart, that *is* he not" (*AE* 291). Hegel has so little to say about individual artistic practice because he considers beauty to be largely the product of cultures, not individuals.

So while Nietzsche may have thought Homer to be "three-quarters convention," Hegel would have to find the poet *wholly* unoriginal. But, of course, it is not a matter of quantity. Whereas Nietzsche and Hegel might both be said, in some sense, to liken history to art, their notions of artistry are so different as to be largely incompatible. For Nietzsche, the beautiful is always something new; for Hegel, it is only a rendering of what is already "cut and dried."

Hegel often anthropomorphizes and speaks as if art itself were an actor: "[I]t is the vocation of art to find for the spirit of a people the artistic expression corresponding to it" (*AE* 603; cf. 72). From this it is but a small step to seeing the nation itself as the source of all art. And, when we leave the realm of fine arts and consider actuality in general, this is exactly what Hegel does:

> The history of a nation consists solely of that process whereby the nation impresses on all the spheres of its activity the spirit's concept of its own nature. In other words, the state, religion, art, the system of justice, and the relationship of the nation to other nations—all of these are aspects [of this process]. . . . As such, [the nation] is like an artist who is impelled to project his own being outside himself and to satisfy himself in his own work. (*IPH* 101; cf. 58)

This last clause indicates that Hegel thought he could reconcile the romantic notion of creativity with his own idealistic view of artistic beauty. He hoped to incorporate the image of the creative soul into that of idealism by identifying the universal with the spirit of a nation, or of the world. Given the overall place of the artist in his system, we must pronounce this attempt flawed. For every instance where Hegel praises creativity, there are two more where he insists that the artist adds nothing to the beauty that already exists in the world. Rather than give of themselves, artists absent themselves in order to be creative. His portrait of the artist seems indefensibly thin, and it is certainly unsatisfying as an account of creative production. For we must either accept an uncreative "creativity" at the individual level or hold that the nation does something creative that individuals do not—but this would violate the thought that the universal comes into actuality through individual labor. The tension can only be resolved through an implausible account of poiēsis, which rests on an even more implausible metaphysics, where beauty descends to us from a higher sphere: implausible not so much for positing a transcendental source of beauty as for positing a single, rigid meaning of *beauty*, so narrowly fixed that whole cultures (indeed all pre-Hellenic cultures) failed to grasp it. This is an important tension, however: important because it points again to the nation as the seat of beauty. And thus, in our reading of Hegel's history, it should indicate to us the central role of aesthetics in his understanding of the past.[29]

The Shape(s) of the Past: The Temple of Mnemosyne

"Beauty can devolve only on the shape" (*AE* 124). But how are we to know the shape of the past? What shape or form can ancient civilizations (or current ones for that matter) be said to have had (or have)? Hegel responds to this challenge he has posed for himself in two (slightly circular) ways. At the level of the particular nation, he uses the art of that nation as a guide to its historical meaning. Thus, for example, the Pyramids and the Sphinx come to stand for Egypt, and, indeed, for all pre-Hellenic history. Although it often appears ad hoc, this procedure allows Hegel to relate history as the evolution of forms. At the level of history as a whole, however, Hegel does not rely on preexisting shapes but constructs his own: the Temple of Mnemosyne. Mnemosyne is the Greek muse of memory, and it is in her honor that Hegel puts together his narrative. He uses Mnemosyne (as opposed to her daughter Clio, the muse of History) to emphasize the way in which we possess the past, as the product of Spirit's labor. Memories (as opposed to "the past") must always be *someone*'s memories, residing in a particular mind, contributing to a personality. It is in memory that history and character fully overlap—and Hegel is acutely aware of this, as his account of history as "property" demonstrates. The Temple of Mnemosyne is an expression of this view. Where Clio represents the exploration of an alien terrain by the historian, with Mnemosyne we are always reminded that in her temple, we explore nothing so much as our own past, and what we find there is nothing but ourselves. This recognition is vital if the beauty of that temple is to seduce us to dwell within it. For Hegel, Mnemosyne is not just a Muse, but also a Siren.

The Temple of Mnemosyne is a kind of repository, a kind of art museum, where the goddess keeps the artifacts of history for the perusal of the present. But it is more than that. It is Hegel's image for the totality of the historical process itself. And it is this totality, rather than the image of the last (Germanic) state, that is the goal of Hegel's story. It is the sum of images that is the fundamental thing. Spirit is evidenced in the *series* of shapes it assumes, and not just in the final shape, or any of the intermediate ones. It is the history of the world as a whole that is "universal" (*PR* 344, 340; cf. 259a). Spirit "accomplishes [its] end in the history of the world; it produces itself in a series of determinate forms, and these forms are the nations of world history" (*IPH* 64). It is for this reason that the perspective of the absolute present becomes necessary. The Temple of Mnemosyne sits in the middle of a time warp, from which point all of the past is equally near or far—it can be viewed as a whole: "Last of all comes the discovery that the whole evolution is what constitutes the content and the interest" (*LG* 237n). The temple is not just a container of past shapes; it is itself the center of the exhibit.

Hegel describes the temple thus: the "Symbolic age" constructs the building, the "Classical age" carves the gods that inhabit it, and the "Romantic age" ushers in the congregation that worships there: "Now when architecture has built its temple and the hand of sculpture has set up within it the statues of the god, this sensuously present god is confronted, *thirdly*, in the wide halls of his house by the *community*" (*AE* 85). This passage appears near the beginning of the *Aesthetics*, but deciphering it requires knowledge of the whole structure of that book. Although Hegel admits that each of the historical eras he discusses contains all kinds of art, he nonetheless believes that each period has a kind of art most typical of it, which produces its characteristic shapes. The Symbolic period, embodying everything pre-Hellenic, has architecture as its representative kind of art. Sculpture is the form connected to the Classical age. Painting, art, and poetry all satisfy the spirit of the Romantic period (*AE* 82). The Classical age encompasses both Greece and Rome, and everything that follows is termed (somewhat confusingly) Romantic. The structure of the *Aesthetics* reflects this division, with the course of world history being covered, in effect, twice. In the first half, Hegel recounts the history of art, and the history of the worlds that produced it, in the order of ages: Symbolic, Classical, Romantic. In the second half, he proceeds by covering different forms of art. But the effect is the same, since the forms correspond so well to the ages: architecture, sculpture, and the "romantic arts" (*AE* 791).[30]

Through the picture of the temple, Hegel captures a moving story in a static image. Nor is it just the story of art. "For in art we have to do . . . with an unfolding of the truth which is not exhausted in natural history but revealed in world-history" (*AE* 1236). The image of the construction of a temple is Hegel's ultimate distillation of the process of history. It captures both the simplicity and power of his argument, as well as its reductiveness. When a nation's era ends, "Memory alone then still preserves the dead form" and "sets it up in the Temple of Mnemosyne, thereby investing it with immortal life" (*PS* 545; *IPH* 12). The three eras, through architecture, sculpture, and (let us say) poetry, provide us with temple building, its idols, and its congregation, respectively. Each stage contributes one shape to a composite image. It is the three stages of the *Aesthetics*, and not the four stages of the *Philosophy of History*, that form the true structure of Hegel's narrative. It is consistent with his syllogistic account of beauty that the beauty of history should be found in a three-part image.

It should also be noted that from a certain perspective, Hegel can reconcile his own activities as a philosopher of history with the passive account of artistry that he gives. The shapes that represent each era, he can say, are designated by him but contributed by the era itself—for example, the Pyramids by the symbolic age. Hegel does no more than call attention to them and their "natural" relationship with other shapes. He acts, as I wrote before about artists, as magnifying glass. His action "alters nothing and opposes nothing." His narrative merely reveals a structure that was, he thinks, there all along. His history only executes "what is already cut and dried." Rather than *fashioning* a meaning for history, he claims only to reveal a meaning that already exists. Of course, from our perspective, it seems questionable, to say the least, for Hegel to claim "objectivity" for a "universal" history that ignores whole continents and takes events out of order to suit its purposes (about which more below). What I want to emphasize here is how Hegel's aesthetic perspective on history is consonant with, indeed even incumbent upon, his attempt to view history from the perspective of objective philosophy. The artist, as Hegel conceives of him, has much in common with the philosopher (as well as with the historian). Both of them, in a sense, are mere unveilers. But both of them, also, work from memory.

Yet as we use this framework to investigate Hegel's lectures on history, we must ask ourselves whether he has succeeded in creating an attractive temple. For if the structure is already complete when we arrive there, the only task left to us is that of maintenance. Hegel thinks that "to dwell in what is substantive" will allow us "to enjoy the present" (*PR*, Pref., 12). But we must wonder whether Hegel's philosophy of history has the very quality he condemned in nature: "in nature there is nothing new under the sun, and in this respect its manifold play of forms produces an effect of boredom" (*IPH* 124).

Art as History

I shall not run through Hegel's narrative in as much detail as I did for Locke and Nietzsche. In those cases, I was attempting to draw a hidden story line into the light. Here, the plot—one of spiritual and intellectual development—is well known, and my purpose is merely to alter how it is understood. In a general way, this should already have been accomplished in the account of how Hegel's history lies on top of his aesthetics. In what follows, I shall pursue that theme in a more topical way than in earlier chapters. First, I shall explore some of the difficulties that appear as a result of Hegel's attempt to erase the boundary between art and history. The use he makes of Sophocles' play *Oedipus Rex* will be of particular importance here. Next, I look at how we should understand each of the three eras Hegel describes. Finally, I shall consider how an aesthetics that ends with the "dissolution of art" must lead to an equally bleak history.

Time seems most like an illusion in Hegel's writings when it is considered as the process of reason following its one idea through to a conclusion: "temporal duration is something entirely relative, and the spirit belongs to eternity. Duration, strictly speaking, does not exist for it" (*IPH* 209). He also speaks of history as a "day's work" in which "man has constructed a building" in which he houses an image of himself. He even speaks of time as nature "for itself"—that is, as something subjective—while the shapes that exist within space exist in themselves (*PR* 10n). All of history, then, even though it contains acts of labor, seems compressed to a wink in God's eye. The aesthetic view only offers a series of images that, like a film, can be run at any speed, producing either a serious or a comic effect. And yet Hegel insists that each stage must be "*lingered* over, because each is itself a complete individual shape." The whole sequence, he says, cannot be understood without a detailed comprehension of every shape. But this is quite different from Locke and Nietzsche, where the stages themselves were time-consuming and were not viewed from a point outside historical time. For those authors, each step was a process that itself demanded time. In Hegel, each stage is just a frozen shape, and if *we* do not pause and linger, the whole process could be recapitulated instantaneously. Lingering, he hopes, will allow time for the beauty of the shapes, and the structure as a whole, to seduce us. His call to linger is more of a plea than an argument. History, he says, "presents a slow-moving succession of Spirits, a gallery of images" (*PS* 808). The effects of this gallery depend on our consideration of each of its images in a deliberate fashion. Where Locke and Nietzsche wanted us to consider the past for the future it projected, for Hegel the lingering is its own purpose and reward. The past is beautiful by itself and, apparently, complete as well. If viewed at the appropriate pace, the images cohere into a beautiful whole. But, we must ask, at what point does this captivation with the images of ourselves and our past become a genuine narcissistic captivity? Hegel may value the past more than Locke or Nietzsche, but perhaps at the expense of the future.

It is the shapes of the past then, the basic elements of the Temple, that are of significance, not the weak mortar that holds them together. Hegel's attention is on nations as a whole; neither the individuals who make them up nor the processes that move them along are as important. The bulk of his lectures in the *Philosophy of History* are concerned with the social structures, customs, religions, and constitutions of the nations discussed, taken as static wholes. Little attention is paid to connections between nations, and only slightly more to the evolution within them. The "heroes" of Hegelian history are, then, not so much an integral part of the Hegelian narrative as they are notably perfect epiphenomena. A hero can "make no distinction between himself and the spirit of the nation" (*IPH* 52; cf. 76, 82). Rather than standing apart from the nation, the hero typifies it, even if, in the perfection of his personification, he is not a typical *individual*. (In this sense, they resemble the ideal artist, special not for his individuality but, precisely, for his capacity to absent himself from the creative process in favor of an unveiling of the already-existent.) Heroes do not link the ages, they only help usher in the mature period of their age.[31] Indeed, the thrust of Hegel's historical description would seem to indicate that Marx was right when he said he had put Hegel back on his feet. Given Hegel's description of societies as wholes of greater and less integration, it really makes the most sense to think of large social forces and their labor, rather than individuals, as the drivers of history. Although he cares much less than Marx about the means of production, Hegel is predisposed to view society in terms of classes and their relation to one another as groups, rather than as single people (e.g., his description of Indian castes in contrast to Persian classes [*PH* 144–54, 174–76] or his description of the Roman social structure [*PH* 285–88]). This is where the "shape" of each era is to be found.

Sometimes it seems that Hegel would rather talk about anything but historical development or the passage of time. Recounting the victories of the Romans would be too "wearisome," he tells his students (PH 304). Rather it is their constitution and their spirit that merits attention—these are the true results of their labor. In the second of three sections on Rome, he runs through the military history in a single paragraph, and then turns his attention to the political arrangements of the empire (PH 306–13). The manifestations of spirit remain the societies themselves and not the flow of events or singular personalities.

As an example of the difficulties this static, aesthetic account of states leads to, consider the transition between the Oriental and the Greek eras (PH 219–22). Although Alexander is one of Hegel's heroes, he actually spends more time with Oedipus than with the Macedonian king. The true transition between the two periods seems actually to occur in Sophocles' Oedipus Rex, which Hegel treats here as if it were as good as fact.

The dialogue between Oedipus and the Sphinx is where Hegel locates the end of the Oriental spirit and the beginning of the Greek. For he has described the Great Sphinx of Cheops as the piece of art that best captures the spirit of the Asiatic era. Half-human, half-animal, it represents the effort of spirit to emerge out of nature. To Hegel, all of Egyptian society exists mostly to pose a question it is incapable of answering. Thus Hegel seems to think that the Sphinx does not know the answer to the riddle it poses to Oedipus (a perversely brilliant thought, really). The question (as is well known) is "What is it that walks on four legs in the morning, two in the afternoon, and three in the evening?" For Hegel, Oedipus's answer, "Man," precipitates both the end of the Egyptian era and the beginning of the Greek. The former is captured in the self-destruction of the Sphinx (it throws itself from a cliff) and the latter by the replacement of the Sphinx with Apollo, and the Sphinx's riddle with the Delphic command "Know thyself" (cf. AE 361). Human self-awareness supplants a sphinx culture that could not fully distinguish human from animal.

An ingenious reading of Sophocles, all will agree. But slightly bizarre to us as a description of a historical transition. Yet this use of Sophocles is in line with Hegel's general approach to nations as shapes. Since the Sphinx had come to stand for the Orient, the destruction of its form was much more important in Hegel's narrative than, say, the defeat of the Persians at Salamis.[32] Similarly, the single god Apollo (Athena might have served as well) represents the Greeks in their emphasis on the single human form. As much as Greece over Asia, we have in this recounting the ascendance of sculpture over architecture. Lest anyone suffer under the illusion that the Sphinx is itself a sculpture, Hegel assures us that it has "a completely architectural character" (AE

644). He allows at other points that it may represent a transition between architecture and sculpture, but that, of course, dovetails neatly with its position in the story here. It is only through such mythical encounters of shapes that Hegel can describe the change of epochs in a manner loyal to his account of the nations themselves. If the episodes of history are primarily pictured as shapes, then transitions will be marked by the ascendance of new shapes over the old.

But in an important sense, his account of the transition here is *not* loyal to his account of the nations themselves. Although his descriptions are often selective, it is not his normal practice summarily to substitute fiction or drama for fact, or to twist, as he does here, the actual chronology in order to make it fit his scheme.[33] His aesthetic perspective, however, has strongly suggested this option for such transitions. By depicting the nations as stable, self-subsistent wholes, Hegel has left himself little basis for explaining their evolution. In depriving cultures of the fluidity embodied in the master/slave dialectic, he has made it difficult to explain the transitions between stages with reference to the stages themselves. This is what makes the pages on Oedipus, as brilliant as they may be in themselves, appear incongruous in comparison to what has preceded them. The problem is not just that Hegel must ignore the fate of Oedipus or misread the Sphinx as a work of architecture or ignore actual historical events. It is rather that the discussion of Indian castes or Persian despotism or even of Egyptian architecture in no way prepares us for finding a point of transition such as this in an Attic tragedy rather than in the historical conflict between Greeks and Persians. Although Hegel often uses art to represent cultures as a whole, he does not normally use fictional literature to describe actual *events*, as he does here. He needs a confrontation of shapes to describe a transition that is in some sense loyal to his descriptions, but his retreat into drama (and his ad hoc use of it) only reminds us that any movement through the gallery of images is something of our own making and not driven by the images themselves. The seamless dialectical progression of the *Phenomenology* has been replaced by a parade of sphinxes and statuary, where each image does not seem to touch any other of its own accord. It is the visible hand of the historian that sets them in motion, despite Hegel's contention that the historian merely reveals what already exists.

Hegel's aesthetic perspective has, therefore, several disadvantages. First, its minimization of dialectical progression drains the narrative of its ironic power (one of the more attractive things, in my judgment, about the *Phenomenology*). Second, the static nature of the images sharply separates them from one another, so that the narrative, and time itself, seems disjointed. Third, this last problem must be compensated for by the ad hoc use of elements different in character from those normally used—and this makes the narrative appear arbitrary. Why, then, adopt all these disadvantages? For the sake of the creation of a beautiful Temple of Mnemosyne, an image that will bind and reconcile us to the past. In what follows, I attempt to show how Hegel makes this point. But I also contend that the costs involved in building such a temple are probably more than we want to bear.

The Three Shapes of History

Hegel is a thoroughgoing trinitarian. Not only does he think that God is composed of three parts, but nearly everything he does is in threes: his books have three parts each; each part has three chapters; each chapter, three subsections. The foundation of his logic is the three-line syllogism. Ethical life requires three main institutions, and so on. So it is not surprising that his history of the world also furnishes us with three principal shapes: "God is thus recognized as *Spirit*, only when known as the Triune. This new principle is the axis on which the History of the World turns" (*PH* 319). These shapes we find principally in the *Philosophy of History*, although the *Aesthetics* provides considerable help. Thus far, the shapes have aided us in two ways: in seeing the nations *as* works of art and in seeing them *through* works of art, since "in works of art the nations have deposited their richest inner intuitions and ideas" (*AE* 7). I shall continue to use both kinds of insight as I explore each shape in some detail, seeking what attraction it holds for us, as well as how it contributes to the overall attractiveness of the Temple of Mnemosyne as a place to dwell.

Having pointed to some of the difficulties in a history of shapes, we should nevertheless consider what Hegel intends in his selection of various works of art as signifiers for entire historical eras. It is hard to avoid the conclusion that Hegel has fixated on a few shapes from history and then warps both his history and his aesthetics to conform with them. Despite a broad display of erudition, the Pyramids, the Sphinx, Greek sculpture, Raphael's Madonnas, and tragic Shakespearean characters form a small inner circle of figures, to which Hegel returns almost obsessively.[34] They form the elements of the Temple of Memory: Symbolic architecture raises the building; Classical sculpture forms the gods; and the Romantic arts provide the spiritually complete human beings who compose the congregation. This is the three-part structure Hegel's history creates, and unlike Locke's or Nietzsche's, it invites us to dwell in the figured past, reconciled to it, rather than pursue an uncertain future. If we can be reconciled to our past in the "absolute present," no redemption of the past in the future is needed. The absolute present, however, makes redemption impossible as well. This, I argue below, is its principal danger—especially if redemption turns out to be necessary after all.

THE SYMBOLIC

Hegel begins his account of history with an appraisal of the early Chinese and Indian civilizations. But he also says that they are outside the scope of history proper, and that it is only the Persian empire that "constitutes strictly the beginning of World-History" (*PH* 174). This corresponds to a lack of attention to the arts of these civilizations in the *Aesthetics*. There it is asserted that "the thorough elaboration of symbolic art, both in its special content and in its form, we have to seek in Egypt" (*AE* 354). His early appraisal of these cultures in the *Phenomenology* reveals that he believes them to have, "the 'shape' of 'shapelessness' " (*PS* 686). It is this odd, in-between characterization of the Far East as both shape and not-shape that allows it to have the position in history that it does—both a part of it and not a part of it. We might compare it to the ground upon which the Temple of Memory is built: it contributes nothing to the structure, yet it is a necessary predecessor. Only after this point does human labor occur and make shapes that are incorporated into the temple.

So it is Egypt, and only Egypt, wherein Hegel locates the heart of the first age of world history, whether called Oriental or Symbolic. Egypt receives over two-thirds of the space purportedly devoted to Persia in the *Philosophy of History*. Over and over again, Hegel describes both the Oriental and Egyptian spirits as characterized by a "riddle" or an "enigma." Although he seems to waver as to whether the Pyramids (*AE* 356) or the Sphinx (*AE* 360; *PH* 199) best typify this condition, he describes the condition itself consistently: "Spirit has still, as it were, an iron band around its forehead" (*PH* 207). Humanity is still struggling to emerge out of nature, and this in-between position is reflected in the "actualization" that takes place at this stage. Instead of freedom, we have "Spirit sunk in Nature, and the impulse to liberate it" (*PH* 218). Although the Egyptians themselves seem not to have known this, Hegel asserts that all their society presents us with is "the enigma of its being" (*PH* 207; 220).

The riddle-posing Sphinx thus becomes the best representation of this condition (see *PS* 697). Even when he considers the Pyramids for this role, it is not so much for their shapes per se as because they "conceal in themselves an inner meaning" (*AE* 356). The riddle sums up the Symbolic age—which gets its name from the idea of one thing standing for another, that is, "symbolically." A riddle, as Hegel understands it, is a question about a symbol, the referent of which is unknown: "What is it that . . . ?" What Oedipus does is to give the simple name for the series of traits that the Sphinx has listed; a name Hegel believes the Egyptians themselves did not know. He solves the riddle and thus destroys the basis for Symbolic existence by ending the separation between symbol and referent. But it often seems as if Hegel has reasoned backward: he seeks to make the half-animal, half-man, riddle-posing Sphinx into the shape of the Symbolic—so he describes it as architecture and then makes architecture the typical Symbolic genre.

He likens architecture to the Sphinx itself by arguing that it is the form of art closest to nature: buildings rise out of the earth and must, in their construction, obey the laws of nature. (One can disobey the law of gravity in literature or painting, for example, but not in architecture.) Yet works of architecture are nonetheless products of human labor as well as artworks. Thus, on the ground of prehistoric nature, the Egyptians have constructed the first element in Hegel's image of the past—the walls of the temple itself. Since the Greeks solved the Egyptians' riddle, it falls to them to shape the next element in the composition.

THE CLASSICAL

"Then into this temple, *secondly*, the god enters himself as the lightning-flash of individuality. . . . This is the task of *sculpture*" (*AE* 82). And of the Greeks. Hegel finds that sculpture is "so much the centre of the classical form of art that here we cannot accept" a division of its study into different periods; he dismisses *all* earlier and later sculpture as poor relations to the Greek period (*AE* 708). And this identification of sculpture and Greece runs both ways: "Greece is not to be understood at its heart unless we bring with us as a key to our comprehension an insight into the ideals of sculpture" (*AE* 719). The ideal forms of Greek sculpture are at the root of his interpretation of the Greek period, and for that matter, the Roman as well. Although he does not fixate on a single work, as in the case of the Symbolic, his obsession with Greek statuary serves the same function as his concentration on the Sphinx or the Pyramids. Among his favorites are the Elgin marbles and a bust of Zeus attributed to Phidias. But since, as with the Pyramids, he considers the sculpture to be the product of an entire culture, individual authorship is not important to him. Greek sculpture embodies his image of this stage in world history and serves as the Classical contribution to the Temple of Mnemosyne.

Hegel also argued that Greek sculpture was simply the most perfect form of art as such. Among the various kinds of art, it met his standard of beauty most completely; its limitations reflected merely the limitations of art itself. The discussion thus leaves open the possibility that the quality of beauty might be possessed to a higher degree by another product of labor, not an artwork, at a later date.[35] The sculpted human form (and Hegel hardly thinks any other sculpture worthy of the name) is the perfect embodiment of individuality (*AE* 433). "Man" is the Greek answer to the Egyptian riddle—and individuality is the characteristic that best typifies the Classical age as Hegel describes it (*AE* 302; 481).[36] He calls it "Individuality conditioned by Beauty" (*PH* 238).

Now, sculpture is the perfect form of art because it perfectly reflects the stage of spirit that it expresses. Hegel maintains that this is so because sculpture represents the human shape better than all other art (though not perfectly). Architecture, painting, and poetry, although they represent something *about* humanity fairly well, mimic neither the human form nor the idea of humanity relevant to that stage of history, as exactly.[37] But the Classical age is not the highest stage of the world history, since it is still concerned with the external—the body—and not with the spiritual itself. What is perfect about these sculptures is that there is no conflict internal to them, as there was for Egyptian art in the division between spirit and nature; there is no "iron band around [their foreheads]": "the Greek gods, in so far as Greek art represents them as free, inherently and independently self-sufficient individuals, are not to be taken symbolically; they content us in and by themselves" (*AE* 313). Unlike earlier artworks, these sculptures are not symbols. There is no separation of ideal and specific. They exactly mimic individual bodies, Hegel thinks, while at the same time displaying the ideal form of the human body. They render both perfectly—thus they are the perfect "middle term" in Hegel's logic of beauty. They represent an ideal given a perfectly individuated expression.

The society of Greece is supposed to display this same perfection of individual form, as well as this sense of satisfaction. And naturally so, since Hegel contends that art's beauty only reflects that which already exists within a culture. Thus, Hegel interprets the ancient Olympic games as a place where "the human being elaborates his physical being, in free, beautiful movement and agile vigor, to a work of art" (*PH* 242; cf. *PS* 725). The Greeks, at least at times, were as beautiful as their statues. Similarly, the Athenian polity, he claims, was without internal disruption. Like the statue of Athena herself, the city is serene and united (*PH* 252–53). Although it is not the perfect state, it is, like the statue, a perfectly integrated shape. Thus, Greek art merely reflects the stage of history to which it belongs, one in which form and content are perfectly reconciled.

The deficiency is that this perfect union of form and content is not conscious of itself as such. It lacks the inner self-awareness of its own beauty. The Idea is still imperfectly actualized in the real world. Thus, Greek social life is "unreflecting ethical existence" where citizens perform their duties "virtually by instinct" (*IPH* 202, 97). "Of the Greeks . . . we may assert, that they had no conscience" (*PH* 253). This lack of inwardness is reflected in sculpture by the "sightless" eye, the blank stare, that Hegel finds always accompanies the beautiful bodily shape in Greek art.[38] "The light of the eye . . . is absent" (*AE* 520–21; 731). In its "eternal serenity and bliss," the image of the Greek god misses the inner beauty of the human, even as it perfectly captures the outer (*AE* 436). Thus, the limitations of the Greeks and their art are the limitations of art itself: as something material, it must always stop at the surface;[39] it has no inside. Greek sculpture is the most beautiful form of art as such. But the most beautiful *thing*, it turns out, will not be an artwork at all, but a historical shape.

With this in mind, Hegel casts all of Roman history in the same minor role that earlier belonged to Oedipus—that of a transition to the next period. Rome goes nearly unmentioned in the *Aesthetics*, and Hegel claims that virtually all of its art is derivative from that of Greece (*AE* 514). He seems to feel that the Greeks have contributed all the poetry to the Classical period and the Romans all the prose (*PH* 288). Thus, Rome seems like nothing so much as a poor reflection of Greece, save only for the appearance of Jesus Christ. (Of course, Jesus is the real Oedipus figure here. Oedipus proclaimed the age of man, and Hegel calls Jesus "man as man"—that is, man who is aware of himself as man [*PH* 328].) Just as Oedipus destroyed the form of the Symbolic age, Hegel calls Rome "the demolition of beauty and joyous customs"; its only original form of art is satire (*AE* 514–15). Rome leaves no distinctive shape behind in the Temple of Mnemosyne.[40] The contribution of the Classical period is the perfectly carved god who stands in the structure donated by Symbolic architecture. Wholly contented, the Greek god poses no riddle, but he is superseded all the same by a society that, if its *art* is less perfect, nonetheless has a superior beauty in *itself*.

THE ROMANTIC

In this last stage of human history (known as the Germanic age in the *Philosophy of History*), beautiful art is still produced. But the highest beauty "passes over" from the fine arts to individuals and society itself. Where the beauty of the Classical period rested in images of the human body, the Romantic period houses beauty in human beings themselves. The best actualization of the Idea now exists in human society and the human soul. But this does not mean that the Romantic period has no image to contribute to the Temple of Mnemosyne: no single work of art, but the community itself, composed of beautiful souls, is the shape that appears in the image of the past—thus completing Hegel's historical trinity of building, gods, and congregation.

Of course, art still exists in this period, and it has distinctive forms, such as poetry, painting, and music. It even reflects the higher stage of the spirit that has arrived. It is just that it does not reflect that stage particularly *well*, as Classical art did for its stage of the spirit: "[E]xternal appearance cannot any longer express the inner life" (*AE* 527). So the previous expressions of beauty in the fine arts become "something subordinate, and beauty becomes the spiritual beauty of the absolute inner life" (*AE* 518). Humans themselves, rather than images of them, become the locus of beauty, the actualization of the idea. Where the Classical age had the image of man in Oedipus, the Romantic age has Jesus, whose true humanity Hegel never ceases to emphasize (see, e.g., *AE* 536ff.). This highest stage of the spirit is still measured in aesthetic terms: "[B]eauty will now reside . . . in the inner shape of the soul" (*AE* 531).

While modern painting has the "eye" that Classical sculpture lacked, and is thus a window onto this great soul, its form is not the perfect expression of that content as Classical sculpture was for its (lower) content. The Romantic art that Hegel describes with obvious affection,[41] he nonetheless holds to be inferior to both Classical art and modern man. Hamlet, as a fictional character, cannot match the beauty of a real human being. Nor, as a written work, can he reflect a human as completely in form and content as a Greek sculpture. Nonetheless, Hamlet, as one who wonders at the meaning of his own existence, does tell us something of the nature of the Romantic soul that Hegel so values. The moderns have achieved a level of self-awareness that even the Greeks lacked. They can thus form a truly live congregation in a way that the Greeks could not.

For Hegel, the modern perfection of the spirit does not mean that all humans must be identical, any more than all Greek sculptures had to be identical when they reflected the same sort of beauty. It is as a congregation, rather, or as a community, that he thinks of the Romantic population—each soul a beautiful shape unto itself, but each also participating in the larger beauty of the whole (*PH* 416–17). "[T]he *community* . . . has its real vitality in the government as that in which it has an individual form" (*PS* 455). Where Classical beauty was the form of the god, the last beauty in history is "the form of the Self" (*PS* 798). Man's search for beauty, for the perfect realization of the Idea in the actual world, has led him through art back to himself. It is not hard to understand Hegel's obsession with Greek statuary; all along he knew that the highest beauty was in the individual form—Greek sculpture was the best foreshadowing of that modern beauty.

Modern humans form the congregation at the Temple of Mnemosyne. They are the last element in the composition Hegel has made, representing the last period of history. The triune work is complete; nothing could be added to it. And though it is a work revealed by Hegel, he maintains that its composition is really the work of history itself, just as the composition of each element was the work of the civilization, as a whole, that produced it. Indeed, the shape each culture leaves behind is nothing less than that culture itself, as a whole, but also as a memory. In exploring history philosophically, as I described above, we explore our own memories—that is, we explore ourselves. Hegel wants us to understand past cultures as part of ourselves and to find our "lost sense of solid and substantial being" in them. In understanding this history, Hegel contends, we understand ourselves. The philosopher, like the artist, reveals something that is already there. Hegel's account of the past is meant to cure an amnesia that has robbed us of our sense of solidity and substantiality. It "alters nothing," yet draws our attention to memories that have lapsed. There is no firm line between Hegel's sense of history and the memories he wishes to revive in us. Nor is there a distinction between the plot he has devised and the character who has a memory of it. In learning our history, we learn ourselves.

The End of History

At times, Hegel hints that there might be future stages to history, that it is only a limitation of philosophy that it cannot see into the future (e.g., *PH* 350). But it is a note he strikes very rarely, and it is discordant with his overall theme. His major chord is rather heard in statements such as "The end of days is fully come" and "the Christian world is the world of completion" (*PH* 342). He even says flatly that "Europe is the absolute end of history" (*IPH* 197). He only hints at a future because he is unwilling to declare an imminent eschaton. As far as his story goes, it needs only such a finishing touch for an end. The development of man is complete, the Temple of Mnemosyne is a perfect tripartite image. It contains the perfect forms that are the result of the labor of each historical era. The temple they compose should be the beautiful climax to the narrative. In memory, those elements of human activity that have risen above the mundane to merge with the ideal (while never giving up their humanity) combine to form the most beautiful shape of all. Its three elements display, not just the beauty of each stage, but the beauty of history as a whole. R. G. Collingwood (and others) has tried to excuse Hegel's lack of future on the grounds that, in Hegel's view, the future cannot be examined "philosophically" in the way the past can be, because it had not yet occurred.[42] But Collingwood does not come to grips with the way Hegel declares history *complete* in the present. Hegel does not merely plead that he cannot go further—he says there is nowhere else *to go*. The only thing lacking is the ringing down of the curtain.

Or is it lacking? The end of the *Philosophy of History* is wildly anticlimactic. It is hard to take seriously Hegel's laundry-list description of European states as a conclusion or his subsequent declaration that he has completed a "theodicy" (*PH* 450–57). The *Aesthetics* offers an alternative, and more disturbing, account of the present. Art does not culminate at the end of history—it actually ends. As Roman satire ended Classical art, Shakespearean comedy ends art completely. Art is literally dissolved in laughter: "[C]omedy leads . . . to the dissolution of art altogether" (*AE* 1236). When the narrative of art is finished, it does not end in a visible final form, but rather fades to black: "No Homer, Sophocles, etc., no Dante, Ariosto, or Shakespeare can appear in our day; what was so magnificently sung, what so freely expressed, has been expressed; these are materials, ways of looking at them and treating them which have been sung once and for all. Only the present is fresh, the rest is pale and paler" (*AE* 608).[43] No further art will be produced. The dusk of the human day of labor has arrived and no further shapes will be made. But if the activity of all human civilizations has been embodied in their labor, what will the humans of the future do? This haunting line, of a life grown "pale and paler" points to the emptiness of Hegelian theodicy or perhaps of modernity itself (on a Hegelian understanding of it). Having crammed so much into the past, by making the past a *complete* shape, Hegel has left nothing for the future.[44] If we find ourselves entirely in the past, in memory, we leave nothing over to be a part of ourselves in the future. If the plot that composes our character is complete, then that character is complete as well. In a closed narrative, the characters are wholly finished—nothing will be added to them. They will not change or grow; their change or growth is done. That is as it should be in a play. Narrative closure is a virtue in literature; it provides the reader with the desired sense of an ending. In life, however, it appears to be a disturbing stasis, a final holding pattern that we shall never leave.[45] For Locke and Nietzsche, it was the incompleteness of the plot, its openness, that provided the opportunity for change, struggle, and therefore a future different from the past, even if always a product of the past.

This lack of a future will haunt the Temple of Mnemosyne. Or rather, fail to haunt it. Where Marx found in Hegel's teleology the idea of a future haunting the present, for Hegel, no specter haunts Europe at all. History is as complete as art. The world has no future, and although events may continue, none of them will have significant meaning. What does Hegel offer us, then, but a life grown "pale and paler"? Even on its own terms, Hegel's history condemns itself. By declaring history complete, he has reduced it to the status of nature, which he declared earlier must dissatisfy us because it contains "nothing new under the sun." Although this reconstruction of history has the virtue of a beauty that nature lacks, it shares this negative trait of staleness with nature. It is all "cut and dried." And nothing further will ever be cut. Perhaps the reconciliation he offers is enough in the way of compensation for Hegel; but he clearly did not think this to be the case with nature itself. Does the attraction to the past that the discovery of beauty in it creates compensate sufficiently for the threat of boredom that results from lack of novelty? This project of reconciliation is at its most enticing, perhaps, in the *Philosophy of Right*. There, the well-ordered modern state appears as the culmination of rationality, and life within it as the perfect harmonization of freedom. Even here, though, Hegel seems to sense the stupor into which the state may slip ("In peace civil life continually expands; all its departments wall themselves in, and in the long run men stagnate" [*PR* 324n]) and can find a solution to it only by turning back to history itself (*PR* 341–53). This position only underlines the degree to which the modern, Hegelian state lacks a task to which it might apply itself.

Is the Absolute Present Heaven, Hell, or Limbo?

Hegel's position "after" history, in the absolute present, weakens the limitation he places on philosophy in the famous remark that "the owl of Minerva spreads its wings only with the falling of the dusk." That only limits those who engage in philosophy in medias res. For those who stand, not just at the end of history, but after it entirely, in the absolute present, there is no limitation to the philosophy of history. Indeed, it is hard to imagine such an evaluation as Hegel's being written by anyone who did *not* see himself at least at the culminating stage of civilization. As Hegel himself acknowledges, the cost in individual human lives would otherwise seem too great (*IPH* 43, 69). It may still seem so.

Hegel aims, by his history, to seduce us to life, to the lives we are living now, and this in two ways. He wants to *bind* us to our history by his account of it as human labor and, thus, property. But he also wants to *attract* us to it by his account of it as actualization and, thus, beauty. As we saw above, because historical actions are the product of human or national labor, they accrue to those who perform such labor as their property. In describing all of human history as the product of a single human spirit, Hegel makes all of it into our property. But it is our property in the twofold sense I outlined before. Its moments are our *characteristics* as well as owned objects. We can decry history, but we cannot separate ourselves from it. It is not merely our history but our *memory*. Its shapes are ours in the sense that memories are ours—a part of us constitutive of our selves. We are bound to it by an identity that admits of nothing deeper than itself. Thus Hegel answers the romantic cry for "the lost sense of solid and substantial being." His philosophy of history gives its audience back their lost sense of substance by giving them all of human history as themselves.[46] And the shape it arrives in is this three-sided Temple.

But Hegel tries to make his audience *love* this Temple, and themselves, by making it beautiful as well. The aesthetics that underlies his account of history is meant to do just this. Lockean labor is not enough, for readers might reject the past in themselves (might therefore come to hate themselves or opt for that loss of self called amnesia) if they found it too abhorrent. Beauty is also required. The account of action as the transmission of ideas into reality, where they take on the quality of beauty, is the ungainly element of seduction in Hegel's work. Beauty is not just of interest to Hegel as an attribute of art. By gazing on all of history as the emergence of beauty, he hopes that it will replace for us what comfort we found in earlier myths or earlier philosophies. By linking nations to beautiful objects, indeed by *making* them into such objects, he hopes to make us find our history beautiful itself. Austere as his philosophy sometimes seems, his unlikely goal is to help us "enjoy the present" (*PR*, Pref., 12). His philosophy urges us toward no particular future. His temple is meant to be a place in which we can happily dwell.

But Hegel leaves us with nothing to do in the house our predecessors have built and that he has unveiled. The absolute present resonates too well with the eternal present that Nietzsche identified as the dwelling place of the Last Man. The Last Man, it will be recalled, is trapped by his own memory. No longer a resource for his creativity, memory has become a wall that enfolds man in the present, unable to change. "Happiness" is just what the Last Men enjoy. In its perfect completeness, the Temple of Mnemosyne is a perfect prison. There are no doors to the Pyramids. Those interred never leave. This is the result of the attempt to put *all* of history into one form. In his zeal to tie up all the loose ends, to bring every line of plot to a conclusion, Hegel succeeds too well. By putting all of humanity into its own past actions, he as much as says that we have no future. Since man has, throughout history, been a laboring animal, bringing history into existence, the end of this labor must mean the end of man as well. Without a task, man must lapse again into a condition of animality, rather than enjoying the present. Hegel agrees with Nietzsche that where there is nothing new, there is only brute nature. Unwittingly, it seems to me, Hegel's attempt to seduce us to life leads instead to the condition of the Last Man.

Perhaps, because it concludes so thoroughly, we should call Hegel's narrative antipolitical. Hegel says we cannot philosophize about the future, but we see now that this is more than a limitation of philosophy. For it is really the conclusion of his philosophy that there is no future. And it is for this reason that we must declare Hegel's attempt at seduction seriously compromised. He declines to imagine a future. Without it, it is not really "life" that he is seducing us to at all, but the remembrance of life in an ever-repeating picture show. *Life*, even on Hegel's terms, is the production of the new, the actualization of the Idea. He cannot promise that kind of future. A seduction requires beauty, yes, but it also requires promise—a hint, a hope, of something to come. Seduction is something that leads us *on*. What Hegel produces instead is a picture of the past—a series of still lifes that run together as a disjointed film, which always fades to black. It is the process of actualization that Hegel thinks is the real essence of, say, the artist's activity, or that of any other laborer of the Spirit. But there will be no such labor, no such actualization, in the future. There is nothing more to be built. Hence, even on Hegel's own terms, there will not truly be any life.

This is the perspective we gain by considering Hegel's philosophy of history in contrast to that of Locke and Nietzsche. Hegel's narrative comes to a close (as Aristotle suggests narrative should) in the present, whereas those of the other two do not. Paying attention to history, to its meaning for the present, does not require that one become so absorbed in it that the future is effectively abandoned. This is clear in both Locke and Nietzsche. The issue of the past being a threat to the future is especially considered by the latter. Nietzsche finds in the Last Man a kind of death-in-life, which is the result of an excess of memory. This excess leads to an abandonment of thinking itself—understanding is frozen in a single pattern, just as Narcissus was rooted to one spot staring at his reflection in a pool of water.[47] In a perfect reconciliation, the opportunity for redemption is lost because the future is abandoned. Redemption, Nietzsche says, "is something higher than any reconciliation" (*Z* 2.20). Whichever is higher or lower, we can plainly see that redemption and reconciliation are not the same thing. Reconciliation is an attempt to merge oneself completely in one's past, to lose oneself in one's memory. Reconciliation is so concerned with present happiness that it forgets about the future in its attempt to come to grips with memory. I use that phrase deliberately, for remembering the future (no matter how paradoxical it sounds) is just what Locke and Nietzsche do.[48] They do not seek the past in order to make the present happy or in order to make themselves happy; they remember the past for the sake of future. The task of redemption does not have the promise of beauty or happiness, but it does offer the possibility of a real future. Reconciliation crushes the future under the weight of the past.

Hegel's history represents such an excess of memory. The completion of the Temple of Mnemosyne is the perfection of our memory. Nothing need ever be added to it. Without a future, no new thoughts will disturb the structure's stability. A future that contains things new and different rests on the imperfection and incompleteness of all interpretations of the past. (Recall Nietzsche's injunction to consider the past ugly, and the wall of memory in need of another brick, in order to add something new.) Hegel's problem is not (as is commonly said) that he worships the present; it is that he loves the past too much. His is a strangely historical narcissism. It is for this reason that his history issues not in a future but in an eternal present. And without a future, the only life he offers is that of the pale Last Men: where human thought develops to the point that it renders new thoughts superfluous. Without promise, Hegel's seduction seems as hollow as his artists; his citizens are truly Eliot's "Hollow Men": "In this last of meeting places / We grope together / And avoid speech."[49] Narcissus was so beautiful that many would have fallen in love with him. But in the end, he only fell in love with himself.

For once Hegel's trinitarianism fails him. His trinity of historical ages and logic does not correspond to the trinity of past, present, and future. The latter is lacking. His temple reminds us too much of a tomb. Now that history is complete, no human action can be significant enough to contribute to it. Hegel's past, the character he builds, the memory he offers us, leads to no life at all. Aristotle recommended that all narratives have an end. But our exploration of Hegel has concluded with a realization that an end may encumber a political philosophy with considerable dangers. Some of the implications of this are considered in Chapters 6 and 7.

PART IV

Visions of Past and Future

Yet the enchainment of past and future
Woven in the weakness of the changing body,
Protects mankind from heaven and damnation
Which flesh cannot endure.
—T. S. Eliot, "Burnt Norton"

CHAPTER 6

Reconciliation or Redemption?

Besides, if there were more heavens than one, the movement of any of them equally would be time, so that there would be many times at the same time.

—Aristotle, *Physics*

At a very high level of abstraction, it could perhaps be said that each of the philosophers examined in this book attempts to give meaning to history. But such generalizations obscure more than they reveal. It becomes all too easy to lump these projects together and dismiss them as composing a woolly, unphilosophical genre. But each philosopher we have read has had a distinctive approach to this project. That is, it is not just that they happen to find very different sorts of meaning in history—it is that they have very distinct notions of what is *involved* in fashioning a meaning for history—distinct theoretically, distinct existentially, and distinct politically. They have different ideas of what it means to invoke history and of what the relationship is between that invocation, the self, and politics. The use of history, per se, tells us little more than the invocation of "reason" in philosophy. Both tell us something—but more about a philosopher's starting point than his or her conclusions. Locke and Nietzsche, in their own very different ways, invite us to create a meaning for the past as part of our own attempt to alter the future. For Hegel, however, the idea is to seek out *the* meaning of history, with the idea that it is already there, cut and dried, so to speak, and awaiting our inspection. Grasping such a meaning implies only that we come to understand our place in time, instead of, as with Locke and Nietzsche, changing it. I have attempted to encapsulate this difference by speaking of Hegel's strategy as one of *reconciliation*, whereas the other is one of *redemption*. Reconciliation results in a closed narrative in the sense that all the plotlines reach some sort of conclusion. Redemption leads to an open narrative, not in the sense that it lacks structure or direction, but in the sense that its future is not wholly determined; the plot continues.

I should add that I am aware of the apparent irony of imposing what seems to be an analytic distinction (reconciliation/redemption) onto narratives, while simultaneously claiming the centrality of history and time themselves. But this seems to me, at most, a limitation of my view rather than an objection to it. In distinguishing two principal characters of narratives of political theory, I am not trying to reenact an absolute character/plot distinction in my own theory after questioning its existence in that of others. Indeed, it was particularly my practice to examine first the characters of each theory, in a kind of artificial isolation, as a useful prelude to reconstructing the whole. I do no more or less here. Undoubtedly these characters are connected to some plot—but that does not preclude considering them separately, at least at this time.

Reconciliation Versus Redemption

The difference between the reconciliatory and the redemptive approaches to history has been one of the key distinctions toward which my inquiry has led. Hegel does not offer a redemption in the manner of Locke and Nietzsche. In light of these other philosophies, this absence appears to me now as a significant failing. Hegel's deeply considered past cries out for some kind of recoupment. His failure to offer any (because of the absence of a future) only increases our sense of frustration with what Nietzsche called "the stone 'It was,'" which "cannot be moved" (Z 2: 20).

Nietzsche and Locke are very different minds, but they agree at least on a strategy of redemption. Although both offer a recovery, Nietzsche's explicit recognition of this need makes his narrative more open and powerful. Locke only deals with the pressure of the past at a particular moment—that of tyranny and revolution. Nietzsche's discussion of memory, on the other hand, reveals the constant tension between past, present, and future at the gate called "Moment." Where Locke describes a redemptive moment, Nietzsche is concerned that every moment be redemptive. If he does not appear to us to have succeeded, at least he faces the politics of memory squarely. But insofar as either of them manages to grasp the three temporal moments together, it is through redemptive action. So long as the past stands unredeemed, the past and future remain disconnected from the present. Where we have been, our memories, are only fully related to who we are, our self-identity, when they contribute to where we are going. Redemptive action thus brings the three moments of time together, within the individual, in a special way. While certainly not offering a permanent solution to Gauguin's three questions (since the flow of time continually alters past and future, making every solution a transient one), these temporary redemptions ("temporary" also in the older sense of belonging to the temporal realm) at least offer a way to live within time that neither denies its presence nor finds it a crushing burden.

It is this redemptive moment that separates the political theory of Nietzsche (and in a lesser way of Locke) from the approach to time adopted by Hegel and, I argue below, Martin Heidegger. An understanding of this latter approach has been indispensable in coming to appreciate this sort of moment. But although it started with these philosophers (especially hermeneuticists like Heidegger), the path I have taken in this inquiry is not simply an extension of them. The divergence follows from the perspective taken on the past and what can be done with the past. It is here that we find the root of the difference between reconciliation and redemption. Ultimately, I believe, Heidegger (and some who have followed him) have relied too heavily on ideas of time and history that are notably Hegelian. As I argue below, this leaves them, as it did Hegel, with a harshly diminished sense of human potentiality.

In the Introduction, I emphasized the connection Heidegger draws between time and human experience. But Heidegger also emphasizes another element of the human condition that he finds equally basic (or, as he puts it, "equiprimordial"): the condition of "throwness."[1] "Throwness" is essential to the human condition, for Heidegger, because we do not choose our time. We do not choose where or when we live; yet we must always live sometime, in the midst of some tradition. Equally, we do not choose to be born or choose to die, and yet we must always live between birth and death—stretched out between them. If we come to any knowledge of ourselves, we may do so only within these conditions. Thus, for Heidegger, coming to grips *with* these conditions themselves (into which we have been thrown) is the most important kind of self-knowledge. These conditions represent, for him, the very boundaries of our knowledge, hence, of our very being. For Heidegger, accepting one's thrown condition is the most elemental wisdom. To wish to leap outside of one's own time is to live "inauthentically." It is to dream of the impossible rather than truly to live in the world. Such dreams run away from the world rather than facing up to it.

But Nietzsche, as we know, is not quite so hard on the dreamer. And I believe that there is an important lesson here. Certain dreams, we might say, offer an opportunity for redemption that Heidegger's emphasis on our "throwness" does not. For Heidegger, the past is past—it can be avoided or accepted but not altered. Whether one embraces the traditions one is born into or rejects them, one cannot live outside them. But Nietzsche writes: "There is no way of telling what may yet become part of history" (GS 1.34). This flexibility about the past, although it comes with its own set of dangers, which must not be minimized, offers better odds for redemption. If the past can be worked on, by dreaming Greeks or dreaming good Europeans, then all that was "dreadful accident" need not have been in vain. Accepting the past in Heidegger's sense means accepting one's limits, but in Nietzsche's sense it means taking up the opportunity to put right what was horrible, vile, and meaningless, by remaking the future to which it leads. Contained in this is an implicit critique of Heideggerian "throwness," as there is of Hegel's "Absolute Moment." Indeed, the two are closely related.

This critique can best be understood through an exploration of the way in which Heidegger uses the terms *birth* and *death* to limit the world into which we are thrown. Heidegger lays great stress on the fact that all human life must end in death. While the use he makes of this fact is quite unusual, the sense in which he means the word *death* is, I think, quite ordinary. Indeed, what he wants to emphasize is the solitary, unstoppable, brute animal character of death, the death every human experiences. From this fact he gathers some of his deepest insights, and it is not my aim to quarrel with them here. What I want to point out is that his use of the term *birth* is not really the exact correlate of his term *death*—it is not the simple biological fact of birth that Heidegger is pointing to.

Although Heidegger says frequently that human life is that which "stretches along between birth and death,"[2] he does not treat biological birth as he treats death—as an absolute barrier to existence. For the time into which one is thrown, although in a certain sense commencing with one's birth, is in a more important sense, for Heidegger, constituted by the cultural heritage one acquires. The time of one's existence is limited by one's death in an absolute way, but not so by one's birth. Instead, the culture into which one is born, most of which precedes one's birth, is of crucial importance. It is the manner in which one reacts to this pre-birth past, Heidegger thinks, that makes all the difference. To accept one's birth, for Heidegger, means to accept one's place in the culture into which one has been born. This is not simply to acknowledge that one is part of a given community, but actively to affirm it. Coming to grips with birth means actively taking up tradition—as Heidegger puts it, "a handing down to oneself of the possibilities that have come down to one . . . a heritage."[3] Only when one recognizes one's "fateful destiny . . . as bound up with the heritage which has come down to us" does one live authentically.[4] Practically, this means that one is limited in one's life by the culture and time into which one has been born. One cannot leap outside of one's time.

We cannot ignore our heritage, any more than we can ignore the fact that we shall someday die. Our only authentic choice is the "repetition of a possibility of existence that has been"—that is, a form of existence that grows out of our traditional roots—rather than attempting to start from scratch.[5] When Heidegger says we are thrown into a life between birth and death, he means that we are thrown into an existence that ends in death but starts with a tradition that we can choose either to affirm or to deny. Only the former choice, he thinks, is an honest one, because it recognizes our "thrown" condition.

But if it is tradition and heritage that Heidegger is concerned with, why use the term *birth* at all? This usage tells us something important about Heidegger's understanding of the past—something that sharply differentiates him from, say, Nietzsche and unites him with Hegel. The metaphor of birth emphasizes the singleness and unquestionability of tradition in Heidegger's understanding of it. One's culture may have a variety of elements, but what is a part of it and what is outside of it should not, he thinks, be a difficult question. One's heritage, one's birth, is as clear as one's death, if only one faces up to it. There is no real difficulty in recognizing one's past, Heidegger maintains, if only one has the courage to do so.[6] Reconciliation comes from an affirmation of the past, not an operation on it.

It is here that we can see the deep parallel between the approaches to history taken by Hegel and Heidegger.[7] The likeness might best be described as a common vocabulary of "revealing" and "unconcealment" that denotes, for both theorists, our means of coming to grips with the past. Recall for a moment Hegel's characterization of the artist. While undoubtedly a special person, the artist's specialness derives not from any force of personality but from an ability precisely to absent himself from the creative process and to let the beauty that already exists in the world come forth. Art, in Hegel's understanding, only presents the shapes that history itself has produced. Individual artworks, therefore, can only achieve the degree of beauty that history, at that stage, has itself achieved. This attitude toward art presages the approach Hegel takes to history itself, which he perceives as the work neither of the historian nor even of the philosopher of history. At most, the latter can only be said to transpose the shapes Spirit has produced into a more complete composition. This means little more than to reveal the shape events already possess, but that are hardly visible amid the debris of historical detail. Rather than fashioning, or refashioning, a meaning for history, Hegel's philosophy means to reveal *the* meaning of history as "the inwardizing and Calvary of the Absolute Spirit" (*PS* 808).

Notwithstanding the many differences between Hegel and Heidegger, the latter's approach to Being strongly echoes this passive-aesthetic approach to Spirit. Indeed, Heidegger goes out of his way to emphasize the passive manner in which we come to have knowledge of Being in his lecture "On Time and Being,"[8] where it is characterized "as the unconcealing; as the gift of unconcealing."[9] That is, we receive Being as a Hegelian artist receives beauty, as a gift. As with Hegel also, our entire essence is to be found in this gift we receive, as it were, from outside of ourselves: "If man were not the constant receiver of the gift . . . , if that which is extended in the gift did not reach man, then not only would Being remain concealed . . . [but] Man would not be man."[10] Just as, for Hegel, the emanations of Spirit become our property, and we are composed of nothing but such properties, so Heidegger finds that gifts of Being manifest themselves as *Ereignis*, which Heidegger specifies should be understood as "Appropriation," the taking on of properties.[11] On an authentic understanding of Being, then, we have as little say in its content (even when that being is ourselves) as we did in our own births. It only appears to us as a gift, one we are to receive with gratitude, indeed without a murmur of protest, rather than with any sort of critical eye. Heidegger has generalized and radicalized the case of the Hegelian artist. In both cases, rather than an activity of creation, there is only an "unconcealment" before the eyes of the patient waiter. (Recall Hegel's description of action as "a transition from a state of not being seen to one of being seen" [*PS* 396].) As with Hegel, though, we are left to wonder whether Heidegger's strategy of a perfect reconciliation with the world truly deepens our sense of humanity (as is claimed) or, on the contrary, empties it. By equating our humanity with what we receive from the past, we may, simultaneously, endanger the future.

Heidegger often presents this view as if it were an extension of Nietzsche's doctrine of "amor fati"—love of fate. And indeed, a superficial reading of Nietzsche might lead one to believe that this is the case. But, as I have argued above, Nietzsche's approach to the past is quite different. Nietzsche does not consider one's inheritance to be a birth, a particular spot in time, into which one is thrown and that one has no power to change. On the contrary, "Every great human being exerts a retroactive force. . . . Perhaps the past is still essentially undiscovered!" (*GS* 1.34). The past is inherently mutable. It cannot be altered at will. But the meaning of an inheritance can be worked on, just as a dreamer works on his own experiences. Loving one's fate, for Nietzsche, does not mean simply accepting the tradition into which one is thrown, however it happens to present itself. If anything, the opposite is true: true redemption can only come from working on the past, remaking it, retelling it, until some sense, some value has been made of it.

The critique of throwness is contained in this notion of the mutability of the past. To accept our condition as thrown in Heidegger's sense means to limit our understanding of the past to that which is given to us. It is to sanction a passivity with regard to the past that Nietzsche finds unnecessary. It is to accept iron limits to our past and, hence, equally iron limits to our future. Nietzsche does not dispute that the past limits us, even chains us; but he passionately rejects the idea that we are in thrall to tradition to the *degree* that Hegel and Heidegger maintain. We certainly cannot escape our past. But the work of a poet like Homer, or of a philosopher like Nietzsche himself, demonstrates the extent to which the past can be reappraised, revised, and retold so that it can become a path to a different future, one that has not been "handed down" to us.

In this sense, Nietzsche's approach offers us an opportunity for redemption that Hegel and Heidegger cannot. Heidegger wants us to accept our heritage as something as immutable as our births. But the fact that he must make this point through metaphor indicates the willfulness of his position. For it seems much more plausible to think, as Nietzsche does, of our past as a vast (but not endless) variety of possibilities, waiting to be taken up by a political theorist, or a poet, to be fashioned into a redemptive narrative that leads us from past to future. Heidegger's emphasis on the singleness of tradition identifies one's past solely with national history. In this sense, his approach grows out of Hegel's, as does his idea of reconciliation. Not only can such an identification be dangerous, but it is profoundly narrow-minded as well. Not only is the past a foreign country, as L. P. Hartley puts it; it is a myriad of such countries, offering a great deal more material for history than any one person could incorporate. In tying the future to the past, one does not tie the individual's destiny solely to the nation's, but to the multiplicity of pasts that are the sources of our lives. We certainly do not choose the civilization or time into which we are born. But civilization and culture are such multifarious things that they could never determine our lives in the ironclad fashion Heidegger implies with his metaphor of throwness. The possibility of redemption is always there, lying dormant in this multiplicity, even if it is not always grasped. It is this possibility that the philosophy of Nietzsche awakens us to in its audacious attempt to remake the future and redeem the past by retelling our history.

Perhaps we do not feel that Nietzsche has entirely succeeded in this attempt. Perhaps he attempts to swallow too much violence and cruelty in his account of the past and, in the end, is unable to digest them. But this reproach should not be allowed to overshadow what we can learn from Nietzsche. How much redemption, after all, can we really expect?

To say that Nietzsche's redemption is incomplete is hardly to say that it was not worth the effort. If anything, we should draw the opposite conclusion. What Nietzsche's work shows us is the need for redemption that exists among memorious animals—and the extreme thoughts that need to be considered in order even to begin to achieve it. Even in its incomplete condition, the redemption Nietzsche offers is worth embracing—if only because the alternative he reveals, the unredeemed Last Man, is so hideous. It is worth embracing then, but only so that it can be extended, embellished, worked on, worked over, and, ultimately, discarded. That is the attitude Nietzsche takes toward earlier such attempts, and one he encourages us to take with regard to his own work. As time continues to run ahead of us, the redemption of any one account of history must seem increasingly provisional. Even if Nietzsche's history seemed whole in 1887 (something I very much doubt), it would appear incomplete to us today. Its incompleteness should not be held against it. Only histories such as Hegel's are complete. And the sense of an ending they provide ends any hope of future redemptions. When history is over, and we live only in the present, then, as Eliot puts it, "All time is unredeemable."

History and Responsibility

One of the issues that divide the redemptive philosophers from the reconciliatory ones, I think, is the question of responsibility. Which is the attitude toward the past that accepts the most responsibility for it? Each side has a claim: Hegel and Heidegger, it might be said, accept the past as a whole and do not attempt to flee from it. In predicating their philosophy on the condition of throwness, they acknowledge the contribution to our being of all that is great and ugly in the past, or at least, in the past of our culture. This, it could be argued, is a brave and unflinching attitude toward the past, one that does not turn away from what is most repellent within it.

But is responsibility really to be found in so undiscriminating a gaze? It seems to me we should draw the opposite conclusion. Heidegger accepts the past in such a way as to make himself answerable for none of it. Everything about throwness emphasizes the lack of choice on the part of the single human being. The metaphor is passive both syntactically (humans do not throw, but are thrown) and substantively: we are not only acted on but violently *flung*, as if our own efforts were of no account against the power of time (which weaker terms such as *conditioning*, *shaping*, or *placing* might not convey). Throwness is a claim of innocence—the innocence of the weak, who have no power and, hence, no liability.[12]

Paradoxical though it may sound, a greater sense of responsibility is actually to be found in Nietzsche's refusal to accept the past as it is. It is true that rewriting the past might allow one to gloss over anything embarrassing or ugly. (Although Nietzsche himself does just the opposite, others might not follow him in this respect.) But the sense of accountability that Nietzsche fosters actually springs from a deeper, more structural element of his sense of the past. For whoever undertakes to rewrite the past must acknowledge that whatever he places (or omits) there appears (or disappears) by his will and choice alone. Nietzsche does not attempt to distance himself from the primordial violence of the human animals he describes. Indeed, he attempts to redeem such creatures by demonstrating their necessity in the path to something better. Nietzsche accepts the past, then, in a sense that Heidegger does not. The lack of a singular past does not inspire in Nietzsche a claim of innocence or "lightness of being" but, on the contrary, an acknowledgment of indebtedness.[13] He accepts history, not just as an ontological condition (as Heidegger does), but also as a moral debt to be paid off. He may vituperate previous generations for creating this sense of debt, this memory; but he does not shirk it—he attempts to redeem it. His only condition for accepting this responsibility is the denial that we are merely thrown into our time. Nietzsche insists that our time is something we can work on. We cannot change it at will, but we can work on it until we have a past that leads to a future we can be proud of. The mutability of time does not imply a flight from responsibility. If anything, it is braver to accept the flexibility of the past than to paint it as a rigid structure into which we are thrown. Others might rewrite the past to whitewash it, but anyone who truly dares to meddle with the past accepts the onus in doing so for what is there, accepts that the past lives on in one, and that one may be accountable for it. For if this were *not* so, there would be no need to revisit the past at all.

This point can acquire a more political meaning by considering it as a question of freedom, as recent debates have done. In a notable book, Leslie Thiele argues that the Heideggerian attitude toward Being described above is best understood as a kind of freedom—a conception of freedom, moreover, superior to our current understandings of it.[14] Thiele calls this "the freedom to reveal what is," one that "celebrates caretaking rather than mastery."[15] Even leaving to one side, here, the questionable claim that all previous conceptions of freedom celebrate mastery, there still seem to me to be considerable problems with this position, which derive from its Hegelian provenance. Since our purpose as humans, on this understanding, is the revelation of Being, and since we, as individuals, can do nothing to bring this about, our characteristic activity, as Thiele rightly puts it, is "waiting."[16] What is troubling about this account of freedom is not so much its passivity (although that can be disturbing) as the lack of a corresponding sense of attribution (and, in this sense, authorial responsibility). Since whatever takes place through this freedom is not of our own making, it would be hard to say how we could be held accountable for it. As Thiele puts it, humans are "a place for Being to become disclosed."[17] But here again we have largely the freedom of the Hegelian artist to absent himself and become a "living corridor" for Spirit (*AE* 298). Hegel maintained that it would be senseless to hold artists accountable for the beauty or ugliness of their creations—it was the world itself that contained beauty or ugliness. Similarly, it would be difficult to hold humans to account for the results of Heideggerian freedom. They merely make it possible for Being to disclose itself—in whatever form it chooses. This would perhaps make sense if there were a single storyline to history, unalterable in its direction by human actions, as Hegel thought, or if our birth were as singular a source of our being as Heidegger suggests. If the end point of our narrative has not been pre-scripted, however, perhaps different kinds of freedom (ones that allow humans at least a degree of authorship) are more attainable than Hegel and Heidegger allow.

There is something paradoxical about Heidegger's position. On the one hand, it is profoundly concerned with an openness and receptivity to the variety of existence. Yet it is simultaneously closed to the deepest source of that variety—the activity of human beings themselves. *Their* contingency and diversity play no part here (however open Heidegger may be to the variety of nature in other ways). Just as, for Hegel, all of history eventually took on the characteristics of nature, so it is with Heidegger's sense of Being. (It should be no surprise that the "politics" Thiele ascribes to Heidegger are largely environmental.) Just as Hegel's Temple of Mnemosyne eventually comes to seem a prison to the final generations of humans, so Heidegger's gift of Being, in the very fullness of its generosity, exacts too high a price. The completion of the temple is like the perfection of the gift—although intended to replenish a diminished sense of self, it ends up depleting the self of purpose, consequence, contribution, and responsibility. This is not to say that Heidegger's prescription is without appeal, any more than Hegel's is. It is only to question whether that appeal can truly be characterized as a kind of freedom—or whether, instead, Heidegger's position must be understood as a flight from politics, including all claims to freedom and its responsibilities. Again: neither should the redemptive approach be understood to promise freedom, if it is to be understood simply as absence of constraint; the Nietzschean character is profoundly constrained by history. But there may yet be another variety of freedom contained in the redemptive approach that accepts the burdens of history but is not wholly crushed by them.[18]

Heidegger's humans resemble Hegel's artists too much—thinking and dwelling, but never building.

Narrativization and Its Discontents

It is perhaps to be expected that some of those writers who have been most interested in calling our attention to narrative in recent years have at the same time been the most discontented with it. Some of these theorists are inheritors of the Heideggerian theory I have just been criticizing. But their concerns are different and novel enough, I believe, to deserve separate consideration.

Even Hayden White, whose notation of the etymological connection between "narrative" and "knowledge" I drew attention to in the first pages of this book, is far from being a happy defender of narrative. Indeed, he chides his fellow historians (and, by implication, the rest of us) for an uncritical faith in narrative coherence, saying that the "value attached to narrativity in the representation of real events arises out of a desire to have real events display the coherence, integrity, fullness and closure of an image of life that is and can only be imaginary. The notion that sequences of real events possess the formal attributes of the stories we tell about imaginary events could only have its origin in wishes, daydreams, reveries."[19] The very impulse to narrativize, White argues, is an impulse to falsify—at best, a misunderstanding; at worst, an active deception. A more radical version of this thesis is advanced by Jacques Derrida, who claims that narrative itself lacks the coherence we wish it to contain, and that it therefore always sows the seeds of its own destruction. Narratives, he argues, are simultaneously a "possibility and [an] impossibility." The radically specific character of individual events "interrupt[s] the continuum of a narrative that nevertheless they call for."[20]

What these two critiques share is a sense of the underlying futility to narrative. White focuses on the disconnection between narrative and "real events," and Derrida on the instability within narrative itself. If this were the sole basis for their complaints, then we might safely dismiss them (as many have) with the common reply made to many postmodernists. Postmodernism, it is said, complains of the constructedness of things. But since, by its own account, such constructedness is unavoidable, its critique amounts to little more than a redescription, and its criteria can only be aesthetic. But for both White and Derrida, the formal critique of narrative leads to a further point. The flawed coherence of narrative, they argue, leads to an equally flawed moral authority. "The story is thus a trial [*procès*], the process of a trial. . . . [The characters] are *before the law*. . . . What we are saying here of the (narrated) story is also valid for the (narrating) narrative, for narration and textual dissemination in general," Derrida writes.[21] "Where in any account of reality, narrativity is present, we can be sure that morality or a moralizing impulse is present too," White says more simply.[22]

It is often pointed out that, aside from Derrida's vague references to "an entirely other text," postmodern critiques such as these offer no real alternative to the structures in which they poke holes.[23] Whatever flaws narrative representation may have, the rebuttal goes, no system of representation without similar flaws can really be imagined.[24] However cogent such responses may be (especially against cruder versions of these theories), they threaten to miss an important point. The claim is not merely a formal one but appears to have important political implications: if moral authority rests on a narrative endeavor that is ultimately futile, then that authority risks a parallel failure because of its own internal contradictions and "aporias." On this reading, the lack of an alternative becomes less a problem for postmodern theory than a further obstacle for any political theory seeking stability in narrative structure.

Although this proposition poses an interesting challenge for the sort of political theory described in this book, the attack (if that is what it is) falls short, I believe, for a series of interrelated reasons. First, it should be noted that this critique of narrative relies on a certain account of narrative that I took deliberate pains in Chapter 1 to avoid. One of my reasons there for preferring the hermeneutic account of narrative to that proposed by speech-act theorists like Alasdair MacIntyre was precisely that hermeneutics eschews the claim that narrative represents real events in the direct manner that White ascribes to all historical narration. If there is a general claim of hermeneutics, it is only that human *experience*, as such, seems universally to contain a temporal component—and that narrative description is the mode of representation that captures that experience (sometimes well, sometimes poorly). But I made no effort, nor does any seem necessary to me, to locate the source of that experience in some metaphysical account of time. Indeed, in Nietzsche, we find the suggestion that this experience has its roots in history, rather than in nature (although he asserts that history to be one all humans share, as the very mark of their humanity). But this does not lead, at least in Nietzsche's eyes, to a delegitimation of narrative. Indeed, it leads to a reauthorization and reinvigoration of narrative representation—with an avowedly political purpose. In other words, it is far from obvious that *all* forms of narrative carry implicit metaphysical claims of the kind White and Derrida decry, notwithstanding their claims to the contrary.[25] To narrativize means only to claim that humans, at this time, are memorious animals, experiencing life as never ceasing to be related to time.

To put this point another way: the virtues (and limitations) of narrative are political, not epistemological. It is not necessary to contest the postmodern claim of the fictitiousness of narrative to counter the further claim of its futility. Although narratives *may* often claim fidelity to events themselves, that is not, as the postmodernists imagine, the source of narrative's persuasiveness. The power of narrative, such as it is, resides in its ability to capture the experience of human existence in a way that logical deduction, say, cannot. It is the correspondence of narrative to *memory* (and the connection of the latter with identity) that lends narrative its (political) importance, not a correspondence to events themselves (whatever that might mean). If the correlation of narrative and memory is even plausible (and regardless of whether the source of that correlation is natural or historical) then the question of an underlying correspondence of narrative and reality is, from a political perspective, largely moot. Once the political weight of narrative as the best representation of human *experience* is felt (as I discuss in more detail in Chapter 7), political theory can flee from narrative only at its own peril, endangering the freedom of whomever it seeks to safeguard. Perhaps Derrida is right to maintain that all such narratives, in order to retain their coherence, must suppress differences or fail. (Every new memory, Nietzsche would happily admit, requires an obliteration—a partial forgetting—of the old.) But the point remains a formal one, subordinate politically to the implications of each narrative's content (i.e., to the question of *what* is suppressed in each case), unless the further charge (that narrative always contains an implicit and illegitimate moralizing) can be maintained in a strong way.

Here, it seems to me, a more fundamental problem in the postmodern argument emerges, one addressed by the contrast between reconciliation and redemption described above. More precisely, the charge seems to me to confuse narrative coherence with narrative closure and to mistake the effects of the latter for those of the former.

Both White and Derrida link narrative's moralizing quality to its ability to achieve closure. For White, this sense of closure is the feature of narrative discourse that distinguishes it from "annals" and "chronicles," forms of temporal representation that historians often designate as failed narratives.[26] Derrida makes a similar point in his discussion of a short anti-story by Maurice Blanchot that Derrida calls "counter-exemplary" precisely because, in rejecting narrative closure, it rejects "the law" that goes with it.[27] Indeed, Derrida lets Hegel's concept of time, with a necessary element of *telos*, stand in for a discussion of time in general.[28]

As powerful as these observations are, they do not seem to me to describe narrative as such, but merely one variety of it, the reconciliatory narrative. As the examples of Nietzsche and Locke demonstrate, narrative *coherence* does not necessarily require narrative closure. Both of these political theorists constructed narratives that are fundamentally open-ended, without being wholly indeterminate. Their rejection of narrative closure, that is, is never a rejection of narrative coherence or its value. This is not to say, of course, that Locke's and Nietzsche's narratives do not carry a moral, or quasi-moral component.[29] The question here, however, is whether their *form* as narratives carries a specific moral content.[30] But their narrative form does not even correspond to the template White and Derrida have marked out as characteristic of narrative as such. This does not preclude the conclusion that each form of narrative in some sense carries a value content. But once it is apparent that "narrative" as such has no single necessary form, and hence no single necessary content, the force of the complaint is considerably weakened. Narrative as such does not confine us morally, since our formal narrative options are multiple. It is open to us to reject the effects of closure without, as Derrida and White suggest by their examples, rejecting narrative altogether.[31] As apt as the conclusions of postmodernists about reconciliatory narratives may be, and as common as such narratives may be in fiction and historical writing, it is not really narrative as such of which they speak. The redemptive narratives of (some) political theory are clear enough evidence of that.

It bears noting here too (as elaborated in Chapter 7) that the redemptive narratives of political theory do not have a unified moral content, and certainly not a "good" one. We cannot, in a search for formal similarities, overlook the deep differences in content that were canvassed in the first four chapters of this book. If redemptive narrative offers a formal option that White and Derrida do not consider, this does not mean that the value of these stories is always the same or always positive. Rather than attributing an ultimate futility to narrative, then, we should consider it, not as a promise or guarantee, but as no less and no more than an opportunity. The discontents of the postmodern critics of narrative are answered, not by denying their critiques of metaphysics, but simply by acknowledging the phenomenological status of narrative, thereby depriving the metaphysical critique of its supposed political outcomes, while at the same time opening up new political possibilities.

Is human freedom to be found in the act of narration, then, and specifically in the redemptive narrative? Would that it were so easy. Human freedom is a rare and complex achievement, not to be reduced to anything that simple. At best, we might consider narrative to make a contribution to this achievement, and not in any single form, but in the very variety of its existence. Rather than equating narrative with freedom, then, or falling prey to the temptation to equate it with servitude, we might say that there are many types of narrative, and *hence* many types of human life.

So long as we have memories, we face the threat that they may subordinate us. The existence of many narratives serves as a baseline guarantee to our imagination (one that, troublingly, can be forgotten) that alternatives exist. Perhaps this is why Hobbes wrote, seemingly paradoxically, that "imagination and memory are but one thing." Imagination is not, as a simplistic romanticism would have it, a flight from memory, from what we know. Rather, it relies for its vibrancy on the richness and variety of memory, the very force that threatens to crush it. Short of amnesia, a complete and final escape from the danger of memory is, then, improbable—and probably as undesirable as the bump on the head that would deliver it. Narrative freedom, always threatened by memory, can, therefore, only be a relative thing and not a sovereign power. But insofar as we have the ability to narrate actively, to control the time of our lives, we have laid the groundwork for the larger achievement of human freedom in which our plots come to fruition. The independent act of narration is the first, necessary step in opposing those who would control our future by controlling our understanding of the past. Simply telling stories will not make us free; an inability to narrate, however, is an impediment that must be overcome on the path to freedom. It is a failure of imagination in the face of a singularly powerful memory.

If this independent act of imagination occurred only once, though, it would be as if it were not done at all. In this case, the prison would merely be one of our own construction. Human freedom cannot be found in any single, best narrative, but must begin from manifold plots. Redemption and reconciliation both represent powerful efforts to take control of human time, but the very ambition of the latter may prove to be self-defeating, as Hegel's effort was. Reconciliation is an act of imagination that discourages further imagination. As Locke put it in his discussion of religious enthusiasm, it is "to tyrannize over one's own mind."

Reconciliation and redemption, I have been arguing, are not compatible. These are the two possible attitudes toward time that have presented themselves to us, the former through Hegel and Heidegger, the latter through Locke and Nietzsche. Who chooses to attempt a redemption must accept an unreconciled existence, one with loose ends and sharp edges. One gives up the sense of an ending, the good feeling of narrative closure that comes with reconciliation. One gives up, without guarantees for the future, a sense of time that feels solid. One gives up "the freedom to reveal what is" for the unpromising freedom to remember, and imagine, what is not. Both ways, it should be said, are superior to the dishonesty of forgetting (discussed in Chapter 7). My sense is, however, that to attempt redemption is the human thing to do, while reconciliation, its search for perfection, is for beasts and gods.

CHAPTER 7

The Politics of Memory

And time will not fail; for it is always at a beginning.
—Aristotle, *Physics*

At the very center of Mexico City lies its Zócalo, that vast square that has stood at the middle of a culture for something like seven hundred years. An enormous national flag flies overhead from an enormous flagpole. To one side, one may spy the grand national palace next to the ruins of the Great Temple of the Aztecs. And the visitor may remember, at that moment, what Nietzsche wrote, that for a temple to be erected a temple must be destroyed.

Walking past the drilling soldiers into the stony palace, one comes upon the powerful murals of Diego Rivera that cover the interior walls. There are no guards. There are no crowds. There is no glass. You can walk right up to the murals. You can touch them.

Stepping around the inner court, this is what you see: each arch holds a different moment in the history of Mexico. It is a tale of decline and redemption. From the simple, idyllic life of the pre-Columbian cultures, it passes to the destruction of their civilization by conquistadors depicted as demons. Later moments hold the recapture of Mexican autonomy in the nineteenth-century war of independence from Spain and the democratic achievement contained in the presidency of Benito Juárez. Full redemption comes through the Mexican revolution of the 1910s. It is a tale told simply but not simplistically. The church is a lackey to the conquistadors but individual churchmen are not. The pictures celebrate Mexico's Indian heritage but also the industrial power of the country's modern working class, who are taken to be a motor of revolution. In short, the pictures are Rivera's attempt to give back to the country a story of itself, a narrative representation of itself, its past, its historical inheritance, which the previous regime, in its attempt to make Mexico a European country, had stolen from the populace. Where U.S. monuments tend to carve the words of speeches and documents or the names of the dead into their walls, Rivera painted pictures of the past. Like Hegel, he believed that representation of the past could be beautiful; like Locke, he believed it could be revolutionary. The last panel (starring "Carlos" Marx) is called "Mexico's Future."

The murals of the Mexican national palace argue in the same manner as the political philosophies this inquiry has explored: not from premise to conclusion but from past to future. There is not a single, rising crescendo of reason from beginning to end, but a flow of events: accomplishments, setbacks, reversals of fortune, and long, quiet interludes. There is not a single sort of human being, but a cast of characters: a few simply good or venal, but most more complicated than that. What looks good at one time, to one character (e.g., the Catholic church) may seem very different from another side or another point in the narrative. But the lack of a single thread of reason that runs the length of the history does not mean that the narrative lacks coherence. Time does not provide a natural meaning or coherence to events, but the work of a narrator can. That is precisely where the efforts of an artist like Rivera or a political theorist like Locke, Nietzsche, or Hegel lie: they hammer the disparate elements of history into a coherent account. And they do so, not out of an antiquarian concern for the past, but from a deep concern for the future. They address politics not through the morals, but through the memories of its participants. "[T]he strength of the thread does not reside in the fact that some one fibre runs through its whole length, but in the overlapping of many fibres," Wittgenstein writes.[1] Political theorists fashion just such a rope with which to pull us into the future. Their work is necessary just because there exists no natural fiber that runs the whole distance. The coherence of memory is the result of human effort. Time has its threads, but without a sharp tug of a hand to twist them into a line, they would merely lie about. I have discussed political theories generally taken to belong to different "schools" in an attempt to emphasize a common element: they all recall, refigure, and retell the past in an attempt to discuss the present and future. In their structure, they all recognize the necessary link between Gauguin's three nonquestions: "Where do we come from[?] What are we[?] Where are we going[?]." They are all plotters—even if the term resonates slightly differently in each case.

Between the Twin Dangers of Memory

Memory is a political resource, but it is not without its dangers. Nietzsche in particular was sensitive to the burden that memory, as a whole, could pose to its bearer even as it formed the basis for a possible future. And if it is Rivera whose work puts one in mind of a Hegelian temple, then it is Jorge Luis Borges who calls attention to these Nietzschean worries, most acutely in his story "Funes, the Memorious."[2] In this story, Borges describes a man, "an untamed and vernacular Zarathustra" he calls him, who becomes unable to forget any experience or perception. Before the accident that caused this condition, "he had been—like any Christian—blind, deaf-mute, somnambulistic, memoryless."[3] Funes sees his new state as a boon, but the narrator does not find it so. Funes hardly notices that his condition is linked to a physical paralysis so complete that he has not left his house since the accident. Moreover, the narrator describes a certain mental paralysis: "To think is to forget a difference, to generalize, to abstract. In the overly replete world of Funes there were nothing but details, almost contiguous details." Ultimately, this burden suffocates Funes, and soon after the accident that perfected his memory, he dies of "congestion."[4] If reimagining the past is a necessary step toward remaking the future, a too-perfect fixation on the past results in absolute passiveness. This is the structural threat (as opposed to the many particular ones) that confronts any political theory that considers the past. It is the reason I do *not* conclude that a concern for the past is a priori a virtue in a study of politics, but rather that Hegel, the most "memorious" of philosophers, has sketched a role for us that bears a frightening resemblance to that of Funes. However beautiful Hegel's memories, they threaten to suffocate us in their completeness and detail. When our whole life is memory, we have no life at all. Borges helps us to imagine this prison-house of memory.

And yet, if we were to ignore the question of memory in politics, if we were simply to consider the association a tainted one, we would risk other dangers just as great. Not only would we deprive some individuals of their voices, we would leave the field open to others to manipulate history to their own ends. Memory is hardly likely to be neutral in politics: if it does not liberate, it may confine. If the mental congestion of a Funes represents one extreme of memory—its utter immobility—then the dark fantasy of George Orwell's *1984* may describe the opposite end of the spectrum: the complete fluidity and manipulability of memory.

To the "Inner Party" of Orwell's novel, political domination is assured through the unceasing manipulation of the popular memory. When the Party adopts an interpretation of the past, all traces of alternative accounts are eradicated from the historical register by a painstaking revision of the entire documentary record. The purpose of this constant policing of the past is simple: to deny the populace an alternative path of thought. By fixing a single account of the past, the Party means to guarantee a single path in the future—namely, the continued authority of the Party itself. Without even the possibility of a counternarrative, the pseudo-citizens of this novel are unable to imagine an alternative to the political situation in which they exist. It is no coincidence, then, that Orwell's failed rebel character works in the ministry where historical records are constantly revised. Although he is already too much a prisoner of the Party to be able to think outside it, he at least sees the hypocrisy of the historical manipulation. He loses what faith in the system he has when he disbelieves the authenticity of the narrative on which it is based. But without an alternative story, he is easily crushed. One lesson of Orwell's novel is that control of the past is one of the most powerful weapons available to those who would control the future. If we leave control of the past in the hands of others, or assume our immunity from its effects, we shall ultimately find ourselves under the authority of a narrator we have not chosen. History and memory are topics that political philosophy flees only at great peril to itself and to political practice.

These two fictions are extreme. But they dramatize the two extreme dangers of the politics of memory: the urge to remember everything and the urge to remember nothing. Neither pole, they seem to say, would be completely human—although both are well within the capacities of the human race. Philosophers have often remarked, following Aristotle, that to be human means to live between the beasts and the gods. One element of this, we might add, is our status between total recall and total amnesia. We are neither memoryless cows in the pasture nor all-remembering muses, and we should not seek to be either. Yet to live in the middle is only to avoid the structural dangers represented, perhaps, by Hegel on the one hand and Nietzsche's cud-chewing herd on the other. Particular memories may still liberate or oppress on a less universal scale. As Locke well knew, the politics of memory may still have its local dangers, even apart from the Last Man or the Temple of Mnemosyne.

Political theorists, then, have not fled from the topics of history and memory—even if some interpreters have made it seem so. Since this is one of the main points I have tried to make over the course of the book, it may be of some use at this juncture, to summarize what the results of each of these investigations has been.

In the work of John Locke, I have argued, there is an account of history that makes use of a vocabulary of labor, money, markets, and contracts—a spiritual economism that finds both God and man always at work. With these terms, Locke gives his readers an account of political authority from the Creation to the present day. In the first of the *Two Treatises of Government*, Locke disputes the rival narrative of Filmer, given in the language of Genesis and Anglican theology. But in the second treatise, Locke gives us a history in his own terms. There are several stages: a pastoral scene of isolated labor; a second period where money furthers production and commerce but also engenders social conflict of a new type; and a third stage where government is instituted to secure the moneyed economy and the society of property rights. And from there Locke's story continues across the generations with the institution of a new testament between them that passes on political authority in the form of a legal inheritance. The tale of government's decline then becomes a story of the abuse of this contract, of an abuse of the very words and language that make it up. And the revolution that this abuse eventually engenders is not meant to create a new government out of whole cloth, but to reclaim an inheritance that has been held in trust, and then abused, by the current authorities.

Locke views the connection between past and future as a matter of contract. The main question his plot raises for the future is whether the contract will be kept or broken. Whereas Nietzsche at times seems to offer a panoply of futures, Locke's fork in the road has the virtue of its concreteness. His two futures both seem eminently plausible, and the political choices open to his readers are clear-cut. Locke's offer of only two futures may seem to us a minimal sort of openness, but it has a sense of reality to it that few political philosophers can match. In any case, Locke's preference for a future where contracts are kept is clear enough; the real ground of the debate with his opponents is not the future but the past. The topic Locke debated with Filmer (and that revolutionaries debated with monarchists) was whether the history of political authority located ultimate dominion with the people or the rulers. Locke's revolutionary political theory rests on his history of political authority. The future he urges only makes sense as a continuation of the plot he established in his reassessment of the past. That is to say, his narrative is central to his philosophy.

Narrative is as clearly on the surface of Hegel's philosophy as it is submerged in Locke. The implications of this, however, are not often well understood. I have argued that the history Hegel sketches in his lectures on the philosophy of history must be understood through the lens of his aesthetics as outlined in his lectures on the history of fine arts. There Hegel gives an account of beauty as a kind of wholeness arising out of form and content. This account not only grounds the evaluations that take place in the historical narrative; they lend that story its ultimate point. The history Hegel sketches falls into three large stages: the Symbolic, the Classical, and the Romantic. They are arrayed on an ascending ladder of beauty that is also the direction of the flow of time. But it is the beauty of the whole spectacle, and not merely of the last stage, that is supposed to enrapture us and reconcile us to our history. This desire for a kind of wholeness in human history robs Hegel's narrative of the possibility of a future in its search for completion in the past. And this lack of a future leaves Hegel's readers with only the philosophical perspective, the absolute present, from which to contemplate history or themselves. Hegel's account of history as integral to human nature winds up removing humanity from the narrative to which he has tried to wed it. Alasdair MacIntyre was thus wrong in detail (although quite correct in spirit) to write: "History is neither a prison nor a museum."[5] It may be both at once if we (following Hegel) ever love the past so much that, like Narcissus, we lose our future in admiration of our present self-image.

This tension between future and absolute present is the ultimate point of Nietzsche's narrative, and he reaches it by means quite different from those of Locke or Hegel. Nietzsche's discussion of dreams, artistry, and perception leads ultimately to a vocabulary of violence and interpretation. These two terms are inseparably paired in Nietzsche's way of thinking because they are deeply connected in his account of human history. Character does not ground plot; nor does plot ground character. These two elements are merely the two sides of a coin whose entirety is the historical narrative. The narrative Nietzsche gives in *On the Genealogy of Morals* has as its subject nothing less than the creation of memory and the historical consciousness itself, which is to say, the creation of human nature as we know it today.

Echoing the structure of Zoroastrian history, Nietzsche divides the world's history into four periods: our animal prehistory, the period of "the morality of mores," the "Christian-moral" era, and the future. The three periods of the past are characterized by their pattern of increasing violence, pain, and cruelty, but also by a corresponding increase in the depth of the human soul and the human capacity for discipline and creation. He portrays the present as a special time, when the increasing memory that humanity has been accumulating harbors both the prospect of a great future, "even beyond the Greeks," and the threat of an eternal present, which will effectively return human beings to the animal state whence they came.

Nietzsche responds to the question of what our future will be with an even larger question: are we to have a future at all? The set of options he offers is, in its own way, even starker than Locke's. Freedom or submission was the choice of futures Locke offered. But even Filmerian slavery, we can imagine, might have its limits. In Nietzsche's terms, if we make the wrong choice, we arrive at the realm of the Last Man. Here there are no possibilities, only a seamless, meaningless set of pleasures: memory will relieve the mind of the need for thought. The eternal present is the ultimate closure of narrative. If it is not too nonsensical to say so, Nietzsche's narrative is its own subject, and the possibility of its own continuance is its central concern. Nietzsche pictures the story in the figure of Zarathustra to help us see this: his success is that he lives to see another day. Indeed, in becoming a sun unto himself, he is assured that his day will never end. More than any particular future, it is the openness of the future in general that Nietzsche sees as threatened. Not only is redemption of the past in the future not premised on reconciliation with that past, redemption may actually require the absence of such a reconciliation. Once we are reconciled to the past, we no longer seek the future.

If these three theorists are linked by their concern for the future, Nietzsche is set apart by his concern for the future *as such*. This is the reason why, as I indicated in Chapter 1, Nietzsche was the inspiration for this study as much as a subject of it. It is his narrative that suggests *why* the connectedness of Gauguin's three questions feels so natural to us. It suggests why, in questions of human identity, we are drawn to questions of history and time. Whatever answer we may venture to the question of what we are, or (I think it better to say) of *who* we are, depends on all three moments of time: past, present, and future. To be fully human, Nietzsche counsels, we need all three. In recognizing this, he is unlike Hegel, who, preoccupied with past and present, empties the future of all significance. Locke, for his part, fears what the future may bring—but only Nietzsche feels the excruciating pressure of being between past and future.

The Politics of Memory

Apart from helping us understand the efforts of political theorists to grapple with time, an exploration of history and narrative in philosophy offers something more prosaic, but perhaps extremely useful. It gives us some comprehension of a phenomenon I gestured at in the Introduction and at the beginning of this chapter: those political battles over the meaning of history whose importance is easy to feel but hard to describe in the normal terms we use to talk about politics. What I say here about politics is only intended as something partial and suggestive; it is my belief, however, that an understanding of the narrative qualities of political theory yields insights as well into politics more broadly construed. Another example may serve to make this category more concrete:

The revolutions of 1989 in eastern Europe had many causes, but in the case of Hungary, there was one precursor that was particularly remarkable: a public debate that took place, early in that year, between the communist government, then still in power, and nascent dissident groups over "the meaning of 1956."[6] The debate began when a reformist government official announced that the events of 1956, previously termed a "counterrevolution" by the government, had been reevaluated by a historical commission as a "popular uprising." Large segments of the Communist party immediately denounced this new terminology, and opposition groups simultaneously rushed to defend it. The issue consumed the media, and the communists were so torn by it that a meeting of the Central Committee had to be called to settle the question. For the opposition, the political import of this debate was obvious. One leading dissident explained why: "the Party's [historical] assessment is important. This is because if the 1956 uprising was counter-revolutionary, its achievements such as the multiparty system and neutrality [i.e., withdrawal from the Warsaw Pact] are thus also counter-revolutionary."[7]

Ultimately, the new interpretation of history prevailed, and Hungary moved forward into a multiparty system. History, in this case, was both battlefield and weapon. Liberalizers attacked what they took to be historical distortions with a narrative of their own; conservatives appeared paralyzed by a hidden memory they could not acknowledge without destroying their own legitimacy. Their hypocrisy lent an air of unreality to the proceedings.

For us, the importance of the debate is its peculiar form, rather than its particular outcome. In its unusual baldness, it revealed elements of the political process that are common, but unfamiliar. The connections between history and politics are often subterranean, like the system of wires and pipes beneath a great city. Their eruption onto the surface, in this case, was brief, if intense. But the "events of 1956" could only have had the effect they did in 1989 if the connections between history and politics were of a deep and long-standing nature. The necessity of such historical wrangling to *both* sides in this event signals the importance of narrative self-understanding to the political process. Memory, rather than the abstract merits of a social system, was the ultimate power in this debate. As much as the virtues of capitalism, it was the memory of 1956 that threatened, and ultimately overwhelmed, communist rule.

Whether it is Hungarians struggling to recover the meaning of 1956 or Americans arguing over the meaning of 1776, the question is the same: whether and how the past is to be redeemed or reconciled. If nothing else, our long examination of the philosophy of history can yield this insight into ordinary politics: the past is important to politics because it stands ready to be redeemed. If left unredeemed, it can haunt a regime like a spirit, but a heavy one, which can ultimately break the back of those, like the Hungarian communists, who deny it.

Like any ghost, the presence of the past is hard to detect by scientific means, but easily felt by the specter's descendants. Outsiders often have difficulty understanding what all the fuss is about, but family members never do. The everyday politics of memory needs to be understood as an attempt to deal with these specters. These moments of political debate over history are not atavistic episodes. They are attempts to redeem the dead—or to exorcise them. Our understanding of politics is not improved if we label such historical politics symbolic and then dismiss it as a lower form of human behavior— as if narrowing debate to those interests that can be quantified showed an advance in our rationality! Such politics deals with a common element of the human condition—our constant struggle with time. It is Nietzsche who describes the burden memory places on us, and who, in so doing, helps us to understand the politics of memory.

Debates over the meaning of history cannot be exorcised from politics— nor would politics be improved if this were somehow possible. Understanding the politics of memory will be crucial for understanding the sources of political authority so long as human beings are memorious animals. Memory is contentious because it contributes directly to a sense of identity. It is contentious as well because it is flexible, open to revision, modification, improvement, even poiēsis. It is also subject to manipulation, fraud, degradation, exploitation, and sheer coercive power. The emotional appeal of the politics of memory has always been easy to sense, if not to explain. What I hope to have accomplished by this point is to have given a greater understanding of this phenomenon and to have examined some of its potential and its dangers. It has also been my goal to establish how, as politics or philosophy, working on memory is merely work in a different register from work on abstract reason or natural rights—neither higher nor lower, merely different. The politics of memory is dangerous stuff—but the politics of reason and rights, despite many claims on its behalf, has proven equally dangerous. And, as noted above, we flee from the politics of memory, I believe, at our own peril. Whoever abandons work on memory to others may find themselves imprisoned by the results.

Human beings fight over history because they conceive their pasts to be an essential part of who they are. And they are right.

It appears to me one of the main virtues of political theory that it struggles against the sense of "throwness" emphasized by a variety of writers. The feeling that we are prisoners of a history not of our making is not merely something that Hegel and Heidegger were prone to. I venture that it is a very common feeling among all people. It can be fought against in many ways but none more important than in the sort of political theory exemplified by Locke and Nietzsche. They do not accept the terms of the history that their heritage handed down to them. They are "rebels rebellare," as Locke had it, against a tyranny of time.

Locke faced a tradition that reckoned time from the Creation, and, correspondingly, reckoned authority from the parentage of Adam. When he saw that this resulted in tyrannical monarchy, he responded, not merely with a challenge to the king's authority, but by undermining the entire history on which that authority was based. He rewrote history so that it contained episodes of contract rather than parentage.

Seeing the Last Man as the end point of such a story, Nietzsche, in turn, made war on the very notion of progress that Locke outlined. His genealogy set out to recover a greater span of time, perhaps, than did Locke's treatise; but the two efforts are similar in that they both reject the history they have been given. They do not accept that humans are merely thrown into their time without a capacity to alter it. Although they acknowledge the sense of history into which they were born, they struggle against it. They struggle to redeem what would remain unrecovered in history if they had left well enough alone. They struggle to alter the future by recovering some part of the past that has been suppressed or ignored.

Nothing requires us to reexamine the past as it is handed down to us. Indeed, there will always be those who prefer that we refrain from looking into it too carefully. The Pilate-like individual can always wash his hands of the past and say that it is not his concern. All the more reason then, to credit the political theorist who accepts the ugly past in order to redeem it. To plot in the manner of political theory means to take up the challenge of altering the connection between past and future, thereby taking responsibility for both. Nietzsche accepts that he is descended from beasts and cowards in order to give birth to something else—a "dancing star." Birth is not something that just happens to us, as Heidegger makes it out to be. It is something over which we can exert control, if only we plot to do so.

Locke's history may seem less ugly to us than Nietzsche's genealogy, but in its own way it accepts quite a lot of unhandsome conditions. Rather than describing political authority as something God-given, Locke describes a historical actor who is profoundly fallen. Locke's man has little guidance from God, and less from the Bible, on how to organize the state. Locke accepts, then, a highly diminished man and a disenchanted past in order to extricate that man from royal tyranny. His plot is also one of redemption, although certainly on a smaller scale than that of Nietzsche.

The political theorists I have discussed are preoccupied with history and with presenting an alternate account of it. Yet because they are all modern, Western authors, we ought at least to consider the possibility that their concern is one local to postmedieval European culture. There is more than a little to be said for this view; several cultural critics have diagnosed the "sense of history" as a peculiarly modern outlook, which has grown in intensity in the past few centuries.

In *The Past Is a Foreign Country*, David Lowenthal has made an exhaustive attempt to document the increasing concern for the past among all segments of European and American societies in recent centuries. His examples run from intellectual discussions of history to the increasing popular interest in "antiques" and the movement for the "preservation" of historical sites—the last two of which are wholly modern phenomena.[8] If his characterization of Western culture is unconvincing on the broadest levels (that modernity just *is* more historical), he at least succeeds in conveying the sense that the modern industrialized nations are concerned about their pasts in *ways* that are new.[9] Concern with history has taken forms, like the preservation movement, that are themselves unknown to history.[10]

Although Lowenthal offers little in the way of reasons to explain the rising historical consciousness of Europeans, others have attempted to do so. Reinhart Koselleck, for one, has argued that an increasing attachment to the past has come as Europeans have felt themselves further separated from it.[11] In this view, the concept of progress that accompanied the Enlightenment and Industrial Revolution shattered a sense of the unity of past and future that is said to have previously held sway in the European consciousness. Without an idea of progress, Koselleck holds, one expects the future to be much like the past. While one might then use the past to describe the future in a general way, nonetheless there is little reason to value the past *as past*, since whatever it contained will likely reappear in things to come. Only with the discovery of "progress," of the idea that the future would be different from the past, was there sparked an interest in the past itself. Thus, on Koselleck's account, the historical consciousness of Europe is a highly contingent phenomenon, dependent on rapidly evolving technology and an accompanying idea of progress.

In addition to this evidence, we have examples of other cultures that seem to take the past less seriously. Some Native American languages do not distinguish in tense between present and past. In his discussion of medieval annals, Hayden White has suggested that their parataxis can be attributed to a lack of connection, in the outlook of their authors, between present and past. He has also suggested that this may even be a more "objective" rendering of events than the narratives of modern historians—because no narratively based meaning has been projected onto the bare events.[12] Can it be, then, that the sense of history I have identified in political theory is, historically speaking, a local phenomenon? Is the concern with time and memory somehow a reflection of modern European social conditions and little more?

While I think that these concerns are valid and serve to warn us away from a certain kind of forced existentialism (e.g., "Everyone *must* always be concerned with past and future"), I think it would be an odd argument that it was a concern for time that separated modern Western philosophy from other worldviews. Modern culture is usually assailed for its excessive rationalism, not its concern for history. Indeed, it is primarily its disdain for time, philosophers have argued, that sets philosophy apart from the "myths," "tales," or "theologies" of other cultures. One of the purposes of this study has been to stress that this separation has not been as great as some would like to believe. But it would be a strange reversal indeed if we were suddenly to learn that ancient, medieval, or non-Western cultures were bastions of abstraction, unconcerned with time and memory.

It would also, I think, be at variance with the evidence. At present there is a small cottage industry concerned with the universality of story-telling. If anything, we are awash in a sea of claims about the global reach of narrative and the harkening of every group to it.[13] If one cares to seek it out, narrative can appear to be everywhere. Even in the oldest writing, it can seem, the urge to tell a story is universal.[14] It would be just as easy to say that the urge to narrate is simply "natural," and that a concern for time is something elementally human as it would be to claim the opposite—that the historical consciousness is a late-Western epiphenomenon.

I hope it will not seem too soggy a compromise if I conclude that something can be learned from each of these views, and that we are not, in the end, required to choose between them. What those who stress the role of narrative succeed in establishing, to my mind, is that every culture grapples, to some extent, with the question of time. The problem of time is endemic to the human condition, and no individual, culture, or civilization has been or will be exempted from answering it. The reasons for this we can only guess, although we have Nietzsche's speculations to guide us. Nevertheless, we may say, *what* that answer will be is in no sense predetermined and may differ widely from place to place and time to time. It may even be that the modern European sense of time is significantly different from that which came before it and places noticeably more weight on the past than previous Western and non-Western culture(s) did.

But even if this much is true, the investigations of this book at least demonstrate the wide variety of temporal conceptions possible within the modern period—as well as the centrality of questions of history to each of the philosophers I discuss. The answers that these philosophers give to the question of time are all quite different, even if the question is central to each of them. Whether one takes a concern with the past to be a natural impulse or a cultural artifact, either way, the content of an individual *answer* to the question of time is not predetermined. And if, following Orwell, we agree that the question of history is a serious, political question, then it will be the content of these answers that concerns us above all.

What Future Has Memory?

It was once believed that dreams were about the future. What was to come revealed itself only in the clear, although elusive, images of the night. Since Freud, we have all thought that dreams are about the past—every animistic idea of the way sin haunts its doer has found expression in psychoanalysis. It was Freud's genius to turn our ideas around on this subject so completely—to *return* us to a primitive idea of haunting in the guise of a modern science. But every true oneiromancer has always known that dreams *connect* past and future rather than separating them. That is the condition that makes interpretation possible. Dreams are *comprehensible* because they take place in terms of the past. They are *interesting* because they foretell events to come.

In the Introduction, I made reference to the etymological connection between words such as *narration* and *knowledge*. I have tried to stress, in my analysis of three philosophies, how an account of self-knowledge is fundamentally linked to an account of time. This emphasis is intended to parallel the connection between narrative and political identity, which I have discussed by way of a few real-world examples, meant merely to indicate where interesting links between politics and philosophy may be found: the two overlap insofar as each is concerned with memory—where narrative time is contained. The philosopher's knowledge and the citizen's have a common form in narrative. Because of this common form, it may be possible for the philosopher to pass on something of his knowledge to the citizen—but there is nothing certain about this.

Political theory may hatch a plot, but no one can be forced to join it. It may succeed or it may fail. As much as we would like to imagine that plots such as Locke's or that of the Hungarian dissidents must succeed because historical truth is on their side, we must acknowledge that it is easy enough to imagine a world in which they fail. Certainly, many others with plots equally noble have failed and will fail again. Baser plots often win out. But political theory at least offers us the tools to struggle with the tyrants, and the tyranny, of time. It allows us to imagine a future in which the past stands redeemed. And whether we join plots hatched by those long dead or choose to hatch our own, in either case, we do not accept our past as simply a given (whether as a heritage, a tradition, or a paradigm), although we do accept the power of the past in a general way.

Politics about the future is the politics of memory. If a polity is divided about its future, it is probably also at odds about its past. Such was the case when Locke disputed Filmer; such was the case in Hungary a few years ago; such may be our case today. There is nothing unhealthy about this. Indeed, in Nietzsche's view, it is a redescription of the past that defeats the *ressentiment* fueled by the irreversibility of time. Although we are not accustomed to thinking in these terms, the politics of plot and counterplot may be the most open of all. What *would* be unhealthy, though, is an attempt to deny the relevance of the past for the present and future. Attempts to divorce politics from history and argue about the future as if the past were a blank slate result only in a posture of willful amnesia amidst a community of stories. There is always the threat that history will enslave us; but if anything, we increase the threat when we attempt to deny the role of narrative in politics.

In the introduction to *Between Past and Future*, Hannah Arendt discusses a fragmentary story that Kafka left in his notes. It concerns a man caught on a line between two antagonists, one pushing him forward, the other pushing him back. Arendt interprets this parable as a general one for the human condition between past and future and the desire to leap off the fighting line as "the old dream which Western metaphysics has dreamed from Parmenides to Hegel" of a realm independent of time. But, in using this story as a metaphor for modern thought, she describes our thinking as a "diagonal force," the sum of the two vectors of past and future pushing in on the man. In so doing, I think, she deliberately skips over one crucial sentence in Kafka's note. Without it, we would only be prisoners of time: "For it is not only the two antagonists who are there, but he himself as well, and who really knows his intentions?"[15]

Here, at least, Arendt perhaps too closely follows Heidegger's contention that our only authentic choice is "the repetition of a possibility of existence that has been." Although she adds the force of the future to that of the past, still, in this parable, both forces push on the individual from the outside, as it were, as objective forces the direction of which cannot be altered. But if the force of the past reaches us through memory, then every repetition of it is a *re*membering and *re*collecting, an opportunity to reshape it and rework it. For better or for worse, then (and we cannot hide from the fact that this may equally be an opportunity to whitewash and prettify), there is no way to tell what may yet become a part of memory.

A concern for history and one's place in it need never be an abdication of individuality or individual responsibility. We exist in time but are not simply of it. That we are always struggling with time and history is proof enough of that. For Kafka, the past and future pressure us, but *we* are there to be pressured. What freedom we possess lies in this act of repetition or remembering. We can remake the past even as it is making us. That is why the past never finally determines us. And that is why Kafka goes out of his way to emphasize that the individual remains present, in the present, to struggle with these two forces, free in the sense that his intentions cannot be known, and free only *because* those intentions are not reducible to a fixed past or future. For this reason, we can never predict what free, redemptive action would look like. In such a situation, every one must speak for himself or herself.

Here we might revisit Aristotle's notion of narrative in order (immodestly) to suggest some improvements. In addition to his comments on the structure of narrative (discussed in the Introduction), Aristotle also made a claim about the relative importance of plot and character. Drama, he says, is essentially composed of actions. Plot is, therefore, essential to drama, while character is not. "Tragedy," he writes, "is an imitation not of men but of action and life" (*Poetics* 1450a). It is doubtful whether this conclusion about the centrality of plot holds true of drama; it is certainly not true of life. So long as Kafka's man remains on the fighting line, caught between past and future, then there will always be some element of character to push on the plot, even as the plot is pushing on the character. If plot is more basic than character, we are truly prisoners of time. But whether the pushing of a Locke or a Nietzsche succeeds or fails, its very existence, it seems to me, is enough to prove that there *is* a person there, on the fighting line, struggling with past and future, memory and hope. Many, perhaps, will let themselves be pushed around by time, but there is nothing essential about it. We simply cannot say how many will fight and how many will resign themselves to their throwness.

In the end, I think, we need both Locke and Nietzsche: the latter to dream in technicolor, the former to see only waking life, and to see it in shades of gray. We need the one's rebelliousness and the other's time sense. Both qualities contribute to our sense of plot. We need Nietzsche's sensitivity to the role of history and narrative in politics, combined with Locke's close attention to actual political choices and forces. And if Nietzsche occasionally tempts us to retreat into a solo story of ourselves, we must recall Locke's willingness to engage in real-life revolutionary plots when he felt the narrative had gone awry. At the time, his partners were condemned as traitors. But Locke's written plot triumphed even after the cloak-and-dagger one failed— and the efforts of his friends were redeemed, and today are called patriotic. And so they were.

In this light, we might want to take note of an incident and rhyme Walter Benjamin reports about the 1848 revolution in France. Apparently, on the first night, "it turned out that the clocks in towers were being fired upon simultaneously and independently from several places in Paris. An eye-witness . . . wrote as follows":

> Qui le croirait! on dit, qu'irrités contre l'heure
> De nouveaux Josués au pied de chaque tour,
> Tiraient sur les cadrans pour arrêter le jour.

> Who would have believed it! it is said that new
> Joshuas at the foot of every tower, as though
> angered with time, fired at the dials in order to
> stop the day.[16]

Reference Matter

Notes

Introduction

1. Goldwater, *Gauguin*, pp. 110–15. The events described took place in December 1897. The painting is now owned by the Boston Museum of Fine Arts. Despite Gauguin's protest, the questions are invariably used as its title.

2. White, "The Value of Narrativity in the Representation of Reality," in *On Narrative*, ed. Mitchell, p. 1.

3. I explain my use of the terms *history*, *narrative*, *memory*, and *time* later in this Introduction.

4. The term *historicism* has been used in a variety of ways. I employ it here to indicate the view that human beings are *in some sense* historical creatures, as opposed to the view that we are *merely* creatures of history.

5. At the end of *Politics and Vision*, which explores the concept of space in the history of political theory, Sheldon Wolin suggests a similar project for the concept of time. While the scope of this project is more circumscribed, it does, in some sense, attempt to take up this challenge.

6. Gadamer, "The Universality of the Hermeneutical Problem," in *Philosophical Hermeneutics*, p. 9.

7. Gadamer, *Truth and Method*, p. 432.

8. Gadamer, *Philosophical Hermeneutics*, p. 15.

9. In making this statement, I do not mean to be passing judgment on the history of hermeneutic philosophy. This is not the place for a history of hermeneutics, and I cannot pretend to offer one. Rather, I use Heidegger as a jumping-off point for a discussion of certain issues because he seems to me to have encapsulated and restated certain trends in the hermeneutic tradition in their most powerful form. In this, Heideg-

ger was building on the work of his teacher, Edmund Husserl. Prior to the work of Husserl, the most sophisticated treatment of hermeneutics, that of Wilhelm Dilthey, suggested that there were two broad modes of human inquiry, one hermeneutic, the other empirical. Dilthey took hermeneutics to ground the humanities, and empiricism to ground the sciences. Husserl tried to grasp all of human experience within a hermeneutic model, believing that this would ground knowledge, in a way that his inheritors did not accept. See his *The Crisis of the European Sciences and Transcendental Phenomenology* (1936; Evanston, Ill.: Northwestern University Press, 1970).

10. Heidegger, "Being and Time: Introduction," in *Basic Writings*, p. 61.

11. Indeed, debates about interpreting the "cruel and unusual" clause in the Constitution generally center on the question of what time period ought to be used as a frame of reference, the colonial or the contemporary. If anything, this debate highlights the importance of a sense of time to the question of definitions.

12. Heidegger, "Being and Time: Introduction," in *Basic Writings*, p. 64.

13. Gadamer, *Truth and Method*, p. 273.

14. In addition to the writings of Heidegger and Gadamer, see also Ricoeur, *Time and Narrative*, and Carr, *Time, Narrative and History*. And see, too, the discussion of identity and narrative in Arendt, *Human Condition*, ch. 5, which she acknowledged to be indebted to Heidegger.

15. MacIntyre, *After Virtue*, p. 205. The discussion that follows centers on ch. 15 of MacIntyre's book.

16. Ibid., p. 211.

17. Ibid., p. 220.

18. This is not to say that they are not guilty of the sort of hubris to which MacIntyre has rightly called our attention.

19. This is beginning to change. For a more detailed discussion of the secondary literature on Locke, see Part I.

20. Here I am drawing somewhat freely on Frank Kermode's account of narrative secrets. See his "Secrets and Narrative Sequence," in *On Narrative*, ed. Mitchell, pp. 79–97.

21. As a secondary and related purpose, I hope that the analysis may make some contribution to the debate on the relation of John Locke to U.S. political culture. Although the theory of "Lockean consensus" was based on an optimism about U.S. politics that is probably irretrievable, it still makes some sense, I believe, to consider the connection of Locke to the principles of the founding generation. My interpretation of Locke may make that link more tenable precisely by bringing to light a side of this philosopher that, in our overfamiliarity with him, we often overlook. From this perspective, his profile may appear more similar to those of the American revolutionaries than recent commentators have been willing to admit. All these purposes, then, will be served only if I can establish the centrality of narrative to Locke's political stance. See my essay "Between History and Nature: Social Contract Theory in Locke and the Founders," *Journal of Politics* (Nov. 1996).

22. See, e.g., Ricoeur, *Time and Narrative*, 1: 32–51; Victor Turner in *On Narrative*, ed. Mitchell, p. 147; White, "Value of Narrativity," pp. 20–22.

23. See Kermode, *Sense of an Ending.*

24. Wittgenstein, *Philosophical Investigations*, § 438.

25. As we shall see, however, Locke's activity demonstrates that a person may have more than a single role in politics, that of political theorist being only one.

26. In the twentieth century, of course, dramatists such as Samuel Beckett and Luigi Pirandello deliberately tried to frustrate their audiences in this way.

27. Here I draw loosely on Gadamer's essay "On the Natural Inclination of Human Beings Toward Philosophy," in *Reason in the Age of Science.*

Chapter 1

1. For the former, see Dunn, *Political Thought of John Locke*, and Tully, *Discourse on Property*; for the latter, Macpherson, *Political Theory of Possessive Individualism*, and Grant, *John Locke's Liberalism.*

2. I am aware that *Second Treatise of Government* is not, strictly speaking, the title of any of Locke's works. However, given the length and awkwardness of either of the two more accurate titles (viz., "the second of the *Two Treatises*" or "An Essay Concerning the True Original, Extent and End of Civil Government"), I have found it convenient to speak, as many others have, of the *Second Treatise* and of its immediate predecessor as the *First Treatise.*

3. The use of gendered terms in any analysis of Locke is tricky. While Locke spoke often of "man" where he seems to mean humanity and include both sexes, there are other contexts where he clearly says women do not have many capacities to the same degree as men. Most of the material I discuss falls into the first category, but I nonetheless eschew the use of *she* to avoid anachronistically attributing to Locke positions he did not hold. Whatever uses of *man* remain should be considered in this light.

4. Strauss was quite right to say that for Locke "all knowledge depends on labor and is labor" (*Natural Right and History*, p. 249); it is Strauss's overly mechanical notion of labor that needs correction.

5. See Seliger, *Liberal Politics of John Locke*, ch. 2, for a longer discussion of this point.

6. This I take to be one of the severest limitations of Macpherson's interpretation of Locke, not to mention Strauss's. Macpherson takes Locke to have a strictly capitalist conception of labor (à la Marx), as something purely of the body, which can be wholly alienated (i.e., sold) in the marketplace (Macpherson, *Political Theory*, pp. 214–20). In fact, however, Locke's idea of labor encompasses the mind as well as the body. He sees all forms of life as characterized by labor, and there are certain kinds of labor that can never be sold. So, while Macpherson is surely right to refocus our attention on the commercial elements of Locke's thought (it will become obvious how much I owe to this view), he is also quite wrong to depict Locke as a class-interested bourgeois, for whom one sort of person labors while another does not. For Strauss, the notion of labor connects Hobbes and Locke as mechanically minded atheists, but in fact, although Locke separates God from man, he does not thereby deny Him completely. Labor, for Locke, is something that characterizes all forms of life.

7. Although it is anachronistic to accuse Locke of holding a modern notion of class, numerous passages (e.g., *RC* 135, 146; *SCM* 71; *E* 4.20.2; *STCE* 6, 117) reveal his anti-egalitarian sentiments. He seems to have believed that the poor, while not without native intelligence, simply lacked time to reflect on the higher issues of religion or politics. Note the absence, however, of such sentiments in the *Two Treatises*.

8. Andrzej Rapaczynski (*Nature and Politics*, pp. 214–15) makes the point, contra Strauss, that labor for Locke is a very moral concept, and not a nihilistic one. But Rapaczynski has a rather different understanding of what this moral sense is from the one I lay out.

9. Indeed, Locke, rather than Benjamin Franklin, really ought to have been the obvious choice for Weber's profile in *The Protestant Ethic and the Spirit of Capitalism* (ch. 2) of the ascetic Christian—the more so since, in life, Locke hewed much closer to his stated principles than did Franklin. "It is not . . . in any way absurd to look in a slightly Weberian mood at the writings of Locke," Dunn writes (*Political Thought of John Locke*, p. 210), but he takes this insight in a rather different direction from what follows here.

10. See, e.g., Jean-Jacques Rousseau, *Emile, or, On Education* (1762; New York: Basic Books, 1979), pp. 33, 89.

11. It ought to be noted that Locke did not think this education was for everyone. He thought it impossible for any but a few to be liberated from daily labor. The distribution of wealth and labor in Britain seemed largely immutable to him. Indeed, one of the continuous problems that Locke's tutor faces is shielding his pupil from the degrading influence of servants and day laborers.

12. Nathan Tarcov, in *Locke's Education for Liberty*, interprets this self-denying element of Locke's education in a more directly political way, as an attempt to curb a child's yearning for dominion. The ascetic interpretation, it seems to me, makes sense of far more passages; Locke generally uses "dominion" as a subset of "covetousness," which is his main concern (*STCE* 110; cf. 103, 105). Of course, these two readings are not entirely incompatible.

13. "One gets no sense of asceticism from the pages of *SCM*," Karen Iversen Vaughn contends ("The Economic Background of Locke's 'Two Treatises,'" in *John Locke's "Two Treatises of Government,"* ed. Harpham, p. 125). But she offers no detailed reading to back up this startling declaration. Nor does she seem to have consulted *STCE* in her effort to form a picture of Locke's "economic man." In the same volume, Richard Ashcraft's essay "The Politics of Locke's 'Two Treatises'" does a much better job of demonstrating how, for Locke, self-denial is one of the main attributes of reason (pp. 23–26)—although Ashcraft attributes this more to Locke's natural-law perspective than to his Calvinism. Thus while Ashcraft effectively rebuts Vaughn's attempt to assimilate Locke to Robert Nozick, Locke comes in the process to resemble, not Aristotle (as Ashcraft thinks) but rather Augustine.

14. This is in keeping with the standard mercantilist doctrine that the nation is rich whose inhabitants are poor (that is, frugal), since consumption decreases wealth in the mercantilists' zero-sum world. My thanks to Pratap Mehta for sharing with me his deep knowledge of early-modern notions of commerce. Clearly, though, Locke's

words here have a moral edge that will not be felt if we simply label his views mercantilist.

15. In *The Politics of Locke's Philosophy*, ch. 6, Neal Wood pursues this conclusion even more strongly and argues that the "hero" of the *Essay* is "bourgeois man." Wood discusses the influence of the Protestant ethic on this hero, but thinks that the hero's dominant characteristics are derived from Baconian models of human rationality. My account stresses the former, but I agree with Wood that Locke, in his philosophical writings, is attempting to describe a certain kind of character. However, the use to which Locke puts this character (viz., revolution) is, I think, quite different from what Wood takes Locke's political purposes to be ("instauration").

16. Locke does believe there are useless truths. The example he usually gives is that of statements of identity. Statements that take the form $x = x$ (e.g., "white is white") Locke considers both true and useless. He cannot deny their existence, but he ridicules their role in philosophy.

17. This may indicate to us, as well, that Locke did not fully appreciate the difference between authoritarian political rule and literal enslavement, as he ought to have. I have no wish to defend Locke on this point, but it should at least be noted that Locke represents a midpoint in the transformation of the Western understanding of slavery. Writing 40 years earlier, Sir Robert Filmer took slavery as the very model of political obligation and thought all subjects were justly enslaved to their king.

18. See *2T*, ch. 4. Note that Locke, the theorist of property, does *not* consider slaves the property of their master (although he probably thought the *products* of their labor were). His conception of slavery as a power relation, rather than a property relation, explains the equivalent treatment he gives to economic and political slavery (which we would consider distinct).

19. Locke makes these points with what is, for him, an unusual play on words: "[S]ome (and those the most) taking things upon trust, misimploy their power of Assent, by lazily enslaving their Minds, to the Dictates and Dominion of others. . . . Nor is it a small power it gives one Man over another, to have the Authority to be the Dictator of Principles and Teacher of unquestionable Truths" (*E* 1.4.22–24). Whoever directs one's thoughts is, effectively, one's dictator.

20. Some of these parallels are pointed out in the discussion of Caffentzis, *Clipped Coins, Abused Words and Civil Government*. He uses the similarity to explore Locke's theory of money; in what follows, I reverse the direction of inquiry and use Locke's reflections on money to explain his analysis of words.

21. Note the caveat that this applies only to languages that have been "framed," which is of course perfectly consistent with the idea that men apply words to their own ideas and then come to hammer out an agreement on their common use with those they are in commerce with. Of course, Locke would have a difficult time were he pressed to identify just when a language was framed, and therefore no longer open to experimentation on the part of its users, especially given that he holds languages to be constantly evolving.

22. "Locke, who is so tolerant of religious deviation, is almost religiously devoted to the quantitative and substantial 'integrity' of silver and gold," Caffentzis remarks

(*Clipped Coins*, p. 46). Although this captures the spirit of Locke's writings quite well, it is not entirely accurate—the devotion is not truly a "religious" one, based on the worship of money, but a zealously fiduciary one, based on the trust of it. (On the role of trust in Locke's thinking, see Chapter 2.)

23. As is clear here, the parallel between words and coins does not lead to their complete identification. On the economic side, one large difference remains: although the full meaning of words is always, in the last analysis, under human control, and the amount of gold and silver that goes into particular coins (and thus the meaning of words such as *pound*) is a matter of consent, the value of silver itself (e.g., how much of any good a pound's worth of silver will buy) is not set by compact. This complicates Locke's economics (perhaps to the point of incoherence), but it does not alter his analysis of words or the point he makes with monetary metaphors: arbitrarily altering the value of a word without the consent of others is a cheat. It is easy to see that clipping a coin is the same sort of cheating; that is why it is Locke's model. But the seriousness of this act in the economic case is more questionable (and not, as Locke thinks, more obvious) when the value of silver is independent of consent (as his contemporary critics were quick to point out).

24. Aaron (*John Locke*, p. 212) points out that Locke was dissenting from the prevailing view of definitions as proceeding "by genus and differentia." In *John Locke and Agrarian Capitalism*, ch. 4, Wood argues the particular influence of Francis Bacon (1561–1626) in this matter. Bacon, Wood suggests, was the one who first formulated the notion of natural history that Locke seems to employ.

Chapter 2

1. Locke's aside that one cannot argue from "has been" to "should be" (*2T* 103) is, in any case, highly ambiguous, and hardly denies the possibility of all forms of historical argument, as it has sometimes been taken to do. It denies a particular form of historical argument, viz., that what once was good, must still be good. But Locke's narrative, as we shall see, employs a different sort of historical argument, one that describes change over time. For a careful defense of this position, see Waldron, "John Locke: Social Contract Versus Political Anthropology," esp. pp. 14–16.

2. For a detailed attempt to work out Locke's reason-based hermeneutics, see Schouls, *Imposition of Method*, ch. 8; cf. Weinsheimer, *Imitation*, chs. 1–2, where the author claims that this approach, taken to its most extreme conclusions, should mean that Locke cannot defend the practice of reading his own *Essay*. The objection seems more clever than substantive—and also ignores Locke's statements about the positive value of testimony in *RC* and *LT3*. Locke's attitude toward revelation did result in some odd views though. He was against the reading of the Bible by children; instead, he suggested that a summary be made in which the events were set down in their "due order of time." This, he said, would eliminate the confusions that arose from the "promiscuous reading of the Scripture, as it lies now bound up in our Bibles" (*STCE* 189; cf. 158).

3. Eldon Eisenach, after a survey of the relationship of Locke's religious writings to

those of his contemporaries, writes that Locke "sought to purge political and cultural life of priestcraft" ("Religion and Locke's 'Two Treatises of Government,'" in *John Locke's "Two Treatises of Government,"* ed. Harpham, p. 77).

4. By *reason*, Locke here means simply the "Agreement or Disagreement" of our labor-constructed ideas (*E* 4.17). Reason foundered mostly for want of ideas or because of the abuse of words, which are their coin. In other words, reason is always tied to experience and what we can deduce from it, rather than from innate ideas or revelation. Similarly, Locke attacked those (primarily the scholastics) who believed the syllogism was the basis of reason (he called it useless). In practice, it is not clear that Locke actually tried to make ideas "agree," or exactly what such a procedure would mean in any case.

5. Dunn, *Political Thought of John Locke*. Extensive further evidence for this view has recently been given by John Marshall, *John Locke: Resistance, Religion and Responsibility*.

6. Ruth Grant presents, in my opinion, the most serious case for this view in *John Locke's Liberalism*. Grant argues that Locke's political theory is meant to be an ordered deduction on the model of a "geometric proof" (p. 7). Hence she denies that such elements of the theory as the State of Nature have a fundamentally historical character, describing them instead as "a logical necessity" (p. 66). Although Grant's work represents a serious effort to impose coherence on Locke's text, I fear she has done so at the expense of too many details. Specifically, she starts from some of Locke's methodological arguments (while ignoring others, such as those just discussed) and then attempts to demonstrate that all of Locke's work adheres to this method. The two main problems I see with the demonstration are: (1) the role of Locke's vocabulary, which I have just been describing, is ignored. Even if Locke meant to be making quasi-mathematical demonstrations, his reliance on an economic vocabulary means that he may have accomplished something quite other. (One might put the point thus: Grant employs a hermeneutics of respect, I use the hermeneutic of suspicion.) (2) Grant's method assumes a restricted notion of what political philosophy might be. Her approach leads her to an understanding of the *Second Treatise* as a demonstration of abstract moral principles. That, for her, is the nature of a book of philosophy. Hence, she thinks it is a book that attempts to answer the question of whom to obey (p. 53). My interpretation concludes that the book is fundamentally a call to revolution, rather than an attempt to derive principles, particularly rules of obedience (although the latter may certainly be included in the former). My reconstruction of the *Second Treatise* is, then, a long defense of this position. And this conclusion, I think, is outside the bounds of what Grant holds a book of philosophy could possibly be. Hence, I believe, she excludes too many possibilities by definition. However, I am happy to have my position subjected to the rigorous standard that Grant sets for her own: "[U]ltimately, the validity of the approach taken here must be judged by whether the analysis provides a convincing explanation of the text" (pp. 9−10). For a weaker version of Grant's argument, see Schouls, *Imposition of Method*, pp. 191−200.

7. This interpretation is exemplified by Hartz, *Liberal Tradition in America*; Vaughn, *John Locke*; Seliger, *Liberal Politics of John Locke*, ch. 3; and in *John Locke's "Two Treatises*

of Government," ed. Harpham. It has recently been reprised in Diggins, *Lost Soul of American Politics*. See also Kendall, *John Locke and the Doctrine of Majority Rule*, and John Plamenatz, *Man and Society* (New York: McGraw-Hill, 1963), vol. 1.

8. See esp. Dunn, *Political Thought of John Locke*, and Marshall, *John Locke: Resistance, Religion and Responsibility*. The thesis is reiterated in a different form by Tully, *Discourse on Property*.

9. The closest thing to this view that appears in the literature of Locke is the argument that in certain parts of *2 T*, Locke was writing "political anthropology." See Waldron, "John Locke: Social Contract Versus Political Anthropology"; Batz, "Historical Anthropology of John Locke."

10. Richard Ashcraft has been prominent in insisting that the State of Nature does have a historical element, but he generally limits history to the role of "evidence" that "validates" an abstract theory, so that it largely drops out of his final analysis. Still, I am largely indebted to him for debunking the older view that the State of Nature is in no way historical. See Ashcraft, *Locke's "Two Treatises of Government,"* esp. chs. 6 and 9; and id., "Locke's State of Nature." Simmons, "Locke's State of Nature," argues that Locke's history is meant to show that men have always *thought* themselves naturally free, but this halfway position does not account well for the figure of the father-king, as I discuss further on in this chapter.

11. Later liberal political theorists have generally dropped the location of the State of Nature in time. Then, reading Locke through these later theorists, interpreters have dropped it in their understanding of Locke as well. John Rawls's "Original Position," for example, does have the character of a timeless, abstract contract, as accessible to us as to a state's founders, as does Kant's account of social contract as an "idea of Reason." The characterization of either of these as the culmination of liberal theory then leads interpreters of Locke to stress that which he has in common with them and to ignore what differs. The results would be much different if one chose to view Locke through inheritors such as, say, Rousseau.

12. 1 Tim. 6:17. Locke continues that this "is the Voice of Reason confirmed by Inspiration." This is a fairly representative instance of the way Scripture appears in the *Second Treatise*, i.e., as the confirmation of a conclusion arrived at through reason.

13. There is some dispute as to whether Locke's premises here actually justify (or are meant to justify) private property. Tully (*Discourse on Property*, pp. 124ff.) believes that they are not meant to, and that they only justify the system of the English Common. Macpherson (*Political Theory*, p. 202) believes that they *are* meant to justify private property, but that they fail to do so completely—an additional assumption about methods of production, he argues, is needed. I believe Macpherson is closer to the mark here, certainly with regard to the issue of Locke's belief in his argument's establishment of private property. The simplest way to see this is to consider the following: there is no doubt that Locke considers personal labor to be the property of the laborer ("the *Labour* of his Body, and the *Work* of his Hands, we may say, are properly his" [*2T* 27]). Even Tully, I believe, would agree to this. And yet, after products are fashioned by labor and made personal possessions, Locke never distinguishes what one may do with them, as opposed to one's own labor. If labor were

private property in a way that food or land are not, we would expect differential treatment of the latter. But there is none: the provisos apply to both. Full exchange rights precede the introduction of money and governments (the famous barter of "Plumbs for Nuts" [2T 46]) and do *not* follow on them, as Tully seems to maintain (p. 130). What is true is that money vastly increases the possibility and scope of these exchanges.

14. Locke appears to have taken this position quite seriously, even when it leads to absurd ends. He maintained that all peoples made contracts denominated in silver (*FCM* 150), and that national governments, although they minted coins, could not control the value of them (156).

15. That association through contract is the only just kind of association Locke could conceive of is further demonstrated by his use of it as a description of churches (2T 120; *LT1* 13).

16. McClure, "Narrative Investments: Money, Meaning and the Lockean State," lays great stress on Locke's use of the phrase "Golden Age" and argues that his narrative is thus linked to the Renaissance myth of the ages of metals. Despite her best efforts to show this, it seems to me that the textual evidence is extremely thin. And, in a search for Renaissance narrative, her argument wholly ignores Locke's quite original narrative in the latter half of *2T* and the more existential role that gold plays in his theory, which makes his reference to a "Golden Age" seem more than a little ironic, as if to say, "The real golden age is the one that makes use of *gold*."

17. So many commentators have focused their readings on this chapter that they have, to my mind, neglected the balance of the text that follows. Macpherson began this trend, and, ironically, many of those who seek to refute him on the subject of property follow him in this pattern (e.g., Vaughn, Tully).

18. The absence of national sentiment in Locke is really quite remarkable, especially given his cognizance of different languages and the way he connects them to different ways of life. He only uses the term *people* to refer to a group that has consciously organized itself into a society. It never refers to a language or ethnic group. In this vein, Locke was in favor of immigration to England from other countries, which he saw only as a net gain in resources in a zero-sum world. In his edition of *Two Treatises of Government* (p. 368n), Laslett points out that the sentence just quoted is, in fact, the first time the word *people* appears in the book.

19. We might call this thesis, antithesis, and synthesis. Hegel certainly understood social-contract theory this way (see *PR*, pt. 3).

20. This may seem to conflict with the sense of § 99 that the people give up their power to a majority, and hence that government must be democratic (perhaps even to the point of democratic despotism; see Kendall, *John Locke and the Doctrine of Majority Rule*). However, what Locke actually seems to have in mind is a two-stage process where a "People" first decide to constitute themselves as such and agree to invest a government with power and *then*, by majority ("unless they expressly agreed in any number greater") decide (at what we might call the constitutional-convention stage) on a particular form of government. This is the only way to make sense of the statement "That the *beginning of Politick Society*, depends upon the consent of the

Individuals to joyn into and make one Society; who, *when they are thus incorporated* [my emphasis], might set up what form of Government they thought fit" (*2T* 106). Locke's point here is that monarchy may be perfectly legitimate so long as it is not absolute and has a democratic origin. If further evidence is needed of the acceptability of monarchy to Locke, a recently discovered document displays his enthusiastic defense of the crown of William and Mary. See Farr and Roberts, "John Locke on the Glorious Revolution." Interestingly, in this document, Locke desires citizens to swear explicitly only that they do *not* believe in the divine right of royal succession, rather than loyalty to king or country (p. 396).

21. Although Locke sometimes proclaims a "public" community composed of all mankind, it is hard to see where, in his theory, it would ever act as such after (or even before) governments are formed.

22. Americans certainly understood Locke this way and carried out just such a historical effort. See my article, "Between History and Nature: Social Contract Theory in Locke and the Founders," *Journal of Politics* (Nov. 1996).

23. He even thinks we have God's grace as an inheritance from Jesus after the latter "adopted" us (*RC* 107). Even God, it seems, is subject to English common law. Cf. Gough, *John Locke's Political Philosophy*, pp. 65–79.

24. Ashcraft ("Politics of Locke's 'Two Treatises,'" in *John Locke's "Two Treatises of Government,"* ed. Harpham, pp. 26–32) argues quite elegantly that differential property holdings do *not* result in unequal citizenship, because property, for Locke, always means something broader than landholdings. My argument can thus be seen as offering further evidence in this vein.

25. For a contrary view and extensive discussion of the divided literature on this point, see Simmons, *On the Edge of Anarchy*, § 4.1.

26. See Laslett's note at § 74 in his edition of *Two Treatises of Government*. Ashcraft ("Locke's State of Nature," pp. 908–15) expresses similar sentiments.

27. See Seliger, *Liberal Politics of John Locke*, ch. 7, for a similar argument, attempting to bring the account of patriarchy in line with that of contract. My account of contract diverges significantly from that of Seliger, so that, while we agree on how Locke approaches patriarchy, we reach rather different conclusions. See also Waldron, "John Locke: Social Contract Versus Political Anthropology," pp. 16–22.

28. *Patriarcha* was published in 1680, almost 30 years after its author's death. Locke apologizes for attacking one "long since past answering" and says that he would not do so were not the churches proclaiming Filmer's doctrine as truth.

29. As Tully (*Discourse on Property*, p. 157) reminds us, divine-right-of-kings theories were a relatively new phenomenon in England at the time of Locke's writing. Despite being an advocate of revolution, Locke, in believing government to be conventional was, in some sense, "conservative" (although Tully perhaps takes this conclusion too far).

30. As noted above, Parliament's wishes in this matter stemmed from James's Catholic faith and a fear that he would submit his kingdom to the pope and the (Catholic) French.

31. See Laslett's checklist of printings in his edition of *Two Treatises*, pp. 136–45.

32. Ashcraft (*Locke's "Two Treatises of Government,"* ch. 5) notes the difference in style, but is not able to make anything of it. Laslett seems largely unaware of it.

33. Dunn's formulation in *Political Thought of John Locke* (p. 155), "The authority of the prerogative over the individual subject is precisely and exclusively what the individual recognizes it to be," cannot possibly be right. Its extreme voluntarism suggests just the sort of linguistic and political chaos Locke sought to avoid, a Wonderland where each individual could choose whatever meaning of a word suited him.

34. As Ashcraft has noted, the crisis in 1688 *was* a case of the legislature versus the executive. Locke's call here for the overthrow of an enslaving legislature has no direct parallel with the political situation of that year (the Exclusion Crisis is more debatable). In his enthusiasm to point out Locke's poor fit with 1688, Pocock, "Myth of John Locke," seems not to consider that this may make Locke *more* relevant at other times. Dworetz, *Unvarnished Doctrine*, for example, makes a persuasive case that Locke was well known, often read, and much broadcast, especially by the New England clergy, in the American colonies in the revolutionary period.

35. Julian Franklin (*John Locke and the Theory of Sovereignty*, p. 94) argues that Locke merely puts the arguments of George Lawson into a "more English terminology." In some sense, this may be so, but in another, it may be that the terms make all the difference. Franklin claims that Locke's greater influence and Lawson's obscurity were mostly a matter of luck—but it may be that Locke's success in casting his particular vocabulary into a substantive narrative is precisely what sets him apart.

36. On the connection of testament and trust: it was a normal practice under the English law of this period to set up a trust to oversee an inheritance, rather than simply to bequeath the inheritance. This was because there were fewer legal obstacles to such trusts: daughters, for example, could not always be the recipients of a simple bequest, but could be the beneficiaries of a trust. Locke worked for a time at the Chancery, which was in charge of enforcing such trusts, and would have had knowledge of this sort of arrangement in some detail. I thank Jennifer Mnookin for the benefit of her knowledge of the English common law.

37. Dunn, "Concept of 'Trust' in the Politics of John Locke."

38. Ibid., p. 296.

39. Gough, *John Locke's Political Philosophy*, ch. 7.

40. *Two Treatises of Government*, ed. Laslett, introduction, pp. 126–30.

41. Recall that this might include a variety of possible forms of government, even an inherited monarchy. It simply could not include an absolute monarchy, where the people give up their ultimate right to judge. Whatever the form of government, the people will always be Trustor and the governor always Deputy.

42. Of course, I am using the example of Hamlet heuristically here. It is not my belief that this character can be understood by a single adjective or through a single choice.

43. Strauss's formulation "Life is the joyless quest for joy" (*Natural Right and History*, p. 251) is evocative, even poetic, but one might more accurately speak of a joyless quest for redemption.

44. As to the United States, it is not surprising that it should be associated with

Locke. As in Locke's text, Americans became a people (one might say), only through the process of rebellion and contract. The *Second Treatise* helps us to understand how such a thing might be possible. Rebellion did not erase the diverse pasts of pilgrims, colonists, servants, and slaves. But it may have served to implant a new memory, a myth of creation, a common original to overlay diverse origins. For the United States, the past Locke offers is all the more resonant for the lack of any other, more detailed past to provide a common narrative. None of this, of course, prevents us from identifying as well with the latter part of Locke's narrative (nor, for that matter, with more local histories), when we feel that the cycle of government has reached that lowest ebb.

Chapter 3

1. See Derrida, "Interpreting Signatures (Nietzsche/Heidegger): Two Questions," in *Looking After Nietzsche*, ed. Rickels, p. 9; id., *Spurs*, pp. 133, 135; De Man, *Allegories of Reading*. To give Derrida his due, it is necessary to distinguish his critique of Heidegger's Nietzsche from his own understanding of Nietzsche. He aptly notes the ironic, even hypocritical, character of Heidegger's interpretation: "At the very moment of affirming the uniqueness of Nietzsche's thinking, [Heidegger] does everything he can to show that it represents the mightiest (and therefore the most general) schema of metaphysics." This critique of Heidegger does not, however, of itself lead to Derrida's own conclusions about Nietzsche. Derrida argues that what Nietzsche accomplishes is a full decentering of Western metaphysics: Nietzsche questions the necessity of coherence, "If Nietzsche had indeed meant to say something, might it not be just that limit to the will to mean . . . ? . . . There is no 'totality to Nietzsche's text'." In other words, none of Nietzsche's particular views matter so much as their self-deconstruction. I think this is letting Nietzsche off the hook too easily—more easily certainly than he would want to be let off. It is a rescue that does Nietzsche little more good than Heidegger's.

2. Shapiro, *Nietzschean Narratives*, p. 23. I am indebted to Shapiro for this critique and only wish I agreed with him more on the substance of Nietzsche's narratives.

3. Giambattista Vico, *The New Science of Giambattista Vico* (Ithaca, N.Y: Cornell University Press, 1984), § 62.

4. Ibid., § 55.

5. See Boyce, *History of Zoroastrianism*, vol. 1, chs. 7–9; Duchesne-Guillemin, *Symbols and Values in Zoroastrianism*, pp. 65–76; and Dhalla, *History of Zoroastrianism*, ch. 9. In Nietzsche's day, the meaning of Zoroastrianism was being widely debated in philological circles. Many of its important texts, and conflicting interpretations of them, would have been available to him.

6. The understanding of Zarathustra is a good barometer to gauging a reader's reaction to Nietzsche's whole philosophy. In the early part of this century, *Zarathustra* was the starting point for many interpretations of Nietzsche. Its mystical and gospel-like qualities encouraged romantic and poetic readings. Later, as more professional philosophers got hold of Nietzsche, the book became something of a stumbling block. In this development, the understanding of Zarathustra as a character also

changed. Romantic Nietzscheans accepted all of Nietzsche's praise of his character and believed they had found a new god to replace the old. More strictly philosophical readers, on the other hand, were apt to ignore the literary qualities of the book and to read Zarathustra's statements as Nietzsche's views. G. B. Shaw, who called *Zarathustra* "the first modern book that can be set above the psalms of David," is a good example of the first kind of reading, and Arthur Danto of the second. See Thatcher, *Nietzsche in England* (Shaw cited at p. 186); Danto, *Nietzsche as Philosopher*.

7. See Lampert, *Nietzsche's Teaching*, pp. 2–5. But old wine keeps refilling new bottles. Staten, claiming a postmodernist insight, writes, "I also do not hesitate to speak of 'Zarathustra' without distinguishing the textual marker from the one inscribed as 'Nietzsche'" (*Nietzsche's Voice*, p. 3). In imagining that he makes a point about the instability and openness of text and identity, Staten reopens the way to an old-fashioned view of Nietzsche and Zarathustra.

8. See, e.g., in very different contexts, *GS* 5.344; *HH*, Pref., 2.

9. The longer life of Zarathustra can be understood in two different ways. Nietzsche tells us quite directly, on the first page of the book, that Zarathustra is 40 years old when he begins preaching. This is in accord with Persian tradition. Since Jesus is usually held to have been in his early thirties at the time of his death (traditionally 33), this line could be read to mean that Zarathustra is asserting that his seven extra years gave him greater wisdom. But this strikes me as implausible. Zarathustra's tone indicates that the wisdom he claims is one that takes many, many years to grow. Thus, it seems to me, the passage suggests that by "Zarathustra," Nietzsche means a being who is thousands of years "old" and whose existence stretches from Persia to the tip of Nietzsche's pen.

10. Where the two diverge, Freud is often implicitly responding to an agenda that Nietzsche set. It is an important side benefit of this inquiry that it illuminates the relationship between Nietzsche and Freud. While the pattern of influence is by now well known, less systematic attention has been given to Nietzsche's thoughts on dreams. In doing so, this investigation will give a better sense of what Nietzschean resources Freud had to draw on in this area. Freud liked to deny that he had read Nietzsche. But he read at least enough to claim, in 1908, that Nietzsche had more self-knowledge "than any man who ever lived or was likely to live." It is hard to imagine Freud making such a claim without a firsthand acquaintance with the text. See Ernest Jones, *Sigmund Freud*, 2: 385. Later notes will point to places where Freud's claims of ignorance seem particularly implausible. Assoun, *Freud et Nietzsche*, makes the most comprehensive attempt to trace Nietzsche's influence on Freud (pp. 5–80). Assoun traces a variety of paths by which Nietzsche's philosophy may have reached Freud, even if Freud's odd denials of having declined to read Nietzsche out of "an excess of interest" are taken at face value (which I very much doubt they should be). As early as the 1880s, there was a personal link between the two men in the figure of Dr. Joseph Paneth, a close friend of Freud's, who got to know Nietzsche quite well in Nice in 1883 and had long philosophical discussions with him. Later, of course, Nietzsche's one-time disciple Lou Salomé became a student and colleague of Freud's. In addition to this, several papers on Nietzsche were presented to the Vienna Psycho-

analytic Society when Freud was present. Freud purchased a set of Nietzsche volumes in 1900, but he asks us to believe that they rested unopened in his library for the rest of his life; "he refused himself the pleasure of reading Nietzsche," he tells us, even though when he bought the books, he wrote of his hope to find in them, "the words for many things which remain mute in me." If one does not detect in all this an unrelieved "anxiety of influence," Assoun reminds us of another important reason Freud had, after a certain point anyway, to deny Nietzsche's influence: Freud's heretical students Jung and Adler had both adopted a recognizably Nietzschean vocabulary. By denying the father, Freud wanted also to deny the sons.

11. In the biography he wrote of himself at age 14, Nietzsche described two dream episodes from his youth. Significantly, he took one of them to be a premonition of the death of his younger brother, an event that followed soon after. For some discussion, see Granarolo, "Nietzsche et sa vision du futur."

12. I consider Nietzsche's work to fall into the following periods: early connotes the period where Nietzsche was still working in a metaphysical framework and includes *BT* and *UM*; middle comprises the works written after he has abandoned this framework, but has not yet freed himself from the influence of Paul Rée's "English" psychology and has not developed his ideas of genealogy or the overman—it includes *HH*, *AOM*, *WS*, and *D*; the late and mature period then starts in 1882 with *GS* and includes everything else. Of course, a great deal is continuous through these periods, and this is particularly the case with the material on dreams. This material acquires a new aspect, however, after the development of genealogy. My division of Nietzsche parallels, although it does not exactly replicate, that elaborated by Warren, *Nietzsche and Political Thought*, p. xiv, and that of other studies of Nietzsche.

13. *D* 2.119.

14. It is not even clear whether creativity is a single process at all, or a variety of processes that we mistakenly subsume under a single label. At *GM* 3.24, Nietzsche faces the question of whether interpretation has an "essence" with an ironic attitude and lists "forcing, adjusting, abbreviating, omitting, padding, inventing, falsifying" as a few of the things that need to be included in an understanding of interpretation.

15. Nietzsche's position splits the difference between the belief that Homer was a single author and the view, taken by many German philologists after Herder, that the Greek people themselves were the authors of the epics—that is, that they are folk narratives. See Hugh Lloyd-Jones, "Becoming Homer," *New York Review of Books* 34, no. 5 (Mar. 5, 1992): 52–57.

16. Phillipe Lacoue-Labarthe maintains that sculpture is Nietzsche's "model of artistic practice" ("History and Mimesis," p. 218). Although he considers Nietzsche's appreciation of Apollonian perfect shapes, I believe Lacoue-Labarthe neglects the elements of sequence, order, and relation of shapes that Nietzsche discusses in *BT*. Other writers have insisted that music is the most Nietzschean art (see, e.g., essays by Michael Gillespie in *Nietzsche's New Seas* or Sarah Kofman in *The New Nietzsche*). It seems to me, though, that music lacks the element of figuration—a theme is never a *Bild*—and that the figure is the essential Apollonian element in the art that Nietzsche holds in the highest regard.

17. See Oliver Sacks, "The Last Hippie," *New York Review of Books* 34, no. 6 (Mar. 26, 1992): 53–62, esp. 58–62. On Aristotle, see n. 20 below.

18. Sleepwalkers are generally acting out their role in a dream drama when they move about at night. Most people, we now know, are normally prevented from doing so by the release of a brain chemical while they dream that blocks muscles from answering to the commands of the brain.

19. Of course, I do not mean that painting is flawed by this. This description merely points to one of the limits of the genre, which also has unique possibilities— just as any genre does.

20. Although this theory may strike us as odd today, it was not original to Nietzsche. Indeed, it might even be called traditional, bearing as it does considerable similarities to Aristotle's account of dreams in *De somniis* (461b–462b).

21. "It is not that 'life is a dream,' but that humans are always dreaming it through and into their perceptions," Peter Canning writes ("How the Fable Becomes a World," in *Looking After Nietzsche*, ed. Rickels, p. 184).

22. As noted above, this view actually has a close parallel in contemporary neuroscientific explanations of dreaming: "Rodolfo Llinas . . . comparing the electrophysiological properties of the brain in waking and dreaming, postulates a single fundamental mechanism for both—a ceaseless 'inner talking' between cerebral cortex and thalamus, a ceaseless interplay of image and feeling, irrespective of whether there is sensory input or not. When there is sensory input, this interplay integrates it to generate 'waking consciousness,' but in the absence of sensory input it continues to generate brain states, those brain states we call fantasy, hallucination or dreaming. Thus waking consciousness is dreaming—but dreaming constrained by external reality" (Sacks, "Last Hippie," p. 58). See R. R. Llinas and D. Pare, "On Dreaming and Wakefulness," *Neuroscience* 44, no. 3 (1991): 521–35. Of course, the resemblance of Nietzsche's account to that of one neuroscientist proves nothing—but it is intriguing how Nietzschean Sacks sounds in his last sentence.

23. Freud repeats this view as well. In an essay entitled "Moral Responsibility for the Content of Dreams" (*Collected Papers* 5: 154–57), he asks, "[W]ho else [but the dreamer] would be responsible?" This correspondence was called to my attention by Tracy Strong, *Friedrich Nietzsche and the Politics of Transfiguration*, p. 102.

24. Likewise, in a note, interpretation is defined as "the introduction of meaning, not 'explanation' " (*WP* 3.604).

25. Blondel, *Nietzsche: The Body and Culture*, pp. 218–19.

26. Although there are many differences between them, here at least, Nietzsche seems to be making the same sort of point as Thomas Kuhn does with his concept of "normal" science. Nietzsche originally addressed an audience—not only before Kuhn, but also before Einstein and Heisenberg—that had largely Lockean and Baconian notions of the role of observation and was disinclined to believe that any theory is anterior to observation. It might be objected here that even though, in Nietzsche's view, we are inventing the experience of a particular object in front of us, this ought not to be called invention, because we are relying on older images in our construction of the new. This points to the difference between waking and dreaming interpreta-

tion, specifically the heightened role of memory in the former, discussed in the next section.

27. It is in fact the basic way Nietzsche explores social phenomena: "Who interprets?—Our affects" (WP 2:254). He always asks, "From what drive, via what interpretation do these phenomena spring?" In the first book of Beyond Good and Evil, where he examines the history of philosophy, this mode of analysis is especially evident (see §§ 5, 6). He is not speaking, though, of the predilections of the individual philosophers. While he does think each philosophy ultimately rests on its founder's personality, he is speaking also of the general desire to philosophize, which he sees as a sublimated urge to dominate: "[Philosophy] always creates the world in its own image, it cannot do otherwise; philosophy is the tyrannical drive itself" (BGE 1.9). Just as in the case of dreams, this passion acts on the impressions it receives and elaborates on them at length: the sense impressions that lie at the bottom of every experience are obscured by the interpretation piled on top. Indeed, they may not really be that important compared to the interpretation of a drive. In other works, Nietzsche gives further examples of the creativity of passions. Several sections in The Will to Power reflect this approach. The sex drive, for example, is held to be the main power behind the creation of art at WP 3.805. And in what appears to be an outline for an unwritten work, "To What Extent Interpretations of the World Are Symptoms of a Ruling Drive," Nietzsche outlines four main interpretations (artistic, scientific, religious, moral) that he intended to reduce to their basic drives (WP 3.677). Although he never wrote a work with this format, at one time or another he did address these interpretations separately in precisely this manner. (See, e.g., GS 2.87, GS 5.344; D 1.68; and TI pt. 2, respectively.) In The Birth of Tragedy, while still under the influence of Schopenhauer, he had thought that it was such things as "the primordial contradiction" that produced the images of dreams (BT 5). But as his psychology developed, he came to view the human unconscious, in all its variety, as the ground for these images, rather than metaphysical maelstroms (see GS 1.8). "It is our needs that interpret the world; our drives and their For and Against" (WP 3.481).

28. Shapiro (Nietzschean Narratives, pp. 24–27) also points out this connection.

29. Nietzsche drew this lesson early on: "[T]he dream is the seeking and positing of the causes of this excitement of the sensibilities, that is to say the supposed causes. [Here the account of the bell appears for the first time.] . . . the supposed cause is inferred from the effect and introduced after the effect: and all with extraordinary rapidity, so that, as with a conjurer, a confusion of judgment can here arise and successive events appear as simultaneous events or even with the order of their occurrence reversed" (HH 1.13). In "Rhetoric of Tropes (Nietzsche)," Paul De Man pointed out that, in a certain form anyway, this view appears in Nietzsche's notes as early as 1872.

30. Descartes drew the opposite conclusion.

31. Again, Nietzsche often views the theories of others as causes they have invented to make sense of the effects they experience. He casts anarchist theory as a creation/interpretation of those who feel "vile" (TI 10.34). Religious interpretations of pain also fall into this category (WP 2.229). It is the main lie priests tell to their flocks, when the latter cannot explain their own pain, that they themselves are the

cause of it. Fundamentally, he holds, philosophers and ethicists who believe our principles are responsible for our characters have it wrong; it is just the opposite that is true (*HH* 9.608).

32. It ought to be noted at this point that this is the direct opposite of Freud's view that "[m]emory is far more comprehensive in dreams than in waking life. Dreams bring up recollection which the dreamer has forgotten, which are inaccessible to him when he is awake" (*Outline of Psychoanalysis*, p. 23). That Freud should frame the question this way suggests, however, that he is responding directly (if obliquely) to Nietzsche, as indeed his entire discussion does. In fact, there is evidence that Freud was familiar with *HH* 1.12. In *The Science of Dreams*, ch. 7, Freud cites Nietzsche by name, but without attribution to a specific work, to the effect that in dreams we can see "a primitive epoch of humanity that we can no longer easily reach by a direct path." Assoun argues convincingly that Freud is here citing *Human, All-Too-Human* from memory, somewhat inaccurately. If as Freud claims, he could only bring himself to read a "half-page" of Nietzsche, then it was, by wild coincidence, a segment terribly important to Freud's own work. The more likely explanation, of course, is that Freud could not bear to admit his more serious exploration of writings he had declared taboo for himself. See Assoun, *Freud et Nietzsche*, pp. 62—64.

33. The inventiveness of cause-creating lies in its thinking up new interpretations, new meanings for "effects." It does not lie in the false elevation of these to the status of "real" causes. Thus, the repetition of cause-elevation is not, for Nietzsche, a furthering of imagination—rather, it repeats the lie of causality, now without any redemptive imaginary contribution. See *OTL* 250.

34. For all Nietzsche's reverence for the Greeks, he never (or at least not after *BT*) wants to dwell in the past. Although he may despise the present, he is not antimodern in the romantic sense of a yearning to "return." Nor does he resent the "newness" of modernity. On this point, I am particularly indebted to George Kateb.

35. One thinks here of Theodor Adorno's critique of jazz (Horkheimer and Adorno, *Dialectic of Enlightenment*, p. 154). Jazz improvisation, he says, provides the illusion of discipline-breaking and creativity, while actually serving to reinforce rather simpleminded basic themes. I cannot accept this position as an analysis of jazz, but it does help to illuminate Nietzsche's point here.

36. Lacoue-Labarthe calls this "creative mimesis" ("History and Mimesis," p. 227).

37. I owe this observation to Victor Preller.

38. This quotation by itself ought to put to rest the idea that Nietzsche has a romantic view of creativity where "to create is to produce objects in the absence of rules" as S. Kemal has it ("Some Problems of Genealogy," p. 41). In Kemal's sympathetic treatment of genealogy, Nietzsche's defense of interpretation as creative leads to the potentially redemptive power of creation. I argue similarly, but with a major difference: because Kemal sees in Nietzsche an account of creativity not grounded in time, the "redemption" it offers is only a redemption of the moment. In contrast, my account of creativity as "dancing in chains" leads to a deeper connection between creation and history, between past and future. Thus, the redemption to be offered is redemption of the past and not just of the present moment. It seems a more substantial offer.

39. The following cheeky formulation occurs to me: Nietzsche prefers to be tied up so long as he is not tied down.

Chapter 4

1. *GS* 354, which is part of the fifth book of that work, added in the second edition and therefore written around 1887, at about the same time as *GM*, encapsulates Nietzsche's thinking on the subject. The first edition of *GS*, with only four books, had appeared earlier, in 1882.

2. Of course, this image of consciousness as a mirror is an old one. What are perhaps less well known are the roots of this association, along with that of memory, in the European Hermetic and mystical tradition. See Yates, *Art of Memory*.

3. *Distortion* is perhaps too strong a term, since Nietzsche's arguments against the thing-in-itself cut against any notion of an undistorted reality. But the term is apt in one sense: any linguistic representation must include the lie of regular causality.

4. This passage can be usefully compared to Emerson's essay on friendship: "Two may talk and one may hear, but three cannot take part in a conversation of the most sincere and searching thought" (*Complete Writings*, 1: 189).

5. This connection will strengthen the argument that pity is the central herd value. I owe my appreciation of the role of pity in Nietzsche's thought to George Kateb.

6. Kaufmann, *Nietzsche: Philosopher, Psychologist, Antichrist*, pp. 152–53.

7. Their works are cited in subsequent notes as I briefly consider some of their arguments.

8. Another reversal involves the noble morality/slave morality distinction. In *HH* 2.45, Nietzsche gives an early version of this distinction but also states quite clearly (in the last sentence) that he believes our present morality to have "grown up in the soil of the *ruling* tribes and castes" (his emphasis). His famous condemnation of Christian morality as slave morality is thus a complete reversal of this early position.

9. Paul Rée, *The Origin of Moral Sensations* (1877). Nietzsche writes: "I made opportune and inopportune reference to the propositions of that book" (*GM*, Pref., 4).

10. The second meditation was published in 1874. It thus predates all Nietzsche's books except *The Birth of Tragedy*.

11. For an interesting meditation on the contradictions of this essay's "struggling to remember what it was like not to remember," see Comay, "Redeeming Revenge," in *Nietzsche as Postmodernist*, ed. Koelb, pp. 21–38. In this chapter, the term *man* will often be used where what seems to be meant is a person or humanity or people in general. I use this term because it seems to me that terms such as *humanity* and *human race* refer to us as biological organisms, whereas what Nietzsche means to signify here is man as a cultured animal—and I want to recognize that the meaning of this culturation has a definite gendered valence, even if I cannot here give that subject all the attention it deserves. That is, using *man* serves the purpose of *not* glossing over Nietzsche's views on the sexes. Although I believe these are much more complicated than a case of simple misogyny, there is no doubt that Nietzsche associates much of our development and culture with man in the gender-specific sense. See Derrida, *Spurs*.

12. Gilles Deleuze calls genealogy "the value of origin and the origin of values" (*Nietzsche and Philosophy*, p. 2). I admire the formulation but would recast it as "the memory of origins and the origins of memory." Foucault's reversal of Deleuze, "[Genealogy] opposes itself to the search for 'origins'" ("Nietzsche, Genealogy, History," p. 140), goes too far. Foucault also holds that Nietzsche *does* return to the three types of history, but that they are "metamorphosized" (ibid., p. 164)—a characterization that raises more questions than it answers.

13. In his correspondence as well, Nietzsche often refers to, and recommends the reading of, all the *UM* except this one.

14. Mark Warren argues that genealogy is the "heir" to critical history and largely "a form of ideology critique" (*Nietzsche and Political Thought*, pp. 87, 102). My objections to this view can only be partially spelled out here, since they require, in some sense, the whole of my account of the *GM*. But put briefly: Warren does not consider the account of the creation of memory that I describe below. He prefers to see genealogy as a method, rather than confront the *content* of *the* genealogy and Nietzsche's reaction to it (he is not alone in this). Doing so would make clear that genealogy bears little relation to critical history and never has the simpleminded purpose of "investigating" and "condemning" history, which is the purpose of the "critical" method. What genealogy uncovers cannot be condemned and abandoned as Nietzsche had at one time suggested in the *UM*. Warren would have been better served in these sections if he had followed his own insights into the connection of memory and violence and not insisted on assimilating Nietzsche to Marx (see ibid., pp. 141–58).

15. For the opposite view, see Ackermann, *Nietzsche: A Frenzied Look*, who maintains, remarkably, that after the second *UM* "the topic of history largely disappears" from Nietzsche's work (p. 72). He terms genealogy "light history" (p. 81). This distinction strikes me as untenable, not to say ridiculous. The *Genealogy* may be written in an exuberant style, but its content is brutal and its tone serious. If anyone's account is light, it is Ackermann's.

16. Even Gary Shapiro, who makes this point about the form and content of genealogy declines to follow up on his own insight in his essay "Translating, Repeating, Naming: Foucault, Derrida, and *The Genealogy of Morals*," in *Nietzsche as Postmodernist*, ed. Koelb, pp. 39–56.

17. The word Nietzsche uses for "moment" here is *Augenblick* (literally, the wink of an eye), as opposed to *Moment*, which is also a German word. But the "gate called Moment" was also named *Augenblick*.

18. Indeed, it is unclear whether there *is* any*thing* at all apart from the accounts of that thing. This passage, with its references to names and things, would seem to indicate that a distinction is retained. And yet, what sort of "things" can these be when the "thing-in-itself" is so vigorously rejected (*WP* 553–69)? I can only resolve these questions as follows (in a fashion similar to that used before with regard to the body [see Chapter 3]): there is a world that makes impressions on our senses, but there are no "things" in that world if "thing" means a separable element of the world with its own essence or meaning. The only meaning or value of a thing is found in our accounts of it, and in this sense all "things" are the product of our accounts. See

Nehamas, *Nietzsche: Life as Literature*, ch. 3, "A Thing Is the Sum of Its Effects." "In short, the essence of a thing is only an *opinion* about the 'thing' " (*WP* 556). Blondel takes the stronger view: "Reality and life *are* not, they are interpreted" (*Nietzsche: The Body and Culture*, p. 78). But the words "they are" in the second clause of this sentence beg the question. Can interpretation be meaningful without a text? Recall Nietzsche's reference to an "unknown but felt" text (*D* 2.119). This is a text, apparently, that exists without distinguishable words.

19. Despite this, and despite my critique of him in the preceding note, Blondel is right to maintain that "Nietzsche does not reduce culture to the body" (*Nietzsche: The Body and Culture*, p. 206). Foucault, of course, reemphasizes Nietzsche's point and highlights its importance for his own work ("Nietzsche, Genealogy, History," pp. 147–56).

20. Deleuze is just wrong to claim that for Nietzsche "Prehistoric means generic" (*Nietzsche and Philosophy*, p. 133). This is just one of the many ways in which commentators have twisted Nietzsche and the *GM* in order to avoid dealing with it as a historical account. Deleuze's attempt is particularly clumsy, however. It requires almost immediately, for example, that he posit two different kinds of memory in Nietzsche (p. 134)—an assumption nowhere supported in the text.

21. For an alternative account of mnemotechnics, which emphasizes the parallels between the *GM* and Freud's *Civilization and Its Discontents*, but plays down, to my mind, the connections to violence and a sense of time, see Crawford, "Nietzsche's Mnemotechnics, the Theory of Ressentiment, and Freud's Topographics of Psychical Apparatus."

22. The *Genealogy* as a whole is composed of 70 sections, and the earliest period reached is also the midpoint of the essay (2.18—the 35th section). Since the first essay works backwards from concepts of guilt to medieval notions to the conflict of noble and slave, while the third essay works forward along the development of asceticism, one might consider the overall structure to be as follows: the book works backwards in time until it reaches the earliest point it can find, the origin of humanity; thereafter, it runs back forward in time until it reaches the present. It recapitulates or retraverses the course of time armed with the knowledge gained on the reverse trip. This is offered purely as a speculation, but it seems to me superior to the only other account of the structure of the *Genealogy* of which I am aware—Deleuze's contention that Nietzsche was attempting "to rewrite the *Critique of Pure Reason*" (*Nietzsche and Philosophy*, p. 88). If this speculation is correct, the structure of the *Genealogy* is *not* equivalent to the narrative it contains. That is, although readers get an account of the past, their path through that account is not the same as the account itself. It is this latter narrative that I want to focus on.

23. But not the converse: violence is not necessarily creative.

24. *Friedrich Nietzsche*, ed. Bloom, p. 7.

25. Indeed, after the initial event, creativity may have to be *more* violent because preexisting forms must be destroyed.

26. This perspective may lessen the importance of the question of whether there was ever a first imposition of meaning or form. If forms become meaningless, perhaps

even shapeless, when one has decided to alter them, then the shapeless mass the beasts attack may only have been so *from their perspective*.

27. This might cause one to wonder how Homeric myth could be the cause of strong memory. The answer is that Nietzsche considered these myths to be spectacles of cruelty, whose ultimate audience was the gods (*GM* 2.7). It does not really matter that the gods do not exist; it is the victims of cruelty, not the perpetrators, who have the strong memories that result from it.

28. Warren, who elsewhere quotes Nietzsche on the creation of memory, and often perceives with great clarity the threat that Nietzsche sees memory posing to life, writes inexplicably that, for Nietzsche, "the capacities that make subjectivity possible (intentionality and reflexive monitoring of action) are given to the human condition" (*Nietzsche and Political Thought*, p. 9; cf. p. 12). While a reading of the *UM* might yield this view, any consideration of the *GM* must surely contravene it.

29. The suppression of multiplicity in the process of civilization is also a key theme in Freud's work (although usually focused on sexual matters) and, I think, also finds its way into Lacan's account of maturation. See Freud, *Civilization and Its Discontents*, chs. 3 and 4, and Lacan, "The Mirror Stage," pp. 1—7.

30. Wittgenstein's dictum "Whereof one cannot speak, thereof one must be silent" (*Tractatus Logico-Philosophicus*, p. 189) takes on a different tone when viewed from this perspective. Wittgenstein's debt to Nietzsche is, I think, greatly underappreciated.

31. See *TI*, " 'Reason' in Philosophy," § 5. Similarly, Werner Hammacher writes: "Since the will articulates itself linguistically and since it is not a will without this articulation, the will is an effect of interpretation and explication" ("Promise of Interpretation," in *Looking After Nietzsche*, ed. Rickels, p. 40). In other words willing/interpretation precedes *the* will conceived of as a subject, a doer behind the deed.

32. Nietzsche attempted to turn this capacity of language to create souls to his advantage. In the introduction to *Human, All-Too-Human* (§ 2), he claims to have invented the "free spirits" for whom the book is intended. More spectacularly, in *Zarathustra*, he claims: "Companions the creator once sought, and children of his hope; and behold, it turned out that he could not find them, unless he first created them himself" (3.3). The book bears out this claim. At the end of the prologue (§ 9), Zarathustra claims he needs companions, but that the people will not do. Nonetheless, in the 18th section of the first book, companions begin to appear. They have been spoken into existence by Zarathustra's speeches.

33. Some readers may feel that I give short shrift, in this account, to the noble morality of the *Genealogy*'s first essay. But if so it will still hardly be enough to counteract the overattention that the first essay and the "noble" have received over the years at the expense of the second essay and the "morality of mores." This is part of a general pattern of Nietzsche interpretation that obsesses over a few key concepts (e.g., noble/slave, overman) at the expense of hundreds of pages on other topics. So many accounts of the *GM* skip directly from the first to the third essay without any attempt to see how the second essay links them. The time frame given by the second essay indicates clearly that the nobles featured in the first are merely the last generation within the era of "mores" in whatever neck of the woods they happen to live: Greeks on the eve of

Socrates and Plato, Romans on the eve of Jesus and Paul. The reason that the identity of the nobles seems to shift so often in the first essay is that Nietzsche is describing a process that takes place at different moments in different places—although by now all of the West has been Christianized. Yet all nobles are, for Nietzsche, "sternly held in check *inter pares* by custom" (*GM* 1.11). The contrast between noble and slave in the first essay is a pale reflection of that between man and animal in the second.

34. See Crawford, "Nietzsche's Mnemotechnics, the Theory of Ressentiment, and Freud's Topographics of Psychical Apparatus," pp. 290–97, and Comay, "Redeeming Revenge," pp. 21–38.

35. Deleuze's interpretation of Nietzsche on this point is important and has, I think, been beneficial to the study of Nietzsche—but it is also deeply flawed. Deleuze's analysis demonstrated the centrality of genealogy and ressentiment to Nietzsche's project. He also succeeded in extricating Nietzsche interpretation from a Hegelian-Marxist mind-set. But his account of ressentiment is misleading. He identifies it with memory directly, such that the two are inseparable (*Nietzsche and Philosophy*, p. 114–16). This has the effect of flattening out Nietzsche's history. My account demonstrates, I hope, that Nietzsche clearly identifies several distinct historical stages. Memory comes into being in an earlier epoch than ressentiment. But because Deleuze wants to identify the two, he has to depict the two eras as simultaneous in a manner that does not accord with the text. This has the bad consequences I discussed above: (1) the historical nature of Nietzsche's account is lost ("prehistorical means generic"); and (2) Deleuze is forced into the claim that there are two types of memory, because many of Nietzsche's discussions of memory make its identification with ressentiment impossible. Deleuze is overinfluenced by Freud and ends up reading him back into Nietzsche (e.g., ressentiment as "anal-sadistic complex" [p. 116]). Warren's interpretation of ressentiment, on the other hand, is guided by Marx. Although he notes the connection between violence and interpretation, he argues that ressentiment is a "species of bad conscience," and that bad conscience "is the psychology of class society that comes to pervade western culture" (*Nietzsche and Political Thought*, pp. 27, 23). In other words, violence is the result of a class society. But for Nietzsche, as we have seen, exactly the opposite is the case: it is a class society that is the result of violence. Violence precedes society, rather than following from it. It is social forms that are shaped by violence and not the reverse. Nietzsche's brand of radicalism, if it is that, is quite distinct from those of Freud and Marx.

36. For an analytic view of this point, see Schact, *Nietzsche*, pp. 136–38.

37. It seems to me that Kaufmann's translation lapses at this crucial point. Although he points out in a footnote that German uses the same word for "guilt" and "debt" (*Schuld*), he often goes on to translate it simply as "guilt," making Nietzsche speak of "the moralization of the concept guilt" at 2.21, a seemingly redundant process. What concept could be more moral than guilt? It is the moralization of "debt" that Nietzsche speaks of; indeed, that is the point of 2.19–22.

38. In Michael Platt's essay, "What Does Zarathustra Whisper in Life's Ear?" there is a charming expression of Zarathustra's care for the future in terms of his love of Eternity and his desire for children with her, as opposed to his other "women," Life

and Wisdom (p. 190). The essay is all the more charming for its flirtation with the outrageous.

39. Quoted in Jaspers, *Nietzsche*, p. 240; Nietzsche, *Werke: Kritische Gesamtausgabe*, 7, pt. 1: 557, from the *Nachlass* of 1883. Otherwise, Jaspers's remarks on past and future in Nietzsche do not seem very helpful to us today; they are largely, if subtly, directed at the German political situation of the 1930s.

40. See George Grant, *Time as History*, pp. 41–47, cited in Warren, *Nietzsche and Political Thought*, p. 193.

41. See Nehamas, *Nietzsche: Life as Literature*, ch. 5.

42. Danto, *Nietzsche as Philosopher*, pp. 202–3; Heidegger, *Nietzsche*, 2: 49–62. When Danto and Heidegger agree, it gives one pause. Actually, Danto does not even appear aware that it is the animals who speak, rather than Zarathustra, or Nietzsche.

43. Stambaugh, *Problem of Time in Nietzsche*, pp. 42, 54.

44. For a contrary view, see Thomas Pangle's interesting article, "The Warrior-Spirit as an Inlet to the Political Philosophy of Nietzsche's Zarathustra." By focusing on Zarathustra's praise of warriors and castes, Pangle portrays the future Zarathustra wants as a sort of dystopic *Republic*, where warriors engage the masses in endless battles over "taste." By ignoring the much more detailed account of the past in *GM*, Pangle manages to stress Nietzsche's account of time while emptying it of content, until all that remains of it is the idea of recurrence. Set against an empty account of the past, Nietzsche's meddling with the future thus looks wanton and dangerous, and Pangle concludes by asking whether Zarathustra's thinking on these subjects only points out "the problematic character of all such longings." It is an interesting thought. But given Nietzsche's account of the threat posed by the past and memory, it would be problematic *not* to think about the future.

45. This point requires emphasis because so many have maintained otherwise: Nietzsche is *not* nostalgic for the Greeks, although he does admire them. He says we must go "beyond the Greeks" (*GS* 340).

46. Staten describes Nietzsche's project as one of redeeming the past but adds, rather strangely to my mind, "as regards the past in general this affirmation has not been thought through very seriously or in any detail" (*Nietzsche's Voice*, p. 75). Whatever one thinks of Nietzsche's attempt to redescribe the past, I hope my review of it has shown at least that it is detailed and serious.

47. It also points away from "the innocence of becoming" and the state of child-likeness or animality that Joan Stambaugh focuses on in "Thoughts on the Innocence of Becoming." Although she is right to point to the role of childlike "play" in Nietzsche's account of creativity, she is wrong to emphasize "the magic of the present" as an element of Nietzsche's prescription (p. 177). That is, while Nietzsche values a child*like* playfulness, he recoils at the thought of child*ish* innocence, ignorant of past and future, which is stuck in the present. To be children again would be to relinquish the achievement of consciousness, its potential powers, and the possibility of redeeming the past. Picasso often spoke of wanting to paint like a child. But this meant that he wanted to unite a child's innocent spirit with a painter's techniques, not that he wanted to give up those techniques altogether.

48. The "Or?" that concludes *Daybreak* is no accident. Nietzsche calls attention to it in *Ecce Homo*.

49. This note comes with the attachment "manuscript source uncertain," but it has been included in all editions of *WP* and seems an unlikely candidate for forgery. Although useful to my argument, it serves no important purpose in the immediate context where it appears. Its style, both in brevity of expression and in the disjointedness typical of the notes, is recognizably Nietzschean. Nietzsche's early editors have many sins to answer for, including strategic deletions and fabrications, but it is hard to see what motive they could have had in composing this note.

50. Lacoue-Labarthe, "History and Mimesis," p. 214.

51. Lou Salomé (*Nietzsche*, pp. 153–55), at least, perceived that there was some distance between the formulations of the *UM* and those of the *GM*. But she took this to mean that Nietzsche's position had changed from one wholly opposed to the burden of history to the "diametrically opposite" view that only the past could be used for the future. As I believe my discussion of the *BT* and the *GM* has shown, Nietzsche had neither the early nor the later extreme views that Salomé attributes to him. But that is not to say that there was no evolution—and she was acute to pick up on it, where so many others have not.

52. Of course, this is a direct and pointed contrast with Plato's account of the Cave in the *Republic*, bk. 5. Plato's wise man emerges into daylight and a single truth.

Chapter 5

1. See, e.g., Singer, *Hegel*, ch. 2; Taylor, *Hegel*, ch. 15; Findlay, *Philosophy of Hegel*, p. 334; Kojève, *Introduction to the Reading of Hegel*, pp. 130–49. Hegel's teleology has both inspired Marxists and embarrassed many of his liberal and communitarian inheritors. The latter have often tried to jettison Hegel's historicism while arguing that the rest of his philosophy can stand on its own, or perhaps with a little help, as a defensible model of social organization. Smith, *Hegel's Critique of Liberalism*; id., "What Is 'Right' in Hegel's 'Philosophy of Right'?"; and Taylor, *Hegel and Modern Society* are among the more prominent recent attempts in English. The former have attempted to invigorate the teleology with a radicalized politics. See Marcuse, *Reason and Revolution*, and, of course, Marx, *The Communist Manifesto* (pt. 1), and *The German Ideology* (pt. 1), in *The Marx-Engels Reader*, pp. 473–83, 146–200.

2. The analysis that epitomizes this view is, of course, that of Popper in *The Open Society and Its Enemies*, vol. 2 (1950); see also O'Brien, *Hegel on Reason and History*. But I am thinking less of sophisticated treatments of Hegel than of the way in which the term *philosophy of history* is used, with Hegel in mind, as an intellectual placeholder for a state-centered view of inevitable progress—an evaluation that has survived even as much of Popper's work has fallen into disrepute. This situation necessitates that anyone using the term dissociate themselves from this meaning even though they no longer identify it with any particular author. See, e.g., Carr, *Time, Narrative and History*, p. 1.

3. Hegel's texts are cited in this chapter by the abbreviations given on p. xii. Page

numbers in the Sibree, Nisbet, and Knox translations respectively follow the abbreviations *PH*, *IPH*, and *AE*. Numbers following the abbreviations *PS*, *PR*, and *LG* indicate paragraphs in the Miller, Knox, and Wallace translations. The numbers may be followed by the letters "a" or "n" to indicate an addition or note to Hegel's main text.

4. A notable exception here is Desmond's *Art and the Absolute*, which does attempt to connect Hegel's themes of art and history.

5. Anne-Marie Gethmann-Siefert attempts to connect and rehabilitate Hegel's aesthetics and history in *Die Funktion der Kunst in der Geschichte*. She does so, however, by reading Hegel's lectures on aesthetics and history through the lectures of the Jena period and by jettisoning some of Hegel's more difficult positions about the "end of art" in an effort to reconstruct a more coherent and defensible perspective on art and history. Although this approach may construct a more usable Hegelian theory, it does not confront Hegel's most challenging views. It is precisely these views, however, and their implications that I ask the reader to take seriously (although not to endorse). See also Gethmann-Siefert's various contributions to *Hegel Studien*, vols. 16, 17, and 19.

6. Nietzsche discusses the "seduction to existence" and life in the third essay of *On the Genealogy of Morals* in decidedly ambivalent terms. On the one hand, he condemns the pain and distortion that the propagation of the "ascetic ideal" as a seduction to life has caused. On the other hand, he recognizes the necessity and benefits of such a project—a project very similar to the one he himself is engaged in. In making use of the concept here, I share Nietzsche's uneasiness with it and, as will be clear from what follows, hardly mean to endorse it or use it as an unambiguous term of praise. See also *BT* 3.

7. This depiction of social organization as a work of art dates at least from Hegel's Jena period, as Jean Hyppolite has shown (*Introduction à la philosophie de l'histoire de Hegel*, pp. 19, 89). But since Hyppolite's focus is an interpretation of the *Phenomenology*, he considers this theme's subsidiary role there and neglects its reemergence in the later lectures on art and history.

8. *Gestalt* (shape) is the German word that Hegel uses most often in this context, although he occasionally uses *Form* (form) or *Bild* (image). Although "shape" is the best translation of *Gestalt*, the latter is also the word that usually stands in contrast to the German term for "content" (*Gehalt*). It has as well the subsidiary sense of "whole" or "character," which, while perfectly in accord with Hegel's usage, would later be emphasized by the psychoanalytic community to a degree that is not evident in Hegel.

9. "Idea for a Universal History with a Cosmopolitan Intent," in *The Philosophy of Kant* (New York: Modern Library, 1949), p. 119.

10. For an excellent discussion of the development of this idea by Koyré and its subsequent adoption by Kojève, see Darby, *The Feast*, ch. 3; and cf. Kojève, *Introduction to the Reading of Hegel*, pp. 95–99.

11. See Rosen, *G. W. F. Hegel*, pp. 29–34, 43–46.

12. "Calvary" (*Schädelstätte*) is, strictly speaking, the site of the Crucifixion. But it also means a representation of the Passion as the path of the Stations of the Cross and

hence, more generally, a life of suffering with distinct stages. Here Hegel seems to mean that history and knowledge put together form something higher—just as Christ was most human and most divine at the moment of his death, a moment that contained a final understanding of the life that had led up to it. It is this union of events, objects, and knowledge that Hegel considers "philosophy" in the strict sense. Knowledge is always knowledge of the past and knowledge of a completed past is the fullest sort of knowledge. But without Hegel's umbrella of faith to protect us, the image of a Calvary may seem to us simply as one of an ending, of a completion rather than a culmination in something higher. Hegel's *Aesthetics* only reinforces this image by describing the end of art, a description more disturbing than that of the end of history.

13. Cf. Hyppolite, *Introduction à la philosophie de l'histoire de Hegel*, pp. 13–17.

14. This point may be reemphasized by considering the distinction between the *Weltgeist* (World Spirit) and the *Volksgeist* (national spirit). Even the final national spirit, the Germanic, is not as complete in Hegel's thinking as the World Spirit, which contains *all* of the various stages of history and the evolution from one to the next.

15. This double meaning also exists for the German word for property, *Eigenschaft*; if anything, the second meaning is stronger in German.

16. Here my interpretation differs considerably from the influential view of Otto Pöggler (*Hegels Idee einer Phänomenologie des Geistes*), who has consistently attempted to deconcretize Hegel's theory of history by reading his later material through the Jena lectures. Thus he argues that history, for Hegel, is merely a "systematic coherence" and a "struggle of consciousness and self-consciousness" (pp. 353, 354). Not only, I believe, does this argument have problems with material like that quoted above from the *Phenomenology* (where Hegel emphasizes that it is the material world that he is discussing), but it is profoundly weakened by what Hegel says in his later lectures on art and history (which discuss this material world at great length and which Pöggler does not address systematically). It may be the case that the early Jena lectures reflect the more purely intellectual position Pöggler describes, and that this position is more palatable to us today, but that does not, I believe, relieve us of the responsibility of coming to grips with Hegel's later, more difficult views. Pöggler's view has clearly influenced Gethmann-Siefert (cited n. 5 above.)

17. Of course, in Hegel's quasi-platonic idealism, the highest degree of "reality" is reserved for thoughts of "the Idea." My point, though, is that the shapes of history have *as much* reality as all other objects that fall short of this pinnacle. This is what allows Hegel to speak of art and history in the same breath.

18. At *PS* 808, Hegel writes that the passage is slow "just because the Self has to penetrate and digest this entire wealth of its substance." But this is really no answer at all. Why are we to think that this process must be a slow one? Because "digesting" our food takes several hours?

19. I think this image derives mostly from Marx's reading of Hegel, a reading popular among Marxists and non-Marxists alike. Indeed, it may even be more popular among the latter, since it conveniently implicates Hegel in Marx's approach to history.

20. Gadamer, *Hegel's Dialectic*, p. 36.

21. Taylor, *Hegel*, pp. 390–91. Despite this point of disagreement, it will be obvious to any reader familiar with Taylor's work how much I owe to this book, the greatest systematic account of Hegel's works yet to appear in English.

22. Kojève, *Introduction to the Reading of Hegel*, p. 20. He finds the master's role "tragic" (p. 19), but Hegel finds little tragic in the earliest masters among the Persians or the Egyptians. In attempting a Kojèvian reading of *PH*, which Kojève does not, Cooper (*End of History*, ch. 3) only succeeds in reading the introduction of that work, and distorts the structure of the rest of it when he briefly considers it.

23. See Plato's *Republic*, bk. 10. We must leave to one side here the interesting question of Plato's own status as a poet—and Hegel's.

24. See Desmond, "Art, Philosophy, Concreteness," p. 141, and *Art and the Absolute*, esp. ch. 5, where Desmond describes art as the union of the spirit and the sensuous.

25. Kojève is certainly correct to point to the role of labor in the production of culture (*Introduction to the Reading of Hegel*, p. 52). He is simply wrong to associate the development through labor with the political triumph of the slave or worker. In *PH*, work is done by all manner of people, high and low.

26. It should be noted that this account of action accords with the *Phenomenology* in the following way: Hegel also calls action the struggle and dissolution of difference (*AE* 179). But "difference" has a strictly ontological meaning. Hegel calls it a limit or a boundary. It is the point where a thing ends. It is, then, roughly speaking, the boundary between the "is" and "is not" of the thing. But then the dissolution of this boundary would mean, among other things, the joining of what is with what is not. And this is what Hegel means when he speaks of making the implicit into the explicit—what is is brought in where it previously was not. See *PS* 3, 166–77.

27. See Desmond, "Art, Philosophy, Concreteness," p. 138, as well as *Art and the Absolute*, ch. 5. Desmond applies this notion of the concrete universal to philosophical concepts as well as artworks. He holds such concepts to be beautiful wholes; hence "Hegel's idea of a philosophical system . . . has an unmistakable aesthetic ring" (p. 144).

28. Like the *Philosophy of History*, the *Aesthetics* was, of course, assembled after Hegel's death from his lecture notes and those of his students. It is generally felt, however, that the quality of the editing was far superior in the case of the *Aesthetics* and produced a far more coherent and comprehensive text.

29. It is for this reason, and not a general immoralism, that Hegel contends that ethics is not a measure appropriate to evaluating the past. Morality, he argues, applies to individual intentions, and aesthetics to the actual shapes of history that emerge, regardless of intentions. Each category is separate, with its appropriate, separate objects. See *PS* 322, 640, 666; *IPH* 141; *AE* 187–88.

30. One cannot help but recall Marx's observation that for Hegel everything and everyone important in world history occurs "as it were, twice. He forgot to add: the first time as tragedy, the second as farce" (*Marx-Engels Reader*, ed. Tucker, p. 594). What Hegel actually wrote was: "[A] political revolution is sanctioned in men's

244 NOTES TO PAGES 165-73

opinions when it repeats itself. Thus Napoleon was twice defeated, and the Bourbons twice expelled" (*PH* 313).

31. The only heroes clearly mentioned are Alexander, Julius Caesar, Napoleon, and (although it is rarely noted), the Persian king Cyrus (*PH* 187). None of these stand between epochs; rather, they are at the center of them. They do not see the future; they merely see the present more clearly than their contemporaries; indeed, they embody that present. This even applies to Cyrus who, in the perfection of his despotism, is said to typify the Oriental stage.

32. The battle that freed Greece from the threat of domination by the Persian empire. Traditionally, it marks the beginning of the "Golden Age" of Hellenic civilization.

33. Despite the fact that the Egypt of the Sphinx existed at least half a millennium earlier, Hegel places it within his section on the Persian empire. The excuse for this is that, much later, Egypt was occupied by the Persians, but the real reason is that Hegel needs Egypt and the Sphinx to represent the "oriental" spirit that was overcome by the Greeks in their defeat of the Persians. It is all a bit arbitrary (*IPH* 200-201). "The inward or ideal transition, from Egypt to Greece is as just exhibited. But Egypt became a province of the great Persian kingdom, and the historical transition takes place when the Persian world comes into contact with the Greek" (*PH* 221). This distinction between "ideal" and "historical" transitions occurs nowhere else in Hegel that I am aware of.

34. To the reply that the selection is not arbitrary but paradigmatic (as Hegel no doubt believed) the response can only be that the text does not make their paradigmatic status compelling. Hegel does not really discuss, for example, why Shakespeare's characters are more perfectly modern than those of Molière, or for that matter, of Da Vinci or El Greco. He merely repeatedly asserts the centrality of the former. If, of course, Hegel is merely acting as a good artist does, representing what is already "cut and dried," he might have expected the paradigmatic status of these figures to be as obvious to his (educated) audience as to himself. Hegel's position is consistent then; it is just that his consistency no longer appears as convincing as it once did.

35. What I have in mind here are both the state of the Romantic stage and the Temple of Mnemosyne as a whole.

36. It should be clear by now just how much of Hegel's imagery relies on Sophocles' *Oedipus Rex*. And, in fact, Hegel does praise Sophocles "above all" as a rich individual of the Periclean age (*AE* 719).

37. For a discussion of "the romantic arts," see p. 172.

38. Hegel would no doubt have been perplexed by some of the more recent findings of anthropologists and classicists, which indicate that the Greeks probably painted the eyes onto their statues, as well as painting the statues themselves—rather gaudily in some cases.

39. This is Nietzsche's phrase. To him, it was a compliment.

40. This must have seemed odd to Hegel's contemporaries. To us, it seems somewhat less outrageous than the similar conclusions about China and India.

41. Except for music. As many have noted, Hegel's appreciation of music does not

seem to match his love of theater or the plastic arts. This may well stem from the fact that, of all art forms, music is the one most difficult to characterize as possessing shape.

42. Collingwood, *Idea of History*, pp. 113—22.

43. Here Hegel is playing on the contrast between the words *fahl* (pale) and *frisch*, which means fresh but also ruddy or healthy of face: "in the pink," so to speak. Hence, the future of art looks unpromising; its face is pale with the sickness unto death.

44. Shklar's contention that "art is dead" because modern times lack "the religion of Hellas, the religion of art" is too simple. While there is something about Greece that produces the most perfect art, the end of Greece is not the end of art. Art has now ended, as far as Hegel is concerned, but it did have a modern phase; Dante and Shakespeare are poets to rank with Sophocles. Moreover, Shklar's discussion does not consider the three stages of art outlined in the *Aesthetics*; their existence, but especially that of the modern drama, cuts against her argument that "modern life not only destroyed the public, but also offered no material to the dramatic imagination." See Shklar, *Freedom and Independence*, pp. 133—34.

45. Desmond (*Art and the Absolute*, pp. 67ff.) offers an alternative conclusion based on what he call "the inexhaustible character of the art work." While admitting that Hegel speaks of the completion of art, he argues that "this perfection we find in art displays, even in its completeness, an open-ended side," because of art's supposedly inexhaustible character. "The sense of an end that art may offer us, then, need not force us into any spurious 'closure'." It is an ingenious argument; however, it is clear that the "inexhaustibility" of art is something *Desmond* ascribes to it. He makes no argument that *Hegel* viewed art in this fashion and offers no text that would lead us to believe this was the case. His argument then is more in the manner of a response to Hegel, where he accepts Hegel's main point but attempts to deny one of its implications. However, even if the response is accepted, the completeness of art remains as something that marks the present off from the past, and that must therefore have significant historical implications. Although Desmond admits the connections between art and history, he makes no attempt to speculate on these implications beyond the argument that they are not as dismal as might appear to be the case. As it is, however, I fear the appearances are not so deceiving. See also the essays by Knox and Carter in *Art and Logic in Hegel's Philosophy*, ed. Steinkraus and Schmitz, which argue similarly to Desmond in a less systematic fashion.

46. Viellard-Baron calls Hegel's a philosophy of *réminiscence* (*Le Temps*, p. 36).

47. However much I disagree with the way in which Kojève attempts to reconstruct Hegel's history, my view converges with his in viewing the consequence to the end of history as "Man's return to animality" (Kojève, *Introduction to the Reading of Hegel*, p. 160). Tom Darby recognizes that, in this evaluation, Kojève follows Nietzsche, and not Marx (Darby, *The Feast*, pp. xviii, 170—88).

48. If the idea of eternal recurrence, to will the past, strikes us as paradoxical, I do not think that its inverse and correlate, to remember the future, does so in the same way. And perhaps this can help us to see the sense of recurrence since, it seems to me, remembering the future is just the flip side of willing the past.

49. Eliot, "The Hollow Men," in *Selected Poems*, p. 79.

Chapter 6

1. Heidegger, *Being and Time*, p. 429.

2. E.g., at ibid., p. 425.   3. Ibid., p. 435.

4. Ibid., p. 438.   5. Ibid., p. 437.

6. Heidegger's belief in the singleness and solidity of tradition, it seems to me, was a crucial element in the thinking that ultimately led him to nationalism and Hitler. I cannot give this complicated question the attention it deserves here, but the example of Heidegger should serve to counter the notion that Nietzsche's disbelief in the fixed character of traditions was the high road to Nazism.

7. I set aside here the question of the degree to which Heidegger *drew* on Hegel as less important to the matter at hand, viz., the extent to which it makes sense to think of the two together.

8. Obviously, it is my contention here that, notwithstanding his self-proclaimed *Kehre*, the views of the later Heidegger on *these* questions are consonant enough with formulations in *Being and Time* for them to be discussed concurrently.

9. Heidegger, *On Time and Being*, p. 6.

10. Ibid., p. 12.

11. Ibid., pp. 19, 22.

12. Everything we know about Heidegger's political involvement, and about his behavior after World War II, only reinforces, it seems to me, what I have just written about his attitude toward history and the notion of responsibility. I make this point separately, however, both because I do not want to throw Heidegger's philosophy and politics together willy-nilly (and I have offered no evidence or argument on the latter) and because I think that what I have argued can be derived entirely from *Being and Time*, so that even if Heidegger had died long before his later behavior gave his philosophical defenders cause for embarrassment, the case could still be made based solely on his early philosophical writings.

13. Whatever inspiration we gain from the "innocence of becoming" as an ideal, Nietzsche does not mean to suggest by this phrase that we abandon what we have become and remain through memory—any more than he suggests we abandon history and return to the status of cows.

14. Thiele, *Timely Meditations*, ch. 3. Thiele does not stand alone here. Although his formulations are quite original, to a certain extent, he develops points made by George Kateb (*Inner Ocean*) and Fred Dallmayr (*Other Heidegger*). I mention this, not to diminish Thiele's contribution, which is considerable, but merely to point out that, in addressing his work, I am not merely taking on an idiosyncratic reading of Heidegger. Rather, I think that Thiele has, in many ways, accurately depicted the political implications of Heidegger's philosophy.

15. Thiele, *Timely Meditations*, pp. 72–73.

16. Ibid., p. 77.

17. Ibid., p. 72.

18. Thiele's Heidegger rejects this program as a dangerous one of "radical self-

creation" that can easily degenerate into "post-modern hubris." That this danger exists cannot be denied. But Thiele's claim that Heideggerian freedom "do[es] not preclude, but rather invite[s] activity and thought" rests on weak foundations. In order to defend it, he must argue that it is Hannah Arendt's activist politics that are the fulfillment of Heidegger's meaning. This conveniently ignores Arendt's stated debt to Machiavelli here. Indeed, for Arendt, it was Machiavelli's profound *humanism* (a humanism that Heidegger could never endorse) that filled precisely the gap in Heidegger's account of individuals—a true source of *action* in the human world. What defense of activism Arendt (and Thiele) are able to provide is achieved only insofar as they move away from Hegel's purposefully empty account of "action."

19. White, *Content of the Form*, p. 24.

20. Derrida, *Given Time*, pp. 103, 123.

21. Ibid., p. 145; see also p. 97. See also Derrida, "The Law of Genre," in *On Narrative*, ed. Mitchell, pp. 51–77.

22. White, *Content of the Form*, p. 24.

23. Derrida, "*Ousia* and *Gramme*: Note on a Note from *Being and Time*," in *Margins of Philosophy*, p. 65.

24. Since Derrida casts the net of narrative so far as to include "textual dissemination in general," this critique has ample purchase. "Narrative," one wants to say, "as opposed to what?"

25. Derrida: "The concept of time, in all its aspects, belongs to metaphysics . . . an *other* concept of time cannot be opposed to it, since time in general belongs to metaphysical conceptuality" (ibid., p. 65). That Derrida believes this to be the case results, I think, from his implicit and uncritical reliance on Heidegger's account of the history of philosophy. The essay cited follows Heidegger in declaring there to have been one dominant concept of time throughout Western philosophy: "This is what will not budge from Aristotle to Hegel" (p. 52). White arguably does recognize a distinction between history and fiction (at least in terms of their implicit representational claims), but that does not blunt his critique of the former as a basis for moral and political authority.

26. White, *Content of the Form*, p. 23.

27. See Derrida, "Law of Genre," in *On Narrative*, ed. Mitchell, p. 77.

28. Derrida, "*Ousia* and *Gramme*," in *Margins of Philosophy*, p. 52; see esp. n. 32.

29. "Moral" is not really the best term here, given Nietzsche's rejection of morality as such. I use the term merely in White's more general sense of "value-judgment," which Nietzsche surely does not eschew, even as he denies that his values are moral values.

30. This is the charge implicit in the title of White's book, *The Content of the Form*.

31. Of course, Derrida and White might reply here that these theories are "not narratives" since they do not correspond to their model, but I think this reply would strike most as either hairsplitting or an admission that it is not really "narrative discourse" as such that they are discussing. If they disqualify works that have an obvious narrative quality (like Nietzsche's) just because they lack a firm ending, their account seems tailored to suit examples that have been preselected to fit easily into it.

Chapter 7

1. Wittgenstein, *Philosophical Investigations*, § 67.

2. See also Alexander Nehamas, "The Genealogy of Genealogy," in *Nietzsche, Genealogy, Morality*, ed. Richard Schact, pp. 271–72.

3. Of course, it is no accident that Borges picks up the connections that Nietzsche draws between weak memories, dreams, sleepwalking, and Christianity. Borges is always a perceptive interpreter of Nietzsche, although here he skews the metaphors to his own purposes.

4. In fact, there have been several real cases like that described in the story of Funes—people, called "hyper-mnesiacs," who have paralyzingly perfect photographic memories. They are often unable to negotiate ordinary daily life.

5. MacIntyre, *Short History of Ethics*, p. 4.

6. In 1956, of course, a liberal communist group took over the Hungarian government and lifted many political and social controls. When it declared its withdrawal from the Warsaw Pact, the Russians and their Warsaw Pact allies invaded to restore hardline communists to power. Popular resistance continued for some weeks, but eventually Moscow prevailed. The account given in the following paragraphs is based on a variety of sources covering the first three months of 1989: the daily reports of the Foreign Broadcast Information Service; the *Eastern Europe Newsletter*; the situation reports of Radio Free Europe and Radio Liberty; and a number of articles in the *New York Times*, the *Times* of London, and the *Financial Times*. For more details, see my article " 'The Poszgay Affair': Historical Memory and Political Legitimacy," *History and Memory* (Spring 1996).

7. Foreign Broadcast Information Service–Eastern Europe Unit, # 89-039, pp. 27–29.

8. Lowenthal, *The Past is a Foreign Country*, esp. chs. 3 and 4.

9. Indeed, Lowenthal's thesis is so general that it is hard to imagine how it *could* be convincing (after all, how can concern for the past be quantified?). As hypothesis, however, it is very intriguing.

10. Of course, this is one of the central ironies of such movements. Their desire to preserve history is profoundly modern and ahistorical; it would not have sat well with the subjects of their desired preservation (who might desire to be preserved, but not because they are *old*).

11. Koselleck, " 'Space of Experience' and 'Horizon of Expectations': Two Historical Categories," in *Futures Past*, pp. 267–88.

12. White, *Content of the Form*, pp. 6–17.

13. I do not discuss the possibility, although I think it likely, that this episode of cultural anthropology itself results from a dissatisfaction with rationalism and an attempt to flee into its opposite or "other." This discovery of narrative in other cultures or subaltern groups, then, would itself rest on the Western philosopher's dichotomy between reason and narrative and would represent, largely, an attempt simply to reverse the poles of this dichotomy.

14. Ursula K. Le Guin, "It Was a Dark and Stormy Night; or, Why Are We Huddling About the Campfire?" in *On Narrative*, ed. Mitchell. She calls our attention to a one-line story from tribal England, "Tolfink carved these runes in this stone," as well as a variety of other examples (p. 194).

15. Arendt, *Between Past and Future*, pp. 11–12. Despite this minor disagreement, it will be clear to those familiar with Arendt that my approach to time and history is profoundly indebted to that laid out in this book and *The Human Condition*. As my appropriation of her title for a section of the Nietzsche chapter indicates, it would be my contention that on these matters (but certainly *not* on many others), Arendt's perspective grows out of that of Nietzsche. Her account of freedom as "the capacity to begin something new" (*Between Past and Future*, p. 166) captures as well as any I know the sense in which a concern for freedom and a concern for the future must coincide, as Nietzsche suggested.

16. Walter Benjamin, "Theses on the Philosophy of History," in *Illuminations*, ed. Hannah Arendt, p. 262. I have made some slight alterations in the English translation of the rhyme.

Select Bibliography

Aaron, Richard I. *John Locke*. 3d ed. Oxford: Oxford University Press, Clarendon Press, 1971.

Ackermann, Robert John. *Nietzsche: A Frenzied Look*. Amherst: University of Massachusetts Press, 1990.

Allison, David B., ed. *The New Nietzsche: Contemporary Styles of Interpretation*. New York: Dell, 1977.

Andrew, Edward. *Shylock's Rights: A Grammar of Lockean Claims*. Toronto: University of Toronto Press, 1988.

Arendt, Hannah. *Between Past and Future: Eight Exercises in Political Thought*. New York: Viking, 1968.

——. *The Human Condition*. Chicago: University of Chicago Press, 1958.

Aristotle. *The Basic Works of Aristotle*. Edited by Richard McKeon. New York: Random House, 1941.

Ashcraft, Richard. "Locke's State of Nature: Historical Fact or Moral Fiction?" *American Political Science Review* 62 (1968): 898–915.

——. *Locke's "Two Treatises of Government."* London: Allen & Unwin, 1987.

——. *Revolutionary Politics and Locke's "Two Treatises of Government."* Princeton: Princeton University Press, 1986.

Assoun, Paul-Laurent. *Freud et Nietzsche*. Paris: Presses universitaires de France, 1980.

Batz, William G. "The Historical Anthropology of John Locke." *Journal of the History of Ideas* 35 (Oct.–Dec. 1974): 663–70.

Benjamin, Walter. *Illuminations*. Edited by Hannah Arendt. New York: Schocken Books, 1969.

Blondel, Eric. *Nietzsche: The Body and Culture*. Stanford: Stanford University Press, 1991.

Bloom, Harold, ed. *Friedrich Nietzsche*. New York: Chelsea House Publishing, 1987.

Borges, Jorge Luis. *Ficciones*. Edited by Anthony Kerrigan. New York: Grove Weidenfeld, 1962.

Boyce, Mary. *A History of Zoroastrianism*. London: E. J. Brill, 1975.

Bras, Gérard. *Hegel et l'art*. Paris: Presses universitaires de France, 1989.

Brauer, Oscar Daniel. *Dialektik der Zeit*. Stuttgart: Friedrich Frommann Verlag, 1982.

Bremond, Claude. *Logique du récit*. Paris: Editions du seuil, 1973.

Caffentzis, Constantine George. *Clipped Coins, Abused Words and Civil Government: John Locke's Philosophy of Money*. New York: Autonomedia, 1989.

Canning, Peter. "How the Fable Becomes a World." In *Looking After Nietzsche*, ed. Laurence A. Rickels. Albany, N.Y.: State University of New York Press, 1990.

Carr, David. *Time, Narrative and History*. Bloomington: Indiana University Press, 1986.

Collingwood, R. G. *The Idea of History*. Oxford: Oxford University Press, 1956.

Colman, John. *John Locke's Moral Philosophy*. Edinburgh: Edinburgh University Press, 1983.

Comay, Rebecca. "Redeeming Revenge: Nietzsche, Benjamin, Heidegger and the Politics of Memory." In *Nietzsche as Postmodernist: Essays Pro and Contra*, ed. Clayton Koelb, pp. 21–38. Albany: State University of New York Press, 1989.

Cooper, Barry. *The End of History: An Essay on Modern Hegelianism*. Toronto: University of Toronto Press, 1984.

Crawford, Claudia. "Nietzsche's Mnemotechnics, the Theory of Ressentiment, and Freud's Topographies of the Psychical Apparatus." *Nietzsche Studien* 14 (1985): 281–97.

Croce, Benedetto. *What Is Living and What Is Dead of the Philosophy of Hegel*. London: Macmillan, 1915.

Dallmayr, Fred R. *The Other Heidegger*. Ithaca, N.Y.: Cornell University Press, 1993.

Danto, Arthur. *Nietzsche as Philosopher*. New York: Columbia University Press, 1965.

———. *Narration and Knowledge*. New York: Columbia University Press, 1985.

Darby, Tom. *The Feast: Meditations on Politics and Time*. Toronto: University of Toronto Press, 1982.

Deleuze, Gilles. *Nietzsche and Philosophy*. New York: Columbia University Press, 1983.

De Man, Paul. *Allegories of Reading*. New Haven: Yale University Press, 1979.

———. "Rhetoric of Tropes (Nietzsche)." In *Friedrich Nietzsche*, ed. Harold Bloom. New York: Chelsea House Publishing, 1987.

Derrida, Jacques. *Spurs: Nietzsche's Styles*. Chicago: University of Chicago Press, 1978.

———. *Margins of Philosophy*. Chicago: University of Chicago Press, 1982.

———. *Memoires: For Paul de Man*. New York: Columbia University Press, 1986.

———. *Given Time: 1. Counterfeit Money*. Chicago: University of Chicago Press, 1992.

Desmond, William. "Art, Philosophy and Concreteness in Hegel." *The Owl of Minerva* 16, no. 2 (Spring 1985): 131–46.

———. *Art and the Absolute: A Study of Hegel's Aesthetics*. Albany: State University of New York Press, 1986.

——. *Beyond Hegel and Dialectic: Speculation, Cult and Comedy*. Albany: State University of New York Press, 1992.

Dhalla, M. N. *History of Zoroastrianism*. New York: Oxford University Press, 1938.

Diggins, John P. *The Lost Soul of American Politics: Virtue, Self-Interest and the Foundations of Liberalism*. New York: Basic Books, 1984.

Duchesne-Guillemin, Jacques. *Symbols and Values in Zoroastrianism*. New York: Harper & Row, 1966.

Dunn, John. *The Political Thought of John Locke: An Historical Account of the Argument of the "Two Treatises of Government."* Cambridge: Cambridge University Press, 1969.

——. "The Concept of 'Trust' in the Politics of John Locke." In *Philosophy in History*, ed. Richard Rorty, J. B. Schneewind, and Quentin Skinner, pp. 279–301. Cambridge: Cambridge University Press, 1984.

Dworetz, Steven M. *The Unvarnished Doctrine: Locke, Liberalism, and the American Revolution*. Durham, N.C.: Duke University Press, 1990.

Eliot, T. S. *Selected Poems*. New York: Harcourt, Brace & World, 1967.

Emerson, Ralph Waldo. *Complete Writings*. 2 vols. New York: Wise & Co., 1929.

Farr, James, and Clayton Roberts. "John Locke on the Glorious Revolution: A Rediscovered Document." Bodleian MS Locke e. 18, "A Call to the nations for unity." *Historical Journal* 28, no. 2 (1985): 385–98.

Findlay, J. N. *The Philosophy of Hegel*. New York: Collier Books, 1958.

Foucault, Michel. "Nietzsche, Genealogy, History." In *Language, Counter-Memory, Practice*, ed. Donald F. Bouchard, pp. 139–64. Ithaca, N.Y.: Cornell University Press, 1977.

Franklin, Julian. *John Locke and the Theory of Sovereignty*. Cambridge: Cambridge University Press, 1978.

Freud, Sigmund. *Collected Papers*. Edited by James Strachey. London: Hogarth Press, 1953.

——. *Civilization and Its Discontents*. New York: Norton, 1961.

——. *An Outline of Psychoanalysis*. 1949. New York: Norton, 1969.

Gadamer, Hans-Georg. *Hegel's Dialectic: Five Hermeneutical Studies*. New Haven: Yale University Press, 1976.

——. *Philosophical Hermeneutics*. Berkeley: University of California Press, 1976.

——. *Reason in the Age of Science*. Cambridge, Mass.: MIT Press, 1981.

——. *Truth and Method*. New York: Crossroad Publishing Co., 1988.

Geertz, Clifford. *The Interpretation of Cultures*. New York: Basic Books, 1973.

Gethmann-Siefert, Anne-Marie. *Die Funktion der Kunst in der Geschichte*. Bonn: Bouvier Verlag, 1984.

——. "Eine Diskussion ohne Ende: Zu Hegels These vom Ende der Kunst." *Hegel Studien* 16 (1981): 230–43.

——. "Vergessene Dimensionen des Utopiebegriffs. Der 'Klassizismus' der idealistischen Ästhetik und die gesellschaftskritische Funktion des 'schönen Scheins.'" *Hegel Studien* 17 (1982): 119–67.

——. "Hegels These vom Ende der Kunst und der Klassizismus der Ästhetik," *Hegel Studien* 19 (1984): 205–58.

Gillespie, Michael Allen. *Hegel, Heidegger and the Ground of History*. Chicago: University of Chicago Press, 1984.

Gillespie, Michael Allen, and Tracy B. Strong, eds. *Nietzsche's New Seas: Explorations in Philosophy, Aesthetics and Politics*. Chicago: University of Chicago Press, 1988.

Goldwater, Robert. *Gauguin*. New York: Henry Abrams, 1983.

Gough, J. W. *John Locke's Political Philosophy*. 1950. 2d ed. Oxford: Oxford University Press, Clarendon Press, 1956.

Granarolo, Philippe. "Nietzsche et sa vision du futur." In *Nouvelles lectures de Nietzsche*, pp. 111–17. Lausanne: Editions l'Age d'Homme, 1985.

Grant, George. *Time as History*. Toronto: CBC, 1969.

Grant, Ruth W. *John Locke's Liberalism*. Chicago: University of Chicago Press, 1987.

Hammacher, Werner. "The Promise of Interpretation." In *Looking After Nietzsche*, ed. Laurence A. Rickels, pp. 19–49. Albany, N.Y.: State University of New York Press, 1990.

Harpham, Edward J., ed. *John Locke's "Two Treatises of Government": New Interpretations*. Lawrence: University Press of Kansas, 1992.

Hartley, L. P. *The Go-Between*. London: Hamish Hamilton, 1953.

Hartz, Louis. *The Liberal Tradition in America*. New York: Harcourt, Brace, 1955.

Hegel, G. W. F. *Aesthetics*. Oxford: Oxford University Press, 1975.

———. *Hegel's Logic* [Encyclopedia Logic]. Oxford: Oxford University Press, 1975.

———. *Lectures on the Philosophy of World History: Introduction: Reason in History*. Cambridge: Cambridge University Press, 1975.

———. *Phenomenology of Spirit*. Oxford: Oxford University Press, 1975.

———. *The Philosophy of History*. New York: Dover Press, 1956.

———. *Philosophy of Right*. Oxford: Oxford University Press, 1967.

———. *Werke in 20 Bänden*. Edited by Eva Moldenhauer and Karl Markus Michel. Frankfurt am Main: Suhrkamp, 1970–71.

Heidegger, Martin. *Being and Time*. New York: Harper & Row, 1962.

———. *On Time and Being*. New York: Harper & Row, 1972.

———. *Early Greek Thinking*. New York: Harper & Row, 1975.

———. *Basic Writings*. Edited by David Farrell Krell. New York: Harper & Row, 1977.

———. *Nietzsche*. Edited by David Farrell Krell. 4 vols. San Francisco: Harper & Row, 1979–87.

Horkheimer, Max, and Theodor W. Adorno. *Dialectic of Enlightenment*. 1972. New York: Continuum Books, 1988.

Hyppolite, Jean. *Genesis and Structure of Hegel's "Phenomenology of Spirit."* Evanston, Ill.: Northwestern University Press, 1974.

———. *Introduction à la philosophie de l'histoire de Hegel*. Paris: Editions du seuil, 1983.

Janicaud, Dominique, ed. *Nouvelles lectures de Nietzsche*. Lausanne: Editions l'Age d'Homme, 1985.

Jaspers, Karl. *Nietzsche: An Introduction to the Understanding of His Philosophical Activity*. 1935. Tucson: University of Arizona Press, 1965.

Jones, Ernest. *Sigmund Freud*. London, 1955. 3 vols. New York: Basic Books. 1953–57.

Kateb, George. *The Inner Ocean: Individualism and Democratic Culture.* Ithaca, N.Y.: Cornell University Press, 1992.

Kaufmann, Walter. *Nietzsche: Philosopher, Psychologist, Antichrist.* 1950. 4th ed. Princeton: Princeton University Press, 1974.

Kelly, Patrick. " 'All things richly to enjoy': Economics and Politics in Locke's *Two Treatises of Government.*" *Political Studies* 36 (1988): 273–93.

Kemal, S. "Some Problems of Genealogy." *Nietzsche Studien* 19 (1990): 30–42.

Kendall, Willmoore. *John Locke and the Doctrine of Majority Rule.* Urbana: University of Illinois Press, 1941.

Kermode, Frank, *The Sense of an Ending: Studies in the Theory of Fiction.* Oxford: Oxford University Press, 1966.

———. *The Genesis of Secrecy: On the Interpretation of Narrative.* Cambridge, Mass.: Harvard University Press, 1979.

Koelb, Clayton, ed. *Nietzsche as Postmodernist: Essays Pro and Contra.* Albany: State University of New York Press, 1989.

———. "Metaphor, Symbol, Metamorphosis." In *The New Nietzsche,* ed. David B. Allison, pp. 201–14. Cambridge, Mass.: MIT Press, 1985.

Kofman, Sarah. *Nietzsche et la métaphore.* 2d ed. Paris: Editions Galilée, 1983.

Kojève, Alexandre. *Introduction to the Reading of Hegel: Lectures on the Phenomenology of Spirit.* Assembled by Raymond Queneau. Ithaca, N.Y.: Cornell University Press, 1980.

Koselleck, Reinhart. *Futures Past: On the Semantics of Historical Time.* Cambridge, Mass.: MIT Press, 1985.

Lacan, Jacques. "The Mirror Stage." In *Ecrits.* New York: Norton, 1977.

Lacoue-Labarthe, Phillipe. "History and Mimesis." In *Looking After Nietzsche,* ed. Laurence A. Rickels. Albany, N.Y.: State University of New York Press, 1990.

Lampert, Laurence. *Nietzsche's Teaching: An Interpretation of "Thus Spoke Zarathustra."* New Haven: Yale University Press, 1986.

Lloyd, Genevieve. *Being in Time.* London: Routledge, 1993.

Locke, John. *An Essay Concerning Human Understanding.* Edited by Peter Nidditch. Oxford: Oxford University Press, 1975.

———. *A Letter Concerning Toleration.* Indianapolis: Hackett Publishing Co., 1983.

———. "A Call to the nations for unity." Bodleian MS Locke e. 18. Accompanying "John Locke on the Glorious Revolution: A Rediscovered Document" by James Farr and Clayton Roberts. *Historical Journal* 28, no. 2 (1985): 385–98.

———. *Two Treatises of Government.* Edited by Peter Laslett. Cambridge: Cambridge University Press, 1960.

———. *The Works of John Locke.* London: Thomas Tegg, 1823. Reprint, Aalen: Scientia Verlag, 1963.

Lowenthal, David. *The Past Is a Foreign Country.* Cambridge: Cambridge University Press, 1985.

MacIntyre, Alasdair. *A Short History of Ethics.* New York: Macmillan, 1966.

———. *After Virtue.* 2d ed. Notre Dame, Ind.: University of Notre Dame Press, 1984.

Macpherson, C. B. *The Political Theory of Possessive Individualism.* Oxford: Oxford University Press, 1962.

Magnus, Bernd. *Nietzsche's Existential Imperative.* Bloomington: Indiana University Press, 1978.

Marcuse, Herbert. *Hegel's Ontology and Theory of Historicity.* Cambridge, Mass.: MIT Press, 1986.

———. *Reason and Revolution: Hegel and the Rise of Social Theory.* 1941. 2d ed. Boston: Beacon Press, 1960.

Marshall, John. *John Locke: Resistance, Religion and Responsibility.* Cambridge: Cambridge University Press, 1994.

Marx, Karl, and Friedrich Engels. *The Marx-Engels Reader.* Edited by Robert C. Tucker. 2d ed. New York: Norton, 1978.

Maurer, Reinhart Klemens. *Hegel und das Ende der Geschichte.* Freiburg/Munich: Verlag Karl Alber, 1980.

McClure, K. M. "Narrative Investments: Money, Meaning, and the Lockean State." Paper presented at the annual meeting of the American Political Science Association, 1991.

Mink, Louis O. *Historical Understanding.* Ithaca, N.Y.: Cornell University Press, 1987.

Mitchell, W. J. T., ed. *On Narrative.* Chicago: University of Chicago Press, 1980.

Nehamas, Alexander. *Nietzsche: Life as Literature.* Cambridge, Mass.: Harvard University Press, 1985.

———. "The Genealogy of Genealogy." In *Nietzsche, Genealogy, Morality*, ed. Richard Schact, pp. 269–83. Berkeley: University of California Press, 1994.

Nelson, Richard. "Liberalism, Republicanism and the Politics of Therapy: John Locke's Legacy of Medicine and Reform." *Review of Politics* 51, no. 1 (1989): 29–54.

Nietzsche, Friedrich W. *Beyond Good and Evil.* New York: Random House, 1966.

———. *The Birth of Tragedy* and *The Case of Wagner.* New York: Random House, 1967.

———. *Daybreak.* Cambridge: Cambridge University Press, 1982.

———. *Friedrich Nietzsche on Rhetoric and Language.* Edited by Sander L. Gilman, Carole Blair, and David J. Parent. Oxford: Oxford University Press, 1989.

———. *Human, All-Too-Human.* Cambridge: Cambridge University Press, 1986.

———. *The Gay Science.* New York: Random House, 1974.

———. *On the Genealogy of Morals* and *Ecce Homo.* New York: Random House, 1967.

———. *Philosophy in the Tragic Age of the Greeks.* Washington, D.C.: Regnery Gateway, 1962.

———. *Thus Spoke Zarathustra.* New York: Random House, 1966.

———. *Twilight of the Idols, or, How to Philosophize with a Hammer* and *The Anti-Christ.* New York: Penguin Books, 1968.

———. *Untimely Meditations.* Cambridge: Cambridge University Press, 1984.

———. *The Will to Power.* New York: Random House, Vintage Books, 1968.

———. *Werke in Drei Bänden.* Edited by Karl Schlechta. Munich: Carl Hanser Verlag, 1954.

———. *Gesammelte Werke.* Munich: Musarian Verlag, 1926–.

———. *Werke: Kritische Gesamtausgabe.* Edited by Giorgio Colli and Mazzino Montinari. Berlin: Walter de Gruyter, 1967–78.

Oakeshott, Michael. *On History and Other Essays.* Oxford: Basil Blackwell, 1983.

O'Brien, George Dennis. *Hegel on Reason and History: A Contemporary Interpretation.* Chicago: University of Chicago Press, 1975.

O'Hara, Daniel, ed. *Why Nietzsche Now?* Bloomington: Indiana University Press, 1985.

Orwell, George. *1984.* New York: Harcourt Brace, 1949.

Owensby, Jacob. *Dilthey and the Narrative of History.* Ithaca, N.Y.: Cornell University Press, 1994.

Pangle, Thomas L. "The Warrior-Spirit as an Inlet to the Political Philosophy of Nietzsche's Zarathustra." *Nietzsche Studien* 15 (1986): 140–79.

———. *The Spirit of Modern Republicanism: The Moral Vision of the American Founders and the Philosophy of Locke.* Chicago: University of Chicago Press, 1988.

Parfit, Derek. *Reasons and Persons.* Oxford: Oxford University Press, 1986.

Platt, Michael. "What Does Zarathustra Whisper in Life's Ear?" *Nietzsche Studien* 17 (1988): 179–94.

Pocock, J. G. A. *The Ancient Constitution and the Feudal Law.* Cambridge: Cambridge University Press, 1967.

———. *Politics, Language and Time: Essays on Political Thought and History.* New York: Atheneum, 1973.

———. *The Machiavellian Moment: Florentine Political Thought and the Atlantic Republican Tradition.* Princeton: Princeton University Press, 1975.

———. "The Myth of John Locke and the Obsession with Liberalism." *John Locke: Papers Read at Clark Library Seminar.* Los Angeles: William Andrews Clark Memorial Library, University of California, 1980.

Pöggeler, Otto. *Hegels Idee einer Phänomenologie des Geistes.* Freiburg/Munich: Verlag Karl Alber, 1973.

Popper, Karl. *The Open Society and Its Enemies.* 2 vols. 1949–50. 5th ed. Princeton: Princeton University Press, 1966.

Rametta, Gaetano. *Il concetto del tempo.* Milan: Franco Angeli Libri, 1989.

Rapaczynski, Andrzej. *Nature and Politics: Liberalism in the Philosophies of Hobbes, Locke and Rousseau.* Ithaca, N.Y.: Cornell University Press, 1987.

Rawls, John. *A Theory of Justice.* Cambridge, Mass.: Harvard University Press, 1971.

Rickels, Laurence A., ed. *Looking After Nietzsche.* Albany, N.Y.: State University of New York Press, 1990.

Ricoeur, Paul. *Time and Narrative.* 3 vols. Chicago: University of Chicago Press, 1984, 1985, 1988.

———. *Oneself as Another.* Chicago: University of Chicago Press, 1992.

Rosen, Stanley. *G. W. F. Hegel: An Introduction to the Science of Wisdom.* New Haven: Yale University Press, 1974.

Salomé, Lou [Andreas-]. *Nietzsche.* Edited by Siegfried Mandel. Redding Ridge, Conn.: Black Swan Books, 1988.

Schact, Richard. *Nietzsche.* London: Routledge & Kegan Paul, 1983.

——, ed. *Nietzsche, Genealogy, Morality: Essays on Nietzsche's "On the Genealogy of Morals"*. Berkeley: University of California Press, 1994.

Schochet, Gordon J., ed. *Life, Liberty and Property: Essays on Locke's Political Ideas*. Belmont, Calif.: Wadsworth Publishing Co., 1971.

Schouls, Peter A. *The Imposition of Method: A Study of Descartes and Locke*. Oxford: Oxford University Press, Clarendon Press, 1980.

Schutte, Ofelia. *Beyond Nihilism: Nietzsche Without Masks*. Chicago: University of Chicago Press, 1984.

Seliger, M. *The Liberal Politics of John Locke*. London: Allen & Unwin, 1968.

Shapiro, Gary. *Nietzschean Narratives*. Bloomington: Indiana University Press, 1989.

——. "Translating, Repeating, Naming: Foucault, Derrida, and *The Genealogy of Morals*." In *Nietzsche as Postmodernist: Essays Pro and Contra*, ed. Clayton Koelb, pp. 39–56. Albany: State University of New York Press, 1989.

Shklar, Judith N. *Freedom and Independence: A Study of the Political Ideas of Hegel's "Phenomenology of Mind."* Cambridge: Cambridge University Press, 1976.

Simmons, A. J. "Locke's State of Nature." *Political Theory* 17, no. 3 (1989): 449–70.

——. *The Lockean Theory of Rights*. Princeton: Princeton University Press, 1992.

——. *On the Edge of Anarchy: Locke, Consent, and the Limits of Society*. Princeton: Princeton University Press, 1993.

Singer, Peter. *Hegel*, Oxford: Oxford University Press, 1983.

Skinner, Quentin. "History and Ideology in the English Revolution." *Historical Journal* 8, no. 2 (1965): 151–78.

——. "Meaning and Understanding in the History of Ideas." In *Meaning and Context: Quentin Skinner and his Critics*, ed. James Tully, pp. 29–67. Princeton: Princeton University Press, 1988.

Smith, Steven. *Hegel's Critique of Liberalism: Rights in Context*. Chicago: University of Chicago Press, 1989.

——. "What Is 'Right' in Hegel's 'Philosophy of Right'?" *American Political Science Review* 83, no. 1 (1989): 3–18.

Stambaugh, Joan. *Nietzsche's Thought of Eternal Return*. Baltimore: Johns Hopkins University Press, 1972.

——. *The Problem of Time in Nietzsche*. Lewisburg, Pa.: Bucknell University Press, 1987.

——. "Thoughts on the Innocence of Becoming." *Nietzsche Studien* 14 (1985): 164–78.

Staten, Harry. *Nietzsche's Voice*. Ithaca, N.Y.: Cornell University Press, 1990.

Steinkraus, Warren E., and Kenneth I. Schmitz, eds. *Art and Logic in Hegel's Philosophy*. Atlantic Highlands, N.J.: Humanities Press, 1980.

Strauss, Leo. *Natural Right and History*. Chicago: University of Chicago Press, 1953.

Strong, Tracy B. *Friedrich Nietzsche and the Politics of Transfiguration*. Berkeley: University of California Press, 1975.

Taminiaux, J. "Le Temps dans la philosophie de l'histoire." In *Temps et devenir*. Louvain-la-Neuve: Presses universitaires de Louvain-la-Neuve, 1984.

Tarcov, Nathan. *Locke's Education for Liberty*. Chicago: University of Chicago Press, 1984.

Taylor, Charles. *Hegel.* Cambridge: Cambridge University Press, 1975.

——. *Hegel and Modern Society.* Cambridge: Cambridge University Press, 1979.

Thatcher, David S. *Nietzsche in England, 1890–1914: The Growth of a Reputation.* Toronto: University of Toronto Press, 1970.

Thiele, Leslie Paul. *The Politics of the Soul: Nietzsche's Heroic Individualism.* Princeton: Princeton University Press, 1992.

——. *Timely Meditations: Martin Heidegger and Postmodern Politics.* Princeton: Princeton University Press, 1995.

Trìas, Eugenio. *Drama e identidad.* Barcelona: Editorial Ariel, S.A., 1974.

Tully, James. *A Discourse on Property: John Locke and His Adversaries.* Cambridge: Cambridge University Press, 1980.

Vaughn, Karen Iversen. *John Locke: Economist and Social Scientist.* Chicago: University of Chicago Press, 1980.

Vieillard-Baron, Jean-Louis. *Le Temps: Platon, Hegel, Heidegger.* Paris: Librarie philosophique J. Vrin, 1978.

Waldron, Jeremy. "John Locke: Social Contract Versus Political Anthropology." *Journal of Politics* 51, no. 1 (1989): 3–28.

Warren, Mark. *Nietzsche and Political Thought.* Cambridge, Mass.: MIT Press, 1988.

Weber, Max. *The Protestant Ethic and the Spirit of Capitalism.* 1920. New York: Charles Scribner's Sons, 1958.

Weinsheimer, Joel. *Imitation.* London: Routledge & Kegan Paul, 1984.

White, Hayden. *Metahistory: The Historical Imagination in Nineteenth-Century Europe.* Baltimore: Johns Hopkins University Press, 1973.

——. *The Content of the Form: Narrative Discourse and Historical Representation.* Baltimore: Johns Hopkins University Press, 1987.

Wilkins, Burleigh Taylor. *Hegel's Philosophy of History.* Ithaca, N.Y.: Cornell University Press, 1974.

Wittgenstein, Ludwig. *Tractatus Logico-Philosophicus.* London: Routledge & Kegan Paul, 1922.

——. *Philosophical Investigations.* New York: Macmillan, 1953.

Wolin, Sheldon. *Politics and Vision.* Boston: Little, Brown, 1960.

Wood, Neal. *John Locke and Agrarian Capitalism.* Berkeley: University of California Press, 1984.

——. *The Politics of Locke's Philosophy: A Social Study of "An Essay Concerning Human Understanding."* Berkeley: University of California Press, 1983.

Yates, Frances A. *The Art of Memory.* Chicago: University of Chicago Press, 1966.

Index

In this index an "f" after a number indicates a separate reference on the next page, and an "ff" indicates separate references on the next two pages. A continuous discussion over two or more pages is indicated by a span of page numbers, e.g., "57–59." *Passim* is used for a cluster of references in close but not consecutive sequence.

Vaughn, Karen Iversen, 33, 220n13
Violence: Nietzsche and history of, 16,
    77, 117–33 *passim*, 189, 191, 203;
    and Christianity, 128f; as self-torture,
    128; and redemption, 136; and Hegel,
    145
Vocabulary, 4, 6, 15–19 *passim*, 26f, 42, 46,
    52–55, 60–63 *passim*, 67f, 70, 72, 142,
    201f, 223n6

Warren, Mark, 111, 230n12, 235n14,
    237n28, 238n35
Weber, Max, 30, 220n9

White, Hayden, 193–96, 209
"Will to forget" (Nietzsche), 102
Will to Power, The (Nietzsche), 133f
Wittgenstein, Ludwig, 19, 199, 237n30
Wolin, Sheldon, 217n5
Wood, Neal, 221n15
Words, 40–46, 53–56, 62, 69f, 85, 107f,
    222n23

Zarathustra, 16, 78–85 *passim*, 96, 106,
    125, 131ff, 137, 204, 228n6, 229nn7–9,
    237n32
Zoroastrianism, 79–83

Library of Congress Cataloging-in-Publication Data

Dienstag, Joshua Foa.
'Dancing in chains' : narrative and memory in political theory /
Joshua Foa Dienstag.
p.   cm.
Includes bibliographical references (p.   ) and index.
ISBN 0-8047-2818-6 (cl.)
ISBN 0-8047-2924-7 (pbk.)
1. Political science—Philosophy.   2. Narration (Rhetoric)
3. Memory (Philosophy).   4. Hermeneutics.   5. Locke, John, 1632–1704—
Contributions in political science.   6. Hegel, Georg Wilhelm
Friedrich, 1770–1831—Contributions in political science.
7. Nietzsche, Friedrich Wilhelm, 1844–1900—Contributions in
political science.   I. Title.
JA71.D52   1997
320'.01—dc20   96-44652 CIP

⊗ This book is printed on acid-free, recycled paper.

Original printing 1997

Last figure below indicates year of this printing:

06 05 04 03 02 01 00 99 98 97

Another Homecoming

Also by T. Davis Bunn
in Large Print:

Gibraltar Passage
The Messenger
The Music Box
Rhineland Inheritance

Also by Janette Oke and T. Davis Bunn
in Large Print:

Return to Harmony

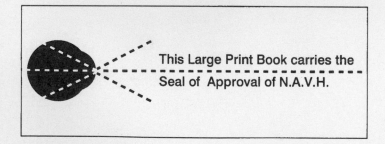

This Large Print Book carries the
Seal of Approval of N.A.V.H.

Another Homecoming

JANETTE OKE
T. DAVIS BUNN

G.K. Hall & Co.
Thorndike, Maine

Published in 1998 by arrangement with Bethany House Publishers.

G.K. Hall Large Print Inspirational Collection.

The text of this Large Print edition is unabridged.
Other aspects of the book may vary from the original edition.

Set in 16 pt. Plantin by Al Chase.

Printed in the United States on permanent paper.

Library of Congress Cataloging in Publication Data
Oke, Janette, 1935–
    Another homecoming / Janette Oke and T. Davis Bunn.
      p.   cm.
    ISBN 0-7838-8332-3 (lg. print : hc : alk. paper)
    1. Large type books. 2. World War, 1939–1945 — Fiction.
I. Bunn, T. Davis, 1952–   . II. Title.
[PR9199.3.O38A82   1998]
813´.54—dc21   97-31794

Dedicated to
all those who have helped and
prayed us through this creative process,
with our heartfelt gratitude.

The first fiction collaboration between novelists Janette Oke and T. Davis Bunn resulted in a delightful story set in North Carolina in the early 1900s, *Return to Harmony*.

This second joint effort, *Another Homecoming*, unfolds with World War II. Characters come to life through heartbreak and hope and discovery. Once again, the complementary strengths and creativity of these two gifted writers provide a compelling reading experience.

Janette Oke and her husband, Edward, live in Calgary, Alberta, where she writes her well-loved stories and enjoys her grandchildren. T. Davis Bunn and his wife, Isabella, make their home near Oxford, England, where he continues his award-winning research and writing.

CHAPTER ONE

The Baltimore train station was awash in khaki. Soldiers crowded every nook and cranny, their faces taut with the excitement of travel and adventure and war. Uncle Sam pointed fiercely at them from every wall, exhorting them to go and do their duty.

She was one of a thousand weeping women that day, her quiet misery a single drop in an ocean of noisy chaos. Martha clung to her husband, feeling his strength as he held her close, so tight she could scarcely breathe. "Take care, my love," he said to her ear, having nearly to shout just to be heard. "I'll be back soon."

"But what if —" The question she had dared not voice during their nine short weeks of marriage now was cut off by his lips finding hers with urgent passion. Even here, amid the tumult of a world going to war, with the tooting whistles and the blaring brass bands and the shrilly, excited kids, Martha felt herself once again overwhelmed by Harry's kiss. It had been that way since the very first time. Before, really, though she could not have explained how, even to herself. Back when Harry had simply been the young boy who had returned from boot camp a man, back when they were walking out to picture shows and taking ices beneath the softly greening trees of spring, back when she felt her heart first begin to sing with love. Even then she knew that if ever he kissed her, even just once, she would be lost forever to loving him.

Harry released her, and the world jarred back into painful focus. "Don't even think it," he ordered. "Just remember, I'll be back soon as I can. With the good old US of A in it now, we'll have them Krauts ducking for cover in no time flat."

His jaunty strength and confidence was overpowering. She managed a wobbly smile and a nod. But the tears kept coming. He was leaving and going off to war. And what if —

The whistle shrilled another time and was joined by a single, impatient chuff from the distant engine. The soldiers who were not already on board surged forward. Martha's sob was lost in the khaki tide that plucked Harry from her embrace.

This time he did not return to her and silence her fears with his lips. This time he shouldered his kit and turned just long enough to give her a grand flashing smile and blow her a kiss. This time her arms reached out, but he was not there to fill them. She could only stand, one in an endless line of weeping mothers and wives and lovers and children. They watched as their men raced for the slowly moving train, flinging their bags and then themselves into the doorways. They saw the men fight for a crack of space to stick out heads and one arm and shout farewells. Martha's last image of Harry's departure was of

8

a train smothered in smoke and made even more blurry by her tears, a train that had grown a thousand arms of its own.

There were three enemies in Harry Grimes' war — the Germans, the heat, and the desert.

Harry tried not to show his discomfort. He was a master sergeant, after all, and Sergeant Grimes had a reputation for not showing anything. But as far as he was concerned, the desert was a lot harder to take than the Germans. He had seen the Jerries only twice during recent skirmishes. But Harry was surrounded by the desert night and day.

He stretched out in the trench, the camouflage netting overhead offering a hint of shade. Though it filtered out the worst of the blistering sun, it also kept out any breeze, trapping the heat and turning the trench into an oven. He looked up and noted the sun slowly sinking toward the ochre hills. He glanced at his watch, then held it to his ear. Even when he heard the ticking he had trouble believing it was keeping proper time.

"Aye, the last two hours are the longest, and the last five minutes longer still." The boy with the British accent to his left was named Harry as well, which was good enough for a laugh now that Sergeant Grimes had been tested under fire and found acceptable. The Brits were a scrawny lot, mostly wiry and small, but they fought as if the world's future depended on them alone.

Harry Grimes asked, "You really think we'll

find them this time?"

"Not a doubt, Yank. They're out there. They're ready, and *they'll* find *us*," he corrected. Harry the Brit was only eighteen, three years younger than Harry Grimes. But he had been fighting in Montgomery's North Africa Campaign for ten long months. His face was a taut mask tainted by sun and war and desert sand. His eyes looked a thousand years old. "Old Rommel's a wily foe. He's kept shifting and turning and running back and forth until he has us right where he wants us. Now he'll be on us like a pack of wild dogs."

"Ease up, Harry, yer a right one with the gloom and doom." The man farther to their left was a heavyset Londoner with a cockney accent so thick Harry Grimes could hardly understand him. "Pay the bloke no mind, Yank. All them Lancashire lads've got porridge between their ears."

"Aye, wait 'til you've been out here long as me, then we'll see how you hold up, sitting here on Rommel's flank."

" 'Ang on, let me go find Monty, tell 'im me mate's got word on how to fix the Jerries up proper."

Harry Grimes slid farther along the trench and shut his ears. The grousing would go on for as long as they were forced to sit and wait. That much was the same here, but not much else. He had been assigned liaison duty with the Brits, and he felt like the proverbial fish out of water — a fish in the desert, no less. But the Brits had been here for a year already and had learned the lessons of desert warfare the hard way. The Americans were just getting started, and everything was in chaos — no surprise, given the speed with which their army had been plucked together.

Harry pulled pad and pencil from his pocket. He had been working on this particular letter to Martha for almost a month. But he never had been much with writing. Besides, there was so little he wanted to say — could say — from such a dislocated distance. The fact that he was thrilled to bits that Martha's pregnancy was going well had been good for a paragraph. Harry desperately wanted that child. The thought of being a father fueled his homesickness. Home to Martha, home to a son. Or a daughter. It really didn't matter one way or the other to Harry.

The fact that he was to become a father made this war even more important. He wanted a safe world for his child. Sure, it would be harder moving from base to base with a family in tow. But many men did it. It gave added stability to army life. And Martha was so excited. He could feel her anticipation even across the miles. It flowed from every line of her letters, and she said it gave her something to look forward to in his absence. "A little bundle of you," she called the child she carried, but he knew it was not just him. The new baby would be a part of each of them.

He had been totally unprepared for his inner

excitement at the news of the coming baby and wished with all his being that he could be there with Martha to share their joy.

Martha's letters were full of bittersweet anticipation. She looked forward to the coming child. Yet she so longed for him to be there with her. It didn't seem right that she had to face each day alone. Harry sighed and tapped his pencil. Even though he felt so deeply, he found no way to put the words on the stiff, trench-dirtied paper.

The stuff the Brits called chow had made for another couple of sentences. But there was little else to report except the heat and the dust and the waiting. He didn't want to talk about this second world war. Days and weeks of endless boredom were followed by seconds of noise and terror so fierce he felt as though he had been permanently wounded down deep, where only he could see the scars.

He had come from the wrong side of the tracks, raised in a home without a father and with a mother turned shadowy by hardship and hard work. In high school, girls like Martha had seemed as far away as the moon. He had joined the army because it had been a way out. He had not minded the drill and the marching and the training at all. In fact, Harry had loved everything about the army. The order and the discipline had been reassuring. At long last, Harry Grimes had found himself a home. He had been sure nothing would make him happier than spending the remainder of his days wearing khaki.

Then the Japs had attacked Pearl Harbor and America entered the war. Suddenly Harry Grimes was being hailed as a visionary, one of the few who had seen the coming tide of events and had signed up before any draft notices were sent out. He had already learned the army's lesson of keeping his lip buttoned, and so said nothing to the contrary when they awarded him with stripes and a medal and orders to help train the newly drafted recruits.

He gladly would have spent the entire war as a drill sergeant, but word came of the battalions they were sending to fight Rommel in North Africa, wherever that was, and Harry found himself volunteered. He did not think he would mind.

And then there was Martha. She was the best thing that had ever happened to him. Along with the army. So if he could get this North Africa stint safely behind him, he would go back to Martha and the baby, and he would cheerfully drill soldiers the rest of his life.

A whistle sounded far down the line. One shrill blast, then nothing except the sound of the wind. Harry the Brit hissed at him, "It's time, Yank. Get your kit together."

Harry Grimes buttoned the letter into his left pants pocket. He checked his pack for water and ammo, then slid the greasy rag over his gun a final time. There was nothing worse for fouling a gun than this desert silt. It was so fine it worked into everything, his water, his food, his —

"Good luck, matey," whispered Harry the Brit,

13

then scrambled out.

"Never fear, Yank." The Londoner jumped up from the trench alongside Harry. As they hustled across the baked desert sand, he hissed, "The Krauts're long gone. We'll just reccy over the other side of those hills, then be back in time for another fine breakfast of eggs and tea and sand."

Harry started to speak, but another whistle sounded. This one was much louder and did not stop. Instead it grew more shrill and closer. Then a roar of noise and light and dust and pain blacked out his world.

Dr. Howard Austin raced up the stairs and into the little apartment, not even bothering to knock. "I came as soon as I heard, Martha. Is it . . ."

He stopped midway across the floor. The yellow telegram lay on the floor at her feet, telling him the news was true. Her motions halting and uncertain, she looked toward him. But her eyes did not see him. Her face was void of expression.

"Oh, Martha." Howard walked over and scooped up the telegram to stare at its message. Somehow the words, pasted on the flimsy sheet, looked even more cold and impersonal in their long lines of capital letters that spelled out such devastating information: WE REGRET TO INFORM YOU THAT YOUR HUSBAND MASTER SERGEANT HARRY GRIMES IS MISSING IN ACTION AND PRESUMED DEAD STOP

"They came in a big brown car," Martha said

14

from her place on the worn davenport, her tone as blank as her face. "Two of them. With medals and uniforms and salutes. One of them was older. He looked like he had done this a thousand times. I felt sorry for him. Can you imagine? They bring me this news, and I'm feeling bad for him."

"Because you've got a heart of gold," Howard Austin replied. He pulled a chair over close and seated himself. "It does say 'presumed,' you know," he said gently, knowing even as he said the word that its tiny offering of hope had already been snatched away from her.

"They told me —" She stopped, her face a bewildered mask, then started again. "They said that battle in North Africa was so . . . was so awful that there wouldn't be any survivors." Howard had to lean forward to catch her last words, barely a whisper. He had heard the news reports and knew the officers were correct in not leaving her with false hope.

"Is there anything I can do?" he asked. "Anyone I can call?"

"I don't have anyone, you know that." A single tear trickled down her cheek. She did not bother to wipe it away. Her unseeing gaze returned to the window. "I'm all alone in the world now." Her voice sounded drained of all energy. All feeling.

Howard started to protest, to tell her that she could always count on him. But he couldn't honestly say that. Just that morning he had received his own induction papers. Every glance at the yellow telegram in his hand left him chilled to the bone. "Anything at all," he repeated. "Isn't there something?"

"I don't know." For the first time Martha seemed to find the strength to bring the world into focus. She turned to look at Howard with eyes so full of haunting pain and fear that his heart twisted. "I'm eighteen years old. I have nobody in the world." She crossed her arms over her distended belly. Martha was a small woman, and the child was scarcely three weeks away from term. Even seated as she was, her lightly boned frame seemed scarcely able to support the load. "What am I going to do, Howard? How will I take care of this baby?" Now her tears fell freely, as though she were weeping on behalf of her unborn child who would never know a father's love.

The deliberate way she pronounced the last sentence left him unable to draw on his doctor's training or his usual good cheer. Howard leaned back in his chair and studied this stoically calm woman. And woman she was, no matter how few the number of years she could claim. Her marriage and pregnancy and now the loss of her husband had left little of the child he had known for most of her life.

A few years apart in age, they had been raised on the same Baltimore street, in a section of the city that had been almost entirely Irish in their youth. Now it was much more cosmopolitan. To Howard it seemed as though while he had been

16

away at college and then medical school, other parts of the world had invaded and taken over their old neighborhood. And during that same six-year stretch, knock-kneed little Martha O'Leary had grown into a willowy young lady, lost both her parents, fallen in love with a man from a different social class, a soldier, and wed. Howard could not help but wonder how things might have been had he stayed in Baltimore as his mother had wished and attended a local college.

"What am I going to do?" Martha was asking again. Her quiet voice held to a single note, droning out words heavy with feeling.

"Martha," Howard started, then hesitated. Suddenly he found himself taken by a desire to ask her to wait for him, to let him send her money until he could return from his own army stint. But something held him back. How could he say such words the same day she had learned about her husband? It was impossible. And what if he didn't return? Howard Austin felt as though his heart was humming with the tension of not being able to say what he wanted, while his country pressured him to leave and prepare for war. He swallowed hard and said, "Wait a few days — maybe something will turn up for you." He hoped the words didn't sound as empty to her as they did to him.

"I know what I have to do."
Something in Martha's voice filled Howard

17

with apprehension as he looked at her across his desk. She had come in for a final examination before her baby's delivery. He watched the play of emotions across her delicate girl-woman features, deep pain and sorrow along with determination.

"I want you to find a family who will adopt my baby."

Howard's breath left him as if he'd been struck in the stomach. "You don't really mean that, Martha."

"You said you would help me, Howard." Her voice was pleading.

"Wouldn't it be better — well, a child would be such comfort to you now."

"And wouldn't that be a fine, selfish reason to deny my baby a decent chance at life?" Martha rose from the chair, easing herself up in careful stages. She walked over to the office window and traced one finger along the trail left by gently falling rain. Her other hand caressed the baby. "I couldn't do that, Howard."

There was no anger to her tone, nothing he could hang an argument on. His heart ached for her and the unborn child. It was at times like this that he wished he did not care for his patients as much as he did. Being colder would have made him a much better doctor. And his personal feelings for her made it even worse. "If you say so. But I still think —"

"A good home," she said and turned back to him. For an instant her features crumpled despite

18

her resolve. Howard watched as she swallowed and seemed to gulp away the tears, making a huge effort to regain control — not for herself, but for her child. "A mother and a father who can give everything my baby deserves to receive."

"Sergeant, hello, can you hear me?"

The voice was as soft as the light. He struggled to open his eyes. He looked up at a golden haze. Strange how the light could be so brilliant and so soft at the same time.

"Can you hear me, Sergeant?"

He licked dry lips. A hand slid beneath his head, lifted, and a cup touched his mouth. When he had sipped a few mouthfuls, the hand lowered him back to the pillow. A voice said, "There, is that better?"

A tent. His eyes focused enough for him to see that he was lying in a tent. The sun struck the canvas overhead and turned it into a sheet of brilliant gold. He turned his head and saw that a nurse was seated beside his bed. She smiled at him. "Nice to have you back among the living, Sergeant."

She kept calling him "Sergeant." Was that his name? He could not think. His mind felt so foggy. And there was something about the way she spoke, something strange.

"You're in a British field hospital. You've been wounded." The nurse hesitated a moment, then continued, "Nod your head if you can under-stand what I'm saying, Sergeant."

19

He nodded his head, though he could make little sense from her words. They seemed to dance through his mind and then disappear before he could lay hold of them. Strange how he could hear her and understand her, and at the same time understand nothing at all.

"You lost your identification in the battle. We don't know who you are. There seems to be no record of you." When he did not respond, she raised her voice. "Can you tell me your name? What regiment are you from?"

A dull drumbeat sounded at the very back of his consciousness. Steadily it grew louder, until he realized it was not a sound at all, but rather a pain. A dull agony that beat to the steady rhythm of his heart.

Another voice approached the end of his bed, one that spoke with authority. "Any word who he is?"

"Not yet, doctor. He seems to just come and go."

"Just as well." The deep voice spoke with clipped brusqueness. "No need to have him awake enough to feel his leg."

His leg. As though the words were a cue, he felt the dull beat of pain center down to his left leg. It did not hurt too badly yet. But there was something about the pain that scared him, even in his confused state. As though the pain was only the slightest hint of what was to come.

The terse voice demanded, "Any word from HQ?"

"Yessir. Still no idea who he is."

"Well, let's see what we can do about this leg. There probably was a letter in his back pocket, but the scraps that are left don't tell us anything. We can worry about his identity later." The deep voice drew nearer. "Help me shift his bandages so I can have a look."

Harry felt movements around him. Then the pain focused. It became not just a feeling, but a white-hot light. He groaned.

"How long has it been since his last injection, nurse?"

"Just under two hours."

"Well, no need to chafe him any more than necessary. Hurry and give him the morphine before we go any further."

Hurry. *Harry*. The pain shot through the fog in his mind, bringing every thought into crystal clarity. Perhaps that was his name. But maybe it was the name of someone else, another friend out there in the heat and the dust and the war. He wanted to speak, to ask if he was the Harry or the other guy. Then he felt the needle's jab, and soon a new wave of confusion swept through him. He did not mind. The pain receded with the sound of his heart, until it was nothing more than a shadow on the distant horizon of his consciousness.

The last words he heard were, "Now let's see if we can save this leg."

The administrator of Baltimore General Hospital stepped into Dr. Howard Austin's office. "Got a minute?"

"No." He did not want to be disturbed. Packing up and preparing for his departure was harder than Howard Austin had expected.

But the administrator did not move. His normally unflappable calm had deserted him. "I told you, leave all that. We'll just lock the office up and hold it for your return."

Howard finally said the words that surrounded him, clawing at his throat until it was hard to breathe. "And what if I don't come back?"

Instead of arguing, the administrator slumped in defeat. "Howard, this is a terrible time to be asking, but I need a favor."

"You are joking."

"I wish I were."

"My train leaves in exactly" — he glanced at his watch, then continued — "four hours."

But the administrator still did not budge. "You know the baby you delivered yesterday morning."

"The Grimes girl?" His attention finally shifted to the man standing in his doorway. "What about her?"

"We've been in contact for quite some time with a couple who wants to adopt a baby girl." It was the administrator's turn to avoid Howard's gaze. "They want to speak with the doctor in charge of the birth and prenatal care. They insist on it."

His movements stilled, Howard demanded, "What are you *not* telling me?"

"This couple," the administrator said, with a sigh, "they're, well . . ."

"Rich," Howard guessed, his tone flat.

"You know we urgently require donors to keep going and buy new equipment," the administrator replied, his voice rising defensively. "They've offered to help build our new wing if we find them a proper baby."

A *proper* baby.

"How much?"

"Half a million dollars," the administrator replied, awestruck. "No strings attached."

Right, no strings — but a baby.

Howard rose to his feet and started toward the door. Despite all he faced, he very much wanted to meet this pair. He had a deep feeling of obligation to Martha and her baby. The baby she had refused to see. She knew that once her eyes settled on her baby girl, she would never be strong enough to carry out her resolve. It would be so much easier for her to know that her child had been well placed. "Where are they?"

The hospital entrance was a product of a bygone era, a tall, swooping dome of brick, crowned by brass lights. The floors were marble and worn into soft waves. The wooden walls probably had once been very grand, but now looked faded and in dire need of varnish. Howard was halfway down the stairs when he drew to a halt, his attention caught by the Rolls Royce automobile. Just outside the glass-topped entrance doors, a uniformed chauffeur stood patiently beside the long, low-slung vehicle.

The administrator backed up a step to ask nervously, "What's the matter?"

"Nothing." Howard started forward once more. "Let's get this over with."

He passed through the long corridor too quickly, granting him little time to form some kind of picture of what this couple might be like. Old? Young? Dark? Fair? Tall? Short? Just where was he sending Martha's little girl?

The administrator pushed open a door, and Howard found himself face-to-face with the prospective parents. One quick sweep was enough to work a knot in his stomach. The woman was as erect and cold as the Statue of Liberty. She stood by her husband's side, gazing at the baby with an expression of utter bafflement. The husband was big and gray and hearty, his face creased by unbounded joy as he cradled the little one in clumsy yet gentle arms.

At the sound of their footsteps, the woman stiffened even further. "Lawrence."

"What, oh — excellent." The big man took a step forward. "You the doctor?"

"That's right. Howard Austin."

"I'm Lawrence Rothmore. This is my wife, Abigail."

"Charmed." The woman's single word was as cool as her demeanor. As she adjusted the mink stole draped about her neck, the double strand of pearls was fully revealed and the diamond on her finger glinted in the light. "Don't you think we should speak with the doctor alone, dear?"

"Sure, sure." He gave the administrator a hearty smile. "You don't mind if we have a quiet chat with the doc here, do you? Sorry, doc, I've forgotten your name already."

"Austin. Howard Austin."

"No, no, of course not." The administrator gave the couple a little half-bow, followed by a look of genuine entreaty to Howard. Then he backed from the room. "I'll just be in my office."

The woman turned her full attention on Howard. "Doctor, can you assure us this is a proper baby?"

The directness took his breath away. "I beg your pardon?"

"Proper," the woman repeated, drawing out the word in an exaggerated fashion. "A proper baby. Not one from — well, pardon me, doctor, but we don't know a thing about the family, do we?"

"Abigail," her husband said. But the word did not carry heat. His attention remained focused upon the tiny child in his arms. "The administrator has already told us —"

"The administrator wants our money," she replied crisply. "There is absolutely nothing wrong with wanting to know that our baby is healthy and comes from parents who aren't, well, deranged or anything."

Howard Austin's sudden anger brought a grating depth to his voice. "The baby's mother is one of the finest women I have ever known."

25

Abigail Rothmore faltered momentarily under the doctor's glare but managed to draw herself together to demand, "And the father?"

"Sergeant Harry Grimes," Howard Austin began, and then stopped. He had broken one of the primary rules governing adoption, which was to never let the adopting couple know the names of the parents.

"Yes, doctor?"

Howard Austin sighed. Put it up to the day's stress and strain. "He was killed on the North African front."

"Hey, that's tough." The gentleman lifted his graying head at the news. He was an older man, and probably had twenty years on his society wife. Genuine sympathy shone from his face. "How is the mother holding up?"

"Not well." There was a sincerity to the gentleman that the woman lacked. Howard focused his attention on Lawrence Rothmore. It was easier than allowing himself to think of Martha Grimes, lying upstairs in a private room. She had been moved out of the obstetrics wing, where her sobs had been upsetting the other mothers and newborn babies. "Not well at all. She's young and doesn't feel that she can take care of the child on her own. But that doesn't make it any easier to give Katie up for adoption."

"Hey, I'm sorry to hear that." The man had the gruff voice of a hale and hearty type, big across the shoulders and a paunch from good living. "Think maybe we could help out?"

"I'm sorry," Abigail interrupted. "Did you say the child's name is Katie?"

"It's nice of you to offer," Howard responded to the husband, "but actually I was breaking the law in mentioning the father's name. Besides, she'll hopefully have a war pension coming to her." He then turned to Abigail and continued, "Katherine is the name given by the birth mother. But you have the right to change that if you wish. Just as the child's birth certificate will list you as the actual parents."

Both adults showed genuine relief. Lawrence Rothmore spoke first. "I'd sure like Katie to think of us as her real parents."

The man, Howard noticed, had an unhealthy flush to his complexion. Too much rich food, high blood pressure, and not enough exercise. Definitely a heart patient in the making. "That is entirely your choice."

"Let me just be perfectly clear on this point," the woman said, her cool aloofness fully restored. "You are saying that there is no chance that some pestering journalist might ferret out details some-time in the future?"

"None at all," Howard replied, understanding her perfectly. "If you want to claim to all the world that you have borne this child, that is your decision."

"It's just like Randolf told us. The secret lives and dies with us," Lawrence concluded. He added for the doctor's benefit, "Randolf Crawley, he's our lawyer. My wife's cousin. Getting on in years, but sharp as they come."

Abigail fingered her pearls and murmured, "I still say we would be better off selecting a proper male heir."

"We've been through all that," Lawrence said, hugging the baby closer to his chest. "If you want to adopt a second child —"

"Simply out of the question." Abigail's tone closed that door permanently.

"I want a baby daughter." There was a sudden power to his voice, a revealing of the force that had carried him to the top. "And that's final."

Abigail opened her mouth, must have thought better of it, and changed tack. "Very well," she said. "But this name, Katie, simply won't do. I mean, really, it's just too — well, too ordinary."

As swiftly as the man's power had been revealed, it vanished. Lawrence Rothmore's attention returned to the little bundle sleeping in his arms, and his features softened. "What did you have in mind?"

"Kyle," Abigail announced. "It was my maternal grandmother's name, as you know. And Elizabeth from my mother."

"Kyle Elizabeth Rothmore." He nodded his head. "Sounds good to me."

Howard Austin glanced at his watch and gave a start. Where had the time gone? "If you'll just step into the administrator's office, he will have the papers ready for you to sign."

"Yeah, he mentioned you were off today for a year's duty." Lawrence Rothmore allowed himself to be ushered across the foyer. "Any idea where?"

"Three months' surgical duty on a hospital boat — after that is anybody's guess."

"Well, good luck to you, doc. And thanks. Thanks a million."

Or half a million. Howard accepted the man's hand, while he returned the woman's perfunctory nod. He then raced back up the stairs. But instead of heading for his office and the pile of unfinished paper work, he continued up to where Martha Grimes lay on the third-floor private wing. It was the least he could do, a last gift to a woman for whom he wished he could do more. A lot more.

Perhaps it would help her to know that little Kyle Rothmore was going to receive everything that Martha herself could not give.

CHAPTER TWO

"Now, Bertie, don't you dare drop them."

"No, Miss Kyle, I wouldn't dream of it." Bertrand Ames shut the manor's tall oak door, which was difficult given the load he carried, and turned sideways to make sure Kyle Rothmore, nearly three, was coping with the broad flagstone stairs. Her two teddies kept her from seeing the steps. "You be careful, now," he cautioned in return.

If anyone had ever suggested to Bertrand Ames that his job would include responsibility for the well-being of a Raggedy Ann doll, three stuffed bunny rabbits, and an enormous pink elephant, he would have turned in his resignation on the spot. But here he was, taking the curving front steps very slowly, so as to be there in case his small charge lost her balance. The doll and stuffed animals were crammed together in a colorful bundle up against the chest of his immaculate uniform.

And then Jim, the head gardener, chose that moment to come around the corner of the house. As with all the servants, Jim answered directly to Bertrand Ames. Jim was a fine gardener but an impossible man to deal with. He had an acid wit and complained with every breath he drew. It did not help that Bertrand and his wife were, like all the staff, relatively new to the Rothmore household. For some unknown reason, the entire household staff had been fired and new people hired three years ago. He and his wife had come shortly after that. At times Bertrand still felt as though he were struggling to establish his authority and position.

It would not do at all for the gardener to go back to the kitchen and start making caustic remarks at Bertrand's expense. Dignity was a vital part of his position.

Bertrand wore three hats within the Rothmore household — butler, chauffeur, and head of the household staff. He managed the tasks by rising before dawn, working hard all day, and keeping himself aloof from the other staff. His habitual expression was a disapproving frown. As Jim walked toward them, Bertrand prepared a frosty response to any remarks about his unusual bundle.

But Jim did not pay him any mind at all. Instead he doffed his ancient cap and gave a creaky bow. "Morning, Miss Kyle. Great day for going out and about."

"I'm taking Mr. and Mrs. Teddy for a drive," she announced.

"Now ain't that a grand thing." He hustled over to the gleaming Rolls and opened the front door.

"Bertie has all their friends so they won't get lonely," Kyle continued.

Bertrand winced at the announcement. Only Maggie, his wife and the Rothmores' head chef, called him Bertie. But like all the servants, Maggie's heart had long been lost to the charms of this child. Their own children were long gone, grown up and off leading their own lives.

Bertrand readied his coolest voice, preparing for the snide comment on his nickname Jim was bound to offer. But to his surprise, the gardener only nodded and agreed. "Always a good thing to have your friends around."

Bertrand stepped forward and began settling his load onto the front seat's posh leather. Kyle handed him the teddies. "Thank you, Bertie."

The gardener had eyes only for the little girl. He asked eagerly, "Anything I can do, Miss Kyle?"

She gave that one careful thought. "They might get a little cold."

"There's a lap blanket in the trunk," Bertrand said cautiously, handing him the key.

"Right you are." The old man scurried around, came swiftly back with the checkered alpaca cover. "Want me to set it in place?"

Bertrand reached over. "I'll take that, thank you."

"I was the one got it out."

"That will do, James." There was a momentary tug of war before seniority won out and Bertrand had the privilege of tucking the blanket around the row of fuzzy passengers. He backed out and straightened. "Will that do, Miss Kyle?"

Inspecting the arrangement meant climbing onto the Rolls' running board and peering inside. The action hiked her little skirt up high enough to reveal the row of blue ribbons in her panta-loons, ones that matched the pair in her honey-colored hair. "Does Mrs. Teddy have room to breathe?"

The question required both Jim and Bertrand to fit in around Kyle. They gave the passengers a careful examination before Bertrand reposi-tioned the pink elephant over closer to his seat. Then he solemnly proclaimed, "I feel certain Mrs. Teddy will be most comfortable, Miss Kyle."

"Yep," Jim agreed. "Looks mighty fine to me." He retreated, waited until Kyle had climbed down and straightened her skirt, then asked, "Seems I've heard talk about some big day com-ing up, Miss Kyle?"

"My birthday," she announced proudly. "Mama says we're gonna have a party."

Bertrand started to dismiss the gardener but was held back by the gleam in the man's eyes. There was a genuine affection in Jim's tone as he said, "A party. Now ain't that nice. Think maybe it'd be a garden party?"

When Kyle seemed perplexed by that question, Bertrand found himself offering, "Perhaps if the weather is nice."

"Then you oughtta come out and show me where you'll have your guests," Jim said eagerly. "Maybe I can put some pretty flowers around, dress things up a little."

Bertrand was hard pressed not to smile. The gardener had a thousand excuses for avoiding

33

any extra work. But the little child had this effect on the entire household. There was something special about Kyle, as though a glorious light shone from her heart, even at this early age, something so special that it lit up the lives of everyone around her. Everyone, that is, except for —

"Ah, good, there you are. For once you're ready on time." Abigail Rothmore carefully swept down the steps on her high heels. "James, I noticed the flowers in the front hall are wilting."

"We were just talking about that very thing, Mrs. Rothmore." The gardener shifted over far enough to block Bertrand from view as the butler ducked into the front seat and flipped the blanket up and over the stuffed animals. "I believe the roses are ready."

She dismissed him with a flick of her gloved hand and inspected her little girl. "Turn around and let me see you, child. Well, it appears you've managed to keep yourself clean for once. Very well, Bertrand, you may open the door."

"Yes, madam." He bowed lower than necessary, the only way he could hide the glint of anger as he saw the child freeze under her mother's austere gaze. When they were both settled, he shut the door and found himself facing the gardener. Jim was still watching Kyle through the car window. He caught Bertrand's eye and gave a slight grimace before turning away.

Bertrand walked around to his door, reflecting that he and Maggie had only two reasons to put up with Abigail Rothmore, and those were her husband and her daughter.

Before he even started the car, Abigail was off on her usual litany of instructions. "Sit up, child. Straighten your dress. And just look at your hair. How on earth do you manage to —"

"Where to, madam?" Bertrand asked, putting a bit more bark into his voice than necessary.

"What? Oh, the dance academy, of course. It's Thursday." But his question had the desired effect and deflected Abigail from further berating the little girl.

"I don't like ballet," Kyle said very softly. "It makes my toes hurt."

"If I've told you once, I've told you a thousand times, dance will teach you both proper posture and an appreciation of music. Besides, it will introduce you to our kind of people."

"I don't have any friends there," Kyle quietly persisted.

"Of course you do. I just heard that the Crawleys' lovely daughter is being sent there as well. She will make an excellent friend."

"I don't like Emily Crawley," Kyle said. Her voice was so quiet as to almost go without noticing. "She's mean to me."

"Nonsense. Emily Crawley comes from one of the finest families in Chevy Chase. Not to mention the fact that her father sits on the Rothmore board. Even if the idea of him having a daughter at his age is positively scandalous." Impatiently Abigail tapped her fingers upon the polished burl

35

of her armrest. "Bertrand, I have a luncheon in town. You shall need to drop me off, go back and pick up Kyle, and bring her home on your own."

"Very good, Mrs. Rothmore." At least there was that to look forward to. Kyle liked to sit up front with him, hugging one of her animals and asking all the questions that she kept to herself whenever her mother was around. Bertrand had never known another child of her age to be so bright and inquisitive.

And yet nothing could please her mother. "Nanny says you have finally managed to learn all your alphabet."

"Yes, Mother." A hint of eagerness. "Can I 'cite them?"

"Recite, child, recite. You really must practice your elocution. And no, it is quite enough to hear a positive report from Nanny for a change."

Bertrand clenched down hard on his irritation as he observed the little girl through his rearview mirror. Kyle gave a little frustrated kick, then commented, "I wish I could have a baby brother."

Abigail gave her daughter a look of genuine horror. "Where on earth did you come up with such a notion?"

"Maggie says her daughter's just had a new baby. A little boy. Can we, Mama? Please?"

"Absolutely not. Out of the question. As if you were not already more than I can manage. Oh, do stop swinging your legs, Kyle. Can't you be still for an instant?"

Bertrand's heart lurched as he watched her subside into a shadow of the bright little thing who had chattered with them earlier. But Abigail was not finished. "Really, you must stop treating the staff like they were family. It just isn't proper to call the cook by her first name."

"But she's . . . she's my very best friend," Kyle protested.

"Don't talk nonsense. Help are not friends. You are a privileged young lady, and you must learn to act the part. I don't see why it is so much to ask, expecting you to be at least a little grateful for everything that has been given to you."

"Thank you, Mama," Kyle said dully.

"That's better." Abigail Rothmore adjusted the fold of her skirt. The diamonds in her bracelet caught the sunlight and shimmered little rainbows round the car's interior. "Now if only you could learn how to behave in a way that reflects your social standing and family position, I will be satisfied."

Kyle's chin quivered a moment, but she brought it under control. When her mother's attention was caught by something outside her window, Kyle gave her eyes a swift little wipe. She raised her gaze, and Bertrand attempted all the warmth he could manage into the smile he gave her through the rearview mirror. Then and there he decided he would treat her to her favorite snack, a chocolate malted milk and a box of animal crackers. They would stop by the sweet-shop on the way home, no matter what Maggie might say about the child's appetite being ruined. He would give anything to see the little girl smile again.

Howard Austin removed the stethoscope from his neck and fitted it into his black carrying bag. He forced a cheery tone. "Fit as a fiddle, heart big as a mule's. Nothing's going to keep our Harry down for long. I want you to start walking with just one cane — see how far you can make it."

Harry gave a silent nod, the expression on his face not changing. When he had first arrived home, he had been wasted down to skin and bones, but now he was beginning to put on weight. His leg was mending well. But nothing could be done about the eyes that looked empty of everything, or the flat, toneless voice that expressed the few words he chose to say. At the moment, he chose not to speak at all.

As Howard backed toward the doorway, he tried to find some cheerful note to end the visit. He could only think of the news that was on everyone's mind that summer. "Looks like we've got the Japs on the run once and for all. Can't be long now."

Harry looked up from his chair. It was placed just beneath the bedroom window so as to catch whatever breeze the sultry day might bring. Sunlight falling through the lace curtains turned his face into stark lines and shadows. The words he spoke now carried deep feeling. "Wish I were over there with them, Doc. That's where I belong. The army's the only thing I ever found worth doing."

"Where you belong is right here with your family," Howard responded, feeling his smile was as false as his hearty tone.

"America's finest hour," Harry mumbled, as though the doctor had not spoken at all. "And here I am, trapped in this chair with a gimp leg."

"You've done your part," Howard insisted stoutly, more because Martha was standing there beside him than because he thought the words might do some good. "Now you're home, where a lot of our boys wish they could be. And your leg was saved. Count your lucky stars, Harry."

When Harry did not respond, Howard started down the hall, saying to Martha as he passed, "There's no need to see me to the door."

But Martha Grimes pushed one hand into the small of her back, making her belly protrude even further, and moved slowly along behind him. Still a small woman, she was carrying this second baby very low. Two weeks until term, and he wondered if her size indicated twins. Only when the screen door had shut behind them did she speak. "He's not getting any better."

"Of course he is."

"Even when one of his old buddies comes by, all Harry does is sit around. There's no fire left."

"Just give it time, Martha."

"And when he does talk, it's about the army.

How much he misses it. How he hates his leg. How his wound has kept him from staying with the one profession he'd ever like. That's his name for it, his profession." She sighed deeply and absently rubbed the curve of her belly with her other hand, as though able to adjust the load she bore. "Talking like the army was a calling, like being a doctor or something important."

"It is important — or was," Howard Austin replied quietly. "At least to Harry."

"He's been mourning the loss for way too long as it is." Her hand kept moving, as though she sought comfort from the child she carried. "I just don't know how much more I can endure, Howard."

"Be patient," Howard said, the words coming automatically. He seemed to be saying them a lot these days. "Be strong. He'll come around."

Instead of arguing, Martha carefully examined his face. "You've changed too, Howard. You look the same as before you left, except for some new lines on your face. But your eyes — they look a hundred years old."

He did not try to deny it. From somewhere down the street, a radio blared out a marching tune. Another house was full of revelry, and at five o'clock in the afternoon. It seemed as though Baltimore had been one vast party ever since the Germans had surrendered three months earlier. "He's been through a lot, Martha. It will take him time to come around. The scars on the outside are easy to see. They'll always be there,

I'm sorry to say. The ones on the inside, who knows how long . . ." Howard let his voice trail off. Martha did not need to hear all the details.

Howard found himself recalling the one time Harry had let down his barriers since returning from North Africa. Frustration and anger and bitterness had poured forth from the lips of a broken man. Howard had stood helpless and silent, listening to heartrending accusations directed at Martha for giving away his child. He wanted their daughter, he had shouted over and over. He wanted his baby back. Harry had wept with uncontrollable sobs when Howard had told him firmly that there was no way to undo what had been done. It had been an ugly scene, one that had left Howard with nightmares.

Harry had never spoken of his lost child again.

"He just sits there and stares at nothing," Martha went on, almost to herself. "For hours on end, he won't say a word."

The thousand-yard stare. That was the name Howard had heard. He had seen a lot of that during his time at the military hospital. And a lot of other things he would rather forget. He pushed away the memories that suddenly began crowding forward and produced a tight grin. "This is something, isn't it, how I've gotten back in time to deliver your second baby?"

But Martha did not respond as he had hoped. She brushed away a wisp of hair matted to her forehead, her face flushed from the exertion of bearing such a heavy load. "Tell me the truth,

Howard. Will my Harry ever come back to me?"

Howard fought back a sudden longing to reach forward and take her into his arms. He had thought he was over his yearning for her. After all, he had returned to find that Harry Grimes had not been killed. Upon hearing the news about Harry's return, Howard Austin had stamped down tight on his dismay, locking away his feelings for Martha along with all the other emotions the war had left as a legacy, things he never wanted to think of or feel again.

But here he was, caught flat-footed and open-hearted by a single look.

"Martha," he sighed, wishing for all that was impossible to have. "I can't lie to you."

"That's why I'm asking," she responded, her tone as quiet as his. "I need somebody I know will always tell me the truth."

"The truth," Howard said quietly, his heart aching. Once again he was glad he had not poured out his feelings to Martha before he left, and that he had held to a friendly tone in his few letters. He had wanted to wait and confess his love for her face-to-face. He had owed it to her, if for no other reason than because she had already lost one man to the war, or so he had thought. Now his disappointment was an acrid twisting to his heart, but at least it was private, something he had shared with no one. "The truth is, your husband is home."

"Is he?"

"He has returned with his body relatively intact. His mind is okay, as far as I can tell."

"It doesn't seem that way to me."

I care too much. The accusation had been leveled at him time after time on the front. Other doctors had taken him aside and told him repeatedly that if he did not grow a tougher hide around his heart, he would not survive. Howard drew himself up. "Martha, Harry was a man made for soldiering. You've told me that yourself. And now he's got to learn to accept that there are other occupations for him than the army. He needs to count his blessings, find a job, raise his family. Having a new baby will help bring him around."

The dark brown eyes did not waver in their careful inspection of his face. Martha asked quietly, "What about my needs, Howard? I lost my husband and then my baby. I spent almost a year mourning the pair of them, thinking my husband was lying dead some place with a strange-sounding name."

"El Alamein," Howard said quietly. "A lot of good men didn't come back from there, Martha. You should count your blessings."

"Blessings." Her mouth pinched down, as though she had tasted something bitter. "What about my baby girl? I dream about her, you know. After all this time, I wake up and wonder where she is, and I feel like my heart is going to break."

"Blessings, like the child you're bearing," Howard plowed on determinedly. He fought down the urge to tell her about Harry's bitterness over losing the baby girl. It would serve no purpose, other than perhaps ease his own nights. "Blessings, like having your husband home from the war."

She stared hard at him, the gaze carrying the force her words did not. "Tell me where my baby is, Howard. I'm begging you."

"For the last time, Martha, I can't. And even if I could, it wouldn't do you any good. The child is theirs. And that's final." He tipped his hat to her and turned for the steps. "I'll see you in a day or so. Call me if anything changes."

Briskly Howard started down the sidewalk, pausing for a final wave before turning the corner. Up where the street joined a main thoroughfare, a young man hawked papers, shouting more news about the war. Howard tuned him out, the action having become automatic.

I care too much, Howard repeated to himself as his shoulders slumped in defeat. It was a flaw he really had to overcome.

CHAPTER THREE

Kyle raced around the corner, one hand holding her leather satchel, the other her hat. Her long dark blond hair and the cap's blue ribbons flew out behind her as she hurried toward the car. Her brown eyes sparkled with anticipation.

The chauffeur stood stiffly at attention as he waited for her, his face set in downward sloping lines. "I'm sorry, Bertie," she said breathlessly, "but Miss Pincushion made me stay after class again."

Bertrand opened the front passenger door. He could not keep an aggrieved tone from his voice as he said, "I do wish you would permit me to wait for you in front of the school, Miss Kyle."

At the sight of the front door open and waiting, Kyle gave off a little exclamation of delight, swiftly stifled. She gave the empty rear seat a quick glance, then asked, "Where's Mother?"

"Mrs. Rothmore felt it necessary to remain behind and prepare for her charity function this afternoon," Bertrand replied stiffly.

"Oh, Bertie, don't be like that." Kyle slid into the seat and straightened the blue skirt of her school uniform. When Bertrand shut her door and started around the car, she allowed herself a smile. Mother couldn't come after all. The day was already wonderful and would soon be even better. A lunch with her father, all to herself, was one of her favorite things in the world.

When the chauffeur opened his door and climbed in, Kyle gave him a look of utter appeal. "Bertie, I've told you how the other girls make fun of me when they see you waiting out front." Further protest was diverted when she glanced at the little round clock set in the burl dash. "Oh, look. You'll have to hurry. Daddy doesn't like to be kept waiting."

"I am well aware of your father's attitude toward time," Bertrand replied. "And I am certain that the young ladies of St. Albans have seen a chauffeur before."

"Now you sound just like Miss Pincushion." Miss Pincus taught eighth-grade math at the exclusive St. Albans Preparatory School, and she was the bane of Kyle's existence. "Not in a *Rolls*. And not the way you wait for me."

"And just what, pray tell," Bertrand demanded, "is the matter with the way in which I wait for you?"

"Oh, you know. Standing there by the door with your gloves and hat and everything. You look like a soldier at attention."

"I merely intend to show proper respect."

"You look like you're waiting for . . . for a princess." Kyle laughed, a musical sound. Then she confessed, "I don't like the other girls to know, that's all."

"There are many wealthy young ladies at St. Albans, Miss Kyle. And if memory serves me correctly, young Miss Emily Crawley is collected in a Rolls."

"But the other girls are nicer, the ones that aren't so, you know, well off." She avoided the additional point, which was that Emily Crawley and her cold, aloof ways frightened her. "If they see you . . . well, I'm afraid they won't like me."

"Anyone in her right mind would like you," Bertrand responded reverently.

"The others don't. The ones Mother says I need to socialize with. They don't like how I talk to . . . to everyone." The tone dropped as she added the word Emily Crawley used most often to describe her. "They call me *common*."

"They wouldn't dare," Bertrand said hotly. "Not if you allowed me to meet you out front like you should."

She gave him a smile that carried warmth and appreciation, then changed the conversation by reaching into her satchel. "Look what I made for Maggie's birthday."

Bertrand slowed long enough to glance over. What he saw caused him to turn the car to the side of the road and stop. "Kyle, what can I say? It's lovely."

Neither of them noted that he had not included "miss" with her name, a misdemeanor that would have brought Kyle's mother to the point of banishing him forever. "It's a watercolor of 'The Praying Hands,' " Kyle explained. "It's Maggie's favorite."

"Twelve years old, and already you're a mar-

47

vel." Bertrand's heart nearly burst with pride. "Maggie is going to love this."

"I'm thirteen — remember?" The young girl's face shone with delight. "You really think she will?"

"I know so. I've been wondering what to get her myself, and now I know. I will arrange to have this framed."

Kyle drew up her shoulders in pleasure. "We'll be giving her something together."

"Indeed we will." They shared a smile until Bertrand glanced at the clock and jerked upright. "I've forgotten the time. We're already late."

But Kyle did not look worried. Carefully she replaced the painting into her satchel, then leaned back with another smile. "Lunch with Daddy, all by myself. Then I can be in his office all afternoon. And guess what? *I Love Lucy* comes on tonight."

Her sigh of pleasure warmed Bertrand's heart. "I'm certain your favorite program does not come on until tomorrow," he said as he watched her from the corner of his eye.

Kyle frowned, ran through the days of the week on her fingers, then caught sight of Bertrand's teasing glance. "Oh, you."

"Here's your father's street, Miss Kyle," Bertrand said, returning to formality. "Perhaps you should think about —"

But before he finished, Kyle took a quick glance around, then in a flash was over the seat into the rear. She settled back, then leaned forward to snatch up her hat. A few seconds of straightening her clothes and hair, putting the hat on and her face into proper lines, and the car slowed to a halt.

As Kyle waited calmly as Bertrand cut the motor and came around to open her door, she caught sight of her father. He was standing just inside the Rothmore building's brass-lined glass doors, talking to someone she vaguely recognized. Then she saw what he was holding as he stood grinning and waiting for her to alight. Kyle's breath came out in a gasp, and she scrambled out the door Bertrand held for her, positively at odds with what her mother would have called ladylike behavior.

She ran to her father. "You got it! Oh, Daddy, it's *beautiful!*" she exclaimed.

"A Schwinn," Lawrence Rothmore declared proudly. "Won't be released until next summer, but a buddy in their head office wrangled this one for me. Get a load of those white sidewalls, will you."

"And colored tassels, and I love the silver and blue," she enthused. "Oh, Daddy, can we take it for a ride?"

"Later, my daughter," he said, putting his arm around her shoulder as he motioned Bertrand forward. "Put this in the trunk, will you?"

"Very good, sir."

Kyle watched as the bicycle was wheeled away. "Promise you'll ride with me, Daddy?"

"Soon as I get home." He waved forward a

young man who hovered just out of range. "You remember Randolf Crawley, don't you?"

Kyle stopped watching intently as Bertrand maneuvered the bicycle around to the back of the car and turned back to her father. As she had been taught, she lifted her skirt lightly and gave a graceful curtsey. "Good day, Mr. Crawley."

"Call me Randolf, please." Her father's associate sounded surprisingly friendly to Kyle's way of thinking. "There's not that much difference in age between us."

She looked curiously at him. His hair was a shiny blond, combed up and back in careful folds. His chin was cleft, his nose straight and long, his teeth perfect. Randolf Crawley was ancient as far as Kyle was concerned. At least twenty-four or five. "There isn't?" she asked frankly.

Her father patted the younger man on the shoulder. "Randolf's going to become my protégé. It's your mother's idea. He's got a law degree from Yale, and insurance law's becoming trickier by the minute. Besides that, I'm not getting any younger, and I need a pair of strong shoulders and a good mind to carry some of the load. Abigail thinks he's perfect for the position."

Kyle had not understood all of what was just said. But she did not like any suggestion that her father was not well. And she *really* did not like the way that man was smiling at her. "You're fit as a fiddle, Daddy. That's what you're always saying."

Lawrence Rothmore's laugh was as big as the

rest of him. But nothing could disguise the sudden flush that crept into his face as he stopped and the heavy breaths that followed. "My little lady. Loyal to the end," he puffed.

"I am pleased to see my young sister becoming friends with you, Kyle," Randolf commented. "She talks about you quite a bit."

"How nice." Kyle used the phrase she heard her mother say whenever she was displeased but didn't wish to show it. In truth, Kyle was uncomfortable around Emily Crawley. She was as beautiful as her older brother was handsome. Emily was leader of the group of wealthier girls at St. Albans, and this group was the biggest reason Kyle did not feel like she belonged. The Crawleys were her mother's distant relatives, and Emily seemed to have Abigail's ability to make Kyle feel as though she did not measure up, could never be as correct and superior as she was supposed to be.

Kyle felt she had been polite to Randolf Crawley long enough. "Where are we having lunch, Daddy?"

"The boardroom, where else?" Dining in the boardroom was one of their little rituals, whenever they had a time alone. "I believe I heard the chef say he had managed to make your favorite dessert."

"I bet it's banana cream pie!"

Lawrence squeezed his daughter's shoulder and said to Randolf Crawley, "You've never seen anything like it," he boasted. "All my little lady has to do is smile, and she could get the Statue of Liberty to lend her the torch."

"I don't doubt it for a minute," Randolf agreed. "I've heard Emily say something about Kyle's friendliness."

But Lawrence had already turned away. "Come on, princess. On to the top."

He handed over a key to Kyle, a ritual they had played out from when she was a tiny girl. There was a private elevator for members of the board. Her father had let her operate it since she had been old enough to reach up on her tiptoes and fit the key into the special hole. Kyle stepped into the wood-paneled elevator, and as the polished doors closed she caught a final glimpse of Randolf's smile directed at her. She wondered why it made her uneasy.

As though reading her mind, Lawrence asked, "So what do you think of my new protégé?"

"I think he's — well, he reminds me of his sister," she said, speaking her mind as was only possible when she and her father were alone.

Lawrence chuckled fondly. "He's going to be the youngest member of our board before long, taking over the seat from his father. When I was just starting out, old Crawley helped bankroll me. His father and your mother's grandfather were brothers, but I suppose you know that. He probably did it out of family loyalty, but he's done well by it. Very well. He has ten percent of the company stock and a permanent seat on our board."

Kyle did not ask him to explain what all that

52

meant. She had no interest in Randolf Crawley. Instead she announced, "Maggie's kitty had six babies."

"Is that a fact." He regarded her fondly. "Don't I recall your naming that cat Benjamin?"

She nodded. "Yes, that was back when I was too young to know better. So now she's called Ben-Hur." When her father laughed again, she worked up nerve to ask, "Daddy, do you think I could have one of the kitties?"

"No pets, my love. We've already been through that with your mother when Jim's golden retriever had puppies."

"Oh, Daddy, *please*. They're such precious little white fluffballs."

"No pets," he repeated, his tone regretful but firm. "Your mother's really put her foot down on that. I'm sorry, princess." He steered the subject back around with, "She thinks very highly of young Randolf." He hesitated a moment, then added, "She says it would be a good idea if you were to get to know him."

Kyle looked up at her father in utter bafflement. "But why, Daddy?"

For some reason, the question made him laugh a third time. He stroked her fine silky hair once more as the elevator doors opened before them. "Why indeed, my princess. Why indeed."

Joel Grimes sat on the parlor floor, his birthday present opened in front of him. Light from the setting sun spilled through the louvered windows, framing him in sharp lines of gold and shadow. He unfolded the large page of plans, being as careful as he could. It was important not to grow impatient, even now when he was so excited he could hardly sit still. Experience had taught him that the plans would be opened time and time again, and the crease-lines needed to be followed very carefully, because when the paper became old it would easily tear. And it was always in the creases that there was some important connection he couldn't figure out without the plans. So he unfolded the white paper, big as a road map, very carefully, noting how the folds went so he would know how to put it back later.

Beside him was the magnifying glass Dr. Austin, his parents' friend, had given him for his last birthday. Save his eyes from squinting over those tiny lines, was what the doctor had said. And now he had a brand-new tube of epoxy glue that was from Grandma. And a new razor blade in the little metal holder that his father had brought him from the tool shop. His mother always left the room when he started working with the blade. She was back in the kitchen now, preparing his tenth birthday dinner. Which meant he only had a few minutes left to look over the plans.

Joel's father sat on the other side of the small front parlor in their Riverdale home. Joel had been born in Baltimore, but the family had moved the fifteen miles south soon after. This was the only home Joel had ever known. He sat on the floor and watched his father listening to news over the radio. The announcer was talking about something called the Cold War. And some man called Nikita Kruschev. Whenever the news started on about those things, his father would always clam up and lean over, his face so tight he looked hungry.

His father was quiet most of the time. He would come home from work, sit there in the front room, and say hardly a word. His distant gaze suggested he saw another world, one that really was just for him, one where Joel had no part at all. It made him feel so small, being in the room with his father and knowing that the man did not see him or even realize he was there.

There was something which lurked deep inside his father, something frightening. Joel had seen it surface that very morning when his father had stomped out on the back porch and argued with the milkman. The veins had stood out on his father's forehead and neck like whipcords. His voice had sounded like an angry lash. All over a missing pint of milk. Joel had sat with his breakfast cereal and known with wisdom far beyond his ten years that it was more than milk that made his father so angry.

Sometimes, though, his father roused himself, and he would look at Joel and say something. Joel's whole world seemed to light up when it happened.

The announcer started talking about baseball, and his father cut off the radio. Washington's baseball team, the Senators, was at the bottom of the rankings, and Baltimore wasn't doing much better. The only time his father was interested in baseball was when the Yankees or the Red Sox were in town.

His father turned to him, watching him cut the first balsam piece free of the wood strip. "What you got there, sport?"

"A B-29 Superfortress," Joel replied with a grin. His father knew that. An illustration of the plane in all its glory was on the box front, flying through a sky filled with dark gray flak clouds, its machine guns spouting flames.

"Ain't that something," his father said calmly. "How many does that make now?"

"Eleven." The gift had been from both his parents, but Joel knew his mother had saved from her household money to buy it. Even so, his father recognized the plane. His father knew all about planes. He worked as a mechanic at the Baltimore airport. It was one of the few subjects that would occasionally light up his eyes, especially if he was talking about military planes.

"I had two more," Joel explained, "but I messed them up and so they don't count. But that was when I was little."

"Listen to this guy. Ten years old and he's not little anymore." His face's deep creases tightened slightly, as close as Harry Grimes ever came to a smile. "Can you understand the instructions, son?"

"I think so." It was so rare to have his father

actually say the word "son," that Joel knew a little thrill. In a sudden rush of insight, he picked up the plans and crossed the room. "I've read them, but I'm not sure I get what to do first." The large sheet rustled as he spread it on the small table by his father's chair. He pointed at a paragraph above the first drawing and asked, "Will you explain that to me?"

"Why, sure." Harry spread the plans smooth, squinted, and slowly began to read and comment. Joel listened carefully, but in truth he didn't need help. Joel wanted a reason to stand near his father. Most of the time it seemed as though his father had an invisible barrier around him, keeping everyone from coming close, even his own son. Joel hesitated, then reached up and put his hand on his father's shoulder. It felt hard as a rock. He moved a little closer so he could lean against his father's arm.

His mother chose that moment to walk into the room. When Joel looked over at her, she appeared to be holding her breath. Her face ran as if it were made of wax, just melting into soft, sad lines. It was so strange to stand there, leaning against his father, feeling so happy and so sad at the same time. His mother struggled to make a little smile for him, then turned and silently left the room.

When his father stopped his explanation of the paragraph, he sat and examined the plans for a while. Joel remained content to stand there and lean against him. Harry pointed at the turrets appearing on the drawing's underside and tail and asked, "How are you supposed to make these?"

Eagerly Joel leaped for the box, pulled aside the balsam strips intended to form the plane itself, and came up with an oddly shaped piece. It looked like a slender tree sprouting rigid gray fruit. "They made them out of plastic, Pop."

"Well, ain't that something. Here, let me have a look." Harry's strong fingers moved across the pieces, comparing them to the scale drawings. "Getting more complicated all the time, aren't they?"

"Sure are."

"Good training for a mechanic. You aiming on coming over, working on the planes with your old man?"

"That sounds great, Pop." But in truth, Joel had no idea what he wanted to do when he grew up. Whenever he thought about the future, it all felt flat to him, as though there was something important he was missing. It was the same way his family was. Everything seeming to be in order, but something was missing. He knew it in his heart.

Harry let the plans slide from his lap. Joel knelt and began the folding process. Then Harry said, "Yeah, the Superfortress and the B-17, they made all the difference. We ruled the skies after that. Had 'em on the run." He was silent a moment longer, then asked, "You heard about the new one?"

"You told me about it, remember?" The other

night, the paper had printed an article on the new army bomber. "The YB–52 Stratosphere. That's what they called it."

"You sure got some memory, sport." Harry reached over and tousled his son's hair. "Mind like that, you'll go a long way."

The moment was so special, Joel decided to risk it. He kept his head bowed over the plans as he asked, "Pop, can I get me a puppy? Bobby Benson's spaniel, she had six pups. Please, Pop. They're the cutest —"

"No pets," Harry Grimes said. More than the words cut off Joel's pleadings. The cold grating sound was back in his father's voice.

Joel felt his heart fall to his stomach in fear that he had ruined the rest of his birthday. That his father would sit over to one side of the table, staring out the back window, saying nothing to anybody the whole time. Meals like that were excruciating.

Steps scraped up their front porch, and a heavy voice said through the doorway, "Are we late? We better not be. I get cranky if I don't get my share of the birthday cake."

"Haven't even got started," Harry replied. "Come on in, Howard."

Dr. Howard Austin stepped through the door, followed by his wife, Carol. The Austins had also moved down from Baltimore, and Dr. Austin ran a very successful family practice. Joel found himself thinking as always how incredible it was, the similarity between Carol Austin and his own mother. They could have been sisters. They even had the same soft, sad smile. Dr. Austin demanded, "Hey, it's the birthday boy. What you got there?"

"A model of the Superfortress," Harry replied for him. To Joel's enormous relief, the coldness was gone from Harry's voice as he rose and limped over. Favoring his left leg, Harry picked up the model box and showed it to the doctor. "Get a load of all those pieces. Some are made of plastic. It even says how many on the front cover. Look at that — two hundred and seventy-three pieces. Worse than the real thing."

"And he puts them together with the precision of a surgeon," Howard agreed. "I've seen those others he's got strung up in his room. They look like they're ready to take off and fly away, all on their own. How you doing, Joel?"

"Fine, sir."

"Happy birthday, Joel," Carol said. Even her voice had the quietly resigned tones of his mother. She handed over a smaller box. "I hope we got what you wanted."

"Gee, thanks, Mrs. Austin." Joel made swift work of the wrapping. "An acrylic paint set. It's perfect. Thanks a lot."

"Thank your mom. She's the one who told Carol what to get." Howard shifted his bulk as Joel's mother entered the room. "And here's the little lady now."

Martha Grimes stood for a moment in the doorway, her face soft and unreadable as her eyes

60

drifted over the scene. Joel seemed to be able to stand there beside her and see what she was observing. Her husband stood smiling, the model box in his hands, her best friends smiling in return. They looked like a regular family. It happened so seldom, it was worth remembering. Finally his mother said, "To the table, everybody. The food is getting cold."

CHAPTER FOUR

Kyle stole down the servants' stairwell at the back of the Rothmore mansion. She had been ordered to appear for her mother's inspection, but first she felt the need to check with Maggie. Quietly she pushed open the door and waited for Maggie's head to lift. "How do I look?"

Maggie offered her a small, wistful smile but did not speak. Kyle prompted, "Well?"

"I was just wishing you didn't have to grow up so fast, is all."

"Oh, Maggie." Kyle moved quickly to hug the older woman. "I don't know what I'd do without you."

"Look at what you've done now — you've gotten flour on your pretty dress front. Brush it off. There, that's better." Maggie's eyes were as quietly happy as her voice. "I can scarcely believe my little darling Kyle is already fifteen years old."

"Sixteen in eight months. Say it that way. It sounds better."

"Just look at you, standing there in your lovely blue silk dress, high-heel pumps, and with your grandmother's pearls."

"It scares me to wear the pearls. I'm so afraid they'll break and spill all over the floor," Kyle confessed quietly. She cast a rapid glance at the door to the front rooms, then added, "But Mother wants me to wear them tonight."

"Then there's no use complaining, now, is there?" Maggie's voice turned brisk. "Besides, this is a formal do, and you might as well get used to dressing the part."

"Emily Crawley is coming tonight," Kyle sighed. "Mother invited her. She told Randolf the invitation came from me, but Emily knows how likely that is," she added darkly.

"That's quite enough, Kyle."

"Anyway, Mother says I could learn a lot from Emily. I don't see what."

"Miss Emily is a . . . a very lovely young lady," Maggie replied carefully.

"But she's not very nice. At least not to anybody who doesn't have as much money as she does. And she only speaks to me when she wants something."

Maggie coughed discreetly, then reminded her, "The Crawleys are an important family, and Emily's brother sits on your father's board now that his father has retired."

"I know, I know. Mother's telling me that every time I turn around. But that's *business*. What has business to do with friendships?" She looked appealingly at the older woman. "Mother keeps bringing Randolf's name up and encouraging me to be friendly with him. But what on earth for?"

"There are some answers that you will simply have to obtain from your mother," Maggie replied firmly.

But Kyle was too distracted to notice the warning. She lowered her voice and whispered, "It scares me."

"Who, young Mr. Randolf?"

"No — well, yes . . . sort of, I guess."

"Which is it, young lady?"

Kyle leaned back and settled her hands on the big kitchen's wood-block central table, then remembered how she was dressed. Hastily she dusted the flour off her hands, checked the back of her dress, and said quietly, "I'm frightened by how Mother won't tell me what she means. It's like she's planning something about . . . about me. And Randolf knows, and maybe Daddy, but nobody will tell me."

"Oh, child," Maggie sighed, wiping her hands on her apron. "I love you like I do my own, and that's the honest truth. But all I can advise you about such things as this is to pray for strength, pray for protection, and pray for God's will."

"That's the same thing Bertie told me," Kyle said, searching Maggie's face.

"My husband is a wise man and a good Christian, if I do say so myself."

"I try to pray. Sometimes, anyway."

"And have you been reading the Bible I gave you?"

"I tried. But I don't think I understood very much of it. Mother says that the pastor will explain such things at church and not to worry about it."

Maggie's chin jutted out and she took a deep breath. "How about coming back to my little sitting room and reading there? Maybe I can help you with some parts you don't understand."

"Thank you, Maggie." But the offer did not brighten Kyle's mood. "It still doesn't help me know what they've got planned."

"Talking to God and reading His word to us will bring you peace," Maggie replied stoutly. "Try it and see."

Kyle avoided replying by leaning forward and kissing Maggie's cheek. Then she turned and quietly left the kitchen.

Abigail Rothmore frowned as she stood before the antique mahogany sideboard at the library's entrance. On the wall rose a full-length portrait of her in a gilded frame, wearing a ball gown by the nation's most famous artist. At least he had been the most popular society artist when the portrait was done. Now that his star was waning, she had wanted to move the portrait to the back stairway, but naturally Lawrence would not hear of it. He was so provincial when it came to such matters.

Idly she rearranged a spray of pink roses arrayed in a silver tureen. But her thoughts were not on the flowers, nor the painting, nor even the coming party. Her thoughts were on Kyle.

The girl was growing up, at least in some respects. Physically she was becoming quite a fetching young lady, though at times Abigail had difficulty admitting it, even to herself. The presence of a daughter approaching womanhood only accentuated Abigail's own age. Just the other day, one of her charity friends remarked on how well Abigail was managing to hide the years.

But why couldn't Kyle grow up emotionally, Abigail fumed. She was such a child when it came to things that mattered. She made friends with the servants, of all things! Kyle smiled and charmed everyone who did not matter, and avoided even speaking to those who did. She cared nothing about clothes. She hated attending charity functions. She yawned through her classes in etiquette. She —

Stifling back a cry, Abigail dropped the rose. She had been so caught up in her concerns about Kyle that she did not realize how hard she had been gripping the thorny stem. Abigail turned and inspected her reflection in the tall side mirror. Her own smooth, blond, patrician beauty had enough characteristics mirrored in Kyle that no one had ever questioned their relationship. And Lawrence and Abigail had traveled enough during those early years of marriage that the appearance of the little baby fifteen years ago had not caused questions or comment.

Abigail sighed and impatiently turned away from the mirror. Emily Crawley, now, she would have been the perfect daughter. *She looks, acts, and thinks like I do* was Abigail's bittersweet conclusion. Which was hardly surprising, given the fact that Emily's and Abigail's grandfathers had been brothers. Which made them second cousins — such a cold way to describe a bond that went far beyond mere ancestral ties. If only she could mold Kyle into the proper kind of daughter.

It was a good thing that Abigail had inherited her grandfather's ambition. Lawrence had not made such a bad job of his insurance company, but he did not have that nearly ruthless instinct required to transform his middling-size business into a national power. No, her husband unfortunately shared his daughter's softness, which was remarkable, given their utterly unconnected backgrounds.

Abigail was all too familiar with the threat of softness. Her own father had been a weak, ineffectual man. Kind to his family, but weak. And it had cost their family everything. Her father had taken over a thriving business established by her grandfather and driven it into the dust.

Abigail moved closer to the sideboard and picked up the little silver bell. There was one in every room of the house, and all the servants knew the immediate summons of its ring. The bells were available for all the family, but Abigail was the only one who ever rang them. Lawrence preferred to call out his requests, and Kyle . . . well, Kyle would just do the task herself. As though the silly girl was concerned not to trouble the servants with extra work.

The doors to the main hall opened, and the maid curtsied. "You rang, ma'am?"

"Has my daughter finished dressing?"

The woman hesitated an instant before replying. "I haven't seen her, ma'am."

Which was probably a safe way for the maid to avoid saying that Kyle was back in the kitchen, against Abigail's express orders, talking with that chef again. It was only because Lawrence had put his foot down that the woman and her know-it-all husband were still in the household. "Never mind that now," she said crossly, speaking her thoughts out loud. "Go tell my husband I need to speak with him. Privately. And at once, before the guests arrive."

"Yes, ma'am." The maid quietly shut the door behind her.

Randolf Crawley. Yes. Here was a man who shared her ambition and her drive. Pity he was twenty years younger than she. The two of them would have made a formidable team. But that was impossible. No, what needed to be done was to make the proper arrangements, so that at least the next generation would rise to the ranks of *true* power. It was not that Abigail was after more money. She already had more than she would ever be able to spend. It was the power to shape and control people's lives, to bend them to her will, to see them bow and scrape and acknowledge her as the leader she had been born to be.

It was her destiny to rule.

Kyle entered the grand formal hallway at the front of the house, then stopped. Voices resounded in the distance. Loud voices. Hesitantly she walked forward, not because she wanted to, but because of her mother's orders to present herself before the guests arrived.

The closer she drew to the tall double doors leading to the library, the more it seemed as though the entire house was holding its breath. Even through the stout oak portals, Abigail's voice sounded very angry. "I simply cannot fathom why on earth you would invite that — that *boy* into our home!"

"Kenneth Adams is twenty-five years old, hardly a boy. As a matter of fact, he's only two years younger than Crawley." Lawrence Rothmore's voice sounded both tired and stubborn. "And he is more mature than some men twice his age."

"And just what is that supposed to mean?"

"Nothing, Abigail. I am simply trying to end this silly discussion."

"Silly, is it? You are choosing to bring a common office worker into my house, and you call it silly?"

"His father is a respected pastor. Ken graduated with honors from Princeton at the age of twenty, played quarterback on their varsity squad, and has been an exemplary employee of ours for almost five years now. I hardly call that common. To be honest, I am amazed that my choice of an assistant can leave you feeling so . . . so threatened."

"Threatened? Me?" Abigail's laugh sounded brittle. "Don't be absurd."

"Like it or not, he is my new personal assistant. You're always telling me I need to slow —"

"What's the matter with Randolf?"

"Young Crawley? You know quite well, Abigail, Crawley's father has retired. Randolf has been appointed to take his seat on the board. I can hardly expect our newest board member to run my errands, now, can I?"

There was a moment's hesitation before Abigail changed tack with, "In any case, you must admit this Kenneth person is a poor substitute for the real thing."

Kyle knew her mother, should she open the door, would be furious to find her listening there. But she could not move. She felt glued to the spot. Though her name had not been mentioned even once, she had the feeling that this entire quarrel had something to do with her. Something bad.

Her father's voice rose a notch. "What on earth are you talking about?"

"You know very well what I mean. You're always forming these absurd attachments with protégés. We should have had a son, just like I said."

Kyle stiffened. A son! She had always dreamed of having a baby brother. But her mother had never allowed her to even mention it. Kyle could scarcely believe her ears. Her mother had wanted a son?

Her father's astounded laugh rang through the closed doors. "Like *you* said? In case you have forgotten, Abigail, *I* was the one who begged you for a son after Kyle —"

"Don't be petty. I meant *instead* of —"

"That is more than enough." A new tone had entered her father's voice. A dangerous coldness. "I want no more of that. Not ever."

Clearly Abigail realized she had gone too far, for her voice took on a conciliatory note. "But to invite him into our house, especially tonight when so much hangs upon —"

"Our daughter is just fifteen years old." A trace of anger grated in Lawrence's voice.

"And growing up fast," Abigail retorted.

"That's right, she is." Behind the closed doors, Kyle was able to visualize her father's determined strength in standing up for her. "Which means that in time she will grow into handling her own affairs."

"Oh, really, Lawrence." Scorn dripped from Abigail's voice. "She doesn't have the faintest inkling of how to handle relationships *or* money. Do you know, I have even had to stop her allowance. She has the absurd tendency of giving it away to the first poor person who comes into sight."

"There's nothing wrong with a little charity," Lawrence said, but a note of doubt had crept into his tone.

"Let us be realistic, please. It is high time this issue be settled in everyone's mind. Which makes it even more bizarre that you would even dream of inviting this other young man —"

"The matter is closed," Lawrence replied stonily.

71

Her father's heavy footsteps started toward the library doors, with Abigail's continuing argument in close pursuit. Kyle inched her way along the dark paneling, then flew up the stairs.

Once in her own bedroom, she shut her door on the words that seemed to have followed her. She turned on the radio and waited impatiently as it warmed up to the strains of the new hit song, "Only You." Shakily she seated herself at her little vanity and studied her reflection. She was certainly not pretty, not like Emily Crawley, who had even the oldest boys stopping to watch as she walked by. Kyle's nose turned upward slightly, almost like a miniature ski jump. She always felt that her shoulder-length hair was too thick, even after she had brushed and brushed until her arm ached. And it seemed such a strange color — not brown and not blond, just a sort of butterscotch.

Whenever Kyle examined her reflection, like now, she felt as though her mother's disapproving gaze was there as well, pointing out all her flaws. Large eyes stared back at her from a face that was shaped like a reversed teardrop, descending from a broad forehead to a pointy chin, which of course made her mouth look even bigger than it really was. Especially tonight, when her mother had personally selected an odd peach shade of lipstick, then had made her paint her fingernails so they matched. It was almost as though Abigail wanted to make her look years older than she was. Even the dress had been personally selected, and Kyle was wearing Gran's pearls for the very first time.

Some girls would have been pleased with the chance to seem older and mature. Not Kyle. What with the constant lessons in etiquette and speech and dance and on and on and on, Kyle felt she was constantly on display. Constantly being prepared for something, being formed into an ornament to be polished and set upon a mantelpiece. Kyle picked up her brush with a sigh. No, growing older held nothing for her but a vague foreboding. As Kyle brushed with swift, hard strokes, her mind went back over the quarrel. What had her mother meant when she said "instead"? Instead of what?

The doorbell rang. Before the chimes were silenced, Kyle had stood, turned off her radio, and started for the bedroom door. Her mother would scold if she was not there to greet their guests. Besides, her mother would never dream of continuing an argument in public. Abigail always presented her loveliest smile to the outside world when she was angry. As Kyle hesitantly moved down the stairs, she wondered if perhaps that was why she herself smiled so seldom. Her mother made the act seem like a lie.

As she entered the living room, Randolf Crawley approached. Inwardly she quailed that he, the last person she wished to see, should quite naturally be the first guest to arrive.

"Kyle, good evening." He flashed a smile.

"How beautiful you look."

"Thank you, Mr. Crawley," she said, feeling her mother's eyes upon her. "How are you tonight?"

"You really must call me Randolf, please." He tugged on the starched cuffs to his shirt, pulling them down below the sleeves of his tuxedo so that the heavy gold cufflinks glinted in the chandelier's light. "We're almost family, you know." He laughed at his own quip, then added, "I suppose you've heard the news. Father has retired, and I have taken over his place on the board."

"Yes. Congratulations." Kyle managed the words with a courteous smile, though she felt little interest in the man's promotion.

Randolf's gray eyes swept over her form. "You look truly spectacular," he said warmly. "That blue in your dress complements your hair beautifully." He didn't seem to notice her blush of embarrassment. "Let's see, you must be seventeen, isn't that right?"

"Fifteen," Kyle corrected. She felt terribly uncomfortable and out of place. "Just barely fifteen."

"Of course. She's the same age as me, aren't you, dear Kyle?" Emily Crawley moved up beside them, her eyes appraising Kyle from top to toe. "I must say, you have made quite an effort tonight."

Kyle tried to put a little brightness into her voice as she asked, "How are you, Emily?"

"Oh, almost as bored as you, I imagine," the girl replied, giving her sleek blond hair a pretty toss. But she did not look bored. Not at all. She surveyed the rapidly filling room with shining eyes. "Why on earth my brother wanted me to accompany him tonight, when there's nobody but old fuddy-duddies around, I shall never know."

"Almost the entire Rothmore board is here tonight," Randolf replied. "Not to mention Senator Allenby over there." He gave Kyle another look and a little bow. "If you ladies will excuse me, I must go and say hello."

Emily watched her older brother walk away, then said, "Isn't it exciting, how this is all working out? In just a couple of years, we will be sisters."

Kyle stared at her. "What are you talking about?"

Emily Crawley had the ability to look particularly beautiful when amazed. "Don't tell me you don't know."

"Know what?"

Emily lifted her perfect little chin and let out a peal of laughter. "Kyle Rothmore, you are positively too droll!" She regarded Kyle with eager eyes. "Think about it for a moment, my little innocent sister-to-be. How your mother has been urging you to come and spend time with my family — at my house with my dear older brother. Pushing you to attend certain meetings, making certain you are seated next to each other. Doesn't she speak of him a great deal?"

Kyle took a step back in genuine horror. "Not Randolf. No, I, it's . . ."

"Whyever not?" Emily followed her, stepping closer, her gaze eager to observe every shred of Kyle's reaction. "Randolf is a prize, don't you think?"

With great effort Kyle struggled for the most polite reaction possible. "But he's so . . . so *old*."

"Dear Randolf is hardly *that* ancient, although I do admit he's getting a bit long in the tooth." Emily's laugh was shrill. "But never mind. In ten years or so age won't matter hardly at all, will it?"

"I didn't, I never . . ."

"Yes, imagine, me being the one to break the news. Isn't that positively delicious?" Emily studied Kyle's face and showed a moment's disappointment that there was no further reaction. She pressed, "I've heard it said that Randolf is one of Washington's most eligible bachelors. You must be *so* excited."

"Yes," Kyle said quietly. She had quickly determined to keep everything she was thinking from showing. Especially here. "Well, if you will excuse me, I must greet our other guests."

Emily's obvious frustration gave Kyle the strength to turn and walk to her father. He reached out an arm to encircle her as he proudly introduced her to the people standing nearby. Kyle forced herself to smile and make all the expected responses. She continued on around the room, speaking to everyone in turn, doing it so well that even her mother stopped her to say how nice it was to see Kyle making an effort. Just how much effort Abigail would never know.

Even though Kyle tried to concentrate on the guests' conversations, her thoughts were constantly turning to Emily's words. *Randolf.* She was to be traded for a union between two powerful families? She felt as if there were a ball of ice where her heart should have been. As she continued about the room, she glanced over to where her father stood laughing with his group of cronies. Surely he had not been a part of this plan, surely not. It hurt more than she could bear to think otherwise.

Then her father broke away from the group and hurried across the room to the door. She watched as he walked up to a newcomer, a young man with dark hair and a grave, hesitant air. Lawrence's arm circled the young man's shoulders as he led him into the room to begin introducing him around. A brief moment of attention was granted his arrival, but as soon as Lawrence was pulled elsewhere, the young man was left standing alone.

Kyle felt drawn to him and to his slightly bewildered demeanor. He looked no more comfortable with the gathering than she did. Kyle imagined herself seeing the grand chamber through his eyes, the curved ceiling almost three stories high, the four grand chandeliers lighting yards of polished wood and precious carpets, the glittering people, the servants in their best uniforms, the sparkling platters and crystal.

As she started across the room, suddenly Emily was at her elbow. "That's the plebe Randolf was telling me about, isn't he, the one your father has pulled up from the masses to stand at his beck and call?"

"He's to be Father's new assistant," Kyle commented mildly.

"Doesn't he look so utterly ordinary," Emily remarked. "I suppose it will be my duty to have him escort me into dinner. No doubt he will bore me to tears with a discussion of actuary tables and the like."

Kyle ended further comments by walking away. She approached the young man, reached out her hand, and said, "Good evening, I am Kyle Rothmore."

"Kenneth Adams." He had a charming smile. "Mr. Rothmore mentioned that he had a daughter. I am very happy to meet you."

The familiar courtesy was spoken with a natural sincerity. Kyle found herself drawn to this pleasant young man. Before she could think of something else to say, Bertrand appeared in the doorway to announce, "Ladies and gentlemen, dinner is served."

"May I take your arm?" Kyle whispered to Kenneth.

"I'm sorry, I didn't —"

"Quickly, please." She was so startled by her boldness that she could scarcely breathe. She reached for his extended elbow, then motioned him toward the dining room.

Four faces confronted them in quick succession. Randolf was halfway across the room and headed toward her when he stopped abruptly. He looked shocked, but swiftly gathered himself. He gave Kyle a formal smile and a slight bow before casting a wrathful glance at Kenneth. Emily was moving their way as well, and showed genuine astonishment at Kyle's maneuver.

The next face Kyle caught sight of was her mother's. Abigail's gaze burned so fiercely Kyle had to turn away. She had never dared to deliberately cross her mother before. The realization of what she was doing left her knees weak.

"Well, look at this, would you." Lawrence Rothmore's ruddy features beamed with genuine pride. "Leave it to my daughter to make our newest guest feel right at home."

That's right, Kyle thought silently. The perspective her father placed upon her actions granted Kyle the strength to straighten her shoulders. *I'd do anything for you, Daddy.*

As she thought the words, Kyle knew they were true. If her father wanted her, *needed* her to marry Randolf Crawley, the reasons did not really matter. Then and there, Kyle knew that if her father asked, she would do it. Even though the thought alone was enough to send ice water through her veins, she would do it for her father.

Lawrence's breath wheezed noisily as he beamed at them both. "Not many people are lucky enough . . ." He broke off to cough. Beads

79

of perspiration spotted his forehead.

"Are you all right, Daddy?"

He waved away her concern. "Working too hard. That's why I need myself a young man — borrow his legs." Lawrence straightened, pulled a spotless handkerchief from his pocket, wiped his brow, then signaled a hovering Bertrand over. "Go out there and rearrange the place cards so these two young people can sit together."

The butler whispered discreetly, "But Mrs. Rothmore specifically ordered —"

"Go ahead and do it." His voice was strong enough to be heard by both Randolf and Abigail. "Make it snappy — people are coming in."

"Right away, sir."

Kyle reached for her father's arm. "Shouldn't you lie down?"

"I'm fine, little princess, don't you fret." He gave her a look of such love and pride that she put aside her fears. "Now you two go and enjoy yourselves."

Kyle led Kenneth over to where Bertrand was holding out her chair. As she settled herself, Bertrand leaned down to whisper, "Well done."

Before she could ask him what he meant, her mother entered the chamber upon the arm of the senator. Abigail's glance flitted over Kyle as if she were not even there. Kyle dropped her gaze to her lap.

"It was very kind of you to accompany me," Kenneth said, obviously uncertain of what was taking place.

But Kyle was not about to go into that. He was an employee of her father, she reminded herself, someone her mother would have referred to as the "office help." As the guests settled around the great oval table, beneath a gilded chandelier from a castle in France, Kyle sought a suitable subject. "What do you do for my father, Mr. Adams?"

"Anything he wants me to. And please call me Kenneth." His smile, warm and broad, creased his features, accenting the vigor and strength of his face. His eyes were dark green, full of life and curiosity. "Right now I am head of his investigating services. I'm responsible for making sure insurance claims are genuine. And sometimes I have to hunt down people to whom claims have been assigned." He glanced down as a flat bowl rimmed in gold was placed before him, then soup was ladled in. "But I shouldn't bore you with business."

"Lobster bisque," Kyle said, not needing to even look at her own bowl. Her mother always arranged for every formal dinner to start with the same dish. Kyle found it rather rich for her own tastes. She went on, "Maggie says there's almost a whole cup of cream in each bowl."

"Maggie is the cook?"

"That's right." Kyle hesitated, then ventured, "And my friend."

"Sounds like a smart woman," Kenneth said, glancing about the room.

Again there was the sense of seeing the cham-

81

ber through his eyes. She looked around with him, taking in the men in their tuxedos and the women in their gowns and jewels. She saw the fancy Wedgwood china and the polished silver and all the fine possessions standing upon the antique sideboards. She felt as though she were seeing everything for the first time. She also understood the expression on his face. Sometimes she did not feel as if she belonged here either.

"Pick up the round spoon," Kyle murmured quietly. "Do what I do. Just raise it up and touch it to your lips. That way you won't look impolite."

"You don't like it?"

Kyle decided to confess what she had not told another soul, not even Maggie, for fear of hurting her feelings. "Melted shrimp ice cream would taste better."

When Kenneth laughed out loud, several faces turned their way. Kyle decided to deflect the attention by turning to her other neighbor, one of Rothmore's senior board members, and asking about his family. But in truth her mind remained on the young man seated to her other side.

She waited until the second course was set in front of them before turning back. Kenneth met her with another of his appealing smiles and said, "Tell me about yourself."

"Me?"

"Sure. What do you like? Do you ever listen to rock and roll?"

Kyle felt uncertain how to respond. She had

never had a dinner guest at one of her mother's events speak *with* her. Everyone politely spoke *down* to her, doing their duty, until they were allowed to turn away and discuss something that really interested them. Kyle decided to risk more honesty. "Sometimes. I'm not sure I like it, though."

"Yeah, there's a lot of strangeness out there. But some of it is powerful." Kenneth ate his filet mignon with gusto. " 'See You Later, Alligator' — have you heard that one yet?"

"Yes." Kyle was unsure what to think now. He looked like an adult, or sort of. He certainly carried himself like one. But adults weren't supposed to be interested in this music. Or were they?

"Then there's 'Que Sera.' I think it's a terrific way to think about the future."

Her eyes widened as she nodded. She had heard the song for the first time the week before.

He smiled his thanks as his plate was removed. "But it's too bad the singer didn't point out that confidence in God is the way to accept each day as it comes."

The informal yet intimate way he spoke of God reminded her of Maggie. "Maybe that's not what the singer had in mind," she ventured in response.

"Well, she should have." He gave her another smile. "Only way to make a philosophy like that really work."

When Kyle did not respond, he gave a little

shrug and asked, "Have you been reading about Grace Kelly's wedding plans?"

It was the perfect question. "Oh yes, isn't it wonderful? Princess Grace, that's what she's going to be called. It's like out of a fairy tale."

"It sure will be something," Kenneth agreed.

"She's going to keep her American citizenship. I saw it on television last week."

"That's right," he nodded, his smile flashing.

"I wish I could see it. Don't you?" Then Kyle met her mother's gaze from across the table, and she felt her enthusiasm fade into a chill of apprehension. She dropped her eyes back to her plate, her appetite gone.

Kenneth asked, "Is something the matter?"

"No, everything's fine," she murmured. She was always doing the wrong thing, talking to the wrong person. She was supposed to keep the proper distance from people like Kenneth. She shivered as she pictured the coming confrontation with her mother.

Kyle leaned forward and glanced at where her father sat at the head of the table. He was laughing at something the senator's wife was saying. Would he really ask her to marry Randolf Crawley?

She risked another glance at her mother. The afternoon's discussion between her parents came back to Kyle's mind. Once again, she found herself wondering what on earth her mother had meant. *Instead* of what?

CHAPTER FIVE

Joel lay in bed, unable to sleep. The moon was high and bright in the clear night sky, and silver light shimmered across his little upstairs room. The house's second floor he had to himself. Well, almost. His father did not like stairs, so his parents slept in the converted back parlor. There were four rooms downstairs, and two upstairs under the eaves. Joel had one. The other was called the guest room, which was strange, because his family never had guests. Gramma Grimes lived only fifteen miles away, and they didn't see much of anybody else except Doc Austin, and he lived just up the road.

His mother had placed frilly pink touches in the guest room that had no guests, items that Joel thought would have looked better in a baby's room. She went in at least once a week to tidy up. She would sit on the room's little bed for a while and stare out the window with a faraway look in her eyes. And when she came back downstairs, her eyes sometimes looked puffy and red and her voice was distant. Often she avoided other family members for a time. It puzzled Joel.

Once in the middle of the night he had thought he heard sobbing. Troubled, he had crept quietly across the little hall that joined the two rooms and peeked through the door. The light from the streetlamp spilled through the room and out into the hallway, touching as it passed the pink cushions on the perfectly made bed. He had expected to find his mother weeping, but to his surprise and bewilderment, it was his father who sat in the chair by the bed, his face in his hands, his shoulders shaking. His father never climbed the stairs. Never. What would bring him to the guest room in the middle of the night? Joel had had a difficult time returning to sleep and had shivered under the warmth of his comforter. But though he had wondered, he had never dared to voice the questions that troubled him so.

Joel now lay and listened to his heart. It was pounding over-loud again. But it did that now and then. Usually Joel ignored the occasional pains and the odd sounds his heart sometimes made. But tonight every rapid beat seemed etched in absolute clarity.

He craned his head and through the screened window watched the stars wink at him. Down below, a solitary car drove by, its passage disturbing the crickets and wind and night owls, but only for a moment.

He glanced at the ticking clock. The hands seemed stuck in place. He rolled over, closed his eyes, and finally drifted off.

The whistle of an early bird jerked him back from sleep. He reached for the clock. His alarm was set to go off in twenty minutes. He tried to lie there, but the anticipation was too great. Finally he rose and slipped into his clothes, tiptoed down the stairs, grabbed the sandwich and apple he had set out the night before, then quietly left the house.

The early dawn was a gentle wash across the sky, the light beginning to dim the stars. The April morning was chilly enough for him to see his breath, but Joel was too excited to feel the cold. The moon was a lustrous circle in the west. As he stood on the corner and ate his sandwich, he imagined that the man in the moon was smiling down on him.

Right on time, the square van chugged down the street and stopped in front of him. A cigar-chomping man stuck his head out of the van's side door and demanded, "Are you, hang on a second, I got your name somewhere. Yeah, here it is. You Joel Grimes?"

"Yessir. Good morning, sir."

"You don't gotta 'sir' me, kid." He slid a thick work-gloved hand under the tightly wrapped wire and tossed the bundle out of the van. It landed at Joel's feet with a heavy thunk. "You bring pliers?"

"Nossir, I didn't —"

"Here, use mine today. Snip the wire and peel it back, careful, otherwise it'll jab you like a knife. That's it. How old are you, kid?"

"Thirteen, sir. Almost fourteen."

The man studied Joel for a moment, as though deciding whether to challenge his statement of age. Joel knew that he was smaller than other boys of thirteen. In fact, that was one of the reasons why his father had agreed to the paper route. "Might build some muscle, put some meat on those bones," he had said. Any reason was good enough for Joel. He wanted the route.

Joel was relieved when the man finally gave a curt nod and returned to his previous argument. "I told you, you don't need to say sir to —"

"Lay off the kid already," the driver called from his place in the front of the van. "Nothing the matter with manners." The driver was as heavy-set as the first man, but his features were bright and smiling. "Thirteen's pretty young for a route all your own. Think you can handle it?"

"Yessir, I sure hope so," Joel replied, handing back the pliers.

"Sunday's the worst," the first man allowed. "Gotta remember to put a magazine and comics into each paper — they come separate. And don't try to carry them all. Find some place to stash them where they won't be seen from the road, otherwise some wise guy'll come by and steal a couple."

"I'll remember that," Joel said, breathless with the fact that it was really and truly happening. "Thanks."

"Don't mention it." The gruff man pointed a gloved thumb at his chest. "Name's Hank. The smart aleck up there driving is Julius."

"Nice meeting you, sir."

"Likewise, kid. And good luck." Hank pounded the side panel, and with a gust of black smoke the van pulled away.

For a moment Joel stood there, taking it in.

The dawn was his and his alone. Finally he hefted half the bundle and carried the papers behind the nearby hedge. The others he coiled using the bag of rubber bands he had brought, then set the awkward rolls into his bike baskets. He had two of them now, one in front of the handlebars and the other over his back tire. He had borrowed money from his mom for them, promising to pay it back from his first paycheck.

In the days leading up to this moment, Joel had done his best to prepare. He had mapped out his route and discovered that it was split in two, with the collection point set almost in the middle. He had spoken to the young man whose route he was taking over, a friend of Doc Austin's who was headed for medical school up north. The young man had described the difficult people, especially the ones who called and complained to the paper's circulation office. They were the ones who could cost him his job. Joel had also called the office himself, though the act had scared him.

Joel mounted his bike and moved out on the route he had already committed to memory. A lot of his tosses didn't land right, which meant stopping his bike and walking up the lawn, sometimes hunting through bushes, pulling out the paper, wiping it clean, and setting it on the front porch. Then he came to the first problem house, an old man who complained his papers were being stolen. Quietly Joel climbed the stairs, opened the screen door, and slipped the paper down where it couldn't be seen from outside.

Another block included the house of old Mrs. Drummond; he already knew about her from Doc Austin. She was not a complainer, but her arthritis was so bad that walking to the edge of her porch was very difficult for her. Joel did what Doc Austin had suggested, which was to slide her paper through her mail slot. As he walked back to his bike, he remembered what else Doc Austin had said, how the woman amazed him with her cheerfulness, how despite her pain she met each day with a smile and a prayer. Doc Austin said he could never understand how someone so afflicted could hold on to faith. Joel wondered what that meant, "hold on to faith." But he didn't ask.

Joel finished the route's first half and hurried back for the second load. His tires whispered down the empty street, and his speed blew up a gentle breeze. He pulled the papers from behind the hedge and began rolling them up. As he bundled them into the rubber bands, he wondered what it was about some people that made them believe in God like that. His parents never talked about religion. Never. His father worked almost every Sunday because he picked up time and a half for weekend work. Joel had seen people going to church, all dressed up and looking stiff and formal. To him it seemed like a strange way to spend a Sunday.

Joel began the second sweep, not bothered by how long it was taking him. He was ready to spend as much time as it took in the beginning, determined to get things right. Besides, he loved having the morning to himself. As he biked down one quiet street after another, his thoughts stood out fresh and clean in the quiet air, and he could think clearly about things. It was even better than being alone in his small upstairs room, working over a new model plane at the desk beneath the window.

His teachers at school said he was too quiet for his own good. He had overheard one of his teachers tell another that his withdrawn nature was a sign Joel did not feel things. Joel did not agree with that at all. As far as he was concerned, he felt things too much.

He finished the route, almost sad that it was done. But school would start soon, so he gathered up the wire and the scraps of paper and started home. As he did, he thought about the call he had made to the newspaper office. The woman had been astonished to hear from him. She had dug up the complaints and read them over the phone to Joel. She said it was the first time she had ever been called for this information by a new paper boy, and that she was going to mention his name to her boss. Joel felt anew the glow over that and resolved that everything was going to go well. There would be no complaints on his route. Not one.

When he turned onto his street, for some reason Joel found himself thinking about old Mrs. Drummond. Strange how she could be so sick and still be happy. Joel parked his bike on the front walk and wished there was some way he could make his parents happy. He'd give anything to have people speak about them the way Doc Austin had talked about the elderly lady.

CHAPTER SIX

Martha stared with unseeing eyes out her kitchen window. The morning sun had pushed up to a sitting position and was taking stock of the brand-new day. Seeming pleased with what it saw, it rose on the eastern horizon to flex its muscles of warmth. But Martha had no interest in the day's beauty. She seldom did. From her place by the sink she turned back to her morning duties. Joel would soon be home from his paper route. Already the smell of breakfast coffee wafted on the morning air. It was her way of getting her day going. It was also the silent signal that drew Harry from his bed to dress for another day of work. A day he never seemed to look forward to with any kind of anticipation. And his mood splashed over on Martha, burdening her with the same sense of resignation.

Martha saw Harry exit the bedroom, still tucking in his shirt and stifling a yawn. She turned away from him in pretense of stirring the morning porridge. Joel would be hungry and perhaps just a bit chilled. The sun had not yet warmed the outside world.

Silently, Harry poured himself a cup of coffee and took it outside to the back porch. The sun struck there first and warmed their postage-stamp backyard before the rest of the house. Harry had come and gone before Martha had time to sense the mood of the morning. Would he be simply taciturn, or would he be surly and quick to criticize? Joel usually returned from his morning route seeking for the signs that would give him the same information. He would stop by the porch, eyes quickly flicking over his father's face.

A sudden thought pulsed through Martha: *Joel's getting so tall. He's growing up — my little boy.*

The thought caught her totally off guard. She'd had no intention of starting her day with maudlin thinking. She had no intention of thinking at all. She did not like to think. She found it far too painful.

She tried to force her attention back to the softly bubbling porridge. She nearly swished the steamy contents from the pot with her vigorous stirring. But even with the increased activity she could not divert her thoughts. *I should have two of them. He should not have been an only child. My little girl — my Katie . . .*

In those chance moments when she did consciously think of her vanished daughter, she was amazed and devastated anew at how deeply the loss still hurt. Martha had been so certain that the passing of time would dim the pain of her heart, ease the emptiness of her arms. But the agony remained so intense it was a physical wound. Her tightened heart seemed to pinch against her rib cage. Her arms literally ached with the absence of a bundle of life, even years after she knew that the little bundle had grown to girlhood. Her throat constricted so she could hardly swallow back the threatening tears.

At such times Martha became even darker of mood than her husband. Even more testy and cutting. It was her only line of defense.

"He's late again," she heard her own harsh voice chiding her absent son. "How on earth am I supposed to have breakfast ready when he won't hold to a proper schedule?"

From the back porch, Harry spoke his first words of the morning. "Sounds like you're riding the boy pretty hard."

She turned to where he sat at the back table and through the open door gave him a hard, cold look. There was no use trying to explain to Harry that it wasn't the time that bothered her. Not the time at all.

It was the high chair tucked away in the pantry — though why she kept it there since Joel had outgrown it, she would not have been able to explain. The high chair that first should have held a baby girl. The high chair that should have been pushed up close to the table, holding another chortling infant thumping an impatient spoon as she waited for her morning porridge.

But Martha could not put her deep feelings into words. She could scarcely form coherent thoughts. At such times the pain was so gripping that she felt she would smother with its force.

She sighed hard, pushing the thoughts and the feelings away as she would a lingering nightmare. "Never mind," she said dully. "I'll make do.

That's what I'm best at, I suppose. Making do with what I have."

After a year of delivering papers, the work had become routine, the time cut by two-thirds. By now his bicycle seemed like an extension of himself. Had he been given to whistling, Joel might have sent a quivering tune into the stillness of the spring morning. There was a song running through his mind in time to his pumping legs, "Oh Yes, I'm the Great Pretender." It already felt like the song was written for him. But Joel made no sound. He had spent his years learning to hide all emotions.

He tossed out the last few papers, his arm cocking and throwing in smooth, automatic sweeps, the papers landing perfectly on the front porches. A year of biking through every kind of weather had brought him a very special knowledge of his little town.

Riverdale was located midway between Baltimore and Washington and had no historical past or town center. It had probably begun as an intersection of Kenilworth Avenue and Riverdale Road, then sprawled out to take over adjoining farmland. Now it was the center of a postwar building boom. Hundreds and hundreds of square saltbox houses lined consecutively numbered streets. With time, the houses became different; people added on summer terraces and winter sun-rooms and patios. The white clapboard exteriors were trimmed with different colored paints. A bush sprouted, another hedge was cut back. But there remained a sameness to the streets and the houses and the neighborhoods.

It was a family town, set in the Maryland countryside about twenty miles north of Washington, D.C. Many were second-generation folk, brimming with the memories of grandparents and great-grandparents having arrived from the old countries to make a new life.

In Riverdale it was probably best to be Irish and have an Irish-sounding name. Joel Grimes was close enough to fit in, though his own ancestors had come from Germany, at least those he knew about. Fathers mostly had jobs the kids could understand. They clerked in hardware stores, fitted pipes, worked at gas stations, put out fires. Some traveled to the iron and steel works in southwest Baltimore, willing to put up with the long commute to give their families a better place to live. The mothers mostly stayed home to mind the children. Laundry hung out behind the homes, and fences were places for neighbors to lean on and gossip.

Joel left his bike on his front walk and picked up his last paper. His father was working the middle shift, which meant Harry left the house after Joel did. Joel usually scanned the paper before he got home and tried to find something in it to talk about. It was a way of testing the waters, passing over some bit of information, seeing if his father felt like talking. Most mornings Harry replied with a grunt, but occasionally his father would continue the conversation. Those days, Joel felt as though he had won a secret battle.

Joel entered the house and heard his mother moving about the kitchen, preparing their breakfast. He gave her cheek a quick kiss as he passed, and she responded with her quiet little smile. Everything was the same, just another morning in their silent house. Yet for some unexplainable reason Joel had the feeling that something was different. Something very big. Maybe even something good.

When Joel entered the kitchen he could see his father out on the back veranda, a steaming cup of coffee on the small table at his elbow, the latest issue of *Argosy* magazine opened in his lap. Harry read *Argosy* and the paper, nothing else. He called *Argosy* the only real man's magazine.

Joel set the paper down on the table and pushed open the screened veranda door. "Pop, did you hear? The Fairey Delta 2, a British plane, it's set a new speed record. One thousand, one hundred and thirty-two miles per hour."

A frown furrowed Harry's forehead until the eyebrows met. "I don't need to know anything about a Limey plane."

Usually a response like that was enough to push Joel back inside. But today the feeling of something important happening kept him there, fishing for whatever it might be. "But, Pop, you're always saying the Brits were good fighters."

His father slapped down the magazine and

rattled the paper open. The tall sheets hid his scowl. "Maybe so, but mark my words, the good old US of A will have that record back in a jiffy."

Joel returned to the kitchen, wondering why he still felt a sense of specialness to the day. He slid into his customary place at the kitchen table, where his mother had already placed a steaming bowl of oatmeal. Joel felt her hand brush against his shoulder as she put two slices of buttered toast at the side of his plate. It was so rare, a touch like that, it seemed as though it was intended to confirm that the day was indeed unique. He nearly started whistling.

He left for school without hearing a single sharp word, a single whiff of discontent. Surely this day held something good in store.

But when he came around the final corner, and his school stood just ahead, the song in his heart was squelched as completely as the one on his lips. Before him, almost blocking the concrete path leading to the building, was a cluster of boys. As soon as he saw them, Joel knew they were up to no good. His stomach knotted in response to the sight, and for one awful moment he feared they were waiting for him.

He wanted to stop, to run, to fly. But he did none of those things, though he could not understand why. His steps faltered, but something kept him going, walking toward them, his whole body tensed in anticipation of what might come.

To this point he had avoided the nasty gang that teased and tormented other kids. They loved to prey on the smaller, the quieter, the more introspective, the loners. Joel was all of those things and would have made good prey. By dodging them at every opportunity and ignoring them whenever they were close, he had so far managed to escape notice. But now he was walking directly toward them, for reasons he could not fully understand. He steeled himself, hoping with all his heart that whatever was drawing their attention would continue to hold their focus.

They were laughing, the kind that rang with a hateful sound. Joel knew it was not shared mirth over some boyish joke. Nor was it good-natured banter. It had a bitter quality. One that left a bad taste in Joel's mouth and formed a knot in the pit of his stomach.

"Hey, farmer," Joel heard one of the larger boys jeer. "Where'd you come from?"

"Looks like he crawled out of a haystack," said their leader. Herman Gadsby was a red-faced bully, a slow-moving football player with a misshapen nose. "Either that or from under some rock."

The laughter rose like a dark ominous wave. "What do you think we oughtta do with him?"

It was then that Joel spotted the object of their ridicule. A boy stood almost surrounded by the crowd. His dark suspendered pants met a simple blue shirt. A black felt hat was pulled down, almost covering the squared haircut. A battered tin pail was clasped tightly in a white-knuckled hand.

Joel had never seen the boy before. For a moment he wished he was not seeing him now. He did not like the feel in the air. All the bullies wore their hair in elaborate pompadours, with the hair in back slicked into flat ducktails. Most kids knew to disappear whenever guys with hairstyles like that came into view. Obviously this guy didn't know any better.

Joel had no idea what to do. He stood quietly, licking dry lips, working to swallow saliva that wasn't there. He felt tension crawl up his spine like a garter snake shivering through meadow grasses. Clammy moistness dampened his hands.

Deliverance came with the loud donging of the school bell. The tangle of boys unravelled and spilled toward the schoolhouse steps at about the same rate that the knot in Joel's stomach unwound.

The next thing he knew, he was staring into a pair of solemn gray eyes. Neither boy spoke a word. They just stood there, measuring each other. In the background the bell stopped ringing, and the silence fell in around them like a living thing. It stirred something in Joel, that silence.

Together they turned and moved toward the red brick school. If they were late for class, there would be trouble. Their steps quickened, and side by side they hurried off to join the clatter as students pressed down the dusty, dark-paneled halls. Joel stopped only long enough to hastily toss his cap toward his assigned wall hook. He saw the boy remove his black hat and look about for a place to deposit it.

"There." Joel pointed at an empty spare peg, and the black felt settled with a gentle rocking motion. The two boys surged ahead to pass through the classroom door, just as Mr. Murdoch stretched out a hand to close it against latecomers.

Joel slid into his assigned seat. The new boy stood silently by the door. As Mr. Murdoch turned to address the new student and assign him a place, the two boys' eyes connected. Some sort of communication passed between them, though Joel was not sure about the message.

It seemed like the most natural thing in the world to fall into step with each other after school. They walked in silence for a moment before Joel finally asked, "Want to go to the soda fountain?" Instantly he regretted it, for this young man in his strange clothes would not be comfortable there. But the fountain in People's drugstore was a gathering point for almost the entire school.

"No, I think," the boy said. He had an accent as strange as his clothes.

Joel thought a moment, then asked, "Want to go see my model planes?"

That met with instant approval. "Yes. I will like to."

Simon was the boy's name. Simon Miller. After giving his name to the teacher at the beginning of class, he had said scarcely a word the entire day. Yet both times the teacher had called on him, Simon had offered the correct answer without hesitation. Joel had spent much of the day observing Simon out of the corner of his eye. There was an unusual stillness about him, attentive yet reserved.

"What are you doing here?" Joel asked. "I mean, it seems kinda funny, starting school a month before the year's over."

"My father has diabetes. Last year they took his leg from — here." He pointed to a spot just above his own knee. "They gave him a make-pretend leg, but sometimes it hurts much." There was a calm acceptance to the way Simon spoke. "Now there are more problems yet, circulation this time. He has to come down and be near the hospital."

Despite the matter-of-fact way Simon spoke, Joel could not help but feel a lance of sympathetic understanding. "Hey, that's tough. My dad has a problem with his leg, too."

"He is diabetic?"

"No. He got hurt in the war."

"I am sorry. Hard it is to see much suffering."

"How come you talk like that? You sound like you're reading off a page."

"I am Pennsylvania Dutch," Simon said simply, as though that was all the explanation required.

"A what?"

"Pennsylvania Dutch. Cherman. You have

never heard of us?"

"I don't think so."

"Papa will explain. He calls us the people apart." Simon grinned at the thought. "You think I talk funny, you wait. Papa did not learn English until he was a full-grown man. He talks English fine, but he thinks Cherman."

Further questions were cut off by turning onto Joel's street. He knew a moment's qualm. His father should still be at work. He rarely came home from the middle shift before six. But what would Simon think of his home or his mother? He had never brought a friend home before. Joel's pace slowed as he reflected how odd it was to have suggested this stranger accompany him home.

"Something is the matter, Choel?"

"No." He hoped he was telling the truth and led Simon up the walk to his front door. Cautiously he opened the door and called out, "Mom?"

The house was silent in reply. Joel gave a relieved sigh and said, "She must be at the market. Come on."

He led Simon up the stairs and into his bedroom. The boy followed him into the room, holding his hat before him with both hands. Joel saw him looking around and said, "Just drop it on the bed."

Carefully Simon set down his black felt hat and took off his coat. His eyes grew large as they took in every aspect of the display — from the suspended airplanes that gently fluttered near the ceiling to the simple shelves lined with painstakingly constructed models. "Ach — so nice," exclaimed the boy.

Joel grinned, his eyes following the eyes of his guest. It was the first time that he enjoyed pride in sharing his hours of work.

"Ach, they are some beautiful! Never have I seen anything like this!"

"They're models. I made them myself. I've got a paper route. Most of the money goes into my savings. I need to save all I can, if I'm going to go to college. But I buy some models, too."

"They are some beautiful." Simon lowered himself to the floor rug and let his eyes wander up and over each plane above his head.

Joel squatted down beside him. It was the first chance he had to closely examine Simon's clothes. The shirt had neither collar nor cuffs. The fabric was coarse, the stitching broad and even. Even the suspenders looked homemade, fastened to the trousers by pairs of buttons. "Does your mother make all your clothes?"

Simon nodded, his eyes still focused on the planes. "We do not buy from the store anything we wear, except the shoes."

"Why not?"

"It is the Mennonite way," Simon said simply.

"Mennonite?"

Simon nodded. "That is what we are."

"I thought you said you were Pennsylvania Dutch — or German or something."

Simon lowered his gaze and laughed good-naturedly. "Pennsylvania Dutch — yes. That is our background. Cherman — that is our tongue. Mennonite — that is our belief — our faith — our whole way of life."

Joel frowned. It seemed a lot to keep track of. He really couldn't understand it all.

They sat there for quite a while as Joel explained about the models and how one had to have the sheet of instructions and carefully unfold it so that the creases would not be damaged, and then follow each step, using the sharp razor blade to shape each section from the paper-thin balsam wood. Later came the gluing and finally the painting and decals. Simon listened with the same quiet attention he had shown in class.

Finally he rose reluctantly to his feet. "I must go. I have chores, and Mother will worry."

"Okay. I'll walk you home." Joel led his new friend back downstairs, then together they started down the street. As they walked, Joel found a strange sense of pressure building up inside his chest. As though all the thoughts and feelings he kept hidden from all the world suddenly demanded release. He found himself saying quietly, "My father isn't happy."

Simon stopped at the corner. His face seemed to mirror Joel's own sorrow. Joel had never before known this in someone his own age. Doc Austin could do it from time to time, sharing the hurt even though something in his gaze said he did not really want to. But Simon just stood and listened and *absorbed*. The pressure continued to build inside Joel, as though all the words and feelings he had tried not to think of must suddenly come out.

"He was injured in the war, like I said. He had to leave the army, and he wanted to stay in. I *think* he wanted to, anyway. He doesn't ever talk about it. But there are a lot of little things."

"Signs," Simon offered. "You watch and see them."

Joel nodded, wondering at how it was possible to be so comfortable with someone he hardly knew. "I guess a lot of what he thinks is about what he never had."

Simon nodded slowly, as though something this important needed to be taken down deep inside. They walked down several more blocks before he finally said, "The book of your name says it is only in the day of the Lord that all God's purposes for man will come true."

The strange words were so confusing that Joel did not know which question to ask first. "Which book?"

The question stopped Simon a second time. "It is in the English as well as the Cherman. Your Bible must say it."

"*My* Bible? I don't have a Bible."

"Well . . . your Family Bible. Your father must read —"

"He never reads it."

The words astounded Simon. He stared at Joel for a moment before he spoke. He sounded puz-

107

zled. "You have a name like Choel and your folks did not choose it from the Bible?"

"Joel was my grandfather's name. I'm named after him." The boy thought a moment. "I think there's a Bible in the house somewhere. But I've never seen anybody reading it."

Simon seemed at a loss to know what to say. Finally he turned and pointed. "This is my house, Choel. I will not give you welcome now, because Mama is still making empty the packing crates. But come home with me soon next week."

"Sure, that'd be swell."

"You will come and have dinner with us," Simon said, almost as though he was talking to himself. "You will speak with Papa over all these things. He will know what to say."

That night Joel lay on his bed, utterly tired, yet not ready to sleep. He felt as though he were floating on a cloud. The day had been so good, better than any day he could remember in a long while. And yet there was nothing really grand, no tremendous earth-shattering event. It was just that he had made a new friend. Someone utterly different from anyone Joel had ever known. And something more. Joel laced his fingers behind his head and smiled up at the unseen ceiling. There was definitely something more to this strange young man. Something very, very good.

CHAPTER SEVEN

Making herself enter the church for her father's funeral was the hardest thing Kyle had ever done.

It was not all the eyes watching her, although there must have been a thousand people facing her as she moved forward. It was not that the family came in last or that her mother had organized a little procession up the church's central aisle. Nor was it the heat, though the July morning was sweltering and its warmth was trapped by her veil and made each breath steamy. It was not even the coffin with its beloved contents that left her feeling so helpless as she slowly walked alongside her mother.

What filled her with dread was all that lay beyond this day and this ritual. The prospect of a life without her father's booming laugh, his hearty voice, and his love left her legs so weak they felt scarcely able to carry her.

The relatives followed behind them, a procession made up mostly of people Kyle had only seen once or twice before in her life. At the news of her father's heart attack, however, they had started showing up, as though word had been passed by telepathy. But even as they had pressed her hand or hugged her close, they had remained strangers.

The whole church was full of strangers. Kyle kept glancing through her dark veil, searching for

109

a familiar face. Occasionally she caught sight of someone she recognized from one of their many dinners, or one of her visits downtown. But most of them she had never seen before.

The church was huge, the grandest in all Washington, D.C. It had been her mother's idea to hold the service here. Kyle had never entered before, and the chamber seemed cold and alien. Honey-stone walls rose to meet stained-glass windows depicting scenes quite foreign to Kyle. High above, the ceiling soared into a series of stone-vaulted arcs. The shining pipe organ poured out a colossal amount of sound. The choir stood and sang words Kyle could not understand even when she tried.

Once they were seated, the minister rose and spoke. His voice rolled out in sad tones, more words Kyle didn't bother to hear. She did not know him, so how could he talk about what she was feeling? She sat there, still and silent, going through the motions set in place by her mother, just as she had been doing ever since the doctor had come out and announced to them that her father had slipped away in the night.

A man she recognized from visits to their house, Senator Allenby, walked to the dais. She asked herself against the backdrop of words she would not hear, why, why? Why did it have to happen now? Now, just as her father was beginning to talk with her as an adult. Kyle sat and pretended to be part of the rite, and remembered the last serious conversation she'd had with her father.

It had been three weeks earlier, on the occasion of her seventeenth birthday. By then the tradition had been well established. They had celebrated together, just the two of them, with a lunch in the boardroom. The preparations for yet another of her mother's high-society parties was not even mentioned. That day, as Kyle and her father had been finishing their dessert, she had asked how he had started his insurance business.

"The telling is easier than the deed," Lawrence had replied with an affectionate smile. "I can't say I started with nothing. My family had enough money to give me a leg up, and the Crawleys helped even more."

"What about Mother?" Kyle already knew her mother's family had been wealthy.

Lawrence shook his head. "They were against it from the start. Abigail's father, once he realized that Abigail had made up her mind that she was marrying me, wanted me to come in and take over his operation — he had no sons. But I saw insurance as the coming thing and wanted to give it a go. And between you and me and the gatepost, Abigail's father had pretty much run the family business into the ground. Her grandfather was quite a businessman, an important wholesaler. But her father . . . anyway, they didn't give me a penny, didn't let me take on any of their own insurance work, not even when it looked like I might go under."

"Did she ask them?"

"Your mother . . ." Lawrence stopped, waving it aside. "Abigail wanted a big house, and they gave us the money for that. They gave us that fancy car, even paid for our first servants. Couldn't see their little girl going without."

"That must have been awful," Kyle said quietly. "Them not helping you with the business, I mean."

"They had their reasons," Lawrence said, cutting off that line of conversation. "In the end I made out all right."

"You sure did," she said, so proud of him she could burst.

He was quiet a long moment. "Beginnings can be terrible times, especially in business. Twenty hours a day, six days a week, living and eating and breathing it, and knowing if it didn't happen, I'd never get another chance."

"But it happened," she offered.

"So slow it was hard to believe I was going anywhere but under," he replied, his normal ruddy features grim with the task of remembering. "To be honest, I don't even know when we actually turned the corner. But one day I forced myself to realize that I didn't need to ask anymore whether we'd make it. Now the question was, how far and how high."

He had looked at her then, a thoughtful, searching gaze. As though he was trying to decide whether to say something or not. Finally Lawrence coughed and told her, "Nobody makes it on their own. You ring up all sorts of debts, and the hardest ones to carry are the ones you can't pay back in coin."

Kyle felt her stomach freeze up. She dreaded what might be coming, more from his tone than his words.

"Your mother has been an asset. She is intelligent and shrewd and knows her way around the upper class. I'm wise enough to know that she has brought a good number of clients to the firm. And I appreciate that. She's been good for me as well. Stimulating. I've not regretted my choice. But there may have been times, especially in the early days of our marriage, when *she* wondered if she had done the right thing."

He seemed so solemn that it made Kyle shiver with foreboding. But because her father was the one talking, all she said was, "I understand, Daddy."

"Do you?" He smiled then, but his expression was touched with deep sorrow. "Your mother . . ." He stopped, the internal argument working its way across his features. "Well, we both know your mother, don't we?"

Kyle nodded. All her thoughts and fears were a huge ball in her throat. But this was her father. And he needed her help. So she forced herself to say, though it was the hardest thing she had ever done in her entire life, "Tell me what you want me to do, Daddy."

He seemed able to see what she was feeling, because his ruddy features turned solemn. "You'd do it for me, wouldn't you, honey?"

"Anything," Kyle said miserably. "Whatever you want, I'll do for you."

"What I want." The words sighed out with such force that all the breath drained from his body. "What I want."

Kyle waited through the longest moment of her entire life. Even her heart seemed unable to beat, the atmosphere was so heavy with anticipation.

Then Lawrence straightened and drew in a breath that seemed to bring with it a new resolve. A strong new determination changed his entire demeanor, from somber and resigned to angry and obstinate. "What I want," he said, measuring each word with force, "is for you to be happy."

The pronouncement was so unexpected, Kyle drew back from the table. "Daddy?"

"Happy," he repeated. "Is there anything so strange about that?"

"No, Daddy, if you're sure —"

"I'm sure." And he was. His eyes glowered as he stared through the door, out beyond the hall and the offices and the building, to whatever foe he saw in the invisible distance. "And I'm going to fix things so that you can do just that." Then he abruptly changed direction, giving her a conspiratorial smile, and said, "Since it's your birthday, I wonder if Chef might have another piece of banana cream pie for me?"

When the funeral service was over, and they had started back down the aisle, Kyle spotted Randolf Crawley standing two rows back looking appropriately solemn. Farther on was her father's former protégé, Kenneth Adams. His eyes were held by the coffin, carried by six men just ahead of Kyle and her mother. Grief was etched in his face and expression. Kenneth chose that moment to look at her, and the depths of his gaze caused her to look away. His eyes mirrored all the pain and sorrow she held deep within herself. Nor did she allow herself to even glance toward where the coffin was being carried down the church steps. She could not do that and maintain her control. There would be time enough to give in to her loss once she was no longer on display. Right now, she was grateful for the numbness, the scattered thoughts.

In a strange way, it was reassuring to be thinking of little things, like the way the trees and shrubs looked as their limousine wound its way through the streets. Or the way a motorcade of police motorcycles cleared the road ahead. She concentrated on how the sunlight danced between the branches overhead, or how fresh the grass looked, as though someone had come out and scrubbed it clean just for them. It was comforting to have such thoughts, especially after last night.

She had accompanied her mother back from the funeral home, where Abigail had gone to take care of last-minute details. Kyle had not spoken a word the entire journey. She had known her mother had said things to her from time to time, but it had been too hard to even hear the words, let them take shape in her mind. Kyle had walked in the front door, knowing Maggie was there and saying something, but again there was nothing but a blur of sound. She did catch a sense of concern behind Maggie's words. But she could not even acknowledge her friend's loving anxiety.

Kyle had climbed the stairs and gone to her room and lain on the bed with her clothes still on. Her mother had come in to say something, then she had left. But Kyle had paid no mind. She had lain there and stared at the ceiling, watching the light from outside fade until the pale blue walls were a dusky gray, and then to black. And she had felt as though she had died with her father, only her body had not realized it yet.

Now, at the cemetery, Kyle allowed herself to be guided into a chair in the front row. She was grateful for the veil, as it helped to hide her face and her thoughts from all the prying eyes surrounding them. She kept her attention on the pastor, but only because it helped to avoid looking at the ugly hole in the ground, the one ready to take her as well as her father.

Did other people have such thoughts? As she sat and watched blindly as the ancient ritual concluded, Kyle wondered if she was the only one in the whole world who felt as though she did not belong anywhere or to anyone. Was there anyone as alone as she was? Had anyone ever felt so helpless, so utterly out of place?

CHAPTER EIGHT

Summer gave way to autumn, and autumn had begun to drift into winter's cold embrace, yet Joel still had not gone to Simon's house for the promised dinner.

Not that he hadn't spent a lot of time at the Millers' home. His reluctance about the meal was not due to the strangeness of some of their ways, although the Miller household was certainly different from anything Joel had ever known. Even so, he felt comfortable with them. But though they had often invited him to share a Sunday dinner, Joel held back.

The Miller household held many mysteries. Everyone was busy all the time, and yet a sense of calm overlay all the activities. Mr. Miller was so sick they had been forced to leave their farm in Pennsylvania and come to live in this strange town near Baltimore, and yet they all seemed happy. He had lost his leg, and sometimes his stump was so sore he could not even strap on the prosthetic limb, and yet he moved about all the time. Even when he was sitting still, he was talking or reading or balancing the baby, or all those things at once.

Mr. Miller did not even seem to realize he was handicapped. He kept up a successful business as a custom cabinet and furniture maker. He moved about the back shed where he kept his tools and wood, deftly carving and shaping and hammering and sawing, supporting himself on one leg and a crutch or a wall or a table, whistling and happy. Yes, *happy*. Not some artificial smile pasted over his sorrows. The man was genuinely happy. The whole family was. And Joel simply could not understand it.

Yet the biggest reason why Joel had not accepted their invitation was that he was afraid to ask his parents. The littlest things could set his father off. The issue of pets, for instance. The second time Joel had dared to ask for a puppy, his father had stayed angry for days, as though the asking itself had been a very bad thing. Joel never could tell what would ignite another bout of anger and shouting. So he chose to remain silent and ask for nothing at all.

But more than Joel's naturally reserved nature was at work here, he knew. Joel felt as though the visit could hold some special significance. Without working out exactly why, Joel sensed that joining them for the meal and the promised talk with Mr. Miller would catapult him into something new. Something alien. And Joel was not sure he was ready for that, or if he ever would be.

A month after his fourteenth birthday, Joel waited as usual for Simon after school. But when his friend appeared, his normally spirited expression was downcast. Joel fidgeted nervously, avoiding Simon's eyes. "What's the matter?"

"Nothing," Simon replied glumly.

"Is it your father?" Mr. Miller had gone through a bad time earlier that summer, something about the doctors not being able to adjust his insulin correctly.

"No, Papa is fine." Simon scuffed along the road, kicking at stones. Finally he said miserably, "A letter from home this morning came. Missy has foaled. And Daisy has another litter. Six this time."

Joel had to think a moment. Daisy was the dog, he knew that much. Simon's sister Sarah talked about little else. That was another amazing thing about this family. They had over two hundred animals, counting the dairy herd. But all of them had names. And the children talked about them as if they were all family. "I forget. Which one is Missy?"

"Papa's horse. He promised me the foal would be mine for raising up myself."

Joel felt a stab of envy. His father would not allow him one small puppy, and the Millers had everything. Four dogs, three cats, cows, four horses, two mules, thirty hens, a bad-tempered rooster, and seven nanny goats. There was even a squirrel that had fallen out of the nest as a baby and Mrs. Miller had bottle fed; she now lived in the tree back of their farmhouse and would come and bring her own family whenever Mrs. Miller called to her. "So, that's great. What's the matter?"

"So now somebody else sees after my foal. Somebody else curries him. Somebody else watches him learn to stand and walk and run." Simon seemed ready to cry. "I want to see him. To do for him myself. I miss home. I miss our farm."

Joel did not know what to say. He had never known another town except Riverdale. His parents had taken him to Washington one afternoon to see the White House and the memorials. But he had never even been to Baltimore. He could not even begin to picture the Millers' Mennonite community outside Lansdale, Pennsylvania. From everything Simon had said, it was an utterly different world from anything Joel had ever known.

They walked the rest of the way to Simon's house in silence. Before they had even climbed the front steps, Joel heard the wails from inside. "Sarah, she makes tears," Simon said forlornly. Sarah was Simon's younger sister. "She wants the puppies. All of them, here with us now. Mama says no, there is not the room. And we could not get them down here to us. So Sarah, she wants to go home. We all want to go home."

Mrs. Miller pushed open the door and tried for a smile, but she could not raise one today. She was dressed, as always, in a dark blouse and printed skirt, with a kerchief tied over her hair. "I am sorry, Choel. Today is not so good."

"Sure, I understand." Mrs. Miller's accent was a little stronger than Simon's, but nothing compared to her husband's. According to Simon, his mother's family was progressive, whatever that meant. "I'll see you later, Simon."

"Perhaps you will come and choin us for worship on Sunday, yah?" The words had been spoken by Mrs. Miller every week since she had met Joel. And every time he had come up with another excuse. The woman did not press. And Joel had never delved into his reasons for delaying.

Today Simon did not even wait for Joel's response. He trudged up the front steps, his shoulders slumped in misery. Joel felt a sudden yearning to do something for his friend, something that would make him happy again. "Sure, Mrs. Miller. I'd love to come."

His unexpected assent astonished them both. Mrs. Miller's anxious expression gave way to a beaming smile. Simon whirled about. "You will? Really?"

Joel was so surprised at the effect of his words that he could only nod.

"That is good." The word off Mrs. Miller's tongue sounded like *goot* to Joel's ears. "Welcome you, we will. Come at ten, and stay you must for the Sunday meal."

"This is very good, Choel," Simon said, and his grin upheld the words.

"Sunday next," Mrs. Miller said and reached forward to pat Joel's head. "It is good to have reason yet to smile today."

Joel walked down the block, turned, and waved back to where Mrs. Miller and Simon stood on the porch watching him. Sunlight and shadow played over the street as a brisk autumn wind

121

sent clouds scuttling overhead. For some reason, he felt lighter than air, able to skip forward, as if just barely tracing his way along the earth.

But the closer Joel got to home, the heavier he became. He tried to sort out in his mind the best way to approach his parents. His first urge was to not talk about it to them at all. Rather he would just do his paper route, then slip over to the Millers'. But much as he hated the thought of conflict, he decided he had to meet this head on. To do otherwise would taint the way this day felt.

As he headed up his street, he concluded that the direct approach would be best. He would simply lay his request before them and hope they would understand.

The next big question was which parent to tackle first. His mother would probably be the most likely to give permission, but his father detested what he considered playing one parent against another. Harry interpreted it as an act of deceit and reacted with denial of the request, no matter how reasonable it might be.

No, Joel decided, it was best to face them both at once and take the consequences. But when? They were so seldom together. Family fellowship was unknown in Joel's household. He had never experienced an atmosphere like that of Simon's home. There the father read near the room's big lamp while the mother tucked up close on the other side of the small table, knitting needles clacking in rapid succession, keeping time with her chattering tongue. And all about the room, children of various sizes hovered over homework while the smaller ones amused themselves with homemade toys. The baby cooed from the cradle, near enough to one parent or the other so that an outstretched foot could continue the steady rocking.

No, Joel's home could not be more different. His father either hid behind his newspaper or *Argosy* magazine or just sat in his corner chair, staring out at the black night. His mother often retired early, giving Joel a quick brush of a kiss and telling him to be sure to finish his homework. Sometimes she would read in bed her dime novels from the corner drugstore. His father called them "your mother's trash" and always tossed them out if he came across them.

No, Joel decided, heading up the front walk, it would have to be at mealtime. Certainly there would be little competition for their attention if he were to voice his request then. Mealtimes were silent at the Grimes home. But the very thought of the coming ordeal made Joel's stomach knot.

Joel did his evening chores and tried to formulate the right words. But every idea he had was met with images of frowns and headshaking. As he trudged into dinner, he resigned himself to the fact that there was no good way to say it. He would just have to blurt it out.

They were halfway through another silent meal before he cleared his throat, swallowed, and dove in. "Simon has invited me to his house for Sunday morning."

Heads did not even lift.

"His folks have a sort of worship every Sunday."

His mother looked up.

"He's invited me to join them," Joel pressed on. His mother's eyes were on him now. He wanted to speak directly to her but feared it would not please his father.

"What do you mean, worship?" Martha asked.

Joel wasn't sure himself but repeated what little he knew from Simon. "They read stories from the Bible and stuff. They sing, too. Together."

His father's head lifted now. "You mean, at home?"

"In their house," Joel confirmed.

"Why? That's what churches are for."

Joel could not recall his folks ever setting foot in a church, but now was not the time to be pointing that out. "They don't have a church here."

"There are churches all over Riverdale."

Joel was skating toward the edge of his knowledge. "Not their kind."

The frown on his father's face deepened. Joel could see he wasn't pleased. "What are they, some kind of weird sect? I don't want any son of mine getting hooked up with a bunch of crazy fanatics."

He sounded so angry. So final. Joel felt his heart sink. He lowered his head.

"I'm sure Simon's family aren't fanatics," he heard his mother saying. "It just doesn't fit."

"They sure dress funny," his father shot back.

"They are Mennonites. That's the way they're supposed to dress."

"It looks goofy."

"You might not like it," Martha replied in her quiet, flat voice, "but it doesn't mean they are strange."

"So what does it mean?"

"It's a sort of uniform. Like the army."

His father's tone sharpened further. "It's not like the army at all. That's a stupid comparison. The army has a perfect reason —"

"So do they," Martha cut in. "They choose to be identified in such a manner."

Joel listened as the angry words swirled about the small room. He wished he could just take it all back. He had not wanted to cause another argument. He hated these quarrels worse than anything. He should have just stayed silent, as always.

But his father was not finished. "So where did *you* get all this information?"

"I read about them," his mother replied.

"In one of those trashy books of yours, I guess. Well, if that's the kind of folks they are, then it's settled —"

"For your information, I found out about Mennonites in the public library. I looked them up when Joel started keeping company with that young boy." She flung the words like a well-

125

aimed lance at her husband. Joel looked up in surprise. It was a rarity that his mother would stand up to her husband over anything. But Martha was not finished. She tilted her head, a defiant look in her eyes, and said, "At least I am interested in what goes on in Joel's life."

Silence again. Joel's father seemed too angry to even respond. Joel turned back to his half-finished plate. He had to eat all that remained before he could leave the table, but his appetite had vanished. All he wanted was to flee the room.

At length his father stirred slightly and demanded, "What are they asking you to do?"

Joel found himself reluctant even to respond, not wanting to start the whole controversy over again. "They just wanted me to join them for the singing and reading time, then stay for a late lunch. They call it dinner."

Again silence. At long last his father spoke again. "Don't suppose it would hurt anything," he said without even looking up. "Might give us a chance to catch up on some sleep around here, with you out of the house."

Joel let his astonished gaze travel from his father's lowered head to his mother's still-flushed face. She simply nodded.

As an afterthought she added, "Make sure you wash your face and brush your hair before you go. Folks are supposed to look their best for church."

CHAPTER NINE

"Mrs. Rothmore will be with you directly, Mr. Crawley," Bertrand announced solemnly, leading him into the library. "She asks that you wait for her here."

"Fine, fine," Randolf replied absently. When the tall double doors closed behind the departing butler, the young man resisted the urge to pace about the room. It was not like him to suffer from nerves when meeting with Abigail. But something about her summons worried him mightily.

When he had taken over his father's position on the Rothmore board, Randolf had discarded many things. One had been the 'Junior' attached to his name. Another had been the deferential attitude he had formerly used around Abigail. The first time he had addressed her as an equal had been in this very room. She had noticed it instantly, of course. Very little escaped Abigail's notice. She had acknowledged the change in his attitude and its intended message with a regal nod.

There was much that remained unspoken between the two of them. Which was fine with Randolf. As far as he was concerned, some of life's most important matters should never be spoken of aloud. Such as the hunger for real power they seemed to share. The kind of power that could be theirs, *would* be theirs, once the reins of Rothmore Insurance were firmly in Randolf's grasp.

Randolf lowered himself into the leather armchair and glanced about the room. The Rothmore library had always fascinated him. Whenever he saw himself taking over control of the family assets as well as the family company, it was to this room that his daydreams took him. If any chamber of the Rothmore manor spoke of opulence, it was this room. The rich wood of the oiled wall panels, the enclosed shelves heavy with leather-bound volumes, the hunting scenes and the full-length portrait of Abigail that graced the walls, the Oriental carpets strewn across the polished floor — somehow the room managed to be both masculine and elegant, a marvelous combination in his eyes.

His reverie was interrupted by Abigail's entrance. "Ah, Randolf, so good of you to come," she said as she swept toward him. "I hope it wasn't too much of a bother to join me so early on a Saturday morning."

"Not at all." Something about her tone brought a new surge of nerves. Yet Randolf managed to hold to his outward calm and languidly rose to greet her. "Your call sounded rather urgent."

"No, not urgent. Just desirable. With the reading of Lawrence's will set for the day after tomorrow, this could not be put off any longer." Rather than settle upon the sofa opposite where he had been seated, she marched to the other side of the hand-carved cherrywood desk. "Won't you be seated?"

He had no choice but take the high-backed chair across the desk from her. "Thank you."

"I've been doing some thinking." She hesitated, toying with the open ledger on the desk before her. Then she added, "About Kyle." Another long moment of silence before Abigail offered, "She's still very young."

Randolf had the sudden impression that all this was staged. Making him wait, seating herself behind the desk, the hesitation — all of it was simple theatrics. No, not simple. Not with Abigail. Everything had a purpose. Even this. And the implications of where this was headed filled him with foreboding.

"I know I have been pushing you to seek, well, some sort of commitment." She picked up the gold-plated dagger used as a letter opener and rolled it back and forth between her fingers. The light flickered directly into his eyes. "But recently I have been experiencing second thoughts."

"Second thoughts," he echoed, his mind racing.

"I have been rather demanding at times, I'm afraid." Abigail sighed dramatically. "And this loss of her father has been most difficult for her."

Randolf knew he was expected to respond, but he could not. The words would not come. His one chance to wrest full control of Rothmore Insurance was suddenly slipping through his fingers. And yet he could not fathom why. He studied the woman seated across from him, searching for the purpose behind her actions.

"I've been wondering if we should not push her so," Abigail continued. "Perhaps Kyle should be given more time to grow up."

Randolf resisted the urge to scream, to tear his hair, to leap to his feet and rage from the room. *But what about our plans?* he wanted to shout. *What about all my ambitions?*

He took a breath. Another. Only when a semblance of calm was restored did he say, "But I thought you were concerned that she might . . ." He was uncertain whether he should even mention out loud what had never before been spoken. But with all his dreams going up in smoke, he had no choice. He pressed forward with, "I thought you wanted to be certain that she had no opportunity to . . . to select a husband of her own choosing."

A small smile flickered around the corners of her mouth, though she tried hard to disguise it. "That is not so pressing now. With her father gone . . ."

"Ah." The word was a release of both pent-up tension and hope. It was clear to him now. Bitterness tainted his voice as he demanded, "So you are severing me from any relationship with your daughter?"

"Oh, my dear Randolf." She leaned back in the big desk chair. Her small figure looked dwarfed by its size, yet a new sense of authority gave the impression that she was quite at home there. "Quite the opposite. I would be perfectly thrilled if Kyle were to choose you. But I also feel that we can now allow her a bit more freedom. After all, she *is* little more than a child."

"That scarcely concerned you before," Randolf pointed out acidly. It no longer mattered, though. Nothing would change Abigail's mind. He knew that for certain. She was going to run the company. She would make her own rules.

Abigail studied him carefully for a moment before replying coldly, "Think what you might, Randolf, but the fact is that all I have done for Kyle has been done with her best interests in mind. She is such a child. She thinks the world is made up of sugarplum fairies and doting fathers. I have had to take a firm hand because no one else would."

Randolf hesitated. She sounded so sincere. Perhaps she cared more for the girl than he had realized. "But I care for your daughter as well, Abigail," he ventured. "She is attractive and intelligent, a rare combination. And her sweet sense of innocence is most refreshing. Business was far from my only motive, I hope —"

"Of course I knew that." She waved a dismissive hand. "I would not for one moment have encouraged you if the business had been your only motive." Abigail's gaze held a new quality, a sense of realized power. "Your qualities are well known to me, Randolf. I will continue to require them, both as an ally within the company as well as a suitable gentleman for my daughter."

His shoulders slumped with sudden relief. All was not lost. Not entirely. Just postponed. Perhaps. "You mean —"

"I meant just exactly what I said." She held him with this new, powerful gaze of hers. "I intend to take a firm hand within the company, and I expect another firm hand to take over when I depart. I know full well how quickly fortunes can rise and fall. My grandfather had wealth, as you full know. My father managed to lose almost all of it, not because he was not intelligent, but because he was weak. I cannot permit either this family or this business to fall into weak hands."

Randolf pushed himself to his feet. He felt drained. Trapped. Abigail was so incredibly in control. "So I should still continue to see her."

"Of course, my dear Randolf." She looked directly into his eyes. "But there is no need to press. Not for the moment, at least."

He nodded mutely and turned to go. He knew the words were his dismissal.

Kyle had begun the habit of rising with the sun. She found it gave her a much-needed respite from her mother, as well as time for quiet reflection. She would dress and walk through the garden, occasionally stopping for a chat with old Jim, but usually preferring solitude. Those winter walks became her refuge, when frost covered the grass with diamond shards and all the world seemed to hold its breath.

Dawn came late and slowly on those mornings, and the sun's arrival formed stark etchings in the frozen yard. Everything was either bathed in frigid shadow or sparkling with a myriad of tiny rainbows. Each of her footsteps whispered through the thawing grass, marking her passage with dark imprints. She carried bread with her, feeding crumbs to every bird she saw. By early December, the birds had come to expect her and would flutter about with quietly drumming wings as she sprinkled the glittering lawn with food.

Afterward, Kyle went into the kitchen and had her breakfast with Bertrand and Maggie. They sat down together, said grace, and ate as they discussed plans for the day. Then Bertrand left to do his morning rounds of the house, and Maggie took out her Bible and read quietly. Several times she offered to read out loud, but Kyle shook her head. She was happy to just sit there and feel the peace as Maggie read to herself.

Kyle avoided the house's big rooms as much as possible. They echoed with her father's absence. There was nothing left to keep the cold, precise emptiness of her mother's style and personality at bay. Whenever Kyle walked through the great hall or the formal chamber or the dining room, with their beautiful paintings and sparkling chandeliers and waxed floors and polished silverware, she felt as though she had wandered into a strange and empty museum.

That first Saturday in December, when Maggie rose to begin her chores, Kyle donned an apron and worked alongside her. Maggie protested, "Child, you've got a score of other more important things to do than work here beside me."

"I don't, really," Kyle said, holding to her matter-of-fact tone. "Emily Crawley and some of her friends are coming over for tennis, but not until eleven." Several of the wealthy families had built communal courts, one indoors and another outdoors, at the bottom of their garden. "Besides, I didn't invite them. Mother did."

"Speaking of which," Maggie continued, "if your mother found you in here working she would not be pleased."

Kyle's hands stayed busy washing the greenhouse strawberries Bertrand would serve with morning coffee for their guests. "Don't send me away, please, Maggie. I don't have anywhere else to go."

The older woman's tone softened as she asked, "What on earth are you saying?"

Kyle kept her hands busy. It helped her hold to the calm tone. "I don't belong here. I'll never be the proper lady Mother wants me to be."

"Oh, honey, my dear sweet Kyle." Maggie walked over and settled one arm around Kyle's waist. "You are the most wonderful young lady I have ever set eyes on, and that is the truth."

"Not according to Mother," she replied. The sunlight streaming through the back window became a lancing blade, and Kyle had to stop to wipe at her eyes with the back of one hand. "She's been at me nonstop since Daddy . . . since the funeral. Nothing I do is good enough. And she's right."

"No she isn't," Maggie said, her voice quiet yet firm.

"Yes she is."

"Look at me, dear."

Kyle let the berries drop into the plastic strainer and turned to face her friend. The sunlight was revealing as it rested upon the old woman's features. Yet a lifetime of hard work had not dimmed the clarity of those wide-set gray eyes. They regarded her now, the gaze clear and direct and loving. "My dearest child, I love you like you were my own daughter, you know that."

"I know," Kyle whispered.

"Then believe me when I tell you, life will always try to bring you down. If it were not your mother, it would be something else. Do you know why?"

Kyle found herself unable to answer, so she made do with a little shake of her head.

"Because your heart is too big for this world. You hold too much love, too much tenderness. It is clear to anyone with eyes open to the truth." A cloud began tracing its way across the sky overhead, cutting out all the light except for the single ray falling upon Maggie's face. It transformed her gray hair into a shimmering silver crown and made the light in her eyes so strong that they seemed to hold the sun itself. "A heart like yours needs protection, my beloved child. It needs the shield of prayer to keep it from seeking out the shelter of cynicism and hardness. Do you understand what I am saying?"

"I'm not sure," Kyle murmured. She wanted to run away, and she wanted to stay. She wanted Maggie to stop saying these words that left her feeling so vulnerable and shaken, and yet she wanted her to keep talking for all her life long.

"You need to ask the Lord into your life, my beloved little one. You need to have His presence guiding you, showing you the path your feet should be walking." Maggie inspected her with a gaze so penetrating that Kyle felt as though it reached deep into her confused heart.

"I'm not —" Her response was cut off by the sound of the front doorbell. "Who is that?"

Maggie stepped back a pace, bringing her face into the shadows, and once more she became a gray-headed old woman. "I have no idea who that might be. Deliveries always come to the back door."

Kyle listened but did not hear Bertrand's measured tread. "I suppose I'd better go see who it is."

As she turned away, Maggie settled a hand upon her arm. "Here, let me take your apron." After removing it, Kyle handed it over, and the woman said, "Will you think about what I have told you, child?"

"Of course." Yet as she walked through the kitchen door and entered the grand foyer, Kyle felt the words slip from her. Like a cloak left behind after a hard summer shower, she cast them aside. She had no choice. Here in the harsh reality of her beautiful home, as her heels clicked across the polished marble tile, Kyle felt as though the words had no place. Nor the sentiment. She could not survive with an open heart. Not here, not around her mother and her mother's friends. They would grind her down and devour her, unless she somehow could learn to be as hard and as cold as they were.

Kyle stopped in front of the oval mirror and checked her reflection as her mother had trained her to do before answering the door. But she caught herself looking into a pair of sad, hopeless eyes. And she had a fleeting glimpse of a thought: *What if Maggie is right, and they are wrong?*

The doorbell sounded again, bringing her from her reverie. She straightened, turned, and opened the door.

Old Mr. Crawley, Randolf and Emily's father, stood in the entrance. "Hello, Kyle."

"Good morning, sir. Won't you come in?" she invited warmly, remembering this man's years with her beloved father. "Was Mother expecting you?"

"Not exactly. We are planning the reading of your father's will, as you know."

"Of course." It was circled in red in her mother's social calendar and had been for over a month. Abigail's secretary had typed letters to each of the family, inviting them all, as though it was some important social event. Every time Abigail spoke of it, she did so with a spark of barely repressed excitement. It left Kyle reeling to see her father's memory reduced to such crassness. But as always, Kyle had remained silent. And safe. "But isn't that on Monday?"

"It is indeed." For some reason, the old gentleman seemed nervous. "There's a certain matter . . . well, I thought it best to speak with you two in private."

Bertrand appeared, apologetic at having been caught away from his post. "Miss Kyle, excuse me, I was out back making arrangements with the caterer for Monday's reception, and didn't hear —"

"It's quite all right. See if you can find Mother, won't you?"

"Of course, miss. Right away." He gave Mr. Crawley a stiff bow and turned away.

"Perhaps we'd be more comfortable in the library, Mr. Crawley." She held none of the negative feelings for the older gentleman that she had for his offspring. Mr. Crawley had married late and was a good twenty-five years older than his wife. He possessed the stiff bearing and formal manners of another generation. But he had always treated her with reserved courtesy. There was nothing false about him, nor any of the cold deceit she felt from Randolf Junior. "Can I offer you a cup of tea?"

"No, thank you." He entered the library, took the offered seat, set the bulky briefcase beside his chair, and waited in some inner tension. When steps announced Abigail's passage across the marble foyer, he almost leapt to his feet to greet her.

"Why, Randolf, what an unexpected treat," Abigail said, entering with her hand outstretched. The formal smile said that in truth his arrival was anything but a pleasure. "If you are looking for your son, I'm afraid he's already come and gone."

A fleeting expression of alarm passed over the old man's features. "You're sure he's gone?"

"Yes, of course, I saw him off myself." She allowed herself an instant's curiosity over his attitude, but clearly there were more pressing matters on her mind. "I'm so sorry I can't invite you to join us for lunch, but I really must —"

"I'm not here for a meal," the older gentleman said grimly. "And I know how busy you are. But we really must talk."

Abigail lifted her chin a fraction, so as to give the impression of looking down at the taller man. "Really, what on earth can't wait until our meeting Monday?"

"I have asked myself the same thing, and wondered if I am not breaking your husband's instructions by being here," he responded crisply. "But as you have refused to listen to my entreaties for the first reading of the will to be held in private, I feel I have no choice."

Abigail showed an instant of uncertainty. She gathered herself with an effort and said, "Won't you sit down?"

"Thank you." Stiffly he resumed his seat.

"As I have already told you," Abigail went on, "I can see no reason for agreeing to this odd request of yours. Lawrence has no doubt shown his relatives the same generosity that he has always demonstrated."

"My suggestion had nothing whatsoever to do with how Lawrence has treated the others. What you may not be aware of, Abigail, is that your husband retained me to take care of some very private matters."

This time, the woman's surprise could not be masked. "I beg your pardon?"

"Matters so private," Mr. Crawley persisted, "that not even my son was to know of them. By Lawrence's own instructions I was ordered not to divulge them, not even to you, Abigail, until the reading of the will. But because of your persistence in making this a public event, I felt it necessary to speak to you personally in advance."

There was the sudden focusing of energy so potent that time seemed to slow. Kyle felt as much as saw her mother's tension. Abigail began turning toward her, but the movement seemed to go on forever, and all around them rose the invisible swirling cyclone. "Wait outside, please, Kyle."

"As a matter of fact," Mr. Crawley interjected, "this very much pertains to your daughter."

"I said wait outside." Her mother's voice was so flat it sounded metallic.

"Abigail —"

"You may have affected some secret relationship with my late husband," the agitated woman snapped, the cords in her throat standing out. "But I am still mistress of this house, am I not?"

Mr. Crawley observed her as he would a witness on the stand, then turned away with a brief harrumph and began shuffling papers brought from his briefcase. Kyle rose and left the room in silence. Quietly she closed the tall double doors behind her, glad to be away from the gathering storm.

But she had scarcely made it halfway across the foyer when Abigail shrieked at the top of her voice, *"WHAT?"*

Kyle stopped in her tracks. The kitchen door popped open, and she was joined by Maggie and Bertrand. Together they stood and gaped at the library's closed doors.

There was the low murmur of Mr. Crawley's voice, then a long silence, followed by Abigail's shout, *"You cannot be serious!"*

A further low murmur was cut off by Abigail shrieking, *"I will not stand for this!"* But the murmur persisted, rising slightly, yet remaining too low for them to make out the words. Kyle was not sure whether she was sorry or glad to be unable to understand what the old gentleman was saying.

Suddenly the library doors were flung back with such force they banged upon the side wall, knocking down one of the portraits. Abigail stalked out, her face drawn and white, her lips a thin line. She shot a single furious glance at Kyle, then fled in a staccato beat of her high heels.

Mr. Crawley emerged, wiping his forehead with a white handkerchief. He gave Kyle a look of pure sympathy. Yet all he said was, "I can see myself out."

CHAPTER TEN

There were many things that Joel found disconcerting about the Miller household. But they were not why he felt so nervous as he walked up the path and climbed their front steps that Sunday morning. He paused on the porch to adjust his tie and slick down his hair. Before he could raise his hand to knock, Ruthie had already opened the door.

"Hello, Choel," she welcomed in her softly accented brogue. Little Ruthie was what she was called around the house because she had the same name as her mother, but Ruthie was not small. Just an inch shy of Joel's own height, she had the look of a healthy, hearty farm girl. Her height and strength only added to her pleasant attractiveness. As always, she wore the same homespun blouse and long skirt as her mother, but the kerchief in her hair was of a brighter color. She stood straight and tall, her face full of her sweet nature. Ruthie held the screen open for him. "I wish you good Lord's day, Choel," she added formally.

"Thank you," he murmured, uncertain quite how to react. The family became so traditional at certain moments. As he entered, he had a closer look at the sadness in her eyes, and he said, "I'm sorry about . . . about your farm home . . . being so far away, Ruthie."

She rewarded him with a look of such gratitude that it warmed him all the way down. "I am glad you are come, Choel," she replied. "You make happy the whole family with your coming."

"Choel, hello, welcome." Simon approached in his simple clothes and lace-up boots. "It really happened yet. To believe it is hard for me. You have come." Simon's accent was stronger today, and the words came out sounding like *you haff gom*.

Joel allowed himself to be guided into the living room where the family was gathered. They all called a hearty welcome — even the baby cooed a hello. Yet as Joel settled himself into place between Simon and Ruthie, he could feel that sadness still cast a pall over the gathering. He felt his own thoughts sobering. He shuffled and cleared his throat, his eyes passing from one face to another.

He found that Mrs. Miller was watching him from grave, dark eyes. He heard her say, "Such a feel for folks you have, Choel. You come, you sit, and already you know how we ache some more."

Joel was astounded by her words. He stared at the fine-featured woman with her brown hair tucked under a kerchief and wondered how she could know this. He had a lifetime's experience at keeping himself hidden, yet this woman was aware of his thoughts and how he studied others. He lowered his eyes and nodded. "You miss your farm," he said simply.

From her place beside him, Ruthie gave a quiet sigh. Across the room, her younger sister, Sarah, choked back tears.

Mrs. Miller turned to her husband. "Did I not tell you? A tender heart has the young man."

Mr. Miller nodded slowly. He was a big man, his work-hardened hands twice the size of Joel's. His sparse blond hair rose back from a broad face that seemed perpetually sunburned. His beard was reddish brown and cut so it ringed his chin and left his mouth clear. He rumbled in his heavily accented way, "Such a greeting we give to Choel, our honored guest. Such a sadness on the Lord's day."

When Joel first had come to the Miller home, he had found it very difficult to understand what Mr. Miller was saying, since he was missing every other word. But with time Joel had come both to understand him and to feel the same relaxed comfort around the big man as he did around the rest of the family.

The youngest boy, Gerth, whimpered softly, "I want home again, Papa."

"Me too," whispered Sarah.

This was greeted with none of the impatient anger Joel would have found in his own home. Instead, Mr. Miller nodded his head again, the motion slow and measured, the eyes grave. He stroked his long beard a moment. "Yah, yah, this have I heard now many times."

Joel felt his glance drawn to Mr. Miller's right pant leg, which was folded and pinned back above where his knee should have been. The first time Joel had seen the man without his artificial leg, he had felt sick to his stomach. But he had come to pay it as little mind as Mr. Miller did. In truth, the big man moved about his home and carpenter's shed as agilely as any other man would on two legs.

But today seemed to be different, because Mr. Miller bent forward and began massaging the end of his stump. His wife's face instantly showed her concern. "Choseph, something the matter is?"

"Ach, it is chust a little soreness. Nothing. Nothing." But he did not stop his rubbing. Instead, as one great hand massaged his leg, the broad face with its rounded features turned and stared at each of his children in turn. He said nothing, but a sense of growing power seemed to fill the room. A sense of communication on a level far beyond that of words.

"Something to help, Choseph?" Mrs. Miller asked.

"Perhaps my shot should I have early this day," he said.

"Yah. So I think too." Mrs. Miller was up and moving for the kitchen before she finished speaking. The room was silent enough for Joel to hear her open the refrigerator, shut it, and hasten back. "Here now."

"Thank you, wife." Without taking his eyes from his family, he pulled the stopper from the needle, pointed the syringe straight up, tapped the glass base, and pushed the plunger until a

146

little liquid squirted up.

Joel knew from Simon that Mr. Miller had to have these injections several times a day. But when Mr. Miller swabbed a patch of skin, pointed the needle downward, and prepared to plunge it into his arm, Joel had to look away. He turned to his friend. Simon's gaze remained fastened upon his father. His brow was furrowed, as though he was concentrating hard, trying to understand something. Some lesson, some message that he was attempting to grasp.

"Well, now."

Joel allowed his gaze to return to Mr. Miller as he set the syringe on the side table and lifted the big family Bible. "Why do we not show our guest how we like to sing? Ruthie, you choose, why not."

She suggested something that Joel did not understand, and only when they began singing did he realize that the words were in German. But it did not matter. The whole family sang. But it was more than just *singing*. Each took a part of the harmony, even the youngest girl, and made music together with such ease and beauty that Joel could scarcely believe what he was hearing.

He glanced from one face to the next. They sat in a loose circle around the room, some in chairs and some on the floor. There was no accompanying instrument. Some sang with eyes closed, others with eyes gazing unfocused. But there was an effortless calm to each one, a sense of having cast aside all the world and joining with one another in song.

Hymn followed hymn. As the music continued, Joel stared at the bare walls and saw how the lack of pictures and decoration matched the simple majesty of their music. He looked at the plain table and chairs and hook rug and saw in the homemade quality the same strength of spirit and self-sufficiency that he heard in their voices. The home held neither radio nor television. Yet it now seemed complete in a way he could not understand.

Finally the music drifted away, but the calm remained. Mr. Miller adjusted the big Book in his lap and said, "Choel, you speak no Cherman, yah? So I read the Cherman, then another for you to read in English. Who? Ruthie? Yah, you with the lovely voice. Good. We start with Isaiah, chapter fifty-two, verse seven."

Slowly he intoned the unknown language, one that seemed to roll much more comfortably from his tongue. Then Joel listened as Ruthie read carefully from a smaller Bible, " 'How beautiful upon the mountains are the feet of him who bringeth good tidings, who publisheth peace, that bringeth good tidings of good things, that publisheth salvation, that saith unto Zion, "Thy God reigneth!" ' "

"Good, good. And now chust one more, I think, yah." He turned the pages, licking his thumb and tracing one finger down the page. "Here at Matthew, chapter ten, verse thirty-four."

Ruthie waited until he had finished before reading, " 'Think not that I came to send peace on earth. I came not to send peace, but a sword.' "

"Such a dilemma," Mr. Miller said when Ruth had finished. "Such a paradox." He cast an eye to Joel and said, "Such words I understand because they are the same in Cherman. But my English, so bad it is. Can you understand?"

"I understand you fine," Joel said, liking the big man very much.

"Good, good, you listen well, you try, you understand. That is good. So. These verses, do they talk of two men? No, how can it be, for does not Isaiah speak of the one who brings salvation? There is only one who this great thing can do." He smiled down at the little girl at his feet. "And who is that, my sweet Sarah?"

"Jesus, Papa. He can."

"Yah, only Jesus. But He the one is who says He comes with a sword. Such a paradox. How peace and conflict can exist together yet. In one world. In one family. In heaven or on earth? Such a mystery, yah? Such a great problem."

He looked from one face to the next. His expression was somber, yet his eyes were glowing. "So. Let us think. What could this mean? Perhaps it is this. Perhaps peace is not meant to be man's at all."

Ruthie cried out, "But, Papa —"

"Wait, my little one. Chust wait and think. Not man's. *Never* man's. But that does not tell us, peace we can never have. No. It says, peace is only God's. All other peace, it comes, it goes, you cannot hold any more than you hold water with a fork."

He paused a moment, then asked, "So a peace that comes only from what we have, will it stay?"

There was a long pause before Simon quietly responded, "No, Papa."

"And why not, my son?"

Joel was surprised at how Simon seemed embarrassed as he replied, "Because it is earthly peace, not God's."

"Yah!" Mr. Miller cried triumphantly. "Peace to earthly things cannot be tied. Why? Because they come, they go, they are cut from us like with a sharpened sword. We lose this and that, health and puppies and even maybe a farm. But does this mean that saddened we must be?"

Joel watched as one head after another gave a small shake in response.

"But God, peace He has. God says, turn to me, and peace always yours will be. Peace is His to give. A great peace, yah. But also a *dividing* peace." Mr. Miller's eyes continued to search, probe, look from one to the other with a force that seemed to press each to look within, to think, to find the answer for themselves. "God's peace, it is a sword. God's peace says to us, *choose*. Between heaven and earth, we must choose. And those who choose, those who seek, those who for Him live, peace He gives. *His* peace. For us to have. For us to *keep*. For now, for always. Ours, because His we choose to be, and true peace is with Him *only*."

Joel sat at the Millers' big kitchen table, silent and watchful, and waited as dinner was set in place. Here in this noisy family, all was so different from what he was accustomed to in his own home. Mrs. Miller brought her dishes to the table with a beaming pride, as though not just her work but somehow her heart was involved with what she made for dinner. The children, all five of them, chattered and laughed at once, and the father was there in his big chair at the head of the table, inhaling the steam from the dishes and already complimenting his wife.

But it was more than just the words and the smiles. There was something else. Something Joel could not describe, yet he knew was there. The mystery that had seemed to surround their Sunday service was wrapped around them now, even though the solemnness was gone with the sadness, and all was laughter and happy talk.

"All right, now," Mr. Miller said in his funny accent. "Am I forgetting something, maybe? Do we chust eat now? What for is it to do next?"

"The blessing, Papa," Ruthie said as she came over with a huge platter of mashed potatoes, then explained to Joel, "That's a not-funny choke Papa says every dinner."

"All chokes are funny, they chust need good ears to hear them," Mr. Miller said good-naturedly, then motioned for all at the table to bow their heads. Mrs. Miller placed one hand upon her husband's shoulder and closed her eyes. For once, Ruthie was quiet and stood by her chair, her head bowed with the others.

Joel followed their example and listened to the strange words. He strained to understand with Mr. Miller's accent, and he wondered how praying felt so natural in this household.

"Amen," the whole family chorused, and instantly the noise and tumult resumed. Joel looked from one face to the next and could not help but compare it to home. Mother would set the plates down, then take her place across from Father. They would sit there, the three of them, not looking at one another, with rarely a word said among them. Here there was not the slightest hint of discomfort. The baby squalled and was plucked up by Mr. Miller, set on his one good knee, and bounced. The child squealed with delight and tried to catch the fork as it rose and fell. It seemed as though four or five different discussions were going on at once, and everyone seemed genuinely excited about listening and talking and arguing and laughing. Joel ate and watched and wondered. He had never heard so much laughter at one table.

After dinner, Mr. Miller took up his crutches and walked out to the front porch. When Mrs. Miller refused his offer to help clear the table, Joel followed, almost as though he was being drawn by something beyond himself. As he was leaving the kitchen, Ruthie called out, "You're not leaving so soon yet, are you, Choel?"

"I . . ." His voice trailed off. He pointed vaguely in the direction of the front door, not understanding at all the reason.

Ruthie turned from the sink and gave him a smile that seemed to transform her from girl to woman. "Don't leave now — leave next time."

"Sha, child, sha," Mrs. Miller quietly scolded.

Ruthie blushed and suddenly was once again Simon's younger sister.

Even more confused than before, Joel turned and walked toward the front door. He found Mr. Miller seated in the big porch swing. The day had warmed up, so if he sat in the sun, it felt genuinely comfortable. Joel selected the side of the front step that would direct his face toward the sun and eased himself down.

Simon came out for a moment, looked at them, and left. The two of them sat there a long time, looking out at the street. Joel wondered how it was that he could remain alone with the older man and feel so comfortable.

Finally Mr. Miller said, "The things my son tells me, Choel. Things like, your father is not a happy man."

"No, sir." There was no hesitation. The comment seemed to pull an unseen plug deep within his heart, and before long the words were spilling out. How his family was, how his father acted. Mr. Miller sat and rocked and stroked his beard and listened, his craggy features set in somber lines.

Joel talked until he ran out of words. Then he

just sat there, not knowing what else to do or say. He felt as though he had suddenly become connected to someone. The emotions he had kept stored up inside for so many years had formed some sort of barrier. Now that they were out, the barrier was gone, and he could think and feel at a different level.

Finally Mr. Miller said, "Hearts of darkness. Hearts of stone." The words were a gentle rumble, like distant summer thunder arching through a clear sky. "Is such confusion, to think they can ever heal, no?"

"Yes," Joel agreed and found himself trying to swallow a sudden lump in his throat.

"Ach, such sorrow one heart of stone can make. Impossible sorrow. Yah, yah, I know. Impossible pain. But one way there is to find healing. One way, for the hurt and the heart both. For the one who moves in blindness, and for the one who cries deep down. The same One way."

Despite the heavy accent, despite the rolling speech, the words seemed etched in the air between them. There was such a power that even Joel's heart could not suppress the surge of hope. "How?"

"Ach, that I cannot say with words. Such words I do not know. Not in English — not even in Cherman." And yet he spoke with a smile. A soft one, but with incredible meaning upon those broad, strong features. "Perhaps there are no words for such a heart, yah? Only that which is *beyond* words. Only that which straight from God

154

comes. Only His healing miracle."

He leaned over close, his voice falling to a murmur. "What to do, I think, is you must speak with the Master. Perhaps if you are healed, then the healing you to others can give, yah?"

"You mean, pray?"

"Ah, my son Simon, he says you are a smart young man. Smart, yah, I can see. You listen. You think. That is the good sign."

"But I don't know how to pray," Joel said, and somehow saying the words were not hard. Not here. Not with this strange, big, comfortable man.

Mr. Miller stopped his rocking and leaned over until he had brought his face down close to Joel's. "Well, well. An honor it would be, such an honor indeed, if would you let me pray the words with you."

CHAPTER ELEVEN

The reading of the will was postponed indefinitely. The caterer was canceled. Abigail's secretary was hastily summoned and spent a frantic weekend contacting all the relatives and telling them not to come. From a quiet corner, Kyle watched the racing back and forth. She listened to her mother's voice, sometimes on the verge of panic, commanding everyone within reach. For some reason, her mother never called for her or ordered her about, which was strange. Usually when these storms struck the household, Kyle was treated with the same imperiousness as the servants. But not this time. Her mother did not seek her once. It appeared that Abigail preferred not to have her around.

Winter slowly moved to spring, and still the will was not read. Kyle knew only because there were occasional visits from irate relatives, who would arrive unannounced and demand to see Abigail immediately. They would convene in the library, where soon the voices rose to a pitch that seemed to rattle the house's very foundations. Kyle took long walks down along the yard's perimeter whenever the relatives arrived. She hated those bitter arguments. She hated even worse how her father's study was turned into a battlefield. Those visits sent tremors through her, as though their angry words sullied his memory.

By March, gatherings at the house began to take on an even grimmer tone. Groups of dark-suited men arrived, to be instantly met and taken into the library. They sat behind closed doors for hours, their voices droning on and on, punctuated by Abigail's strident tones. Kyle heard Maggie mutter to Bertrand about how business should be taken care of in the office, not at home. But he always shushed her after a quick glance at Kyle.

Kyle was not the least bit sorry to be excluded from those proceedings. Just as she was glad not to have to go down to the office. She did not want to visit the top floor of Rothmore Insurance and view it without her father. She was glad to not be a part of any of it. The little snippets of words she caught whenever the library doors opened and closed were more than enough — those and the harried glances the dark-suited men cast her way. She did not want to know what was going on. She wanted to keep her father's memory detached from all this friction and scheming. He had been a businessman, yes, a good and honorable one. But he had also been a kind and loving father. Kyle wanted to know nothing that would shake her hold on this remembrance.

There were a number of very nice things about that reluctant spring, and Kyle clung to them. Focusing on them helped to ease her through the worst moments of loss and reestablish some feeling of balance. She would be graduating from

St. Albans and had been accepted to Georgetown University. To her surprise, her mother seemed almost relieved at the news. Abigail's concern was apparently not whether Kyle would go to college, but whether she would continue to live at home. Kyle desperately wanted to study at the university. She was willing to continue living at home if that was all it took to avoid a confrontation with her mother.

Another good thing about that winter and spring was that Kyle saw Randolf Crawley almost not at all. For some reason, his visits were now limited to occasional swift meetings with her mother. Whenever Kyle greeted him in his comings and goings, he would glance furtively toward wherever her mother had last been seen.

Emily Crawley had apparently been bitten by the same bug, for she seemed to avoid contact. Yet whenever Kyle saw her at school, Emily cut off conversation and watched her pass, her gaze thoughtful. Could it even be envious? That surprised Kyle as much as anything, for Emily Crawley had never been envious of anyone else in her entire life.

That March, the weather seemed to match Abigail's gale-force moods. Occasionally days would warm up, as though spring was struggling to break free, only to be beaten back by fierce winds and freezing temperatures. The first day of April was marked by a freak snowstorm that brought Chevy Chase and Washington to a shuddering halt. Kyle spent the day building a snow family with Bertrand and Maggie's four grand-children, whose weekend visit had been extended by impassable roads. They rolled up a portly daddy snowman and a smiling snowmom, then made eleven snowkids, from a nine-foot basket-ball player down to a snowbaby only six inches tall.

Kyle was grateful for the company and the reason to stay outdoors, because Abigail paced the front hall and railed against the weather with anger that frightened her. Kyle could not under-stand what the commotion was about. She knew Abigail was supposed to have gone to court that day. Kyle wondered if all the meetings and ar-guments of that winter were coming together, focusing down upon this time in court. The delay caused by the snowfall left Abigail almost speech-less with rage.

Two days later the snow admitted defeat. But as the days and weeks flowed on toward May and Kyle's graduation, the stormy cold continued to do battle with spring. Mornings remained frosty, the days overcast. Jim joined her for early walks, muttering about how his entire garden was a month and more late. Even the tulips seemed afraid to rise above the earth and face the unsea-sonably chilly weather.

April began to approach May, and still spring was held at bay. The weather began to make the news, with announcers vying with one another to describe the freakish weather. Kyle continued the ritual begun by her father, joining her mother for the evening news. Secretly she glanced over from time to time and noted that often Abigail seemed not even to be watching. Her mother remained strangely silent. Even at dinner Abigail did not take up her normal criticisms of how Kyle sat or ate or talked. She said almost nothing at all.

Finally, the first week of May, the bitter weather faded so swiftly it was as if it had never existed. Warmth blasted in, and overnight everything blossomed. Kyle's morning walks became explorations of wonder, for the entire garden bloomed at once. Colors were so brilliant that she felt ready to cry aloud with joy.

By this time, the birds knew her so well they awaited her arrival just outside the kitchen door, chirping irritably if she was a few minutes late. Even the shy sparrows would flit in and land on her fingers, accepting bread from her hands. The household staff took to gathering at the kitchen window, sipping their morning coffee and watching as Kyle coaxed everything from cardinals to tiny finches onto her outstretched arms.

On Tuesday afternoon, Kyle had returned from St. Albans and was upstairs changing when she heard Maggie exclaim, "Mrs. Rothmore, are you all right?"

"Where's Kyle?" came her mother's flat reply.

"Upstairs, madam. Should I —"

"No, never mind. Has Randolf arrived?"

"Mr. Crawley? No, madam, there's nobody here except Kyle and the staff."

Something in her mother's voice drew Kyle out of her room and down the stair's sweeping curve. She held back, able to observe while remaining unseen. Her mother had a wild-eyed look about her. "He should be here," her mother said. Abigail's voice sounded rough, hoarse, as though filed with a rasp. "Why hasn't he come?"

"Madam, I don't know. Should I call someone?"

Kyle could scarcely believe her eyes. Her mother, whose whole life seemed built around looking impeccably polished and perfect, was in total disarray. Her eyes scattered glances every direction. Her hair was coming down in sparse strands. Her clothes looked haphazard. "He'll be here. He said he had to stop by the office. But he'll come. He has to. We must plan. This can't be final. It can't be."

"No, madam," Maggie said doubtfully. "Should I call the doctor?"

The question seemed to help Abigail focus. "Don't be silly. I'm perfectly all right. When Randolf arrives, show him out to the back veranda."

Friday Kyle came out of St. Alban's to find the family Rolls parked directly in front of the school's main doors. Bertrand stood beside the open door, his face blank and stony as Kyle hurried over. "I thought you promised —"

"Your mother's express orders, Miss Kyle." Bertrand ignored her unease and the whispered

161

comments of other students who gathered and watched. He walked around, slid behind the wheel, and continued, "She wants you to join her down at the office."

"But it's Friday," she protested, knowing it was a feeble objection but not able to come up with anything else.

Bertrand shared a somber look with her before repeating, "Your mother insisted."

"Well, at least take the long way," Kyle begged.

Bertrand hesitated, then swung the big car around and headed toward the city's center, not the Rothmore building. Kyle settled down with a sigh. "Thank you, Bertie."

They cruised in front of the White House before heading down Constitution Avenue. The Jefferson Memorial and The Mall were surrounded by hundreds of cherry trees, which the Japanese had sent over to symbolize the end of the war. The trees had grown over the ensuing years until many of the branches met overhead. Bertrand slowed so he could turn and look with Kyle, for in the sudden explosion of a delayed spring, all the trees had bloomed together. The walkways were thick with people, all captured by the glory of the moment. The sun was bright and hot overhead, the trees so ephemeral their blossoms belonged more to the clouds than to the earth.

When they finally turned toward the Rothmore building, Kyle became increasingly uncertain and agitated. As Bertrand pulled up in front, he turned to her and said, "It's all going to be fine, Miss Kyle."

"Is it?" She searched the familiar face, saw the genuine concern. But it only seemed to make it worse. "How can you be so sure?"

"Because I know you," he replied. "And I know you will do the right thing."

"I'm so scared, Bertie."

He hesitated a moment, then said, "I find Maggie's wisdom fits such times very well. Perhaps you should try to find comfort in a time of prayer."

Kyle glanced up and through the front windshield. She could feel her mother's presence and all the unanswered questions there waiting for her. "Prayer doesn't belong in this place," she murmured.

"That is not true," he protested. "The Lord saw Daniel out of the lion's den. He could be with you here, if you let Him."

The words tugged at her heart, but the dark shadows reached out from the high unseen floors and grasped at her. "I have to go," she said through wooden lips.

Before Bertrand could come around, Kyle slid from the car. She did not want to wait, to hesitate even a moment. There was too much risk that her nerve would fail and she would not be able to enter at all.

But once inside, the reactions that greeted her were so unexpected she found herself pushed beyond her fears. A pair of secretaries coming out of the ground floor soda fountain stopped to smile and wish her a good morning. She could only vaguely remember having ever seen their faces before. Then the elevator operator tipped his hat to her and kept up a cheerful chatter about the weather. The elevator clanked up the floors, and as others came and went, all of them seemed to have some kind word for her. Kyle had never known such a greeting before. For her father, certainly, all the employees knew him and seemed to have genuinely liked him. But this was directed at *her*.

When she reached the top floor, a passing secretary greeted her with yet another smile and said that she had just seen her mother down in Randolf Crawley's office. Kyle thanked her but found her footsteps turning toward the far end of the corridor.

She did not hesitate, not even when she pushed through the tall outer door and Mrs. Parker, her father's secretary, greeted her by bounding to her feet and giving her the most brilliant smile Kyle had seen that day. Instead, she went into the inner sanctum and closed the door behind her.

She stood still, her hands on the knob behind her, and leaned against the door. This, she knew, she had to do alone.

She turned slowly to look at the long-familiar broad chamber. The office was so much like her father, she could feel his presence surround her again. At each step, her heart collided with her chest. She traced one finger along the edge of his desk. She looked at his high-back leather chair and mentally heard the heavy tread as he walked into the room behind her.

She closed her eyes so as to hear more clearly his booming voice, smell the English Leather cologne that he always used, feel the weighty pressure of his hand on her shoulder. But when Kyle reached up, she felt only emptiness as her hand touched nothing but the fabric of her jacket.

Carefully Kyle checked her compact to obliterate any trace of tears before opening the outer door. Mrs. Parker was still standing by her desk, as though she had not moved. "Your mother came by, Miss Kyle. I . . . well, I told her . . ." she hesitated, "I said I'd send you down . . . as soon as you appeared."

"Thank you," she murmured, avoiding the woman's gaze. This visit to her father's office had shattered her more than she had expected. "Where is she now?"

"Down with Mr. Crawley, I'd imagine. Shall I ring and find out?"

"No, that's all right, Mrs. Parker, I'll go down."

"Miss Kyle," the woman started, then stopped. Mrs. Parker was a professional woman who had been with her father for as long as Kyle could remember. But now the astringent features suddenly softened in genuine concern. "I just wanted to tell you, madam, that all of us here are rooting for you."

"Thank you," Kyle said, but she didn't know what the woman meant. She entered the hallway, returned the greetings of several people she did not recognize, and started toward Randolf's office. But her legs did not want to carry her. Her limbs felt leadened, as though all her strength and focus had been drained away. She felt utterly alone.

Kyle faltered and reached out a hand for the side wall. But instead she touched a door, which pushed inward as she leaned.

"Why, Kyle, hello, how are you?"

She recognized the voice before she remembered the name. Kyle watched her father's former assistant rising from his desk. "Hello, Kenneth."

He walked over, searched her face, and in that moment his own smile slipped away, swallowed by a mirror of what she felt in his own heart. "It's so hard," he said quietly. "I still can't get over the fact that I'll never hear his voice booming out for me again."

The hollowness in her chest was filled with a soft fire. Her tears began again, leaving warm trails across her cheeks. "I miss him so much," she whispered.

"I know you must. He loved you so." He took her arm, guided her inside, and shut the door behind her. "I never heard such happiness in his voice as when he was talking about you."

Each word seemed to unravel another thread of her control. Her shoulders shook with the sorrow that seemed to always hover nearby. She put her hands over her face, trying to push it all back inside, feeling as though her whole body was crumbling.

Kenneth's arms seemed to just appear, wrapping her up in strength and comfort she had not known since her father's passage. She heard the voice murmur in her ear. She felt a hand stroke the hair out of her face, felt the muscles of his arms cradle her with gentle strength.

Gradually she recovered her composure, until she was able to free herself and wipe her eyes with the handkerchief he offered. "I'm so sorry."

"Don't apologize. I think I know how you feel."

She glanced at him, just a quick look. There was too much sincerity in his gaze to hold it for long. But his words seemed to speak directly to her heart. "You miss him too."

"So much. He was a friend as well as my employer. You don't know, you can't know, how rare that is." He guided her over to a chair, seated himself beside her. "He was a genuine man, right down to the core. Every word he spoke, he meant."

She nodded. That was indeed her father. Still she could not look at Kenneth. It was too hard. Those strong features held an immense capacity for compassion. They pulled at her heart, inviting things from her that she tried to keep hidden.

Kyle avoided returning his gaze by looking around his office. She had seen it several times in the past, usually when her father pushed open the door and proudly pointed to his protégé as though he himself had invented the young man. Yet this was the first time she had ever been inside. Then she noticed the plaque set above the door, and it drew her upright.

He noticed the change. "What is it?"

She pointed at the plaque. "Up there."

"The needlepoint? It's very old. My mother's grandmother did it."

The design was intricate and beautiful, a garden trellis supporting wisteria in full bloom. Above shone a four-pointed sun, shaped like a golden cross. And framed by the trellis and the flowers and the streaming light were the words, "My son, give me thine heart."

"That's from the Bible, isn't it?"

"The quote? Yes, from Proverbs."

She turned to him, recalling the conversation they'd had at the dinner table, the only other time she had really talked with him. It seemed like memories from another lifetime. "You're a . . . a Christian?"

The surprise in her voice caused him to smile. "I try to be. No — that's not correct," he quickly went on. "One does not become a Christian by *trying* to be one. But I do try to live up to the standards that Christ set."

Kyle could not bring herself to respond. At a moment when she felt her world so shaken, she was confronted not with mere words but with a *fact*. Here was a man who cared deeply for her father. He showed her the caring concern that her own heart yearned for. He was successful in business; she knew that by the way her father had often spoken of him.

And he was a Christian. Here. In the heart of the place where she thought faith did not belong. Especially now.

Kenneth's eyes turned back to the plaque. "Your father used to come in here sometimes after hours. We'd talk about everything under the sun. Including faith. Toward the end, we began to study the Bible together."

She could not keep the shock from her voice. "Daddy?"

But he was not seeing her. His eyes and his mind seemed fastened upon something very far away, maybe very dear. "He was one of the most open men I've ever met. Most people who find success are *imprisoned* by it. They refuse to consider anything that might challenge their hold on the good life."

Kyle found herself nodding at the words. This sort of person she knew all too well.

"Lawrence was totally different. He was interested in everything. He had no time for fools, and could be quite short with somebody he thought was wasting his time. But he'd sit there and listen with an openness I found amazing. He told me once . . ."

Kenneth stopped. Kyle found her eyes drawn to the young man. His silhouette was a strange mixture of sharp-angled strength and the softening of deep sorrow. He took a long breath, held it, let it out slowly.

"It was toward the end, one of the last times we talked together here in private," he said quietly. "I've found myself wondering if maybe he knew what was coming. Lawrence told me he'd never met anybody who talked about faith like I did. He said the words seemed to spring naturally from whatever it was I had inside — that was the way he put it. I told him nobody had ever paid me a nicer compliment. That night we prayed together. He received God's gift of salvation. And there was such a wonderful feeling here."

Kenneth turned to her then, the move unexpected, and seemed to catch them both with aching transparency. Kyle stared into his eyes and felt as though heart was speaking directly to heart. Finally he said, "I miss him."

"So do I," she whispered. "So much." After a pause she said, "Thank you for telling me about this."

A sense of need finally stirred within Kyle. As though a thought had been planted inside her mind, Kyle sensed that here was someone she could ask. Someone she could trust.

She sat straighter and asked, "Please tell me. What is going on around here?"

She would think back over that moment many times in the days and weeks to come. For Kenneth did not disengage and withdraw behind an official barrier. Instead, he stayed right there with her, comfortable with the closeness, willing to go wherever she wanted. "What do you mean?"

"Everybody is so nice to me. They've always been kind, but not like this. It's different."

He nodded slowly. "You haven't been back here for some time, have you?"

"Not since the funeral. I just couldn't."

"You wouldn't have heard at home, of course," he went on. "Around here, though, rumors fly faster than the speed of sound."

"What rumors?"

Again, there was no sense of Kenneth playing calculating games. He examined her face, then asked, "Are you sure you want to know?"

In that moment she began to understand. Not just the day, but all the events of the entire winter. Even before the words made things clear, she felt a dawning sense of clarity. As though she had not wanted to search out what had always been there for her to see.

Kyle did not turn away. Not now. She nodded her head, very slowly, her eyes not leaving Kenneth's face.

He sighed his acceptance. He took her hand. It was the act of a friend, one who was giving her an unspoken assurance that she would not be alone. "Your mother has been contesting the will. Do you know what that means?"

"Yes." She was her father's daughter. She knew the words of his world. To contest meant to challenge in court.

"Your father surprised everybody. He set up a trust in your name. He put all of his stock, the controlling interest of Rothmore Insurance and all its subsidiaries, into this trust. For you."

Kyle sat totally still for a moment before rising to stare out the window.

"I understand that you might be shocked, even frightened," he said. She slowly turned back to him. His face was creased with the power of comprehension. "But this is what your *father* wanted, Kyle. Nobody could have structured this so carefully, or so secretly, unless it was something very important."

He motioned to the seat beside him and waited until she had resumed her place before he continued. "The two trustees will vote your stock until you turn twenty-one. Then you have power to do what you will, except that you cannot sell the shares until after your twenty-ninth birthday."

Her mind was a swirling tumult of questions, so many she did not even know what to ask. Kenneth went on, "Your mother has tried to nullify the will. But your father left enough assets to her, things other than the company, that she has no real basis for a suit. None of her own family's money was used in setting up the firm; that is all on record. Last week the court threw out her case. The company is now yours."

"No," she whispered. "I don't want it."

"The head trustee is old Mr. Crawley." Kenneth continued to speak with gentle insistence. Now that he had started, clearly he wanted to tell her everything. But his voice continued to hold to its kindness. "There have been some real

172

battles on that front as well. When Mr. Crawley heard that your mother had tried to enlist Randolf Junior into her challenge, he threatened to cut his own son off without a penny. And he would have. I'm sure of it."

Kyle remembered the hurried visits, always done in secret. She recalled the glances he had thrown her way, the silence, the sense of fear. "I don't —"

The door was flung open with such force that they both jumped. Her mother looked in, saw her, took in the scene at a glance, and seemed electrified with horror. "What are you *doing* here?"

"We were talking." For some reason, her mother's agitation seemed to only make Kyle more calm.

"Come out of here this *instant*." Abigail almost stamped her foot with rage. "I forbid you from ever speaking with this . . . this *meddler*."

Kyle rose from her chair and started to follow her mother from the room. But just as she was moving through the doorway, she turned back and asked, "Who is the other trustee?"

"*NOW!*" her mother commanded.

Kenneth Adams stood in the center of his room, untouched by Abigail's rage. His voice remained gentle as he said, "If you are ever in need of anything, anything at all, just give me a call."

173

CHAPTER TWELVE

That spring and summer were the fullest and most memorable Joel had ever known. Throughout those mixed-up seasons with their crazy weather, he was up before dawn delivering papers. The April frosts were the worst — not the coldest, but still the hardest, maybe because he was expecting warmth that did not arrive.

As soon as the school day was over, he met up with Simon. Usually they went back to the Miller home, where he grew accustomed to helping in Mr. Miller's workshop. The broad-shouldered man was a good teacher and introduced Joel to all his carpentry trade. Joel grew as comfortable with the lathe and drill and sander and broadband saw as he had with the smaller instruments of his modeling days.

At the beginning of summer, Mr. Miller declared the boys ready to begin work on their own furniture. Joel was as delighted as Simon and started on a rocker for his mother. The two worked in a corner of Mr. Miller's shed and learned to move about the cramped space with ease.

When evening shadows lengthened, Joel found it harder and harder to put down his tools and head for home. Toward evening, Mr. Miller would often look at him, his gaze filled with a thoughtful sadness. But he seldom spoke of Joel's homelife, except for their continued discussions after Sunday services. Sometimes Mr. Miller prayed with Joel about a specific need or a particularly bad day at home.

Joel's life at home became more and more a world apart. He found it increasingly difficult to slip into his silent role as he journeyed home. The Miller household was so full of laughter, of talk and life. Ruthie was always in and out of the carpentry shed, bringing lemonade, a word, and a bright smile. Joel found himself increasingly drawn to the shining-faced country girl. And she seemed to save her warmest smiles just for him.

The first day of August, Joel arrived home just in time for the evening news. He had found this the easiest way to slip back into his home. Walter Cronkite supplied the comfortable conversation his parents lacked. That night was a special treat, because the Ed Sullivan Show would be on later. Joel found himself in hopes that the little mouse, Topo Gigio, would make an appearance. The puppet always made his father laugh. It was such a rare occasion that he and his mother shared a smile behind his back.

He parked his bike behind the house, came in through the kitchen door, and kissed his mother as she stood over the stove preparing dinner. He entered the living room in time to see Elvis Presley being shorn like a lamb, while his drill instructor stood and observed. The entire world had watched as Elvis had been inducted into the army. For some reason, it had made his popularity grow even stronger. The day he had left for boot camp, millions of teenagers had written and wished him well.

At his mother's call, Joel rose and went to set the table. He returned to watch as Marines landed on the sands of Beirut. His eyes on the television, Joel's father murmured, "Look at the leathernecks go."

"What are they doing?"

"Ah, some king got shot," he said. "Over in Jordan or someplace."

"Iraq," Joel quietly commented, remembering now having seen it on that morning's front page.

"Wherever." He waved it aside as unimportant. "Boy, do I ever wish I were . . ."

The words were cut off by a loud thump and breaking glass in the kitchen. Joel and his father stiffened, then leaped toward the hallway at the sound of a long moan.

They raced into the kitchen to find Joel's mother on the floor, one leg outstretched, the other trapped back under her. Her face was contorted with pain. "Oh, I slipped. I can't . . ."

With surprising speed his father limped his way through the broken glass to kneel beside his wife. "Where does it hurt?"

"My back," she moaned. One hand pulled feebly at the trapped leg.

With a gentleness Joel would have not thought possible, his father eased the foot free and stretched the leg out straight. Then he turned to his son and said, "Go get Howard. And fast."

Joel accelerated down the hall and out the door, leaped over the front steps, and flew down the street. At the end of the block he skidded through the turn, caught himself on one hand, and sped on. He raced across the street, ignoring a car that screeched on its brakes and blared an angry blast of its horn. He ran up the front steps of the Austin home, tore open the screen door, and found Doc Austin seated in an almost identical position to his father, watching as Cronkite declared that's the way it was, on that first day of August.

"You gotta come," Joel gasped, fighting for breath, his heart pumping so wildly that he felt nauseated. He thought he was going to be sick and fought hard against it as he sucked in air.

Howard Austin drew his focus away from the screen. His tired gaze spoke of having been disturbed by a thousand pressing calls. When his eyes fell on Joel his demeanor quickly changed. "Slow down, take a deep breath. You're pale as a ghost. Are you okay? That's better."

When Joel could catch his breath enough to form words again, he repeated his message with more urgency, "You gotta come quick."

"Easy now," Howard said. "Now, tell me what's the matter."

"It's Mom," Joel managed. "She's fallen and it's bad."

Alarm spread in rapid stages across the middle-aged features. Howard Austin scrambled from his chair. His wife appeared in the hall entrance, her face creased in sudden concern. "Is she all right?"

"Where's my bag?" he said to answer her question.

"Right here on the table where it always is," she said, holding it out to her husband. "I'll put dinner in the oven. Joel, tell her I hope she's all right."

"Thanks, Mrs. Austin."

"Okay, sport, let's take my car."

Doc Austin drove with practiced haste. Joel sat beside him, his heart still pounding erratically, making his breathing rise and fall in funny little flutters. As always, he ignored the stabbing pains in his chest that came with too much exertion. Soon the doctor was pulling up to Joel's house and easing from the car before the motor had stilled. He bounded up the steps, opened the door, and hurried through to the kitchen. In the doorway he stopped so suddenly Joel collided with him. There was a sharp intake of breath, then Doc Austin crossed the room in three quick strides and knelt beside Martha. Joel felt a chill spread through his belly at the sight of blood spread over the linoleum.

"Where are you bleeding, Martha?"

"It's me," Harry replied, holding up a hand wrapped in a dish towel. "She dropped a glass when she slipped and fell. I was trying to pick it up."

"For Pete's sake, I've got enough to do without you going and making more work for me."

Howard Austin slipped a hand under Martha's neck and deftly felt around. "Does that hurt?"

"No, farther down," she murmured.

Harry asked, "Want me to lift her up?"

"No, hang on a minute." As gently as he could, the doctor continued his examination until he grunted softly and stopped.

"What's the matter?" Harry's face was a mixture of alarm and fear. Joel found himself staring at his father. He had never seen such emotion on that normally impassive face.

But Howard did not respond. He felt a moment more, then raised up slightly and asked, "Can you move your toes?"

"I think so."

"Don't lift your legs. Good, that's good." He then turned to Harry and said quietly, "Better go call an ambulance."

Harry stared at his friend for a minute, then rose and moved for the hall phone.

Howard turned back to Martha and asked, "Do you have any tingles running up and down your legs? Any shooting pains? Numb spots?"

"No."

"Good," Howard sighed, his tension obviously easing. "That's good."

Joel's mother chided, "All I did was slip on a puddle by the sink."

Doc Austin looked down and said quietly, "It appears you've injured your spine, Martha. But you can move your feet, so apparently there's no serious damage to the nerves."

Harry slammed the phone back into its cradle and reappeared. "They're on their way."

"We shouldn't move you," Howard said to the prone woman. "But I can slip a pillow under your head. Would that help?"

"I'll get it," Harry said before Martha had a chance to respond. He hurried down the hall and returned with one of the sofa pillows. As Doc Austin lifted her head, Harry knelt and gently slid it into place.

Joel stood by the door, frozen to the spot. He was caught as much by his father's reaction as by his mother's pain. There was such concern on Harry's features, such caring. It was as though Joel was confronted with a totally different person, someone he had never known except maybe in old photographs. A person who felt, who showed, who cared.

In the days after his mother was settled into the hospital, Joel's homelife went through a subtle transformation. Joel spent an hour every afternoon in her hospital room, as much time as he was permitted. His father, however, spent more time there than at work. At home, Harry remained silent and withdrawn as always, but occasionally his face was softened by worried glances at the phone and a milder tone toward Joel.

Joel found himself amazed by it all. Howard Austin continually reported progress, assuring them that Martha was healing nicely. She was responding so well to traction that surgery probably would not be required. Joel's father remained in his new world of concern, one that stripped away his stony mask and left him openly vulnerable.

Yet when Joel was there in the hospital room with the two of them, his parents were still uncommunicative. To Joel's eyes, it seemed they had become so accustomed to their mute roles that they did not know how to break out of them.

In the evenings when Joel was home alone, he liked to look at the pictures from his parents' very early days. Back before he was born, even before the war. Before everything became shadowed by what he saw on their faces now, like the heavy clouds of an overcast day.

Back then, their eyes seemed to shine with excitement and love and hope. His father had a jaunty smile. Joel could see the traces of that smile still today, only now the lines were twisted downward, the face too quick to grimace and sneer. And his mother . . . back then her eyes looked at the camera with such trust and joy. Such happy times. Why couldn't they have lasted? Was it because of him? Was he at fault? Joel would go through the pictures one by one, wishing there was some way he could make things go back to the way they had been.

During those evenings alone, the quietness of his home had a different quality. The stillness acted like a mirror, drawing him to look at himself and his isolation in ways he had never before

181

experienced. He found comfort in the Bible, ashamed by how even the littlest Miller girl knew the Scripture stories better than he did. By the second week of his mother's hospitalization, Joel was reading the Book every night. And though words still came hard when he prayed alone, he tried to talk with God every night before going to bed, asking first for his mother's healing. But in time, he found the prayers being extended, almost of their own accord, to include an inward healing for his father as well.

Toward the end of that second week, while Joel and his father watched television together, there came a firm rap on the door. The knocking brought a surprised look from his father, who sat slumped in his well-worn chair. He nodded toward the front. "Answer it."

Joel moved to obey. At the door he stopped in surprise. It was Mr. Miller, his huge frame drooped slightly over his crutches and his good-natured smile on his face. Joel was unsure what to do. They had so few visitors, only Doc Austin and his wife. His heart began to beat a nervous rhythm. As he moved to open the door, inwardly he uttered a short, disjointed prayer. "Don't let it be something about Simon. Please."

Mr. Miller stumped through the open door and asked, "Is your father been to home yet, Choel?"

A voice from the back of the house called, "Who is it, boy?"

Joel swallowed hard. He worked his mouth for a moment, but the words were hard to form. "It's . . ."

"Choseph Miller," the big man called back and started down the hall, lightly brushing past the bewildered boy. The crutches made a dull thud, thud, on the bare wooden floor.

Joel followed Mr. Miller down the hall and saw his father push himself upright from the chair's lopsided cushions. He half stood, half leaned on the chair arms, as though uncertain whether or not to raise himself and greet this man who had disturbed his evening.

But Joseph Miller was not an easy man to dismiss. Joel watched as his father stared openly at the big man. The staccato rhythm of the crutches echoed in the still room. His one good leg moved easily in time to the crutches, his other pant leg fastened at the knee. His father watched as the shortened leg swung with each forward thrust of the man's body.

"Sorry to be cutting in on your evening," the man said, ignoring the chattering television. "But the boy here's been saying you have some problem to yourself. The wife to town took herself today and came back saying I was to bring myself by."

His father glanced toward him, then back to the shortened leg. Harry looked bewildered and even a little angry. Joel could feel his slight frame shiver with discomfort. Surely, he cried inwardly, surely his father would not make a scene. The

183

very thought made him want to dash from the room.

But to his relief his father stretched out a hand in greeting. Joel was pleased that his father did not wince as Mr. Miller gave it a hearty shake. "Have a seat," Harry offered, nodding toward a neighboring chair.

"I thank you." Mr. Miller crossed to the chair and seated himself, placing his crutches carefully together and lowering them to the floor. The pleasant expression did not leave his face. He carefully studied Joel's father before saying, "A hard lot it is, when one's wife is wonderful sick. Makes a man know not where to take himself next. My Ruth stopped by the hospital, says the doctor wants your good wife to stay to her bed when home she comes. And quiet she needs as well. 'How can a growing boy live quiet?' I ask. Boys were made for noise yet. So my Ruth, she says, 'You go and tell the poor father that Choel can come make his noise to our house.' He can stay until the Missus be fine on her feet. No hurry to push her back on up. Choel be chust fine."

Joel's breath caught in his throat. Was he hearing Mr. Miller correctly? Was Simon's father really issuing an invitation for him to live with the Miller family? But he couldn't. He was needed at home. He was the one who ran the errands. Who helped with meals and washed up the dishes. Who soothed his mother when she sank down in quiet despair. Who ran to the store

184

for tobacco or cigarette papers when his father's nerves and hands demanded something to do.

Then another thought came to Joel. A longing to be part, just a small part, of that big, bustling, loving household. Where laughter was common, and teasing was done in good-natured fun. Where food was tasty and plentiful, and laid out for hearty appetites to devour at will. Where prayer was offered to a God who was so real that He seemed to be standing in the very room, somewhere just beyond natural vision.

He would never be able to go, Joel thought despondently. There was no use even dreaming.

But Joel's father chose that moment to speak. His voice was deep and unnatural, and his hand fidgeted restlessly with the frayed chair arms. "Well, the doctor's told us about this place up-state. It's a veteran's hospital — they've done all sorts of work with back problems. Howard said it would do her a world of good. I was wondering how we could —"

Mr. Miller smacked his hand loudly on the knee of his good leg. The big smile lit his face again. "There," he exclaimed. "That does it good. You give your Missus a rest to make better the way she is, and we keep Choel with us for this time."

He beamed from father to son and back again. Joel felt himself squirming on the hard-back chair. What would his father say? Would he agree to such an arrangement? He could hardly bear the moment of suspense.

"That's mighty kind of you," his father said and rubbed one thin hand against his shirt sleeve in a nervous gesture. "It would sure help us out, but I understand you already have a lot of mouths to feed. It seems a lot to ask —"

"Yah," said the big man. "Yah, seven we got. Such a household. My Ruth, she says a pack of hounds chasing the chickens not so much noise makes." Mr. Miller gave a hearty laugh, one that started deep in his barrel chest and rumbled forth in joyous ripples.

Joel's father cut in, as though the sound of untempered good humor unnerved him. "So you've already got enough to care for without —"

"So what is one more on top with so many? Besides, Choel is a good helper, already he shows that." He waved a carefree hand. "He chust fit in fine with the rest of all of them. He won't be hardly of notice."

Mr. Miller reached down and retrieved his crutches. "Simon comes to help Choel bring his things to the house over tomorrow. You think nothing of. Chust fix better your good wife."

Joel's father watched Mr. Miller heave himself upright and settle the crutches under his arms. For some reason, the action seemed to silence whatever further protest Harry was planning.

Mr. Miller proceeded across the room. "I not keep you more from the chores that take up your time before bed yet." His crutches thumped toward the front doorway. He swung it open, then turned and nodded, first to Harry and then to

Joel. "Good night to you, and God's peace rest on the house and all who live the roof under."

Joel watched, eyes wide and heart pounding, as the big man eased himself out and closed the door softly behind him.

Silence. Dead silence. Joel did not even stir. He was afraid that his father might hear the frantic thumping of his heart, but the man said nothing. He seemed to be in another world as his fingers picked at the threads of the chair arm. His eyes did not appear to be focused, but rather stared off into emptiness. Joel found himself wondering what thoughts were churning around in his father's head.

But when at last his dad did speak, Joel was totally unprepared for his statement. "You didn't tell me the man was missing a leg."

Joel gulped. What should he say?

"Why not?"

"I . . . I never thought of it," Joel managed.

His father's eyes looked angry. Joel found himself mentally scrambling to try and figure out what he had done to upset him once again. He stumbled on in a hurry, "I . . . it, well, just didn't seem important, I guess."

His father swung around in his chair. "A man is without his leg, and you don't think it's important?"

Joel knew he had to respond, yet found it impossible to meet his father's gaze. His head began to dip, until he remembered how much his father hated it when he hid his eyes like that.

He had to be a man, his father often said, and learn to face things head on. Joel lifted his chin. "It . . . I mean . . . Mr. Miller, he never says anything about his leg. He just sorta forgets it. I guess, well, I sorta forget it too. Nobody in the family notices it, hardly ever."

He knew it was not a good answer. But it was the best he could do. Joel held his breath, dreading his father's reaction. He was bound to come back with one of his angry blasts. He was sure of that.

But it did not happen. His father pushed himself up from the lumpy chair and limped his way to the small front window. With a sweep of a hand, he flipped back the simple curtain and stood staring silently out at the gathering night.

Joel remained on the edge of his chair, mute and still, stifling even the sound of his breathing.

When his father finally broke the silence, it was with a softer voice. "You'd better go get your things together and get to bed. Tomorrow will be a big day if you're moving over."

Joel's breath came out in a shaky little gasp. He caught his lower lip between his teeth as he rose and left the room. It seemed that the impossible was to happen. He was to be allowed to become a temporary member of the Miller household. He could scarcely wait to see Simon in the morning.

CHAPTER THIRTEEN

College was far more exciting than Kyle had ever imagined. Her days were filled with a sense of discovery and challenge. College meant an opportunity to broaden, to expand beyond the boundaries of the Rothmore estate and her mother's friends. She took as many business courses as she could fit around her required freshman classes and mostly found them baffling. But she was determined to learn. She owed it to her father and to his legacy for her.

Years of her mother's manipulation and subtle put-downs had tempered her spontaneous spirit, however, and she made few friends. Kyle watched the other students meet and laugh, and she yearned to be a part of their easy life. But she did not know how to react when they tried to speak with her. And with the need to return home as soon as classes were over, she remained separated from the college social scene. The few free hours she had on campus were spent at the edge of things, watching and listening. The other students were drawn from every strata of society, and their conversations were as great an education for Kyle as the classes themselves.

She knew she did not have a natural aptitude for business. Lessons that seemed to come easily to other students took her hours and hours each night to grasp. But her teachers seemed to recognize her as someone who was genuinely trying, and they showed a willingness to help. Besides that, she loved the *challenge* of learning.

That spring, she began appearing at the Rothmore Insurance building once each week. Her Wednesday classes ended at noon, and her mother did not expect her home before four. She enjoyed the place and the feeling that she might someday become a part of her father's work. She began writing down questions before she arrived, then finding people who could answer them. Some employees seemed suspicious or at least perplexed, a few genuinely hostile. But most met her with a smile and kind words of encouragement. She tried hard to ask intelligent questions, to be honest if she did not understand the answer. The majority responded with a real willingness to teach.

For the first month, however, she did not go to the top floor. Earlier that winter, Randolf Crawley had been elected the new chairman and had moved into her father's old office. Kyle did not want to walk down that long hallway, see the big mahogany door at the end, and know that someone else was now sitting behind her father's desk.

But Kyle found her thoughts continually returning to Kenneth Adams, and in early March she gathered her courage and took the elevator straight upstairs. She walked the long hallway, trying not to look at her father's office. Yet when she paused at Kenneth's office, she found her eyes drawn unwillingly to the end door, now bearing another nameplate. She felt the familiar sadness flood over her.

Hurriedly she knocked and pushed open Kenneth's door without waiting for his invitation, as though blocking the scene from her sight might soothe her aching heart.

"Kyle!" The young man's face broke into a delighted smile. He rose from his desk and hurried over. "You didn't tell me you were coming."

"I didn't know it myself until I was downstairs," she admitted. "How are you?"

"Busy," he said, sweeping a hand over his cluttered desk. Forms and reports and correspondence rose in scattered bundles from every free surface. "Sometimes I think our new chairman intends to bury me in work."

"Then I shouldn't disturb you. I just wanted to stop by and say —"

"Nonsense." He grasped her arm and drew her forward, closing the door behind them. "Come, sit down and tell me how you've been."

Conversation was such an easy matter with him. He seemed to draw her out far more than she would ever have expected — or her mother would have called proper. Abigail had continued to keep a tight grip on Kyle's activities, and Kyle was determined not to give her mother any reason to pull her out of school. But here with Kenneth, what her mother thought seemed to matter a lot less. They sat and chatted with the easy manner of old friends. Within minutes it felt as though she had seen him just the week before rather than months earlier.

They discussed everything — Kyle's studies, her work here within the various departments, and the memory of her father.

There came a comfortable pause in the conversation, and Kyle found her attention caught by the *Washington Post* newspaper dropped by the side of Kenneth's desk. She pointed at the headline that she had heard students discussing for several days now. "What's so important about Fidel Castro?"

He glanced around and saw the newspaper. "Are you following this in the news?"

"I try. He's the new leader in Cuba. But it's such a tiny place, I don't see how it can be very important to America."

"It's not Cuba's size," he explained. "It's how close it is to America. Added to that is the fact that nobody knows what to expect of Castro. Will he allow the Soviets to set up a military base? That's what has everybody frightened."

Kyle loved the sense of being able to discuss anything with him, from world politics to her situation at home. "I read about the Shah of Persia taking power. That's another problem like this one, isn't it? Nobody knows what he's going to do. And he could destabilize the whole Middle East."

"You're exactly right," he said, observing her with some surprise. "Your father would be proud of you, Kyle."

She blushed, then asked the question that had been at the back of her mind ever since she had decided to come upstairs. "The last time I was here, you said if there was anything you could do for me, all I needed to do was ask. Do you remember?"

"Very clearly."

"You told me there were two trustees." She took a breath. "You're the other one, aren't you?"

"Yes." Kenneth instantly sobered. "Yes, I am."

"Why didn't you tell me?"

"It is not always correct for . . . for a minor to know who is responsible for managing a trust," he said, choosing his words very carefully.

"But that's not the real reason, is it?"

"No." His voice turned quiet. "After you were here the last time, I was ordered not to call you, not to approach you, not to write you. Since I could not come to you, I hoped you would come to me. The same applies to what has been happening in regard to your trust."

He seemed to wait for her to ask the next question, but suddenly she could not remain in her seat. Kyle rose and crossed to the window. From the executive floor of the Rothmore building, she looked out over the tops of neighboring white stone buildings. In the distance rose the needle-point of the Washington Monument. Below her, the tree-lined streets were brightly decked with spring foliage. People walked back and forth, stopping below burnt orange awnings to peer at window displays. They were free to come and go, live where they pleased, marry whomever they loved. Kyle sighed, wondering if anyone else in the whole world felt as trapped as she did.

"I didn't want Rothmore Insurance," she said quietly. "Not ever. I hate how all these possessions only imprison me tighter and tighter. I feel so . . . so manipulated. And Daddy's memory — they're all so busy twisting things around, turning the goodness he showed me into dollars and cents. I hate it."

There was a long silence, until Kenneth said quietly, "I have been praying for you."

The words were so unexpected that Kyle found herself staring at him before she realized she had even turned around. "What?"

"It is the only thing I know to do for you." His gaze was as steady as his voice. "The only gift I can give."

Kyle struggled to cast off the sudden feeling of having been caught defenseless and vulnerable. Her eye caught sight of the framed needlepoint still hanging over his door. "I remember something about your father being a minister."

"He was. He's retired now."

She found herself still struggling to bring the fact of his faith into perspective. "I suppose it's natural that his beliefs have been passed on to you."

"His beliefs?" Kenneth smiled. "I was raised with Bible knowledge, of course, and am very thankful for my upbringing. But that doesn't mean that God offers us a family savings plan."

Kyle found herself drawn to Kenneth's deep-seated calm. "What do you mean?"

"Salvation is not simply passed down from one generation to the next," Kenneth said. "It is something that each one must find for himself or herself. Just having a pastor as a father is not a guarantee of God's presence and blessing here on earth or a place in heaven. Only belief in Jesus can do that."

Kyle could not keep the bitterness out of her voice as she said, "I can't see much room for God in everything that's happened to me."

"I understand," he said, his voice so mild there was no sense of conflict. "You feel as though your whole life is caught up in random winds. All around you blow storms so great they push you back and forth without any hope of gaining control."

The words held such insight they threatened to draw tears from her eyes. "I don't understand any of this. I don't know why I'm even listening."

"Because your heart hungers for something, and I believe what you are looking for is the Lord's strength and guidance," he replied. "And I pray that you will find it."

In the distance, a church bell chimed the hour. She glanced at her watch and was startled to see that it was four o'clock. "I have to be going. Thank you."

Kenneth rose to his feet to see her to the door. As she turned to leave, he said quietly, "Whatever you need, whenever you need it."

"I know," she replied. "And again, thank you."

"Miss Kyle!" Mrs. Parker's brisk voice stopped her at the elevator. Her father's former secretary looked both pleased and surprised. "Were we expecting you today?"

"No, I was just . . ." Kyle allowed her voice to trail off. She had heard downstairs that Mrs. Parker was now acting as Randolf Crawley's secretary, and she was not sure whether she should say anything of her visit with Kenneth.

"Of course," Mrs. Parker said, misunderstanding her. "Well, your mother is already in with Mr. Crawley."

Kyle took a step back. She was not sure she had heard correctly. "My mother?"

"Yes, she arrived earlier than expected, but Mr. Crawley canceled an appointment so they could get started." She held up the tray she was carrying with the empty pot. "I was just going to make some fresh coffee, but if you like I could first show you in."

"There's no need," Kyle said weakly. She was trapped. She could not leave now. Her mother would hear about her visit and grill her about what she was doing. No, it was better to simply go straight in. "You go ahead, I know the way."

Mrs. Parker smiled brightly. "Yes, of course you do."

But when she entered the outer office, the raised voices behind the inner door stopped her

196

cold. Kyle stood in the middle of the room and heard her mother say, "I am telling you, Randolf, this situation must be resolved *immediately*."

"First you say, 'Don't rush,' now you insist I do."

"You know things have changed since that foolish will was brought to light!"

"Yes, I most certainly do." His voice carried a tone of strange smugness.

"Don't be difficult, Randolf," Abigail cut in.

"I wasn't being difficult. I'm just frustrated. There are too many people telling me what I can and cannot do."

"It's quite simple. We mustn't dally. Time is of the absolute essence."

"And I am telling you," he lashed back, "that I can do absolutely nothing about it."

Kyle found herself remembering another overheard conversation and all the discomforting questions it raised. She started to turn and leave, but some unseen force seemed to hold her in place.

"What on earth are you talking about?" Abigail was demanding harshly.

"Haven't you heard a word I've been saying?" Rather than his usual forced friendliness, Randolf Crawley's tone had an edge that sounded razor sharp even through the closed door. "My father has forbidden me to have anything to do with Kyle. Do you hear me? I am *forbidden* to even approach her."

They were talking about her. Why was she not

surprised? Kyle moved closer to the door. She heard her mother snap, "What utter nonsense."

"Nonsense, is it? How would you like all my shares and voting rights to be returned to my father? Would you care to see him demote me and resume his place on the board? Because that is *exactly* what he has threatened if I so much as call your daughter."

There was a lingering silence. Kyle's gaze flittered around the room. Randolf's absence from her mother's little parties made sense now. Along with how there had been less mention made of him in discussions with Abigail. Instead, Kyle had simply been kept on a short leash, allowed to attend college classes so long as she did not have time or space to make new friends.

"That old fool," Abigail muttered. "I thought his meddling was only temporary, that he would leave you alone once the business with the will was finished."

"So did I." There was a loud creaking, and Kyle's hand flew to her mouth. She knew that sound. It was her father's chair. Randolf Crawley was leaning back in her father's chair. His cultured voice went on, "His health is not good, you know, and —"

Before she fully realized her intentions, Kyle grasped the doorknob and flung it open. The shock on both their faces was reward enough for her boldness. Her mother had been standing by the side panel, holding a crystal plaque given to her father at some honorary banquet. It fell with a crash and shattered on the hardwood floor. "You!"

"Good afternoon," Kyle said evenly. Seeing Randolf leap to his feet gave her the strength to remain calm and continue. "Excuse me for disturbing you. I was here doing some research for school and heard you were here, Mother. I'm downstairs in the coffee shop whenever you're ready to leave."

She turned and left the room, closing the door quietly behind her. The absolute silence that marked her departure granted her a sense of satisfaction all the way back downstairs.

Abigail sat musing. It was not a pastime that she readily allowed herself. She did not like to reflect. One could get oneself in a state of morbid discontent if one thought too deeply. No — action was more her style. Quick, decisive action that left no room for sentimentality or self-pity.

Not that she had much reason for self-pity, she admitted, as her eyes traveled over the expanse of the elegant library.

But it had not always been so. With a grimace she thought back to the fear she had known in her teen years, when her father's inept business dealings had whittled away at the family fortune. And that had been followed by those tough, struggling years of her early marriage. The scrimping to make last year's wardrobe look fresh for a new season. Even now her face flushed with the humiliation.

Somehow, Lawrence by his sheer will and hard work had pulled them out of that morose state and provided them with more than an adequate lifestyle. Their success had been a matter of great importance to Abigail. She had enjoyed showing off the new wealth in front of her father, the man who had blustered and fumed when she had announced her intention of marrying a man who had little, as far as her father was concerned, and not much chance of changing those circumstances.

Why had she been drawn to Lawrence? Abigail dared for the first time to ask herself that question. Had it simply been to challenge the authority of a weak-willed father? The father who spoke forceful words, prefaced always with, "For your own good," and then followed with demands that indicated only his own desires?

Certainly she had been drawn by how utterly different Lawrence had seemed from her loud and blustering father. There was a gentleness to Lawrence, despite his rough masculinity. There had always remained an underlying sense of strength and genuineness in his hearty manner. One never could have called him weak. He was decisive and firm when the situation called for it. Even her complaining father eventually had been forced to admit that.

Lawrence.

Abigail paused in her reverie, one delicate finger tracing the rim of the gold-edged cup. Lawrence. It seemed so strange without him. She hadn't expected to miss him so much. It wasn't that they had been really close. Yet it was not the same house without his energetic presence. He had always been so generous with his praise, so easy with his encouragement, so much the protector and provider. He had not been one bit like her dark-browed, scowling father. Even his hearty disagreements had added spice to her life, keeping her alert in seeking ways to best him.

She stirred herself and brought her thoughts back to the issue at hand. Kyle.

Kyle was not cooperating. In fact, she was most exasperating. Abigail wondered how much longer she could keep Randolf on a tether. He must be as tired of the delay as she was herself. Perhaps he was even tired of Kyle. And now there was this unwelcome interference by his dotty father.

The very thought made her stir in irritation. What would happen if Randolf now decided that Kyle was not worth the wait? That the company money and position was not worth the effort of trying to win Kyle? Would he give up? But he couldn't. They would both be losers. Dreadful losers. The way the exasperating will was set up, neither Randolf nor Abigail would acquire control of the company that they wanted. It would be horrible. Just horrible. No — even worse. It would be disastrous. There was only one way for Abigail to maintain any control of the company. Kyle had to marry Randolf. She had to. There was no other way to work out the situation.

Abigail stirred again, her hands trembling on

the cup between her fingers. She had to find some way to convince the girl — to force her if necessary.

But how? She had tried everything she knew. Was she going to lose it all now? Lose it because of this girl who wasn't even of her own blood — nor Lawrence's? Why had she let him talk her into an adoption? Why? She should have known it would come to no good.

Then a new idea came to her with such clarity that it stiffened her shoulders and lifted her chin. "Ahh," she heard from her own mouth and her eyes took on a new glitter. She wasn't done fighting yet. There were still ways that she hadn't explored.

She set her coffee cup on the marble-topped table with such force that it rang out in sharp protest. But Abigail did not notice. She was done with musing. Now was time for action. She lifted her head and reached for the bell.

When Bertrand appeared, her words were clipped, curt. "Bring round the car immediately. I need to go to the office."

"Very well, madam." He gave a slight bow, but she was already heading for the hall and the long, winding staircase. She would freshen her makeup, grab her handbag, and be off for another session with Randolf.

CHAPTER FOURTEEN

Joel climbed the Millers' front steps, his heart racing in its painful flip-flop fashion. Was it just his sorrow, or was today's wild flutter from some other unknown reason? These bouts, whatever they were, had been coming more often lately and seemed to leave him shorter of breath. Much as he dreaded the thought, maybe he should talk it over with Doc Austin.

Once on the Miller porch, he found himself unprepared to enter and face what waited behind that door. He turned and leaned against the weathered banister. The morning was clear and fairly cool for July. Birds sang from every tree. A lone car slid quietly down the street, one of those new sporty Corvairs. The Corvair had been a hit from the start, a sort of affordable T-Bird. Small, low, and well balanced with its rear engine, all a guy had to do to wow his friends was to claim to have driven one. Joel watched the car roll by and listened as the radio blared out "Smoke Gets in Your Eyes." Joel sighed. The song certainly fit his mood.

Normally Saturdays were great. Ever since he had stayed with the Miller family that previous summer, weekends were spent with them. He would finish his paper route, return for breakfast at his house, then leave for a day of carpentry and fellowship and laughter, returning home only after the Sunday service and meal the next day.

Those weekends, and the three weeks he had lived with them, were a retreat from a world in which he mostly felt alienated. The Millers were so full of life and hope and fun that his own home, school, and the rest of the world seemed like a different planet.

Along with watching no television, the Millers never went to the movies. In a year when Danny and the Juniors took all of America to the hop, the Millers remained completely untouched by popular music and its accelerating influence on society. Nor did the strife and strained silence so familiar to Joel have any parallel in their joyful, boisterous household. He looked forward all week to these times of work and laughter and worship.

But today was very, very different.

"Ah, Joel, what do you say, sport." As Doc Austin pushed his bulk through the front door, Joel was not surprised. It was not unusual for Doc to be at the Millers'. He checked on his patient frequently. Doc Austin's tired-looking eyes regarded Joel with mild interest. "Over for a last visit?"

"Yes, sir." There was no escaping it. Squaring his shoulders, he turned to face the front door. "I guess I am."

"Never would have expected it, the son of Harry Grimes becoming friends with the Millers." Doc Austin stuffed a prescription pad in the side pocket of his rumpled jacket. His clothes looked perpetually slept in, which was kind of strange, for the doctor's face looked as though he rarely slept at all. His cheeks were puffy, his eyes lined with dark smudges. Joel's father said the man was destined to an early grave. "Cheer up, son. You'll make other friends."

"Not like these," Joel said simply.

"No, perhaps not. The Millers are one of a kind."

It surprised Joel to hear the doctor agree with him. He found the strength to say what was on his heart. "I feel as though I'm losing my own family."

Eyes far older than the man's years regarded Joel. "Your mother tells me you've gotten quite caught up in their religion."

Joel met the doctor's gaze. "It's the most wonderful thing that has ever happened to me."

"Ach, such a fine parting gift Choel gives the family, to hear how simple faith he values." Joseph Miller pushed open the screen door and stepped carefully out on the front porch. His normally broad smile was tempered with sadness. "You are well, Choel?"

"I guess so." Seeing the sorrow in Mr. Miller's face made his own heart ache even worse. "Well as I can be."

"Yah, yah, a hard day it is for all." Joseph offered the doctor his hand. "To you I owe more thanks than words there are."

"Don't mention it." Doc Austin accepted the hand, yet seemed embarrassed by the man's openhearted tone. "I've been real glad to see you respond so well to this new medicine. I'm thinking about writing up your case, sending it in to the *Journal*."

"Yah, with patience and skill, years of life you give me. Strength and time to see the farm again. Such a debt we carry back with us. Glad we are to be able to go home again. Now my brudders can care for their own fields and stock and let me take over the work of mine once more. Too long we have kept them over busy. And the children — they miss their cousins, many that they are, and their pets." His somber nods spread his beard down flat across his chest. "This debt to you, we will never be able to pay it still."

"I've already been paid." Doc Austin fumbled with the strap to his black bag. "Not to mention the porch chairs and table you made for me and my wife. The finest things I've ever seen. We're much obliged."

Mr. Miller stumped over and placed a hand on Joel's shoulder. The strength of that grip brought a lump to the boy's throat. Mr. Miller went on, "Prayers we will say. May you hold the gift of life, Doctor Howard Austin. That gift only One can grant, and for that we will pray."

The doctor's nervousness increased. "Never had much time for religion."

"Speak with Choel. Here is one who has found the time. He has learned well."

"Not yet, but I'm trying," Joel mumbled.

"Yah, yah, lessons of faith are there for all our

206

days." The grip tightened. "But salvation is yours. This you know."

"Yes," Joel said, lifting his head to find the doctor's gaze upon him. "That's right. I do."

Doc Austin opened his mouth, closed it, nodded absently to them both, then turned and shuffled down the front walk. Mr. Miller waited until he was around the corner before saying, "Such a man, he does not know his heart cries to the Savior."

"I wish he'd listened to you," Joel agreed.

"Perhaps," Joseph Miller said quietly. "Perhaps it is you who he listen to."

The door opened behind them. A teary-eyed Ruthie appeared, her hands in a tight knot before her. "Mama says come to the table."

"Yah, the first furniture in to come, the last out to go." Mr. Miller turned and moved into the house. "Mama has made the house a home and given our kitchen a heart."

Joel tried to return Ruthie's wobbly smile, but felt as though his face merely twisted into a different shape. He followed the two of them inside. His heart thumped in his chest as he surveyed the empty rooms. Nearly everything was already packed and loaded into the two trucks, even the pallets they had spread out to sleep on last night. Joel had skipped two days of school to help with the loading. Their silent acceptance of his gift had been the finest thanks he had ever known.

The table and few chairs still in the kitchen somehow made the room look even emptier.

Mrs. Miller turned from the stove long enough to give him as big a smile as she could manage, but she did not say anything. Joel asked, "Where's Simon?"

"Moping in the shed," Ruthie said. "Sit yourself down, Choel."

But before he could settle himself, Ruthie's younger sister Sarah grabbed his hand and pulled him toward the back door. He did not resist. Together they moved to the back stoop, where Sarah looked up in a silent challenge to him before calling toward the carpentry shed, "Simon, come from your work in, the coffee soup's on the table and Choel's about to et himself done already!"

"Hush yourself," Joel countered, continuing a game that Sarah had started the day he had moved in with them. At first, he had found their speech among themselves to be utterly baffling. But by the time his three weeks in their boisterous household was drawing to a close, he had picked up quite a few of the phrases himself. "Sarah, go comb yourself wunst, you're all strubbly," he added.

"Am not!" For a brief instant her lively face lit up with the joy of playing a game of her own making. "Talk like that, Choel Grimes, you ain't so fer schnitz pie!"

"And change that terrible schmitzig apron, wunst," Joel said, wondering how it was possible to joke when his heart was cracking.

She pretended to look down at herself. "Been

layin' over the dough, got to get my bakin' caught after."

"Then hurry up wunst, and go smear me all over with jam, a piece of fresh-baked bread."

She slapped little hands over her face. The first to giggle lost the game. She gave a little high-pitched laugh, but just as swiftly her sky blue eyes filled with tears, and she turned and fled through the back door. Her forlorn wail sounded through the empty rooms.

Simon walked over, cleaning his hands on a rag. "Never did I think we could be so sad over going back to the farm."

Ruthie pushed the door open, stepped out and stood there, her hands still gripped tightly together. "Mama says come to table now."

Joel looked at her and repeated the words she had said to him after his first meal there, then said again the day he had left to go home the summer before, "Don't leave now. Leave next time."

She swallowed and tried to smile. A single tear traced a lonely path down one cheek. "You must promise to come visit, Choel."

He nodded. "Next summer." It seemed a life-time away.

When they were all seated and the prayers said, they ate in silence until Mr. Miller finally set down his fork. "Choel, such sadness my family shows because of one thing only. You do not come with."

All eyes turned his way. Joel stopped pretending to eat food he could not taste. "I will miss you. All of you. So much."

Mrs. Miller reached over and rested a work-hardened hand on his. "You are like another son to me, Choel."

Joel could only nod in reply.

"Choel." Mr. Miller waited until he raised his gaze, but then could not seem to find a way to express himself. He glanced at Ruthie, who turned pink and looked at her plate. Joel glanced in confusion at Mrs. Miller, who was smiling gently at her husband. Mr. Miller cleared his throat and tried again. "Choel, at our table a place waits for you."

"Thank you," he managed, unsure exactly what was meant but finding himself blushing just the same. "Thank you very much."

Before the sky had given itself over to night, Joel excused himself and went upstairs. He closed his door to the murmuring television and stretched out on his bed. He missed the Millers with an ache that left him hollow. Their laughter, their smiling concern, their simple acceptance of him. Never before had he felt such a sense of belonging. Now they were gone, and their absence was a ballooning void in his heart, so great he could scarcely draw breath.

He climbed out of bed. There was no use trying to sleep. Lying there in the darkness only made the loss worse. Joel seated himself at his desk and turned on the lamp. He pulled over his Bible and opened it to the Old Testament.

He loved the ancient words. He loved the sense of divine history displayed before him. He loved belonging to something so strong that it had borne the test of time. A long parade of people, marching down through the centuries, had learned from God and passed on the lessons, step by step, until *he* was able to sit there and read their stories and hear their messages. No matter how hard this moment might be, still they were there in spirit with him, letting him know he was part of a huge and loving family, united by the Spirit of God.

The next day was the first Sunday he had spent without the Miller family in almost two years. Even so, the ache was not as bad as he had expected. After lunch, Joel carried his Bible out on the front porch. He knew he would need to find a church of his own, but not yet. Right now, the Millers' absence remained too strong. But the sense of being surrounded by a comforting presence was there with him still. The best part of the Miller family was a part of him forever, and this knowledge took the edge off his sorrow.

He was so caught up in his reading and his thoughts that he did not hear the door open. Only when a shadow fell over the page did Joel look up to find his father watching him.

"What's going on here?" his father demanded.

For some reason, his father's irritation did not touch him. Not this time. "What do you mean?"

"This religion thing." He flung a hand toward the Bible open in Joel's lap. "Seems like every time I see you, you're all wrapped up in that book."

Joel studied his father. The situation was so similar to all their other arguments. His father's voice held both accusation and anger even before Joel said a word.

Yet there was a difference, too.

This time his father's bluster did not appear backed up by genuine anger. Instead, there was a nervous indecision, as though Harry was not completely sure he wanted to have his question answered at all.

And Joel knew a sense of comforting isolation, of protection, even while encountering his father's ire. He sat calmly before his father and realized he was neither alone nor defenseless.

Joel sent a silent prayer lofting upward and instantly knew what was needed here. "Pop, how many friends do you have?"

"I've got lots of pals." His father's retort lacked his usual heat over being challenged. "Buddies at work, men down at the Veterans' hall, lots of them. Howard, old Doc Austin, he's around here almost too much."

"That's not what I mean," Joel persisted, both thrilled and awed by the sense of guidance. "I mean, a friend you can trust to be there whenever you need him. Someone you can always rely on, through thick and thin."

"That's the problem with kids these days, they

212

got their heads up in the clouds," Harry blustered. "You can't expect too much from people. They'll let you down every time. Just like life."

"But I've found a friend like that."

"Simon?"

"No — not him. None of the Millers. That's not what I mean," Joel countered with quiet confidence. "Another friend. Someone I can trust with everything I am and everything I have. Someone who loves me, who will always be there, who will always guide me. Someone so great and powerful that I can trust my entire life in His hands."

There was a long silence, then Harry asked gruffly, "You're talking about God?"

"Yes, I am," Joel agreed. "I'm talking about the Lord Jesus Christ."

CHAPTER FIFTEEN

Kyle was dreading the summer.

School let out four weeks before her twentieth birthday, leaving her with no reason to escape from the house. Three long months stretched out before her like an endless void.

Abigail had adamantly refused to grant her permission to take summer classes. Her mother's grip on her life had continued to tighten over the last several months, until now it threatened to choke her. Kyle found herself thinking of running away. The fact that she had no money would not have stopped her, though her mother kept her almost penniless. Abigail measured out just enough to pay for meals at school, refusing to let Kyle take a job, even locking up her jewelry unless she was wearing it. But money was not the problem. Kyle knew she could borrow enough from Maggie for a bus ticket. What kept her back was school. She loved her classes, loved the thrill of learning. She was determined to hold out and earn her degree.

But it was not just the emptiness of a summer without school that so worried Kyle. At the beginning of May, old Mr. Crawley had passed on. Ever since the old man's funeral, Abigail had paced the house like a hungry tiger. Her attitude toward Kyle had sharpened. Kyle could feel something was being planned. Something she knew she would hate.

And Randolf Crawley had been appearing more and more frequently.

The last week of May, Maggie called Kyle in from her early morning time in the garden. When she stepped through the door, Maggie handed her the phone with a curious look. Kyle accepted the receiver and said, "Hello?"

"I'm sorry to be calling you so early," a familiar voice said.

"Kenneth?" She accepted the cup of coffee from Maggie's outstretched hand with a smile. "I thought you weren't supposed to be in contact."

"I'm not supposed to, but I was hoping to catch you before —" he paused, then continued — "before the rest of your house woke up. I haven't seen you around here recently, and we need to talk."

"Mother has ordered me not to come to the office." She made no attempt to keep Maggie and Bertrand from hearing. They already knew all about it. "I don't have school as an excuse for getting out anymore."

There was a long pause, then, "I don't want to get you in trouble, Kyle, but we really do need to talk."

The quiet urgency to Kenneth's tone stilled further questions. "Just a minute." She held the receiver to her shoulder and asked Bertrand, "Can you run me downtown?"

She did not need to finish with *before Mother*

wakes up. Bertrand glanced at the wall clock and decided, "We'll need to leave immediately, Miss Kyle."

She raised the phone and said, "I'll come right now."

"Good." Relief rang loud over the line. "I hated the idea of your hearing this from someone else."

"Hearing what?"

"I'll tell you when you get here."

Kyle had Bertrand drop her off a block from the insurance company. She did not want anyone seeing him and bringing trouble down on his sweet, graying head. The light changed, and Kyle allowed the crowd to almost carry her across the street. The capital city had changed so much in the past few years. Every time she came into Washington, D.C., there seemed to be another huge building going up somewhere near her father's. When she was a child, she had often thought Rothmore Insurance was the biggest building in the whole world. Now it wasn't even the largest on their block.

"Kyle, good, come in." As soon as she appeared in the doorway, Kenneth Adams was up and out of his chair and coming around to usher her into the room. "How have you been?" he asked as he closed the door behind her.

"All right," she said as she sat down. "But I wish I could come down and work."

The words brought a glint of anger to Kenneth's eyes. The muscles in his jaw bunched up tightly. "I asked you here today because I feel you need to know what is going on."

She took a tight grip on her purse to give her hands something to do and gave a little nod.

Kenneth hesitated a moment longer, then said, "Your mother is pushing to have Randolf Crawley named head trustee over your estate."

She felt her whole body clench at the news. "Can they do that?"

"Probably. Old Mr. Crawley apparently left no instructions. I suppose he thought he had more time to take care of those matters." Kenneth sighed. "And your mother's voice carries a lot of weight. After all, she is your sole guardian."

She searched his face. "But you'll still be around, won't you?"

The internal struggle showed on his features. "I have debated for weeks over what I should tell you, Kyle. But to remain silent at this point, I feel, would be terrible. So I have decided to ignore your mother's instructions and the orders of my own chairman."

She could feel a chill grip her heart. "Tell me."

"If Randolf is appointed, or perhaps I should say when," Kenneth said slowly, "he will most likely seek to have me dismissed."

She stared at him. "What?"

"Legally, you have just over a year left before you come into your inheritance," Kenneth persisted grimly. "But I am afraid that if they do manage to have me discharged, they may seek to extend that period. Or change the particulars.

Theoretically, anything could happen."

"Can they do that?" she asked again.

"They *shouldn't* do it," he responded. "But they might try. I have no evidence to indicate that it would happen, but I'm afraid —"

"Daddy went to all this trouble for a reason," she said, tension raising her voice a notch. "To change it would be *wrong*. Can you stop them?"

"If you are very sure this is what you want," he said with a slow nod. "But it will mean defying your mother."

The chill crept through her body. Kyle forced herself to rise to her feet. "If what you say is true, then I have to try and stop it. But I need to be sure." Though she dreaded the prospect of confrontation, she declared quietly, "I'll talk to her today."

"Yes." Kenneth rose with her. "Do you want me to come with you?"

She shook her head, wishing he could come, wishing she could rely on his strength, but knowing she needed to do this alone. She was almost at the door when she stopped. "I don't have any money. Can you lend me cab fare, please? I —"

"What?" The question seemed to shock him.

"Mother says there's no use indulging me from her monthly allowance," Kyle said, too burdened by what she had just heard to worry about revealing such news. "She says I'll only just give it away."

"Kyle, don't you know the trust pays you a monthly income?"

It was her turn to be shocked.

"Last month you received — wait, I have the exact figures right here." He leaned over his desk, ran a finger down a list of numbers. "Yes, last month your dividends totaled thirty-four thousand, seven hundred dollars. A check was deposited in your account, just like always."

Kyle managed a weak, "What account?"

He stared at her a moment longer, emotions running across his features. Then he sighed, shook his head, and reached for his wallet. "Here," he said. "I've got, let's see, a hundred and twenty dollars." He handed her all but one of the bills. "Will that do?"

She watched herself reach out and accept more money than she had held at one time in her life. "But this is yours."

"Please take it. We'll work out the money side later."

"Thank you." She seemed to move in a fog of confusion. So much was hitting her all at once. But when her hand touched the doorknob, the world flashed into focus with a startling thought. Again she turned back, this time to ask, "What — why are you helping me, Kenneth?"

The question did not seem to surprise him at all. He replied quietly, "Because of your father. It's what he wanted. . . ." His gaze deepened, until Kyle felt as though she could see into his very soul. "I hope you understand," he said quietly, "I have not done any of this for my own personal gain."

She nodded slowly. It amazed her, how even in all of this confusion, there could be such a moment of clarity. "I trust you," she said softly.

But when the taxi dropped her off at the entrance to her drive, Kyle saw a cream-colored Cadillac convertible in front of her house. The car belonged to Randolf Crawley. Kyle knew she could not face the two of them, not together, not with this. She skirted the house, walked through the gardens, and followed the sound of balls striking rackets. Her steps led her down to the communal tennis courts. The courts were tree-lined and fronted by a slate-tiled veranda. Kyle loved the game, but she still felt out of place and uncomfortable with the players from wealthy families who used these courts.

Emily was playing singles with a man Kyle had met at one of her mother's little soirees. As Kyle approached, Emily left the court and walked over. She flashed Kyle a sardonic smile. "Well, the little princess has decided to join the lowly masses."

"You're the princess," Kyle countered feebly. Emily did look regal. She even had the ability to perspire prettily.

The blond girl patted her face with a towel. "Has your mother found you?"

"I didn't know she was looking for me."

"She's sent the penguin in a tuxedo over twice looking for you." That brought a titter from the lounging girls. "Whatever is his name?"

"Bertrand Ames," Kyle replied and felt ice congeal in her middle.

"Why, Kyle dear. You would think you actually were a friend of the *butler*. I mean, excuse me, but is he not simply one of your help?"

Kyle turned and walked away, certain that something had ended. She crossed the garden toward the waiting figure of Bertrand, thinking, *They are like actors on a stage. They never show what is real, what is important. Not to each other, and not to themselves.* Never again would she put up with their petty, cutting ways.

"Ah, Miss Kyle, Mrs. Rothmore wishes to have a word with you." Bertrand pointed at the veranda where her mother was seated. "I asked down by the club courts, but —"

"Thank you, Bertie." She stopped there beside him and placed a hand on his arm. She didn't care who saw. She stared into his eyes, willing herself to show enough affection to wipe away all the slights and insults he had borne on her account. "You are a dear, dear friend."

"Miss Kyle." He faltered. "Perhaps I should serve tea."

"That would be fine," she said. "And thank you. For everything."

Her mother was seated alone on the veranda, the metal chair turned to face out over the formal gardens. Abigail was dressed in a blue cashmere day suit, with a cream Shantung silk blouse and a single strand of pearls. Kyle noted her mother's customary look of faint disapproval, and something else. As Kyle seated herself across the table, she detected an unaccustomed nervousness. "Where is Randolf?" she asked. "I thought I saw his car . . ."

"He just left. Some emergency at the office." She focused beyond Kyle. "You may bring in the tea service and set it here, Bertrand."

"Very good, madam."

"Kyle, be good enough to serve us."

Kyle did as she was told, carefully handling the silver pot without spilling a drop. Abigail accepted her cup with a hand that seemed as fragile and transparent as the china. Her spoon made a musical tinkling sound as she stirred. "I never thought you would ever manage to properly learn the art of pouring a cup of tea."

Kyle kept her face utterly impassive. She stilled her hands from betraying any impatience by clasping them in her lap.

"Aren't you joining me?" Abigail asked.

"No thank you, Mother. There was something you wanted to talk with me about?"

Abigail shot her daughter a glance. "Obligations, young lady. A word you have had as much trouble with as you did the tea service."

Kyle's calm features and lack of response only seemed to irritate her mother further. "Obligations," Abigail repeated sharply. "They come with the territory, the name, the house. You are not a free spirit, young lady. You have responsibilities to uphold."

The words were so familiar that Kyle did not

even bother to respond.

"Life is full of unexpected change. And responsibility. And the fact is, you shall never be able to live up to your responsibilities alone. You need someone to take care of them for you."

"Mother," Kyle said quietly, gathering herself for what she had planned to say. "What do you and Randolf plan to do about the trust?"

Her mother sat in silence, staring at her. There was no change to her features that Kyle could see. But inwardly Kyle felt as though a choice had been made, a change begun.

"So," Abigail said finally. "Randolf was correct."

"I want to know," Kyle said quietly.

"Yes, I see that you do." Her mother's normal poise seemed exaggerated into a new stiffness. "Kyle, I want you to brace yourself for some very bad news."

She nodded. Apparently Kenneth's suspicions were right. It was hard to say why she was not surprised.

Abigail's features were abnormally stony. "My dear, I am afraid I must inform you that you were adopted."

"I do not want you to change Daddy's . . ." Kyle's voice sank to nothing as her mother's words hit home. "What?"

"Yes. I did not want ever to tell you, but circumstances are such that now the truth has to come out." The words were evenly spaced and spoken with a metallic clip, as though Abigail was reading off an unseen script. "The welfare of your heritage, and that of our family, demands that you know."

Kyle gripped the chair's arms to stop herself from trembling. "What . . . what do you mean?" She could not control the quaver in her voice.

"I could not have children. Your father wanted a daughter. He — that is, we chose you." She glanced over, then away. "But never mind that now. The reason I am telling you is that your inheritance has been brought into question. There are apparently some discrepancies with the adoption documents. Fortunately, Randolf has unearthed them in time. He has offered to take care of everything and make sure that none of this ever comes to light."

Kyle would have risen to her feet, but she could not force her body to move. Tiny tremors shot through her muscles, little electric shocks in time to the ones bombarding her mind.

"Randolf is offering to become your guardian, Kyle. To take care of all your needs. Both in regard to your inheritance and your future. *Our* future. The future and welfare of Rothmore Insurance."

Feebly Kyle raised a hand, silently begging her mother to stop.

"In return," Abigail pressed on doggedly, "you will marry Randolf. He is a most capable young man, quite handsome, an enviable catch. Really, Kyle, I don't see why we should be having this discussion at all. He has courted you quite properly for years. And even though these discrepancies could mean that you would be totally disinherited if brought to a court of law, he still wishes to go through with marriage. You should be grateful."

At Kyle's look of sheer panic, Abigail continued. "You are so exasperating, I am honestly at the end of my rope." She took a deep breath. "You shall marry him, and that is that. Your twentieth birthday is coming up in a month's time. It will make a perfect occasion to announce your betrothal. Then you shall have a year to complete your schooling. On your twenty-first birthday we shall organize a gala event. You shall be wed on the day you receive your inheritance."

Kyle had to leave. She *had* to. Her only hope was to get up and walk away from this terrifying encounter. She focused all her attention on moving her legs, bringing her feet up and under her, readying herself for the effort of trying to stand.

Abigail's hands moved nervously about, touching her hair, her pearls, twisting her gold bracelet. "It's *your* fault it has come to this, I hope you realize. If you had only shown the good sense to realize marrying Randolf was the only *proper* course, that the family *demands* you do this, it would *never* have been necessary to speak of it. But no, you have dillied and dallied, and now I've reached the end of my tether. The *absolute* end, Kyle. I hope you realize what you've put me through . . . Kyle? *Kyle!* Where are you going? Don't you *dare* walk away from me! I'm not through, do you hear me? Come back . . ."

Without knowing where she was going, Kyle walked down the back stairs and away from the veranda. Her feet seemed to know where she needed to go, for her mind could not move beyond the single word. *Adopted.* She had not been born into the Rothmore family, did not belong to Lawrence Rothmore. Not really. Had never been his true daughter. The thought hit her with such solid impact that it left her weak and drained.

Her entire being felt uprooted, torn away from everything she had ever known. She wandered aimlessly down the graveled walk lining the back garden, her frantic thoughts tumbling about in utter confusion.

Suddenly she recalled a storm that had struck many years earlier. She had been only seven or eight. That night the wind had been so fierce that the rain had struck her window with driving fury, fighting to break in. Lightning had blasted from every side, flickering so constantly that everything in her room had come alive and danced with the blinding light. Kyle had been absolutely terrified. She had hidden, whimpering, under her covers until her father had come and taken her in his strong arms, quieting her fears with love and calm words.

The next morning, they had walked outside to a world transformed. The garden, normally so neat and precise, was a jumble of trash and debris. Limbs had fallen from trees, and almost every bush had lost its flowers. Kyle had walked along, her hand tucked safely in her father's, and listened as he had consoled Jim. The gardener had been numbed by the destruction. Together they had walked over to where one of the grand old elms had been uprooted. The tree, almost as tall as the house, had lain there on its side, the bundle of roots sticking up in soil-strewn defeat. Kyle had stared up at the great twisted wreckage for a long time. She had felt as though only her father's strength had protected her from the storm.

But now, when this new storm raged and tossed her about, her father was no longer there. She did not have a father. Had never really had one. Why had he deceived her — the one person she had felt she could trust? Why? Kyle shivered with the loneliness and the fear.

Adopted.

CHAPTER SIXTEEN

The years had not treated Dr. Howard Austin very well. He did not need a mirror to realize this. Reaching up to his head meant encountering more bald patches than hair. A glance downward meant he was confronted with an expanding paunch. Whenever he caught sight of his reflection, he could not help but see the dark half-moon pouches below his eyes.

I care too much. The thought came unbidden to his mind. But the words had been repeated so often over the years that they no longer held the power to ease his burden. Especially today.

As Joel sat on the edge of the examining table and rebuttoned his shirt, Howard fiddled with the papers in his hand. "I've known you since before you were born," the doctor said, surprising them both.

Joel grinned. "You delivered me. I remember Mom talking about that once."

"That's right." Suddenly tears pressed against the back of Howard's eyes. It was not a giving in to today's sorrow. Rather he felt as though all the loads he carried, all the pains and discomforts and illnesses he had seen, all suddenly crowded up in a mighty wave, hitting him when he least expected. He swallowed hard. "That's right, Joel," he said again. "I was there from the beginning."

"You may as well go ahead and say it," Joel

said quietly. And though the voice was only that of a young man, the calmness Joel showed seemed to Howard Austin to be coming from beyond time. "I can see on your face that the news is not good," Joel probed.

A young man cut down in his prime. Howard wondered if perhaps he should put off telling him until Joel's parents could be summoned. But the young man sat there, his peace and inner strength so evident that Howard found a calm for his own troubled mind.

Which gave him the strength to say, "The results of your tests have come back. And this examination verifies the diagnosis."

Joel searched his face. "Not good," he repeated.

"No." The word was a long sigh, drawing all the breath, all the resistance from his body. Telling the boy was a defeat, both for Howard and the body of medicine as a whole. "You have a degenerative heart condition."

Joel gave a slow nod, his eyes suddenly fastened on nothing. "I knew it had to be something," he said quietly. "I've been feeling so tired lately. And my chest hurts a lot. It's been worse the last six months."

"*Last six months?* You've had this a long time?"

Joel nodded. "I guess so."

"Why didn't your folks bring you in earlier?"

"I never said anything about it." Joel looked down. "I didn't know anything was wrong — really. It wasn't until the pain and weakness got bad that I thought . . ."

The silence hung between them. At last Joel spoke again. "Would it have made any difference if I'd come earlier?"

"In all honesty, probably not. You have degenerative heart disease, and your condition is inoperable," he replied. Howard was flying directly into the face of his normal habit, which was to give very little information to the patient at all. But this strength about Joel — a strength that transcended the problems of his body — was something Howard had recognized whenever they were brought together. Even here, even now. "I've seen this before, and I have to tell you that your condition will only grow worse."

Fathomless eyes looked across the chasm that now separated them, and Joel asked, "How long do I have?"

Why was he doing this? Why had he even started talking about it at all? Despite his desire to cover over with platitudes, Howard continued with his chosen course. "Hard to say, son. Six months, a year, two at the outside."

As though he understood the struggle inside the doctor, Joel said quietly, "It's okay, Doc."

The words were so strange, coming from a young man who had just heard of his own approaching death, Howard felt himself jerk back a step. "What?"

"I really appreciate you being straight with me. It'll give me time to do some things. Prepare as best I can."

The words left Howard feeling indignant.

"Doggone it, Joel, I'm the one who's supposed to be consoling *you*."

Joel's grin came and went very quickly. "Mom will be the one who'll need consoling. We'll need to tell her together. And Dad."

"Your father doesn't feel much of anything." The words were out before he could think, and he wished he could take them back.

Slowly Joel shook his head. "I used to think the same thing, but I've decided it's not true. He feels too much. That's his problem. He's never been able to get over his sorrows. He cares too much about things."

Another wave of sadness swept over the doctor. "Here you are, just graduating from high school next week. All your friends will be heading off to college."

"Not so many friends," Joel said without remorse. "I got to be known as Simon Miller's buddy. Most of the kids couldn't understand him. They felt really uncomfortable about his clothes and his attitudes. Even since the Millers left, the other kids still see me as an oddball. I don't really mind. It has helped me to rely more on the Lord."

Howard found himself shocked by the easy manner with which Joel talked about God, as though He was a close personal friend. Howard stared at this young man, seeing him with new eyes. "You've grown, son. So much it makes me feel older than I already am."

"It's the Lord's doing, not mine," Joel said. "I

feel like I never really lived before coming to know Him."

In the silence that followed, a shadow of grief passed over Joel's young features. "I've been saving my paper-route money for college," he said quietly. "Plus I want to go see the Millers. It's going to be hard to tell them."

Howard found himself unable to respond. There were so many levels to this young man, such a sense of timeless maturity. He was less than half Howard's age, yet already he had the strength to accept as well as the strength to honestly grieve.

"It doesn't seem fair," Joel said with a sigh. "Why should I be struck down now? Why do I have to suffer from a bad heart?"

Howard stood and watched as the young man sorted through his thoughts and knew Joel was coming to grips with his own death. And doing so with a strength that left the doctor feeling incompetent. All his life he had cared but had run away from caring. Why? Because he did not have the strength required for the responsibilities of caring.

"I hate bringing pain to my family," Joel mumbled. "I hate missing out on all the things I wanted to do. But life isn't fair, is it? That's what Pop's always saying, anyway."

For some reason, the moment held a reflective power for Howard Austin. He observed the young man seated on his examining table, but in truth he was paying more attention to his own mind and heart. He had hidden behind a hopeless yearning for another man's wife, and never given as much as he should to anyone else. Not to his wife, not to his patients, not even to himself. Why? Howard Austin did not need to search for the answer. It rested there directly in front of him, as clearly as though the words were being spoken straight to his very soul. He had run away from caring because he had always cared from an empty heart.

Joel seemed to gather himself. He straightened, and the hollow lines of his face filled with renewed calm. Howard stood there and watched it happen. "As long as I'm prepared to go," Joel went on determinedly, "death is nothing to be feared. The Lord has shown me that. I think in a way I've known what you were going to tell me, and He has helped to make me ready."

For the first time in his life, Howard had the feeling that what Joel spoke of was something genuine. In the past he had always used his trained mind to dismiss what could not be seen. But here in the calm strength of this young man, in the shining eyes and wisdom beyond his years, Howard found himself accepting the reality he had always refused to consider before.

Howard felt the young man's gaze rest on him and struggled to find words to fit the moment. "I'm so sorry, Joel. If there's anything at all I can do . . ."

The words drew Joel outward, in a way that spanned the distance caused by Howard's news.

"There *is* one thing, Doc."

"What's that?"

"Pray for me." A veil lifted from Joel's eyes. "Pray I'll be strong enough to see this through to the end. And pray that I'll do what the Lord wants with what I've got left."

There was a crumbling inside, a silent acceptance of Howard's own defeat. "All those wasted years," he murmured, not even aware he had spoken.

"Nothing is wasted," Joel replied quietly. "Not if in the end it brings you to your knees."

"You don't know," Howard said, no longer speaking to the boy. He could not be saying these things to someone so young, especially not Martha's son. *Martha.* Howard released a long, aching sigh. The yearning was with him still, for what might have been.

"No," Joel agreed quietly. "But God does."

Howard raised his head. The light in Joel's eyes was as clear as summer sun, a breathless promise of all that his own life had lacked. Mutely he nodded his head. Once. And in the act, he felt another unseen barrier lower, and he found himself looking into the void at the center of his being, the one he had always refused to see, the endless, aching hunger that had consumed him and left him bereft.

"I wish I could pray with you, son. I really wish I could. But, well, life — your God, if you will — hasn't dealt too kindly with me. I'm afraid there is nothing left inside that can . . . can reach out in prayer . . . even for you."

There in the whitewashed doctor's office, with its smells of disinfectant and iodine, Joel spoke quietly, yet sincerely. "Then *I'll* pray for *you*, Dr. Austin. Every day that I have left."

Martha Grimes paused in the front room and examined herself in the mirror hanging above the scarred table. It was a nice face with pleasing features and clear eyes. Yet there was something missing. Maybe it was the light she had seen for months in her son's face. It had been there even as Joel had sat with Howard Austin and delivered the news. Such a peace and light that even as she had cried over the coming loss of her boy, she had felt the serenity reach out with his hand and gently touch her, easing her sorrow.

But over the hours, the days, that followed, Martha had been tossed to and fro, one minute accepting, the next collapsing in uncontrollable sobs. It couldn't be happening. It couldn't. She would never be able to bear the loss of another child.

Harry did not — could not — help. He had curled his emotions into an even tighter ball. He came home only to eat and sleep. Martha did not know where he went, never dared to ask. Did he just walk the streets, or was he trying to dull his sorrows at the local bar like many of his army buddies? She never smelled liquor on him when he did finally come in. But that didn't prove anything.

In between her bursts of tears and desperation she watched Joel. *He must feel it — this dreadful horror of what the future holds, but he looks so calm. So settled. How can he be this way?* she asked herself over and over. *He has so much to live for. How can he bear the thought of dying?* Martha had no answer.

She lifted her eyes again to the mirror. *What is missing inside me?* she wondered, running her fingertips down her cheek. Whatever it was, she had learned to live without it for so long that she had not given it thought. But now it was here before her. All she had to do was close her eyes to again see the light shining from Joel's face. It seemed as though the light grew stronger with each day. He did not need to say anything. Anyone who looked at him with honest eyes had to see the growing strength from inside even as his body gradually weakened.

Martha glanced down the hall to where her husband sat at the kitchen table. She found herself wondering if he could see the changes in Joel as well. She walked down the hallway, entered the kitchen, and seated herself across from her husband. Martha examined Harry. There was a small scar on his forehead, one he had brought back from the war. The thin line had been joined by a dozen others and now had deepened until she could no longer tell which one was the actual scar. The skin of his face looked gray, as though the silent exertion of keeping so much inside had aged him beyond his years.

She seemed to see him for the first time, as though all the years and all the memories and all the sorrows had been washed away. It only lasted a moment, yet it was long enough for her to observe him with crystal clarity. This was a gift from beyond herself, of that she had no doubt, both the vision and the compassion that filled her heart. He had known such a hard life. Working every day at a job that was as close as he could ever come to his dream. Bringing himself back home, staying here with her, doing the best job he could. It was not all that good, no, but he had tried.

She found herself reaching across the table, taking his hand. The move was so alien that Harry jerked upright and stared down at her hand.

"I think Joel has found something that can help us," Martha quietly told him.

He looked over at her. Instead of the barrier of old disappointments and bitterness, there was only confusion. "You mean, this religion thing?"

She nodded. "I feel as though, well . . ." Martha stopped and gathered herself, as though just saying the words was enough to push them both over the edge. New beginnings loomed before her, strange pulses ran through her veins. It took a long moment before she realized what she felt was hope.

She took a breath and went on. "I think maybe we could start over, you and I. If we ask God to help us."

There was no cutting response. None of the acrid mockery that normally greeted anything she said. Instead, his gaze dropped back to her hand resting upon his own. He murmured, "I don't know what to do."

"Maybe —" she whispered, her breath catching in her throat, "maybe you could ask Joel to teach us how to pray."

To her surprise, tears formed in Harry's eyes and dropped unheeded onto her hand. He said nothing, just turned his palm upward and enclosed her fingers with his own.

"It seems too much," he said when he was able to speak. "First our baby girl — now this."

For a moment Martha's eyes showed her surprise. Then they too filled with tears.

"You miss her, too?" she asked quietly.

His tears increased. He nodded.

"I never knew. I mean — you never talked about her. I thought I was the only one . . ."

"I visit that upstairs room, too, when no one is around."

Martha was weeping openly now. "I didn't think . . . I mean, you never said —"

"I couldn't. Not without . . . blaming you. You shouldn't have done it, Martha. Shouldn't have given away our little girl. There would have been a way. Some way. My mother . . ."

"I couldn't ask her, Harry. I barely knew her. I couldn't ask. I felt so alone — and scared. All I could think about was that I'd lost you and I couldn't bear to . . . I didn't even want to live."

He reached a hand to her cheek. "You cared that much?"

"Oh, Harry, I thought I'd die with the pain of it. I wished that I'd been in that battlefield. That I'd died, too."

"But when I did come home you were so distant." There was puzzlement in his voice.

"I was numb by then. Dead inside. And you were so changed. I felt I didn't even know you anymore."

"Guess I was numb, too." Ancient pain creased his features. "I'd had a tough time out there in the field hospital. It was really bad, Martha. A lot of pain. Took almost three months before I remembered my own name."

"It should have been different, Harry. We should have clung to each other. Through our sorrow. We could have helped . . ."

He brushed at her tears with a clumsy hand. "This time we will, Martha."

"I'm still hoping, praying that Doc is wrong. That Joel will be all right. He's such a good boy. Surely God . . . Doctors have been wrong before, you know."

Harry shook his head. "I'd like to hang on to that, too, but those x-rays look bad. Doc showed them to me. You don't have to be a doctor to know. He says it's a wonder that we've kept Joel this long. That he could do his paper route and all. He's been hurting for some time, Martha. He must have known."

"Why didn't he tell us?"

Harry cleared his throat and pushed back from the table. He ran a shaking hand through his thinning hair. "Isn't that we've been easy to talk to, Martha. We've both shut ourselves away."

"We need to pray," repeated Martha with a strength of conviction in her words.

Harry walked out to the back porch and seated himself in his customary chair. The afternoon shimmered with the year's first heat wave. Suddenly Harry was consumed by a memory of another time, another place of heat and dust and light. And noise.

He was back in the desert, preparing himself for the first big push. Beside him was a young man who spent his last hours before the battle in prayer. There had been such a sense of peace about him, such a sense of light drawing down and near. Harry had intended to speak with him about it, about the way he spent his time reading the Bible, even when the coarse humor and arguments echoed about him.

But when the young man had been killed in the skirmish, Harry had shrugged it off, thinking that the man's faith had not helped him at all.

Harry shook his head to clear it, and once again he was surrounded by birdsong and his own back garden. But the lingering light from the young man's eyes remained with him, joining with the memory of how his son had been over the past months. The light from both pairs of eyes now touched his heart like gentle fingers prying open the long-closed recesses inside him. Then the light seemed to grow until it surrounded him on all sides, flooding into his mind and heart. And Harry knew that what his wife had said was true. That if he wished, he could start anew. He could be healed within. He could begin again. It was not too late. Not even for him.

Had anyone been watching all they would have seen was a single nod. He would speak with his son.

CHAPTER SEVENTEEN

As soon as the familiar voice answered on the other end of the line, Kyle felt a tremendous flood of relief. "Kenneth, it's me."

"Kyle." The warmth with which he said her name made her think of her father. "Where are you?"

"At the Economy Inn out by the airport."

"Why on earth did you go there?"

She looked around the shabby room, then waited for an aircraft to pass overhead before replying. "I needed to have some time to think. I had your hundred dollars less the taxi fare, so I came here. I've even got money left over for meals."

"This is crazy," he muttered. "Look, stay right there, and I'll come pick you up."

"Thank you." She did not want to go home, but the money was running out. Calling Maggie and Bertrand meant making them risk their jobs, which she knew they would do for her, but still she did not want to chance it. "Thank you so much."

It was more than relief she felt when she saw him enter the hotel lobby. She stood and watched him cross the room. Unlike Randolf, he was not particularly handsome. Yet an honesty shone from his face, a strong vitality. His direct gaze seemed to reach straight to her heart. "I'm sorry to have dragged you into this."

"Kyle," he said, taking her hands in both of his. "There is nothing I would rather be doing. Nothing at all."

Coming as they did after five lonely days of soul-searching and sorrow, the words were met with a burning behind her eyes. She could not speak around the lump in her throat.

Kenneth seemed to understand. He released one of her hands to pick up her small case, then led her toward the doors. "Come on, let's get out of here."

On the way back across the river, he told her, "I've reserved you a suite at the Mayflower."

She stared at him in alarm. "I can't afford that."

"Yes you can." He stopped at the light by the Fourteenth Street Bridge and turned to smile at her. "You might as well start getting used to it."

"The money is not mine," she protested. "It's Daddy's."

She knew that Kenneth had no idea what the reclaiming of her father's relationship meant to Kyle. She had spent days struggling to sort out who her father really was. Who *she* was. Finally she had come to accept the truth that Lawrence had *chosen* her. Had given her his name and his love. She really did belong to him. Perhaps, she had ventured to think that very morning, perhaps they were bound by even stronger ties than if she had been his blood child. The knowledge had brought tremendous relief and freedom. Adopted? Yes. But she was still her father's daughter.

"It's Daddy's money," she repeated.

"And he left it to you. Just as he had every right to do."

"Kenneth, did you know I was adopted?" It was the first time she had said the word aloud since hearing it from Abigail, and she was almost afraid to see the shock in Kenneth's eyes. But when she looked into his face, she realized before he spoke that he already knew.

"Randolf told me the morning after you disappeared. Probably his attempt to scare me off. But it will take more than that." He handed her a bulky envelope. "Here."

"What is it?"

"As trustee to your estate, I've arranged a small withdrawal from your account. There's a paper in there you need to sign."

She opened the envelope and gasped at the bills. "Small?"

"It's better not to draw attention too often to your account, not until everything is cleared up. Your mother . . ."

When he did not finish the sentence, Kyle said, "She's worried."

"No," he replied slowly. "Abigail left 'worried' behind right after you disappeared. She's crossed the great divide and entered the land of 'frantic.' "

She found it nice to have a reason to smile. It

was the first time she had done so in what felt like weeks.

"She's even spoken with me — well, shouted really. She accused me of kidnapping you."

"I've made more trouble for you," she said. "I'm so sorry."

"Abigail has made no secret of how she feels about me." Kenneth turned onto Massachusetts Avenue and asked, "Where would you like to go?"

"To the office, please," she said, steeling herself for what had to come.

He glanced at her. "Are you sure?"

She nodded. "And please cancel the reservation at the Mayflower. That's my mother's kind of place. I want to find something nice, simple, and within walking distance of Rothmore Insurance."

He studied her more closely. "You're not going back home, then."

"When Mother stops fighting against what Daddy wanted us to do," Kyle replied, forcing herself to keep her voice steady, "then I will go back home."

Kenneth did not say anything further until they had stopped in front of the Rothmore building. Once there, however, neither had much desire to leave the car's safety. It was Kyle who finally spoke. "I don't know what I would do without you, Kenneth. You are a true friend."

He lowered his head and stared at where his hands gripped the wheel. It took a long moment before he was able to reply, "I would like to be more than that."

"I know," Kyle said, and found herself not at all surprised by his admission — or her own. It had been there between them for a long while, never said but there just the same.

Suddenly she was very uncertain. Nothing in her past had prepared her for the affection that rose within her. It was so real, so *genuine*. She did not know how to act, what to do or say.

But Kenneth kept his head lowered and did not see the nervous uncertainty that gripped her. He said quietly, "Ever since the first time I walked into your house, and you came over to welcome me, I have been head over heels in love. You were so kind. You tried to hide it and be just like the others, aloof and sophisticated. But I could see it in your eyes and hear it in your voice. You were different than the rest of them. You didn't really fit there."

"No," Kyle agreed softly. "I never belonged."

He looked up then, instantly contrite. "I'm sorry. That's not at all what I meant."

"I know." The need to reassure him gave her the strength to reach over and take his hand. She felt a little thrill run through her as he released the wheel to enfold her fingers. "It's the truth. I've always known I never fit in."

"Perhaps," Kenneth told her, "that is why your father loved you as he did."

It was the perfect thing to say. She pressed his hand tightly, feeling that she could tell him anything, ask him whatever was on her mind. "Why have we waited so long to talk like this?"

"Your mother has been against me from the first day we met," Kenneth said. "It was frightening to see how strong her reaction was."

"I know."

He went on, "And I wanted to be sure you understood that what you possessed, or what your name was, had nothing to do with how I felt."

My name, she reflected, and felt the hollow sorrow bloom again within her chest as it had done over and over those past few days. Her father's love was not enough to erase the questions from her mind. *My name. What is my name? Who am I really?*

But Kenneth was not finished. "There was something else." Kenneth regarded her a moment longer before saying, "At times like this, I have to keep in mind what is most vital in my life."

"You mean, your religion?"

"My faith, yes." He searched her face, as though looking for something, yearning to find it. "It is something which I absolutely must share with, well . . ."

For once, the words did not unsettle her. In accepting him, she was coming to accept what made him the man he was. "I would like it very much," she said quietly, "if you would teach me."

His face seemed to crumple in relief and joy.

"Thank you. From the bottom of my heart, thank you."

"Kyle!" As soon as she stepped from the elevators onto the executive floor, Randolf Crawley hurried down the hall toward her. "Thank goodness you're all right!"

"Hello, Randolf." She squared her shoulders, and with only a brief backward glance to where Kenneth stood, she allowed Randolf to lead her toward his office. She needed to get this over with, and she needed to do it in private.

"Miss Kyle!" Mrs. Parker sprang to her feet, relief written over her features. "We've been so worried."

"Call Abigail," Randolf barked, not slowing down.

"No." Kyle shook off his hand so abruptly that he continued on another step before coming to a halt. She said to Mrs. Parker, "I will call her myself in a few minutes."

Mrs. Parker looked from one face to the other, then made her decision. "Very well, Miss Kyle."

"Thank you," she said, then passed before an astonished Randolf and entered her father's old office. She seated herself across from the desk and felt the familiar pang as she stared at its massive polished surface.

Cautiously Randolf circled the desk and took his place. Clearly her actions and attitude were not what he had expected. "Has Adams had anything to do with your disappearance? Because

I am seriously thinking —"

"Kenneth has done nothing but what I asked him to do, which was to bring me here," Kyle said sharply. "And I consider him to be not only a dear friend, but a highly valued associate. Just as my father did."

"Of course, of course," he agreed warily. "It is only that we have been so concerned for your welfare."

"I am fine. I merely had some things to think over."

"Yes, your mother informed me of your discussion." His handsome features creased into an expression of sorrow. "It is so unfortunate that you were ever forced to find these things out. However, I want you to know that I have everything under —"

"I want to find my parents," Kyle stated flatly.

"Your . . . ?"

"My birth parents."

"My dear Kyle, that doesn't matter. Whoever they might have been makes no difference to you now." He presented her with one of his professional smiles. "Or to us."

"It matters to me. Very much."

The pronouncement drew him up sharp. "Why? You are doing fine as you are."

"No, I'm not. I'm all alone in the world."

"Of course you're not." His refined manner made the words sound as though he listened to them first in his mind before saying them aloud. "Why, your mother and I are very much here

249

with you, you know that."

"I want to know, Randolf."

The words came more slowly. "Whatever the reason behind their giving you up for adoption, you can be certain it wasn't a happy one. Don't you think such sadness should be left alone?"

"No, not at this point in my life — or theirs."

"You disappear without a word for five days, then return and start making these astonishing demands." He turned quite patronizing. "Really, Kyle. Your mother has always said you were a trial, unwilling to listen to a thing she said."

"Which means," Kyle said, "you are not going to help me."

He spread his arms. "There is actually very little I can do. Your adoption papers are sealed."

"What does that mean?"

"Your parents gave you over to the state. Your records are sealed by law." He talked with pedantic superiority. "They cannot be opened."

She struggled to keep her voice calm. "Mother told me you knew enough to take care of some 'unsettled' matter. Which means you also know enough to give me something to start on."

Her persistence finally rattled his composure. "Really, Kyle. I have heard about enough of this. Let it go. They have their life, whoever they are. You have yours."

She rose to her feet. "I decided I had to give you one last chance, Randolf. This was it."

He rose with her. "What on earth are you talking about now?"

Kyle turned toward the door. "This conversation is over."

She walked into Kenneth's office, as tired as she had ever been in her entire life. She shut the door and said in a voice ragged with weariness, "I've just gotten off the phone with Mother. She said basically the same thing as Randolf. They won't help."

She crossed to the window behind his desk. "I've known people like them all my life," Kyle began. "They're powerful and they have money and they have all the wonderful things of life. They are focused on power, and they are ready to leap at whatever opportunity comes their way. They're in control."

She glanced back at the closed door and went on, "But they're lacking something. They seem empty inside. All that hardness, all that brilliance and drive, is wrapped around . . . around an empty void. They would never understand that outside their fancy houses and their boardrooms is a wonderful world full of sunsets and trees and people. People with needs and cares and concerns." She looked back at him and smiled ruefully. "Sorry for the lecture."

"Not at all, Kyle." Kenneth's voice was as reassuring as his words. "You are talking about something very important. About that empty place inside everyone — rich, poor, greedy, generous. Any person who doesn't know God's love."

There was a sense of moving in harmony with him, of feeling a comfort and closeness she had not known since her father died. "I want to know that love," she said quietly. She looked at him, reveling in the quiet strength she found there.

"There is nothing I want more than to introduce you to Him," Kenneth said. "Is there anything else I can do for you, Kyle?"

She took a breath and replied, "Help me find my parents."

CHAPTER EIGHTEEN

But finding a place to start the search proved much harder than Kyle had imagined. Summer slipped into autumn, then winter had begun spreading its cold blanket over Washington, and still Kenneth could come up with no information as to who had given her up for adoption. Any tiny lead quickly turned into another disappointing dead end.

As the weeks changed to months, Kyle found it best to avoid even thinking about the lack of progress. Impatience too easily led to bitter frustration. Thankfully, there were many things to occupy her mind. An overwhelming amount of newness flooded into her life with each passing day. Learning to live one pace at a time was crucial to making it through this period of change.

The week after her confrontation with Randolf, Kyle had signed up for the final term of summer school and moved into a dormitory room. Arriving in the middle of summer had been good, for the dorm had been almost empty, thus granting her a way to experience this transition in gradual stages.

Since then, days were split between school and the company. She became increasingly comfortable around the work and the terms used in the insurance business. Yet her interest did not grow as she had hoped. When she lay awake in her little room at night and listened to the laughter and music ringing up and down the dorm's hallway, Kyle knew that she would make an adequate businesswoman. But the spark of enthusiasm, of interest, that had made her father so special in his field was missing. And try as she might, this was not something she could learn.

Throughout all this time, her mother and Randolf remained strangely quiet. Kenneth assured her that there had been no direct action taken against the trust. Kyle was not sure how she felt about their silence. Her emotions were so confused and tumultuous, she found it easier not to think about that at all.

Twice there had been attempts within the boardroom to have Kenneth Adams dismissed. The first time, Randolf had tried a frontal assault, accusing him of gross negligence in his duties. To Randolf's surprise, every other working executive had spoken up in Kenneth's defense. When Kenneth had told her about it the next day, his voice had been full of emotion and awe at the compliment paid him.

Then in November Randolf had tried a more indirect approach, proposing that the board take the cost-saving measure of eradicating Kenneth's entire department.

Kenneth called her that night to break the news. "Randolf was at his most persuasive, painting pictures of enormous profits to our stockholders. The vote was put off a month, pending a report from the accountants."

Kyle found herself as concerned about him as she was about the action. "You sound exhausted."

He did not deny it. "Things have not been very pleasant around here for me."

"But all this is going to work out, isn't it?" When he did not reply, Kyle pleaded, "Kenneth, tell me you're not leaving."

"I have been offered a directorship with another company," he replied slowly.

She fought down rising terror. "You'd leave me all alone?"

"Kyle, I never want to leave you. But . . ." He hesitated a long moment, then continued, "You've been so quiet, I haven't been sure how you feel."

It was true. She could not deny it. She had kept her distance from him, building walls to keep him at arm's length ever since their talk in the car.

"There's been so much happening," she replied, knowing it was inadequate even as she said it. A girl she vaguely knew came down the hall and gave her a knowing little smile. Kyle grimaced in reply, then rested her forehead on the wall beside the phone. It was as much privacy as the dormitory's hall phone could offer. "I feel as if I'm just barely holding on as it is."

"I understand," his voice was sympathetic. "And I've tried to be patient. I really have. But, well, I feel as though I've spent most of my adult years waiting for you to decide."

Kyle opened her mouth, but the words were not there. In truth, she did not know how she felt. And she could not shake the honesty between them by pretending otherwise. "Kenneth, I . . ."

"I would still be there for you. But not inside Rothmore Insurance." He sighed. "There's something else. I'm pretty sure all this cost-saving hokum is merely a smoke screen. Randolf thinks if he can get rid of me, you will be more . . . well, amenable to his plans. He's very shrewd, make no mistake. He knows I'm concerned about all my staff losing their jobs. So he's bargaining. If I went to him and offered to leave, he'd probably be willing to drop the whole thing and leave the other employees in place."

She found herself so weak with pending loss that her knees threatened to give way. "What will you do?"

"I don't know," he breathed. "Pray. That's all I know to do."

"I . . . I've wanted to tell you." She had to take another breath to steady her voice. "I've been going to church with Maggie and Bertrand."

"Kyle, that's wonderful." Enthusiasm rang in his voice. "How was it?"

"Good, I think." A tear escaped to trickle down her cheek. He was so happy for her. He had done so much, given her such warmth and kindness and friendship and strength. Why could she not respond? "Please don't leave me, Kenneth. I need you."

There was a long silence. Then, "Do you?"

"Yes." But even this admission seemed wrenched from her. She had to change it. She could not leave it without further explanation. "The company does." It sounded lame even to her.

"I see." The tired flatness returned. "I have to travel to some of our other offices these next few days. I'll think things over and speak with you when I return."

Kyle replaced the receiver and staggered back to her room. From the open door of her neighbor's room came the tinny sound of a little phonograph. "Somewhere beyond the sea, my lover waits for me," the voices sang. Kyle felt as though the music was heckling her. She closed her door and sank down onto the floor.

Kenneth was going to leave. She could see it happening with absolute clarity. What reason had she given him to stay?

She covered her face with her hands and suddenly found herself recalling a conversation she'd had with Maggie after church the Sunday before. As they had left the vestibule, Maggie had busied herself with her Sunday gloves, then commented, "I notice you don't bow your head when the pastor invites us to join in prayer."

"I'm trying to be honest," Kyle had replied.

Maggie had stopped, waving Bertrand to continue on without them. "Honest? Or are you trying to hold on to your independence?"

The woman's quiet perception had rocked her. "I don't know what you mean."

"I think you do." Maggie chose her words carefully. "You have had to fight hard to reach a point where you could think and act for yourself. And I am proud of you. But this does not mean you can go through life by yourself. Not with any sense of real peace or real success. You think upon what I have said."

Kyle remained curled up on the floor of her little dorm room, her face hidden behind her hands. Gradually her breathing slowed, and the words seemed to form of their own accord. *Help me,* she said, and felt something inside flowing out from behind the self-made barriers, reaching out and into the unknown. *Please help me.*

She stopped. There was more to be said. She could feel the thoughts hovering about her mind and heart, waiting for her to open further and accept. But she could not. It was suddenly all too much. She sighed herself up from the floor, only to sprawl upon her bed and close her eyes to the world.

She was awakened the next morning by a knock on her door. "Kyle?" The voice outside her door sounded both sleepy and irritated. "There's a call for you. A Kenneth Adams, I think that was his name."

She raced down the hall, grabbed up the receiver from where it swung upside down, and stammered, "Hello?"

"Success!" Triumph rang in his voice. "At least, a little bit. The first step, and they say that's always the hardest."

Kyle focused upon the wall clock. It was a quarter past six. "Where are you?"

"The office. I've got to get some things done before I leave town. And lucky thing, too. There was a message on my desk from a contact in the state government. Do you have a pencil?"

"No, wait, I don't . . ." Kyle tried to force her fuzzy mind awake. She fumbled in her pockets, came up with a lipstick holder. "Okay, yes."

"Riverdale. That's a little town just over the Maryland border." He seemed a half-breath away from laughter. "The fellow had time for only a brief glimpse at the notes related to your case. They contained an enquiry made a year or so after your adoption. The man claimed to have been the doctor attending your birth. The notes were in pencil and so smudged my friend could not make out either the doctor's name or street. But the town was definitely Riverdale."

"Oh, Kenneth." Electricity seemed to zing through her system, and her heart took wings. "Are you sure?"

"This guy has never failed me yet. I'm sorry it's not more."

"It's a start," she breathed. Finally. "How can I ever thank you?"

"Say you'll come out to dinner with me.

He had asked many times over the months, and almost before she could think, the standard denial was there on the tip of her tongue. That she wasn't ready. That it wouldn't be right until she was sure of what she wanted and who she was. But she stifled the impulse and instead said weakly, "Yes, please, let's do that."

"What?"

"I said yes."

This time the laugh broke through. "Do I have the right Kyle Rothmore on the line here?"

"Thank you," she said again. "With all my heart. Thank you."

"You're welcome," he said softly. "With all my heart."

The instant she set down the phone, Kyle knew it wasn't enough. She hurried back to her room, dressed in haste, and rushed to call a taxi. Impatiently she waited in the chill misting rain until the cab arrived. She flung open the door and said, "The Rothmore Insurance building, please. Massachusetts Avenue."

She was out the door before the cab rolled to a halt. The elevator seemed to crawl up between floors. As soon as they opened upon the executive floor, Kyle was out and running down the hall. She almost collided with Kenneth as he came out of his door, overcoat in one arm, briefcase in the other. He stared at her in astonishment. "What are you doing here?"

"I had . . . I had to speak with you," Kyle puffed.

"Wait and catch your breath." The smile broke

out again. "Maybe it really was you I spoke with this morning."

She took one step inside his office, impatient to speak, to get out what was pushing up from deep inside. "I wanted to say thank you, Kenneth. For everything."

"You're welcome," he said, the smile still tracing through his voice and eyes.

But she was not done. "All my life, I've hidden myself away. I've never even realized how much time and effort I've spent holding myself apart from everything and everybody."

The smile faded as he searched her face. "You have had as much reason to do it as anybody I've ever known."

"But not now," she said, rushing on. Fearful that if she stopped her courage would drain away and she would not be able to start anew. "Not with you."

"No," he said quietly. "You don't need barriers with me. Not ever."

"I know that now. It's just that, after all this time, it's so hard —"

"Kyle! How wonderful it is to see you again." Randolf Crawley pressed his elegantly dressed form through the doorway. "Could you join me in my office, please?"

"No I cannot," she replied. She pushed down her irritation and said evenly, "I have no intention whatsoever of going anywhere with you."

The firmness of her tone and manner shocked them both. Randolf tried to dredge up a pasty smile. "Kyle, you don't mean that."

"Yes I do. And right now Kenneth and I are having a conversation," she responded. "A private one."

Randolf gave Kenneth a very hard look, then turned back and pulled his face into more polite lines. "Don't tell me you are intending to continue with your silly pursuit."

"Searching for my parents is silliness?"

"Your *mother* is very concerned about your welfare. As I am." Randolf strained to hold to his smile. "I really must urge you. Don't take this dangerous course."

She inspected him carefully. "How is it dangerous?" she asked finally. "Are you afraid to find out who I really am? If so — why? What could it possibly mean to you?"

The false smile slipped away, revealing a coldness in his eyes. He retreated, pausing at the door long enough to shoot Kenneth a venomous look.

Kyle stared at the space Randolf had vacated for a long moment. Part of her mind wondered where she had found the strength to stand up to him. Perhaps it was the knowledge that her back was to the wall, that she could retreat no further.

She turned back to Kenneth and found him watching her with that same patient regard she had seen so often before. "Oh," she said dispiritedly. "That special moment, it's gone now."

"No it's not," he said quietly. "It won't ever be, not if you want it back."

"Help me," she pleaded. "Show me what to do."

"You don't know," he softly replied, "how often I've dreamed of hearing those words."

She placed both hands on his arm, feeling the softness of his overcoat and the strength of his shoulders. Her heart beating like a humming-bird's wings, she raised up on tiptoes. He stood stock still as she drew nearer and gave him the softest of kisses. "Hurry back," she whispered.

His breath a lingering sigh against her cheek, he put his arms around her and held her for a long moment.

CHAPTER NINETEEN

Kyle was frightened, yes, but she was also determined. She felt as though she had been forced to shed one skin, only to discover something utterly different underneath.

She prepared as best she could. Leaving the office, she went straight to Woodie's, Washington's oldest and most popular department store. It was the first time she had been shopping since all this had begun.

Her mother had always taken her to Garfinkel's, a woman's shop that catered to Washington's upper crust. Kyle had always sought out dark-colored clothes, feeling that they helped her escape attention. A two-piece suit of navy blue or dark forest green would allow her to drift more easily along the edge of things, observing but remaining as isolated and unnoticed as possible.

But not today. She found herself choosing a two-piece outfit in dark gray, with an ivory blouse and simple gray pumps. Things were changing. It was time she changed with them.

As she studied her reflection in the mirror, she wondered if perhaps she ought to smile more. Smiles had always seemed part of the falseness that she had hated so. But she had always loved Kenneth's smile. It warmed her, even the memory of it when he was so far away. Yes, she decided, an honest smile would be a nice gift to share.

"Turn signal, Miss Kyle. There on your left."

"I know where the signal is."

"Then use it, please." Bertrand's tone was sharp, and she turned her head to stare at him in surprise. "That car up ahead is going to stop," he said, tension raising his voice from its usual somber tones. "Please watch the road, not me."

"Well, of course," she told him, turning back to the task at hand. "I can see the stop sign."

"Then you must prepare now. Take your foot off the gas and begin pressing the brake."

"I've already done that." After turning the corner, she said, "Maybe this wasn't such a good idea after all."

"I am quite happy to give you driving lessons," Bertrand said stiffly.

"No, you're not. You're scared silly I'm going to scratch your precious Rolls."

"Don't even speak of such a thing." Nervously Bertrand pulled a handkerchief from his pocket and mopped his brow. "Besides which, it is your car."

"No, it's Mother's. I wouldn't dream of owning such a thing."

"Stoplight, Miss Kyle."

"It's half a block away," she complained. "Give me a chance to see these things for myself. And stop calling me 'Miss.' Please."

"But . . ." Bertrand struggled a moment, then

gave a little smile. "I suppose it would be all right, wouldn't it?"

"Of course it would. And calm down. You're making me more nervous than I already am."

"All right, I'll try." He settled back and crossed his arms determinedly. But at every intersection, she could see his foot pressing on the floorboards, reaching for pedals that were not there.

To take his mind off her driving, she asked, "When did you and Maggie start working for Daddy? It was after I was . . . after I was born, wasn't it?"

"You had just celebrated your first birthday." Bertrand smiled at the memory. "You looked like such a little angel. You stole our hearts the first time we saw you." He hesitated, then said quietly, "I was so distressed to hear of, well, everything. And shocked. It came as a complete surprise to both of us. But it changes nothing as far as we are concerned."

"Thank you."

"The house is so quiet without you. So empty." He glanced over. "Is there any chance you might reconsider and move back?"

"If Mother agrees to leave things as Daddy wanted," Kyle said, but in her heart she wondered if that was still true. After all that had happened, she was no longer sure she could ever have any place there again. The thought left her empty.

"Yes. I understand," he said, as though he could read her thoughts. He turned to watch the

Riverdale city limits sign sweep by, then asked, "What exactly are we looking for?"

"I don't know. Maybe nothing. Kenneth will try to find out something more when he returns. But that could take months. I just thought . . ." She sighed. Now that she was here, the task seemed impossible. "I don't know what I thought."

"You're driving very well, Miss . . ." Bertrand stopped himself and smiled. "That will be one difficult habit to break."

Kyle turned long enough to give him a fleeting smile, then resumed her search of the Riverdale streets. The town did not look old, yet already the houses seemed tired and defeated. There was a weary sameness to the little white clapboard houses, many in dire need of paint and repairs. She drove down street after street, unable to find an area that felt like a center, some place from which to begin her search.

Kyle sighed, pushing at her growing tension and frustration. Her stomach felt tied in knots. She stopped at a traffic light and found herself repeating the brief prayer, *Help me*.

On impulse Kyle pulled into the parking lot of a Hot Shoppe restaurant. She cut the motor, then sat looking at the entrance until Bertrand asked, "Are you hungry?"

"Not at all." She'd had nothing to eat all day and it was now past the noon hour, but she did not feel like eating. Steeling herself, she opened her door. "Would you wait here for me, please?"

"Of course," Bertrand said, giving the restaurant a doubtful glance.

She walked in and seated herself at the counter. To give herself something to do, she picked up the menu but could not concentrate on the words. What was she doing here?

The waitress walked over, a sturdy woman with an expression that said she'd seen it all and heard even more. "Ready to order?"

"Just coffee." Kyle waited until the cup was filled and placed in front of her, then asked, "Do you know everyone in this town?"

"Know more than I'd ever want to, honey." The waitress turned away. "But that don't make me a talker."

"Wait. Please. I'm looking for someone."

"Sorry. Can't help you."

"They're my parents." Just like that. Blurted out.

The waitress turned back, took a step toward Kyle, inspected her with eyes the color of gray marbles. "You don't say."

"No, really. I was put up for adoption. I just learned about it." A quick breath. "I don't even know their names. Just that some document has placed them here in this town. At least, they used to live here." She looked down at the cup, feeling the desolate futility swamp her.

The waitress set the coffeepot back on the burner. "I've traveled about a million miles since the last time somebody caught me flat-footed." Another careful inspection. "You eaten today?"

Kyle shook her head. "I'm not hungry."

"You look hungry. All wore out to boot. I'll have Jimmy fix you a plate."

"Really, I couldn't eat a thing."

"Wait 'til it's sitting there in front of you and tell me that." She pointed behind them. "Go have a seat in that booth by the window. And lay off the coffee. Your nerves are already so tight I can hear them humming."

Kyle did as she was told, then motioned through the window for Bertrand to join her. Her offer was declined with a shake of his head.

The woman brought over a steaming plate. Kyle started again to protest, but as soon as she smelled the food, she felt faint with hunger. The woman watched her eat with satisfaction. "There, what did I tell you?"

"This is delicious."

"Slow down, honey. It ain't going nowhere." She glanced out the window, then stared harder. "That battleship on wheels out there belong to you?"

Kyle glanced over, saw her staring at the Rolls. "My mother — yes, yes it does."

"Well, if this don't beat all." The waitress observed her a moment longer. "You say you don't even know what your last name was?"

"No."

"That's tough." She mulled it over, then pulled out her order book and scribbled a moment. She tore out the sheet and laid it beside the plate. "You could try talking to this fellow.

269

He might be able to help."

Kyle turned the slip of paper around and read aloud, "Dr. Howard Austin."

"Been here even longer than me, knows almost every secret there is. His office is halfway down the next block. Might as well leave the barge here, keep from holding up traffic."

Kyle read the woman's name tag. "Thank you, Stella. From the bottom of my heart."

The waitress offered her first smile, and the years dropped away. "What's your name, honey?"

Kyle hesitated, then gave the only name she knew. "Kyle. Kyle Rothmore."

"Well, I sure hope you like what you find. Think maybe you could stop by, let me know what happens?"

Kyle set down her napkin, slid from the booth, and offered Stella her hand. "I promise."

Kyle sat in the corner of the doctor's office for hours. She leafed nervously through magazines whose pages had been wrinkled and torn by countless hands before her. People of every sort and description came and went. Most seemed to know one another, especially the mothers with infants. They sat and dangled the children, or let them play with the blocks scattered across the floor, and gossiped. Kyle, isolated by her nerves and her purpose, wondered what it would be like to feel as though she belonged so clearly to a place and a group of people that she did not even need to think about it.

"Miss, ah, Rothmore?" The nurse was a heavy-set woman with strands of graying hair falling out of her starched white cap. "Did I get that right?"

"Yes." Kyle had to use both arms to push herself up, she had been seated so long. "Yes, you did."

"The doctor can see you now," the nurse said doubtfully. Her expression said volumes about what she thought of strange young women who appeared and asked for an appointment, then refused to give any reason. "But he's extremely busy and can only give you a minute."

Kyle tried to ignore the questioning glances from the other people filling the waiting room. "I understand."

"This way, please."

Kyle followed her down the hall and into the office, where a man with a tired face and heavy paunch sat writing in a file. The nurse pointed her toward the examining table, but Kyle stood nervously in the center of the room. She was positive they could both hear her wildly beating heart.

Finally the doctor folded the file shut, put it on the counter beside him, and said, "Yes?"

Kyle glanced to where the nurse stood. In response, she crossed her arms and set her jaw. Clearly the woman was going nowhere.

The doctor looked Kyle over. His eyes were rimmed with great dark circles, yet his gaze was as kind as his tone. "Are you pregnant, young lady?"

"What?" Kyle took an involuntary step back. "N-no, that's not it at all."

"Well, you're obviously not here representing a drug company." He motioned toward the table. "Wouldn't you be more comfortable over here?"

"No . . . no thank you." She swallowed, then stammered, "M-my name, it's . . ."

When she could not continue, the doctor reached a hand to where the nurse was standing. She passed over the single sheet of paper and said irritably, "Like I told you, she just gave her name and address. Refused to fill in the history."

"I see," the doctor said doubtfully. He looked at the page, said, "Well, Miss Rothmore . . ."

He stopped, looked up, and stared at Kyle. "Rothmore," he said softly.

The nurse started forward. "Doctor, is anything — ?"

"No," he said, his eyes not leaving Kyle's face. "Leave us a moment, will you, Miss Grant?"

"Doctor, I'm not supposed . . ."

"It's fine." The doctor tore his gaze away from Kyle long enough to say as reassuringly as he could manage, "It's all right, Miss Grant. I won't be long."

The nurse paused long enough to give Kyle a final hard look, then left. When the door had closed behind her, the doctor turned back and said quietly, "How did you find me?"

CHAPTER TWENTY

Weakness flooded through Kyle in a sudden shocking wave. *It's really happening.*

"Hang on," Dr. Austin said, reaching out with alacrity. "Okay, steady now, just come on over here, that's it."

Kyle felt gentle arms guide her over to the examining table and settle her down. The doctor turned away and came back with a cup of water. Gratefully she accepted it and sipped. He watched her with a startled, kindly gaze. "Now, feel like maybe telling me how you got here?"

In bits and pieces she explained how she had come to be in his office. The doctor's amiable questions drew her further and further, until she was revealing more than she had ever expected. About her father's death, and the trust, and how she had found out about the adoption. Even bringing Kenneth into the discussion, and what a help he had been.

Finally the doctor was satisfied, at least enough to step back and regard her with a bemused expression. At length he said, "If you had come in here a year ago, I would have clammed up and sent you on your way. What's done is done — that would have been my reaction. No use in digging up the past."

She found herself tensing once more. So close.

But there was no way she could rush things. "And now?"

"Now, well," Dr. Austin let out a noisy sigh. "I'm beginning to find the Lord's hand at work in more and more things these days. Do you have any idea what I mean?"

"Yes," she said, and her answer made her look deep inside and find it was true. "Yes, I think I do."

"Well, it's all still a big mystery to me. But these days the strangest things just seem to be worked out before my eyes." He offered her a small smile. "I still don't understand much of anything. Once I would have dismissed it as mumbo-jumbo. Now I'm not sure *what* is touched by God."

She tried to answer his smile with one of her own, but it was hard. "Can . . . can you tell me something about them? My family, I mean." It sounded so strange, saying those words. Her *family*.

"I'm not sure," he replied slowly. "To tell the truth, I don't exactly know what my role in all this should be."

She gripped the starched sheet covering the table's padding. But she remained silent. Something told her now was not the time to press.

He rubbed one hand up and down his cheek, pondering a moment longer. Then he lifted his gaze and said quietly, "I need some time to sort this through. Could you come back tomorrow and —"

"I . . . I . . ." Kyle started to agree, then stammered quickly, "No, I . . . I can't."

He seemed taken aback by her response. "Why not?"

"Because," she replied slowly, "I broke rules to come today. Bertrand brought me. Mother would be furious if she ever found out. I can't take that risk again, not so soon. It could cost him and his wife their jobs."

He nodded his head thoughtfully, then reached for his prescription pad. "Tell you what. Give me a while to think this over. Call me at home this evening. That's my number."

"Thank you." She accepted the paper with numb fingers.

Dr. Austin hesitated a long moment, then looked down at his hands and said, "It so happens that I do know your parents. They have not forgotten you. The sorrow of losing you nearly ruined their lives. I'm just not sure that bringing you back into their lives is the right thing to do."

There was an awful instant when she felt certain he was going to refuse her then and there. Instead, he remained as he was, his head bowed so that she stared at his bald spot, and murmured more to himself than to her, "Then again, they sure could use some good news right now, what with Joel . . ."

When his voice trailed off and it appeared that he would not go on, she quietly pressed, "Who?"

He raised his gaze and shook his head at her question. "I promise to give it careful thought.

Perhaps it wouldn't do too much harm, after all." He offered her his hand. "Nice to know you've grown up and turned out so well."

She walked back down the hall and reentered the waiting room. She did not feel as though she had turned out well at all. She felt lost and utterly alone. Suddenly she was filled with an overpowering need to contact Kenneth, feel his strength, and hear his wisdom make sense of the tumult in her mind and heart. She turned to where the nurse was regarding her from behind the receptionist's counter. "May I use your phone, please?"

"I suppose so." Her tone was disapproving.

"Thank you." Kyle dialed the office, then asked for Kenneth's secretary. When the woman came on the line, she said, "This is Kyle Rothmore. Do you happen to have a number where I can reach Mr. Adams?"

"Miss Kyle, why, yes, hello." The woman seemed tremendously flustered. "I was just trying to reach you at the dorm."

"Why, what's wrong?" The alarm in her voice brought the nurse back around.

"Nothing, that is . . . Mr. Adams is back here. He's in with Mr. Crawley." There was a moment's hesitation, then, "And Mrs. Rothmore has just arrived."

Alarm bells jangled along every inch of her body. "Slip him a note," she said, not trying to hide her apprehension. "Tell him I'm coming. Tell him I'm hurrying just as fast as I can."

The journey downtown seemed to last forever but in truth took less than an hour. Bertrand took the wheel himself and expertly maneuvered the big car through the city traffic. His normal caution was cast aside in answer to her urgent pleadings for speed.

At the Rothmore building, Kyle was out of the car before Bertrand even had his door open. Barely controlling her impatience up the elevator to the executive floor, she flew down the hallway and flung back the door to her father's former office. She took one look at Kenneth's face and exclaimed, "Don't let them do it!"

"Really, Kyle," her mother said peevishly. "What on earth are you thinking? Rushing in here and spouting off nonsense. Honestly, it's just too much."

Kyle glanced at her mother. It was the first time they had seen each other since the start of the school term. She turned back to Kenneth and pleaded, "Don't let them push you into anything."

He turned to her, the entreaty clear in his eyes. "They say they'll keep my entire staff in place, if I —"

She could not let him say the words. "No! I will not allow it."

"Oh, stop it. Stop it right now!" Her mother slapped the arm of her chair. "Sit down and behave yourself."

Kenneth kept his gaze upon her. "That's almost

two hundred jobs we're talking about, Kyle."

"Really, Kyle. This is nothing you need concern yourself with." Randolf Crawley was at his most polished. He moved swiftly around the desk, walked over, took her arm, and said, "Here, why don't you —"

She pulled her arm free. To Kenneth she pleaded, "There must be something we can do to stop them!"

"Oh, do be quiet," her mother snapped. "I won't allow you to interfere in something you know absolutely nothing about, do you hear me? I forbid it!"

"I suppose we could challenge the act in court," Kenneth mused aloud. "After all, I am still a trustee."

"But a secondary one," Randolf said, not returning to his seat. His poise slipped a notch. "Really, I must warn you —"

"Please," Kyle said to Kenneth, "please do that. I'll help any way I can."

"*You'll* help?" Abigail gave a shrill laugh. "Oh, this is just too much."

Kenneth turned his attention to Abigail. "Kyle is less than six months from coming into her full inheritance. This includes, as you know, voting rights for over sixty percent of the stock. I would imagine the least we could do is have a holding order placed upon such a decision until she reaches her majority."

Abigail stiffened as though slapped. She glared at Kyle. "You wouldn't *dare*."

Kyle forced herself to remain fully erect. "There's a lot I've been daring to do, Mother."

"Whatever is that supposed to mean?"

"I've just come from Riverdale," Kyle replied. "Where I met with Dr. Howard Austin."

Her mother's face turned absolutely white. "I'll not have you inherit my company just to turn around and hand it over to a family of *peasants*."

"It is not your company, Mother," Kyle said, glad that her voice did not betray her turmoil. "It was Daddy's, and as far as I'm concerned, it still is." She paused, then said, "What do you know about my birth parents, Mother?"

"Nothing." Her voice was a lash. "I had no interest whatsoever in knowing anything at all. Why should I mix with rabble?"

"I am that rabble," Kyle said softly.

"All that is behind you," Randolf said, heading off Abigail's retort. But his soothing tone was marred by nervousness. "Really, Kyle, don't you think we would all be better off if you trusted us to look after your best interests?"

Firmly Kyle shook her head. "I think it's time I started trusting myself."

Abigail leaped to her feet. She snapped at Randolf, "I *knew* it was a mistake to try your roundabout maneuvers. I've had all of this I can stand." She wheeled around to face Kyle. "Young lady, I am *ordering* you to stop this nonsense *immediately*."

Kyle stood with shoulders squared. She felt as though an immense distance was separating them, at the same time hurting her but also sheltering her. "I'm sorry, Mother. But I can't do that."

"Then I will have the courts declare you incompetent," Abigail ground out. She spun away and started for the door. "Come along, Randolf. We have work to do."

When they were alone, Kyle felt her strength and resolve drain away. She sank into a chair.

"I think they are going to find that very hard going," Kenneth mused aloud. "The first time they contested the will and the trust, the courts rebuked them for even trying. Not only that, you're attending college and doing well in your studies. You are six months from your majority, you have been spending time here in . . ." He noticed her expression. "What's the matter?"

"I feel ill." Standing up to her mother had drained the energy from every fiber of her body.

"Do you want something?"

"A glass of water, please." Gratefully she accepted the glass, took a sip, and felt slightly better. "That was dreadful."

"I hate arguments," he agreed. "But you handled it very well."

"Do you think so?"

"I was so proud of you," he said quietly.

She reached over, took his hand, and said, "I could not have done it without you."

"I didn't do anything."

"You were here. That was the most important thing." She felt strength flow through his grasp, up her arm, and warm her chest. "Don't ever leave, Kenneth. Not ever."

He leaned closer and said, "I want nothing more than to be here for you."

CHAPTER TWENTY-ONE

Joel lay in the barn loft's snug room and listened to the noisy tumult of another dawn. Whoever thought living on a farm was quiet had never been near one. Dogs and roosters and cows and horses were all competing to make the most racket. He had never known a place as noisy as this — or as pleasant.

The Millers had offered him a place in the big house, but he had declined. He required so much sleep these days, he needed a place to come and shut the door on the family noise and the activity. His chest hurt almost all the time, a dull ache that had become as familiar to him as breathing. A constant reminder of what lay ahead.

Joel shifted restlessly, making the rusty springs of his ancient bed squeak and complain. The room had last belonged to a farmhand, brought in back when the Miller children had been too small to take on many of the chores. The little room's dresser lacked the two middle drawers, the mirror was cracked and held together with masking tape, and the bed was twice his own age. Yet Joel had never felt as much at home as he did here. Which made his impending departure even harder to bear.

Two days a week, he did light chores around the Miller farm. It was the only payment the family would accept for his room and board. The rest of the time was spent working with a youth mission connected to a Lansdale church. Lansdale was the nearest thing to a city the Pennsylvanian Dutch region could boast. In recent years, it had gained a reputation as a stopping place for kids on the move. And there were so many of them these days. Runaways, college kids taking a semester off, or kids just roaming around. The Lansdale church work had given Joel an opportunity to give, to share, to love. He had never known such a feeling of completeness. Even when it made him so tired.

For some of the young people he was meeting, he represented their only chance of knowing love. Not the love of the streets, where they bartered their bodies for what they so desperately yearned to have — a sense of belonging. Joel had found he could reach to them on a deeper level, giving from the peace and joy in his own heart, and speak of One who would grant them unconditional love. *Real* love.

Joel had discovered an ability to share that love. He knew this was his gift, his calling, as clearly as he knew his own name. He could not explain why he had been chosen to serve in this manner. He did not understand how someone like him had been selected from a world of believers to have the glory of such a mission. Except for perhaps having come from circumstances with a similar lack of love and acceptance.

Joel heard the farmhouse door slam and took it as a signal to roll from his bed. Today was a chore day, and he had promised Ruthie to hitch up the buggy and take her to town. As he slipped into his clothes, he gave thanks anew for this gift of understanding, the gift of renewal, the gift of purpose.

If only there was some way he could give a little longer.

Normally Joel enjoyed urging the horse and buggy to a brisk pace. The animal was a trotter and loved to run. Joel usually gave him the freedom to do so, as he loved to feel the energy of a racing thoroughbred passing through the leather reins. But today he deliberately slowed him to a gentler gait. There was no need to hurry. They had not managed to leave the farm until late afternoon, what with one chore after another keeping them busy. Ruthie had delivered the cartons of eggs to the local merchant and purchased the few supplies from her list, and now they were headed home.

The afternoon drive seemed a perfect time for slowing life's busy pace. A time for reflection. For enjoying a little leisure, a rare commodity for people who worked so steadily. Even the horse sensed it and settled into a slow, even trot, so different from his normal pull against the reins. Joel relaxed, his arms resting lightly on his knees. The cool breeze gently played with his uncovered hair. The day was warm for fall, and his dark cap lay on the seat beside him.

Ruthie, close at his side in the buggy's confines,

leaned back with a gentle smile playing about her lips. Clearly she meant to enjoy every moment of the rare respite from her household responsibilities.

On the road toward them moved another buggy, the horse traveling much faster than their own. Little puffs of dust lifted with each clip-clop of hoof and spin of buggy wheel. Joel pointed and spoke with a smile. "Someone's in too much of a hurry for such a fine day."

Ruthie peered ahead, then replied, "It's the Enns' black. He must be forgetting something up to town."

Joel nodded. Just as some folks knew cars, Ruthie seemed to know every horse in the entire neighborhood. They continued to watch the distance close between their two buggies. There was no other traffic on this road, and the sound of the horses' hoofs fell into a pleasant rhythm in the crisp autumn air.

Ruthie was right. It was indeed Henry Enns, a neighbor to the Millers. He nodded in their direction and called out with a broad grin, "Strange time of day to be courting out!"

Joel frowned. He knew the words were good-natured teasing, but he wondered if there was more to them than that. Yes. Henry likely meant his words. Joel stole a sideways look at Ruthie. What he saw made him stir with uneasiness.

He had grown to know her well over the months, and he could see that the girl's thoughts were taking her in the same direction as Henry's.

She blushed and smiled, then shifted slightly on the leather seat. Her arm brushed up against Joel's sleeve. He felt the color rise in his cheeks.

He had to do something. Say something. But what? What could he possibly say without hurting the one he had come to care for so much? He worked his dry mouth and tried to formulate some words. Nothing reasonable came to mind.

Ruthie stirred again. He heard a little sigh escape her lips. She seemed so totally at peace with herself and with their relationship. But maybe she was thinking that the relationship held more promises than Joel was prepared or able to make.

Again he fought for some way to broach the subject. At last he straightened and turned slightly. "Do they really think we're courting?"

The smile on Ruthie's face was a little embarrassed, but she nodded.

"Why is that?" The question sounded much too abrupt, he knew as soon as the words were out.

Her smile wavered, but her eyes did not fall before his. "Because, Joel, we are together much. And we enjoy our times together. This all can see."

"Yes, but . . ." Joel could not deny the fact that he spent a good deal of time with the young girl. Nor would he have tried to deny the fact that he enjoyed her company. But to court her? His sigh seemed to come from the bottom of his soul. No. Courting was a privilege of young men with a future. Men with promise. He had nothing to offer Ruthie, not even time.

"What is it, Joel?"

"You know that . . . that I can't . . ."

The girl's eyes clouded. "You do not enjoy?" Ruthie asked frankly.

"You know I do. It's just . . . you know my circumstances. I'm not well, Ruthie." He glanced at her with painful appeal. "I don't even know how long I have."

Timidly Ruthie slipped a hand over his. Joel could feel her press close to his side. He dared not look at her again. "I know about your heart that makes you sick," she said her voice clear, confident. "I know, and I pray."

"But, Ruthie —"

"Wait, Joel. No one knows the time of parting. The hours, or the days, those are God's to give. We are not to know. Just to live, and thanks to give to Him our Maker. To make good what we have."

The words and the feelings began tumbling out. "But they wouldn't be good, can't you see that? At any time I could — be gone. I can't promise you anything, Ruthie. Not even to live long enough to marry. To build a home. To raise children. I wouldn't do that to you, Ruthie. I wouldn't do that to anyone. I will not make promises that would only be broken."

"Have I asked for promises yet?"

"No, but —"

"And I will not do. But we can dream and

plan, Joel. Plans can change — without being broken. And if God wills . . .”

But Joel was shaking his head. The agitation that filled his whole body transferred down the reins he was holding. The horse threw up his head and quickened his gait. Joel had to give quick attention to his driving, but he welcomed the change of pace. Suddenly he wished to have the ride over. To be freed from his difficult position. He straightened and lifted his hands to control the horse that now had broken into a full run. Ruthie’s hand withdrew and joined the other in her lap.

“I cannot make plans,” Joel declared with a firmness that sounded almost cold. “I have no tomorrows to share. I will not unload this on anyone else.”

A quick glance showed him the tears in Ruthie’s eyes. Her chin was lifted, her jaw set. “You are a stubborn man, Joel Grimes.. Do you not leave room still for love — or miracles?”

“No,” he said, and immediately realized he was proving her statement to be true. Maybe he was stubborn but he repeated, “No, I don’t expect miracles. And you’d be wise not to be looking for one either.”

Kyle’s heart soared and plunged a dozen times during her second drive back to Riverdale. What if they did not want to meet her? What if they did not like her at all? Why had they given her up for adoption in the first place? What if the reason was a bad one? Could she survive the news?

Finally Kenneth stopped on a street very much like others they had traversed and pointed to a house ahead of them. "Up there, the second on the right."

Kyle's breath came in quick little gasps. She looked up at the small home. "You're sure this is it?"

"If the address the doctor gave you is right, it is." He stared through the front windshield. "I don't see anyone."

"No." She pressed a hand against her rib cage, willing her heart to slow its frantic pace. She looked up at the house, trying to gather a feeling for who lived there. The narrow yard fell in three grassy steps to the sidewalk. Shrubs colored by late autumn frosts formed a neat border. A picket fence held it all together. "I'm so scared."

"I understand." He reached over for her hand. "Are you sure you're ready for this?"

"I think so." She looked at him. She hesitated, then asked, "Would you . . . would you pray with me? Please?"

"You don't know," he said, still holding her hand, "how often I have dreamed you would say those words to me."

She bowed her head and heard him say, "Heavenly Father, we are so grateful for this moment. Grateful that we are sharing it together, and sharing it with you. Be with Kyle, precious Lord, as she steps into this new part of her life. Guide her, shield her, comfort her. In Jesus' name we pray. Amen."

"Amen," Kyle murmured and raised her head. The first thing she saw when she opened her eyes was a slight, dark-haired woman standing on the house's front porch. The woman held the door with one hand, as though fearful to let it go and step away. She stared down at the car. Kyle whispered, "Oh, Kenneth."

Suddenly her fingers were unable to work the door handle. Kenneth reached across her and pushed it open. "God will go with you, sweetheart."

The words gave her strength to stand. At her appearance, the woman on the porch raised one hand to her mouth and started down the steps. Kyle took a tentative step forward.

The woman made it down the steps, walked hesitantly forward, and finally whispered, "Katherine?"

Kyle felt her heart twist painfully at the sound of that name. "Mrs. Grimes?"

"Oh, Katie . . ." The woman ran forward, then halted, her arms halfway raised, tears streaming down her face. She reached one trembling hand out, uncertain, helpless to go farther. Kyle found herself unable to see the woman's features any longer for the tears in her own eyes. She took another tentative step, and suddenly the two of them were hugging, and the woman was stroking Kyle's hair and her back and crying over and over, "Katie, oh my little Katherine."

And suddenly Kyle was crying, too. Partly because the search was finally over, partly for all the sadness that had brought her to this place, partly because she had never even known that her name had once been Katherine.

"So this is your young man," Martha Grimes said for the fifth or sixth time. "How nice. You make such a handsome couple."

"Thank you. It's all very new to us," Kyle admitted with a flush to her cheeks. She shifted, flustered and shy over her discovery of love. While getting her feelings back under control, she let her glance travel about the room. Everything in it spoke of age and hard use. The covers to the sagging furniture were worn, the coffee table scarred. The bookshelves were almost bare, the television an older model with a huge cabinet supporting a small corner screen.

"And you brought him for us to meet." Martha beamed at Kenneth. "I am so happy for you both."

"It is an honor to meet you, Mrs. Grimes."

"Call me Martha, please. What do you do?"

"I work in Kyle's company. Rothmore Insurance."

"How nice. It's wonderful to have things you can share, isn't it, Harry?"

"Absolutely," her husband agreed.

Kyle looked from one to the other. It was remarkable, how little interest they seemed to have in the Rothmore wealth. Despite their obvious lack, they listened to her speak about her family, her growing-up years, her experience as the daughter of a successful businessman, with interest only because it was *her* they were happy for. They looked incredibly satisfied with what they had.

She turned back to the woman seated beside her. Martha had not released her hand since embracing her outside. Not even the room's dimness could disguise the light that shone from the woman's face. And from that of her husband. Kyle glanced over at the silent man, saw the same gentle light as she had found in the woman's gaze. "You both look so happy."

For some reason, her words caused Martha and Harry to exchange a long glance. Harry finally replied with, "Yes. We are. Finally."

"At long last," Martha agreed.

Harry turned to Kyle and explained, "It was all Joel's doing."

"It was God's doing," his wife corrected quietly.

"True, true." There was another shared glance. "But it was Joel who showed us the way."

"You're believers," Kenneth said. "This is wonderful."

But Kyle's mind was still back grappling with the previous statement. "I'm sorry," she stammered. "Who is Joel?"

The question brought fresh tears to Martha's eyes. "Oh, my dear, sweet child. You don't know."

"How could she?" Harry murmured.

"No, of course." Martha sniffed loudly and tried to collect herself.

Kyle demanded weakly, "Know what?"

"You have a brother," Martha said softly. "His name is Joel."

"A brother?" The word rocked Kyle. A brother? She had always longed for a brother. Had begged for a brother, and now she was discovering she had a brother that she did not even know. It was all so overwhelming. "Where is he?" she finally managed.

"Oh, he's not here," hurried Martha. "I know he'd be as excited as we are if he only . . ."

When Martha's voice dropped off, Kyle had to take several breaths before she found the strength to whisper, "Doesn't he know about me?"

Martha's head lowered and she fiddled with the hankie in her lap. "No," she said and there was anguish in her voice. "No . . . we never told him."

"But why . . ." Kyle could not finish her question.

Even so, the words brought a fresh rush of tears from Martha's eyes. "Losing you was too painful to even talk about."

"Even between us," Harry added quietly. Lines like jagged furrows etched his face as he sadly observed his wife. "All those wasted years," he murmured.

"We could not even talk to each other . . . until . . . recently." Martha wept as she said the words. "And only after Joel brought us face to face with our need. After the doctor . . ." She could not go on. Sobs shook her shoulders.

Harry crossed to her and put a protective arm about her, comforting her with clumsy yet gentle pats. He looked over at Kyle and said, "It truly is God's doing, bringing you here now."

Kyle could sense that something was wrong, something more than the emotion of all the lost years. There was an underlying current of sadness in the home, even amid the evident feeling of peace and the joy of reunion.

"Oh, Harry, must we speak about that now?" Martha said, trying to stop the flowing tears.

"I think so, but if you'd rather . . ."

Martha hesitated, then dropped her eyes and sighed, "No, no, I suppose she should know it all."

Kyle felt a chill. "Know what?"

"Your brother," Harry Grimes replied quietly. "He's not well."

"His heart," Martha said and wiped her face anew. "The doctors — they say there's nothing they can do." The last part of her sentence was spoken so softly Kyle wondered if she had heard correctly.

No. No. Kyle fought against the fact of finding a brother and then losing him in nearly the same breath.

"Is he in the hospital?" she heard Kenneth ask on her behalf.

"No, he's . . ." began Martha.

"Honey — I think we need to start at the beginning and tell her everything."

Kyle sat and heard the full story. The meeting of two young people just as the country was going to war. The marriage and their few short but happy weeks together. The war. The injury and loss of Harry's ID. The anguish of a young mother, seemingly widowed, giving up the baby she wanted and loved. Harry's return to an empty cradle and a grieving wife, suffering through the loss of his health and his profession and the daughter he never knew. The arrival of Joel, whose presence in the home was unable to heal the deep rift that had driven them apart. Martha's accident and the gradual breaking down of some of the unseen walls. Joel's friendship with the Millers. His finding a faith that he shared with his parents when they needed it the most. The doctor's diagnosis had been cruel, crippling, yet with God's help they were somehow managing to bear it. Now Kyle — their little Katherine — had been brought back into their life. Surely it was God's doing.

Kyle wiped away tears as she listened to the story. Why had it happened? Why the strange circumstances and twists of fate that had ripped them all apart? And brought them together?

And a brother. A younger brother. As the story wound its way toward her presence here in this room, Kyle found she could hear no more. She simply could not emotionally face anything further. She rose to her feet, shaking her head as if that would help to put things into some kind of focus. "I . . . I need to be going," she stammered.

"Oh, must you?" Martha rose with her, holding Kyle's hand as though not wishing to ever let her go. But there was no conviction behind Martha's protest. Clearly they all felt overwhelmed by the day's events.

Harry's wounded leg was giving him trouble as he pushed himself erect. "When will we see you again?"

"Soon," Kyle promised. She would be back. Just as soon as she could catch her breath and sort things out. But she had to see Joel. Her brother. She had to. "Where will I find Joel?"

Martha looked to her husband for guidance and stammered, "Oh, Harry, might this be too much for his poor heart?"

But Harry was shaking his head. "Emotionally he's the strongest man I've ever met. He wouldn't be able to do what he's doing if he wasn't. He'll be all right."

Kyle's attention was caught and held by a single word. *Man*. Harry had called the baby brother she had never known a man. Again she felt overwhelmed. "I really must be going." Kenneth held her arm protectively.

The Grimes led the two out to the front porch. Harry's slight limp continued to pull at Kyle's attention, as though that leg contained the mystery of the missing years. Kenneth walked alongside her. He did not speak, just remained close enough for her to draw from his steady strength.

"He's been staying on a farm in Mennonite country, north of Philadelphia," Harry explained. "He and a fellow from the family, they do charity work together, I guess you'd call it."

"Joel's such a wonderful boy," Martha said proudly. "I'll show you his letters next time you come. They're so full of love and warmth they just make you want to weep."

"Last time we talked, Joel said he's found needs he didn't even know existed." Harry leaned against the pillar by the front steps, one strong arm around his wife's shoulders. "Joel came home for a while, but he couldn't settle back in here. Kept on about the needs out there and something he wanted to do before — while he still could."

"A mission, he said it was," Martha added. "A calling from God. His last letter said he felt he had discovered what life was really all about."

"They work with some group that helps all these kids piling into the cities," Harry said. Clearly he was troubled by the thought. "Runaways and the like."

Kenneth spoke for the first time. "My church has become involved in that as well. It's a growing problem down here in Washington."

Martha was still unwilling to let go of Kyle's hand. "I miss my boy," she confessed quietly.

"He's doing God's work," Harry intoned quietly. "You can't read his letters and doubt that

297

for a second. But it's hard on both of us, him being gone when we don't know how long . . ."

"Here." Martha reached into her cardigan and brought out a pencil and a scrap of paper. She released Kyle's hand long enough to scribble hastily, then hand over the paper. "This is the address for the Millers' farm. They don't have a phone. I'll be sending him a letter today, telling him everything, but why don't you write to Joel yourself?"

"Thank you," Kyle said, accepting the slip, yet knowing she could not wait for an exchange of letters.

"I know how busy you folks must be," Martha said. "But do you think we could invite you back for a meal next week?"

Kyle saw the entreaty in the woman's eyes and knew she could refuse her nothing. "Whenever you like," she said, squeezing the small hand. "That would be wonderful."

The trip back to Washington was made in nearly absolute silence. Kyle had so much to absorb, she felt as though she could not hold on to any thought for more than an instant. The impressions and feelings and images whirled through her mind as she leaned her head against the back of the seat.

Kenneth obviously felt her need for quiet. Every once in a while he would reach over and pat her hand, not speaking, just reminding her that he was there. Each time, she felt her mind and her spirit calmed by his understanding and care.

Gradually, a single thread began to run more clearly through her thoughts. Over and over she returned to how faith had such impact in the lives around her — in her father, Lawrence, in her adored Bertie and Maggie, even when she didn't recognize it. In Kenneth, and now in the Grimes family. . . .

Strange how she would think of this now. Or perhaps not, she reflected, staring out at the city. The power of God had been reflected in so much that day — the way Harry and Martha described the change in their relationship, for one. She did not doubt for a moment that what they had told her was true.

This power of faith also was evident in Kenneth's peace, his silent understanding, his patience. All of these were offerings in a way. She had never thought of them in that sense, but it was true. He offered to her what he had learned through faith.

As they drove beneath trees dressed in the final flecks of autumn gold, she decided it was time she offered him something in return. But what? She looked over at Kenneth, this dear man who had seen her through so much, and wondered what on earth she and this fragile faith of hers had to give.

As Kenneth pulled up in front of her dormitory and cut off the motor, he said, "You're not going to wait and write Joel, are you?"

His ability to understand her thoughts and direction were another precious gift, especially now. "I can't."

"It won't be possible for me to take another day from work this week," he said apologetically. "I have to meet with the lawyers first thing tomorrow. The best way to halt Randolf and Abigail is to be there first. I must —"

"I understand," she said quickly. No matter how urgent those matters were, she did not want to discuss them. Not now. "I can take the train."

Kenneth did not object. "When do you want to go?"

"Tomorrow," she said, without hesitation. *A brother.*

"Perhaps it would be best after all," he said slowly, "for you to go up there alone."

She tried to echo what her awakening heart was feeling. "You will be there with me," she said quietly. "In my heart, where it counts most."

His gaze into her eyes offered her a glimpse to the depths of his spirit. "With all that you've gone through, what a wonderful thing to say," he said. "Thank you."

And she knew she had been able to offer a small gift of her own. "It's a lesson you taught me." She reached across and took his hand, felt the strength and the warmth and the spirit. Here was a truly good man. "Would you pray with me now?"

CHAPTER TWENTY-TWO

"It's very kind of you to invite me in like this," Kyle said. She was seated at the Millers' kitchen table, feeling out of place but very welcomed.

"Choel's sister," Mr. Miller repeated and shook his head once more. "Never did I think such a shock could be such a happiness."

Mrs. Miller rose and reached for Kyle's plate. "Here, let me some more pie bring."

"No, really, I couldn't." Kyle glanced around, taking in the big, bare-walled kitchen with its finely crafted table and chairs, and the people with their curious dress and speech. Despite the strangeness of the setting, Kyle could not help but feel the peace that permeated the room. And something more. The same light shone from their faces as had from Martha and Harry Grimes.

She had taken a train up to Philadelphia, then to Lansdale, not sorry that pressing issues in the company had forced Kenneth to stay in Washington. It was good to be alone for this journey of discovery. The time of travel and solitude gave her an opportunity to sort through her thoughts and emotions. So much was happening and so fast.

As the train had clattered on, Kyle had found herself praying. It had come with the quiet naturalness of a thought about Kenneth, seeing his smile and his strength and his concern for her,

301

feeling the closeness even when every minute of her journey took her farther away. She had closed her eyes, pressing her forehead against the train window, and heard the words drift into her mind. *Help me, Father,* she had prayed, and this time she had felt the words fill her being, running into those that she had earlier pushed away, yet which now stood out as if written in light before her mind's eye. *Help me to come to know you. Help me to understand. Help me to know the life and the joy and the light that I see in other believers' eyes. Help me to understand what salvation truly means.*

The lingering peace had stayed with her, through the remainder of the journey and the long taxi ride out to the Miller farm. She could not call ahead since they did not have a telephone. But it had not mattered, for they had accepted her with hugs and cries of delight, and drawn her into the kitchen for coffee and fresh pie and talk and smiles. They had explained that Joel was not there right then but was doing mission work in town.

The young man named Simon rose to his feet. "Perhaps you would like to walk the farm now."

"Yes, thank you." She returned their openhearted smiles; only the young woman called Ruthie remained quietly sad at the table's other end, watching her with an unreadable expression. "You've all been so kind."

Simon walked with her toward the paddock. "I stayed home from the mission church to help with the chores this day," he said to her unasked

302

question. "Papa, he has good days and bad days. Today is not so good."

The late autumn sun turned the pasture a glistening gold. The horses spotted their approach and came trotting over to the fence. The most persistent was a chestnut mare whose nose was flecked with the gray of age. "This is Missy. My father bought her the year before I was born. She is old now. We let her be lazy. She no longer works on the farm."

The mare seemed to realize they were talking about her, for she tossed her mane and snorted before walking up and resting her chest on the top post. She muzzled into Simon's open hand, then turned her attention toward Kyle.

Kyle lifted both hands to the great head and stroked the neck. The horse nuzzled gently against her shoulder. "She's wonderful."

Simon watched in mild surprise. "She looks for sugar. It is a game we play. Never did I see her do this with a stranger. Can you ride?"

"I used to. I haven't in years."

"Sometimes I think horses, they understand things better than people. Dogs too. They have such a simple way of living, as though we could look at them and remember things we have forgotten. Or maybe never really learned."

"You have held to a lot of the simple things in life."

"Yes." He watched as she lay her cheek against the horse and was rewarded with a soft whinny. "You share your brother's way with animals.

303

They must see a good heart in you."

She turned to face Simon. The horse, disappointed by her movement, shoved at her gently. She reached out again to stroke her and asked, "Where is my brother, Simon? I must see him."

"He went to the mission church in Lansdale without me today." He nodded slowly. "I think it is very good that he sees you. Joel needs us all to help him at this time. He is very brave — but he hurts within, more than from the heart that does not beat right."

He stared out to where the fields joined with low-slung hills. Kyle shifted from one foot to the other. She had the feeling that Simon wanted to say more about her brother, but she didn't feel she could press him.

At length he sighed. With a nod back toward the house he went on. "Our Ruthie — she loves your Joel. It is no secret. She cannot hide it. And Joel, he returns the love. Only Joel asks me, what can one give with so few days left? 'Love,' I say. 'For as long as God allows.' But that is not good enough answer for him. So Joel, he has not only a bad heart — but a broken one."

Kyle felt the tears rise in her eyes. Tears for the brother she did not know. "I wish I could do something for him," she said, her voice little more than a whisper.

"That sounds just like what our Joel would say." Simon smiled with surprising sweetness for such a hearty-looking face. "He is quite the man, your brother. He can say more in silence than most folk can with a year of words." He turned to stare out over the paddock. "He understands these people, the wanderers. He knows their distrust of voices. But still he speaks to them. Heart speaks to heart. And their own hearts, they listen."

Kyle felt as though she were reaching through the mists of lost time, struggling to understand a man she had never met. Her brother. "Why do you think he can do this?"

Simon was a long time in answering. "Because," he finally replied, "Joel is an orphan of the storm — the storm of this life — just like them. It has left him alone too much and too long. He understands their sadness, and he speaks to their need."

"I —" Kyle stopped as she saw Ruthie approaching. She had a new appreciation, a new empathy, for the young girl. She wished she could reach out to her, ease the pain of the heart that loved — and sorrowed.

The young woman walked over, stopped in front of Kyle, and in her lilting English asked, "You go to Joel?"

"Yes," replied Kyle with a slight nod.

"Would you give him a message for me?"

"Of course," Kyle responded, but she heard her voice crack on the simple words.

Sadness turned her smile crooked. "Tell him, don't leave now, leave next time."

Kyle wasn't sure she had heard correctly. "But he's already in town."

"He'll understand." Abruptly Ruthie reached out, hugged Kyle fiercely, then released her and turned away, but not before Kyle caught sight of the tears. "And give that for him from me yet."

Kyle stood and watched Ruthie return to the house, saw her hand reach up to brush at her cheeks. Kyle could not stop her own tears from flowing.

Late that afternoon, Joel braved the brisk wind to help with what the church folk had come to call the street patrol. In the early morning and again just before dark, they searched out new faces huddled under blankets or sleeping inside the limping vehicles that had brought them to town.

Lansdale was often called the gateway to the Pennsylvania Dutch country. It was a picturesque place of Revolutionary War–era buildings and grand, tree-lined avenues. Young people headed into New York, Boston, or Washington — or just moving — often stopped here. A few days or weeks — or months. "Beatniks" had for years been the word to describe such young people. Joel shared the feeling of the other church folk that something needed to be done for these lost ones.

Shadows were lengthening and the night was drawing its cold cover over the town when Joel's eye was caught by a lumpy form huddled in a doorway. He crossed the street and identified three bodies shivering under a shared blanket.

He made as much noise as he could in approaching. One of the heads popped into sight, then another. A trio of young girls, the oldest no more than sixteen, stared at him with sleepy eyes. Fear seemed to have been etched permanently into their young faces, a sign he had come to know well. It meant they had been on the road long enough to sample the harshness of life alone.

"Good evening," he said, giving them a gentle word and a wave, but no smile. By now they would have learned that smiles could mask danger and deception. People often lied as easily with a smile as their voices.

The girls watched him with eyes that were swiftly clearing of sleep. Their bodies tensed, ready to flee if he made a sudden move. "My name is Joel. Have any of you heard of the Lansdale Mennonite Church?"

There was a long pause before the middle girl gave a little shiver of a headshake.

"We run a local mission outreach. There's hot soup there. Have you eaten recently?"

The hollowness of their cheeks told him everything. Joel did not wait for them to respond. "Everything's cool," he said, using the language of the street, but knowing it was more important they feel his concern than hear his words. "You can stay as long as you like, have a shower and a bed for a while if you need it. Hot food, there's a doctor, too. If you want, we'll let your folks know you're okay, but we won't say where you are unless you want us to."

Joel waited a moment, long enough to give a silent, open-eyed prayer that the Lord would speak to their hearts. Then he offered them his hand. "It's so cold this evening the streets are white. Feels like it might even snow later. Wouldn't you like to come in and get warm?"

Joel set up rows of chairs, preparing for their evening service. The church was on the outskirts of town, and the mission occupied the ground floor of a neighboring building. They had left the floor open and set the worship area in one corner. They had discovered early on that few of these wary young people would accept the word of God outright. These kids first needed to observe from a distance. They could sit in the lounge area, or help in the kitchen, or talk among themselves. It never ceased to give Joel a thrill of pleasure the first time one of the newcomers would hesitantly walk over, after a few days of careful observing, and sit down and listen to the Word.

A flicker of movement caught Joel's eye, and he stopped to turn and stare with the rest of the room.

Not that the girl was beautiful. No, the features were too definite, the shoulders too square, the bearing too erect. But this was certainly not a person who had come looking for shelter.

She stood there and searched the faces turned her way. Joel walked toward her. The young lady was definitely not a social worker, not the way she was dressed. She wore a winter suit of palest yellow, with matching pumps and purse. Her hair was brushed to a warm glow, and her skin was smooth as peaches and cream.

Obviously she was looking for a runaway. It happened from time to time, but usually the searcher was someone older. As he approached, he wondered if there wasn't something about her. Something oddly familiar. Something that raised the hair on his arms and brought a shiver up his spine.

"Can I help you?"

She just stared at him, her eyes big and glowing. "Joel?" There was a faint tremor to her voice. "Are you Joel Grimes?"

For some reason he found himself unable to answer. The shiver grew stronger, until his whole body seemed to quiver. He gave her a rather abrupt nod.

She tried for a smile, showing the same trembling nerves that he himself felt. "Is there some place we can talk?"

Joel shook his head. "I can't believe this. . . . Why was I never told?"

"I asked the same question. They said it was all too painful. That they couldn't even talk about it between themselves."

They sat in the mission's upstairs office, as bare and rundown as the rest of the center. Thankfully, they had the place to themselves. When they first came to the room, Joel had seated her by the window, offered her coffee, and started with a few practiced questions — until he realized that Kyle was not there looking for a runaway.

Kyle gave Joel silent space to grow accustomed to the idea of a sister. She spent time inspecting his face. There was the same shape to his eyes, his forehead, and his chin, as she saw when she looked in her mirror. On him it looked good, she decided. He was a nice-looking young man. A bit too thin and pale, but nonetheless attractive — and pleasant, especially his eyes.

"You're sure?" he said at last.

"Yes. I'm sure."

Silence. Absolute silence. He picked up his spoon and began to stir his coffee. Round and round — his eyes staring into a past only he could see. "The guest room," he murmured as though answering a question.

Kyle frowned. "Pardon?"

But Joel did not explain. He lifted his head and studied her closely. At length he nodded. "I guess it explains a lot of things. Sort of." The spoon continued round and round. "My sister. I can't get over this."

"Dr. Austin delivered us both."

"You're kidding."

"No. . . . He's the tie that got me to your — *our* parents." Kyle watched a range of expressions cross her brother's face.

"So where have you been hiding?"

"A family in D.C. adopted me."

He appraised her. "And they are well-off, by

the looks of things."

Kyle nodded. There was no use denying it.

"Did the folks decide to look for you?"

"No, I began to look for them."

"And you found them. How?"

"It wasn't easy. I've had a friend looking for months. The adoption records were sealed. We had to gather hints here and there. I finally found Dr. Austin. He decided to break some rules and contacted . . . contacted Martha."

"Why didn't Mom tell me?"

"She just found out, and she's writing you a letter. They said it's not possible to contact you by phone. I suppose you could call them, though . . ."

"Already she's trying to boss me around," he said to the world at large, and they both laughed. "I *have* been busy."

"Well, they sure would love to hear from you, especially with —"

His gaze swung around to her. "With what?"

"You know." She paused for a breath. "They just miss you, that's all," she finished lamely.

But he understood her deeper meaning. "So you've been told everything, is that what I'm hearing?"

"I'm your sister, Joel. They felt — they thought I should know."

Joel looked away. Clearly, having a stranger know about his illness had unsettled him. Kyle wondered if she should have first warned him. Maybe a letter would have been better. Perhaps he could not understand her longing for family. Maybe she would never be able to explain.

But she had to try. She needed to be open and honest and risk his rejection. "I want to know my family. I really do," she began slowly.

He raised his eyebrows, a small smile tilting the corners of his mouth. "Was there ever anything you wanted in your entire life that you couldn't have?"

She stared at him, wondering if he was dismissing her as merely frivolous and empty-headed. How could she explain her life in just a few words? Kyle was tempted to give up the attempt with some pleasantries and hope for a better opportunity in the future.

But something in his eyes made her take a deep breath and speak the truth. "I used to wish to be accepted . . . loved for who I was. Spoken with, rather than *ordered* to sit up straighter or hold my teacup properly. My father . . . he loved me . . . just as I was, but he's — I lost him. Mother . . ." There was no use trying to explain to him about her mother. "I was lonely," she finished in a whisper.

It took a moment for her halting words to sink in. She watched it happen, watched as her simple explanation settled down deep, wiping away his doubts.

A sense of rightness came between them, and Joel nodded slowly and said, "Then we have a lot in common, after all. More than I thought."

And to her surprise he reached across to take

her hand and give it a little squeeze. He looked at her evenly, the questions now gone from his eyes and replaced by a soft, genuine smile. "I'm very glad you were determined enough — brave enough — to find us. To come find me. I really am."

CHAPTER TWENTY-THREE

That evening, she called Kenneth. "I miss you more than I thought could be possible."

He was silent long enough for her to wonder if she should have spoken. Then he murmured, "Oh, Kyle."

"Everything I see, all that's happening, I want to tell you about, describe to you," she said in a rush. The doors that had been opened in their last conversation were not to be shut again. Not ever. "I wish you were with me."

"Your words sound," he said quietly "as though you had looked right inside my mind and knew what I longed to hear."

"I have so much else I want to tell you," she confessed. "I need your perspective and experience, Kenneth."

"How are things going?"

"Good, I think." She recounted the events, her visit with the Millers, and the meeting with her brother. She finished with, "Now I feel, well, I feel like we're all just beginning to know each other, learning how to communicate. I look into Joel's face, which seems so *familiar* to me. And yet it's so strange to *feel* like we know each other, yet really to know so little — we have so many years to catch up on. . . ."

"Give it time," Kenneth assured her after a moment. "Remember, he's not even known about you, and you've been searching for months. All of you need time to adjust to this discovery."

"Yes," she said, still sounding pensive.

"Where are you now?"

"I've taken a room in the Lansdale Hotel." She gripped the phone tightly. "I wish I could see you."

"Would you like me to come up?"

"Could you? Oh, Kenneth, that would be wonderful. But I thought —"

"Things have changed around here," he said, a chuckle in his voice. "I have some news of my own."

"What is it?"

"Randolf and Abigail," he announced, "are dropping the court case."

"What?" She leapt to her feet.

"Apparently their lawyers have advised them against attempting to disinherit you. That is what our own people think. Bad publicity, risking loss of whatever clout they still have, and a case they don't have a hope of winning — whatever the reasons, the case has been dropped, Kyle."

"You mean, it's over? Really and truly finished?"

"We will have to work out a number of details, but you can leave those to me. Yes, if you want my opinion, I would say we are home free."

"Dear Kenneth," she said softly. "Thank you. Thank you for helping me."

"I would like to keep doing that," he said, his

tone matching her own. "For the rest of my life."

The next morning, Joel once again rode the bus to Lansdale alone. Simon was still busy helping his father with farm work. Joel found himself glad for the chance to travel in solitude. The day before had left him very unsettled. All night he had relived the encounter with his sister, trying to come to grips with what it all meant.

He stared out the bus window at the bright blue sky of a country autumn morning, and all around him the world was painted in colors of fire. Each bend and rise brought a new scene into view, but Joel scarcely noticed. He reflected that it was not just this newfound sister that had left him so unnerved.

As the bus wound its way into Lansdale, Joel felt a tugging at his heart, as though his parents were reaching out across the distance through Kyle. He stepped from the bus, waved to the driver, and started down the street to the mission. He spotted Kyle walking toward him, leading a tall young man by the hand. Joel had a pang of envy over the man's obvious strength and vitality.

Kyle halted in front of him and said shyly, "Joel, I'd like you to meet Kenneth Adams. This is my brother, Joel."

Kenneth shook his hand, a calm, compassionate light in his eyes. "This is a true honor, Joel. You are doing great work here."

"Thanks." Joel heard the warmth and concern in the young man's voice and immediately felt ashamed at his first response. "Why do you say that?"

"Because of what your parents told us. I think we're seeing just the beginning here." Kenneth's voice held the same quiet power as his face and his grip. "Everywhere I go these days, I'm hearing about a new restlessness among young people. New challenges to the established order of things. We may not be able to stop or redirect the rebellion, yet someone needs to remind them that the ultimate authority is God. But that His is an authority based on love."

The three walked into the building, and Kyle said, "I'll let you two get acquainted." She backed away and asked, "How about coffee?"

At Joel's nod, Kenneth said, "Make that two, please." He then motioned toward nearby chairs. "Do you want to sit down?"

Gratefully Joel accepted the invitation and moved toward a seat. "It sounds like you're a Christian."

"Yes." Kenneth looked around the vast hall. "When I come to a place like this, it challenges me to make my faith a living, breathing part of everything I am, everything I do."

The honest humility touched Joel, and he sank into the chair with a long sigh. When he looked up, Kenneth was watching him with an expression of grave concern. "Kyle tells me you are not well."

"It's a heart condition," Joel admitted.

"Kyle told me. I'm sorry." The silence fell

between them for several minutes before Kenneth spoke again. "Kyle and I both wonder if perhaps there is something more that can be done. There are some amazing discoveries about the heart recently — but I'm sure you are aware of this."

"I've lost count of all the tests I've had. If there had been something — anything — that could be done, I'm sure Doc Austin would have seen to it."

"Would you — and your doctor — be willing to undergo further testing?"

"I'm not sure." Joel offered a small smile, not just to the question, but also to the fact that he was talking so comfortably with a stranger. "Maybe I'm just a coward," he admitted slowly. "Any thought — any faint hope — and I'm afraid I would grasp at it."

"That's natural. God created us to fight for survival."

"It's not just for me. Though I've had hopes and dreams that I would love to see fulfilled. It's more than that. It's my work here. I feel that with these young people I am finally doing something important. Something *lasting*. And the irony is that it's about to end."

Both pairs of eyes drifted over the room where ministry for body and soul took place daily. "Sometimes it seems so unfair," Joel said.

Kenneth nodded slowly. "I understand."

The bonding between the two young men was something beyond the mere words they were exchanging. Joel realized this was no stranger. Kenneth was a *brother*. A brother in *heart*. "Sometimes, when I'm alone, I feel like death is standing in the corner of my room, watching and waiting — taunting me." He lowered his head and his voice. "There's so much I want to do. So much left to learn."

Kenneth was quiet for a long moment. His gaze filled with a sorrow that mirrored the anguish spilling from Joel's heart. "The Lord's hand is truly at work in your life, Joel. Whatever happens, He is still at work."

Joel nodded slowly. He already knew this, but had not wanted to accept it. He now realized that the reason he had fought against the truth of God's hand, even in this, was because he had seen it as a defeat. Yet who was he to question God? His love, His will, or His timing.

At Joel's slow nod, Kenneth continued, the warmth in his voice removing any hint of a lecture. "Perhaps you have been seeing this as *your* ministry. Not *His* ministry. If it is truly His — and truly important — don't you think He will care for it? Perhaps the Lord is asking you to prepare yourself for handing over your responsibilities here to someone else." He stopped and searched Joel's face. "But I can't say that for certain. I'm not sure I should be saying anything at all."

Joel struggled to find words. "I feel like you are saying what my heart has been trying to tell me for weeks."

"Then I'm glad I spoke," Kenneth replied quietly.

Joel straightened his shoulders and looked directly at Kenneth. For the first time in a long while he felt at peace. "I'm afraid I have been taking myself far too seriously. It is God's program, after all, isn't it?"

Light footsteps signaled Kyle's return. Joel raised his head to see Kyle a few paces away, steaming coffees in both hands. She glanced from one face to the other. "I'm sorry, am I interrupting?"

The two smiled at each other. "No," Joel said. "Not at all."

Kyle handed over the coffees and settled onto a chair. She hesitated a long moment, then said, "I called your home this morning. They said to tell you . . ." There was a hesitancy, as though she was uncertain how to continue. "They miss you, Joel."

He nodded, both at the words and at what was unsaid. That he was nearing his own end, and his parents needed time with him. "I need to go home," he acknowledged. "But I don't like the thought of leaving here" — he looked around — "and the Millers. They have been such a strength to me."

"That reminds me." Kyle hesitated, then said carefully, "Ruthie said to tell you, 'Don't leave now, leave next time.' "

"Yeah," Joel said quietly. "If only I could."

Kenneth quietly offered, "You know, you

could take your mission work home with you."

Joel looked up, his question unspoken.

"My own church has an outreach program, trying to help young runaways in the Washington area," Kenneth went on. "They could always use experienced help."

Joel felt a newfound surge of hope. "You really think so?"

"I'll take you over and introduce you myself." Kenneth set aside his coffee cup, looked for a moment at Joel, then said, "I would consider it an honor if we could pray together."

Joel found hope rising still, a gift that gave strength he could not receive through words. He nodded his acceptance and said quietly, "I'm so glad my sister found you."

Kyle did not miss the words. Tears formed in her eyes at the acceptance and the open affection they carried. "So am I," she agreed, reaching for Kenneth's hand, then Joel's. "So am I."

That night Kyle lay in her hotel bed and thought back over the events of the last few days. She had never felt so happy, so filled with a sense of anticipation. *God is at work,* she exulted. She felt His very presence with her, deep in her heart. She never wanted to lose this, not ever. She wanted it to grow inside her, getting bigger and stronger every single day. *Please, God, stay with me and let this . . . this feeling of knowing you are here never leave me. Not ever.*

She reached out to touch the wall between her

room and Kenneth's. He was part of all this — God's plan for her life, she realized. He had somehow brought peace and a new sense of direction to Joel. Joel had even agreed to further medical opinion. Perhaps the diagnosis would be the same. They all had to face that fact. But at least they would have the comfort of knowing they had done all they could. It was important for her to do anything that she could, anything that her resources could arrange for, to ease their parents' hearts.

She no longer had to worry about the will that her father had left, about repercussions from those who had tried to contest it. Kenneth possessed the business expertise to give direction to the company; his faith would help her mold Rothmore Insurance into an organization operating in a way that honored God. He shared her sense of calling — to God, to her father's wishes, and now to her new family.

In the search for her roots, she had knocked on many doors. She had been searching for herself and began to realize it really was a search for God. For the first time in her life, she was coming to see who she truly was. Not the proper society lady Abigail wanted. Not even the girl Lawrence had loved. No, it was something far deeper, far richer than that. She was a child of God. And the realization was another door through which she would enter and continue traveling.

Nor would she go through this journey alone. She *knew* it. No matter that her beloved father had died or that Joel might leave her just as she was coming to know and love him. There was a new vision that calmed her heart and filled the void of loneliness that had been so much a part of her life.

For her earthly family — families — had been joined to an eternal one. The heavenly family was a part of her now. Nothing could ever take that away. She *belonged*.

Martha held Joel for a long time when he first arrived home. Joel could feel the tremble of her body as she fought against tears, but bravely she tried for a smile as she pushed back and placed her hands on his arms. "I think you've put on some weight," she said. "Maybe you like Mrs. Miller's cooking better than your mother's." Joel could tell she was teasing, and they both laughed.

It was Harry's turn then. Joel had never been hugged by his dad before, as far as he could remember. Mr. Miller gave him an occasional bear hug, but this was different. Harry drew him close and held him snug against his chest. "We've missed you, son," he said with a husky voice that hinted at all the lost years.

Kyle had traveled with Joel and was welcomed by loving embraces, too, and soon the bittersweet emotions turned to joyous reunion. Almost without realizing it they fell into easy conversation.

"I made your favorite dessert, apple crisp," Martha informed Joel as she led them to the little kitchen where the table had been carefully set with the best they had. She turned to Kyle. "Had I known your favorite, dear, I would have made it, too." The words touched Kyle's heart in a strange but warm way.

"I'm sure your apple crisp will quickly become my favorite," she said. The two looked at each other without speaking, but the message that passed between them brought joy to both.

"Well, now," Martha said finally, "let's get supper on the table."

In a very few minutes the four were gathered for the meal. Harry said, "Take your usual place, son, and, Kyle, you sit here in this spot that has been vacant for too many years."

Kyle accepted the seat and looked around her at her family. *Her family.* Harry reached out his hands, one to his daughter, one to his son, and Martha took their hands on the other side.

"I think we need to thank God for far more than our food today," said Harry. "He has blessed us beyond our dreams. Our son" — he gave Joel's hand a squeeze — "and our daughter" — he turned to Kyle — "are both here at our table." His voice sounded husky. Kyle wondered if he would be able to continue. "Our family. Our *whole* family — together at last."

Kyle could hear Martha sniffing. She choked back her own tears.

"Let's thank God. Then let's make the most of this very special day," said Harry.

As Kyle bent her head to join in the prayer she felt a little nudge against her foot. She looked up

to meet Joel's eyes, misty but filled with joy.
"Thanks, my sister," he mouthed to her across
the table. Kyle's heart had never felt lighter.

CHAPTER TWENTY-FOUR

Kyle stepped from the taxi, paid the fare, then stopped a moment to gaze down the long drive. Taking her time, she strolled through the gate, examining the lawns and the house with a fresh new eye. The day held a surprising warmth, as though trying to make up for the previous week's hard frost. As Kyle approached the house, happy childhood memories flooded back. There had been some good times here. Her father's love. The devoted care of the Ameses and the rest of the household staff. Even the training of her mother, though often misplaced and exaggerated, had not been wasted. In her mother's own way, perhaps she had cared.

Not even the cloud of apprehension about what was coming could take away Kyle's feeling of rightness, of renewal.

"Miss Kyle!" Her reverie was interrupted as a familiar figure took a long moment to rise from his work at the flower bed. "If you aren't a sight for sore eyes!"

"Hello, Jim." She hurried over and embraced the bent old man. "How are you?"

"Better, after that hug." The old gardener cackled. "They keep thinking I'm gonna give up the ghost, and I keep surprising them."

"Don't you dare." She took a step back, looked around her, and said, "The place looks wonderful

— better than ever!"

"Yep, that's the sign of a good garden. Tend it well and let it kinda grow into itself." The lined face had grime worked deep into the folds, but the eyes were clear and the grin genuine. "You're looking pretty good yourself."

"Thank you," she replied. "I'm doing just fine."

"Glad to hear it. Been awful quiet around here without you."

She glanced toward the house. The high stone edifice looked as regal and imposing as it had when she had been a small child.

"When you gonna bring that young feller of yours around?"

"Soon. I promise."

The front door of the house was flung open and a portly lady in a faded kitchen apron hurried down the stairs. Jim cackled again. "Look at them old bones move, will you."

"Kyle, oh, my baby, it's been so long!" Maggie enfolded her in a warm embrace.

"Hello, Maggie. I'm sorry I didn't call ahead, but —"

"This is your home, child. Why on earth would you need to call?" She held Kyle back at arm's length. "You look absolutely marvelous."

Kyle inspected the dear, familiar lines of her face, and the lump in her throat returned. "So do you, Maggie."

"Oh, look at what I've done." Maggie began brushing her off. "I've gotten flour on your beautiful jacket."

"I'll let you two get on with it. I'm sure I'd not get a word in edgewise," Jim said with a twinkle, tipping his battered cap to the pair of them. "Come on out and chat with me 'fore you leave."

"Come inside," Maggie said, pulling her toward the door. "Bertrand has gone to the shops, but he won't be long. How *are* you? Tell me all about your new family. I can't wait to find out *everything*."

"All right." Kyle couldn't help but smile at Maggie's enthusiasm.

She entered the vast front foyer, looked around, and felt all the old memories surging up. But now she was able to push aside the old anxieties. She was not alone.

Maggie pointed toward the kitchen. "Come join me for a cup of tea."

"Not just now, Maggie." Kyle knew the purpose of her visit could be put off no longer. "How is Mother?"

The woman faltered a moment before replying, "She's out on the veranda."

"How is she, Maggie?"

The woman's forehead creased. "It's nothing I can put my finger on. But the past few days, it seems like all the starch has gone out of her."

"Let me go talk with her. I'll come in after and we can have a nice long chat."

Maggie reached up and patted Kyle's cheek. "You always were a good girl, a good daughter."

Kyle felt a flutter around her heart. "Pray for

me, Maggie. And pray for her."

"I always have, child," she replied, her eyes shining. "And I always will."

"Kyle!" Abigail half rose from her seat, light springing into her eyes as one hand reached out toward the girl. Quickly she checked herself and settled back in the chair with an uneasy clearing of her throat. "Well, I was not expecting you," she said in her usual controlled manner.

Kyle longed to rush to her mother, throw her arms around her as freely as she did with Martha, and sob out the long years of loneliness and hurt. But her mother's return to formality kept her from it. "Hello, Mother."

"I suppose you've come back to crow over me in triumph."

"Oh, Mother." Kyle mourned as she walked out on the veranda and pulled one of the heavy metal chairs up closer. "How are you?"

"How do you think?" Abigail answered sharply. "I am faced with watching everything I have spent my life trying to build be reduced to ashes."

"Please, Mother. Nothing is going to be destroyed." Kyle folded her hands in her lap, took a deep breath, and nestled within the gift of calm. Not even her racing heart could overwhelm her sense of being sheltered and guided. "I have not come here to gloat — or to argue."

Her mother took the reading glasses off her nose and put them and her magazine on the table at her side. "Soon it's all yours. All of it. I suppose you're going to bring vengeance on us all."

"Neither Kenneth nor I want vengeance in any way, Mother. He is an honorable, God-fearing man, and he will be directing the company. He will do what is right for us all."

Her daughter's calm seemed to leave Abigail even more rattled. "I hope you aren't expecting me to crawl and beg. The house is mine. Mine, I tell you. Lawrence —"

"Of course it's yours. I wouldn't dream of trying to take anything from you. Most especially your home."

Abigail's gaze scattered across the back garden, and her finger nervously picked up her glasses, then laid them down again. "Well, you had better not have come down here expecting an apology. What I tried to do was the best thing for the company. And for you. You have no idea how to run a company."

"No I don't," Kyle agreed. "But Kenneth does."

"My own daughter," Abigail interrupted. "Turning against me."

"I haven't turned against you, Mother. I've come to see you and find out how you are."

"I thought you had gone to your *other* family," Abigail retorted. "They have no money, no family heritage. But I guess you found that out for yourself. I told Randolf that you'd be back. I told him that you'd soon discover that they couldn't give you anything you didn't already have."

"But they did. The most worthwhile things that life can offer. Love. Acceptance. Family. I haven't turned from them, Mother. I love them dearly and expect to spend a good deal of time with them in the future. I have come back because of you."

"Me?"

"I've come here to say that I love you and I don't hold anything against you."

For once Abigail was brought to an astonished silence.

"If you want it, Mother, I forgive you."

Abigail finally managed, "Forgive?"

"For everything." The surge of love that flooded Kyle's being was like a light descending from above, a power so strong it *demanded* that it be shared.

Kyle reached across the emotional chasm that had separated her from Abigail all their lives, even as her hand reached across the table and took the slim, trembling hand of her mother in her own. "I have discovered salvation, Mother, and the wonderful gift of forgiveness. God has forgiven me and expects me to hold no bitterness toward others. It is *His* gift, a gift of love that I want to share with you. I do love you, Mother. I truly do. God has filled my heart with a love that I cannot even explain. Please don't turn it away. We have so much to share with each other. So much."

There were no words forthcoming from Abigail. Kyle might have wondered if her offering was received had she not felt the clasp on her hand undeniably tighten.

Abigail was looking at her with a strange expression on her face. She gave a tight nod, then quickly said, "Well, don't expect miracles."

Kyle smiled softly and quietly replied, "Oh, but I do."